FINANCE AND EMPIRE

By the same author

BANKERS AND DIPLOMATS IN CHINA, 1917–1925

Finance and Empire

Sir Charles Addis, 1861–1945

Roberta Allbert Dayer

MACMILLAN
PRESS

The author and publishers would like to thank Athlone for
permission to use extracts from R. Dayer, 'The Young
Charles S. Addis: Poet or Banker?', in Frank H. H. King
(ed.), *Eastern Banking: Essays in the History of the Hongkong
and Shanghai Banking Corporation* (London, 1983).

First published 1988

Published by
THE MACMILLAN PRESS LTD
Houndmills, Basingstoke, Hampshire RG21 2XS
and London
Companies and representatives
throughout the world

Typeset by Wessex Typesetters
(Division of The Eastern Press Ltd)
Frome, Somerset

Printed in Hong Kong

British Library Cataloguing in Publication Data
Dayer, Roberta Allbert
Finance and empire: Sir Charles Addis,
1861–1945.
1. Addis, *Sir* Charles   2. Capitalists
and financiers—Great Britain—
Biography
I. Title
332'.042'0924   HG172.A3
ISBN 0-333-44464-7

For my husband, Dr Roger S. Dayer,
whose faith and love sustained me

Contents

List of Maps

List of Plates

Preface and Acknowledgements

Charles Stewart Addis is hardly a familiar name either to historians or the public at large. Yet he was one of the world's most important international financiers and policy-makers in the first half of the twentieth century, one who shaped history in two major areas – Far Eastern international relations and monetary policy.

I first became interested in Addis fifteen years ago, when I began my doctoral research on British and American policy in China.[1] Research in the diplomatic archives in London and Washington convinced me that Addis was very powerful, yet no one seemed to know much about him and a search for private papers proved fruitless. After revising the dissertation for publication as *Bankers and Diplomats in China, 1917–1925: The Anglo-American Relationship*, I learned in 1978 that there were Addis papers which were still at the family home at Woodside, near Tunbridge Wells.[2] Since my manuscript had not yet been published, I left immediately for England.

In London I met Sir Charles Addis's daughter, Miss Robina Addis, OBE, who, with her brother, Sir John Addis, KCMG, controlled access to the papers. She took me to Woodside, the family home near Tunbridge Wells, where (in Sir Charles Addis's study) I found a complete set of diaries, begun in the 1880s and continued up until 1945. In addition there were stacks and boxes of letters, articles, scrapbooks, pictures, and so forth, which had been collected and preserved by Addis's wife and their daughter Robina. I was able to read the relevant Addis diaries and to include this new information in *Bankers and Diplomats*.

Many people have asked me why Addis kept a diary, or how such a complete collection of his letters and correspondence happened to survive. I asked Miss Addis if she thought her father (who was a gifted writer) might have intended to write an autobiography. She had no knowledge of such plans. If he did intend to write his memoirs, the fact that he continued to be active in the City almost until the end of his life precluded such an undertaking. Fortunately Lady Addis and her husband's best friend, Dudley Mills, early recognised the likelihood that Addis would become an important figure and carefully preserved the correspondence, speeches, news-clippings and so on.

My work on the biography began in 1979 when Commander C. P. Addis, RN, MBE (encouraged by his Aunt Robina) invited me to see the family materials he had collected at Chatham and permitted me to read the family histories which he has written.[3] Since that time Commander Addis has continued to advise me and in addition has generously supplied many of the pictures which are included in the biography.

My motive in agreeing to undertake the project was a desire to continue my investigation of British and American policy in China. I viewed the biography as a convenient vehicle for such a study. However as the research progressed I discovered that I had under-taken far more than I had anticipated since Addis also followed a career in the field of international monetary policy. This fact forced me to master a whole new area of expertise, enlarged the scope of the biography and meant that what I had hoped to finish in two or three years took seven. In retrospect, I realise that an additional reason why I pursued this research was to satisfy my basic interest in power – how it is acquired and implemented. A further interest concerns international conflict, both its sources and solution. Since each new letter or document I read helped me to understand the interrelationship of all these questions, I found the research fascinating. In other words my interest in researching Addis's career has been to find how he influenced his times. I knew he was important, my aim was to find out why. I discovered far more than I anticipated.

The person who is most responsible for this biography is Miss Robina Addis, who somehow decided (without my being aware) that I was the proper historian to write her father's life. Without her steady encouragement I could not have completed this work. From 1979 she generously shared her home, memories, friends and family with me, but most of all, her own indomitable fortitude. While she patiently read and commented on each draft as it appeared, she always insisted 'you must write what you think is true'. To me as to all who knew her, she was an inspiration. After I had written the above, I learned that Miss Addis had died on 7 September 1986, and thus would never see the published work. I find comfort in the fact that she knew Macmillan had accepted the manuscript, and in June had helped me and Commander Addis in the selection of pictures. Her last letter to me (22 July 1986) described her pleasure with the catalogue. Thus I feel that she has given not only her approval but her blessing to what follows. I shall always be grateful for the privilege of her friendship, the gift of her affection.

Through Miss Addis, I became acquainted with her best friend, Lady Norman (the widow of Montagu Norman, and herself another remarkable woman) who in many conversations has provided information and insights concerning her husband (the Governor of the Bank of England [1920–44]) and some of his associates.[4] In addition she permitted me to read both sets of Norman diaries which are at the Bank of England.

The other Addis children who kindly granted me interviews and provided hospitality are: the late Sir John Addis; the late Lady Bernard (Elizabeth); Lady Lawrence (Susan); Mrs Booth (Etta); the Hon. Mrs M. K. Geddes (Margaret); Mrs Pownell (Jean); Mrs J. F. Cornes (Rachel) and Mrs Michael Warr (a daughter-in-law who lives at Woodside). I have also benefited from interviews with Mrs Huxley (the daughter of Col. Mills), Miss Jean Stewart (the daughter of Gershom Stewart and niece of Murray Stewart) and Sir Dallas Bernard (a grandson). Although a thank-you to family members and friends seems terribly inadequate, I think they know the gratitude it represents.

In 1981 Miss Addis and Sir John agreed to donate the Addis papers to the School of Oriental and African Studies where the cataloguing began. After the original donation, additional materials were discovered, so that the collection continues to expand.[5] For this reason, the reader will notice that some of my notes have a document number while others do not, reflecting the different times I read them and/or the timing of their discovery.

My task would have been far more difficult had not the Hongkong and Shanghai Bank agreed to finance the cataloguing of the Addis papers and to host a Conference on the History of the Hongkong and Shanghai Bank (HSBC) which took place in Hong Kong in 1981. Professor Frank H. H. King, who is writing a history of the Bank, invited me to contribute a paper on 'The Young Charles Addis' which I have incorporated into Chapter 1.[6] Professor King deserves the credit for recognising the value of the papers and convincing the HSBC Bank to finance the cataloguing. He and Stewart Muirhead (then the Controller of the HSBC archives) have been invaluable sources of information concerning the Bank's history. In addition, Professor King and his wife Catherine have been gracious hosts to me, in both Hong Kong and Oxford, which made my research far more pleasant.

After finishing the first draft of the biography (in the summer of 1984) I circulated various chapters to recognised authorities – Stephen Clarke, Donald Moggridge, Philip Williamson, Richard Davenport-Hines, Stephen Schuker, Parks Coble, Olive Checkland and Frank H. H. King, all of whom responded with trenchant remarks, helpful suggestions and encouraging enthusiasm. Stephen Clarke, Philip Williamson and Richard Davenport-Hines read and commented on the entire manuscript, while Clarke and Williamson volunteered to read further drafts as well. Such a sharing of precious time and hard-won expertise demonstrates the finest aspect of scholarly endeavour. Needless to say, the biography is far better for these experts' contributions, even though I must hasten to add that I doubt if any of them will agree fully with my conclusions. At a later stage, I turned to the professor who had guided my dissertation, John F. Naylor, for a 'final reading', and once more received the benefit of his outstanding editorial skills and knowledge of British political history. Shortly before his death, Sir John Addis (who had served in the Foreign Office in the late 1930s) read and gave his approval to an earlier version of Chapter 11. Naturally I alone am responsible for errors which remain in the text, despite all this assistance.

Other historians and archivists who have contributed to this study are: Professor Richard Sayers, who helped me to gain early access to the Bank of England archives, where John Keyworth answered many of my questions; David Steeds, who shared the Lampson papers with me; John Orbell, who permitted me to use the Revelstoke papers at Barings; Leslie Hannah and David Jeremy at the London School of Economics, who made the Business History Unit's resources available; Everett and Josephine Young Case, who permitted me to use the Owen Young Papers at Van Hornesville, New York, and shared their memories of Mrs Young's father; Dorothy Hamerton, honorary archivist at Chatham House, who explained that organisation's history; Robert Wood (the former Director of the Herbert Hoover Presidential Library at West Branch, Iowa) who is unfailingly helpful and encouraging to historians; Carl Backlund at the Federal Reserve Bank of New York, who helped me to research the Strong and Harrison papers; the late Murray Mindlin (my former editor), Kathleen Burk and D. C. Watt.

I wish to acknowledge the invaluable assistance of archivists and librarians at the Marshall Library, the King's College Library and the University Library, Cambridge; at Rhodes House Library, Oxford; the Thomas Fisher Rare Book Library at the University of

Toronto; the Hoover Institution on War, Revolution and Peace, Stanford University; the Baker Library at Harvard University; the Butler Library at Columbia University; the John M. Olin Library at Cornell University; the Seeley G. Mudd Manuscript Library, Princeton University; the Bancroft Library at the University of California, Berkeley; Morgan Grenfell & Co. Ltd, London; the Public Record Office, Kew; The British Library, London; the National Archives and the Library of Congress in Washington DC. These patient and knowledgeable individuals provided both permission to quote from their collections and gracious help in utilising their resources. Quotations from the Lloyd George Papers are made with the permission of the Clerk of the Records, House of Lords Record Office. Quotations from the Addis Papers, the Aglen Papers and the Maze Papers appear by permission of the Librarian of the School of Oriental and African Studies.

The capable and cooperative librarians at my own Lockwood Library at the State University of New York, Buffalo, efficiently obtained documents for me and kindly permitted me to keep hundreds of their books on my own shelves for several years. Without the resources of this great institution, the research for *Finance and Empire* would have been far more difficult. Credit for these resources belongs to the long-suffering taxpayers of the State of New York. Rarely are their contributions put to such worthwhile purpose.

Finally, I wish to make special mention of Rosemary Seton, the Archivist at the School of Oriental and African Studies, who over the past five years has borne the major burden of my research needs, never failing to respond with both expertise and good humour.

My notes demonstrate the degree to which we historians depend on the work of those who have gone before, but there is no way I can indicate adequately my gratitude for the warm hospitality, academic help and encouragement which so many individuals have given me over the course of the past seven years' work. Suffice it to say that the British scholars have made their own particular contribution to improved Anglo-American relations.

As most historians know or belatedly discover, there is very little monetary reward for historical endeavour. Support for the research and publication of this biography has come from the American Philosophical Society (encouraged by my first mentor, Professor Lewis White Beck) and from my patient and sympathetic husband, Dr Roger S. Dayer, to whom I dedicate this book.

ROBERTA ALLBERT DAYER

List of Abbreviations

AIC	American International Corporation
B&C Corp.	British and Chinese Railways Corporation
BDI	*Biographical Dictionary of Internationalists*
BIS	Bank for International Settlements
Cab/	British Cabinet papers
CER	Chinese Eastern Railway
CHC	*Cambridge History of China*
DAB	Deutsch-Asiatische Bank
DBB	*Dictionary of Business Biography*
DBFP	*Documents on British Foreign Policy*
Diary	Addis diary in the Addis papers, SOAS
EAC	Economic Advisory Council
FO	Foreign Office (Great Britain)
FRBNY	Federal Reserve Bank of New York
FRUS	*Papers Relating to the Foreign Relations of the United States*
HSBC	Hongkong and Shanghai Banking Corporation
IG	Inspector General
JMK	*The Collected Writings of John Maynard Keynes*
KMT	Kuomintang
RIIA	Royal Institute of International Affairs (Chatham House)
SDCGK	Society for the Diffusion of Christian and General Knowledge among the Chinese
SDF	United States Department of State Decimal Files
SMR	South Manchuria Railway
SOAS	School of Oriental and African Studies
T/	British Treasury Papers

Introduction

'The Altogetherness of Everything.' – Blackett, 1931, quoting Hegel

The question which led to my interest in Sir Charles Addis was: 'Why after the First World War did the United States not succeed in supplanting the British influence in China, when such was the intention of the State Department, which possessed the financial muscle to enforce its will? In 1976 I concluded that Addis, as the London Manager of the Hongkong and Shanghai Banking Corporation, was largely responsible for Britain's success in combating American competition in China.[1] This biography shows how Addis attempted to block the American initiative not only in China but throughout the world. In brief Addis can best be understood as a defender of Empire; his weapons were those of the international financier – capital and financial expertise.

Addis's career demonstrates the complex interrelationship of financial and diplomatic issues, which caused Sir Basil Blackett (a Treasury official who had shared many undertakings with Addis) to remark in 1931 that 'The Cabinet Room in 10 Downing Street ought to have prominently emblazoned on its walls the Hegelian motto: "The Altogetherness of Everything." How many of our troubles are due to our insistence on thinking and acting piecemeal.'[2] In focusing on Addis's life, I became aware of the interrelationship of seemingly disparate topics and recognised the continuity of British policy, connections and patterns which to date have gone unnoticed as we specialists pursue our own narrow subjects, whether they be limited by geographical area or brief spans of time. Because Addis lived such a long life and approached issues from an imperial (or world-wide) perspective, I was forced to see the 'altogetherness of everything'.

What this biography reveals is the close working relationship between the various British governing bodies (formal and informal) in the interwar period and the fact that British leaders shared a common goal – to win American cooperation in ruling the world. This is not meant to suggest that there was unanimity; indeed some like Lord Curzon bitterly opposed sacrificing the Anglo-Japanese Alliance for the 'temporary conquest of the *beaux yeux* of America'.[3]

But for the most part, Great Britain in the 1920s sought to accommodate its policies to those of the United States.[4]

Addis's uniqueness was the result of his participation in all four centres of British financial power – the City (as a leader of the HSBC), the Bank of England (as a member of the Committee of Treasury), the Government (as Cabinet Advisor and Treasury representative), and academe (as author and a member of the Council of the Royal Economic Society, Chatham House and the Tuesday Club). In Professor Sayers's words, he was 'a host in himself'.[5] The breadth of his contacts and the personal influence which he commanded enabled him to serve as a liaison between these various centres of power, to some extent as a coordinator of policy.

What the Addis papers (particularly those at the Bank of England) make clear is that Addis, Norman and the Treasury adopted and pursued a common strategy in the 1920s aimed at regaining Britain's prewar supremacy.[6] But American mistrust of Great Britain as well as Washington's belief that it could remain independent of Europe doomed all efforts at Anglo-American cooperation. In recent years many historians have emphasised the significance of the Anglo-American relationship between the wars, describing the shift of power from London to Washington.[7] The reason the relationship is considered so important is that many scholars feel successful Anglo-American cooperation might have prevented the outbreak of the Second World War.[8] One of the chief aims of this biography is to examine Addis's role in shaping and implementing British strategy.

This biography is divided into three parts, only the first of which deals in any detail with Addis's personal affairs. Part I traces the young Addis's early development – where he got his ideas, what he believed, his philosophy, training, goals, relationships, how he learned the 'rules of the game' and became part of the British ruling class. It describes Addis's experiences in East Asia where, as an employee of the Hongkong and Shanghai Banking Corporation (HSBC), Addis acquired the financial and diplomatic skills which would determine his future. In addition Part I analyses the financial techniques of empire which Britain developed in the nineteenth century to exert influence. After becoming Manager of the London Office in 1905, Addis, in cooperation with the Foreign Office, began to organise an international consortium of banks to cooperate in financing the needs of the Chinese government. When the First World War broke out in 1914, he became a government advisor on international exchange and by the war's end, he had been elected to the Court of the Bank of England.

Part II explores Addis's efforts to win American support for cooperation in China and on reparations and war debts. In addition it shows the development of the friendship between Addis and Montagu Norman, revealing Addis's influence within the hierarchy of the Bank of England. It also explains the influence which Addis exerted over domestic monetary policy, especially regarding the return to the gold standard, and over reparation questions. Britain's departure from the gold standard in 1931 demonstrated the failure of the cooperative policy which Norman and Addis had laboured to achieve.

Part III traces Addis's role in shaping the government's new sterling strategy, both in preparing for the World Economic Conference of 1933 and in wooing trading partners such as Canada. Although I think the ideal biographical approach is chronological (because it helps to prevent inaccuracies and actually reflects the experience of the subject) I found attempts to explain Addis's China activities and his monetary role simultaneously produced too much confusion. Addis may have been able to keep track of everything at once, but we cannot. Furthermore, since it is impossible to understand the China policy of the 1930s without first understanding the financial background of the 1920s, I decided to postpone a discussion of Addis's role in China after 1922 (when Anglo-American Far Eastern cooperation began to decline) until after I had described the monetary and financial negotiations. Thus Part III deals with the failure of the World Economic Conference (1933) and Britain's default on war debts (1934) before returning to Chinese affairs in the 1920s. China became one of the countries which the British Treasury (with Addis's help) succeeded in luring into the so-called 'sterling area'.[9]

Although this organisation forces the reader to do some mental backtracking, I think it ultimately provides improved clarity and deeper understanding of events and their significance. In tracing Addis's influence on China policy one is struck with the continuity of British policy from the nineteenth century to the late 1930s, despite the vast political changes which occurred during these years. One can also see patterns which continue to shape international affairs.

Since Addis dealt with many of the problems which remain dominant and unresolved issues of our own time – such as currency stabilisation, or aid to the underdeveloped world, his career offers more than an explanation of the past – it provides insight into the present. Most significantly, it reveals the methods by which investment bankers influence and control government policy.

Investment bankers look at the world through a single lens which does not distinguish political or cultural differences. Whether the applicant for a loan is Chinese, Latin American, Russian or German, or whether the application is filed by a government or a business, the question is the same – namely, how creditworthy is the applicant? The answer is determined by an estimate of the applicant's assets and liability and the likelihood of repayment (security). Important considerations for the financier are control of revenues and the ability to enforce this control. When loans to foreign governments are under consideration, political factors cannot be avoided, especially when bankers are requested by their governments to make loans for political purposes.[10] Because Addis was not only an international financier who served the interests of his corporation, but also a central banker who served the interests of his government and in addition a committed internationalist, who sought to promote world peace, his career inevitably involved great complexity and continual conflicts of interest. Furthermore, since he did not look through a single lens nor pursue the simple objective of getting rich quickly, his career is neither easy to understand nor simple to assess. But it is fascinating.

This study comes to new and startling conclusions regarding the Bank Crisis of 1931, the Pacific War and the administration of the Bank of England which will no doubt be challenged and cause controversy. In anticipation of this, and also because Chinese politics, international banking and monetary policy are all esoteric subjects, I have attempted to fortify my arguments with the most recent scholarship available. I make no claim to final answers but instead hope that my views will be treated more as hypotheses than final conclusions, as an attempt to move a little closer to that ever-elusive goal of the historian – understanding the past. Since I was trained as a diplomatic, not an economic historian, I approached monetary questions with much apprehension and confess that I smiled in silent agreement when I read Addis's diary comment, written after twenty years service in banking – 'I shall never understand banking.'

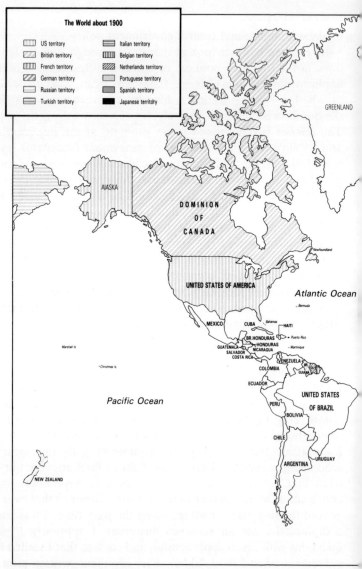

The World about 1900

US territory	Italian territory
British territory	Belgian territory
French territory	Netherlands territory
German territory	Portuguese territory
Russian territory	Spanish territory
Turkish territory	Japanese territory

GREENLAND

ALASKA

DOMINION

OF

CANADA

Newfoundland

UNITED STATES OF AMERICA

Atlantic Ocean

Bermuda

MEXICO   CUBA   Bahamas
                    HAITI
          BR.HONDURAS   Puerto Rico
GUATEMALA   HONDURAS
    SALVADOR   NICARAGUA   Martinique
       COSTA RICA   VENEZUELA
                    GUIANA
          COLOMBIA

Marshall Is.

Christmas Is.

ECUADOR

Pacific Ocean

PERU   UNITED STATES
BOLIVIA   OF BRAZIL

CHILE

ARGENTINA   URUGUAY

NEW ZEALAND

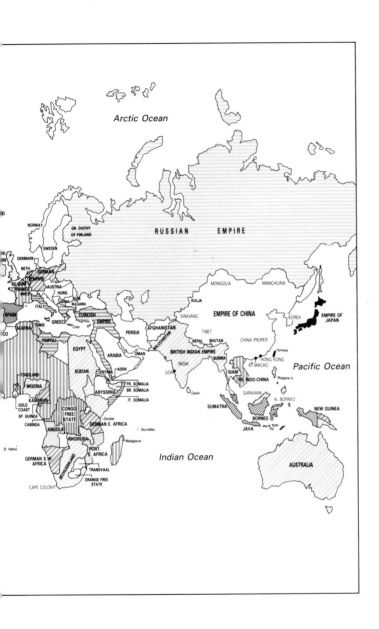

Arctic Ocean

NORWAY

GR. DUCHY
OF FINLAND

SWEDEN

RUSSIAN   EMPIRE

DENMARK

NETH.

GERMAN

EMPIRE

BELGIUM

FRANCE

SWITZ.

AUSTRIA

HUNG.

SPAIN

ITALY

RUM.

SERBIA

BULGARIA

GREECE

Crete

TURKISH

EMPIRE

ALGERIA

TUNIS

TRIPOLI

EGYPT

PERSIA

AFGHANISTAN

MONGOLIA

MANCHURIA

KULJA

SINKIANG

EMPIRE OF CHINA

KOREA

EMPIRE OF
JAPAN

TIBET

NEPAL

BHUTAN

CHINA PROPER

Formosa

ARABIA

OMAN

BALUCHISTAN

BRITISH INDIAN EMPIRE

BURMA

HONG KONG

MACAO

Pacific Ocean

SUDAN

ERITREA

ADEN

INDIA

GOA

SIAM

FR. INDO-CHINA

Philippine Is.

TOGOLAND

NIGERIA

FR. SOMALIA

BR. SOMALIA

Ceylon

SARAWAK

N. BORNEO

NEW GUINEA

KAMERUN

ABYSSINIA

IT. SOMALIA

SUMATRA

BORNEO

GOLD
COAST

SP. GUINEA

CONGO
FREE
STATE

Zanzibar

Seychelles

JAVA

CABINDA

ANGOLA

GERMAN E. AFRICA

St. Helena

RHODESIA

Madagascar

Indian Ocean

GERMAN S.W.
AFRICA

PORT.
E. AFRICA

BECHUANALAND

AUSTRALIA

TRANSVAAL

CAPE COLONY

ORANGE FREE
STATE

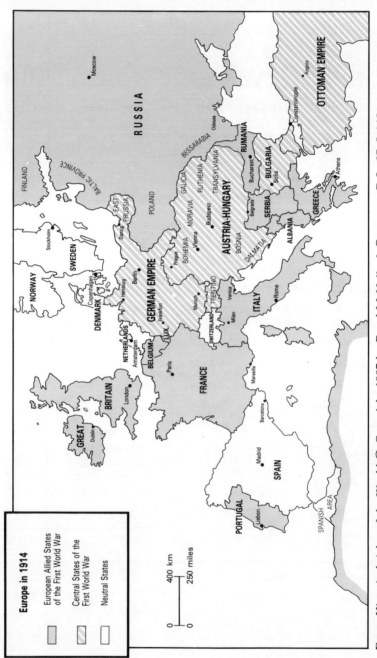

Europe in 1914

European Allied States of the First World War

Central States of the First World War

Neutral States

400 km

250 miles

GREAT BRITAIN

Dublin

London

NETHERLANDS

Amsterdam

BELGIUM

LUX.

FRANCE

Paris

PORTUGAL

Lisbon

SPAIN

Madrid

Barcelona

Marseille

SPANISH AREA

NORWAY

SWEDEN

Stockholm

DENMARK

Copenhagen

Hamburg

GERMAN EMPIRE

Berlin

Frankfurt

Munich

SWITZERLAND

TRENTINO

ITALY

Milan

Venice

Rome

FINLAND

BALTIC PROVINCE

RUSSIA

Moscow

EAST PRUSSIA

Danzig

POLAND

Prague

BOHEMIA

MORAVIA

Vienna

Budapest

AUSTRIA-HUNGARY

GALICIA

RUTHENIA

TRANSYLVANIA

BESSARABIA

Odessa

RUMANIA

Bucharest

BULGARIA

Sofia

SERBIA

Belgrade

BOSNIA

DALMATIA

ALBANIA

GREECE

Athens

Constantinople

OTTOMAN EMPIRE

Angora

From *Historical Atlas of the World* © Copyright 1987 by Rand McNally & Company, R.L. 87-5-145.

Part I

The Development of a Man and His Career

1 The Young Charles Addis, 1861–95

'After eighteen months in Peking I begin to think that diplomacy is just another name for lying.' — Addis to Etta, 1887

While there is much disagreement as to the degree to which genes or environment determine the individual, there is no doubt that human personality amounts to the sum of the two influences. The young male child, Charles Stewart Addis, who was born to the Rev. and Mrs Thomas Addis in Edinburgh on 23 November 1861, was generously endowed in both respects. From his parents he inherited high intelligence and good looks; from his environment he absorbed classical learning and the cultural self-confidence characteristic of the high Victorian era. Although Addis left school at the age of 16, he soon became part of a firm which provided him with the skills and contacts which made possible his future success.

CHILDHOOD AND EDUCATION, 1861–80

Thomas Addis (1813–99) was a clergyman, the son of a plumber, educated with the aid of scholarships at St Andrews University where he studied mathematics, Greek and Latin. After being licensed in the Presbytery in Edinburgh, he went to the nearby community of South Leith to assist the Rev. David Thorburn and was ordained in 1841. The next year he married Robina Scott Thorburn, the daughter of a tea merchant in South Leith and the niece of the Rev. David Thorburn. Robina 'came from a family whose typically lowland Scots characteristics were a tough constitution, high spirits, a pawky and rather malicious sense of humour, and a lively interest in everything.'[1] In 1843 the Rev. Thomas Addis joined the 'Disruption', when 500 ministers 'came out' of the Established Church of Scotland to form the Free Kirk. After a year of meetings in temporary accommodations, including the home of the Rev. Dr Thomas Chalmers (the creator of the Disruption) the Rev. Thomas Addis and his followers founded the Morningside Free Church, in a small village in the southern suburbs of Edinburgh. Here he was to serve as minister until his death in 1899. St Andrews University recognised his achievement by awarding him an honorary Doctor of Divinity in 1885.[2] The Rev. and Mrs Thomas Addis had twelve children, six sons and six daughters, Charles being the youngest son.[3]

. As was the custom in those days, Addis as a child was compelled to spend many long hours at church and many more at home reading the scripture and hearing prayers, activities which, like most children, he often resented. Yet this Calvinist heritage provided him with a permanent store of memorised scripture and a command of the English language which would enable him to become an accomplished public speaker. Like his clergyman father, he committed material to memory easily and expressed his thoughts and ideas confidently.

The Addis household was poor in material things but rich in spirit. As the youngest son of twelve children Addis was surrounded, not only by siblings but by many relatives. On the Thorburn side there were uncles who had gone out to the Far East to make their fortune and whose tales of adventures may have awakened a desire to travel in the young boy.[4] Later a homesick young man in Peking would recall a typical family scene in which his mother and sister Susan sat knitting and darning, while his father 'pored over his sermon'. Cropp (a younger sister) worked at her lessons and he sat reading:

> My father stops now and again to poke the rather dull fire, an opportunity for a broken conversation in which we all join; prayers and supper afterwards – how clear & distinct the old room seems. And those lovely Sundays – I only remember the bright ones – when my father and I sat on the garden seat and watched you & Etta making the beds & mother coming out to feed the dog & the crows too.[5]

This memory contrasts sharply with a bitter account which Addis wrote in his diary in 1887, where he recalled his childhood and early education. He described his father as 'at bottom a kind-hearted man', but 'a strict father of the old Scottish type'. He blamed his father for being 'too vain of me' and for demanding too much from him after he entered the Edinburgh Academy at age 11:

> Dazzled by my success my father insisted upon my passing over the 2nd and entering the 3rd class the next term. He conceived the bold plan of compressing the work, which, in natural order of things, I should have done in the following year into the short space of the midsummer holidays. For three years after that I never had a genuine holiday. My old companions would clamour for me

at the gate of a Saturday, but I was chained to my desk. On Sunday we did Greek Testament in the morning. There were two long services in church. After the Sunday school and in the evening we had catechism and questions on the sermons. Every evening I spent in the study where often my tea was sent in to me to drink alone. I could hear them laughing and talking in the next room and sat alone nourishing such thoughts of bitterness as I hope few boys experience. My father never relaxed. Often and often I have gone to him and told him I had prepared my task and was able to repeat it perfectly. 'Go back to your study and revise' was the invariable answer.[6]

Because of this unhappiness, Addis insisted on leaving school and becoming an apprentice in order to get away from home. In this same memoir he admitted: 'It was a great blow to my father who had destined me to follow my brother, David, in the India Civil Service.[7] I am sorry now to think how keenly I relished my father's disappointment.'[8] Ultimately Addis forgave his father and dwelt on happier memories, but both the stern parental training and the warm family life shaped his character.

It is clear that the Addis family life encouraged intellectual endeavour, as well as the enjoyment of music and society. Addis later recalled that he read Tennyson, Cowper, Swinburne, Rossetti, Meredith, Praed, Moore, Longfellow 'and occasionally Austen and Long. Then for a year or two Coleridge was everything and I admire him very much.'[9] Much later, in a speech to the Edinburgh Academy Dinner in 1932, Addis would recall that 'Latin and Greek were our staple fare', subjects which he claimed 'trained the mind'. He believed that a classical education was the best education for a Banker.[10]

While the Scots were less class-conscious than the English and social mobility was greater, there was nonetheless a sharp division between the middle class and the working class.[11] Although not wealthy, as a member of the clergy, the Rev. Thomas Addis and his family enjoyed the prestige and the privileges accorded those of the upper middle class. A good description of the Manse in 1889 was provided by a close friend, Dudley Mills. Mills seems to have found the Addis family life quite different from his own, describing it in vivid and amusing detail to his mother:

Susan is in the elderly settled down condition but very bright and pleasant. 'Croppy' is more about 25 – been highly educated in Germany very good at music – but not above cooking and household work. Both of them nice natural straightforward unaffected as the daughters of a 'meeneester' and as the sisters of my friend should be.

After describing Addis's other brothers and sisters at length, Mills summed up the picture of the Addis family:

So the Free Church minister without a penny to start with, with such feeble business ideas that he has chucked away all his savings, with such stupid educational ideas that he gave neither sons nor daughters even such advantages as he could have given them, the younger ones only getting what the elder ones managed to insist on for them, my friend in particular having been let loose on the world practically at 14 years of age – only one servant being kept in the house and the daughters having to do and doing cheerfully the household work though the grown up sons were ready to supply money for a proper establishment – the Free Church minister with all this against it has planted out 5 sons and three daughters with great success.[12]

Another influential individual in Addis's youth was a preacher named Kippen. Addis recalled that 'it was from him I drew whatever little taste I may have for literature or poetry . . . I had never read a line of Newman's until I took down the *Apologia* from his library shelf and hardly stopped until I had finished it'.[13] Addis's older brother William, who had been part of the Oxford Movement and had become a Catholic priest, later recanted, married and become a Unitarian minister.[14]

As an apprentice at Peter Dowie & Co., General Importers, Addis came in contact with boys from a much different background, or as Addis expressed it 'below me in station'. For three years, Addis, according to his own account, strayed from the strict standards in which he had been drilled, spending his time 'drinking and in theatres and music halls'. Then, after being reprimanded by Peter Dowie and spoken to by his sister, Addis mended his ways, stopped drinking and started studying again, returned to the church and began teaching Sunday School.[15] Another apprentice friend, John Leathe, wrote Addis saying that he was glad to hear about Addis's new behaviour: 'I hope you gave up cards & betting at the same time, those things *always* go together.'[16]

One of Addis's closest friends during this apprenticeship period was Johnnie Fleming, with whom he attended elementary school. Fleming, who came from a working-class background, always emphasised how much he appreciated Addis's friendship and loyalty. Writing from South Africa, he recalled: 'I always admire you for this, when good friends of yours such as Richie and Inglis cut me, you, it always seemed to me stuck closer.'[17]

Although Addis briefly revolted against what he felt were the excessive demands of his father, he never doubted the validity of the Calvinist ethical system. Nor did he ever question the inherent superiority of either his culture or his class. American egalitarianism (on which he would later comment) was quite different from British beliefs concerning the rights and duties of a gentleman, and the distinction between those who ruled and the others who served.

In the 1870s (when Addis was growing up) British influence, which had already penetrated East Asia and Africa, was supreme and still expanding. Queen Victoria presided over an enormous empire where opportunity seemed unlimited: wealth there for the taking. As the young man grew to maturity, so too did the empire. By the time Addis left school, he had no doubt imbibed the assumption that the British were born to rule, as well as the conviction that privilege carried with it responsibilities; that those who went abroad had a civilising mission – to raise the less fortunate of the world to British standards. These beliefs, which were fundamental to the Victorian era, formed as significant a part of the Addis heritage as did his Scotch ancestry or the free-church tradition of his clergyman father. Similarly, the Calvinist teachings of thrift, hard work, moral uprightness and devotion to duty formed the core of both the Victorian era and the Addis family ethic.

After finishing his apprenticeship, Addis, on the advice of his older brother George, applied for a clerkship with the Hongkong and Shanghai Bank in London, in hopes of travelling.[18] His appointment as a clerk in the London Office of the HSBC joined him to an institution which served as a key instrument of the expanding British empire. Strictly speaking, China of course was part of what some historians call Britain's 'informal empire', meaning that China was not a British colony but was within the orbit of British influence.[19] Nonetheless, the employees of the HSBC and other Britishers behaved in China much the same as they did elsewhere in the colonies, treating the 'natives' as subjects and establishing their own customs, law, churches, institutions and currency. Europeans were able to establish these foreign enclaves because of the privileges which foreigners enjoyed under the treaty system which Great Britain had forced upon the Ch'ing rulers following the First and Second Opium Wars.

THE BRITISH, CHINA AND THE HONGKONG AND SHANGHAI BANKING CORPORATION

By the late nineteenth century the Chinese Empire, which had been one of the world's longest enduring and richest civilisations, had fallen behind the Western Powers in terms of industrial development.[20] Convinced of their superiority and confident of their self-sufficiency, the Manchu rulers had at first resisted all Western demands to establish commercial relations except for the trade permitted at the southern port of Canton. In the late eighteenth and early nineteenth century, the British East India Company, with the connivance of Chinese officials, had developed a highly profitable (though illegal) opium trade with Canton.[21] When the Emperor appointed Lin Tse-hsu, the Governor-General of Kiangnan and Kiangsi, as High Commissioner to suppress the opium trade, the stage was set for a conflict between the world's two great empires.[22] After Commissioner Lin seized and destroyed the illegal opium, the British attacked Canton, quickly defeating the Chinese forces.[23] In the Treaty of Nanking of 1842, which concluded the First Opium War, the Emperor's representatives were forced to open five Chinese ports to trade, accept a fixed tariff, concede the right of extraterritoriality to British citizens, and cede the island of Hong Kong to Great Britain.[24] Thus began the so-called 'Treaty system', whereby these two great cultures sought to accommodate their different traditions to each other. Each believed the other to be inferior and in need of civilisation.

The succeeding years were marked by continual disagreements and in 1858 the British and French went to war a second time to force China's rulers to open more ports to trade. The foreigners' demands included: diplomatic representation in the capital of Peking; trade with the interior; the right to own Chinese land; and the right to establish Christian missions.[25] The combined forces of France and England swiftly defeated the Chinese, and forced them to sign the Treaty of Tientsin which opened still more ports to trade, granted the foreign powers the right to representation in Peking, legalised the opium trade and included war indemnities which were to be paid by instalments out of the customs collection.[26] When the Emperor refused to accept this treaty, foreign armies invaded

Peking and burned the Imperial Summer Palace. Only after this disaster did the Hsien-feng Emperor realise the need for modernisation.[27]

After the signing of the second Tientsin treaty in 1860 British officials recognised that their future interests lay chiefly in trade and thus would be best served by supporting a unified China and buttressing the central government.[28] They therefore cooperated with the Ch'ing officials in suppressing the Taiping Rebellion and in beginning a programme of 'self-strengthening', while at the same time encouraging the efforts of Sir Robert Hart, the British Inspector General of the Imperial Maritime Customs Administration, to make that organisation a model of Western efficiency and good management.[29]

Hart was to become a legendary figure, dedicating his entire life to the efficient and honest administration of the Customs.[30] Throughout his long tenure (1863–1908) Hart maintained the position that the Inspector General was the servant of the Chinese government.[31] Yet, despite Hart's unquestioned loyalty to the Ch'ing, the foreign-managed Customs administration was to become the single most important source of foreign influence over the monarchy. Since the customs revenues were used as security for foreign loans to the Ch'ing rulers, they provided a means of political pressure. Gradually, over the next quarter century, the Dynasty became dependent upon customs revenues, and Sir Robert Hart 'came to enjoy more influence with the Foreign Office than did the British Minister'.[32]

In the 1870s the Hongkong and Shanghai Banking Corporation (HSBC) was one of the foreign banks which was eager to provide loans to the Ch'ing.[33] Founded in 1865 by a group of European merchants in Hong Kong, the HSBC from its inception had directors of various nationalities.[34] It had expanded rapidly, establishing agencies in the major cities of Asia, as well as San Francisco, New York, London, Hamburg and Lyons.[35] The bank's success in China was due to its ability to meet the specific needs of the China trade: namely to form a bridge between two very different economic systems, becoming a kind of institutionalised comprador. The comprador was the Chinese employee of the foreign businesses in China who spoke sufficient pidgin English to communicate with both Chinese and English and who sometimes exercised great power and authority.[36] At first the HSBC primarily filled Western needs for international exchange and credit but before long it became the source of capital and credit for both foreigners and Chinese, with its notes functioning as currency in the treaty ports.

When young Addis joined the London HSBC office in 1880, the life of a clerk was neither demanding nor well paid. Addis's salary was £60 per annum.[37] Addis was later to recall that he had often been hungry while a clerk, and after achieving a management position in the Bank, he insisted that the Bank provide a subsidised meal for its trainees and staff.[38] In London Addis continued to enjoy reading, history and economics, taught Sunday School, participated in a Shakespeare Club's amateur productions and made the most of his time and opportunities. He attended French classes at the Birkbeck Institute, where for 18 shillings he could use the library facilities and go to lectures and entertainments.[39] He began studying Chinese under Professor Robert Douglas (at King's College on the Strand) with classmates Harry Thomsett and Gershom Stewart and attended the Gilbart lectures on Banking by Leone Levi, for which he was awarded a certificate.[40] In 1883 Addis welcomed the news of his appointment to the Bank's Eastern staff.

SINGAPORE AND HONG KONG, 1883–6

A young bank employee's first trip out to the East was naturally an exciting adventure. Travelling out by the overland route, Addis embarked at Brindisi and arrived in Singapore on 7 April 1883 where he was welcomed by his brother George, the Manager of the Mercantile Bank. Life in Singapore formed quite a contrast to what Addis had known in London. One of his London friends wrote to him: 'How calmly you talk of keeping a pony and trap and any amount of "boys" . . . I am glad that the climate agrees with you.'[41]

In November Addis was transferred to Hong Kong where he was to spend the next two and a half years living in the Bank Mess with ten or eleven other young men. Thomsett, who had preceded Addis, described life in Hong Kong:

> There are eight of us there [at Beaconsfield, the Bank mess] – Johnson, Coombs, MacTavish, St John, Hawkins, Gaskell, Stewart and myself. The house is one of the largest in the island, & nice & cool. We live like princes, in fact rather too well, for I find I am getting a 'belly' – I am on a current-a/c ledger, there are three of them, & the work is pretty easy just now.[42]

Obviously, even the lowest of the HSBC staff enjoyed a happy, carefree and luxurious life in Hong Kong. Addis formed close and lasting friendships, both with men his own age and with his superiors, namely Thomas Jackson, the Chief Manager of the Bank. Jackson and his wife took the young bank clerks under their wing, treating them more like sons than employees.[43] One of the most able managers in the Bank's history, Jackson set a high example for the new recruits to follow. Addis simply idolised him.[44]

The other Bank officer most influential in Addis's career was Ewen Cameron, the Manager of the Shanghai Branch and later, of the London Branch of the HSBC. Addis was later to describe himself as Ewen Cameron's heir, in the bequest of securing for the Bank 'a paramount position in the London market in respect of the finance of China'.[45] He credited Cameron with several key appointments in his banking career.[46]

Life in Hong Kong was anything but dull. Addis described it to his mother: 'Gaieties continue apace. We are living at high pressure. I begin Chinese at seven every morning except on Tuesdays – mail days – when I start work in the office before seven.'[47] Although Addis does not describe his duties at work, other accounts suggest that they may have involved such mundane activities as overseeing the weighing of silver bars, or counting old bank notes. One former employee recalled being:

> shown into this big cage where there were about, I suppose, fifteen other juniors who had been in Hong Kong probably a year or more . . . you sat down there, and you counted old notes which were going to be destroyed, and as you counted them, the fleas and the bugs and other things like that jumped off and onto you. It was a very nice introduction to banking in Hong Kong![48]

An incessant round of parties occupied the evenings.

One of Addis's most treasured activities was the Chinese Reading Club. He described the President, Dr Robert Chalmers (who had been a missionary in China for over thirty years) as 'one of the greatest living sinologues':

> We meet every Tuesday night at 9 o'clock at Chalmers' house and there seated round a large table with paper and pencil beside us, while the centre of the table is littered with dictionaries and the works of different authorities . . . I enjoy it very much . . . It does one good after days of small talk and small things to breathe even for so short a time a loftier and purer atmosphere.[49]

As the above comment suggests, Addis was disturbed by the materialism which dominated European society in East Asia. He observed to his mother: 'I sometimes think we Bankers are like Doctors – we always see people at their worst . . . Money has a dreadfully hardening influence on most of us.'[50] Addis hated the way Europeans treated the Chinese – simply as a source of profit – and, recognising that the European presence in China had been achieved by force, he felt shame at the memory of his government's past actions. In a letter to his sister (written later from Peking) he described the beauty of the Western Hills, and next observed:

> Not thirty years ago the Christian nation of England planted her guns on that little hill to the West and shelled and shattered the antique towers, the gorgeous palaces, till not one stone stood upon another. I do not think that one of us can look down on the scene, lovely in desolation, without a bitter feeling of shame, that we should ever have had a hand in an act so shameless, so barbarous. No wonder they hate us. They tell a crying child as I pass that if he does not be quiet the 'foreign devil' will come to him.[51]

From this time on, Addis aimed at making the British influence beneficial to China.

Unlike many of his contemporaries the young banker interested himself in Chinese culture and beliefs. Part of his sensitivity to the Chinese may have been produced by his Chinese teacher, An Yeung-wai, whom he deeply revered. He described An Yeung-wai:

> For two years morning after morning we have sat together teacher and scholar. An old man with huge goggle spectacles but as keen in his wits as many a younger . . . He always spends the whole of Sunday forenoon with me. He comes after breakfast and with tobacco and those little Chinese covered cups of tea we talk over our different customs or he tells me story after story of China's old heroes and I sometimes tell him a story of our Land – he listens rather incredulously, though too polite to express his incredulity – and somehow I think we always finish up with the belief strengthened that folks with [pig] tails are very like those without and that a strong chain of human sympathy binds together the children of one father.[52]

When Addis was appointed to Peking, An Yeung-wai gave him a portrait of himself which Addis kept on his wall for the rest of his life.[53]

This conviction that despite their cultural differences, all people shared common characteristics and needs would serve as the foundation of Addis's philosophy throughout his life. He was to remain open-minded, unhampered by the petty prejudices and rejecting the racial feelings characteristic of most Europeans in China. Addis's interest in religious questions was quite typical of his times. He wrote to his sister: 'perhaps you agree with John Bright, as I do, that religion and politics are the only things worth talking about'. Addis believed that all great religions shared a common truth, and as for practice, he loved to quote the verse from the *Book of Micah* in the Old Testament: 'And what doth the Lord require of thee, but to do justice, love mercy and walk humbly with the Lord' as the 'perfect ideal of religion'.[54]

Nowhere does the contrast between high-minded Victorian morality and degrading colonial exploitation become more obvious than in the area of sexual relations. While the evidence is not conclusive, what there is suggests that as a young bachelor Addis behaved according to the accepted beliefs of the day which reflected the well-known double standard of the Victorian era – men were permitted premarital sex while women were to be kept virginal. Although there is much scholarly disagreement on this subject of Victorian mores,[55] there is little doubt that since the young bachelors of the Bank were forbidden to marry until after their second tour, it was taken for granted that they would indulge their desires through relations with prostitutes or 'native women'. For instance, in a comment obviously not meant for outsiders' eyes, Leathe wrote to Addis: 'You must have settled down by this time, with half a dozen black women as bed warmers, how do you like them?'[56] Unfortunately, if Addis answered this letter, it was not preserved. However another letter, from a friend who followed Addis to Singapore, suggests that Addis had advised him to stay away from the prostitutes.[57]

What Victorian morality strictly prohibited was sexual contact with young, unmarried women of one's own class, who were to be kept pure and totally ignorant of sex until marriage. Insight into contemporary male attitudes regarding sexual practice are reflected in a letter which Fleming wrote to Addis from Port Elizabeth, South Africa: 'I'm glad to hear that you have got some decent women in your "City". Here the commodity is scarce, hardly to be had at any price, all the best women get snatched up as Keeps of Kaffirs & Hottentots, bastards of all shades & low Dutch "f'lows". There are any quantity at prices ranging pretty much like those we used to have "plaisir" from at home.'[58] Addis's letters and diary comments lead one to suspect that while he may have indulged in such practices, he was never comfortable with his behaviour.[59] Given the contrast between what was preached and what was practised in Victorian society, it is hardly surprising that Addis's correspondence reveals two different aspects of his personality, the one side highly disciplined and idealistic (the aspect which came to dominate his adulthood) the other reflecting the more physical, pleasure-loving and self-indulgent concerns characteristic of youth.

The friendship with Lieutenant Dudley Mills (who was stationed in Hong Kong with the Royal Engineers) emphasised the more intellectual interests. Mills came from an English family which had been less shaped by religion and was better supplied with worldly goods.[60] Mills was a thinker rather than a doer. But the two young men shared similar interests in literature, politics and Chinese culture. Mills, who was a geographer, persuaded Addis to take trips with him exploring the Chinese countryside, visiting temples and learning more about the customs and beliefs of the Chinese people.[61] When Mills returned home, he frankly told his countrymen that the Chinese were not slow to understand the importance of new ideas (as the English liked to believe) but rather feared 'the foreign bondholder, the concessions he endeavoured to obtain, and the rights on which he would insist if he got them'.[62] This rare type of intellectual honesty suggests one of the reasons why Addis valued Mills's friendship.

After Addis was transfered to Peking, he and Mills began a correspondence which continued over the next forty years. In these lengthy letters, the two young bachelors confided their dreams, ambitions, motives, doubts and disappointments. When Mills was about to leave Hong Kong, Addis wrote to him: 'It is possible that what interest I had in China might have died a natural death but for your sympathy and the infection of your energy.'[63] Mills, who early perceived the important future role which Addis would play in world affairs, became a self-appointed recorder of Addis's career, saving all the letters and news clippings, helping him to get his first articles published and criticising drafts of speeches and articles.[64] Because the two friends trusted and respected each other so completely, they discussed all manner of questions and concerns without pretence. Surprisingly, they were able to preserve their close relationship despite long-term separation and the wide divergence of their careers.

As is often true in friendships formed during the early years, the frankness, earnestness and lack of pretence characteristic of youth continued to shape this special relationship even after both men had experienced the depressing realities and disappointments which inevitably accompany maturity and the responsibilities of career and family. Mills would dare to say things to Addis that few others would dream of, and did not hesitate to question overstatement or challenge possible hypocrisy.[65] Since Mills lacked the drive and ambition of his friend, and occupied no public position, he remained the perfect confidant, content to serve as a sounding-board or critic for Addis's ideas. Much later he wrote to Addis: 'I have had no difficulty [finding my level] as my ambitions were very limited – In fact I have always been keener to *understand* the world than to make any impression on it.'[66] Not so his good friend Charles Addis.

PEKING, 1886–8

In 1886 Addis's knowledge of Chinese led to his appointment as Acting Agent in Peking.[67] Naturally excited and thrilled by the honour and the opportunity which the appointment offered, Addis reported to his father that it 'lifted him over thirty of his seniors'.[68] The 25-year-old Scotsman set out from Hong Kong in May, sailing north to the Treaty port of Tientsin and then travelling the last eighty miles inland by pony – a long and dusty trip. He described his arrival:

At three in the afternoon I drew reins under the walls of Peking. What a thrill of wonder and delight went through me as I saw for the first time these frowning walls and decaying towers. Under the Chinese city wall we rode and down by the moat to the gate that leads into the tartar City where the Imperial pleasure parks were green with Spring and the palace roofs flashed yellow in the sun.[69]

The Peking years proved to be of seminal importance to Addis's future career. Here he gained the diplomatic experience which was to serve him so well in the future and became acquainted with the Chinese and British officials who were to dominate the scene for years to come. He described the Inspector General (IG), Hart, as 'more affable than I was led to believe' and the British diplomat, John Jordan (then a student interpreter in the legation) as 'a cultured and clever man with a capital foundation of strong common sense'.[70] Situated on the northern edge of the Empire, the capital of Peking was the seat of the Hsien-feng Emperor, the 'Son of Heaven', and his mother, the Regent Empress Dowager, Ts'u Hsi. Only a few outstanding officials, such as the Viceroys Li Hung-chang and Tseng Kuo-fan, recognised the threat which the Europeans represented and the urgency of adopting Western technology.[71] The Ch'ing court no doubt expected to deal with these latest foreigners as had its predecessors – obtain whatever knowledge they had but keep them on the periphery. Segregated behind walls in the 'forbidden city', the imperial court followed the centuries-old practice of isolating the barbarian foreigners, allowing them to have their own institutions, and refusing to recognise the necessity for change.

Since Peking was not a treaty port, the foreign community was small, including mostly diplomats, missionaries and officials of the Maritime Customs. As Englishmen had done in cities throughout the empire, they established their own institutions and way of life – churches, racecourse, dinner parties. Since contact between most Westerners and the Chinese was limited to contact with Chinese servants, the foreigners remained ignorant of the country or people in whose midst they dwelt.[72]

Officially the Hongkong and Shanghai Bank had no legal right to have an agency in Peking, since the Ch'ing rulers had refused to open Peking to foreign commerce. But Addis predicted:

> If we can gradually get in with the Chinese by means of loans and such like business, make ourselves indispensable to them and ultimately be permitted to do business openly we of course shall be first in the field and a magnificent field it will be when the resources of this great country in the North are thrown open.[73]

The above comment reveals a keen awareness of opportunity, both for the Bank and for himself. Although Addis admitted that there was not much business in Peking at the moment, he predicted: 'In the next few years if China begins to open up there will be a great future for Peking. If I can get a grip of things now, my foot will be on the bottom rung.'[74] Clearly this was an ambitious and self-confident young man, keenly aware of the significance of Chinese developments and determined to have a role in shaping them. His ideas reflected assumptions which were shared by the Bank's competitors, Jardine Matheson & Co., one of the oldest and most powerful British trading companies in China, which for decades had been providing funds to various Chinese officials in order to gain influence and favour thereby.[75]

While at first the inexperienced young Bank Agent felt somewhat overwhelmed by his new position of responsibility and authority, before long he revelled in it. Fortunately, a saving sense of humour prevented Addis from becoming unbearably impressed with his own importance. Only a few days after he had established his office in the back room of a small hotel, where the Agency would escape detection, Addis described his position: 'Well, here I am in my little office, monarch of all I survey, despatching and receiving telegrams, issuing drafts, etc. – alone in Peking, except for my Chinese staff.'[76] To a friend in Hong Kong, he confessed:

> It tries my gravity to sit back in my chair and look wise while I discuss business with some man who is old enough to be my father. However, I talk learnedly about the market fluctuations and the future price of silver and as I am the only banker here, there is no one to contradict me. Then I get daily telegrams of the London and Shanghai market so that I know more than most of them.[77]

Addis interpreted his primary purpose in Peking to be political – to gather information and establish contacts with Chinese officials. He wrote to Alexander Leith, the HSBC Agent in Tientsin who was his immediate superior and who earlier had negotiated loans to the monarchy: 'I take it I am sent here as a sort of watchdog, a picker-up of unconsidered trifles, and my field must be almost entirely in social intercourse.'[78] From the beginning Addis established close relations with the British Legation which demonstrated its willingness to cooperate with the Bank by secretly sending Addis translations of their documents.[79]

For the first twenty years of its operations in China, British interests had dominated the field of Chinese investment but by the time Addis arrived in Peking (in 1886) competition among international banking groups was beginning to threaten Britain's special position, making diplomatic support of increased importance. Replying to an enquiry from Cameron in Shanghai about a possible loan of taels 300 000, Addis explained:

> O'Conor of the Legation would prefer to wait a day or two; [he] wants [the] Chinese to act spontaneously. All loans (ordinarily all) take their rise in Peking. Now that we have German syndicates and French Syndicates & a host of others eager to snatch up business it is of immense importance to acquire daily information. You can only get that from the Chinese. Besides my boy I have ten Chinese in my employ, none of whom speak a word of English except one shroff who speaks a little pidgin English.[80]

Thus Addis employed Chinese to keep him informed of Ch'ing politics, whose complexity and secrecy continued to mystify Europeans. Addis described the Chinese method: 'They are fond of waiting until such matters [as loans] are extorted from them, as if they were favours.'[81] In addition to the Chinese whom he employed, Addis courted good relations with local bankers and compradors, accepting their invitations to dinner and returning their hospitality. Some years later Addis recalled that the Marquis Tseng (Tseng Chi-tse, son of Tseng Kuo-fan) had 'dined at my table, the only private table, I believe, he ever sat at in China'.[82] The benefit of these personal contacts was demonstrated that autumn when a loan for taels 700 000 was completed. Despite his success Addis had found the complicated manoeuvres and lengthy negotiations very frustrating and was relieved when they were finished.

One additional responsibility of the Acting Agent was to purchase gold for the Bank. He informed his brother: 'We do a fair trade in gold and have been a source of excellent business to many of the Chinese and so we are winked at and if we can only hold on long enough we become an established fact and far too much a necessity to be packed off.'[83] After his first six months in Peking, Addis proudly reported that Bank business had more than doubled and could even boast of a small profit.

As the Acting Agent of the HSBC in Peking, Addis fulfilled several functions. By establishing good personal relations with Ch'ing officials, he was encouraging them to borrow through his bank. These loans were exceedingly profitable because they were heavily discounted. By buying gold Addis was obtaining the metal which was used as a basis for British currency. Most important, he was learning the great profits to be made in the field of international exchange. Since trade in China was largely done in silver, those who knew the relations between the various types of taels, as well as the relationship between gold and silver on the world market, could be very useful to both banks and governments.

Nor was Addis's success in Peking limited to business matters. The handsome young bachelor found himself much sought after in the elaborate round of teas and dinners which characterised social life among the foreigners in Peking. In the social world, where women's preferences mattered, Addis's attractive physical appearance and outgoing personality provided important advantages. Tall, curly-haired, possessing sparkling blue eyes, Addis appealed to both the matrons and the young ladies in the Peking Western community.

Then, too, because he had been close to his sisters, mother and aunts, he was not in the least ill-at-ease among women. Thus the hostesses in the diplomatic community were delighted to include him in their dinner parties and planned activities, especially when they found that he could sing, recite poetry and would participate in theatrical productions. In addition to these activities, Addis enjoyed riding, tennis and hockey.

Since the foreign community was small and isolated for several months in the winter, its members could hardly avoid each other. And so the normal social barriers, which in England would have prevented the young banker from being received by State Ministers, were absent. Addis soon became acquainted with many important people informally, thereby gaining experience and insights into human behaviour as well as self-confidence in diplomatic society. As one might predict in such a situation, there was no such thing as a secret – gossip and rumour ran rampant; flirtations and romance eased the boredom of the long, cold, winter months. Blessed with high intelligence, great energy and considerable leisure, Addis took an interest in everything around him in the Ch'ing capital city. His natural curiosity, combined with good writing ability, made him an ideal reporter, as Alexander Michie, the editor of *The Chinese Times* (an English language newspaper published by Jardine, Matheson & Co. in Tientsin) sensed upon meeting Addis for the first time.[84]

Michie asked Addis to send him some news of Peking. When Addis complied with a long letter describing recent social events. Michie proceeded to publish the whole letter anonymously, under the title of 'Peking Notes'.[85] Flattered to see his words in print, the fledgling author continued to supply material to Michie, reporting on both the foreign community's activities and on Chinese politics, customs and beliefs.

Michie, a Scotsman who could boast of long experience in Chinese politics, acted as a special agent for Jardine Matheson's in negotiating loans.[86] Michie encouraged Addis to write, commenting: 'By exercising your pen quietly in this way you will gradually gather strength, confidence and concentration which is all you want.' Addis, who greatly admired Michie, described the editor to his mother: 'I have seldom met anyone so wise or so full of interest as he.'[87] What began as a father–son relationship gradually developed into a close friendship between equals, as each man learned from the other.

Since Addis was involved in a great variety of activities in Peking, he was able to supply first-hand accounts and news in abundance, making frank comments, safe in his anonymity. He found that he enjoyed writing, demonstrating a sharp eye for detail and a keen sense of humour, often poking fun at both social pretensions and religious bigotry, as well as assembling information formerly unknown to the Europeans about Chinese beliefs and practices. Some of the latter included articles on 'Animal Worship', 'Chinese Bathhouses', and 'Recycling the Soul'.[88]

Michie, who was delighted with his new protégé, wrote: 'It seems to me that we are only now beginning to make honest observations of the Chinese.' And somewhat later, 'I have several times noticed a remarkable coincidence between your ideas and my own.' Shortly thereafter Michie wrote: 'as I grow older I am more & more conscious of a sort of Disraeli-like faith in young men'. He observed that Addis's writings 'all possess one special charm which I told you of long ago – genuineness & sincerity'.[89] By June Michie was employing Addis as a critic as well as a reporter, seeking his advice on other articles and his comments on books.[90] The more Addis learned about the beliefs and practices of his host-culture, the more did he admire the Chinese. Writing to his Aunt Mansfield he said that he would trust the Chinaman over his European counterpart.[91]

Since Addis served as both society editor and sports reporter, his accounts provide a good view of what daily life in Peking was like for the European. In a description of the fancy-dress ball, Addis outdid himself, writing several paragraphs describing the various outfits, the dancing, the food, the decorations. Addis readily admitted that he had a tendency to let his words run away with him, and tried to curb it. His friends teased him about his verbosity and preachiness and one acquaintance, J. O. P. Bland, referred to him irreverently as the 'Light of Asia'.[92]

Undaunted, Addis also used the *Chinese Times* as a means for advocating change. Hardly had he become a member of the Peking Oriental Society than he began criticising its proceedings. In one article he criticised a recent presentation on the 'Evolution of the Chinese Language' as a topic undeserving of attention:

Now, if ever, when the air is thick with rumours of railways and postal unions and the general advance of China on the path of Western progress, now, if ever, when we believe the oyster is about to open, is the time to acquaint ourselves with the present throbbing life of the empire.[93]

While Addis's comments demonstrate the impatience and intoler-
ance typical of youth, they also revealed larger concerns than were
characteristic of most young bank clerks. Addis helped to organise a
Young Men's Literary and Debating Society which provided him
with another forum for his opinions. In his first speech, 'Our
Intercourse with China', he explored the relations between merchants
and consular officials in China.[94]

Another area of interest (which may have been sparked by Michie)
was the relationship between the foreign missionaries in China and
the other Europeans. Michie wrote to Addis that he desired a
cooperative relationship with the missionaries, who were generally
disliked and shunned by the European merchants and diplomatic
personnel, and he encouraged Addis to write a series of articles, saying
that he thought the *Quarterly Review* might publish such a series.
Michie advised him to avoid the fault of 'trying to be too deep . . .
Our business is to be superficial, but true.'[95] Addis explained to Mills
why he had undertaken the series on the 'The Missions of Peking',
observing that 'the ignorance of missionaries and their work shown
by foreign residents in China is deplorable and I should be glad if
any feeble efforts of mine could enlighten their darkness'.[96] Throughout the summer of 1887 the *Chinese Times* ran Addis's articles
describing each Church Denomination's work in China.[97] To his
clergyman-father Addis explained the reason why missionaries were
hated, writing: 'What I have seen in the South holds true in Peking.
They have the best houses in town and the finest temples in the
country. It seems to me something very much like embezzlement.'[98]

During his first summer in Peking Addis had spent several hours a
day studying Chinese but once the autumn social season got under
way, with its endless round of dinners, balls and athletic events, the
study of Chinese received less and less attention. Addis complained
to his brother George: 'if Cameron really wants to have men to be
of use in Chinese he must treat us as students and give us a clear two
years (like the Legation students) to do nothing but work at Chinese'.[99]
One suspects that Addis simply found too many other subjects more
attractive, that he was too extroverted to spend his days in study. He
was certainly a joiner, belonging to the Royal Asiatic Society, the
Tract Society and the hockey team, and in addition taking a role in
the local dramatic productions.

Before long Addis began to experience doubts about his various
activities. He feared that his journalism might cause him to 'drift
away too much from his career as a banker'. At the same time he

criticised the diplomatic aspects of his work, confiding to his sister: 'After 18 months in Peking I begin to think that diplomacy is only another name for lying.'[100] He described himself as tired of the 'unreality and worldliness' of the diplomatic life and exhausted by the demands of entertaining constant visitors. To his good friend, James Stewart Lockhart, he confided:

> My position here is certainly a unique one. I am in the crowd and yet not of it, and no doubt my independent position brings me a lot of confidences from all sides which no one else enjoys to such an extent. But at what a cost! I feel as if I had become a machine which someone inside me was working: as if I had a dual personality . . . the tea duties; opium; the duties of consular officers in connexion with trade; the establishment of a national bank; a mint: a note issue: a post office: contracts: imperial loans: loans to departments & sub-departments: the telegraph amalgamation: syndicates – oh! the hours . . . I entered upon diplomacy with a zest. I succeeded in it (excuse the arrogance. I am writing you frankly) and the fruit has turned to ashes in my mouth, I am weighted down with the utter futility of it.[101]

Lockhart, who had earlier advised him against taking two years off to study Chinese, reminded him again: 'Be careful to make Banking come first in all things and your love for Chinese second.'[102]

Regardless of these doubts and uncertainties, the fact was that during these first few months in Peking Addis had laid the foundations for a successful career as an international financier, gaining experience in the complicated field of international exchange which was to be of lasting importance.[103] Although he complained and expressed misgivings, he was well-aware of the significance of what he had accomplished. Furthermore, the first year had produced a sobering effect on the Acting Agent, who admitted that 'increased responsibility etc. has taken a good deal of the wild spirit out of me'.[104]

A new distraction developed when Addis found himself more and more involved with a pretty young woman, the daughter of the American Minister in Peking, Col. Charles Denby.[105] Addis described Miss Harriet Denby, as 'very fair, medium height, speaks with a drawl rather than a twang, exquisite hands and feet, waltzes divinely, has a sweet, innocent expression, and is extremely natural and sensible withal'.[106] Addis suspected the ladies of the diplomatic community of plotting to marry him off to Miss Denby. But while he appreciated her intelligence, beauty, charm and character, Addis did not think he was really in love with Miss Denby. Although sorely tempted, he did not allow the relationship to become too intimate, despite many opportunities and much encouragement from the young lady, which demonstrated a remarkable degree of self-control on his part.

After much agonising and soul-searching Addis determined to wait until after his first leave home before considering a proposal of marriage. Clearly it was with some regret and misgivings that, following their last evening together, Addis sadly confided to his diary: 'Well, it is all over. What a pleasant friendship it has been. But only friendship? I hardly dare to answer that question now. And yet I did rightly. I am glad I am free. A year at home will let me know better.'[107] Both Addis and Miss Denby left Peking in the spring of 1888. He journeyed home by way of Australia, where he visited his sister Etta and her family, and then travelled across the United States, stopping in Logansport, Indiana, to see Miss Denby. With relief he definitely decided that she was not the one he wished to marry. Shortly thereafter, she wrote to him that she was engaged to a Mr Wilkes, whom Addis had met in Logansport.[108]

Before leaving China for his year at home, Addis had talked over his future with both Michie and Cameron. Michie advised Addis to set his goal on the London Managership and wrote to one of the London officers that Addis was 'thrown away in Peking'. Michie seems to have recognised that Addis could aim at even greater heights than the Chief Managership in Hong Kong – that the greatest opportunities existed in the London office, whose Senior Manager made the decisions and reaped the profits from China loans.[109] As parting counsel to Addis the editor predicted good fortune and success for Addis, but cautioned him to 'Seek it seriously but never worship it. Make it your slave, never your master.'[110]

TIENTSIN, PEKING, SHANGHAI, 1888–91

Encouraged by Michie's advice Addis decided not to spend his entire leave visiting friends and family. While in Scotland he wrote an article on 'Railways in China' which he submitted for consideration to the *Contemporary Review*. Addis explained his motives to Mills, writing that if the article were to be published, 'it would of course be a great puff for me at an important time as it would be read in China just prior to my name coming up there for a new appointment'. The next day he added: 'I confess the object is not a high one – self advertisement. But it is an honest motive at any rate. In a less degree my object is to arouse the British trader.'[111] This last comment reflected the fear of many Britishers that they might lose their position of predominant influence in China in the anticipated competition of other governments to gain railroad concessions from the Ch'ing.

In seeking contracts to build Chinese railways the Europeans had two motives: profits and political expansion. Since the Franco-Prussian War of 1870–1, both Chinese and European leaders recognised the military potential of railways – that their construction could serve as a stepping-stone to gaining political control.[112] In China the leaders of the 'self-strengthening movement' argued that only if the government built its own railways would it be able to 'resist humiliation' from the foreigners.[113] In addition, Addis predicted that railways would produce 'an entire reform in the Chinese currency', and warned his countrymen that French and German businessmen were better acquainted with Chinese language and culture.[114]

Unfortunately for Addis, the publication of the article did not have the desired effect – that is, it did not assure his promotion. When Addis returned to China in the spring of 1889 he found that the Bank's leadership had shifted to F. de Bovis and G. E. Noble, neither of whom seemed to appreciate his abilities. Or perhaps they feared the potential rivalry of this energetic, self-confident and articulate young author. In any event, Addis did not secure the kind of assignment for which he had hoped. Appointed to Tientsin, the Treaty Port which served as the sea outlet for Peking, he described the daily routine:

> I rise at 6.30 a.m. My Chinese teacher comes at 7 and we read till 8 or a little after. Then breakfast and a smoke and perhaps a stroll to the shipping office to see what steamers have come in but more generally to the office at once, say 9 a.m. Tiffin at 12.30 and office again till 5. Then a ride or tennis and a chat at the club or a visit and so home to change for dinner. At night and on Sundays are the only chances for reading. One must read the newspapers Chinese and Home, a banker cannot afford to be ignorant of anything transpiring either at home or abroad which may affect his business – and what does not?[115]

After his experiences in Hong Kong and Peking, Addis found Tientsin dull and confining. Although bored, he did not lose his enthusiasm or optimism concerning China's future. The news that H. Hewat, the Agent in Peking, was feeling 'seedy' and needed someone to take his place for a while, came as a welcome opportunity for Addis to return to the Capital. During July and August, he was able to renew his old friendships with former associate, Jordan, who was still serving in the Peking legation, as well as meet new officials, such as Francis Aglen who would succeed Hart as IG.[116] Regardless of the fact that Peking was hot and dry, there were stimulating people with whom to talk and week-ends could be spent in the beloved Western Hills, where since the 1860s the foreigners migrated every summer to escape Peking's heat and dust.[117] There they rented Buddhist temples, using them as summer homes, picnicked and played games, oblivious to their Chinese hosts and the resentment of their presence.

Although Addis had been bored in Tientsin, he had not wasted his time there. He read extensively, wrote a regular column called 'Tientsin Notes' for the *Chinese Times* and succeeded in having two leading articles published. These articles dealt with the two subjects which would form his major interests for the rest of his life – international exchange and Chinese railways.[118]

Addis began the article on exchange by explaining that 'the merchant who most skilfully collates his facts and infers from them the probable future of exchange is – *ceteris paribus* the most likely to be successful'.[119] He continued that the subject of exchange was of interest to merchants only as long as the relative value of silver and gold remained stable, but when these began to fluctuate, then the topic of exchange became a matter of concern to all Europeans living in China, who saw their salaries which had been quoted in silver, suddenly depreciated with the decline of that metal in relation to gold.

Addis blamed governments for this situation because they interfered with the laws of political economy: 'You may drive political economy out at the door but it will enter again by the window.' He traced the monetary history of the various world governments, placing most of the blame on the United States and its excessive coinage of silver:

As long as there is this coquetting with Government intervention, as long as men neglect the natural laws of supply and demand and look to extraneous factors for the establishment of a non-natural ratio between the metals, just so long will the day of deliverance be delayed. The laws of political economy will not cease to act because they are ignored.[120]

In this article Addis clearly identified himself with the teachings of the classical economists, Adam Smith and John Stuart Mill. He observed that the chief evil was not the low price of silver but its instability: 'Fluctuating prices and unstable exchanges impair credit and paralyse all trade.' This clear and frank expression of his views showed Addis's commitment to the principle of free trade and suspicion of governments' attempts to regulate currency.

The article on railways discussed the reasons why Viceroy Chang Chih-tung's proposal for a railway from Peking to Hankow had been stillborn, pointing out the great difficulties in the construction of such a line, while predicting that eventually '"the iron horse" will run all the way between Peking and Canton'. Thus Addis drew his contemporaries' attention to two of the chief issues which would dominate East Asian affairs over the next half-century – international exchange and railways.

While in Tientsin Addis continued his friendship with Michie who wrote to him: 'It is a source of unfailing pleasure to me to think of the good you are destined to do in the world with your fine constitution, physical and mental, and capacities far above the common'.[121] Michie introduced Addis to Professor Alexander Williamson, a Scot who had founded the Book and Tract Society for China which later developed into the Society for the Diffusion of Christian and General Knowledge among the Chinese (SDCGK).[122] Michie's and Dr Williamson's liberal approach towards religious questions expanded Addis's horizons, helped him to escape the prejudice of the merchant or the narrowness of the Calvinist tradition. To missionaries Addis stressed the need for Westerners to understand China, confidently stating to one acquaintance: 'We don't want the Church of Scotland here – we want the Church of China. And we shall have it.'[123] In addition, Addis welcomed religious controversy, commenting that controversy produced discussion and 'we all want more light'.[124]

That autumn, Addis learned with great relief that he was to be named Corresponding Clerk in the Shanghai office. The International Settlement in Shanghai resembled a British city with its large European-style buildings along the Bund or waterfront, its own governing council, taxes, parks and gardens, clubs, racecourse and policemen. The policemen were Sikhs, brought by the British from India. Here Addis found an opportunity to pursue all his interests, employ to the full his energies and talent. Almost immediately be became a director of the SDCGK, and the Secretary of the Shanghai Library. He wrote Mills: 'I like meddling with books and to control such a big library takes my fancy.'[125] Out of a sense of duty he also joined the Shanghai Volunteers. Writing to thank Addis for the syllabus from the Literary and Debating Society, Michie commented: 'It is truly a great thing to wean Shanghai from its dinners and its conversations, from whores and horses, which was really about all I ever heard among my contemporaries.'[126]

An important new experience was public speaking. In May 1890, Addis debated the topic 'On Educating the Chinese' for the Shanghai Literary and Debating Society. Addis argued that it was the duty and obligation of the International Settlement to provide education for Chinese children. He reminded his audience: 'We claim to point the way to a higher civilisation and to do that there is but one way – education.' As to the claim that Europeans should not interfere with the Chinese, Addis dismissed this argument with characteristic candour: 'Not interfere? Why, what is the whole history of our intercourse with China but one long succession of interferences?'[127] Describing the debate to Mills, Addis expressed surprise at how much he enjoyed addressing several hundred people:

> I spoke rapidly for a little over half an hour. It was a very delightful sensation. There was not a trace of nervousness. I felt the people were interested. I had them in hand from the start and I do not think their interest flagged for a moment.[128]

This desire to influence others, essentially a missionary impulse without the religious dogma, formed a major component of Addis's personality. In Shanghai Addis began writing an anonymous weekly column called 'Quidnunc' for the *China Herald* and the *North China Daily News* dealing with current events and activities. Occasionally he wrote articles of more substance as well, such as an article on the 'Death of Tseng' in the *North China Daily News*. At the same time Addis continued to worry lest his interest in journalism might interfere with his career in banking. In a long letter to Mills, Addis explained his ambition to 'some day be Manager' and stated that: 'to do anything now which might impair my future usefulness, nay, to neglect anything which might increase my capacity for being useful is therefore a sin'.[129] In a reassuring letter Mills replied that the 'Quidnunc' column could do no harm but the public interest questions were more productive and went on to observe:

The fact is you and I are priggish and pedantic – you are in addition able, influential etc., . . . but we are both inclined to be didactic and priggish – this is to some extent unavoidable with self-conscious self-analyzing people.[130]

Although Addis enjoyed the busy and stimulating environment which Shanghai afforded, he was not happy with the slow progress he was making in his banking career. Understandably he was very tempted to make a change when two different firms offered him positions.[131] But first he sought the advice of his brother George, explaining that Jackson and Cameron had encouraged him to expect his own agency in five years but the new leadership had returned to the seniority system. 'As things go now I shall be lucky if I am made accountant within 5 years. And then my pay is only $300. The best years of my life will be gone before I can possibly be an Agent.'[132] On the other hand, Addis continued, he hated to 'throw over 8 years of service in a fine bank'.

The process by which Addis decided to stay with the Hongkong and Shanghai Banking Corporation revealed much about his character – in particular his straightforwardness and loyalty. First Addis decided to 'talk the whole thing over with our manager and asked his advice as a private friend.' He wrote of not wanting 'to desert the HSBC,' which suggests that in Addis's eyes, staying or leaving involved a question of loyalty. When considered in those terms, he chose to remain with the Bank. Given the nature of his future career, it is somewhat ironical that Addis gave as an additional reason for staying, his reluctance to become involved in the China loan business again: 'I am sick of those endless negotiations with Chinese which never come to anything.'[133] In time it would be such negotiations which would facilitate his emergence as a world-famous financier.

Despite his decision to remain with the Bank, Addis continued to be dissatisfied feeling that he was not being given a fair chance. 'We have Leith, Veitch, Cook, Rickett, Broadbent, Balfour, Oxley – all sticks, all tried and found wanting, but all young and likely to hang on for another quarter of a century.' Furthermore he felt overworked, and foresaw no likelihood of improvement:

Every year the claims of business seem to grow more exacting and one pursuit after another falls within the range of the tentacles which suck the life out of their victim or leave it so maimed that it is incapable of seizing its old food and dies of inanition. I see now that the time is not far distant when I shall never open a book at all from one Year's end to the other . . . I call it sweating.[134]

Nevertheless, despite these notes of desperation, Addis remained in the firm.

CALCUTTA AND RANGOON, 1891–3

When Addis received the news of his appointment to Calcutta as Acting Accountant he felt encouraged regarding his future with the Bank.[135] It took him three weeks to travel by boat from Hong Kong to Singapore and Penang and then by train from Diamond Harbour, which was 40 miles from Calcutta.[136] Although India was a completely new cultural experience he did not show the same interest in the language or customs which he had previously demonstrated in China. Perhaps it was that he was older or maybe the lack of language training explains his disinterest. He confided to Mills: 'I feel in a way that I have passed youth's grand climacteric and am settling down into the ordinary banker.'[137] In any event the Indian experience would not shape Addis's career in the way that China had, except to provide useful knowledge of Indian exchange. He wrote to Mills: 'The only plans I have are, first, to get hold of the way business is done in India . . . and second to get a talking acquaintance with Hindustanee.'[138]

Nor did Addis form friendships in India such as those which had enriched his early years in China. With the exception of J. R. M. Smith, his business associates remained just that. Perhaps because of the lack of other interests, Addis became enthusiastic about golf. When his sister Croppie suggested that his talents were wasted in business, Addis responded with the explanation that 'Business is the beefsteak of life; the *belles lettres* are its *sauce piquante.*' He continued with the remainder that 'Our life, our real life, is after all lived within', and quoted Pippa's first song: 'All service ranks the same with God.'[139]

While temporarily in charge of the office, Addis experienced one of the most frightening events which can occur in a bank – a run on the deposits, following the failure of the Oriental Bank. Addis wired to the London office, where Jackson, then Senior Manager, responded by wiring £100 000 sterling through Coutts.[140] It was a terrifying experience for the young banker. Even though the cashier kept saying: 'we must stop', Addis kept saying 'pay out'. Sheer nerve carried the day. The depositors became convinced that there was no cause for concern and the crisis was over. But Addis never forgot the episode, which to him demonstrated the importance of public confidence in banking.[141]

For a while, Addis carried almost total responsibility in the office, which naturally proved exhausting. He wrote to Croppie: 'My work day begins with the telegrams at half past six in the morning and ends with the last telegram at nine o'clock at night.'[142] Fortunately, a new accountant, Jeffrey, was sent out to share the load. Finding the heat in Calcutta almost unbearable, Addis was thankful to get leave in October 1892. He spent the next few weeks travelling, after which he was appointed acting agent in Rangoon.[143]

Addis described Chittagong on the Bay of Bengal: 'The customs officer had been out 27 years and was just as narrow-minded and ignorant as we all become in India.' He concluded: 'apparently civilization has always got to fight it out with barbarism and in the burdens thrown upon her. England pays the penalties of a high civilization.'[144] After a year's service in Rangoon, he finally attained the rank of full Agent 'after so many aching billets', but as had been the case in Calcutta, he found the assignment boring, since the major occupations were golf, whist and drinking.[145] One interesting new responsibility he assumed was to become the Treasurer of the Dufferin Hospital, where he regularly visited patients. In one particularly poignant account, he described the case of a German female patient who had been a prostitute. Recognising that she was close to death, Addis speculated about her history, picturing her as a victim of a vicious social system which was particularly cruel to women. This account reveals Addis's sensitivity and compassion, as well as his recognition of the iniquities of the male-dominated society of which he was a part.[146]

This was a very introspective period for Addis, a time when he discussed his views on women with both Mills and Croppie, challenging the Biblical view of marriage. He felt that St Paul held the married state 'lower and inferior to the celibate'. In his customary self-confident manner, Addis claimed that rather than raising the status of women, Christianity had actually 'been the chief instrument of asserting their inferiority' and that it was 'doing its best to accomplish the separation of the sexes'. He continued:

> women are our equals, different but equal; that far from degrading a man she is fitted in the highest place sense to draw out and cherish his inner life, to be in a very real sense his spiritual

comforter and sustainer; that marriage and not celibacy is the ideal state.[147]

After a discussion with the American doctor and empire-builder, E. H. Parker, on the practice of concubinage (Parker defended the practice), Addis wrote to Mills that he believed the custom was wrong because it allowed 'men generally an easy method of escaping their social obligations'.[148] In one unusually frank discussion with a friend from Peking, Addis wrote: 'I take it that a virgin has no more *inside* difficulty in maintaining his continence at 25 than at 15. For us now there is but one remedy, as far as I can see – marriage.'[149] He reported to Mills that 'during a recent period of depression I fell back on the Waverley Novels'. Later the same month he commented: 'Let us be something before we try to do anything. To influence young men is not our business. Our business is to be good men ourselves.' Discussing Browning and Wordsworth with Mills, he wrote: 'I prefer Pippa's other song: 'All service ranks the same with God-With God, whose puppets best and worst, Are we. There is no first nor last.'[150]

While to the modern reader Addis's seriousness and conscientiousness may ring false, and sound both hypocritical and most improbable, such idealism was not unusual for that era. The widespread belief in European racial superiority combined with the acceptance of Rudyard Kipling's concept of the 'white man's burden' to raise the heathen, remained virtually unquestioned and unchallenged assumptions in Western culture. Social Darwinism added the so-called scientific evidence for this belief in the survival of the fittest. The problem of course was the inability of most human beings to live according to the high standards which their religion preached, especially in colonial or semi-colonial situations, where power produced unrestrained privilege for white people. And so one concludes that compromises such as concubinage and prostitution flourished to bridge the gap between high ideals and lowly human nature.

Addis, who apparently had more difficulty than most young men in reconciling the contradictions between his high ideals and customary behaviour, was eager to marry a woman who would make it possible to live according to his ideals. Of course the most telling evidence of sincerity, the real demonstration as to how committed Addis was to the virtues he extolled, would be his behaviour over the next fifty years. For as he wrote later: 'we owe little to what people say, but much to what they are. One consistent life is a more potent influence for good than bushels of words.'[151]

The fact that Addis's close friends regarded him as exceptional is the most telling testimony to his high character at this stage in his life. That so many of them considered him their best friend, the one to whom they confided their innermost thoughts, speaks for his sincerity, sympathetic concern and trustworthiness. Moreover, his contemporaries as well as his superiors all seem to have recognised that he was an exceptional person, destined for greatness: not only Michie, Jackson and Cameron recognised the potential of the man, but also his own closest associates, such as Mills, Lockhart, Jamieson, Stewart, Sundius and Leith.[152] For instance, Leith wrote in 1893:

> I steadfastly believe your dialectic skill, combined as it is with a vast capacity for work & reading, will, if cultured, place you in some grand position some day. Often I doubt if you have chosen the best sphere of life, either for your own self-development (to say nil of advancement) or for the interest of our fellow men. Bunkum apart Addis! you are in many ways finely endowed for political life.[153]

By the end of his Burma assignment Addis had matured a great deal, had determined his goals and objectives. One of the most central of these was to find a wife. Travelling home by the Eastern route, Addis left Rangoon at the end of November, stopping at Calcutta, Aden, and continuing on through the Suez Canal, arrived at Charing Cross station on 16 December, in time to celebrate the Christmas season with his family. On 27 December he exclaimed: 'It is grand to be at home again.'[154]

COURTSHIP, MARRIAGE AND RETURN TO SHANGHAI

Early in January Addis attended a dinner-party at Saltcoats (a small seaside town near Glasgow) with his sister Croppie and her husband, the Rev. Robert Adamson, at the home of Provost McIsaac.[155] The Provost had two daughters, Annie and Eba, the latter of whom swept Addis off his feet. Afterwards he described Eba in his diary, saying that her 'pure beauty & manifest goodness melted my heart. She sang with marvellous truth & sweetness . . . I prayed that I might win her love but checked myself to pray I might be made worthy of it.'[156] The next day he noted: 'It is Eba I am thinking of all day. I can never be worthy of her. She is too pure, too good.'[157]

Soon Addis was 'Off to Glasgow at 4.37. I go to prove my soul. I know my path, etc., that is to say I go with the intention of seeing Eba and asking her to be my wife. And the result? – is with God.'[158] A week later, he dejectedly commented: 'I am making no progress whatever.' Eba met and exceeded Addis's highest standards and expectations. As the daughter of Provost McIsaac, Eba came from a well-to-do home, was educated and intelligent and had a mind of her own. Unfortunately it appeared that she had not been similarly smitten by the young banker from China. On 24 February, Addis complained: 'I have seen her 7 times but I never can be alone with her nor can I bring myself to say anything pointed.' Finally he decided to ask Eba's parents formally for permission 'to pay my addresses to Eba'. While the McIsaac's did not object, they said Eba must decide for herself.[159]

At last, on 7 March, Addis saw Eba alone and told her that he loved her. Unfortunately, Eba replied that she did not feel she could love him! Characteristically, Addis refused to give up. He begged for more time. After his initial rejection, he wrote her a passionate letter, both apologising for causing her pain but at the same time imploring her to give him a chance. Summoning Divine help, he argued:

> The strange sudden joy of love, that, after thirty years, burst so unexpectedly into my life could only (so it seemed clear to me) have come from God. The consequences were not in my hands. I refused even to consider them. I waited to be led . . . So far my path has been made plain to me, and yet, do what I will, my heart never ceases day and night to cry out for you. That may be denied me and the future be dark indeed; but one bright spot at least there will always be – my love for you . . . I confess I shrink from thus laying bare, even to you, motives sacred and personal to myself alone, but the respect due to you claims complete frankness.[160]

While Eba did not encourage her ardent suitor, Addis apparently had won the favour of her parents, for they invited him to join them for an Easter holiday in Jersey.[161] Once alone with Eba in Jersey, Addis made rapid progress. On 26 March he reported to his diary: 'No spooning or anything approaching it & yet alone so much! How will it end?' In less than two weeks time he rejoiced: 'Eba promised tonight at 10.10 p.m. to be my wife! Victory at last!! . . . Thank God!'[162] And two weeks after that he exclaims: 'Never have I known such happiness!'[163]

And so they were married on 6 June 1894, establishing a union which was to last over fifty years and never lose its lustre. However, once having won his beloved, Addis resumed his interests in things more rational. The summer was spent in relaxation and travel, but by October the young couple set off for Shanghai, where Addis had been appointed sub-manager. Delighted by the appointment, he wrote that he liked Shanghai better than any other place in the East.[164] The newly-weds stayed temporarily at the Astor House Hotel until their house was ready for them at 26 The Bund. Although only two rooms were furnished, the whole was lit by electric lights.[165] At the end of the year Addis exclaimed as if in wonder: 'And we are still happy.'[166]

In Shanghai Addis quickly resumed his membership of such organisations as the SDCGK (of which he became a Director) and the Shanghai Library. His old friend, the famous missionary Timothy Richards, welcomed him back with the kind comment that 'you invariably leave each place better than you found it'.[167] By January 1895 Addis was once again writing for the *North China Daily News*, reporting that he had sent his first 'leader' in.

A far more exciting event was the birth of the young couple's first child – a boy, whom, in correct Scottish tradition, they named Thomas after Addis's father. With excusable pride, the new mother exclaimed: 'Our son is beautiful, like a delicate shell. His eyes are a deep violet colour, and his hair looks rather dark, and lies in a ringlet on his forhead.'[168] When Addis was sent to Peking, Eba noted: 'It is our first separation only for a night. I hope it will be our last.'[169] While Addis was in Peking he began a practice which he continued for the rest of their married life – that of writing Eba every day when they were separated.[170] Despite her hopes, Eba's diary entry a few months later gave evidence of what lay ahead for the couple: 'Charlie is having a very busy and exciting time in the office and things are going well. They and the German Bank divide the New Chinese loan between them.'[171]

The new loan to which Eba referred was the second indemnity loan after the Sino-Japanese War. As Addis became involved in these negotiations, he no longer had time for self-analysis or literary exploration; he was hard-pressed even to find time for his family. For China was undergoing enormous changes which Addis was determined to influence.

2 Widening Horizons, 1895–1904

'You grow to be the Bagehot of the Far East.' — M. Stewart to Addis, 1902

'The ultimate basis of all economic conceptions is ethical.' — Addis, 1903

The assignment to negotiate the indemnity loans (which the foreign banks issued to enable China to pay Japan after the Sino-Japanese War) placed Addis at the heart of the international competition for empire. As he observed the competition among the Powers to gain control of China and the way which this competition affected China and world politics, Addis became convinced that only international cooperation could prevent war. He recognised that British interests could best be served by preserving China as a single market.

During this ten-year period Addis's horizons expanded beyond China as he began formal studies in Political Economy at Edinburgh University and became acquainted with American politics and finance during a brief assignment in the New York office. Returning to Shanghai after the Boxer uprising, Addis became even more convinced of the urgency to bring about currency reform in China. As sub-manager of the HSCB Shanghai office, he gained increasing prominence and esteem among the members of Shanghai's international community.

INDEMNITY LOANS, 1895–8

Japan, like China, had been forced to open its doors to trade with the West, but unlike China, quickly adopted the technological skills which made the Westerners strong.[1] The world suddenly became aware of Japan's rapid progress in modernisation when the Japanese navy scored a complete and humiliating victory over the Chinese and forced the defeated Ch'ing (to which it had formerly paid tribute) to sign the Treaty of Shimonoseki.[2] China's swift defeat called attention to her weakness and served as a notice to other imperialistic nations, such as Russia, Germany and France, that Chinese territory and resources were 'up for grabs'.

The 1890s were a period of keen international competition for empire, when the newly unified and industrialised states, such as Germany, Italy, the United States and Japan, sought to acquire territory as a demonstration of their power.[3] Since Britain's rulers' chief objective was trade, they had preferred to support the Ch'ing rulers in order that China might remain a united state, meaning from a commercial point of view a large unified market dominated by the British trading in British ships financed by British loans.[4] This international competition between the Powers to gain control over areas of Africa and Asia was accompanied by the development of an alliance system.[5] In 1895 France and Tsarist Russia signed an alliance, which led Kaiser Wilhelm of Germany to negotiate an alliance with the Austro-Hungarian Empire. Great Britain remained aloof from this system of alliances until her leaders became convinced that she could no longer protect her Empire in 'splendid isolation'. Once Japan had demonstrated just how weak and defenceless China was, Britain was unable to stop the other Powers from following Japan's example in seeking spheres of influence in China.

The technique which the European governments used to achieve influence in China was that perfected earlier by Great Britain – loans to Peking. In 1895 the governments of Russia, Germany, France and Britain all encouraged their bankers to compete for the first Chinese indemnity loan.

The bankers were quite willing to cooperate with their governments' wishes since they expected that these loans would be highly profitable and they were adequately secured on revenues like the Chinese Imperial Maritime Customs. Thus there was brisk competition in 1895 to provide the Ch'ing with the first indemnity loan. Shortly after his return to Shanghai, Addis supported a loan to China as a means of assuring continued British influence: 'This is England's opportunity. It will not remain open long. Have we a statesman who can see it and seize it?'[6]

The answer was 'no'. In the competition to float the first indemnity loan, Russian and French bankers, with the active support of their diplomatic representatives in Peking, succeeded in offering better terms than their British and German competitors. Addis blamed Britain's diplomatic representatives in Peking for the failure. Writing to Mills, he described the British Minister, Sir Nicholas O'Conor, as 'in every way little; a vain man, an intriguing man and unsuccessful in intrigue', forever, as Michie put it, 'hunting rats in the drains while there were eagles in the air'.[7] Addis described the negotiations, as involving the merger of high finance with the higher politics, but observed 'happily commercial supremacy is not fought out in Downing Street although O'Conor seems to think it is'. He also reported that Hart, the Inspector General, had been 'thrust aside because he allowed himself to become identified with British interests'.[8]

Both the above observations provide valuable insight into Addis's views – that the politicians were of little help in commercial matters, and that the Inspector General should not become identified with any national group, despite his British nationality. There is little doubt that Addis's views were typical of his time in that he had little sympathy for the Chinese government, writing to his father: 'nothing you have read can have exaggerated the absolute failure of China. It is complete.' But he viewed the Chinese defeat as an opportunity for China to learn her lesson and now submit to modernisation. He stated that the war had demonstrated 'the absolute supremacy of Great Britain in the East . . . The Yangtze is untouched. We have shown Chinese we are the only power who can protect them.'[9] Furthermore, Addis assured his father, 'the amount of the indemnity will be financed in London', and predicted that such financing would enable Britain 'to have a voice in reform of tariff and a development of the material resources of China.'[10]

Addis hoped that the Chinese would agree to abolish their inland taxes (liken) in return for an increase in the tariff.[11] As an enlightened imperialist, Addis believed that British interests and Chinese interests were compatible: in assisting China to become a strong nation, British citizens would also be promoting British interests, which were commercial rather than territorial. He was typical of most Westerners in China in his impatience with the Chinese and their reluctance to develop their resources, not appreciating the fear of Chinese leaders that the foreigners would gain permanent control over Chinese mines and property. Thus he wrote to Mills that the Chinese should 'place the entire railway administration in the hands of a strong board with a first-class foreigner at the head of it'.[12] This view did not change over the next forty years.

When a Russian banking syndicate succeeded in capturing the first indemnity loan the British government (alarmed about Russian intentions in North China) became more willing to provide diplomatic support for its bankers in China when the time came to negotiate a second loan.[13] In February 1896, the *North China Herald* reported

that the HSBC had offered Peking a loan at 5 per cent at $89\frac{1}{2}$.
Evidently the Chinese rulers did not consider these terms sufficiently
attractive for the negotiations continued. The Chinese loan negotiations were complex because they involved so many competing
interests. On one side were the Chinese, represented by the venerable
Ch'ing statesman, Li Hung-chang, who served as Governor-General
of Chihli for twenty-five years, and the Inspector General, Hart, who
naturally aimed at securing funds on the most advantageous terms
and with the least political commitment. On the other side were the
foreign bankers and their governments, sometimes working together
but just as often working against each other. The intrigue was beyond
belief, and the fact that negotiations were conducted across a distance
of thousands of miles and in several languages did not simplify the
situation.

A disadvantage which hindered the British government was its
espousal of the doctrine of *laissez-faire*, which meant that the
government was neither to intervene nor to provide assistance to
businesses in their dealings abroad.[14] However, having lost the first
indemnity loan to the Russians, Whitehall could not afford to be
caught napping when negotiations for a second loan began. In this
situation, Ewen Cameron, now the London Manager of the HSBC,
succeeded in convincing the British government that a proposed joint
loan by the HSBC and the Deutsch–Asiatische Bank could not be
placed without the support of the Bank of England and its counterpart,
the Konigliche Suhandlung.[15] The final arrangement was that the
Bank of England agreed to inscribe the bonds.[16] Addis wrote to John
Walter at the HSBC that technically the Bank of England could call
it what they liked but 'practically, it is one of the best guarantees'.[17]

In convincing the British government to make these arrangements,
Cameron had expanded the relationship of the HSBC with the
Foreign Office in a way which was to prove of far-reaching importance.
Henceforth, the HSBC was to serve as the chief financial agent of
the British government in China, despite the inevitable public criticism
which such a relationship would involve. Nor did Inspector General
Hart particularly like the HSBC calling it a 'provincial institution'.[18]
However, Hart did not have a much better opinion of the Bank of
England. When that institution refused to issue the loan itself, Hart
complained that 'the BE must be governed by people as excruciatingly
pigheaded as the H'kong Bank lot are careless'.[19]

Judging by the profits which the HSBC was reporting, it knew
what it was doing. In 1896, the half-year dividend was equivalent to

18.73 per cent per annum.[20] On 13 March the *North China Herald* reported a sudden rise in HSBC shares which it explained as 'due to the news of the favourable conclusion of the negotiations respecting Anglo-German loan to China'.

Addis felt that with the second indemnity loan to China of £16m at 5 per cent, 'the high-water mark of Chinese government borrowing has been reached. Some new form of security – railways for choice – must now be devised.' He also expressed concern that the Russian loan had given the Russians a lien on the Chinese customs prior to the British.[21] However, one of the conditions of the second indemnity loan was that the Inspector General would continue to be an Englishman.[22] Addis wrote a memorandum, 'A New Way to Pay Old Debts', in which he pointed out that China:

> had borrowed over twenty million pounds that year and would have to borrow twenty million more; that the annual service would cost about three million per annum and that sum would nearly absorb all her maritime customs revenues, of which formerly six tenths were used in the provinces, four-tenths for the imperial exchequer.[23]

Since the customs had been exhausted as a source of security for loans, the financiers and diplomats began the search for new Chinese revenues which could serve as security for new loans. Later this period was described by historians as the time when China was carved into spheres of influence. The difference between a sphere of influence and a colony was that Chinese sovereignty continued to be recognised but economic control had to a large extent shifted to the foreign powers. Although the international competition and intrigue continued, after the successful negotiation of the second indemnity loan, Addis gained a temporary respite from Chinese loan negotiations when he was appointed the HSBC Agent in Hankow.

HANKOW, KOREA, CALCUTTA, 1896–8

Actually Hankow was but one of three adjacent cities known collectively as Wuhan, located in the Yangtse in central China, the other two being Hanyang and Wuchang.[24] Situated on the Yangtse 1000 km from Shanghai, Hankow served as the central link between the trade of the interior and that of the sea. Here the British had established a Bund, just as they had in Shanghai, but they experienced far more difficulty in winning acceptance of their presence so far in the interior, where the Chinese were much less accustomed to foreigners. Much of Chinese hatred and resistance to the foreigners was understandable and hardly irrational, since the European steamships interfered with and undermined native trade traditionally carried by junks and sampans while the missionaries undermined the officials' authority.[25] In Hankow, as in other Treaty Ports, the British established their own institutions and ignored the customs and rights of the millions who surrounded them. Here one of the late Ch'ing's most able statesmen, Chang Chih-tung, served as Governor-General at Wuchang, where he had first outlined the plans for the Peking–Canton railway.

Initially, Addis and his wife were relieved to escape the pressure of life in Shanghai. However, before long the intellectual young couple found Hankow society to be vulgar and boring.[26] Eba's comments suggest that she shared her husband's dislike for the shallowness of the typical expatriate. At the Bank the only busy time was during the tea season. That summer Eba and Tom went to Japan to escape the heat, where Charles joined them in August. From Japan Eba wrote to her husband describing a dinner-party which she had not enjoyed because the conversation was 'silly' and then commented: 'I hope I am not a prig.'[27] One suspects that many of their contemporaries might have considered both Eba and her husband almost too conscientious, too upright, too serious. However, they were happy with each other.

By this time Addis found that his attitude towards China affairs had changed, reporting to Mills that his interest was not 'nearly so keen' as formerly. He wondered if:

> this is what they all come to, these bright dreams of the days of our youth! All that was to be done and learned and achieved concentrated, after soaring to world-wide benefits, on making one home happy, sinking from mankind to a mannikin.[28]

Perhaps it was because his primary interests now centred on wife and child that Addis no longer showed the interest in Chinese local customs or beliefs which had marked his tenure in Hong Kong, Peking and Shanghai. Or perhaps his increased responsibility as Agent or simply the fact that he was growing older explained the decreased interest in such matters. Whatever the explanation, Addis did not demonstrate any awareness of the Chinese discontent and growing resentment of the foreign presence. Nor did he become acquainted with Governor-General Chang Chih-tung.

In all likelihood, as Addis's responsibilities grew, his attention increasingly focused on the growing international competition for influence in China. Although the Sino-Japanese war had demonstrated Japan's determination to replace Chinese influence in Korea, it had not settled the question as to whether Russia or Japan would control China's former tributary state. In September Addis received orders to go to Korea to provide advice to McLeavy Brown, the financial adviser to the King of Korea, on the possible formation of a national Bank.[29] In September 1896 Addis, Eba and their young son Tom, travelled from Japan to Seoul where they spent the next six weeks.

After studying the situation, Addis advised Wade Gard'ner, against a loan to Korea for the establishment of a national bank, explaining that:

> the present condition of the country is altogether too unsettled and its political future too uncertain to offer a favourable soil for the reception of so delicate a product of our modern civilization as a national bank.

Addis speculated that Japan had 'loaned Corea [sic] money at low rate in hope of default as excuse to take over customs.' While he acknowledged that such a loan would enable a foreign bank to 'obtain the handling of the Government funds and probably a fair share of the imports as well', he did not think the risks were worth it, primarily because he saw Russia as possessing 'all the advantages in Corea [sic]'.[30] These comments demonstrate Addis's recognition that a country's currency and banking system were intimately involved in political issues.

Upon returning from Korea, the Addis family found Hankow even more trying.[31] During this period both Addis and his wife were seriously ill, he with hepatitis, she with pneumonia. They were therefore pleased to learn that Addis had been promoted to Calcutta, where he was to proceed as soon as their second child was born.[32]

The Hankow assignment however did provide the leisure for Addis to write an article about Korea, which he entitled 'Korea Under the Russians'.[33] The article, which was finally published in the *United Services Magazine*, described Korea as 'the Issachar of the East, crouching down between two burdens, Japan and Russia'. For those readers less familiar with the Old Testament, Addis explained that in Genesis XI, 14–15, Issachar was a strong ass.[34] Fortunately, this was the last time Addis attempted biblical allusions to explain international politics.

With the birth of a daughter, Elizabeth, on 31 January 1897, Addis was amazed to find how his happiness could grow. He exclaimed: 'How infinite is love. And thus we learn of God and his infinite love.'[35] Shortly thereafter Addis set out alone for Calcutta, stopping first to consult with Gard'ner in Shanghai, and Chief Manager Jackson in Hong Kong. While in Hong Kong Addis learned that Eba had pneumonia. Only after twenty-four anxious hours did he and the Jacksons receive word that the crisis had passed. These months of separation were to be one of the most difficult periods of Eba's and Charles's married life. *En route* to Calcutta, Addis developed fever, which lasted a couple of weeks and left him weakened. Throughout the spring he was ill and lonely, trying to console himself by reading Lord Chesterfield's *Letters* and Burns's poems. But not until Eba arrived in June did he feel that 'the winter is past'.[36] And the chills and weakness continued. Eba was very worried about him, feeling that he was working too hard and resenting the demands the Bank made on him.[37]

The most valuable aspect of the Calcutta experience for Addis's career was first, that it demonstrated the confidence of the Bank management in his judgement,[38] and second, that it provided him with additional expertise in international exchange. During this period he witnessed the effects of Japan's establishing a gold standard, and also observed at first-hand the way political decisions can affect a nation's currency.[39] Since all these questions would be of vital concern to him the rest of his career, it is clear that the Calcutta experience was very important, even though unpleasant.

Evidence that the Bank appreciated his service was provided when the Directors voted Addis a $1000 bonus for the last six months service.[40] However, when the news arrived that he was to be appointed sub-manager in Shanghai, Addis was delighted.[41] Of course this assignment meant a return to loan negotiations, but it also meant a return to old and cherished friends, and the cultural advantages only possible in a large foreign community. By the end of April, the young family had settled back in their old house at 26 The Bund.[42] Given Addis's ill-health and Eba's pregnancy, they had arrived none too soon. He continued to look weak and thin, while she delivered a second son, Charles Thorburn, on 2 July 1898.[43]

SHANGHAI, 1898–9

In all likelihood, Addis was reappointed to Shanghai because of his demonstrated ability to negotiate loans. In March 1898 Cameron (the HSBC London Manager) had signed a contract in Berlin for the third Chinese indemnity loan and began discussions concerning a possible joint railway loan to China.[44] Cameron doubtlessly wanted his most able and experienced associate to be in Shanghai to handle the Chinese end of the arrangements. By September Addis described himself as 'immersed in railway negotiations, night and day'.[45]

In 1898 the foreign penetration of China was gathering momentum, while the Ch'ing's authority had been further weakened by an abortive attempt by the young Emperor, Kuang-hsu, to institute drastic reforms in the government.[46] The 1898 reforms were quickly crushed by the reactionary Court officials and the Empress Dowager, Tz'u-hsi, came out of retirement to reassert her authority. In October 1898 Eba wrote that the Dowager Empress was 'chopping off reformers' heads' and that her husband thought China was 'on the verge of a great crisis'.[47] After this abortive attempt at reform, the remarkable Empress Dowager forced the young Emperor and his advisor, K'ang Yu-wei, to flee for their lives.

Europeans generally assumed that China was about to undergo the same kind of divisions which were taking place in Africa at that time, with each Power carving out its own colony. In order that they should not be left behind in the scramble for concessions, commercial interests in London had dispatched Lord Charles Beresford, a British Admiral, to China to investigate and report on the situation. After his visit, Beresford wrote a report entitled, *The Break-up of China*, which announced to the world the imminent demise of the Chinese empire. Addis, who had several conversations with Beresford during his China visit, told Beresford that he favoured 'a commercial alliance of England, Germany, America and Japan to maintain spheres of influence which would provide preferential but not exclusive rights'.[48] Addis did not think much of Beresford, describing him as 'always playing to the gallery'.[49]

The policy of spheres of influence represented a compromise between the British espousal of the open door and the establishment of colonies, which Japan, France, Russia and Germany favoured.[50] In this great struggle to determine China's future, Chinese opinion was ignored, her powers of resistance underestimated. Europeans (Addis included) remained unaware that there was such a thing as

Chinese national self-consciousness.

In expectation of eventual Chinese dismemberment, the European governments became even more eager to obtain railway concessions, on the assumption that building railways in a specific area would ensure control of the area.[51] By October 1898 Addis happily reported to Mills: 'We signed the Peking–Shanhaikwan–Newchwang [*sic*] railway agreement yesterday. Apart from the HSBC it is a great coup politically.' He continued that although the Americans got the Hankow–Canton concession, they 'are almost certain to want our finance. The Canton–Kowloon portion of it comes to us alone.'[52] A few months later he reported that the loan had been 'a grand success. The non-alienation clause right up to Newchwang was a great coup. I certainly never thought we should get it beyond Shanhaikwan.' 'Non-alienation' clauses provided that China would not grant another Power special rights in this particular area.[53] Addis continued that 'It was a mercy we got the loan out before Beresford got home . . . he is not to be taken seriously.[54]

This provision to which Addis referred formed a vital portion of China's developing railway system in Manchuria, which the HSBC was helping to finance. Connecting with the Chinese Eastern Railway (CER) was a southern extension to Port Arthur or Darien, which hooked up to an extension to Shanhaikwan.[55] In April 1899, Britain accepted Russian exclusive rights to build railways north of the Great Wall, while Russia recognised similar British rights in the Yangtse region.[56]

Beresford strongly criticised the British government for not adopting a more aggressive role in China. He recommended the foreign control of China's army to protect British interests. Frustrated by the government's refusal to follow his recommendations, he turned to the press, writing to George Morrison, the influential *Times* correspondent in Peking, that 'We are ruled by a society clique, who are ignorant amateurs.'[57]

One development which made the British more competitive with other national syndicates was the formation of the British and Chinese Railways Corporation (B&C Corp.), jointly undertaken by Jardine Matheson & Co., and the HSBC, which hereafter made the two old British firms partners rather than competitors. At an important meeting held in London on 1 September 1898, representatives of the HSBC and the B & C Corporation agreed to delimit respective spheres of influence for railway construction and to share profits on construction.[58]

At this time, the British government was still uncertain as to its attitude toward Russia. Evidence of this uncertainty was demonstrated by the Chancellor of the Exchequer's proposal that Britain should offer to share the third indemnity loan with Russia on the basis of division of spheres of influence, 'each of us extracting from the Chinese what we wanted within our spheres. Russia acting by land, we by sea, could completely control China, and defy any other to interfere with us.'[59]

The evidence suggests that the experienced Ch'ing diplomat, Li Hung-chang, once again used one barbarian to fight another, securing better terms from the Anglo-German syndicate than Russia offered.[60] In any event, by successfully obtaining the third indemnity loan, Great Britain had won an important diplomatic victory, one which further cemented the relationship between the HSBC and the Foreign Office. Sir Claude MacDonald, the new British Minister to Peking, stressed that 'the main value of the loan' lay not in the accompanying concessions but 'in the hold it gave Great Britain on the revenue machinery and the chance it allowed of effecting financial reforms'.[61] This loan, like its predecessor, went through inscribed by the Bank of England. Despite that institution's recommendation, the loan found a much greater welcome in Berlin than in London, which might suggest that British investors had wider and more attractive choices than had their German counterparts.[62]

Evidence of the prominence which Addis had achieved in the Shanghai international community was provided by the frequent requests for him to speak. In a long and detailed address to the Young Men's Christian Association of Shanghai on 'How to Spend Money', Addis set forth his basic philosophy of life as well as his views on the challenges ahead for the British Empire. He not only lectured on political economy but on the purpose of life, stating that man is here 'to make the most of himself intellectually and morally', and that 'the sacrifice of money is the highest ideal of all'. He concluded this address by quoting Burke's 'solemn admonition to the English people':

> If we make ourselves too little for the sphere of our duty – if on the contrary, we do not stretch and expand our minds to the compass of the object, be well assured that everything about us will dwindle by degrees, until at length our concerns are sunk to the dimensions of our minds.[63]

Addis's participation in so many activities combined with the stress of his work doubtless contributed to his health problems at this time. Nonetheless, he refused to make banking his exclusive occupation. While in Hankow he had written to Stewart, warning him to avoid a 'literary or sinological taint', indicating that Lockhart, now the Colonial Secretary in Hong Kong, had told him that such charges against Addis had resulted in his being 'shelved'. Addis continued:

> I am told that success in banking demands an entire devotion to business concerns to the exclusion of all that you and I sum up in the world 'culture'. I reply that I decline to sell my soul for any such pottage. The life is more than meat . . . I would rather be damned for my best than praised for what was not my best.[64]

At last, in the spring of 1899, the young couple received orders for home. It had been a very strenuous tour, with Addis gaining further experience not only with the Chinese currency but with that of India and Korea, and further political experience in railway negotiations. Meanwhile, Eba had produced three children in four years. Both husband and wife had been ill, but nothing had altered their love for each other. Eba worried about her husband's health, feeling that he was working too hard, but she appreciated his devotion, commenting: 'His love for me is wonderful.'[65]

Eba continued to marvel at how much responsibility her husband undertook: she described him as the one to whom everyone else turned for advice. She thought he needed to assume fewer responsibilities. Her letters to him testify to the joy of their relationship as well as to her feeling that he was a superior person.[66] Earlier, in a letter which she intended him to receive upon arrival in Calcutta, she wrote: 'As always you are teaching me what love is.' But then, as if to reassure him in the face of their long separation, she told him that she had been:

> re-learning the metrical version of the CXXI Psalm and I am going to think of it all the time we are separate – and you will think of it for us when we are travelling. It has often lately come to our 'trusting in Providence' and it hasn't failed us yet.[67]

Eba was the calmer, more self-contained person in the marriage, the one who provided the peaceful atmosphere of serenity and contentment in the home. At one point she wrote: 'If Charlie could only take even his novels easily; but he can't. He just devours them & his scientific books as well.'[68]

HOME LEAVE, 1900, EDINBURGH AND NEW YORK

Despite the bravado of his comments to Stewart, Addis was determined to succeed in banking, but on his own terms. One of the things he thought most important was to 'gain some understanding of the larger issues involved' in banking.[69] To do this he read political economy on his own, and when they returned to Scotland, he enrolled at the University of Edinburgh. In May 1900 he wrote to Mills: 'I am reading many books on currency, etc. w/o [without] much perceptible clarification of ideas . . . I shall never understand banking. And babies are not conducive to sustained mental effort. Matrimony is bad, but babies. . . !'[70]

Despite his discouragement, this third home leave, which Addis succeeded in having extended for six months, proved to be an important turning-point in his career. In addition to enrolling in Professor J. Shield Nicholson's course in Political Economy, Addis decided to seek the position of sub-manager of the London Office. In August 1899 Addis wrote to Cameron to ask 'if there was any use in my applying for the post of sub-manager'. After consulting with Cameron, Addis decided to ask for a six-month extension. This evidence strongly suggests that Cameron was grooming Addis as his successor in the London Office. Upon completing his course on Political Economy at Edinburgh University, Addis continued to study books dealing with currency, although to Mills he repeated his fear that he would 'never understand Banking'.[71]

Then too, in addition to professional plans, there were personal reasons why Addis wanted his leave extended – Eba was pregnant again and in April delivered a daughter, Robina Scott, named after her maternal grandmother. After her christening in June, Addis noted in his diary: 'the child of many pious memories and hopes. May she live to be like her Grandmother.' A few months later, when A. M. Townsend (the New York Agent) went on leave, Addis received orders to fill in for him in New York for two months.[72]

Part of the reason for Addis's appointment to New York was to give advice to the Americans regarding the establishment of a currency for their newly acquired colony, the Philippine Islands, which the United States had annexed after its victory over Spain in the Spanish–American War of 1898.[73] Addis explained the situation to Eba: 'The American officials in the War Department have got mixed up over their currency payments to the troops in the Philippines . . . now I am off to see them in person and see if I can explain matters.'[74] The next night he described his interview with the American 'colonial secretary', who was a 'fine straightforward fellow and with ability too'. After two interviews, Addis said: 'Well, admitting this difficulty of exchange between American gold and Spanish silver dollars, our desire is to put it right. And my first step is to ascertain just what your wishes are.' To which the American official admitted that 'he really did not know quite enough about an intricate subject to say just exactly what his wishes were'.[75] They decided that the Treasury would have to formulate its views and then Addis would return. Addis concluded by remarking that 'they are a very nice lot' and that he was 'more in love with Americans (above a certain class) than ever. But oh! the spitting!' Addis does not seem to have recognised how determined the Americans were to assert their own financial control in the Philippines.[76]

Addis found New York to be quite fascinating, worthy of admiration, but not without its faults. To Mills he commented: 'I agree with Bryce. America marks the highest level, not only of material well being, but of intelligence and happiness which the race has yet attained.'[77] However, he was astonished at Americans' apparent lack of any aesthetic sense and at their vulgarity. Nevertheless, he concluded that he 'would rather live in America than in any British colony'. He was impressed by the egalitarianism he observed and by Americans' 'organizing faculty', but he was not so certain about their 'business faculty', commenting that the top American officials 'should seclude themselves in order to think. Americans [are] always accessible, always rushing.'[78]

When Eba and the children joined him late in August Addis was content. Early in October they set off for China, catching a brief glimpse of Niagara Falls as their train made its way west, and a few days later, the Grand Canyon and Salt Lake City. By November, they had reached Shanghai.[79] Despite Addis's complaints to Mills about babies interfering with business, he was a devoted father and husband who hated to be away from his family. After only one day's separation, he confided to his diary, 'A day away from her is a day lost!'[80]

THE BOXER AFTERMATH, 1901–4

The China to which the Addises returned had been rent by an explosion of violent anti-foreignism – the Boxer Rebellion. Members of a Chinese Secret Society (who were called 'Boxers' by the foreigners because of the exercises they performed) had attacked and killed foreigners in North China, cut off the railway line to Tientsin and surrounded the foreign legation in Peking. Worst of all, the uprising had won support from the Empress Dowager, who had declared war on the Foreign Powers. After a seige lasting fifty-five days, the foreign expeditionary force succeeded in battling its way to Peking and rescuing the legation, while the imperial court had fled to Jehol. Once again, foreign troops were turned loose in retaliation on the helpless Chinese peasants, unleashing a wave of rape and pillage, and burning the Summer Palace.[81]

While the worst of the violence had been confined to the North, the entire world was stunned and frightened by the episode which demonstrated the intensity of Chinese hatred for their foreign 'teachers'. Peace had been preserved in the central provinces by Viceroy Chang Chih-tung, who in August signed an agreement with British Consul E. H. Fraser, and the Peking Agent of the HSBC, E. G. Hillier, whereby the Viceroy promised to maintain order in return for a loan of £75000.[82] This agreement further demonstrated the close cooperation practised by the British legation and the HSBC in China.

After his return to Shanghai Addis expressed both horror and disgust at foreign behaviour during the Boxer uprising, condemning the looting which had occurred. In a letter to Mills he asked: 'Why have we no white troops in the North? The answer is the jealousy of the Indian staff corpsmen who seem to look upon China as their peculiar province.'[83] Referring to the Christmas spirit, he posed the question: 'I wonder what the Chinese think of our practical illustration of it [peace on earth, good will toward men] in the North?'[84] Addis quoted Admiral Bruce as saying that the British Minister, Sir Claude MacDonald, 'took 170 tons [of loot] out of China'. Addis continued: 'it is sickening that at such a time a man in his position should have set such an example'.[85]

In addition to being revolted by the immorality of such actions, Addis worried about the political effects which the Boxer indemnity would have. The foreign powers intended to force the Chinese government to pay greatly inflated claims for the damages to foreign property and the expense of the Allied Expedition. Addis feared that the 'extravagant assessments' would lead to rebellion and predicted: 'Every Chinaman will know that the foreigners with their preposterous indemnity are the direct cause of his troubles.'[86] Michie wrote to

Addis, discussing the Mackay commission (which had been appointed to revise the tariff), saying that China might not pay the indemnity.[87]

In a debate at the YMCA, Addis discussed possible ways by which China could pay the indemnity, proposing a tariff increase.[88] Addis argued that the tariff could be raised to 20 or 30 per cent, but recognised that the Manchester merchants would oppose any such measure, since they could never 'see beyond their noses'.[89] Such views could hardly have endeared Addis to many of his countrymen in Shanghai. Because of his expertise in international exchange, he understood that the declining value of silver would add about 20 per cent to the burden of the Boxer indemnity.[90] But most foreigners did not share these concerns. Even Stewart showed the more typical attitude when he wrote from Hong Kong that the Boxer Indemnity might force the Chinese to permit mineral exploration, and thus 'prove a blessing in disguise'.[91] Such comments reveal the underlying assumption that the Chinese must be forced to accept modernisation, which ultimately would benefit them.

A matter of greater moment to the Foreign Office at that time was the Russian presence in North China, since those troops which had come with the Allied Expedition had not been withdrawn. The fear was that Russia would soon annex Manchuria. Stewart wrote Addis that he was disgusted 'with the feebleness of the Government's protest re Russian activities in Manchuria'.[92] However Addis did not share this concern, predicting that Britain would benefit from greater trade.[93] Nor did he share the anti-German feelings then so prevalent. In this age of increased national consciousness Addis clung to the view that there was enough trade for all. No doubt his views were shaped by the international nature of the HSBC's activities.

By this time Addis had emerged as one of the most respected leaders of the International Settlement in Shanghai. He served as the President of the St Andrew's Society, a trustee of both the Cathedral and the Chinese Hospital, Chairman of the Public School Committee and Vice-president of the SDCGK. In these various capacities he frequently gave speeches and toasts which often caused controversy, since his views were not usually shared by the majority.[94] One area of disagreement centred on the missionary question. Addis continued to favour the development of a Church of China 'rather than the imposition of a foreign ecclesiastical system'.[95] In addition to public speaking, Addis continued to influence those around him through his writings for the local newspapers.[96]

Perhaps what was most unusual about Addis was his combination of financial expertise and moral commitment. For instance, in a speech to the Literary and Debating Society, in February 1903 on 'The Daily Exchange Quotations', Addis explained the intricacies of foreign exchange and monetary theory, but then concluded with the statement: 'For the ultimate basis of all economic conceptions is ethical, and when all is said and done in the way of material considerations, the question of national character remains as the prime element in national welfare.'[97] This comment reflects a belief that shaped Addis's entire career – that not only good banking relations but peaceful international relations could be achieved through establishing relationships of trust with men of good character. Nor was Addis alone in this assumption.

From Hong Kong, Stewart, who was Secretary of the China Association in Hong Kong, revealed the same approach. He hoped that Addis would be appointed to the sub-manager's position in Hong Kong and commented: 'Here, where the Directors are, is the power. Were you known to them you would be the Heir-apparent without a doubt.' Continuing, Stewart observed:

> The place needs you. It needs a man to stem, as T. J. [Jackson] has stemmed, the baser tendencies of modern commercial life . . . it needs men with clean hands who will keep them clean. Unless a few such show up Hong Kong will tend more & more to become a Johanissburg [*sic*] -a Jew-run & ridden gambling den without morals or manners. Come over & help us![98]

After Addis prepared a 'Note on Chinese Currency' for the American Commissioners who had been asked to make recommendations for Chinese currency reform,[99] Stewart commented: 'That they should have come to you is surely a great compliment . . . You grow to be the Bagehot of the Far East.'[100]

Soon the HSBC management demonstrated its approval of Addis by giving him (Addis) a bonus of $3000 and additional salary of $200 a month.[101] Addis also received permission to take early leave the next spring in order that he might 'settle his boys in school'.[102] The trip home in April provided time for reading all three volumes of Morley's *Life of Gladstone* and a second reading of Marshall's *Principles*, as well as Shakespeare and Wordsworth.[103] On the 11 May 1904 the Addis family arrived at Albert Dock. Little did they suspect at this juncture that they would never again reside in China.

3 From Eastern Banker to Financial Diplomat, 1904–14: 'Playing the Game' in China

'Under modern conditions the intrusion of politics in commercial affairs is inevitable.' — Addis, 1912

A combination of circumstances led to Addis's appointment as joint manager of the London Office of the HSBC in 1905. This position enlarged Addis's perspective, enabling him to become more than an Eastern banker. In the next few years he worked closely with the Foreign Office regarding the negotiation with other national groups of railway loans for China, and succeeded in creating an International Banking Consortium for China.

During this same period, Chinese nationalists began to demand that the Manchu rulers resist foreign encroachment and provide representative institutions. Ultimately Chinese nationalism led to the overthrow of the Manchus in the Revolution of 1911. As Manager of the Consortium, Addis helped to ensure the success of the Republican leaders by providing financial aid to the new government.

In addition to enlarging his business responsibilities, the London appointment enabled Addis to expand his contacts with academic society. He became associated with economists at Cambridge University and assumed new administrative positions on University boards in London.

THE LONDON OFFICE, 1904–5

Addis's first years in London coincided both with major shifts in the European alliance system and important political changes in China. Japan's humiliating defeat of Imperial Russia in the Russo-Japanese War of 1904–5, profoundly affected events in both Europe and Asia.[1] The first thing that struck Addis when he returned to London was the British investor's enthusiasm for Japanese loans. In May 1904, he noted that a Japanese loan had been subscribed '30 times over'.[2] Obviously the British expected that in the long-predicted struggle with Russia for control of Northern China, the Japanese would succeed.

Of course the outcome of the Russo-Japanese war, perhaps even the occurrence of the war, had been foreshadowed much earlier by the signing of the Anglo-Japanese Alliance in 1902.[3] Addis conceded as much when he wrote to Murray Stewart that the alliance with Japan had been a necessity and that the Foreign Office was 'fully alive to danger of too powerful Japan . . . England virtually let loose the dogs of war and it was England who finally chained them up'. Addis indicated that this was the impression he had gained as the result of many visits at the Foreign Office. He continued: 'My own view is that Japan will have enough to do with her own finances for many years to come and that we have nothing to fear from her.'[4]

By ending the Russian threat in Asia, the Japanese shifted the focus of international competition back to Europe.[5] After 1905 the British Foreign Office became increasingly hostile towards Germany, which created complications for the HSBC, since for the past ten years it had been cooperating with the Deutsch–Asiatische Bank (DAB) in Chinese finance. But in 1905 the Foreign Office let the Bank know that its German alliance was 'incompatible with the Bank's standing as *persona grata* with British officials'.[6] One of Addis's first tasks was to solve this diplomatic difficulty.

Not only had the European balance of power shifted but the attitude of Chinese leaders had also changed since Addis first went out to the East in 1883. To Chinese nationalists, Japan's defeat of a European power demonstrated the importance of modernisation in promoting national interests.[7] When the Empress Dowager Ts'u-hsi returned to Peking from Sian in the north-west (whither she had fled from the Allied Expedition), she began to put into effect the reforms long advocated by forward-looking Chinese leaders.[8] Ironically, these belated reforms in combination with the enforced collection of the new taxes made necessary by the Boxer indemnity payments, further undermined the Manchu dynasty and accelerated the development of nationalism among the educated Chinese.

Addis described the new nationalism to Mills, saying: 'The problem before us is how to reconcile the conflicting claims of China for the Chinese and foreign control for foreign capital.'[9] This conflict between Chinese and foreign interests concerned Addis for the next thirty-five years. He consistently argued that it was in Britain's interests 'to have a strong China to deal with. It has all along been China's weakness, not her strength, that has been at the root of her troubles and ours.'[10] Here Addis underestimated the potential conflict between a strong China and the interests which he represented.

In 1904 Smith telegraphed Addis that he would like him to visit the bank's Hamburg branch and discuss the possibility of opening an office in Tsingtau in the province of Shantung, which was the German sphere of influence. He indicated that the German representatives in Hong Kong wanted the HSBC to open there.[11] After his German investigations Addis recommended to Smith that the Bank should wait to open an agency in Tsingtau until commercial considerations made such a move attractive. He wrote that he was suspicious of the 'political factors'.[12]

In February 1905, Addis learned of his appointment as junior manager in London, and also as Director of the B&C Corporation and of the Chinese Central Railways.[13] Both he and Eba were delighted with the appointment. She exclaimed 'We can by no means realise yet this wonderful news that we are to remain at home, and are done with the East. What goodness and mercy.'[14]

The London Office of the HSBC, because it managed the issuing of foreign loans, commanded great authority:

> Whatever was done in the way of preliminary negotiations on the other side, whether in Pekin [sic] or in Hong Kong, the arrangement of the issues in London necessarily fell to the task of the London manager. Many delicate matters had to be arranged, and in consequence of this circumstance those who have filled the position have always been men of exceptional standing in the bank.[15]

With his appointment as Joint Manager of the London Office, Addis began a new style of living, one which both pleased and alarmed him.[16] His schedule included many dinners, receptions, and luxuries with which the Scottish minister's son was not completely comfortable. Addis began taking riding lessons and studying French. He and Eba leased a large house in Primrose Hill north of Regents Park for their steadily expanding family, which now included six children.[17]

In addition to the social and economic changes which the appointment brought to his life, the new position also involved partnership with individuals whose past record in China Addis could not have approved. Neither the B&C Corporation nor the Pekin [sic] Syndicate exemplified the ideals which Addis had preached to date. Since he makes no reference to such issues, one must conclude that he accepted these conflicts as inevitable in business life.

But while he feared the materialism surrounding his new position, he soon found that he not only enjoyed the authority but aspired to even more. By the end of May, after Townsend (who had succeeded Cameron as Senior Manager) had been away for several weeks, Addis confessed: 'I must own I like running the office by myself.'[18] Nevertheless, management worries took their toll. Eba wrote that 'Charlie can't sleep properly.'[19] To Mills, Addis admitted that he liked London and liked the work but was not sure that 'I have not bitten off more than I can chew'. As in the past, he worried that he might never have time for the other pleasures of life.[20] These normal worries and self-doubt proved to be only a passing phase. For the most part Addis revelled in his new responsibilities and repeatedly savoured the joy of success. The first real challenge came in August 1905 when the Foreign Office asked Addis to try to obtain a modification of the Bank's agreement with Germany regarding China loans.

RAILWAY LOANS, 1905–9

The fundamental problem resulted from Britain's new diplomatic relationship with France and the effort of reconciling new friends with old business partners. In 1904 the Conservative Government, led by Prime Minister Balfour and Foreign Secretary Lansdowne, had formed an *entente cordiale* with the French.[21] In 1905 Morrison condemned 'the alliance between the British and German banks for the sharing of all Chinese Government business'.[22] Morrison, an Australian journalist of strong and outspoken views and an enthusiastic defender of both the British Empire and the Chinese, believed that war with Germany was inevitable.[23]

Unlike Morrison, Addis hoped that war with Germany could be avoided. He wrote to Mills: 'the real contest with Germany is in efficiency, in education, in training, in a new way of life'.[24] In October he succeeded in reaching a modification of the agreement which satisfied both the Bank and the Foreign Office.[25] Addis suggested that the agreement provide for independent negotiations rather than joint, but that 'any business that may result is equally shared by both'.[26]

Thus Addis began a major effort to bring the German and French banking groups together in a working agreement to cooperate in issuing loans for China's central railways, which were known as the Hukuang railways. Between 1905 and 1910 a large percentage of Addis's time was spent travelling between London, Paris and Berlin in an attempt to find terms which would satisfy all concerned. All these negotiations took place with the cooperation and consent of the Foreign and Colonial offices, so that Addis's role became not only that of international banker but financial diplomat as well.[27] Regarding events in China Addis wrote to Stewart: 'I am an opportunist in China. The factors are too uncertain, too inscrutable, too unstable to permit of a definite policy. It is better to deal with events as they arise.'[28]

No one was more surprised by his success than Addis himself. In a long and reflective letter, Addis wrote: 'I never cared for any useful branch of study and between ourselves how I ever evolved into the manager of a bank is a mystery that I have ceased expecting to solve on earth.'[29] While this disclaimer might be dismissed as false modesty – the ambition had been there from the start – yet it was also true that throughout his life Addis retained an inner humility in the midst of success.

What became apparent to both Addis and the Foreign Office over the course of these negotiations was the impossibility of separating business and politics in China, despite the national ideology that the two should have nothing to do with each other. Speaking before the China Association, Addis argued 'An imperial policy is essentially a commercial policy and to resent the intrusion of politics into business is to do injury to both.'[30] Already Addis was attracting attention as a leader in imperial policy as the press began to report his views.[31]

Addis faced three sets of conflicts in negotiating railway loans for China: first, there was the competition between rival national investment groups, backed by their respective governments; second, there was growing Chinese opposition to the expansion of foreign investment in China, and third, there was domestic opposition in Britain to the favoured treatment which the HSBC received from the government regarding China loans.

Despite the competition between national syndicates for railway loans, there were powerful motives of self-interest pushing the Powers to cooperate in China.[32] The consolidation of foreign financial interests in China began in the early 1900s, when first the Pekin Syndicate allied with the British and Chinese Corporation in 1903 and the next year the Chinese Central Railways, Limited, was organised to admit French interests.[33] Addis feared that continued competition among the Powers would lead to war and/or the dismemberment of China. He reasoned that not only Britain but all the Powers had a stake in preserving the central government of China, since all the loans were secured on the revenues of the Maritime Customs. If these revenues were not collected, ostensibly for the credit of the central government but in fact to pay the foreign bondholders, the loans would default. Addis's task became to convince the various banking syndicates and their government backers to see that cooperation in China would be more beneficial than continued competition.

The second set of rivalries was between the Chinese and the foreigners. A 'Rights Recovery Movement', led by such powerful officials as Chang Chih-tung and Hsi-Liang, the Governor-General of Szechwan, who opposed the increasing foreign influence and control in China, gained momentum in the early 1900s, now supported by both the monarchy and the provincial gentry assemblies which had been established as a result of the 1905 reforms.[34] Although the foreigners were for the most part unaware of the extent of the nationalist opposition, China was in the early stages of a fundamental revolution. One goal which united all Chinese was to stop the foreign take-over of Chinese resources.[35] In addition, various leaders and organisation called for the overthrow of the Manchus or the establishment of a constitutional monarchy.

The most obvious manifestation of this new nationalism was the effort of Chinese patriots to regain control over China's railways. A popular campaign began to buy back the concession for the Canton–Hankow Railway, which had earlier been awarded to a group of American investors, precisely because Sheng Hsuan-huai, the Director-General of the Chinese Railway Bureau, believed that the Americans represented the least threat to Chinese sovereignty.[36] But the American investors, had allowed Belgian nationals to gain a controlling interest.[37] Since the Belgians were aligned with the French and Russians, Chinese Viceroy Chang Chih-tung feared that China would lose control of the central railways and he therefore led a movement to redeem them with Chinese funds.[38] Yet, despite heroic efforts on the part of patriotic Chinese, insufficient funds were raised.[39] In this situation Viceroy Chang Chi-tung turned to the British who were eager to gain control of the Hankow–Canton line, since it traversed their sphere of influence.

Because the British feared American plans to develop a port at Whampoa (near Canton) which would compete with Hong Kong, they sought a concession from the Chinese to build a railway line connecting Hankow directly to Hong Kong with a loopline around Canton, connecting Hankow to Kowloon, thus assuring Hong Kong's continued monopoly of trade. In 1905 the British Colonial Office arranged for the HSBC to lend £1 100 000 to the Government of Hong Kong, which then provided Viceroy Chang Chih-tung with the necessary capital to buy out the American interests in the Hankow–Canton Railway from J. P. Morgan & Co. Part of the agreement provided that China grant to the British the Canton–Kowloon concession.[40] The Foreign Office naturally turned to the HSBC as the likeliest source of capital, and in August Addis assured William Tyrrell in the Foreign Office that the B&C Corporation was ready to float a £3m bond issue for the Chinese government to redeem the Hankow–Canton Railway.[41]

A third area of conflict involved in negotiating Chinese loans was the reluctance of the Foreign Office to admit what was in fact the case – that the HSBC was entitled to diplomatic support, since it was serving Britain's political interests in China. Complicating the situation was the relationship between the B&C Corporation and the HSBC. Would support for the HSBC require that the B&C Corporation have a monopoly over purchasing agreements? Any government could expect a public outcry if it gave exclusive support to one British firm. The interaction of all three areas of conflicts made Addis's task extremely difficult.

For instance, in the spring of 1908 Addis negotiated a joint loan with the German bankers for the Tientsin–Pukow Railway loan and one with the French for the Chinese Central Railways.[42] Although Addis consulted constantly with the Foreign Office regarding these negotiations, his French counterparts were evidently not so careful to inform their government of the transactions. In June Addis noted that the French had 'got into a hole through not advising their FO of the German participation in the Peking–Hankow loan'.[43] As a result, there was a great furore and Addis had to interrupt his vacation to go to Berlin, where the DAB obligingly declined participation in the new loan. Addis wrote: 'This was just what we wanted and it was a double coup to get our end without friction and indeed with gratitude for our consideration in making the offer.'[44] Next Addis went to Paris where, he met with the representatives of the Banque de l-Indochine, then to a French Treasury conference and finally to the Foreign Office, where his agreement was approved. But this was only one battle and the competition continued.

It is impossible here to examine or explain all the issues involved in the railway negotiations of this period.[45] For Addis one of the most trying aspects of the whole struggle for advantage in China loans came when his own appointee and erstwhile associate, Bland, turned against him. This episode provides a glimpse of the difficulties surrounding railway loans in China. Earlier, Bland had asked Addis to help him to get the appointment as the B&C representative in China, and Addis had complied. He explained his support for Bland to Murray Stewart, saying that even though he had never thought too highly of Bland, he felt his previous experience in China would make him well qualified for the post.[46]

As representatives of the B&C Corporation, both Addis and Bland bore the burden of bad relations produced by earlier B&C policies. Morrison wrote to his editor, Valentine Chirol, that Bland's 'negotiations for the Kowloon–Canton railway have come to a deadlock', and observed that 'the tactics in the past of the British and Chinese Corporation guided by that sinner Wm. Keswick' put them at a disadvantage. He continued: 'Look at the way we have swindled the Chinese in the case of the Pekin Syndicate and still worse in the case of the Chinese Engineering and Mining Company.'[47]

In 1908 Bland accused Hillier, the long-time Peking agent of the HSBC, of being pro-German and of engaging in unfair practices in China. Both Bland and Hillier appealed to Addis for support. When Addis refused to take his part, Bland denounced him as well, claiming that the 1908 loan was political rather than strictly a railway loan and that it benefited the HSBC at the expense of the interests of the B&C Corporation.[48] Stewart, who had recently visited Peking, and who was a friend of Bland and Chirol as well as of Addis, blamed E. Fraser, the British Consul-General in Hankow, for what he called the 'vagueness of the treaty language'.[49] After additional exchanges, Stewart finally concluded that Bland had been fairly treated by the B&C, 'even generously in the matter of salary' and that he should not have made it a personal matter.[50] Addis wrote to Stewart on 20 June 1909 saying that he had secured an English engineer for the whole of the Hankow–Canton line, and that the Germans had agreed to waive the demand 'to supply all the material for the Hankow–Ichang section'. He blamed Bland for lacking skill in negotiations, a criticism sustained by the leading scholar of this topic.[51] There seems little to explain Bland's reckless attack except bad advice and inexperience.

However, Bland's accusations against Addis naturally aroused the suspicions of the Directors of the B&C Corporation, threatening their confidence in him. But in a meeting with the Directors Addis convinced them of the falseness of Bland's accusations. Elated at his success, Addis afterwards described the meeting to Mills, saying that Keswick was 'amazed' at the outcome, since prior to the meeting most of the Directors were against him. Addis concluded: 'It is clearly this power, the power of dominating others (first experienced in Bible campaign Shanghai 1903) which is the secret of success.'[52]

The HSBC junior manager emerged from this unpleasant episode with increased esteem on all sides, while Bland remained permanently bitter, indicating that nothing would induce him to have anything to do with Addis ever again. He was recalled by the Board of Directors but continued to write for the *Times*.[53] Bland's mistake was to attack publicly someone in a much stronger position than his own. In such a situation, Addis had no recourse but to fight back or see his own reputation ruined. But he did not enjoy such personal controversies and had very few similar experiences in his lifetime. This was one of the rare occasions when his own integrity was even questioned. The crisis left Addis's reputation not only intact but enhanced.[54]

Seen from a larger perspective, Bland's attack on Addis really represented an attack on the entire system of spheres of influence in China which the Foreign Office had so carefully developed over the past decade. On 31 March 1910, Eba noted that Bland was home from China and that he had told Lord ffrench: 'he is going to smash the B&C C & H&SB. He surely must be mad'.[55] Lord ffrench [*sic*] had been the agent of Pauling & Co., the railway contractors, who in 1907 had negotiated a loan for Manchurian railway development which was opposed by the Japanese since it would have challenged the Japanese-controlled South Manchuria Railway (SMR).[56] Lord ffrench (in cooperation with the Chinese official, Hsi-liang and the American representative of E. H. Harriman, Willard Straight) was attempting to compete with Japanese interests in Manchuria.[57] Such a challenge conflicted with Foreign Office wishes and with the Anglo-Japanese alliance. Lord ffrench continued to be a bitter opponent of Addis through the First World War.[58] On 24 November 1910, Addis noted 'Bland's bombshell turned out to be a damp squib at B&C annual meeting. Found no support.'[59]

After this distressing affair with Bland, it was particularly reassuring for Addis to be nominated by the Foreign Secretary, Sir Edward Grey, as British Censor to the State Bank of Morocco.[60] The Censors served as advisors to their respective Governments in questions where 'conduct of State Bank in relation to finances of Morocco might be prejudicial to the interests of the foreign powers'. Walter Langley, of the Foreign Office, told Addis that his experience in the Paris and Berlin negotiations had led to his appointment. Morocco, like China, was an area where European governments were using financial pressure to achieve political ends. The Foreign Office thus recognised the unusual abilities which Addis possessed: tenacity blended with the ability to conciliate; self-assurance and most of all good judgement as to when to stand firm and when to compromise.

THE CHINA CONSORTIUM

By 1909 Addis had become convinced that the three leading European Powers (Great Britain, France and Germany) should form an '*entente generale* for railways in China', a proposal which he made to the Foreign and Colonial Office officials in February.[61] Despite the fact that such an arrangement would involve 'the abandonment of British preference for materials on the Hankow–Canton railways line', Addis argued that it was desirable, and he succeeded in convincing British officials, at least provisionally. Next came the more difficult task of convincing the Germans and the French. After very trying negotiations, an agreement was finally reached in May 1909 between the representatives of the three National banking groups, to share the financing of the Hukuang Railways.[62]

Hardly had this achievement been recorded when the American government, led by President William Howard Taft and Secretary of State Philander Knox, demanded a share in the financing of China's railways.[63] The Taft administration appointed the House of Morgan to represent the American Group, which included, in addition to Morgans, the National City Bank, the First National Bank of New York and Kuhn, Loeb & Co. While Addis did all he could to limit the American participation, the combined pressure of the Taft Administration and the vitriolic denunciations of Chirol of *The Times*, who claimed that 'Addis has lied all through like a Cretan', prevented the hoped-for Consortium agreement in 1909.[64] Ultimately Chirol's anti-German policies discredited him with the Foreign Office but not before he had done considerable damage to international relations. After breaking with Chirol, Morrison quoted Grey as saying to Addis that 'Chirol was a man who would not hear the truth'.[65] In July 1909 Stewart wrote to Addis from Hong Kong, discussing the possibility of war with Germany, favouring American admission into the Chinese railway agreement, saying: 'We here [in Hong Kong] would never have bought the Americans out [in 1905] to let the Germans in, and, as the latter have got in, my view is that it would be desirable to have the Americans back. Maybe the Russians too.'[66] Clearly Addis's friends were not as sanguine as he about German cooperation.

The succeeding negotiations with the Americans proved most exasperating.[67] Addis commented: 'Of all the negotiators with whom I have had to deal the Americans are the worst.'[68] While the Hukuang negotiations were still pending, Straight, the American Group representative, had proceeded to Manchuria and signed an agreement with Viceroy Hsi-liang for the construction of the Chinchow–Aigun Railway which Lord ffrench had assured Straight would receive British support.[69] Of course the Foreign Office was unwilling to support any agreement such as Straight's, which was so clearly aimed at competing with its Japanese ally's sphere of influence.

By November 1910 the Inter-bank agreement among the four national banking groups (the USA, France, Great Britain and Germany) was finally concluded and signed. Addis commented: 'now that the Americans are in I hope they will play the game', suggesting that he may have had some doubts about that likelihood.[70] 'Playing the game' in China meant cooperating in the total treaty system which had been imposed on the Chinese over the previous sixty years, a system which ultimately depended on the willingness to use force to back up agreements. Soon the Americans would demonstrate that they did not understand the rules of the game.

In addition to cooperating in the financing of China's railways, the four banking groups were also discussing sharing a loan for Chinese currency reform. The Ch'ing had originally negotiated a currency loan agreement in 1908 with Straight, while he was representing Harriman. Harriman had dreamed of developing a worldwide transportation system, by buying the CER from Russia.[71] This currency loan proposal had been part of an over-all American scheme to compete with Japanese and Russian influence there.[72] However, after Harriman's death in 1909, no other American investors were willing to challenge the spheres of influence policy which the European powers and Japan had established in China. Morgans preferred to cooperate with the system in which it was closely involved, having heavily invested in Japanese bonds during the Russo-Japanese war.[73]

What was being considered by the Consortium bankers in 1911 was a large international loan to the Ch'ing to enable that government to go on to the gold standard. In 1904 an American monetary commission, headed by Professor Jenks had recommended a gold exchange system, similar to that of the Philippines and India.[74] Like China, both the Philippines and India used silver currency which had a fixed rate of exchange with gold and was protected by a reserve fund in New York and London respectively.[75] In 1911, the Chinese government invited Gerard Vissering, the President of the Bank of Java, to act as its adviser on monetary reform.[76] Vissering proposed the gradual adoption of a gold exchange standard and the establishment of a central bank.[77]

The terms of the Chinese Currency Reform and Industrial Development Loan Agreement of 15 April 1911, provided for control over Chinese revenues such as the wine and tobacco tax and the salt tax. Its provisions for advances to the throne further ensured the Ch'ing's dependence on foreign support.[78] Not only the Chinese but the Russians and Japanese were alarmed by the implications of these Chinese currency negotiations. They demanded to be included, since the terms involved the 'pledging of Manchurian revenues and monopoly of industries' which they regarded as their 'special interests'.[79]

Addis suggested the importance of the proposed currency loan to the Foreign Office and asked for government assistance in examining the Chinese proposals.[80] In September, the Group representatives, meeting in Berlin, agreed to issue a currency loan to China.[81] In a cover letter forwarding the minutes of this Conference to the Foreign Office, Addis explained the agreement and reasoned:

> the four Banks have agreed to give China virtually a free hand to carry out her scheme of Currency Reform and to provide her with the funds to do so. It is a tremendous experiment, but possibly in this case the bold course is the wise one.[82]

Addis seemed to be saying: 'We'll see if Chinese officials can be trusted to use the loan for the purposes for which it was intended, namely, currency reform.' If instead the revenues were used for other purposes such as bribes or squandered, then this would demonstrate the inability of the Chinese to manage their own affairs and the consequent necessity for foreigners to control any revenues loaned to China.

But in 1911 China lacked the strong government and political unity which its Japanese neighbour enjoyed. The political situation in China had continued to deteriorate after the death of the Empress

Dowager in 1908, followed shortly thereafter by that of her nephew, the Kuang-hsu Emperor. This left the monarchy in charge of a Regent, ruling on behalf of a child Emperor, Pu-yi. Opposition among the provincial gentry to the nationalisation of China's railways was so strong that the Peking officials did not sign the Hukuang Agreement until 24 May 1911.

To many patriotic Chinese, the Ch'ing's submission to foreign demands had deprived it of its legitimacy. In the words of one revolutionary leader, 'China's present situation is that if it is not conquered by partition it will be lost through invisible financial control by foreign powers.'[83] The event which dramatised the ransoming of China's resources was the signing of the Hukuang Railway agreement, in which each of the Four Powers was given the right to develop one stretch of the railway, using foreign engineers, accountants and materials.[84] This hated agreement became the spark that ignited the Chinese Revolution of 1911.

THE REPUBLICAN REVOLUTION OF 1911 AND THE REORGANISATION LOAN

The outbreak of revolution in Wuhan in October 1911, although long expected, caught both the monarchy and the foreigners off guard.[85] Since it was not clear that the monarchy would survive, the Banking groups were forced to reconsider their agreements to provide advances to Peking. What was important from the bankers' point of view was to ensure that whatever government emerged from the revolution would continue to honour the debts of the past. Not surprisingly the Powers did not agree on policy: should they continue to support the monarchy, aid the revolutionaries, or stand aside?[86] Meeting in Paris, the four Group Representatives agreed 'not to lend any money to China till responsible gov't established.'[87]

Shortly thereafter, the Chinese revolutionary leader, Sun Yat-sen, who had been in Denver, Colorado, when the revolution began, arrived in London seeking money for the revolutionaries. Sun Yat-sen was already well-known to the British leaders and the public in London because British officials had rescued him from a kidnapping attempt in 1896, after which he described his ordeal in a book published in London. Sun Yat-sen's *Kidnapped in London* made the Chinese revolutionary an international figure and won foreign sympathy if not support for the Chinese revolution.[88] In the intervening years, Sun had worked with Chinese secret societies and revolutionary organisations in a continuing effort to overthrow the Manchus.[89]

Although Sun had won the admiration of the British public in the late nineteenth century, in 1911 his position had changed dramatically – he was returning to China to assume the position of Provisional President of the Republic of China. How he contacted E. C. Grenfell (a partner of Morgan Grenfell, the London representatives of the American Group) is not clear, but in November Grenfell told Addis that Sun was in London but 'dare not be seen coming to my house'. Addis suggested that Sun should come at night, and reported the matter to the FO who approved.[90] On 13 November, Eba recorded 'General Homer Lee – a little, pale, hunchbacked American missionary – and Sun Yat-sen, the future President of the proposed Chinese Republic, dined with us in great secrecy for Sun Yat-sen's life is at stake.' She described Sun as 'a man of say 35, gentle, quiet, thoughtful & with the sweetest smile imaginable, he looked little like a rebel leader.'[91] Sweet smile or not, Addis informed the FO that he would not lend Sun money until 'a proper government was established'. However Addis also warned the FO of the 'grave danger of lending Yuan Shih-k'ai party money'.[92] Yuan Shih-k'ai, the former commander of the modern Pei Yu army, had been dismissed by the Ch'ing in 1908, only to be recalled in 1911 to defend the Empire and put down the rebellion. Yuan next approached the Group representatives in Peking for a loan.[93] Thus Addis was counselling a policy of neutrality.

Addis's advice differed with those reports coming from the British Minister in Peking, Sir John Jordan, and also from that of HSBC representative, Guy Hillier (then in London), both of whom recommended a loan to the Ch'ing.[94] Despite the contrary advice from Peking, Addis succeeded in convincing Foreign Secretary Grey to adopt a neutral stance, until the Ch'ing abdicated in December. Yuan Shih-k'ai then joined the revolutionaries as Provisional President, while Sun Yat-sen volunteered to step aside, on condition that Yuan Shih-k'ai establish his capital in Nanking and hold elections.[95]

Once Yuan Shih-k'ai had taken command (in February 1912) the HSBC began advancing funds to his government. After 26 February, Tang Shao-yi, the Premier, who had had long experience in dealing with foreigners, took charge of the negotiations with the representatives of the Consortium banks – the HSBC, Banque de l'Indochine, Deutsch-Asiatische Bank and Morgans.[96] The arrangements for the advances were made by Chou Tzu-chi, Acting Minister of Finance in Peking.[97] The agreement reached provided that the 'Banks should have a "firm option" to provide the further monthly requirements of the Chinese Gov't', as well as 'a larger loan for general reorganization'.[98] Obviously, the foreign bankers (in supporting Yuan) still regarded Chinese loans as desirable investments.

At the same time Addis suggested to the FO that Russia and Japan be invited to cooperate in China finance.[99] As indicated earlier, the Russian and Japanese governments, eager to protect their spheres of interest in Manchuria, had been demanding inclusion in the Consortium since 1910, despite the fact that they did not have money to lend.[100] In proposing that Russia and Japan be admitted, Addis was recognising their political/military presence rather than financial capability, which was to be supplied by their British and French allies. In May the six banking groups began meeting to plan a large reorganisation loan for the Republic of China, despite the fact that there were already indications that Yuan would not adopt democratic policies in China.

When news of the proposed Reorganisation Loan became known, it was adamantly opposed by Chinese revolutionary leaders who viewed it as further evidence of foreign determination to control China. The opposition of Chinese nationalists to the Reorganisation Loan led Yuan to break off negotiations in May 1912.[101] Meanwhile, by June the HSBC had advanced £1 200 000 to Yuan's provisional government, with the understanding that these funds were to be part of a large Reorganisation Loan to be issued by the Consortium banks.[102] Naturally the bank was concerned that such advances would be repaid.

After a tough fight Addis had obtained the Foreign Office's assurance for exclusive support to the HSBC regarding China loans. After one session at the FO, he wrote: 'Had rather a scene at FO with Langley and Max Muller over Bank's claim to exclusive gov. support. I went for them straight.'[103] Addis's insistence on diplomatic support strained relations with the FO that spring.

Seeking some way to escape control of the Consortium bankers, Yuan negotiated a loan with an independent group of British investers led by the financier, Charles Birch Crisp.[104] Since such an independent loan would enable Yuan Shih-k'ai to evade the controls which the Consortium and the foreign powers were attempting to impose on the new Chinese government, the Foreign Office told the Crisp Syndicate that the government could not permit such a loan.[105] Crisp (whom Straight described as 'a clever little fellow, sharp and weasel-like') responded by denouncing the FO not only for supporting a monopoly but even worse for giving exclusive support to an institution which was regarded as 'not wholly British' (the HSBC had four German directors).[106] The Crisp Syndicate included Lloyds and London County & Westminster.[107] What appeared to be government favouritism toward one bank led to widespread public criticism in the press. When Crisp ignored Foreign Office warnings and provided a loan to Yuan Shih-k'ai, he was informed that only the HSBC could obtain diplomatic support.[108]

Meanwhile, under pressure from the FO, Addis agreed to enlarge the British group, but further ill-feelings arose when Addis rejected the applications of the Chartered Bank and the Eastern Bank.[109] Those participating in the British Group were the HSBC, 33.5 per cent; Baring Bros, 25 per cent; London County & Westminster Bank Ltd, 14 per cent; Messrs Parr's Bank Ltd, 14 per cent; J. H. Schroder, 14 per cent.[110] There is no doubt that this apparent favouritism created ill-will and enemies for Addis, both in the City of London and among the British community in China in such instances as when Addis refused to permit Russia to issue its loans in London through Schroder's.[111]

At the same time, the various Consortium groups, anxious to protect their special interests, began quarrelling among themselves as to the terms for the loans. In these negotiations, Addis proved more determined than Foreign Secretary Grey to resist the demands of the Russians and the Japanese to exclusive rights in their spheres of interest. After what he described as a 'full dress interview at FO', Addis wrote that 'Grey is evidently ready to give way to Russia's claim to Manchuria. I told him that from the Group's point of view that would be to betray China.'[112] Finally Addis succeeded in devising language whereby Japan and Russia would be reassured that their interests were secure. The exact language (which had been used since the Anglo-Japanese Alliance, and would be used repeatedly in future diplomatic agreements with Japan) took this form:

Japan agrees to take part in loan on understanding that nothing connected with the projected loan should operate to the prejudice of the special rights and interests of Japan in the regions of South Manchuria and of the Eastern portion of Inner Mongolia, adjacent to South Manchuria.

The Russians delineated Northern Manchuria, Mongolia and Western China as the areas of their special interests.[113]

When Hillier and Sir Newton Stabb (the Chief Manager in Hong Kong) urged independent action by the British Group, Addis insisted: 'We must stand by our own gov't.'[114] One student of these complex negotiations concludes that Addis was the only person who 'behaved with integrity'.[115] Having received the firm support of the Foreign Office, the Consortium resumed the negotiations for the Reorganisation Loan.[116]

Yuan Shih-k'ai faced increasing opposition from Chinese nationalists, who believed he was conceding too much foreign control and that he was using foreign backing to make himself a dictator and crush opposition.[117] In March 1913, Yuan Shih-k'ai ordered the assassination of his leading opponent, Sung Chiao-jen, just as Sung had succeeded in leading the Kuomintang (Nationalist) Party to an electoral victory and was departing for Peking to lead the National Assembly. This assassination led to a second revolution in China in 1913.[118] When the Kuomintang protested against the Reorganisation Loan, Yuan responded by attacking Nanking, 'the bastion of Kuomintang power'.[119] Sun Yat-sen warned Addis that 'civil war would ensue if we signed the loan w/o [without] consent of Chinese National Assembly'.[120] He predicted that the Loan 'would be repudiated by all of the Provinces south of the Yangtze as well as by Shansi & Shensi' and begged the Group banks to reconsider. As a result of this telegram, the Peking representatives of the Groups were instructed not to issue an advance until they heard from their governments.[121] Evidently the various foreign governments did not take the Kuomintang (KMT) opposition too seriously, for on 9 May, Eba reported: 'That awful & difficult Loan at last settled; but Charlie is too tired to be happy.'[122] Members of the Kuomintang were purged from the Assembly. In December 1913, Sun Yat-sen fled to Japan.

Meanwhile, the Americans had once again launched a diplomatic attack on the European bankers. Formerly, under the Republican President William Howard Taft, Washington had insisted on being included in China loans. Now, under the self-righteous leadership of the newly elected Democratic President, Woodrow Wilson, and his anti-imperialistic Secretary of State, William Jennings Bryan, the American government emphasised its independence from European policy and its support for Chinese nationalism. First Wilson condemned the Reorganisation Loan, and second, the government unilaterally recognised the Republic of China.[123] Since the Europeans had insisted that Yuan Shih-k'ai could not obtain recognition for his government until he signed the Reorganisation Loan, the Americans action seemed to offer a powerful source of new support for the Chinese rulers. In a public statement (which Foreign Secretary Grey denounced as a 'diplomatic outrage') President Wilson condemned the Reorganisation Loan as an unwarranted interference in the internal affairs of China. Having lost the support of the State Department, the American Group withdrew from the Consortium.[124] Clearly the Wilson administration was not going to 'play the game' in China.

While the American President couched his denunciation of the Reorganisation Loan in the idealistic terms of anti-imperialism, his announcement really signified a new American initiative in China. By publicly allying itself with Chinese nationalism, the American administration sought to convince the new Republic leaders of China to do business with Washington rather than London. Thus began American competition to replace British leadership in China, a challenge which the British both resented and feared.[125]

If Addis had any personal misgivings about the morality of the Reorganisation Loan, he did not record them. Certainly it was a huge success in the City.[126] In all likelihood, Addis believed that China would be better off with this kind of arrangements than with continual squabbling among the Powers for special advantage in China, which could only lead to constant strife and perhaps even political disintegration.

Nor surprisingly, Addis's view differed from that of the Chinese nationalists who had broken with Yuan Shih-k'ai. They believed the Reorganisation Loan enabled Yuan to remain in power and to establish a dictatorship, financed by foreigners.[127] One thing seems certain: the ability of the HSBC to provide and channel funds to particular political leaders made it indispensable, both to Yuan Shih-k'ai and to the British Foreign Office.

From 1913 on China was in reality divided by civil war, the Republican government in Peking dependent on foreign support for its very survival, its budget based on customs and newly reorganised salt revenues controlled by foreigners.[128] Furthermore, the foreign Bankers in 1912 had created an International Commission of Bankers which took charge of the collection of customs receipts, depositing them in foreign banks and reserving the surplus for a *recognised* government. Hereafter, the Diplomatic Body (the Ministers of the Foreign Powers in Peking) would decide *which* Chinese government would receive customs revenues and require that Peking explain in detail what it intended to do with the funds.[129] Whether or not China would have been better off without the Reorganisation Loan, with each competing leader free to make his own bargains with foreign lenders, remains problematic. The possibility of any central government effectively replacing the monarchy in the period 1911–13 was probably remote, and Addis may have been right in his belief that foreign military intervention might have ensued. Certainly Addis had protected British interests very effectively.

Addis's role in the Consortium negotiations was personally acknowledged by the Foreign Secretary who wrote to thank him for obtaining the Consortium's consent to exclude industrial loans from coverage by the Reorganisation Loan agreement, saying that he 'very much appreciate[ed] the good will and the public spirit, that made you respond so promptly to my appeal' and recognising that Addis's 'personal influence in the groups has been invaluable and has, I believe, been the decisive factor in reviving British freedom as regards industrial loans'.[130] It was this 'personal influence', which transformed Addis from an Eastern Banker to a government policy-maker.

In terms of his own career, the Reorganisation Loan marked a milestone for Addis, who was knighted in recognition of his service in the field of finance.[131] The ceremony took place at Windsor Castle on 15 November 1913. Eba was astonished when it was announced, since her husband had kept news of the honour a secret.[132] She confided to the diary that it was 'very curious to be addressed as "My Lady": it seems like a play that must shortly be over'.[133] The investiture marked the culmination of ten years of steadily increasing success and prestige in London, both for Addis and the London Office of the HSBC of which he was now the senior manager, having succeeded Townsend in 1911.[134] Recognition of the extent to which Addis's opinion affected the City was demonstrated when Stephen complained that Addis's pessimism about China was having a bad effect on the market: 'what Addis thinks is of great importance to Chinese credit in London'.[135]

Addis resisted the efforts by competitors of the HSBC to woo him with offers of a higher salary. First came an offer to head a Scottish bank. Stabb, the Chief Manager in Hong Kong, expressed his relief that Addis had decided to stay with the Bank, saying: 'I can well understand how tempting the offer must have been – in refusing it you have acted right loyally to the Bank and I trust you will never have any occasion to regret the choice you have made.'[136] Later

Addis was offered the Chief Managership of Union of London–Smith Bank 'with a salary of £5000 or more if necessary'.[137] After Addis told Jackson of the offer, Jackson wrote to Stabb that he did not 'know any Banker in the City of London who stands higher in public repute than Addis', and that he 'would look upon it as a calamity if Addis were to leave us'.[138] With Jackson's prodding, the Head Office finally increased Addis's salary to £4500.[139]

Addis's position as Manager of the British Group of the Consortium brought increased contact with such influential financial leaders as Lord Revelstoke, the head of Barings, and Gaspard Farrar, also of Barings.[140] Lord Revelstoke served as a kind of mentor to Addis in later years.[141] These contacts in the City, in addition to his experience with Foreign Office officials, enlarged Addis's vision, training him to think not only as an Eastern Banker but as a national leader. As his perspective widened his priorities began to change – he gradually began to weigh and estimate not only the particular interests of the HSBC, but the larger interests of the British Empire.

FAMILY, FRIENDS AND INTELLECTUAL MILIEU

During these first years in the London Office Addis had also enlarged his circle of acquaintances in the British academic world. One important friend was Ferdinand N. Schiller, whom Addis had met in India and included among that small select group of friends who received copies of 'Leaves from a Diary'.[142] In 1903 he wrote to Schiller, saying that he envied the world of Oxford men: 'Our commercial life seems such a horrid contrast.' Then he quoted from the 'lines to the Professor':

> Your path and mine lie wide apart,
> For you the things of head and heart
> The level of that loftier plane,
> Where soul draws near its source again.
>
> For me the sordid street and mart,
> Your choice has found the better part,
> And Martha-like, I feel the smart,
> And oft contrast, with secret pain,
> Your path and mine.[143]

Schiller may have introduced Addis to his friend, the highly esteemed scholar, Goldsworthy Lowes Dickinson. E. M. Forster, Dickinson's biographer and friend, described 'Goldie' as: 'not merely intelligent, affectionate, charming and remarkable; he was unique'.[144] At King's College, Cambridge, Dickinson commanded a devoted following of promising undergraduates, including John Maynard Keynes. There Dickinson held regular sessions of a discussion group, which emphasised just the sort of conversation which Addis had earlier enjoyed during his years in Peking and Shanghai.[145] Its members also shared the high ideals, liberalism and concern with truth and duty in which Addis so fervently believed.[146] Addis hated the social world of the Bank, writing after a Bank smoker concert: 'I loathe these functions', and he longed to be part of a more intellectual society in London.[147]

Schiller, who was Dickinson's closest friend, invited him and Addis to join him on a mountain-climbing holiday in Switzerland.[148] Later Dickinson wrote an account of the three men's conversations in the form of a symposium, which was published as *Justice and Liberty*.[149] The discussion provides considerable insight into Addis's thinking about political and philosophic issues of the day.

In the following dialogue from this book there are three speakers, Henry Martin, a professor; Charles Stuart, a banker; and Sir John Harrington, a gentleman of leisure. The conversation deals with the question of the ideal society, involving discussions of love and marriage, property, and the possibility of improving society. (The bracketed page numbers refer to the 1908 edition.) Throughout Martin sharply challenges Stuart's assumptions and views, accusing him of reflecting a class bias, which leads Stuart to challenge the professor to convert him. Martin is the idealist, the self-proclaimed democrat, who roundly condemns 'the rich class that really governs our own society' (p. 19), while Stuart and Harrington defend privilege and aristocracy. Martin seeks to convert them to his belief in the equality of opportunity, stating that at the present, 'opportunity is the monopoly of the well-to-do.' (p. 59) In an attempt to exempt Stuart from being identified with the hated business world, Harrington says: 'You belong yourself to the most leisured, and therefore the most honourable and cultivated class of business men. Yet it is from you that I have heard some of the most striking illustrations of the mental and moral decadence of the commercial world.' (p. 75)

Throughout the dialogue, Stuart is treated as the defender of the *status quo*, while Martin is its chief critic. For instance, in discussing the distribution of the products of labour, Stuart is made to say that 'Roughly speaking, a man gets what he deserves' (p. 82), which leads Martin to a long denunciation of the evils of inheritance and interest. Stuart is portrayed as the practical businessman, content to take life and men as he finds them, while Martin is the zealous reformer. When pushed, Stuart admits that the present system of distribution is inequitable, but doubts that it is possible to devise a better system (p. 104).

Martin then goes on to describe the ideal society, one in which 'no able-bodied person ought to receive anything except as the direct reward of his labour' (p. 104). But Stuart argues that progress comes from the profit incentive (p. 119). This comment initiates the most fascinating discussion, as Martin launches an attack on the financier and capitalism, picturing government as the instrument of the capitalists, as the maintainer of 'economic unfreedom for the great mass of citizens' (pp. 124–5, 137, 143). However, both Stuart and Harrington feel that the kind of government Martin favours would lead to an unbearable collectivism (pp. 158–62) a comment which inaugurates a discussion of the meaing of liberty.

Stuart defines liberty as 'freedom from governmental regulation'. Martin gains Stuart's support for the concept of equality of opportunity, and then affirms that in the present system there 'is hardly even an approximation to equality of opportunity' (p. 182). Next Martin succeeds in converting Stuart to support for his view of the ideal society based on equity, but Stuart remains unconvinced that such a society can be achieved (pp. 197–8, 214). Stuart insists that 'Ideals are not a cause, they are an effect; they are not an inspiration, they are a pretence' (p. 219). Stuart argues that it is impossible to change human nature, while Martin preaches the possibility of conversion (p. 247). On this note, the dialogue ends.

Although the dialogue is portrayed as fiction, since it is based on a real experience, in all likelihood it reflects Addis's mature ideas, as well as suggesting Dickinson's influence on Addis. Dickinson challenged his friend to face the contradictions between his ideals and the life which he lived and offered views which contrasted sharply with those of his business associates. Like Mills, Dickinson encouraged Addis to question the smug assumptions of the City. Addis cherished Goldie's friendship, and continued to be impressed with his moral commitment.[150] Dickinson may also have introduced Addis to some of his other Cambridge colleagues, but it is also possible that Professor Alfred Marshall invited Addis to Cambridge.

Marshall was working to inaugurate a new degree which 'would give economics a place in the University curriculum alongside classics, history and the other great subjects of study'.[151] Addis favoured a university education for Bank employees, having himself long ago felt the need for more education. In 1899 he had remarked: 'It is absurd that I should be engaged year after year in the conduct of large financial operations, sadly with an eye to the pecuniary profit, and without any adequate comprehension of the larger issues involved.'[152] During this period Addis was one of the prime movers in the establishment of the University of Hong Kong,[153] and early became involved with the management of the University of London. So it seems likely that both similar interests and common friends drew Addis into London and Cambridge academic circles.

The friendship with Col. Mills continued to be one of the most valued aspects of his life. Eba described the two of them riding off on bicycles together, writing that they were 'like two boys together'.[154] It was to Mills that Addis continued to confide his intellectual and personal concerns, frequently discussing a book he was reading, or international politics. Although Addis had joined the Anglican church, he continued to feel an outsider. Again to Mills he commented: 'I was born in the atmosphere of protest and was not confirmed till I was 40, and will probably never acquire it, the real sense of communion.'[155] By 1910 Mills had retired, leading Addis to remark enviously: 'He is now a retired R[oyal] E[ngineer], rich, clever, free.'[156]

By maintaining his contacts with the China Society and missionary organisations Addis continued to champion Chinese reforms.[157] Frequently invited to speak on China, Addis always emphasised the responsibilities which the Western powers had to the Chinese, and the richness of that ancient civilisation. Early in 1911 he prepared a lengthy address on 'Western Culture as a means of Chinese Reform', as a speech to the Stepney Readers Union. Eba described the audience as numbering 'some 60–70 working men & women many without even a collar on; but so interested, so intelligent. Charlie enjoyed himself.'[158] After a trip to China, Lowes Dickinson organised an 'Anglo-Chinese Society' at Cambridge, and invited Addis to address the group.[159] Addis spoke on 'Revolution and Reform in China'.[160]

There is no doubt that these years took their toll in the sense of not having time for the reading or family events he so much enjoyed. For instance he wrote on 12 April 1910: 'Another busy day. How my life is hustled. So little time to pause and think. And the years are passing swiftly by. Such things to be, So little done.'[161] This sense of time passing, of wanting to accomplish more than time would allow, was ever present. Nonetheless, Addis still found time to devote to his ever-growing family, never failing to comment in his diary on important family events or concerns, and relishing the annual holidays when he could bicycle and play tennis with his children.[162] On one occasion, when his oldest son, Tom, had left to return to school, he commented: 'We may be wrong in lightening the atmosphere of fear and dread in which my boyhood was passed but surely there is great compensation in the love of our children and their trust in us.'[163] His relationship with Eba continued to be a source of strength and joy. On 20 April 1911 Addis commented: 'The intimacy of married life at its best is a wonderful, an incomprehensible thing.'[164]

Schiller, who was a bachelor, was occasionally included in Addis family events and thus had a chance to observe his friend in informal circumstances. In the autumn of 1912, Schiller offered the toast to the Senior Manager at a Bank Dinner, commenting that the 'most distinguished quality' of Addis's character was 'his essential humanity – a humanity of the heart and of the mind'. He continued by recounting an experience with Addis while on the mountain-climbing trip in Switzerland, when Schiller asked if the great peaks did not make him realise the insignificance of mortals. After some thought Addis said: 'the snows pass and perish – only man abides'. Finally Schiller spoke of Addis's 'romantic imagination' which he felt was another quality making him a remarkable banker.[165]

Schiller's remarks provide further evidence that even though Addis had emerged as one of London's most esteemed bankers, he had not lost the inner spiritual qualities – a philosophical approach to life and sensitivity to human needs, which had so impressed his contemporaries in Peking and Shanghai and had been evident in his early writings. Now that every minute of every day was spoken for, self-analysis and philosophical discussions were luxuries which he could rarely afford. But they were very much missed.

In the face of growing criticism and alarm from writers and businessmen concerning Britain's foreign policy,[166] Addis continued to express optimism about Britain's future. Speaking to his Bank colleagues, he explained: 'Under modern conditions the intrusion of politics in commercial affairs is inevitable.' While he recognised that 'the politics of the Great Powers have been reshaped with a view to securing for their nationals a place in the markets of the world', he assured his audience 'Happily there is room enough and to spare in the world for us all.'[167] However Addis's complacency did not ring true to those like Bert Crisp who had been shut out of China loans by what appeared to be government favouritism.[168] There was rising criticism at home that the government was not doing enough to protect British traders against the American and German commercial threat. To those less favoured by the government, Addis's optimism resembled the smug complacency of the insider, naturally causing resentment, even hatred.

Nor were the Chinese content to remain passive while the foreign powers distributed their assets and chose their leaders. In all likelihood, Addis's failure to appreciate the extent of Chinese nationalism would have caused major problems for the Consortium, even had the First World War not begun in 1914.

Addis's optimistic approach, the tendency to 'play down' obstacles and exaggerate agreements, was both a strength and a weakness, a tendency which would later create difficulties with the Foreign Office. Whether such optimism should be interpreted as self-deception or simply the negotiating tactic used by a self-confident, successful man who always sought to emphasise the positive, is debatable. In all likelihood, there is some element of truth in both interpretations. This much granted, it seems undeniable that Addis, when compared with his contemporaries, was an unusually large-minded individual, one who habitually took the long view, who when negotiating, took into account both his country's interests and the larger goal of international peace, as well as promoting the interests of his own corporation.

This approach can be seen in the testimony Addis gave in 1914 regarding the proposed State Bank for India. The Government of India had adopted a gold exchange standard which Keynes, after serving in the India office for two years, described as 'the ideal currency of the future'.[169] In the spring of 1913 a Royal Commission had been appointed to enquire into Indian Finance and Currency. While the Commission was taking evidence, speculation in Indian silver began. The failure of the Indian Specie Bank in the autumn of 1913 threatened to produce a crisis, which Addis in cooperation with Thomas Fraser and Thomas Henderson Whitehead, of the Chartered Bank, moved quickly to avoid by forming a syndicate to purchase all the silver at $20\frac{1}{2}$.[170] Afterwards, both the Bank of England and the Secretary of State for India thanked Addis 'for public service rendered in averting a calamity'.[171] Addis noted in his diary on 5 December

1913 'Over a cup of coffee in Bk. of Eng. parlours I sold one million one hundred thousand pounds of silver to the Governor, Walter Cunliffe. A bold coup and, I think a good one.'[172]

Addis's cooperation in this crisis and his knowledge of Indian finance brought him to the attention of the leaders of the Bank of England. Addis wrote to Mills that he was 'to be cross-examined on Monday on the State Bank for India project'. He commented that the Eastern Banks' opposition represented 'too narrow a view'.[173] Keynes, who sat on the Commission, strongly influenced its report.

Although no action was taken at this time regarding either a full gold standard or a central bank for India, Addis's examination of these questions furnished him with additional background and expertise which proved valuable in the future. Since the 1890s when he went to Korea and studied the question of a central bank, he had recognised the political and economic implications of currency and central bank issues.

The first ten years in the London Office had greatly expanded the scope of Addis's experience. He was now recognised not only as an Eastern Banker but as an authority on currency, a respected leader in both the City of London and the associate of leading economists. In 1914 Addis believed that by creating the Consortium for Chinese finance, he had proved the advantages of international cooperation and lessened the chances of war. Unfortunately, the international competition for economic dominance continued in Eastern Europe and Africa. Soon the hard-won cooperation in China would disintegrate as the major European Powers went to war.

4 Becoming a Central Banker, 1914–19

'The financial supremacy of London is based upon the absolute confidence abroad that a foreign bill discounted in London is as good as gold.' — Addis, 20 June 1918

Just as the First World War changed the nature of European society and the shape of the map of Europe, so too did it transform Sir Charles Addis's career. Since in time of war governments must raise huge sums of capital to pay for unusual military expenditures, they require expertise in the area of international exchange and capital mobilisation, and only those individuals familiar with the world of international finance and trade possess such expert knowledge. Thus in wartime, specialists in international exchange suddenly occupy positions at the hub of political decision-making, advising government leaders who usually only barely comprehend the complex world of international finance. And so wartime needs provide international financiers with unusual opportunities to exert political influence. Addis's rare combination of financial and diplomatic ability quickly brought him to the attention of the most powerful political and business leaders in the country.

The First World War not only brought financiers into positions of political influence in London and Washington but it also created a small group of financiers who as a result of their wartime collaboration grew to trust and respect each other and became convinced that postwar Anglo-American cooperation was essential to the preservation of world peace. However, the question not settled by the war was the exact nature of this new Anglo-American partnership, namely, who was to be the senior partner? Put differently – after the war, would Wall Street replace the City of London as the financial centre of the world? This possibility was one which troubled many British leaders, not the least of whom was Sir Charles Addis.

As an investment banker, Addis was accustomed to think from a long-term perspective, to disregard the emotional aspect and to look instead at assets and liabilities. Thus when Addis was asked to advise the government about borrowing money, he did not abandon the training or approaches which had made him successful in the first place. Each wartime decision was examined not only as to its immediate effect but also according to its long-term impact on the British Empire, whether it concerned the China Consortium, the Russian Revolution, or German reparations. Addis's ability to adopt this global approach helps to explain the transformation in his career from Eastern to Central Banker, from a businessman concerned chiefly with profits, to a Director of the Bank of England, concerned with protecting national interests.

In addition, through his wartime speeches and writings, Addis emerged as one of the leading champions of free trade, helping to defeat those businessmen and political leaders who argued that Britain needed to adopt protection to meet the postwar competition of competitors such as Germany, Japan and the United States.

WAR FINANCE

The outbreak of war in August 1914 caught both Addis and the Asquith government by surprise, unprepared for the financial emergency which ensued.[1] In order to prevent panic and a run on gold, the Bank of England imposed a moratorium on bank acceptances and all indebtedness and closed the stock market while officials consulted with leading bankers.[2] Addis described the first week of war as 'such a week of meeting and interviews and discussions that looking back it seems like a month'. He was convinced that 'The Government have done right. On that point Grey's speech was convincing. At least it made a tardy and reluctant convert of me.' But he worried about the outcome: 'I suppose Germany, our best customer, will be beaten and what then? The map of Europe will be redrawn. What becomes then of your Balance of Power? Are we to fight Russia next to redress the Balance?'[3]

Addis recognised that the war raised questions which reached 'the foundations of our financial system',[4] One of his services to the wartime government was to provide advice concerning the importing of *sycee* (uncoined silver) from China to meet the demand for a subsidiary coinage, since the £1 notes which the Treasury had printed were not well accepted.[5]

More than ever before, the structure of the British banking system, which had developed gradually over centuries and without logical planning, was being subjected to critical scrutiny. Earlier calls by

Holden, the Chairman of the Clearing Banks, for a Royal Commission to investigate the subject of gold reserves had been resisted by both the Bank of England and the Treasury. Neither the Chancellor of the Exchequer nor the Governor of the Bank of England wished to see any increase in the influence of the commercial bankers, whose motives they suspected.[6] Immediately prior to the war, the Clearing Bankers had hoarded their gold in the anticipation that gold payments would be suspended.[7] However, Basil Blackett in the Treasury, fortified by a memorandum which he requested from Keynes, persuaded the Chancellor of the Exchequer to avoid suspension.[8]

While both the Treasury and the Bank of England distrusted the commercial bankers they were not agreed as to their own responsibilities. There was no clear division of authority between the Bank of England and the Treasury over monetary policy which created much confusion and misunderstanding.[9] The onset of war simply made more obvious problems which had been developing for a long time but which had been ignored by both the government and the Bank of England. But action on such matters was postponed until after the war.

Meanwhile, Addis made the rounds of government offices, discussing the effects of various financial measures on the Empire. By September he exclaimed: 'The way trade is being directed by Govt nowadays is astonishing.'[10] Addis described one of the early meetings to his wife, saying that he had been 'asked to speak twice, once on the Stock Exchange and again on the moratorium'. He was pleased that 'The bigwigs, Lord St Aldwyn, Inchcape, Holden, etc., listened attentively and in subsequent speeches referred to my views which seemed to command general assent.'[11]

The close relations which Addis had formerly enjoyed with German bankers created difficulties both for himself and for the HSBC throughout the war. In December 1914, after meeting with Straight (the American Group representative of the China Consortium) Addis predicted: 'We are going to have no end of difficulty with the effect of the war on the position of the German group in Chinese affairs.'[12] Two months later Addis posed the question to Mills: 'What, *post bellum*, is to be done with Japan? What does she want? What will she take? What can we give her for valuable service rendered? Voilà! The latest nut the FO have asked me to crack.'[13]

One of the ways Addis kept well-informed on government finance before he himself became intimately connected with the government was through informal contacts at the London School of Economics and the Royal Economic Society. For instance, on 17 March 1915, Addis noted that at the Royal Economic Society meeting, Keynes (who had joined the British Treasury in January 1915) had read 'an interesting paper on French finances during the first six months of war'.[14] Keynes was considered to be 'the ablest theorist on finance in England'.[15] That autumn Addis attended a series of lectures on War Finance at University College, London, which Keynes gave.[16] Although Addis described Keynes as 'intelligence personified', he was rather disappointed by the series of lectures, commenting that Keynes had told them 'little we did not know – so little is known!'[17]

In addition to these activities, Addis was also helping to raise funds for the war effort, both directly, through the HSBC's purchase of war bonds, and indirectly, through speech-making to inspire public enthusiasm for saving. In a speech to the Trustee Savings Bank Centenary at Perth on 3 June 1915 Addis said: 'In a very real sense the savings of the country are become the sinews of war.' He warned that a great war loan would be needed to continue to finance the war and outlined those virtues which must underly any successful effort: 'frugality, diligence, punctuality, veracity . . . the grand fountains from which money and all real values spring for men'.[18] Following similar speeches at the Mansion House and Princess Gate, Addis explained to Mills (who was now a Colonel serving in France) that his purpose in giving speeches was to help the non-combatants realise that 'they have a part to play in the war. We ought not to leave all the sacrifice to you fellows at the front.'[19]

Although Addis had become a highly respected financial leader, whose achievements were beginning to be widely recognised, as demonstrated in a feature article in the *Scottish Bankers Magazine*,[20] he had not lost his sense of fun. In one diary entry he describes himself as 'skipping in front of the house. If only the City could see me, tails flying, jumping over the rope!'[21]

Nor had he lost his competitive instinct. In July 1915 Addis first met the American banker, Benjamin Strong, the Governor of the newly created Federal Reserve Bank of New York, who had been holding discussions with various British and French officials concerning war finance.[22] Strong, who visited London in the spring of 1914 on behalf of the Bankers trust, had become acquainted with such British bankers as Grenfell and Holden.[23] Addis reported to Stabb (the HSBC Chief Manager) that Strong thought the British would be happy to let New York take part of the financial burden. Addis did not agree, saying that London would be able to 'hold its own as centre of international trade', if 'only our joint banks and other large banking institutions in London are prepared to replace the many discredited finance houses in London, and take their share in financing foreign trade'.[24]

This comment suggests that Addis was already concerned about the United States' intentions, since the country remained neutral while its rivals were at war. Furthermore, by the summer of 1915 it was becoming clear that to meet the enormous costs of the war, the Allies were going to have to borrow heavily in the United States. The Wilson Administration was strongly opposed to any government loans to the belligerents and therefore the British and French governments were forced to depend upon private financing from J. P. Morgan & Co. which provided a line of credit and handled Allied borrowing in the United States.[25]

The Morgan firm, through its British partner, Morgan Grenfell & Co., enjoyed access to leading government officials as well as to influential private financiers in London.[26] Addis had earlier worked with Grenfell, as well as with Henry P. Davison (a senior partner in Morgans) and Straight, in the China Consortium negotiations. Late in 1914 Straight and Davison travelled to London with a returning British delegation, which included Sir George Paish (a special advisor to Chancellor of the Exchequer Lloyd George) and Blackett. Davison and Straight succeeded in obtaining Morgans' appointment as the fiscal agent of the British government in the United States.[27] Grenfell, as a Member of Parliament and a Director of the Bank of England, had wide-ranging contacts. Thus his firm became the chief conduit between J. P. Morgan and the British government, providing not only financial advice but information helpful to influencing both the American government and the investment market.[28] Morgans' support of the Allied War effort during the critical period between 1914 and 1917, until the United States became a belligerent, forged strong links between Morgans and the British government, for the Morgan partners refused to obey President Wilson's request that Americans be 'neutral in thought as well as deed'.[29] In September 1915 J. P. Morgan & Co. became the underwriters of the $500 000 000 Anglo-French Loan.[30]

Sympathy and aid to the Allies came not only from the Morgan partners but also from their friend and former associate, Governor Benjamin Strong, and from President Wilson's most trusted advisor, Col. Edward House.[31] Then in 1916 Strong struck up a friendship with Montagu Norman, a relationship which was to have great significance for Anglo-American cooperation in the postwar world.[32]

Norman, a member of a British banking family, had been an apprentice with Grenfell in the investment banking firm of Brown Shipley where he acquired valuable experience with American finance during several years in the United States in the New York office.[33] In 1915 Norman began working full-time for the Bank of England, providing his specialised knowledge of the American exchange situation. By 1916 the continued British borrowing in New York to finance not only its own war needs but those of its allies had caused a crisis in exchange.[34] To pay for wartime purchases and loans in the United States, the British Treasury was regularly shipping large amounts of gold to America from Australia, India and Europe. Such shipments necessarily involved close coordination between the Bank of England and the Federal Reserve Bank of New York, which handled all foreign exchange dealings for the US Government.[35]

Since the beginning of the war Addis had informed both the Bank of England and the Treasury of the HSBC's shipments of gold and silver to ensure that such movements did not interfere with wartime financial needs.[36] In February 1916 he appeared before the Committee on American Exchange, which included such leading bankers as Governor Cunliffe, Sir Felix Schuster and Holden.[37] Afterwards Addis informed Stabb that he had been 'privately assured by both [the] Governor of [the] Bank of England and Blackett of [the] Treasury of no objection to [the] proposed shipment of Gold $2 000 000 from San Francisco to Batavia'.[38]

In all likelihood, the fact that Addis was familiar with specie shipments, and had earlier cooperated satisfactorily with the Treasury and Bank on such questions, explains why Cunliffe once again sought his help when silver was needed for India.[39] After meeting with Cunliffe, his Deputy (Brien Cockayne) and Norman, Addis sold the Bank £500 000 silver in *sycee* and dollars.[40] In August he was appointed to the Treasury's Exchequer Committee as Chairman.[41] From this point on Addis was to remain closely involved with the government's management of exchange and currency, which required the closest regulation while the war continued. The wartime experience convinced Addis, Strong and Norman that Central Bank cooperation was essential to ensure international financial stability.

While Addis's comments only occasionally provide direct evidence that he feared American ambitions to supplant the British as the world's financial leader, the policies which he hereafter advocated suggest that this fear motivated his future strategy.[42] One area of intense Anglo-American competition which was of particular concern to the Foreign Office was China.

THE CHINA CONSORTIUM

Because American government and business leaders viewed the First World War as offering an ideal opportunity to further American interests in China, they were eager to provide loans to the Chinese government.[43] However President Wilson's attitude toward the Consortium was somewhat ambiguous, since he remained suspicious of Wall Street bankers, especially J. P. Morgan & Co., and had earlier denounced the Consortium as imperialistic. One of Morgans' major achievements during the war was to maintain its position as manager of the American Group of the Consortium in the face of State Department opposition. Part of its success stemmed from its British connections. When Strong visited Addis for the second time (in the spring of 1916) he noted that Addis was 'much surprised at our Government's attitude regarding the Chinese [Reorganisation] loan'. Strong noted that Addis recognised 'that there are difficulties in a policy which might later involve the use of the big stick, but China is such an important field of commercial development that he believes we will find it necessary to undertake business of that character if we wish to establish ourselves in the Orient'.[44] Strong described Addis as 'an authority on these matters' and concluded that the 'HSBC enjoyed high esteem', while Addis gained the impression from these talks that 'America was again thinking of taking a hand in China'.[45]

Addis also talked with Straight, who after leaving Morgans became the Vice-president of the American International Corporation (AIC) a company which the National City Bank had recently organised to invest in underdeveloped areas, such as China, Russia and Latin America.[46] Straight came away from the Addis conversation with the impression that 'Addis was the same old fox as always' which suggests that he anticipated that Addis would seek to limit the AIC's role in China.[47] After visiting most of Britain's financial leaders to explore the likelihood of their cooperation, Straight concluded that success depended on establishing good relations with leading banks like Morgans, Barings, Browns, Lazards, and so forth. He continued: 'The houses named particularly are intimately connected with New York and their cooperation in London cannot be obtained unless the relationship between the corporation and their New York affiliations be adjusted also on a cooperative basis'.[48] Furthermore, he commented that the British view of cooperation was that 'the other fellow does what the Britisher wants him to do, takes as much of the profit as he can get and for this, in the Englishman's mind, he ought to be thankful'.[49]

These various conversations in 1916 reveal the underlying suspicions which the British and the American financiers felt concerning each other's intentions in China, even while they recognised the necessity of cooperating, since at that time Japan posed a far more serious threat to both countries' interests.[50] In Washington this recognition led to plans for a new China Consortium.

By 1916 many changes had occured to affect the first Consortium. First and most obvious was the fact that Germany had become the enemy of the other four members – England, France, Russia and Japan. As the Manager of the British Group, Addis was under considerable pressure from the Foreign Office to dissolve the Consortium and reconstitute it without the German Group, a step he resisted, because, as Addis had told Straight in December 1914: 'he did not want to erect any unresolvable differences with the Germans as it would certainly be necessary to take up business with them again after the war'.[51] In May 1915 Addis wrote a memorandum for the Board of Trade in which he argued that 'It would be very difficult to damage German trade in China without inflicting a greater injury upon our own'.[52] Addis predicted to Mills that after the war the British and Germans would be friends again and it was important 'not to make the *rapprochement* more difficult'.[53]

However few individuals in wartime Britain were able to think in such dispassionate terms, since they were daily being exhorted to 'hate the Hun', not to plan for postwar trade with him. Across the Channel, the French were even more emotional than the British since this was the second war with Germany which they had experienced in less than fifty years. They accused Addis of treasonous behaviour and of 'selling the interests of his country and at the same time of the allies for certain vague advantages of his bank'.[54] The French Ambassador informed the Quai d'Orsay (the French Foreign Office) that the Deutsch–Asiatische Bank (the German bank in the Consortium) was 'basically financing the German presence in China on the fifth of the salt gabelle receipts that go to that bank'.[55]

Some of these British and French complaints can be explained as the resentment on the part of British businessmen who had been shut out of China loans, or of French bankers who resented the dominance of the HSBC in China. Nonetheless, the British Foreign Office expressed so much concern about the HSBC's connections with Germans that Addis ultimately decided that, like it or not, he must sever all relations with the Germans. In December 1915 he noted that he was 'subjected to a sharp cross-examination by Russell, a City solicitor, representing the War Trade Committee, who suggested [that the HSBC had shown] leniency towards the Germans'.[56] These kinds of accusations and insinuations convinced Addis that he should make clear the HSBC's total loyalty to the British cause.[57]

As far as Chinese politics were concerned, Addis's approach had not changed, despite President Yuan Shih-k'ai's recent attempt to make himself Emperor. After his suppression of the second revolution of 1913 Yuan Shih-k'ai had consolidated his power, becoming in effect a dictator.[58] Not content with dictatorial power, Yuan became involved in a misguided attempt to re-establish monarchy, with himself as Emperor.[59] In the notes for the Chairman's speech (which Addis wrote for Stabb in December 1915) Addis recommended that the Chinese accept Yuan's monarchy.[60] But Yuan Shih-k'ai had made a fatal miscalculation. Further popular rebellion in China led to Yuan's retirement and subsequent death in 1916. From this point on central government in China was a myth: actual power rested with local warlords.

Addis had little faith in the rebel government which Sun Yat-sen had established in the South, commenting: 'I wish I could see more hope in young China. They seem to get drunk on phrases – to acquire knowledge without assimilating it.'[61] In these circumstances, Addis continued to practise the techniques that the British had developed in the nineteenth century in dealing with Chinese governments, namely, assuring influence through loans. The increased revenues from the reorganised Chinese Salt Administration made the profitability of future loans seem assured.[62] On 30 May 1916 Addis reported to Stabb that since it was doubtful that the Chinese government would be able to make its payment on the Canton–Kowloon Railway he had visited the Colonial Office and asked it to guarantee an advance by the HSBC to make the payment, thereby preventing default. He had also asked the Foreign Office to gain the consent of the other Consortium Powers to the release of the surplus Salt Revenues to meet this payment. Addis reported that the Foreign Office was favourable but that it would take time, and therefore suggested that in the interim the advance should be made.[63] Addis believed that the goal was to maintain the Consortium's presence until the war was over and loans again became possible.

Another concern troubling Addis was the Foreign Office pressure to enlarge the number of banks in the British Group in order that the FO could not be accused of supporting a monopoly. In 1916 he reluctantly gave in to this demand and agreed to admit the Chartered Bank, giving it an 11 per cent share in Consortium business. How much distress this concession caused Addis can be sensed from his account to the Chief Manager, in which he confessed 'that there is no act of my official career which I have performed with less liking than the initiation of a loan partnership with the Chartered Bank'. Addis continued that he 'could not but reflect gloomily, as I took my way home, that at that moment The Chartered Chiefs were probably gloating over our various Intergroup Agreements, now for the first time disclosed to their cupidity'.[64] One HSBC achievement to which Addis does not refer was the transference of the Deutsch–Asiatische Bank's share of the [customs] revenues to the HSBC in 1917, which gave the Bank even more control of Chinese revenues.[65]

DEFENDING FREE TRADE, 1916–17

In addition to Addis's involvement with the China question and problems of international exchange, he was also becoming a leading defender of free trade at a time when many were calling for some form of protection or preference for British goods. Addis, like other City financiers, had little sympathy with the claim of British industrialists that British investors were sending money abroad and were preoccupied with foreign loans to the detriment of home industries. Nor did he accept their argument that foreign loans should include provisions for contracts to be placed in Britian.[66]

By 1916 those who supported government intervention had forced the appointment of a secret government committee to consider trade relations after the war. Chaired by Huth Jackson, the committee was holding hearings 'to consider the extent to which Germans and other foreigners should be permitted after the war to operate in Britain in any aspect of finance, industry, commerce or shipping'.[67] The reports of this committee, which were privately circulated, suggested possible banking reforms to promote British trade interests.

Early in January 1916 the editor of the *Economist*, Francis W. Hirst (a prominent defender of free trade) invited Addis to chair a discussion of free trade at the London School of Economics.[68]

Afterwards, Hirst quoted the speech in the *Economist*, referring to Addis as 'that great authority on Far Eastern Trade'.[69] After summarising the arguments of those calling for protection as indicating that the time had come 'to discard old economic theories and to cast our principles into the melting pot', Addis stated:

> so far as a theory is merely a convenient expression for a series of facts, I agree that when theory and fact come into conflict it is not the fact which was to give way. But when I am asked to abandon my principles, I demur. A principle is a résumé of human experience. It is the embodied wisdom of the ages, hard to come by and not lightly to be parted with. Its essential function is to act as a guide in unravelling new problems, and it would be the height of rashness to substitute empirical methods merely because the conditions happen to be complicated and obscure.[70]

In addition to quoting this speech at length in the influential *Economist*, Hirst also published it as a pamphlet for the House of Commons, where the first edition of 1000 copies was exhausted necessitating a second edition. Eba proudly exclaimed to Mills: 'Surely this is fame!'[71]

In this speech and in a subsequent article on the proposed British Trade Bank published in the *Economic Journal*, Addis left no doubt of his opposition to the proposals for a Trade Bank as well as to the secret plans being made for a postwar Anglo-French *entente*. Addis argued that 'the policy of the Government should be directed to encouraging the efforts and abstinence of the people so as to make the surplus as large as possible while leaving the exporters to look after themselves'.[72] This article was Addis's response to a report by the Board of Trade's committee, chaired by Lord Faringdon, published in September 1916, which recommended that manufacturers, merchants and bankers combine to push British products abroad, through the creation of a British Trade Bank.[73] The Board of Trade had responded by creating a British Trade Corporation.

Addis's article represented a direct challenge to this new approach. While this conflict between the industrialists and the financiers over the way government should serve British interests was temporarily put aside in the common effort to win the war, it did not disappear but resurfaced as a major political issue in the 1920s. For the time being however, Addis's and the City's championing for the principles of free trade triumphed. Addis noted in his diary that J. F. Darling's scheme for an Imperial Bank and currency got 'roughly handled' at the Tuesday Club.[74]

The Tuesday Club was a dining organisation, first organised in June 1917 by O. T. Falk, the head of a stockbroking firm, who assisted Keynes in the Treasury. The original members were: Professor H. S. Foxwell, A. W. Kiddy, (a City editor) Keynes, Geoffrey Marks, F. E. Steel, Hartley Withers, and E. Harvey.[75] Thereafter the Tuesday Club held monthly meetings which brought leading economists, financiers, businessmen and government officials together at the Café Royal on an informal basis to discuss topics of mutual concern. As one member observed after reading the Tuesday Club minutes, 'Many of the discussions which took place must have had an important formative influence on the minds of those present, most of whom then as now held public positions and influenced policy'.[76] These discussions, which often provided inside information to those in the private sector, had the advantage of being 'mercifully free from the intellectual dishonesty of the economist–politicians with an axe to grind . . . at our Club the innovators played with their ideas and, credulous or not, we listened and debated'.[77]

In 1916 many of those arguing for protection and/or imperial preference also supported joint allied action to ensure that after the war Germany could not recover her markets.[78] The Paris Economic Conference of June 1916 approved resolutions providing for postwar economic warfare. In remarks before the Institute of Bankers in November Addis again reiterated his opposition to economic war and commercial boycotts. He told his fellow-bankers 'No Government department, however able, however well-equipped, or well-intentioned, can ever supplant the trained banking intelligence of the country in controlling the movements of capital'.[79]

Probably one of Addis's most persuasive arguments with Whitehall was that the Americans would bitterly oppose Anglo-French economic plans, as they had already informed their friends in London that spring.[80] Whitehall's financial dependence on American loans was forcing British leaders to adopt a new attitude of humility, since by the end of 1916 the government faced virtual bankruptcy.[81]

The Wilson administration was attempting to use British financial dependence to force the belligerents to the peace table. In November, the Federal Reserve Board (with President Wilson's encouragement) issued a warning to American investors about the risk involved in buying Belligerents' notes.[82] This warning made it impossible to raise any more credits in the United States. Although Morgans dismissed the warning as 'an attempt on the part of Warburg and other German sympathisers to counteract the effect of Mr Davison's efforts to impress upon the Bankers and the Public the dangers of inflation' it is clear that the warning represented more than the view of 'German sympathisers'.[83] While it is true that Paul Warburg (an original member of the Federal Reserve Board) was a brother of Max Warburg, the German banker, his views did not reflect sympathy for the Germans so much as concern about the American financial commitment to the *entente* powers.

It seems more likely that Morgans sought to discredit Warburg because he was a member of the rival investment firm of Kuhn Loeb & Co. Unlike Morgans, Kuhn Loeb had obeyed the State Department's advice on neutrality and had not issued loans to either side. Then, after President Wilson severed diplomatic relations with Germany and Kuhn Loeb indicated its willingness to provide loans, Davison informed the British that Morgans would 'resent any attempt by Kuhn Loeb & Co. to insinuate themselves'.[84]

In this situation of financial dependency on Morgans, (who had extended a line of credit which amounted to $400 000 000 early in 1917) the British government could hardly afford to antagonise either Morgans or for that matter, other potential American investors by negotiating secret trade agreements meant to exclude the United States.[85] More than ever it was important to work with those skilled in the art of cooperation. Thus Addis's and Grenfell's recommendations, rather than the arguments for protection and commercial leagues, must have appeared to Whitehall as the only realistic course.

Wilson's declaration of war in April 1917 solved Britain's immediate financial needs, since large loans now became available from the American government.[86] Addis commented on the American entry in a long letter to Mills, praising President Wilson's declaration of war and demonstrating that he shared Wilson's idealism:

> At war with the German government – the enemy of the human race – not with the German people; only democracies fit to be members of the League of Nations; no indemnity territorial or monetary; the aim, the preservation of peace. Ach! All that is good to read – an immense step forward.[87]

Addis made similar comments on G. Lowes Dickinson's *The Choice Before Us*: 'His candour and fairness to his foes, the loftiness of his aim and his passionate love of liberty are at once impressive and persuasive'.[88] Dickinson, one of Britain's leading organisers in support of a League of Nations, in 1916 supported President Wilson's call for a negotiated settlement.[89]

Yet despite the idealistic terms which Wilson and Addis (both the sons of Calvinist preachers) used to describe war aims, neither man neglected his own country's self-interests. The Wilson administration quickly demonstrated its intention to use the war to advance its own position of influence in the world. Throughout the war, the American President would demonstrate almost as much suspicion of his allies as of his enemies, making collaboration very difficult. American financial and business leaders continued to view the war as an opportunity to establish Wall Street as the centre of international finance. Not surprisingly, the British were determined to frustrate this attempt. But their financial dependence made resistance to American demands difficult.

While willing to provide loans, the American Treasury insisted on controls and attempted to prevent the use of wartime loans to pay Morgans' advances to the *entente* powers.[90] Secretary of the Treasury William McAdoo told British Treasury agent Sir Hardman Lever that Morgans had charged 'grossly excessive rates of interest & commission'.[91] Furthermore, McAdoo's insistence that Whitehall furnish the American Treasury with securities to back up the loans infuriated the British Treasury. The Chancellor of the Exchequer, Bonar Law, wrote to Lord Reading, HMG's special envoy to Washington, that the US Treasury action was 'small-minded and unreasonable'. He continued: 'it almost looks as if they took a satisfaction in reducing us to a position of complete financial helplessness'.[92] This would not be the last time that Whitehall would feel this way. Such suspicions would soon be confirmed.

Meanwhile Addis continued to defend the British banking system, through writing articles in leading publications. His article on 'Bank Reserves and Depreciation' had been published in the highly regarded *Economic Journal* in 1917.[93] Such publications widened his reputation and no doubt helped to explain his appointment to an important government committee to consider financial reconstruction after the war.[94]

THE BANK OF ENGLAND AND MONETARY POLICY

The Committee on Currency and Foreign Exchanges after the War was appointed in January 1918 with Governor Cunliffe serving as

Chairman. In addition to Cunliffe and Addis, the Committee included Professor Pigou, and Sir John Bradbury from the Treasury who was replaced by Blackett when Bradbury became Principal British delegate to the Reparations Commission.[95] The Committee was charged both with planning for postwar reconstruction and with considering 'the working of the Bank Act, 1844, and the constitution and functions of the Bank of England with a view to recommending any alterations which may appear to them to be necessary or desirable'.[96] It met twice a week at the House of Lords hearing testimony from many of Britain's financial and business leaders.[97] The Cunliffe Committee's reports were to exert great influence over Britain's postwar monetary policy.[98]

Two important issues were involved: the first concerned the control of monetary policy; the second involved the question of how much inflation could be permitted. Addis took the view of a central banker, expressing concern lest the wartime issue of Treasury notes, unbacked by any reserve, should lead to uncontrolled inflation. Therefore when he appeared as a witness before the Bank Amalgamation Committee in the House of Lords he opposed the proposal to expand the fiduciary limit set by the Bank Act of 1844.[99]

Later Addis noted that he 'fought hard against any modification of the Bank Charter Act but found myself alone. The others agreed with my argument but felt some concession must be made to public opinion'.[100] In his testimony to the Cunliffe Committee in June, Addis told his fellow-members that 'the danger to be feared is rather the elasticity than the rigidity of the English monetary system'. He continued by observing that 'The mercantile community is at heart inflationist', that the primary function of the Bank of England 'is to maintain the gold standard and to regulate the circulation in such a way as to preserve the equilibrium between the supply of and legitimate demand for currency'.[101] Afterwards he confided to his diary that he had been cross-examined for one and three-quarter hours, but he 'held his own' and that he thought he 'shook them a bit'. Such comments indicate both a tough self-confidence and resolute determination to ensure Britain's return to what he regarded as sound banking practice. As a disciple of Adam Smith, Addis naturally opposed Treasury control over the currency, favouring the Bank of England's complete independence from the government. By the summer of 1918, Addis had joined that august body's court of directors.

Addis's election to the Court of the Bank of England in May 1918 testified to the esteem which he had achieved in the highest circles of Britain. Needless to say, he felt very honoured, noting that it was the first time in 200 years that an Eastern banker had been asked to join.[102] Professor Nicholson wrote to his former student to congratulate him, saying that 'I had an idea from Bagehot that no banker could be a Director, which always seemed to me one of our glorious British paradoxes'.[103] On 29 May Addis recorded: 'I was today duly elected a Director of the Bank of England. That I should have lived to see the day'.[104]

Early in 1918, after hearing Addis speak at the Tuesday Club, Harold Cox, the editor of the *Edinburgh Review*, invited him to write an article on British banking for his journal.[105] In preparing his article, Addis was able to draw on all the expert testimony he was hearing as a member of the Cunliffe Committee. Finding the article difficult to write, Addis worried that he was not a 'trained man of letters', complaining that he had difficulty getting his subject in perspective: 'But I keep plodding on and when all is done, then I must try to bring order out of chaos, rearrange and re-write'.[106] He sent drafts of the article to Professors Pigou and J. Shield Nicholson for criticism and suggestions.

In 'The Problems of British Banking' Addis dealt with the relations between industry and finance in the British banking system, comparing it with Germany's, and attempting to assess if the German system offered advantages for industry. He admitted that a closer connection between the two areas might be beneficial, but argued that 'it should be perfectly possible to obtain the desired nexus between industry and finance without sacrificing the independence of either'. He denied the charge that fledgling British enterprises had failed for the lack of credit. Similarly he denied that there was a need for government help in financing foreign trade, claiming that:

> any attempt to interfere with what may be called the natural flow of money to this market would undoubtedly tend to restrict our foreign trade by raising the rate of interest, and so increasing the comparative cost of production on which our power to compete in international trade depends. It might also place in jeopardy the financial supremacy of London as the clearing house of the world.

He emphasised that:

> Freedom is the breath of life for credit and commerce. To interfere by arbitrary and artificial restriction with their free course and development is to stifle them

and concluded that:

> the best service government can render the London money market is to leave its management and control to the bankers, whose business it is to understand it.[107]

While Addis may not have convinced the critics of the City, it is clear that he enjoyed the support of the elite in Whitehall and the world of high finance.[108] After the article's publication in July, he wrote that he was 'not proud or pleased with article in print but I am proud to be an Edinburgh Reviewer.'[109] With obvious pride, Addis described the reception to Mills, saying that 'all copies were immediately sold out and the buzz of comment was endless'.[110]

One other area involving monetary questions where Addis continued to be helpful concerned silver exchange. The British government purchased war supplies in India and paid for them in paper notes, redeemable in silver. This placed a great demand for silver, driving the price up. In September 1917 Addis recommended to the Governor of the Bank of England that the United States should fix the maximum price of silver.[111] A few months later Addis wrote a long memorandum on the silver situation, recommending that London ask Washington to meet China's demand for silver until November 'in order to maintain the rate of exchange at Shanghai'.[112] In 1918 the British Treasury suggested that the United States, which held $490 000 000 silver in its vaults, sell some of it. By the Pittman Act of April 1918, the US Government was authorised to melt and sell up to $350 000 000 ounces of silver at $1.00 an ounce, which ensured a guaranteed price to Western miners for the next four years. In 1920 the world price of silver fell to 60 cents an ounce.[113] The silver question illustrated both the complexity of currency and exchange issues and the necessity for international cooperation in finding solutions to these problems. Furthermore it showed the interconnection of trade and politics; the impossibility of separating them. It continued to cause difficulties in the postwar period.

For the time being, British leaders set monetary questions aside, as they turned their attention to ending the war. Of particular concern in the summer of 1918 was the situation on the Eastern front, since Lenin had signed the Treaty of Brest Litovsk with the Germans and withdrawn from the war. Addis's combined position as both a Director of the Bank of England and the Manager of the London Office of the HSBC made him uniquely qualified to deal with the financial problems caused by Russia's withdrawal.

THE CHINESE EASTERN RAILWAY AND RUSSIAN GOLD, 1918

In July 1918 the Department of Trade asked Addis if the HSBC would open a branch at Vladivostok in order to finance the Allied expedition.[114] The Allied Powers were sending American and Japanese troops into Siberia with the official mission of rescuing Czech prisoners of war who were making their way eastward. Addis explained his interest in the expedition to Stabb, saying that he feared the introduction of the Japanese yen into Siberia, which would 'greatly facilitate its circulation over the whole of Manchuria, and perhaps eventually in North China'. He felt that the Bank must oppose such a possibility.[115] But this was only one of the British government's concerns.

The Allied leaders had been worried about events in Russia ever since the overthrow of the Tsar in March 1917 and the establishment of the provisional government of Alexander Kerensky. Much was at stake – the continuation of the war on the Eastern front, control of the Chinese Eastern Railway (CER), the eastern extension of the Trans-Siberian Railway which linked Siberia to Russia's only Pacific port at Vladivostok, and large supplies of Russian gold.

The British were seeking gold supplies in order to meet their financial commitments to the United States. Since Whitehall was carrying not only its own expenditures but also those of the French and Russians, it felt justified in expecting its allies to make their gold resources available. As early as December 1916 Grenfell had advised the Treasury: 'With the large amounts of Gold in France and Russia, it is hardly believed that those countries should hesitate to part with the metal'.[116] This comment was included as part of a long discussion of the financial condition of HM Government and its dependence on J. P. Morgan for financial support. After the Bolsheviks overthrew the Kerensky government in November 1917, murdered the Tsar and his family, and denounced the former government's debts, Whitehall felt it had a rightful claim on Tsarist gold which might come into its possession.[117]

The situation in Siberia was particularly complicated because of the number of contestants interested in gaining control of the Chinese Eastern Railway, which although built by Russian and French capital, was wholly located in the three north-eastern provinces of China, known collectively as Manchuria and therefore technically under the sovereignty of Peking. In the spring of 1917 the Wilson Administration had appointed American railway engineer John F. Stevens to head a special railway mission which had set up headquarters in Harbin, Manchuria. Although Stevens never seemed to have any clear sense of his precise mission there is little doubt that the British would have liked the Americans to dominate this area.[118]

The fear in Western capitals was that Japan would take advantage of Russian weakness after the Revolution to increase its influence in Siberia. Also of importance were the supplies awaiting shipment from Vladivostok. By the end of 1917, '648000 tons of railway materials, shells and munitions, chemicals, metals, food and the like were awaiting removal'.[119] British fears that these materials would fall into Bolshevik hands led to the landing of Allied forces at Archangel and Vladivostok. Early in 1918 Whitehall began its attempt to persuade the Wilson Administration to join with Japan in dispatching an expedition to Siberia.[120]

There were political as well as strategic reasons for the Allied intervention in Russia.[121] The Bolshevik Revolution of November 1917 had so alarmed the Allies that from the beginning many British and French leaders were committed to preventing the Russian Communists from establishing control over the entire Russian state.[122] Seen from the capitalist's perspective, Russia was an area where investment opportunities must be preserved, which translated into opposing the Bolsheviks.[123] Using the excuse of supporting those Russians who would continue to fight the Germans, the British and French had sent troops into Russia to support rival regimes, one under Admiral Kolchak in the North, with Allied troops centred at the Baltic ports of Archangel and Murmansk; the other under General Deniken in the south. But there was no agreement even within the British War Cabinet on Russian policy. However there is no doubt that one purpose of intervention in Russia was to defeat the Bolsheviks, or that one of the most ardent champions of this objective was Winston Churchill, then Minister of Munitions, who became Secretary of State for War and Air in January, 1919.[124]

President Wilson at first opposed all proposals for the Siberian expedition, fearing that foreign intervention in the Russian civil war 'would risk creating a serious anti-Allied and even pro-German sentiment in Russia'.[125] Since by 1918 the United States was financing the war for all the belligerents, Washington believed it could dictate policy. Understandably, the British did not agree.

Inasmuch as the British Treasury and the Bank of England were vitally interested in securing Russian gold and there were known to be large amounts of Tsarist gold in the interior, it seems likely that one motive for the proposed Siberian intervention was to obtain this gold. Naturally such an objective would be highly secret and the evidence is circumstantial, but the events which followed suggest that gaining control of the gold and the CER were the immediate objectives of the Siberian expedition.

The outbreak of fighting between Bolshevik forces and Czechoslovakian prisoners of war who were making their way eastward to be evacuated, provided the ideal excuse to persuade the American President to approve intervention.[126] By July, 1918 the British had succeeded in persuading President Wilson to support the Siberian intervention, as a 'rescue mission' for Czech prisoners, counting on the humanitarian aspect to appeal to Wilson's idealism. But Wilson was never happy with the expedition and remained suspicious of the British and French motives, not to mention those of the Japanese, who were pouring troops into Siberia.[127] Wilson's worst fears were fulfilled – the Japanese dispatched not 7000 troops but 70 000 troops into Siberia.[128] Nevertheless by September Sir Beilby Alston, the British Minister in Peking, reported that the railway was open and in the hands of the Czechs all the way from the Pacific to beyond the Urals.[129]

Initially, the outlook for British plans seemed bright. In August the White Russians (Kolchak's forces) took Kazan, 500 miles from Moscow, capturing bullion formerly the property of the Imperial Government amounting to £80m in gold bars and coin.[130] Admiral Kolchak took the Russian bullion to Omsk (which was occupied by British troops) and made arrangements with the Vladivostok branch of the HSBC bank to receive the gold.[131] But the question which remained was : would Kolchak be able safely to transport the Tsarist gold to Vladivostok?[132]

The civil war in Russia along with the question as to who ultimately would control the CER awaited the outcome of the war and the Peace Conference. And since the CER was in Chinese territory, it became enmeshed in the question of both China and the Consortium's future. Although the evidence of Addis's involvement in these questions is sketchy, it is difficult to believe that in his capacity as London Manager of the HSBC and Director of the Bank of England, he was not fully informed, or perhaps even giving advice. Furthermore, Addis's appointment to the Court had been recommended by Lord Revelstoke, the head of the House of Baring, which had large investments in Russia.[133]

THE SECOND CHINA CONSORTIUM, 1918–19

The effort to keep the Chinese Eastern Railway under Allied control fitted in well with developing American plans for a new China Consortium in 1918. In Washington, the US Department of Commerce was drawing up plans for the international control of the CER with the expectation that a Consortium loan would provide the capital for necessary repairs.[134] The assumption was that American capital would at last make possible the long-dreamed-of American domination of the Chinese market.[135]

The official British position was that only a revived Consortium would possess sufficient financial power to prevent the Peking government from becoming a client state of Japan. Thus the Foreign Office encouraged British and American financiers to loan money to China. In December 1917 Addis informed Stabb that he favoured an advance to the Peking Administration 'provided the American Group will do the same'. Addis argued that 'the advantages of American cooperation in China are so great, even from the point of view of their indirect effect upon trade, as to outweigh the weakness of the proposal as a business proposition'.[136] But Stabb did not agree. He responded: 'There has never been a time when China was less in need of borrowing than at present and there was never a time when borrowings cost her more both from an exchange and interest point of view.' He felt that a Consortium loan would only 'add to the country's future financial difficulties'.[137] Stabb's admonition to Addis reveals the different perspectives of Hong Kong and London. But the question never required a decision since the Allies' overwhelming wartime financial needs soon preempted China loans, leaving the field to the Japanese.[138]

After the death of President Yuan Shih-k'ai in 1916 no Chinese government enjoyed sufficient national support to resist Japanese encroachment. At the same time the Japanese government changed its tactics in China, adopting financial rather than military means to gain influence.[139] Increasingly the Peking Cabinet (led by President Li Yuan-hung and Prime Minister Tuan Ch'i-jui) relied on Japanese loans to fund its needs. After the United States entered the war the Allied and Associated Powers encouraged the Chinese to become belligerents with the promise that Boxer indemnity payments would be suspended for five years and that China would have a seat at the peace conference.[140] But even after China became a belligerent, the Peking government continued to rely on Japanese funds, negotiating a series of loans with Japanese financier Nishihara Kamezo. This dependence worried American and British representatives in China who feared for the future of their interests in China.[141]

By autumn 1918 the corruption of the Peking government and its dependence on Japanese loans had convinced many of the foreign representatives there that some kind of an international debt commission would have to be created at the Paris Peace Conference to supervise the Chinese government's finance. John van Antwerp MacMurray, then serving in Peking as American Chargé, and soon to be appointed Chief of the Far Eastern Division of the State Department, wrote to Secretary of State Lansing saying that an International Debt Commission 'must be the only alternative to an economic and moral subjugation – perhaps falling only short of outright annexation – by Japan'.[142]

The problem which the Americans encountered as they sought to organise a new China Consortium was the inability of the Banking Groups to agree among themselves. Morgans had gained the Wilson administration's support for its management of the American group, but the Morgan partners had not yet reached agreement with Addis. From Paris Morgan commented on the British government's failure to accept American terms:

> I am inclined to fear that our friend Addis, whose influence with the London Foreign Office has always been paramount, may have persuaded the latter, most unwisely I think, to delay their assent impelled thereto by the interests of his own bank which he would prefer to describe to them as 'British prestige.'

He explained that 'It has always been his bogey that British interests in China, which have hitherto been so dominant, would one day be overwhelmed by the American avalanche.'[143] Shortly thereafter, Strong wrote to Norman (who had become Deputy Governor of the Bank of England) that he was worried about a possible reversion to a 'period of economic barbarism' as businessmen and 'those in political office who claim to represent business, are thinking of the main chance'.[144] Strong wrote that he favoured economic partnership between the United States and England. Addis too favoured partnership. However, each member wished to be the senior partner.

The American State Department rather naively expected that the second China Consortium (which was to include banking groups from the United States, France, Japan and Great Britain) could be organised at the Paris Peace Conference. The plan was for the

Consortium to provide a large loan to China to provide for the nationalisation and unification of all China's major railways, in the expectation that these would be staffed with American engineers who would order American materials and equipment.[145] To pave the way, the State Department had sent John Jay Abbott, the Vice-President of the Chicago Continental and Commercial Trust and Savings Bank, to Japan and China, and J. P. Morgan Jr to London.

In February 1919 Abbott reported from Japan that the Japanese Group bankers, Eiichi Shibusawa and Viscount Inouye were favourable to the American Group plan but that the Japanese government was waiting for the British to become satisfied. Inouye stated that Addis objected to the surrender of all options.[146] Thomas Lamont, the Morgan partner who was to be the manager of the American Group of the Consortium, was already in Paris, serving as an economic adviser to the American delegation. Although the Whitham Report, which outlined these American plans was kept secret, it seems highly unlikely that the British were not informed of American plans, which included the development of Whampoa harbour, near Canton, to serve as a deep-water port, thus challenging the position of Hong Kong. Certainly they were determined to frustrate them. Only on the question of American control of the CER were the British sympathetic, hoping that continued American involvement would prevent the Japanese take-over of Siberia.[147] In May 1919 Addis arranged with Lord Revelstoke for a credit for the Kolchak government, secured on the Omsk gold which had been shipped to Hong Kong.[148]

However, the State Department both underestimated its British rival and misunderstood the Morgan firm's goals in China. It was simply not realistic to expect the British to stand by passively and allow the Americans to supplant them in China, nor were American leaders wise to expect the Morgan firm to challenge the British position, since Morgans in fact benefited from that position. Although the American Far Eastern experts on the American delegation warned Washington that the British were determined to frustrate American plans for the organisation of Consortium, their warnings were either not read or simply ignored.[149] Far more vital and politically explosive issues perplexed President Wilson and Secretary of State Lansing at this critical stage in the peace negotiations.[150]

For Sir Charles Addis, however, there was no more vital issue than China. In 1919 he prepared to meet this new American challenge in China on three fronts; first through Morgans, then through coordination of British offices, finally through influencing the Chinese. First, he met with both Lamont and Morgan in February and accompanied them to Morgan Grenfell's where they 'had a long discussion on Chinese affairs'.[151] Next, Addis invited government and financial leaders to a dinner for Sir Richard Dane, the Associate Inspector of the Chinese Salt Administration. Present were representatives of the Treasury, the Foreign Office, the Overseas Department, the India Office, the Bank of England and other leading bankers. While Addis does not record the conversation, he does comment that it was a 'very successful dinner'.[152] It seems unlikely that he was referring to the food and wine. This coordination of the various government officials and private capitalists in working towards one single purpose – protecting and defending British interests – had long been one of the secrets of British success. Just the day prior to the dinner with government officials, Addis recorded that the government had promised the British Group 'exclusive support'.[153]

Finally, Addis met with the Chinese delegates before they went to the Paris Peace Conference, no doubt impressing upon them the realities of the China political and financial situation.[154] While the Chinese nationalists no doubt liked the sound of President Wilson's call for self-determination and an end to secret agreements, they were also aware, even if the State Department was not, that the HSBC controlled a large part of the Peking government's revenues through its control of Customs and Salt tax deposits. They also knew that Japanese troops occupied the province of Shantung and controlled the South Manchuria Railway, which ran south from the CER through Manchuria. What remained to be seen at the Paris Peace Conference was whether Wilson could implement his promises to bring about change in these unpleasant conditions and could in fact bring about self-determination.

When the Consortium Group Representatives assembled in Paris in May the Americans succeeded in reaching an initial understanding that the railways were to be treated as a whole and initialled a draft Four Power Consortium Agreement.[155] Lamont warned, however, that the British and French 'were worried about their share of supplies and raw materials'. (Under the former system, each National group built a section of the railway, using its own products and appointing its own engineers.) The unrealistic nature of American plans concerning the Consortium soon became evident when the Japanese demanded the exclusion of Southern Manchuria and Eastern Inner Mongolia from the scope of the Consortium. Shortly thereafter,

Lamont announced to the State Department that he was coming home.[156]

American efforts to take advantage of their wartime strength to advance their influence in China had failed. On the highly charged issue of the return of Shantung to China, President Wilson capitulated to Japanese demands, leading to general disillusionment with Wilsonian idealism in Paris, Peking and Washington.[157] The Chinese nationalists forced the Premier to flee Peking and the delegates refused to sign the Treaty.[158] It took over a year of negotiations before the second China Consortium finally came into existence. Meanwhile, the China question was displaced by the far more critical issue of German reparations.

THE GERMAN INDEMNITY

As we have seen, Addis had recognised from the onset of the war that British interests lay in postwar reconciliation rather than punishment of Germany. In advocating this view, he could draw on statistical evidence prepared by Keynes and Professor Sir W. J. Ashley, who in 1916 wrote a 'Memorandum on the Effect of an Indemnity', as well as the moral viewpoint of his friend, Dickinson, who strongly opposed a harsh settlement.[159] Although President Wilson had promised the Central Powers a peace without revenge as armistice terms, there was much sentiment among the allies for a large German indemnity. The British War Cabinet appointed a committee to consider the feasibility of claiming an indemnity, under the chairmanship of Australian Prime Minister W. M. Hughes.[160] After the armistice was declared in November 1918, Addis testified before the War Cabinet Committee on the German Indemnity (Hughes Committee) where he 'was heckled for an hour'. He wrote to Mills that 'Hughes, the Australian Premier, is not at all of my moderate way of thinking'.[161] Years later Addis recalled that he had claimed Germany might 'transfer £60m a year. At this, as was then thought, fantastic reply, the Chairman fell back in his chair. No further questions were asked and an inconvenient witness was got rid of as speedily as possible.'[162] According to one source, Hughes discounted the businessmen's testimony because they had German trading connections.[163] Ignoring such expert testimony, the Hughes Committee came to the conclusion that Germany should pay the whole cost of the war to the allies, estimated at the fantastic figure of £24000m, which would have required an annual payment of £1200m as interest and amortisation on that amount. The British Treasury's investigations indicated that Germany was capable of paying £2000m and £3000m in all.[164]

While the Peace Conference was in session, Addis launched a major effort to persuade British leaders to support a moderate policy on indemnities. In January he addressed the Council of the Institute of Bankers on 'The Economics of a War Indemnity'.[165] The next month he spoke to the Political Economy Club, a small but influential organisation of financial and political leaders.[166] Then on 5 March he addressed a large gathering at the Institute of Bankers, arguing for moderation both from the viewpoint of self-interest and principle.[167] Addis argued that:

> The question of principle which touches the honour of the Allies is not whether or no the loser in a war may justly be called upon to pay the costs, but whether or no such a condition was implicit in any reasonable interpretation which might be placed upon the Allies' own words by the persons to whom they were addressed.[168]

After analysing the various means and effects of forcing a large indemnity on Germany, Addis concluded:

> To secure the maximum indemnity with the minimum injury to the trade of this country it will be necessary to afford Germany free access to raw material, and freedom to arrange her own mode of paying the indemnity, which should be for a moderate amount well within her taxable capacity and on such terms as to keep alive in the debtor the hope of redemption within a reasonable time.[169]

Addis described this address to Mills, as a 'great success', and continued: 'Why don't the Allies mortgage France and make the French work for us for years?' Obviously Addis was not caught up in war hysteria which had captured so many of his countrymen. Addis was too much the practical international banker, who looked at ways and means. He told the Institute of Bankers: 'Suppose that for the total cost of the war is substituted the amount of our foreign debt, say £1500000000, and that the US agrees to take the German indemnity bonds in liquidation of our debts.' Addis felt this unlikely possibility would disturb the normal pattern of trade too much.[170]

One should not conclude from this that Addis was not affected by the war, for he was well aware of its costs, both personal and economic – his two eldest sons were serving in the army and navy, and seven of his nephews had been killed.[171] The difference was that Addis knew that the permanent peace, which all desired, could not be secured by a policy of retribution, nor could British economic recovery be achieved through crippling Germany.

Unfortunately, in the spring of 1919, the English people were receptive neither to rational argument nor to appeals for Christian charity. Their Prime Minister, David Lloyd George had promised them in the election that previous December, that he would support demands for reparations which would 'squeeze the German lemon until the pips squeaked', and that was what they expected him to do at Versailles.[172]

At Versailles, British and French demands for large reparations led to an impasse with President Wilson. The Americans also rejected the suggestion of Keynes (who was the financial adviser to the British delegation) that German bonds be used to pay the Allies' war debts.[173] Lamont advised the President not to accept Keynes's proposal.[174] Unable to reach agreement, the Big Four (Wilson, Lloyd George, Clemenceau and Orlando) left the question of reparations and war debts for later settlement.[175] Thus began an ongoing Anglo-American controversy which fatally crippled all other efforts at postwar cooperation. Addis stayed on an extra day in Paris after the Consortium meetings in May in order to advise the British Delegation's Financial Committee. After attending a meeting with the German delegates, he came away very depressed at the way the Germans were being treated, remarking that some of his old associates were among the delegates.[176]

At Versailles the Germans were forced to accept the total guilt for causing the war.[177] Reflecting on the world situation to his friend, Mills, Addis exclaimed: 'What a pass we have come to in Paris! How much better off we might have been if we had accepted Lansdowne's negotiated peace. It is too late now. The world is ablaze.' Addis felt that only the League of Nations offers a 'sole ray of hope'.[178]

And so the war came to a conclusion, leaving most of the major problems of international relations unsettled – German reparations, allied war debts, revolutionary Russia, Japan's future in East Asia and the international banking consortium for China. While Addis and his financial associates recognised that permanent peace depended on solving these problems, their experience with government officials inspired little confidence that political leaders could be trusted to achieve satisfactory solutions. Aware that international economic competition would continue and could cause future wars, they championed a return to private management of international problems, believing that informal cooperation among trustworthy associates would provide the best means for assuring permanent peace. Addis remained confident that the methods of the past would not fail to solve the crises of the present, that Britain could re-establish London as the financial centre of the world.

Part II

Attempts at Anglo-American Cooperation

Part II

Attempts at Anglo-American Cooperation

Overview: British Postwar Strategy

In 1919 the world economic system lay in pieces; the first task was to put it back together. Most of the world's political and financial leaders hoped to return to the prewar system of trade and credit and believed that government should withdraw from its wartime control over economic and financial affairs.[1] But private control of the economy meant different things in the United States and Great Britain.

In England the three centres of financial power – the Treasury, the Bank of England and the City of London – were more accustomed to working together than was the case in the United States, where sheer geography (with finance centred on Wall Street and government in Washington) prevented the kind of daily discussions which occurred in London. The Bank of England, a private corporation but also Britain's central bank, had traditionally consulted the Chancellor of the Exchequer informally on financial questions affecting the Empire. Two instances already noted – the HSBC loans to China in the late 1890s and Addis's appointment as Censor to the State Bank of Morocco in 1908 – demonstrate this system of regular informal consultation. The Governor of the Bank would seek the opinion of the Treasury when an appointment was pending, or vice versa. Similarly, the Treasury would ask the advice of the Bank when a new securities issue was proposed. This informal system of control enabled the Bank of England to act as a regulator, giving it far more power than the Federal Reserve Bank could exercise.[2] This means of communication formed the inner network of British imperial power, one that Addis penetrated after becoming the Manager of the London Office of the HSBC, then joined when he was elected to the Court of the Bank of England. In the 1920s Addis frequently became the official representative of the Treasury as well.

Years of experience in administering the Empire's financial problems had enabled the permanent officials of the Treasury (recruited from the foremost scholars of Oxford and Cambridge) to become experts in highly specialised fields, such as currency and exchange, stocks and bonds, government debt and so forth. This corps of specialists provided the government with both expertise and continuity. While political leaders came and went, Treasury officials such as Blackett, Sir Otto Niemeyer, Ralph Hawtrey, Sir John Bradbury, and his assistant, Frederick Leith-Ross, remained.[3] These permanent officials shared a common goal: to defend the Empire. In terms of training, knowledge and commitment, they enjoyed considerable advantage over their American counterparts, for in Washington (where an imperial tradition did not exist) Treasury officials usually served brief terms before leaving that department for more lucrative employment with banking firms such as J. P. Morgan & Co.[4] Addis had commented on this lack of expertise when he went to Washington in 1900 to advise the Americans on Philippine currency and during the later Consortium negotiations.[5] As a result of these differences, the British officials felt infinitely superior to their American counterparts, regarding them as naive, inexperienced and unreliable. Furthermore they did not always disguise such feelings which hardly improved Anglo-American relations in the 1920s.

Britain possessed a small and élite governing class, the members of which knew each other well, since they had gone to the same public schools, belonged to the same clubs and often served together on the same Boards and advisory committees.[6] While it is true that Addis had not entered the ranks of Britain's governing class in the traditional manner, by 1919 he had learned to speak their language and commanded their respect and confidence.

In Britain's informal system of rule, much depended on the particular personalities involved. After Montagu Norman became Governor of the Bank of England (in March 1920), he transformed that position into one of much greater authority than it had been in the past. Instead of rotating governors every two years which had formerly been the practice, the Bank kept Norman at its helm for twenty-four years. During this time the Governor assumed enormous personal power and authority. His methods were secret and highly autocratic. In the 1920s Addis played a central role in assuring Norman's continuance as Governor, successfully fending off efforts to unseat him.

For questions dealing with international affairs Norman relied on a small group of advisors, of whom Addis was to become one of the most influential.[7] The Addis–Norman friendship significantly affected both international affairs and the administration of the Bank of England. The two bankers' personalities complemented each other – Addis was frank and outgoing, assertive and energetic, practical and down-to-earth, a fighter who did not shrink from combat. In contrast, Norman was a romantic aesthete – one who relied on intuition rather than carefully marshalled facts in making decisions – a sensitive, highly strung individual who shrank from controversy, who sought to influence events through persuasion in the inner sanctum of his private office rather than from the speaker's podium or the published article. While Norman preferred to manipulate his opponents, Addis was more likely openly to confront them. Addis thrived on controversy and seemed to have nerves of steel, whereas Norman, when faced with crisis, would collapse and seek refuge abroad. Both men possessed commanding personalities, both had what was described as 'the international mind', but they exerted influence over their colleagues in different ways.[8] In the 1920s the two central bankers worked as an effective team to promote British recovery and preserve the independence of the Bank of England.

Addis became important in shaping monetary policy when he was elected to the important Committee of Treasury of the Bank of England in the spring of 1919, only a year after becoming a Director. Normally a Director did not achieve this distinction for years after his election to the Court.[9] The Committee of Treasury was the executive body of the Bank of England, an inner cabinet, with whom the Governor consulted regularly.

Addis seems to have served as one of the Governor's liaisons with Whitehall. Quite naturally there was tension between the Treasury and the Bank of England as to areas of responsibility and authority, and Norman's habitual secretiveness did not improve relations. While Addis shared Norman's determination to guard jealously the independence of the Bank, he was accustomed to working with the Treasury and Foreign Office officials, more experienced in resolving diplomatic conflicts which required the fine art of compromise.

Although Addis had recognised in 1912 that political and economic questions could not be separated, he did not allow this perception to affect his statements on free trade or monetary policy. Perhaps only poor academics and editors can insist on consistency; those who succeed in business and politics must be able to ignore or gloss over such contradictions, to make compromises between beliefs and practices. In any event, in the postwar period Addis strongly denounced the new proposals being advocated by bankers such as McKenna and economists like Keynes, that government should manage the currency and consider adopting tariffs. Instead Addis affirmed his faith in the automatic function of the gold standard and in the teachings of Adam Smith, arguing that recovery could best be obtained through an unregulated market economy.

Addis used his considerable influence to assure the preservation of free trade, the restoration of the gold standard, and the return to the Bank of England's exclusive control over monetary policy. He believed that Great Britain could regain her prewar position as the world's financial leader only by winning the confidence of the international financial community, which required an end to government borrowing.[10] The government must follow a policy of economy; prices and wages must come down. These were the recommendations of the Cunliffe Committee (reported in 1919) which Addis promoted in an article on 'The Victory Loan', published in the *Review of Reviews* in July 1919.[11]

Addis's views were traditional and shared by most leaders. Few economists or statesmen in 1919 understood that the old system could not be recreated, that the secret of the monetary stability of the nineteenth century was not the gold standard but the financial power and unity of the British Empire,[12] a situation which had come to an end when the war transformed the United States into the world's major creditor nation. In currency terms this meant that the dollar now competed with the pound as the primary medium of international exchange. But while financiers like Addis, Norman and Keynes recognised the significance of the wartime changes, they refused to accept them as permanent, believing instead that with proper strategy, Britain would be able to regain her position as the centre of international trade.[13] The key element in this strategy was winning American cooperation.

American cooperation was essential for two reasons: only the United States had the surplus capital available for the foreign loans and investments which would fuel economic recovery and, second, the United States government held demand notes for British war debts which Britain was obliged to pay unless some other arrangements could be worked out. The overall British goal in the postwar period was to persuade American leaders to use their surplus capital cooperatively rather than competitively. Thus two main themes dominate the postwar Anglo-American relationship: cooperation and competition.

In theory the United States' emergence as the world's creditor meant that it should assume Britain's former role in international finance and become the world's major lender. But while American leaders were eager to assert their new power, they were inexperienced, reluctant to assume the responsibilities which that power entailed. Part of this reluctance was political, reflecting the particular nature of the American system of government, but much of the cause of isolationist sentiment reflected popular disillusionment with Wilsonian idealism.

After a bitter political struggle (marked by Republican denunciations of the Versailles Treaty) the US Senate refused to ratify the agreement. Since the Covenant of the League was a part of the Treaty the United States did not join the League of Nations. Thereafter both Congress and the American public became increasingly suspicious of European politics, disappointed by the outcome of the war and determined to pursue an independent path. President Wilson's humiliating defeat by the Senate and the subsequent victory of the Republican Presidential candidate, Warren G. Harding, in the Presidential election of 1920, initiated a period of executive weakness in Washington. Throughout the 1920s the President and the State Department were too intimidated by Congress to attempt to educate the American public to accept the responsibilities which their new wealth and power implied.

The issue of war debts and reparations became one of the chief causes of Anglo-American enmity in the 1920s, since Washington consistently refused to recognise any relationship between reparations and war debts. American policy demonstrates congressional intimidation of the executive branch, but even more significantly, showed American determination to preserve its dominance over Britain. The inter-allied war debts were those debts owed by Great Britain, France, Russia, Italy and Belgium to the United States and to each other. As we have seen, at the Paris Peace Conference in 1919 the American delegation had turned down Britain's proposal that such debts be cancelled. At the same time Lamont opposed Keynes's suggestion that the British and French use German reparation bonds to pay their war debts to America, arguing instead for a return to purely private credits for postwar recovery.[14]

Strong (who was visiting London in the summer of 1919) recognised from the first the connection between war debts and reparations and encouraged his British friends to believe that some arrangement could be made to provide that war-debt payments could be met with German bonds, although he admitted to Blackett that he had no authority to make such a proposal.[15] Addis had told Strong that he felt 'some adjustment of the debt between the various parties could be effected so as to reduce the gross amount'.[16] After conferring with Addis and other British bankers and government leaders, Strong wrote to R. Leffingwell (an Assistant Secretary of the US Treasury) that 'most of the really level-headed able men that I met like Cokayne, and Norman in the Bank of England, Sir Charles Addis and the Chancellor, Mr Austen Chamberlain, do not expect forgiveness of the debt'.[17] Strong emphasised however that all these leaders were concerned about American competition.

Over the next few weeks, Addis, Strong and other British and American leaders, such as Col. House (who had been President Wilson's closest advisor) developed a plan whereby they could pay British war debts to some extent out of reparation payments.[18] The hope was that Col. House and former Foreign Secretary Sir Edward Grey (who with Foreign Office official William Tyrrell was to undertake a special mission to Washington) could persuade the Wilson Administration to adopt such a plan.[19] Unfortunately in the autumn of 1919 President Wilson had a stroke and Col. House never regained his former influence, so Grey did not see the President.[20] Meanwhile the American Treasury remained adamantly opposed to any suggestion that the two topics were connected, a position it maintained throughout the 1920s.

The American Treasury's consistent refusal to recognise any connection between reparations and war debts (illogical and unreasonable as it might seem) could be explained – even defended – from a narrow, nationalistic point of view – as an ideal strategic tactic adopted by American leaders determined to supplant the British as the world's leading power. Since the American financial community hoped to finance the recovery of Germany through new loans (which would necessarily require the security of that country's resources) the Americans opposed the pledging of those resources for reparation payments. Addis assumed a similar position regarding a proposed Consortium loan to China, insisting that it could not be used to pay off the First World War debts to Japan and the United States, whereas the Americans insisted that these debts must be funded from the new proceeds.[21]

In other words, one's view on debt repayment depended on who held the debt. At Versailles reparations had been given a first charge on the German assets, meaning that if the German government defaulted on reparation payments, then the French and British were entitled to collect such revenues as those of the German railway system. Thus if a high reparation figure was established, there would be no security left for further loans to Germany. This explains why the Americans insisted on a generous policy toward Germany (in establishing the reparations figure) while at the same time insisting that the Allies pay their war debts and refused to recognise any connection between the two. The Americans reasoned that if British citizens had to pay high taxes to pay war debts these taxes would make British goods more expensive and thus less competitive.[22] Not surprisingly, Norman, Addis and the British Treasury were determined not to pay any more in war debts to the United States than they received in reparation payments.

What masked the underlying competitive nature of the Anglo-American relationship, making it difficult to discern, were the public professions of friendship and cooperation made by British and American bankers in the postwar years. Nor were these professions necessarily insincere. Initially Addis, Norman and Strong all believed that Central Bank cooperation would assure world economic recovery and international financial stability.[23] Yet despite this agreement and regardless of the fact that Strong and Norman possessed a genuine affection and respect for each other, neither of these two central bankers was willing to concede the primacy of his own financial capital. On the contrary each aimed at establishing his own country's currency as the leading unit of world finance and exchange. However in the immediate postwar years the international situation was so unstable that the bankers temporarily ignored their countries' implicit adversarial positions while they pursued their common goal of restoring monetary stability and establishing central bank cooperation.

In the years immediately after the war Addis became a key figure in Britain's attempt to win American cooperation in both Asia and Europe, making several trips to the United States between 1920 and 1930 in an attempt to persuade American policymakers that Anglo-American cooperation was essential to the world's economic recovery and stability. He succeeded in organising the second Consortium for China in 1920 and the next year (after a visit which he and Norman made to the United States), he thought that they had also won American support for similar financial cooperation in Europe. But he was mistaken. What is not clear is whether Strong and Morgans deliberately misled Addis and Norman concerning the possibility of future cooperation, or whether the American financiers were deceived themselves.

What was certain was the effect of government withdrawal from the arena of international finance – the private financier became far more important in shaping international financial policy. In the United States, the House of Morgan succeeded in expanding its dominance over world credit without the accompanying responsibility which such authority implied.[24] In the 1920s Morgans worked assiduously and successfully to preserve the dominant position which it had won during the war through financing the Allied Powers.[25] In some instances Morgans worked as a partner of the American State Department while in other circumstances (such as China) it opposed the Department's aims. Morgan's interests were global rather than national; its power was so enormous as to make it impossible for the State Department to control.

Much of Morgans' success stemmed from its combined influence with the British government and with Governor Strong. Strong, Lamont and H. P. Davison had been close friends for years.[26] The British continued to employ Morgans as their fiscal agent after 1919 in the expectation that the firm would ultimately be able to change American government policy on the war debts. Morgans encouraged this expectation throughout the 1920s while making use of British influence in Europe and China to block competition from other American investment houses.[27]

Unfortunately for the British, their strategy, – using Morgan influence to win some accommodation on war debts and working with Strong to achieve Central Bank cooperation – proved to be fatally flawed. The Federal Reserve System did not possess as much authority, either with Wall Street or the government, as the Bank of England enjoyed; neither Morgans nor the American Executive branch could control Congress. As a result neither the expected cancellation of war debts nor Central Bank cooperation took place.

After ten years of cooperating with the United States and 'playing the game', by cancelling the Anglo-Japanese Alliance (1922), funding the war debts (1923), accepting the Dawes Settlement for reparations (1924), returning to the gold standard (1925) and agreeing to the Young Plan (1929), the British found that these policies had produced not economic recovery and an Anglo-American partnership, but unemployment, industrial stagnation, a budget badly out of balance, and American hoarding of gold. Faced with economic crisis, Addis fundamentally changed his views in 1929 and supported a policy of inflation and a greater government role in monetary policy.

At the Reparations Conference of 1929 (where Addis served as a British financial expert) he helped to create the Young Plan (which specifically connected reparations and war debts and provided a means to eliminate both) and drew up plans for the Bank for International Settlements which he believed could provide a solution to Europe's credit needs. Shortly thereafter the collapse of the American stock market (in October 1929) and the withdrawal of American funds from Europe led to new pressures on the German budget and the subsequent disintegration of the whole international framework which had been created by the Dawes and Young plans.

At this point, Addis joined with a small group of financial leaders in the Treasury and Bank of England to force a showdown with the United States on the reparations and war-debt questions. When Hoover refused to cancel, speculation on the pound pushed Britain off the gold standard in September 1931. While this humiliating event publicly revealed the deficiencies of the British Treasury, its more important lesson was to show that the strategy of Anglo-American cooperation had failed.

5 Competition vs Cooperation, 1919–22

'Their whole tradition and outlook are provincial – to keep out of European entanglements – and to convince them that the war has made this forever impossible and that no nation can hereafter live to itself alone requires persuasion and persuasion takes time.' — Addis, 24 August 1921

In June 1919, Addis and Eba celebrated their silver (25th) wedding anniversary, with twenty-four relations and friends at dinner. All thirteen children were present 'in health and happiness'.[1] Reporting the event to Mills, Addis quoted the Biblical passage: 'To whom much is given of him shall much be required.'[2] This sense of commitment and duty continued to be the motivation for Addis's behaviour, unlikely as such idealism may seem from the more cynical perspective of the 1980s. There is no doubt that Addis sincerely believed that his efforts would benefit not only his corporation but his country and the world.

During these years Addis's responsibilities as government adviser continued to expand, while his prestige and authority grew in the City, as demonstrated by his 1921 election as President of the Institute of Bankers. Although he officially retired from the position of London Manager of the HSBC in October 1921, the retirement merely marked a new stage in his many-faceted career. As adviser to the Governor of the Bank of England, and to the British Treasury, he helped to shape Britain's position on war debts and reparations. As Manager of the British Group of the Consortium, he presided over the establishment of the second China Consortium. During an extended East Asian trip, he demonstrated his determination to preserve British influence in China.

WOOING THE AMERICANS, 1919–20

In the summer of 1919 respected authorities on international finance, such as Dr Gerard Vissering, Governor of the Netherlands Bank; C. E. ter Meulen, a Dutch financier with Hope & Co. (the Dutch financial agents for the British government); Jean Monnet, the Deputy Secretary General of the League of Nations; Joseph Avenol, the French Financial Attaché in London; and Fred Kent, an American banker on the Reparations Committee, began their search for a plan which would assure world economic recovery.[3] Addis's close contact with Strong began at this time while Strong was in Europe making arrangements for the distribution of German gold to the various victors.[4] Convinced that a large loan would be needed for European recovery, Vissering invited Keynes (who was now out of the government but still in touch with Treasury officials) to a meeting in Amsterdam in October 1919, with ter Meulen from Holland, Kent and Paul Warburg from the United States, and other financiers, to discuss the financial position of Europe and his proposal for an 'international loan to be furnished mainly by America'.[5] Warburg, a recognised financial expert, had resigned from the Federal Reserve Board during the anti-German hysteria of 1918.[6] Afterwards, Keynes (assisted by Warburg) drafted a proposal for an international loan intending to submit it to the League of Nations. The British banker Robert Brand agreed to participate. After consultations with other leaders such as Lord Robert Cecil, British representative to the League of Nations, and redrafting in November, the organising group decided to obtain influential signatures in each country to accompany the proposal.[7]

As originally drafted, the International Memorial called attention to the urgency of finding solutions to the problems of inflation then prevalent throughout Europe as well as those caused by reparations and war debts. It argued that 'the working capital needed is too large in amount and is required too quickly for such channels to be adequate'. Therefore they felt that 'a more comprehensive scheme is necessary'. The Memorial emphasised that 'the interests of the whole of Europe and indeed of the whole world are at stake', and stated that 'if the League of Nations were to recommend cooperative action, there is no action amongst either neutral or belligerent countries which would stand aside from taking its proper part'.[8] But the drafters of the Memorial were too optimistic. Despite the fact that the Memorial provided that the proposed loan would rank ahead 'of all other indebtedness whatsoever whether internal debt, reparation payments or inter-allied government debt', the American Treasury refused to become involved.[9] As a result, the framers decided to direct the International Memorial to heads of different governments and, in the United States, to the Chamber of Commerce.

Meanwhile, the publication of Keynes's *The Economic Conse-quences of the Peace*, which harshly criticised the Versailles Treaty and its formulators, led to the decision that Keynes's name should not appear as one of the signers of the International Memorial.[10] While it is difficult to estimate the effect of such works, there is no doubt that by increasing American antipathy toward the British, it lessened any possibility of winning support for the extension of new credits for European recovery, as Austen Chamberlain and Brand had warned.[11]

As the year came to a close, there seemed little reason for optimism concerning the future. Addis described it in his diary as 'a year of public disillusion' but he was thankful nonetheless that there was 'peace at home. Twelve children with us and Charles expected soon. A year of uninterrupted good health and blessing – Thank God.'[12]

After meeting with Grenfell and the Governor of the Bank of England (Cokayne) Addis agreed to sign the Memorial which was published in all the world's leading newspapers on 15 January 1920.[13] Next Addis discussed the Memorial with Lord Cecil, Brand, and Walter Leaf (at Lazards) then with McKenna, Chairman of the Midland Bank, J. H. Thomas, an influential Labour leader, Chamber-lain, Chancellor of the Exchequer, and Auckland Geddes, the newly appointed British Ambassador to the United States.[14]

The most serious problem remained: how to persuade the Amer-icans to provide loans.[15] Since the United States refused to participate in the League, that body could not carry out the financial role which Keynes envisioned. Despite his government's lack of enthusiasm concerning the proposal, Kent continued to support the International Memorial, writing to Vissering that there was 'no question that our chance to successfully combat Bolshevism may lie largely in an ultimate combination of the neutral nations of Europe and the Allies'.[16] Kent's comment demonstrates the general awareness among both American and European financial leaders that world recovery depended upon some kind of aid to central Europe, reflecting a concern about the spread of Bolshevism. But the American financiers could not convince Washington. In addition, there was disagreement among the financiers as to where the first loans should go and how they should be arranged.

At this juncture Norman (who became Governor of the Bank of England in March 1920) began to emerge as a major formulator of the government's international financial policy, albeit behind the scenes. In May 1920 Governor Norman asked Addis to represent

Great Britain at the Brussels Conference, which the League of Nations was convening to consider the international financial situation.[17] As it turned out, Addis could not go to Brussels as he was going to Washington for the organisation of the second China Consortium, but he continued hereafter to be involved in the question of international credits for Europe, as well as reparations and war debts. The informal, even irregular, highly personal and secret method which Norman devised to solve the problem of the Anglo-French loan provided an early indication of the techniques he practised thereafter.

Repayment of the Anglo-French Loan of 1915 (an obligation due to Morgans in August 1920) was one of the most urgent problems facing the British and French governments that spring.[18] Norman began discussing the topic with Blackett of the Treasury and private bankers in February 1920.[19] Later that month Norman consulted with Avenol regarding means of repaying the loan and found him 'not generally hopeful'.[20] However, new possibilities emerged late in March when Norman met with senior Morgan partner, H. P. Davison, for Davison drew Norman's attention to the Russian gold held in Paris by the Allies jointly. These conversations continued through May, when a complicated British plan (which will be discussed in the next section) was forwarded to Washington.[21]

At the same time, a further conversation with Avenol led Norman to devise a strategy for the war debts. In a long memorandum he summarised his conclusions: first, he did not think that Germany could 'borrow 400 million pounds' and second, he agreed 'with the policy that our dealings over War Debts with the European Allies should be separate from our similar dealings with America'. But Norman saw 'no reason why our (future) ability or intention to pay America should govern our (present) willingness to make promises on that score. Politically America is in no state to make long agreements which will stand or be allowed to stand the test of time'. He emphasised that 'our War Debt to America cannot be wholly disassociated from European conditions, for the idea that we should now begin and repay America in cash which (if we can spare it) is desperately needed throughout Europe, is not reasonable'. Therefore the Governor concluded that 'in any Debt negotiations with America we should just mark time till conditions have cleared on both sides of the Atlantic'. In addition he observed that 'as between England and France the proportion of 5 to 11 is pretty well agreed as regards dividing the indemnity'. Therefore he proposed that:

once the total indemnity shall have been fixed our eventual share in it can be defined and *it would not be out of the way to fix the total so that our share of it would be equal to our War Debt to America.* If that could be done in the near future it would only be a question of time before our War Debt to America could naturally be set off against our share of the indemnity in one or other of several possible ways: e.g. we might forego any share in the proceeds of M. Avenol's 400 million pound international loan and give our proportion of Bonds to America on account, or we might take from Germany a Bond for our whole share of the indemnity and hand it to America in payment of our debt. To put it shortly: we should never pay in cash the principle or interest of our War Debt to America or make agreements when to do so: this debt was not incurred on our own behalf but on behalf of our allies: we need no indemnity for ourselves from Germany: we should discharge our War Debt to America by means of our indemnity from Germany, an exchange which would be approved as right and equitable by the whole world.[22]

Norman's approach and strategy regarding war debts and reparations, which was virtually identical with the view argued by Keynes at Versailles and thereafter, became the government's policy as announced in the Balfour Note of 1922. As such, it created endless friction with the Americans and prevented the kind of cooperation which leaders in both countries recongnised was essential to world recovery.

Not all British leaders supported this policy. Chancellor of the Exchequer Austen Chamberlain protested against the refusal of the Lloyd George government to fund the war debts, ultimately insisting that his dissent from the government's policy be recorded.[23] But a policy of releasing the allies from their debts without first obtaining American cancellation of Britain's debt was not supported either by the Governor of the Bank of England or by the Lloyd George government. Since Addis worked closely with Norman throughout this period and definitely opposed the British debt-funding agreement of January 1923 it seems certain that he supported the Lloyd George Coalition government's policy. In all likelihood Addis believed that his primary duty was to defend British interests, even if that implied a refusal to pay the war debts.

The explanation for the different points of view in London and Washington lies in the fact that in British eyes, the Americans had benefited greatly from the war loans, while in American eyes, only Morgans had benefited, and the American taxpayer had paid. The failure of British leaders to understand how suspiciously most Americans regarded Morgans as the epitome of the 'Wall Street Interests', which they viewed as opposed to most Americans' interests, continued to handicap British efforts at partnership.

While these complicated financial and economic questions were being resolved within the British government, Addis was at the same time working closely with the Foreign Office regarding plans for the second China Consortium. Far Eastern questions appeared to offer more opportunity to woo the Americans, since Washington needed British cooperation to control Japan.

THE CONSORTIUM, 1919–20

Several obstacles had to be surmounted before the second Consortium could become a reality. As the Americans had discovered at the Paris Peace Conference, Japan had to be reassured regarding her 'special interests' in southern Manchuria and Eastern Mongolia, and Addis had to be reassured regarding government support. The State Department expected the British to intervene with their Japanese ally to persuade the Japanese to join the Consortium.[24]

As he had done in 1912 Addis insisted on 'exclusive government support' for the Consortium even though he recognised that such a demand placed the Foreign Office in a difficult position.[25] The British Group included Lord Revelstoke, Lord Faringdon (Governor of the British Trade Corporation); Walter Leaf (President of the London County Westminster and Parr's Bank); and Turner (a financier),[26] representing in Addis's words 'the élite of city finance'.[27] The Foreign Office had insisted in 1919 that the British Group be expanded to include the British Trade Corporation and Rothschilds.[28] Addis continued to defend the HSBC's primary place in Chinese finance. After talking to Addis in June, Lamont wrote to the State Department that 'The Hong Kong & Shanghai Bank is not yet inclined to open up and play the game the way the new plan contemplates.'[29] What Lamont was referring to here was the provision for the surrender of options, concessions granted earlier by the Chinese, which under the new Consortium were to be shared equally with all four groups.

Gradually the areas of disagreement between the American and British groups were worked out and Addis reached agreement with the Foreign Office regarding support for the Consortium. In an article titled 'European Policy and Finance in China', published in Europe in the *International Review* in June 1919 and reprinted in *Living Age* in the United States, Addis explained the purposes of the Consortium.[30] While recognising the dangers of monopoly, he described the Consortium as 'the best solution possible'. He stated that 'The natural remedy for the evils of excessive competition is cooperation', and frankly recognised that the object of the proposed loan to China was 'the reform of the Peking Administration and the rehabilitation of the currency'.

What proved more difficult to achieve was an understanding with the Japanese regarding Manchuria and Eastern Mongolia. Early in 1920 the State Department sent Lamont to Japan and China to try to work out an agreement.[31] From Tokyo Lamont detailed the requirements for Japanese entry, listing the Manchurian railways which would not be included in the scope of the Consortium.[32] Although Addis was not particularly pleased at the exclusion of the Taonanfu–Jehol railway, he accepted these terms.[33] While Lamont was discussing specifics in Tokyo, the British Foreign Office devised a formula (using language from the Lansing–Ishii Notes of 1917) to assure Japan that her special interests would be protected.[34] Not only did the Americans and British reach agreement regarding the Consortium that spring but they also devised a complicated plan for financing the Chinese Eastern Railway (CER).

At this time the Foreign Office (which favoured American control of this strategic railway) was under pressure from the Treasury to remove the British military who had been guarding the railway since 1919.[35] Faced with the need for funds for the CER as well as the repayment of the Anglo-French loan, the Treasury, with the help of Norman (who had earlier discussed the Anglo-French Loan with Davison) devised a plan whereby the Tsarist gold (which had been turned over to the Allies after the Treaty of Brest–Litovsk and deposited in the Bank of France) would be used 'to extinguish a portion of Russia's liability of $100 000 000' which the French and British government had advanced to the Tsarist government. In order to gain Morgans' cooperation with this proposal, the Treasury suggested that $10 000 000 be used as security for a loan to the CER.[36] This must be the proposal to which Norman referred as being 'forwarded to Washington'. Strong was in Tokyo at this time, meeting with Japanese bankers, with letters of introduction furnished by Addis.[37]

Strong and Lamont returned from Japan very favourably impressed with the Japanese bankers whom they visited, convinced that they shared the Western point of view and could be trusted.[38] Strong formed a particularly high opinion of Junnosuke Inouye (who began his career with the South Manchuria Railway Company and then became a Governor of the Bank of Japan) and Eigo Fukai (the Deputy Governor of the Bank of Japan). Strong established a relationship between the Bank of Japan and the New York Federal Reserve.[39] Addis had known Fukai for many years.[40] After Lamont returned from East Asia, American and British diplomats met at the State Department in July and agreed to use the Tsarist gold to finance the CER and also to pay off the Anglo-French loan.[41]

The importance of these Anglo-American–Japanese conversations and contacts is what they reveal about the development of interntional economic policy in the early 1920s – the Japanese bankers were incorporated into that inner circle of financiers who trusted each other more than their own political leaders and who hoped through private cooperation to ensure international stability.

It seems highly unlikely that Addis could have been unaware of these arrangements for the CER, given his involvement in other closely related matters, and his membership in the Committee of Treasury of the Bank of England. While he was not directly involved in the negotiations over the Tsarist gold held in the Bank of France, during the same period he was selling the so-called 'Omsk gold' to the Indian Government, HM Treasury and the Bank of England.[42] As noted earlier, the Omsk gold had been used as security for an advance by Barings to the Kolchak government in the summer of 1919. With the demise of that government in 1920 the Russian Provisional government officials agreed to its sale.[43] Addis was also a member of the Committee to Enquire into Indian Exchange and Currency, appointed in 1919, which provided additional sources of information.[44]

What is important to recognise is the unofficial and secret way in which these complicated financial arrangements were made, for they demonstrate the way in which international bankers operated almost outside the law or government control. Indeed, when Ambassador Geddes informed the Foreign Office that President Wilson found it 'contrary to his conscience' to use the Russian gold for the CER, he added that Norman Davis and Bainbridge Colby (the Under-secretary and Secretary of State) said that 'if gold were received in New York it would not be the business of the Assay office to enquire as to its origin'.[45] To be safe, the British Treasury simply exchanged the Russian gold for British gold.[46]

For the financiers the important thing was that the British, American and Japanese bankers had finally worked out their differences in East Asia. They assumed that once this was achieved, their governments would carry out their plans. One cannot but be struck by the lack of concern about the Chinese point of view. The fact was that all three groups regarded the Chinese as in need of control and guidance, not ready for treatment as a truly sovereign government.

With most of the financial problems resolved, Addis believed that business in China might resume. Early in September he hosted a dinner at the Oriental Club which included most of the British leaders involved in China affairs – Victor Wellesley from the Foreign Office; Aglen, the Inspector General of the Chinese Maritme Customs; Hillier, the long-time agent of the HSBC in Peking; Stevenson, the London representative of the Chinese Maritime Customs; and Sidney Mayers, a Director of the Chinese Central Railways. Addis opened the discussion with a survey of Consortium prospects and noted that 'a lively discussion followed'.[47] In a later speech at the B&C Corporation, Addis supported the principle of open tender for all industrial contracts and welcomed the inclusion of a Chinese banking group in the Consortium.[48] A month later, on board *The Olympic* bound for New York, Addis observed: 'If we fail to achieve our result it will not be for want of preparation.'[49]

As the banking groups assembled in New York, no effort was spared to convince the world that with the organisation of the Consortium a new day was dawning for China. To mark the event, a special service was held in the National Cathedral, where the Bishop of New York welcomed the delegates and blessed the Consortium. Addis described the impressive ceremony to his wife, saying 'There were 700 Chinese present, Thomas Lamont spoke on China, the Stars & Stripes and the Chinese Flag were unfolded and we sang the Star Spangled Banner in English and the Chinese National Anthem *in Chinese.*'[50]

One senses in this description a certain degree of embarrassed scepticism and yet at the same time, a feeling of being caught up in the events, overwhelmed by American idealism perhaps. At a dinner given by Lamont, Addis sounded a familiar theme:

> what kept men apart was misunderstanding and misrepresentation;
> that the causes of war were ignorance and untruth . . . that on us

lay the responsibility by patience and wisdom to make of this Consortium an instrument to bridge the gulf between East and West and to lay one stone of the foundation of that Temple of Peace which somehow or other mankind must erect or see the world plunged in the anarchy of war.[51]

Up to the very last day Addis was not certain whether the French would agree to surrender their options. He wrote to his wife that unless they did, the agreement could not be signed. 'Whether we shall sign or not I do not know. Failure would be a disaster and the responsibility of saying "No" which now depends on me, is a heavy burden to bear. But I have given the French to understand that I shall not shrink from it if necessary.'[52] Addis succeeded, the French gave way, and on 15 October 1920 the agreement was signed by all four Groups.

The Consortium agreement provided that the governments gave 'their complete support to their respective national group' and promised 'collective support of the diplomatic representatives in Peking of the four governments'.[53] Addis had already begun the task of persuading the investment community to buy Chinese bonds. Speaking to the Bond Club Addis described conditions in China, indicated that the frequent revolutions were 'bloodless' and stated that Chinese railway bonds were 'one of the best secured bonds in the market'.[54]

What Addis did not anticipate was how difficult it would be to win the cooperation of the Chinese government, which was expected to accept a Consortium loan with conditions regarding the 'supervision of construction, expenditure, and operation' of its nationalised railway system.[55] In addition to continuing the present controls and supervision, the foreign Powers expected to develop new Chinese revenues such as the wine and tobacco tax.[56] Given the expectation of the Western-educated Chinese that President Woodrow Wilson's promise for self-determination would be carried out through the League of Nations (of which they were a member) it was hardly realistic for Addis and his partners to expect to continue the policies of the past in China. Before long reports of Chinese opposition to the Consortium began to reach the State Department, where they received some sympathy.[57]

A further problem surrounding the implementation of the new Consortium agreement was the question as to which railways were to be included in the scope of the Consortium. In speaking to Professor

Kemmerer's graduate students at Princeton, Addis explained that the Shantung railway, which was the key to the control of Shantung province, could not be taken away from Japanese control, since 'the League of Nations recognised Japan's position there' as a result of the Versailles Conference.[58] In addition, he said that the Chinese Eastern Railway was technically outside the scope of the Consortium, although the Americans and British still hoped that arrangements could be made for a Consortium loan to that line.[59] These difficult questions would have to be settled diplomatically. Meanwhile, Addis took advantage of his time in the United States to do some sounding on the war debts issue.

WAR DEBTS, REPARATIONS AND FAR EASTERN QUESTIONS

It seems likely that Addis, while visiting Federal Reserve officials in New York and Washington, began to explore the questions of British payments of the war debts as well as a loan to the Chinese Eastern Railways.[60] Addis wrote to Eba that he was going to Washington to see William P. Harding, the Governor of the Federal Reserve Board.[61] Addis may also have been making sure that the Bank of England gold sent in payment of the Anglo-French loan had arrived safely. The New York bankers described Addis as 'a most delightful fellow' who had a 'well-developed sense of humor'.[62] Pierre Jay, the Chairman of the Federal Reserve Bank of New York, reported: 'we had a most interesting evening discussing central banking conditions in England and this country . . . He visited Washington . . . and talked with members of Fed.'[63] These American central bankers doubtless warned Addis of the current anti-British views in the United States regarding the war debts and the political effect these views were having on Congressmen faced with an imminent November election.

While he was in Washington Addis took the opportunity to visit the British Ambassador to the United States, Sir Auckland Geddes, who was not optimistic about the political outlook in the United States. He was urging the Lloyd George government to fund the war debts before a new Republican administration came into power, since he felt that such new officials were likely to be less generous than the present Democratic administration of Woodrow Wilson. Geddes warned the Foreign Office that full-page advertisements were appearing urging the necessity for payment of the Allied debts.[64] However, the Foreign Secretary (Lord Curzon) explained to Geddes that the government did not want to fund the debt because 'Any plan which involves our giving the United States Government bonds which they could place with private investors is the most objectionable of all expedients from the British standpoint.' He pointed out that 'from the moment that they passed into private hands, it would be impossible for the US Treasury, even if it should hereafter desire to do so in connection with any general scheme for the treatment of international debts, to remit or postpone any part of the British obligation'.[65] And so, as the American government went to the polls to elect a new President, the war-debt question remained unresolved, and with it, most of the other major issues affecting Anglo-American relations.

Despite the signing of the Consortium agreement and the State Department's commitment to Anglo-American cooperation in East Asia, there were many Americans in both public and private positions who remained suspicious regarding British intentions in China. These feelings were especially strong among American representatives in South China. Many reports came into the State Department regarding the 'Cassel Concession', which was reportedly a contract which the rival Southern Chinese government in Canton had granted to Major Louis Cassel, involving a monopoly over railway building and mine development. Cassel represented the major British firms in China – Jardine Matheson & Co., Butterfield & Swire, Taikoo Dockyard, the HSBC and the Peninsular & Oriental Steam Navigation Co.[66]

When the American Group representative, F. W. Stevens, arrived in China he was dismayed by the extent to which the British dominated the economic scene. Stevens, who did not share Lamont's trust in Addis, especially disliked the practice of sending Consortium communications via London. Lamont, who was very upset by Stevens's suspicions, reproved him for his 'bad beginning'. He informed Stevens that:

> The whole key to the success of the Consortium, and above and beyond all that to the settlement of all Far Eastern problems lies in the joint hands of the US and Gt Britain. Great Britain is our one best bet. We have simply *got* to get on with her.

Instead he said that Stevens had 'started out by slapping her in the face'. Lamont also scolded Stevens for his poor handling of the British Minister, Sir Beilby Alston, and described Addis as 'the Daddy Long-legs of the whole Consortium'.[67] Despite this firm tone,

Lamont did not succeed in convincing Stevens that he should cooperate with the British. Stevens continued to suspect that they were trying to put something over on the Americans, an accusation which Lamont denounced as 'perfect rot'.[68]

Nor was Stevens alone in feeling this way. Julean Arnold, the American commercial attaché, in discussing the Federal Wireless Agreement, warned: 'Our British Cousins are not as kindly disposed toward us as they were while we were helping Germany to keep away from London.'[69]

While the State Department continued to ignore these suggestions, the Department of Commerce, under the aggressive leadership of Herbert Hoover, requested detailed data on 'the effect of the British action on our commerce in China'.[70] At the same time, the powerful Anglophobic Senator William Borah (who most recently had helped to defeat the Versailles Treaty) questioned MacMurray (the Chief of the Far Eastern Division of the State Department) about the monopoly aspects of the Consortium.[71] MacMurray admitted that an independent group would have no chance of succeeding in making industrial loans in competition with the Consortium.

Although MacMurray remained firmly committed to the Consortium and Anglo-American support for the Peking government, other voices in the State Department, such as Economic Advisor Stanley Hornbeck, were not convinced that this was the wisest policy. Hornbeck felt that Washington was making a mistake in channelling all customs and salt revenues to the Peking government, in effect abandoning the rival Southern Chinese revolutionaries in Canton.[72] In other words, while a beginning had been made in forging an Anglo-American partnership for the Far East, suspicions continued and much remained to be done.

In May 1921 A. Stephen (the Chief Manager of the HSBC) suggested that Addis consider making a trip to China. Stephen wrote that Alston had put forward the idea when he was in Shanghai, thinking that it was desirable that Addis should get 'into personal touch with the people in Peking and with affairs generally in China'.[73] While this proposal was under consideration, the government recognised Addis's achievement by the appointment of a KCMG 'for valuable services to HM Government in connexion with finance in China'.[74]

Shortly thereafter Addis announced his retirement as Manager of the London Office of the HSBC, to be effective in the autumn, and indicated that he would be succeeded by Sir Newton Stabb.[75] Addis was to stay on as Chairman of the London Committee of the HSBC, and Manager of the British Group, with a salary of £5000. Explaining the purpose of his China trip to his son, Addis wrote: 'It is supposed my visit may be of some benefit to British interests.'[76] But before leaving, Addis still had some financial questions to attend to.

When Addis returned from America, he had several meetings with Norman and Strong, to discuss the European situation.[77] Norman told Addis that he had been commissioned to offer him the post of organiser of the Ter Meulen scheme of international credits under the League of Nations, which had been recommended at the Brussels Conference.[78] However Addis did not feel he could accept, since it would mean 'giving up a couple or three years to the work'.[79] While it was true that he would be retiring the next year, he had already assumed new responsibilities as a Director of the P&O and the British Indian Steamship Co.[80] With his combined Consortium and Bank of England responsibilities, there was simply not enough time for a League of Nations position.

Furthermore Addis wrote to Mills that he was beginning to feel his years, in the sense of having few close friends left: 'I have always understood that with advancing years one's friends drop out like one's teeth – this is not the fault necessarily of oneself or one's friends – the cure is making new friends – but they must of course be people much younger than oneself.' He continued that he had 'always liked talking with people older than myself – and still do (when I can find them)'.[81]

The situation in Europe had not improved. At a dinner given by Sir George Paish, to discuss the reconstruction of Europe, Addis emphasised that the revival of trade was the 'keystone of European construction'. He explained that 'Central Europe must be furnished with credits to purchase the raw materials required to restart its industries', and continued: 'By the sale of their produce India and China would be able to satisfy their demand for British manufactures. This would in turn by the liquidation of existing stocks of commodities stimulate British production in England.'[82] Shortly after this Addis signed 'An Appeal by Bankers of the United Kingdom' which was published in the *Times* protesting against the regulation of trade.[83] This appeal echoed the classic free-trade argument which Addis had made at the Paish dinner, but it did not provide any immediate answer for Britain's growing unemployment problem.

In May the Treasury sent Addis to Paris to meet with the Reparations Commission.[84] After meeting with British Treasury officials Frederick Leith-Ross and Bradbury, Addis left Paris 'well content'.[85] Norman wrote to Strong that he was pleased that Germany had accepted terms and expected a loan to Austria from J. P. M. & Co.[86] Credits for central Europe formed one piece of the central banker's overall plan for economic recovery. At the same time British financiers and government leaders were continuing their talks concerning the funding of the war debts. Addis noted in his diary of 10 March 1921, that he took the chair at the Tuesday Club where Blackett read a paper on funding the debt.[87]

Meanwhile, the Lloyd George government continued to postpone sending a debt mission to Washington while the Harding Administration sought legislation which would permit the Executive branch to handle the funding. As the plans for a forthcoming naval disarmament conference developed that spring, the possibility that some kind of an arrangement might be worked out with the Americans, whereby they might agree to more favourable treatment of British war debts in return for British willingness to accept naval parity and give up the Anglo-Japanese alliance seemed encouraging.[88] Lamont's presence in London for a meeting of the Consortium Council gave the British an opportunity to exchange views on all these concerns.[89]

The esteem in which his fellow-bankers held him became obvious that spring when Walter Leaf, the President of the Institute of Bankers, told Addis that the Council wanted Addis to succeed him. His delight at the honour is suggested in his brief diary comment: 'That I should have lived to see the day.'[90] Later he wrote to Mills: 'It is the first time the Institute has ever gone outside the charmed circle of the home banks for their President.'[91]

Addis continued to be at the centre of these informal Anglo-American conversations. When the International Chamber of Commerce Conference was held in London, Addis dined with Paish to meet the American bankers who were attending, and discussed the economic revival of Europe. On 14 July he chaired the Tuesday Club dinner where Keynes referred to him as 'one of the most eminent economists in the Kingdom'. That same month, Norman invited Addis to accompany him on a secret mission to New York in order to confer with their American counterparts, in hopes that understandings might be reached and plans made for the Anglo-American cooperation which he felt could alone assure peace.[92] With the Naval Disarmament Conference now scheduled for November and a planned Addis trip to East Asia in the autumn, there seemed reason to hope that the long-awaited opportunity to gain a firm

American commitment to a general scheme of international economic cooperation had arrived. Immediately prior to leaving for Washington, Addis had dinner with Miles Lampson, the former British High Commissioner in Siberia, and W. E. Leveson, the Secretary of the British Group of the Consortium, when they no doubt discussed plans for the Chinese Eastern Railway.

The matter of most concern to the Americans continued to be the CER. Lamont asked Secretary of State Charles Evans Hughes to talk with Addis, saying that Addis:

> realises, from conversations with his Foreign Office people, just as I from you, the political aspects of this matter, and he assures me that the British Group is of his mind. I am particularly *anxious that Sir Charles have an opportunity of conversation with you during his brief stay in this country.*

Lamont informed the Secretary of State that Addis was going to the Far East in the autumn and continued:

> I hardly have to explain to you that his presence there will be of great advantage to the functioning of the Consortium. Sir Charles is an old and valued friend of all of us. He commands our implicit confidence. He has had the advantage of long and intensive study of Far Eastern matters. He appreciates the American point of view, and I cannot recall a single matter on which we have failed to see eye to eye with Addis.[93]

During his Washington trip, Addis was not only received by Secretary of State Hughes but by Secretary of the Treasury Andrew Mellon and President Harding as well.[94] Afterwards he wrote to Eba:

> Their whole tradition and outlook are provincial – to keep out of European entanglements – and to convince them that the war has made this for ever impossible and that no nation can hereafter live to itself alone requires persuasion and persuasion takes time.[95]

After his return to London, Addis reported to Wellesley that both Lamont and Hughes supported a Consortium loan to the CER.[96] With these understandings reached, it appeared that all was arranged for the international control of the Chinese Eastern Railway, which was now put on the agenda for the Washington Conference on Naval Disarmament to be held in November.[97]

In addition to the discussions on the CER, Addis and Norman had discussed the war-debts question and the problems of European recovery. They left the United States convinced that their trip had been successful. Strong wrote to Addis: 'We have all profited greatly by your coming here, and this is especially true of myself because of the better understanding which has resulted all around of the importance of relationships which we have with the Bank of England.'[98] The Morgan partners were encouraged at the improved relations and understanding achieved. Lamont described Addis's talk with Treasury officials and indicated that Morgans was submitting a proposition via Arthur Anderson to Eliot Wadsworth.[99] Norman indicated in his diary that the 'substitution of subrogated securities is now satisfactorily and finally settled'.[100] All expected that at the forthcoming Washington Conference some arrangement would be made for the war debts in return for British cooperation on the Anglo-Japanese Alliance and naval limitation. Yet this optimism proved unfounded. The problem was the strong anti-British sentiment in the American Congress.

In October 1921 the House of Representatives specifically prohibited the exchange of bonds of any foreign government for those of another and forbade the cancellation of any part of such indebtedness except through payments.[101] Such legislation hardly augured well for British hopes. Congress was determined to assert its authority and was highly suspicious of the Executive branch's subservience to the 'Wall Street Interests'. At the Senate Hearings, Secretary of the Treasury Mellon denied that there had been any suggestion that the US should take German bonds in exchange for Allied indebtedness.[102] Nor was Secretary of Commerce Herbert Hoover, who later served on the World War Foreign Debt Commission, sympathetic to debt cancellation. Addis had found Hoover quite uncooperative.[103]

Back in London Addis met the Chancellor of the Exchequer, Sir Robert Horne, and Foreign Office officials to report on his Washington visit and discuss the growing European crisis over German reparation payments.[104] He described Horne to Mills as 'a coarse, kindly, ruddy man and inimitable in the House' but observed that Horne's 'ignorance is astonishing. Apparently he believes, or half believes that Germany is deliberately depreciating her currency and exchanges in order to evade payment.'[105] He continued that the Germans were 'terrified' that, in the case of default, the French would occupy the Ruhr, and that they thought default was inevitable by spring. He concluded this letter with the comment: 'Really the Lloyd Georges and Hornes of the day are a menace to security. They have no sound knowledge and are liable to be blown about by every kind of doctrine.' Addis had obtained information on the German situation from Rudolf Havenstein, the President of the Reichsbank, and his comptroller, Kaufmann, who had come to London for a secret visit to Norman.[106] Shortly thereafter Norman received word from Morgans that a loan to Germany would require a 'lien ahead of all reparations'.[107] This was the price American investors later demanded for helping to reconstruct Europe. However, it took almost three more years before the British finally accepted American terms.

Meanwhile, the American and British bankers continued to collaborate on ways of dealing with the war-debt question. Pierre Jay informed Norman: 'We in the bank are entirely sympathetic to your idea that reparations and debts should be considered simultaneously.'[108] This view, which of course was secret, was not shared by the majority of Americans who little understood the complexity of the issues. Therefore American bankers in the Federal Reserve of New York and J. P. Morgan & Co. acted secretly to find some way whereby the war-debt question could be disposed of. The Norman Diary records a meeting between Norman and J. P. Morgan on 25 November, and indicates that Norman showed Morgan a secret memo on reparations and Morgan suggested the words 'settlement of international indebtedness shd. be arrangement'. On succeeding days Norman met first with Treasury officials, then with bankers Walter Leaf, Vassar-Smith and Reginald McKenna, and finally with the Chancellor of the Exchequer, regarding what he called 'cold storage plans'.[109] The expectation was that Prime Minister Lloyd George would go to the Washington Conference when and if arrangements for payment of the debt were made. Norman wrote to Strong that he would make the secret proposal known to the Prime Minister 'before he goes to Washington'.[110]

THE TRIP TO CHINA AND JAPAN, 1921–2

While Addis was anticipating his first trip to East Asia in nearly twenty years, British and American diplomats made their final preparations for the historic Conference on Disarmament and Problems of the Far East.[111] The diplomats believed that the Consortium's successful organisation the previous autumn had laid the economic basis for these expected agreements. The Lloyd George government was willing to accept naval parity with the United States and surrender the Anglo-Japanese Alliance in return for a more generous attitude toward British war debts by the Harding administration.[112]

Addis had prepared extensive materials for the British Delegation which was to be led by one of Britain's pre-eminent senior statesmen, Arthur J. Balfour, and to include Miles Lampson and Sir John Jordan. He wrote to Mills that he had been 'urged to go' to the Washington Conference by the government but feared it would take too much time, so he had agreed to keep the government informed of his movements and to be prepared to go on to Washington from China 'if & when required'.[113] Addis felt that at Washington Britain had 'a great opportunity of playing the part of the "honest broker" between Japan and the United States: 'The Anglo-Japanese Treaty is no longer necessary but until the new tripartite arrangement is fixed up it may still prove to be of use as a counter in negotiation. It is better to be on with the new love before you are off with the old.'[114]

Before the British Delegation left for Washington, Addis made a point of speaking to his old friend from China days, Sir John Jordan, telling him that he was discouraged and disappointed by his 'silence on the Consortium'.[115] Jordan was not as convinced as the State Department and the Foreign Office that the policy of exclusive support for the Peking government, which the Consortium agreement assumed, would work. As will be seen, Addis was also having second thoughts about this policy even before he got to China. Perhaps Jordan had influenced him. Certainly the visit to China led to a new approach.

31 October was Addis's last day as London Manager of the HSBC. While he wrote that he was 'glad' to retire, he admitted that 'there is always something sad in those changes'.[116] On 11 November 1921 he exclaimed; 'The Great Adventure has begun.' Addis was accompanied to China by his wife and oldest daughter, Elizabeth.[117] The long sea voyage gave Addis the leisure to sort out his thoughts after the heavy responsibilities and high-pressured pace of the last few years. As had been his habit in earlier, more leisured times, he developed his views in the process of writing long letters to friends and family members. To his daughter Robina, he suggested that a federation of states was the remedy for China, saying that China 'must work out her own salvation and in the interim the Powers should stand by to keep the ring and to assist in the maintenance of security while amid the ferment of political ideas the Chinese state is evolved'.[118] Addis's suggestion of a federal system for China was something new, or at

least something different from what the American State Department and Foreign Office had planned. Before long the proposal led to difficulties.

In addition to letter-writing, Addis took advantage of the long sea voyage to read and think. In December he shared his thoughts with his oldest son Tom, describing his reading as including Bryce, Wells and Carlyle, and observing: 'It is well to have the company of books for I don't care for games and, truth to tell, I find the conversation at table very banal.' He went on to wonder 'what it is that infects good, honest, simple, ingenuous natures like the Captain's or my sister Susan's with so low a view of human nature?' He described their philosophy as excluding altruism:

> all men, even the highest, are bent on seeking their own advantage: human progress among the backward nations is not merely an illusion: it is an impossibility contrary to nature, so to speak. Experiments in the self-government of Ireland, India, Egypt, Arabia are futile. Force is the only remedy.

Addis felt such 'fatalism' was the very 'antithesis of the Christianity they profess, the very foundation of which is a belief in human progress', and blamed such views on a lack of education. He himself believed that 'the explanation of the paradox is the lack of culture, of education, of comparative knowledge'.[119] Before long, Addis would have an opportunity to apply his philosophy and belief in human progress to revolutionary China, since his arrival in Hong Kong was followed by the most serious labour uprising in China the foreigners had ever experienced.

THe HSBC Chief Manager (A. G. Stephen) welcomed Addis aboard his launch and over the next few days hosted him at a round of teas, luncheons and dinners with old friends and colleagues in Hong Kong.[120] Next Addis visited the British Consul-General in Canton, J. W. Jamieson, who took him to see the Southern Nationalist leaders, Wu Ting-fang, his son, C. C. Wu, and the Civil Governor, Ch'en Chiung-ming. After these meetings Addis returned to Hong Kong where he discussed the possible recognition of the rival Canton government with the Governor-General, Sir Reginald Stubbs.[121]

At this time Hong Kong trade had been badly disrupted by the seamen's strike which British diplomats considered to be Bolshevist-inspired and instigated by Sun Yat-sen. By mid-February, 40 000 men were out, and by late February virtually all Hong Kong workers had walked off their jobs.[122] Jamieson had written to the Foreign Office, describing the bad relations between the Hong Kong government and Sun Yat-sen and emphasising the need for a 'wise and tactful attitude' toward the government of General Ch'en Chiung-ming.[123] He criticised the 'high-handed ostrich-like attitude of Hong Kong' and its 'failure to realize that the new trade union movements must be lived with'.[124] By the end of March Governor-General Stubbs was suggesting that the British help General Ch'en Chuing-ming against Sun Yat-sen.[125] Alston reminded the FO that Sun Yat-sen had published a book in 1920 on *The International Development of China* in which he contemplated 'with obvious relish the supplanting of Hong Kong as a trans-shipping centre by Canton'.[126] Such ideas hardly made Sun popular with the British.

But Stubbs's proposal was dismissed in the FO as a 'dangerous and absurd policy', one that violated the recently signed Washington Agreements. Instead the FO ordered that strict neutrality was to be observed and no loans made.[127] However, as had often been the case in the past, local British officials and the HSBC were quite prepared to ignore the views of the FO and deal with the situation as they saw fit.

Addis's talks with Chinese and British leaders in Canton and Hong Kong evidently convinced him that the policy of exclusive support for the Peking government was not realistic. After conferring with Stephen and the Bank comprador, Sir Robert Ho-tung (a powerful Hong Kong millionaire), regarding a possible loan to Canton, he took the train back to Canton where he 'discussed the railway and lunched with General Ch'en Chiung-ming, C. C. Wu, Frank Lee, and Sun Fo, the son of Sun Yat-sen. On 9 January he had another interview with Governor-General Stubbs who told him that the British were 'backing the wrong horse in supporting the North'.[128]

The first public evidence of Addis's new approach came when he refused to approve a proposed Consortium loan to Peking of $96 000 000, for which the Peking government applied in January. This refusal was much resented by the Consortium Group Representatives in Peking and also by the American diplomatic representatives in China. The latter interpreted the refusal as further evidence that Addis was promoting British interests at the expense of American.[129] After receiving reports of Addis's activities, Hornbeck, in the State Department, concluded that the Addis visit was 'a British plan to increase their prestige in South China by closer cooperation and encouragement to the authorities of the Canton and provincial government in Kwantung'.[130]

The Americans were also disturbed by the report that Addis was supporting provincial railway loans. In a speech to the Chinese Chamber of Commerce in Shanghai on 26 January 1922, Addis was quoted as saying that 'plans might be framed for proceeding with railway construction in consultation with provincial authorities temporarily independent of the Central Government if Chinese opinion showed that such a course was desired'.[131] This was hardly the policy of exclusive support for the Peking government and a unified national railway system upon which the American and British diplomats and bankers had agreed at Washington! Nonetheless, in his discussions with the Consortium Group Representatives in Peking, Addis indicated that railway loans to independent provinces were 'O.K.'.[132]

In the FO, Wellesley (the chief of the Far Eastern section) angrily complained that a good opportunity to secure Chinese adherence to the Consortium had been lost.[133] As a result of the Consortium's refusal of Peking's request, the Chinese floated their own $96 000 000 loan with the cooperation of Inspector General Aglen, a step which did not please either the FO or the Consortium bankers, since it facilitated Peking's independence of their control.[134] Meanwhile, the Consortium representatives in Peking continued to plan for a large comprehensive loan of $400 000 000, intended to provide for the Chinese government's debt.[135] But the possibility that such a loan would ever be agreed upon seemed far less likely after Addis's visit.

During his visit to Hong Kong Addis was awarded an honorary LL.D. at Hong Kong University. In his acceptance speech, he noted that he had been associated with the University since its inception and affirmed the identity of Anglo-Chinese interests. He stated that the causes of bad feeling were misrepresentation and misunderstanding and challenged his listeners to 'aim high'. He continued:

> The aim, the function of a University is to act as a guide to experience and to life: to enable people to understand each other better, their relations to each other and to the world in which they live; to unfold in the domain of morality and science and art the essential unity of the human spirit and the motives which impel it forward to the pursuit of goodness of beauty and of truth.

In conclusion he told his audience that he envisioned Hong Kong University as becoming an 'Imperial University' in contact with the other great centres of learning around the world.[136]

After arriving in Shanghai on 22 January and meeting Alston, Addis went on to Peking where he gave a highly significant address to the Anglo-American Association on the topic of 'Reconstruction in Europe'. Addis first surveyed the losses incurred by the war and then warned his audience that they could not afford to wait 'for natural economic laws to work'. He said that 'international competition must give way to international cooperation if Europe is to be saved and civilization as we have come to know it prevented from going by the board altogether'. He outlined a plan:

> to establish a new centre of European finance in place of Germany which was formerly the heart of the economic system of Europe . . . upon Austria we propose to establish a new credit centre from which the springs of industry and finance may flow into the surrounding States and draw them back into a common economic system.

He explained that the 'unit of the scheme is of course the State Bank, and the first step is to amalgamate the several units, to concentrate the banks of Europe and America into a consortium . . . on the lines of the consortium for China.' Sounding an optimistic note, Addis reported: 'negotiations are proceeding favourably and may even be said to have already met with a measure of success'. While acknowledging that there were 'Anglo-American differences', he claimed that the British were assured of American support. In fact, he said:

> the stage of complete understanding has already been reached. Between the Bank of England and the Federal Reserve Bank of the United States there is entire unanimity of view. The identity of their international interests is not in question.

In conclusion Addis told his audience that 'the salvation of Europe depends upon the united efforts of our respective countries' and called for the promotion of the 'unity of Great Britain and America in a common effort to restore the peace of the world'.[137]

Since there are no accounts of this speech in the British or American papers, and since it reveals secret and sensitive strategy to achieve goals which had not yet been achieved, it seems possible that the Foreign Office suppressed reports of this speech. The *Peking and Tientsin Times* quoted Addis as saying 'sometime may yet elapse before the American people are persuaded that the wiping out of inter-Allied indebtedness is the only real solution of the problems which the war has left in its train'.[138]

The speech is important because it frankly reveals British goals and also because it demonstrates the extent to which Addis underestimated the difficulties which lay ahead. His mistake was to think that the Federal Reserve bankers in New York possessed the authority and influence which the Bank of England enjoyed, which was hardly the case. While it may have been true that he and Norman had reached a meeting of minds with the New York bankers in August 1921, the latter did not reflect the political thinking in Washington, nor could they determine government policy.

In addition to making this indiscreet speech, Addis proceeded to conduct independent negotiations with Chinese leaders, arranging to meet Premier Liang Shih-i and Yeh Kung Chao, the Minister of Communications.[139] Liang (who was officially on sick leave from his post in Peking) told Addis that he wished to form a coalition between Chang Tso-lin, the Manchurian warlord, and Sun Yat-sen, and asked for an advance of $10–15m for the expenses of the campaign. Although Addis was not convinced that the opposing warlord, Wu Pei-fu, could be 'worsted', he agreed to take up the proposals with the other Consortium members.[140]

Meanwhile, F. W. Stevens reported to Lamont that the Manager of the HSBC in Hong Kong had agreed to grant Chen Chiung-ming $500 000 when the [seamen's] strike was settled. Furthermore he stated that the effect of this loan was to 'strengthen the resolution of the Canton government'. Stevens interpreted this move as a British attempt to 'get permission to connect the Canton–Hankow railway with the Canton–Kowloon railway and thus retard the Canton harbor project'.[141] Addis's diary entries suggest that F. W. Stevens' reports may have been true.

Addis and his wife left China on 19 February, travelling to Japan by way of Korea. They spent the next week visiting various cities of Japan, arriving in Tokyo on 28 February where they were met by officials of the Yokahama Specie Bank. The last event of the Far Eastern trip was a luncheon given by Viscount Inouye, the President of the Bank of Japan.[142] Returning to England by way of the United States, Addis and Eba stopped in California for a last visit to their friend, Murray Stewart, who was dying of tuberculosis.[143] In Chicago they were entertained by John Jay Abbott, the Vice-President of the Chicago Continental and Commercial Trust and Savings Bank, which had provided loans to China during the war.[144]

Addis found little enthusiasm for his proposal to support the Liang–Sun coalition. By the time he reached New York he had decided there was little hope for such a loan, cabling Hillier (who served as the British Group Representative in Peking) that the American Group felt 'there might be grave objection to their joining in any advance that might be construed as designed to furnish with munitions to any one faction in China'. Furthermore the American bankers believed that no 'considerable issue can be offered successfully in their market unless at the same time it is made plain that definite plans are contemplated for looking after American issues now in default.'[145]

At the State Department, MacMurray was quite astonished that Addis would go ahead with such plans without prior consultation. In a long memorandum, he denounced the proposal and suggested that Lamont be advised that: 'It contemplates an unwarrantable partisanship in the internal factional disturbances of China, which would be substantially a repetition of the Japanese championship of the Anfu faction in 1917 and subsequent years'. MacMurray added: 'if we do want to punt on the races, this is not a promising horse to back'.[146]

By this time, the Washington Conference was long since over. The historic Nine Power, Four Power and Five Power Treaties had been signed, naval disarmament agreed, the Anglo-Japanese alliance dissolved, and the Nine Powers with interests in Asia had promised to give China 'the fullest and most unembarrassed opportunity . . . to develop and maintain for herself an effective and stable government.'[147] The convening of a Special Tariff Conference and the appointment of a special Commission to investigate the abolition of extraterritoriality were also promised.

While the Conference had ended in February on a note of great optimism concerning Anglo-American cooperation, there remained serious reasons for misgivings about the future of the partnership which naturally did not receive much publicity. Most importantly, the hoped-for cancellation of the war debts had not occurred. Instead, before the final treaties were signed, the US Congress passed the World War Foreign Debts legislation which made clear that there was little reason for the British to expect favourable treatment on the war debts. Nor had the Chinese proved cooperative regarding the Chinese Eastern Railway proposals. In fact, the delegates had refused either to sign the agreement or to have anything to do with the Consortium.[148] In addition much publicity critical of the Consortium appeared in the American press.[149]

Furthermore, while the Conference was in session, the Chinese government had defaulted on two American loans.[150] Thus the market for Chinese bonds in the United States was hardly favourable as Addis had indicated to Hillier. Indeed there was even talk of the American Group pulling out of the Consortium, although such talk may have been a ploy to gain Secretary of State Hughes's public endorsement for the Consortium.[151] In any event, the British Foreign Office hoped that Addis's visit to New York would encourage Lamont to remain in the Consortium.[152]

Certainly the State Department was not happy with the Consortium's refusal to provide loans to the Peking government, nor did it welcome the limelight which Addis's visit to China had captured. Briefly stated, American leaders felt that they were losing the initiative in China which they had gained during the war and were also losing credibility with the Chinese. Despite all the ambitious plans, the British seemed to be regaining their former dominance.

On 28 March 1922, Addis described to the Downtown Association in New York the changes he had found in China. He did not try to disguise his views, indicating that the future lay with 'Young China', that the *Tuchuns* (warlords) were dividing China, that he would support a comprehensive funding loan for the conversion of the debt. However, he also suggested that the Consortium should consider provincial railway loans and possible recognition of the Southern Nationalists.[153] From Peking, the American Chargé complained that Addis's suggestions were 'highly damaging to American prestige in China',[154] while in Washington MacMurray complained that American proposals were becoming a 'by-word for futility'. In this troubled atmosphere, Secretary of State Hughes attempted to convince American investors of the government's support by publicly endorsing the Consortium.[155]

Stanley Hornbeck, a Far Eastern expert who was then serving as economic adviser to the State Department, was extremely dissatisfied with both the American and British banking groups, describing the American Group as being under British influence. He felt it was doubtful that the American Group was really promoting general American interest in China, and felt that they were not gaining any advantage from the United States' financial superiority, especially in failing to develop 'a great financial port of entry for American influence and commerce in the new "Far West" of East Asia'.[156]

While Foreign Office members recognised that the Americans would oppose Addis's actions, they were powerless to stop him.[157] Addis had simply gone ahead on his own, in cooperation with the HSBC Chief Manager and the support of Governor-General Stubbs, but not with the sanction of the Foreign Office. While nothing immediate developed from Addis's coalition plans (since Chang Tso-lin's forces were soon defeated by Wu Pei-fu) neither did a Consortium loan to Peking occur.

In Peking the American Minister, Jacob Gould Schurman, argued in vain for a Consortium loan, saying that conditions for reunion have 'not been so favorable for years'.[158] But it was the bankers' opinions that mattered. American newspapermen in China, like George Sokolsky, the editor of the *Journal of Commerce Press* in Shanghai, struggled in vain to convince Lamont and others that Americans had a unique opportunity to win the friendship of the Chinese.[159] Meanwhile, Americans in China grew increasingly frustrated with their inability to make any progress. Julean Arnold, one of the most knowledgeable and experienced Americans in China, wrote a long memorandum to the Director of the Bureau of Foreign and Domestic Commerce in July, indicating that 'Many [Chinese] are of the opinion that Great Britain joined the Consortium so as to keep America out of the field in an independent way, while British financiers were recouping from the effects of the War and that so soon as Great Britain is able again to assert an independent position, she will disassociate herself from the American Group.' He explained that:

> The acquiescence of the American Group in loans for betterments and extensions to existing railway lines in China, by the financing interests, is recognized as perpetuating the equity in those lines to the original foreign financial groups . . . Through this method, practically all needed railways in China may be built under the guise of extensions or betterments to existing lines. Thus American enterprise and capital will be precluded from direct participation in railway construction in China, while the present entrenched interests strengthen their position, to the detriment of American and Chinese rights.[160]

Addis's independent actions in China found disfavour not only with the Foreign Office and the State Department but also with Aglen, who denounced Addis in the strongest terms: 'So that was why he kept clear of me. How ridiculous! He is a man of very strong opinions and he had already committed himself to a line before he fetched up here. I fancy he didn't want to hear contrary opinion.' Aglen described Addis's intervention in Chinese politics as 'very characteristic', and observed:

Liang of all people – I could have told him that wouldn't get anywhere. He seems to argue that the 'outbreak of civil war' which spoiled his little plan was an accident. Any one at all conversant with affairs in China knew that outbreak was inevitable. I had seen it coming for a long time.[161]

Aglen, who was working closely with Chinese bankers to establish fiscal stability for the Peking government through the Domestic Loan Fund, doubtlessly resented any other British representative suggesting support for opposing Chinese leaders.

One fact emerges clearly amidst all this complexity – the British goal of Anglo-American cooperation had not been accomplished in 1922, either in China or on financial reconstruction of Europe or on war debts and reparations. While Addis recognised the importance of cooperation, he seemed unaware that his independent actions in China badly crippled the delicate understandings reached at the Washington Conference. One must conclude that Addis underestimated both the American ability to strike back and the Chinese power of resistance. His attitude was probably the same as that of Stewart who, in commenting on the Washington Conference, wrote: 'the clever American-educated [Chinese] youths who do the talking will not face any facts that are unpleasant for China, as a good many are'.[162] It is also conceivable that Addis was angered by the American legislation on the war debts.

While Addis was in New York he received word through Strong that Norman wanted him to serve as a financial adviser to the British mission to the Genoa Conference.[163] With this appointment Addis turned his attention from China to monetary affairs.

6 Monetary Policy and European Reconstruction, 1920–8

'Do not be the Louis XVI of the monetary revolution.' — Keynes to Addis, 25 July 1924

'We feel in fact that America has pretty well let the world down.' — Niemeyer, 19 May 1927

In the years 1920–8, Addis, Norman, Strong and Lamont sought to establish the same principles in international financial relations in Europe and Latin America on which Addis had long insisted regarding China – namely, that governments could not secure new loans without funding old debts and stabilising their currencies. The British believed that sound banking practices would enable London to re-establish itself as the centre of world finance.[1] As President of the Institute of Bankers, Addis became one of the leading spokesmen for deflation and stabilisation. But after his return from China, when the United States pressed the English to settle their debts, Addis began to recognise that deflation might cause economic hardship. To avoid a gold shortage and at the same time ensure stability in international exchange the financial experts at Genoa recommended the adoption of a gold exchange standard accompanied by central bank cooperation.

The policy of deflation and return to the gold standard led to political difficulties at home, with opposition coming from both commercial bankers and industrial leaders, because the British economy failed to recover and unemployment increased. After Britain had funded her debt to the United States in January 1923, the expected central bank cooperation did not develop. Addis still continued to favour cooperation, and supported the return to the gold standard in 1925. But as the deflation continued, Addis began to have second thoughts. Addis became deeply involved in the German reparations question after the Dawes settlement in 1924, when he was appointed British representative on the Reichbank Council.

Addis's views concerning monetary policy and the relationship with

146

America gradually came to correspond more with those of Treasury officials than with Governor Norman. Nevertheless, despite his disagreements with the Governor, Addis refused to cooperate with those Directors who called for his removal. By refusing (despite his dissent) to break with Norman, his trusted friend and colleague, Addis assured Norman's continuance in this powerful position.[2]

MONETARY POLICY AND CENTRAL BANK COOPERATION, 1920–2

Immediately after the war, when prices rose rapidly, financial leaders' concern about inflation and speculation led to the British Treasury's decision to raise the bank rate.[3] From this point on the bank rate became a political issue causing controversy among leaders and economists. While the Bank of England and the Treasury were concerned about inflation, the Clearing Bankers, led by McKenna, opposed a high bank rate.[4] Addis described the Cabinet as divided with regard to the raising of the bank rate and said that a political crisis threatened unless the Chancellor of the Exchequer (who had appealed to him for arguments) could hold his own against Lloyd George and Bonar Law.[5] He believed that Chamberlain was weak in the face of such opposition and exclaimed: 'If only he had the courage to threaten resignation, but these politicans are timorous.'[6] Addis (along with Blackett, Keynes, Niemeyer and Hawtrey) was recruited to write a memo for Chamberlain on money rates.

In his memorandum Addis argued that the only way to continue British financial supremacy was through raising bank rate.[7] Addis recognised that 'The Government will have to pay more for their loans', but felt that the 'increased cost to the Nation is as dust in the balance compared with the restoration of free trade and the removal of social unrest and political discontent'.[8] Addis's views corresponded closely to those of permanent Treasury officials and Keynes, who felt the boom must be stopped quickly.[9]

The purpose of a high rate was to inspire investor confidence and therefore prevent a fall in exchange, but despite the adoption of 7 per cent in mid-April, the pound continued to fall. In July, the exchange fell to 3.71.[10] Although both Addis and Keynes argued for increasing to 8 per cent, they could not convince the Chancellor.[11]

While most financial leaders agreed with the Cunliffe Committee's recommendations on the desirability of a return to gold, a few currency experts, such as Keynes and the Swedish economist, Gustav Cassel, challenged the accepted wisdom, arguing instead that the British pound was overvalued and that if Britain returned to gold, she should do so at a lower rate of exchange, or in other words, she should devalue the pound.[12] At this time, however, such advanced ideas of managing currency seemed almost revolutionary, and they found little support in the City of London.

Hawtrey in the Treasury, had already warned of the need to economise on gold, recommending instead of a gold standard, an Anglo-American convention on gold.[13] In an article in the *Economic Journal* in December 1919, he recognised that 'debtor nations had an interest in holding down the value of gold, while creditor nations might wish to enhance the value of the medium in which the debts were to be paid'.[14] While Addis admired Hawtrey and Keynes, describing the latter as a 'passionate economist', he strongly opposed the idea of a managed currency.[15]

The bank rate was reduced to 6.5 per cent on 28 April 1921, in response to pressure from the Treasury, but Addis and Norman opposed further reductions.[16] In June 1921 Addis told the Oxford Economic Society 'Deflation, like convalescence, should be a gradual process in which the patient has time to recover his strength before he begins to use it again.' He indicated that 'not credit but capital is scarce. Capital can only be made out of savings and the best way to attract savings and capital is to offer a higher and not a lower price for the use of their services.' He continued with the unpleasant prediction that since normal trading conditions depended on 'a return to the gold standard', or the exportable sovereign, that may mean that we have to suffer a further fall in prices of 25 per cent'.[17] It is clear from this speech, as well as from a 'Memorandum on a proposal to Reduce the Bank Rate', which Addis probably prepared for the Committee of Treasury, that he opposed further reduction.[18] Hawtrey's call for a further reduction in bank rate was dismissed by Norman who commented that Hawtrey was 'all theory'.[19] Norman believed that bank rate in England must be kept higher than that in the United States, and only when Strong notified Norman that the rate would be reduced in the United States to 5½, did the latter agree to a reduction.

Meanwhile the Federation of British Industries called for a new currency committee. The issue of bank rate was becoming highly political, since, as Austen Chamberlain recognised, 'The Federation of British Industries is very strong in the House and . . . I shall have a big fight with the Big Bugs'. But he considered them 'a selfish, swollen lot, and if they think they can bully the Chancellor because there are so many of them in the House, they will find that they are mistaken'.[20]

Addis made monetary policy the subject of his Presidential Address to the Institute of Bankers that November. After surveying the argument for devaluation, Addis dismissed the proposal as being too theoretical and quoted Cromwell: 'I beseech you, consider it possible you may be mistaken.' Addis continued by admitting that 'in an ideal work devaluation might be the ideal plan'. But he observed that:

> it is not enough for a principle to be shown to be logically indefensible in the seclusion of the economist's study. We have to take the world as it is. The principle must be brought down into the hurly-burly of the market place and proved in operation there, through the medium of the heart and mind of ordinary men in conflict with their opposing interests, their changing purposes, their unruly passions and their defective wills.

He continued:

> To suppose that a people so conservative by instinct, so tenacious of custom, so careful of tradition, could be induced to trample on their monetary past and to relinquish the dearly purchased gold standard, which rightly or wrongly they believe to be bound up with the prestige of their national credit and their supremacy in international finance, is to live in a world of illusion.

Addis concluded by saying that the economic crisis was similar to those of the past and predicted that 'the old and proven methods of dealing with them' would work. He promised:

> A little more patience, a little more steadfastness, and success is assured. A little longer and the old supremacy of this country as the acknowledged leader in the finance of the world will return. Is this a time to lose heart or to falter in our task?[21]

Before giving the speech, Addis had submitted it for comment to Keynes, Hawtrey and Professor Pigou. In his reply, Hawtrey supplied data on debt payments and budget figures, and raised questions concerning Addis's conclusions about past crises.[22] Keynes commented that he 'altogether dissent[ed] from our conclusions', but had 'no criticism and only admiration for the way in which you have marshalled the opposing arguments'. He continued:

if your conclusions had been that devaluation was the ideal plan, but that the selfishness, dishonesty and idiocy of the business world would prevent it from being adopted, I should not quarrel with you. But you seem to make out that these factors actually make it in itself a bad plan, and are a reason for opposing rather than supporting it.[23]

The financial press treated Addis's speech as the 'voice of authority', as the official response to the recent assaults on monetary policy. In the United States, the influential *Christian Science Monitor* commented that the earlier calls for devaluation 'could not be allowed to pass without remark unless the Treasury and the Bank of England were content to allow it to be understood that they, too, were wavering in their allegiance to the canons of "sound currency" hitherto accepted.'[24]

While most of the financial journals praised Addis's strong and unequivocal pronouncement,[25] some of the more analytical comments questioned how the government could consider a return to gold with such large debts outstanding, especially the debt to the United States.[26] And some reviews were even hostile, criticising Addis as too idealistic, as unfair to Professor Cassel, and as misleading.[27] One critic, writing in *The Times Annual Financial Review*, asked:

What are we going to do about it if we discover, perhaps too late, that the practised and properly trusted operators of our prewar automatic currency are as hopelessly lost as the least pretentious of us in the unchartered ways of post-war currencies of the world, and that their ultimate rule, the 'effective gold standard' proves under current world conditions to be in effect a 'gold brick'?[28]

A few months later, a long-time Financial Editor of the *Daily Mail*, commented on Addis's assurance in the same speech, that 'we know the way', saying: 'I for one do not' and emphatically stated: 'But I do hope it will be a long time before we return to the wasteful system of a gold currency.'[29]

These comments both reveal the wide attention which Addis's remarks commanded and demonstrate that there was not unanimity among financial experts as to the desirability of Britain's return to gold. Furthermore, they reveal a widespread concern about American policy and an awareness of the power which the United States could exert as Britain's creditor. Addis emerged as the chief public spokesman, of 'the cause of conservative orthodoxy'.[30]

Much of what Addis, Keynes, Hawtrey and Cassel were discussing represented unknown territory in the field of monetary theory.[31] Time would soon demonstrate that Addis's underlying assumption – that the problems were not different from those of the past, that Britain could regain her prewar position through thrift and self-sacrifice – while inspiring, was unrealistic. His younger and less-trusted colleague's recognition that Britain's economic problems were too fundamental to be cured by self-denial, while more accurate, found little support in 1922. However, Hawtrey's idea of a gold-exchange standard fared better, receiving official support at the Genoa Conference of 1922.

THE GENOA CONFERENCE

While the Washington Conference was still in session and Addis was in Hong Kong, the Supreme Council of the League of Nations (meeting at Cannes) had invited the German government to send a delegation to discuss the reparations question.[32] Out of these discussions emerged the decision to call an international conference on financial and economic questions to meet at Genoa and to include the Russians for the first time.[33] The Europeans continued to seek a solution to the war debts and reparations question which the Americans would accept. Until they knew what reparations they would receive from Germany, they were reluctant to settle their debt with the United States.

At the Genoa Conference the financial experts faced all the unresolved problems of the postwar era, with the additional complication of deflation, which was beginning to cause concern to Addis and the British Treasury. Thus the Genoa Conference, which was inadequately planned, became exceedingly complicated, encompassing both political and financial questions.[34] An added difficulty was the declining political influence of the Liberal Prime Minister, Lloyd George, whose Conservative colleagues in the coalition government were becoming restive.[35]

At this same time, a Bankers' Committee had been appointed by the Reparations Commission to determine the reparations figure, on which J. P. Morgan Jr was serving as the American representative.[36] Herman Harjes, the Morgan partner in the Paris branch, wrote to Lamont that Otto Kahn of the American Banking firm of Kuhn Loeb & Co., had contacted Blackett at Genoa, complaining that J. P. Morgan Jr had been appointed to the Bankers Committee instead of himself. Harjes continued: 'We shall undoubtedly have to be very careful and try to get all our friends in line to work with us in an endeavor to counteract the strenuous efforts of our adversaries.' Lamont replied: 'I am more than interested in all that you can say in regard to the campaign of the Chosen People against the Christians and I can readily believe that it is all true.'[37] This exchange suggests the behind-the-scenes competition among banking groups for government favour which was constantly influencing decisions and strategy.

Once again official Washington refused to cooperate with British plans. Because it feared that the creditor nations would combine against the United States, the State Department refused to send an official representative to Genoa.[38] In addition, the Americans suspected that the British would attempt at Genoa to organise a Consortium for Russia and Secretary of Commerce Herbert Hoover wanted to keep Russian development for the United States.[39]

Norman and the Treasury had made specific plans for Genoa. The British Treasury official, Hawtrey, who had come to the Genoa conference prepared with resolutions which recommended the 're-establishment in Europe of a stable currency system' as 'an essential condition of the restoration of trade', suggested ways in which this should be brought about through a gold exchange standard.[40] These resolutions recognised that the 'value of gold might be raised by simultaneous and competitive efforts of countries to secure metallic reserves' and so favoured central bank cooperation to prevent such competition.[41] Addis, who had been briefed on Treasury policy by Blackett and Sir Henry Strakosch (a member of the League of Nations Finance Committee) agreed to sign the Hawtrey resolutions.[42]

While Addis was at Genoa, Norman wrote him suggesting that he and Edward Peacock (a Canadian Bank of England Director who was also at Genoa) should see the German, Rudolph Havenstein (the President of the Reichsbank) whom he had met the previous autumn.[43] Norman explained that Havenstein

> is part of the rather loose sort of consortium which we are trying to build up among the principal Central Banks in Europe as well as in America and Japan; and I am anxious to do anything we possibly can to make things easy and pleasant for him both for his own sake and for the sake of the rehabilitation of Europe.[44]

While Addis and Blackett were at Genoa, Norman went to the United States for discussions with Federal Reserve officials and the Morgan partners.[45] Meanwhile, preparations for a conference of central bankers continued at the Bank of England, with the drafting of an agenda and resolutions.[46] The Genoa resolutions recommended that the Bank of England summon a meeting of Central Banks to achieve the necessary international cooperation.[47] Norman believed that the Bank of England had the responsibility, working through the Finance Committee of the League of Nations, to help countries to establish central banks and to protect these banks from the political pressure of their various governments. Norman believed that the purpose of central banks was 'to prevent the commercial banks from mulcting the public'.[48] He believed that London would continue 'to be the main lending Market in Europe' because 'New York would never take the initiative, certainly not in outlying Countries'.[49]

However, other European countries were not so enthusiastic about the gold exchange standard or central bank cooperation, suspecting the Anglo-Saxons of dictating to the rest of the world, of attempting to create a system which would primarily benefit themselves.[50] Thus no conference of central banks was convened, then or thereafter. Since the French government refused to allow the Bankers' Committee to reopen the question of reparations, stabilisation of currencies could not proceed.[51] Each Treasury wished to know what it would receive in reparations before it would promise to pay war debts.

FUNDING THE WAR DEBT TO AMERICA, 1923

In April 1922 the World War Foreign Debt Commission asked those governments which owed the United States money to make proposals for funding their debts.[52] The next questions was: could the British government afford to cancel unilaterally the debts which the French, Belgiums and Italians owed it? Serious disagreement existed within the British Cabinet and among the permanent Treasury officials in 1922 as to what policy to adopt on allied war debts.[53] Blackett (one of the most expert and influential of the permanent Treasury officials) wrote a long letter to Lamont saying:

> I begin to believe that God gave us three years from the signing of the Treaty in which to put Europe back in the path of peace and goodwill and that though we have made progress we have not made enough & God will smash things up in consequence.

He criticised himself and his colleagues, saying that they knew 'what needs doing and could have done it if we had taken our courage in our hands and determined to settle up Inter-European debts without waiting for America.'[54]

But neither Blackett nor Sir Edward Grigg (Lloyd George's private secretary) could persuade the government to change its policy. Blackett warned: 'A sincere policy of funding our debt to the USA preparatory to a settlement with Europe designed to rescue Europe from chaos might well bring the USA in to our help. An insincere policy will have the reverse effect.' And Griggs claimed that Winston Churchill was 'the protagonist of the bargaining policy' which he said 'deepens, if anything could, my suspicion of it'.[55] Despite these private appeals, Lloyd George, Winston Churchill (the Colonial Secretary) and Balfour refused to listen.[56] Disregarding such advice, the Secretary of State for Foreign Affairs, Balfour, issued a note in August 1922 which announced that Great Britain would only charge her debtors what Washington charged London.[57]

The publication of the Balfour note, which implicity blamed the United States for the continuing disagreements on reparations, caused great ill-feeling and resentment in the United States, similar to the earlier reaction to Keynes's *Economic Consequences of the Peace*.[58] Not until Lloyd George was forced to resign (in October 1922) did the British government (now headed by Conservative Prime Minister Bonar Law) finally consent to send a debt-funding mission to the United States.[59]

During this period between August and October, Addis was temporarily removed from policy-making by abdominal surgery. Norman reported on Addis's condition to Strong: 'he got through it well, and has such physique and determination that I hope he will now make a complete recovery'.[60] While Addis left no record of his feelings concerning the American attitude, there seems little doubt that he resented the American refusal to recognise the relationship between war debts and reparations. He thanked Lamont for his efforts to explain the British point of view to American bankers.[61] While recuperating in his beloved Scotland, Addis took the rare opportunity to philosophise:

An idle day. A stroll in the morning through the birches on Marrone where we surprised a herd of deer. A walk in the evening over the brae to Glen Cherry. The sweets of convalescence! What a pure joy it has all been. Infinite love is the alchemy which transmutes the trials we shrink from into life's richest blessings. It is good for me to have been afflicted.[62]

Before discussing the US Debt with the Committee of Treasury Norman visited Addis at home on 3 October 1922.[63] Norman had discussed the British position with Morgan, saying that Britain should 'delay definite funding and merely talk in Washington. He agrees unless Rep. Schedule can be readjusted first. It can't: Poincaré won't.'[64] Throughout the autumn Norman met with Strong, Niemeyer and Morgan in an attempt to find some mutually acceptable plan for funding the British war debts. Strong wrote to Parker Gilbert, Undersecretary of the US Treasury, that he thought Britain could repay 'the entire debt but not within the limitations of the funding bill'.[65]

As President of the Institute of Bankers, Addis may have been responsible for arranging a series of lectures in which Keynes discussed the whole tangled web of war debts, reparations and British monetary policy.[66] Keynes made no attempt to disguise the fact that the British expected important concessions from the Americans.[67] Privately Keynes described the debts as 'diplomatic weapons' and said he favoured cancellation so as to avoid repudiation.[68] In other words, Keynes did not think the debts would ever be paid. After the first lecture, Addis, who was in the Chair, described Keynes's talk as 'most interesting and suggestive'.[69]

However, while Keynes and Addis shared a common perception of the American threat to British interests, their disagreements on monetary policy prevented them from working together effectively. Instead, they became adversaries. What might have been a powerful alliance between two of the very few experts who fully understood the interrelationship of all these topics and who shared a commitment to the national interest became a source of weakness as they instead attacked each other's views. Bradbury submitted a plan to Baldwin on 15 December which appeared to be a modified version of Keynes's proposal to use German bonds in lieu of war-debt payments.[70] A week later, Addis saw Norman and Chancellor of Exchequer Baldwin off for Washington to discuss the war debts.[71]

As the year came to an end, Addis sadly reflected: 'A chequered year draws to a close . . . death of my dearest friend Murray Stewart at San Francisco; sunshine and shadow; joys and sorrows; and through it all the divine thread of eternal love. I will go on in the strength of the Lord, in thankfulness and hope for He will sustain.'[72]

Although Norman may have intended only to talk, after less than a week the American and British missions (meeting at Secretary of the Treasury Mellon's home) agreed on a proposal which Baldwin recommended to the Cabinet as 'a better settlement than the Treasury believed to be possible a few months ago and a vast improvement on the terms offered us under the United States funding act'.[73] The Bonar Law Cabinet did not share Baldwin's enthusiasm. It denounced the settlement as 'intolerably unjust' and ordered Baldwin home.[74]

Addis agreed. On 29 January he noted that Norman and Baldwin were back and were 'committed up to the eyes to $3\frac{1}{2}$ per cent. At Bank of England I alone opposing terms as excessive.'[75] The terms drawn up at Washington provided that the British should pay $161m a year for ten years with interest at 3 per cent, and $184m a year for fifty-two years with interest at 3 per cent.[76] The total debt was set at $4600m. An undated comment in the Addis papers indicates that 'the annual service for 62 years is more than the total burden of our prewar debt' and that the 'Option of paying in gold bullion gives us an interest in the depreciation of gold'.[77] Addis discussed the British debt settlement with Keynes, Strakosch and Walter Layton, the editor of *The Economist*, at the Tuesday Club meeting.[78]

However, with the exception of Keynes, McKenna, Beaverbrook and Addis, the Prime Minister found no support for his opposition to the settlement.[79] At the meeting of the Cabinet on 31 January Bonar Law finally gave way to the combined pressure of American and British financiers and political leaders and accepted American terms.[80] Whether or not the terms were excessive (an issue still debated today) the fact remained that once pledged to pay them, the British Treasury did not believe it could forgive its Allies their debts, and they in turn insisted that they must recover from Germany what they had to pay. And so the whole question of war debts and reparations continued to cause ill feelings and friction between Washington and London.

The British war-debt settlement must be seen as a dubious victory for the American intention to supplant the British as the leader of world finance. Nor had the British Treasury given up its determination not to pay the United States more than it got from its former allies. It arranged that the bonds should be issued in such large denominations as to be unmarketable.[81] One Foreign Office minute explained:

> Our real reason for not wishing the bonds to be marketable is to safeguard the possibility of eventual cancellation. This reason can hardly be publicly disclosed. But I understood from Mr Grigg . . . that the American Commission was more or less pledged to give us some more definite safeguard than is now proposed.[82]

Nevertheless, payments were to begin and the Bank of England faced the task of meeting these payments in either dollars or gold.

The settlement of the debt to America (an obligation fixed in gold dollars) put additional pressure on the Bank of England and British Treasury to make a decision on future monetary policy. By 1923 Britain's major economic problem had become not inflation but unemployment. Thus the concern of the Treasury was to get rates down. But the problem was still the pound, the value of which must be raised before Britain could contemplate a return to gold at the old parity of 4.86 dollars to the pound.[83] One plan which the Bank of England and the Treasury considered was to force the inflation in the United States by shipping them gold. The objective was to 'strengthen the British balance of trade and afford the basis of a sustained rise in the dollar value of the pound'.[84]

British leaders hoped to restore prewar parity between the dollar and the pound so as to facilitate Great Britain's return to the gold standard. Norman felt that arrangements should be made to establish a reserve in New York to provide for American debt payments, before the return to gold was considered. Addis noted that he alone of the Committee of Treasury opposed the Governor's proposal to 'pay off £100m in Currency Reserve gold'.[85] In order to ship such a quantity of gold, Norman proposed to amalgamate the Bank of England notes and the Treasury notes.[86] Such action would require the amendment of the Bank Act of 1844 to increase the Fiduciary Issue of the Bank. At the Committee of Treasury on 14 March, Addis 'spoke strongly against Norman's proposal to ship £100m gold to United States'.[87] Two weeks later Norman wrote to Addis from Nice, asking him:

> to devote some thought to the questions of American debt: gold: the 2 issues, etc. They are parts of a whole which must, I believe, be tackled if not solved, on our side within a few weeks or months: it cannot be avoided altogether. Pray too, remember that our functions include the giving of advice to the State (or Chancellor) as well as directing the bank.[88]

Addis responded with a sixteen-page memorandum, strongly opposing the proposal for amalgamation writing that:

> Never before in the whole course of its history has it even been suggested that the Charter should be suspended with the avowed and cynical object of enabling the Government to lay hands on the

gold in the issue reserve of the Bank of England and make use of it for their own purposes.

He asked:

> Is it likely that suspension for such an object would end there? Is it not certain that it would be followed by renewed agitation for a revision of the Bank's statutes and a demand for such a modification of the Charter as would bring the Bank into closer relations with the Treasury and, in effect, menace the independence of Government control which has hitherto been the characteristic feature and the chief glory of the Bank of England as a national institution.[89]

Addis had discussed Norman's proposal with Revelstoke and gained his agreement to oppose the plan, which he denounced as 'spectacular finance'.[90] In May Addis met Bradbury, Norman, Lubbock, Schuster and Inchcape to discuss the proposal, which Addis alone opposed.[91] The discussion was expanded to include former Liberal Prime Minister Asquith, who asked Addis for a memorandum. On 16 May Asquith, Bradbury, Inchcape, Schuster, Norman and Addis met to consider the memo, which Addis described as having 'shaken them', quoting Asquith as saying it was 'difficult to answer'. The combination of Addis and Bradbury's resistance, with the slide of the pound against the dollar, ended the matter.[92]

Unlike Addis, Niemeyer favoured shipping gold, writing to Norman:

> we should be following what I believe to be our correct policy of using our gold rather than looking at it in the cellar. We have had signs lately that America was beginning to find the burden on her stomach unduly heavy. Is not our policy to increase it and to push them over the edge into expansion and increased prices?[93]

While keeping a close eye on the exchange and planning the Austrian stabilisation loan, Norman was also feeling political pressure regarding the economy.[94] For if he could not protect the exchange by shipping gold, he felt he must then adopt the traditional method of raising the bank rate. Once again Addis disagreed. On 7 April Addis wrote a long memorandum on bank rate for the Governor, agreeing 'that the Bank rate is the appropriate instrument for this purpose.' However Addis recognised that an improved exchange rate:

> can only be achieved through a progressive lowering of prices in

this country. This in turn would operate as a check on trade. *The advantages of a rise in the New York Exchange might be dearly purchased at the expense of retarding the recovery of industrial enterprise.*

Therefore he concluded that:

> Upon the whole it is safer to leave the New York exchange to itself. It was steady up to the middle of June at about 4.61 . . . The first consideration in determining a change in the Bank Rate should be the condition of trade and industry . . . Trade requires all the encouragement we can give it. I agree with PM: 'There is no greater necessity for this country, both for its trade and its finance, than cheap money . . . a rise in the Bank Rate would appear to be inexpedient and inopportune.[95]

But Norman was not convinced. Baldwin, who had become Prime Minister upon the retirement of Bonar Law and was temporarily acting as his own Chancellor of the Exchequer, felt forced to accept Norman's recommendations, despite the fact that senior Treasury officials such as Niemeyer were worried about the effect of high rates on the economy, since unemployment was over a million and appeared to be getting worse.[96]

While his memorandum quoted above makes clear that Addis agreed with the political leaders about the seriousness of the economic situation and the desirability of cheap money, he refused to accept the recommendations of the so-called 'Cambridge school' of economists, namely that the government should devalue the pound and in effect adopt a managed currency. Instead Addis continued to put his faith in the methods of the past, believing that the restoration of the gold standard would bring the stability and the recovery of trade which would enable Britain to regain her former greatness.

In June 1923 Addis, as President of the Institute of Bankers, welcomed Professor Cassel to lecture on the topic of 'The Place of Money in Political Economy'. In his introductory remarks, Addis hardly sounded like a neutral, asking:

> Have we sufficient confidence in the competence of any man or body of men to extend its use to the stabilisation of internal prices in such a way as to arrest the fluctuations of price and to mitigate, if not to flatten out, the declivities of trade cycles which we have too long perhaps regarded like the weather as part of the order of nature. Or are we to close our ears to the siren song of the

Professors of Political Economy and having deliberately counted the cost, bend our steps back to the resumption of the automatic working of the gold standard in all its pristine vigour?[97]

Obviously, Addis slanted the argument; clearly, he had not been convinced by Keynes or Cassel. However, as the economic situation worsened and the Bank of England raised the bank rate, the views of Keynes and McKenna began to win more support.[98]

In December 1923 Keynes sent Addis a copy of his recently published *A Tract on Monetary Reform* in which he called for a managed currency. Addis thanked Keynes for the copy, saying:

> I find myself in agreement with nearly all of it, I think, except the conclusion. A managed currency may come some day, but I do not believe we are ripe for it yet. It would be ill to work except in an atmosphere of confidence and belief which at present is non-existent.[99]

Addis responded publicly to Keynes's proposals in a speech to the Joint Meeting of the Institute of Bankers in Scotland and the Society of Accountants in Edinburgh on 10 December 1923, titled 'Back to the Gold Standard'.[100] Addis denounced the 'Cambridge school' for advocating a managed currency and preached the necessity for more deflation.

In commenting on Addis's speech, one critic, identified only as 'E.J.S.', sharply criticised Addis's views, especially his tendency to present them as ethical questions of right versus wrong rather than theoretical questions of truth and error; righteousness versus sin rather than fact versus fallacy.[101] In the same issue, another writer (Arthur Kitson, President of the Banking Reform League) claimed that those academic critics of the gold standard had lost their jobs as a result of their views. Such comments suggest the emotional atmosphere which surrounded the question of Britain's return to gold and demonstrate that doubts as to its advisability were becoming more widespread.

Economic policy became a matter of central concern as Britain's Labour Party assumed power after the election of 1923, when Baldwin's Conservative Party failed to win a clear majority on the issue of protection. The Liberal Party candidates, divided between the followers of Lloyd George and those of Asquith, trailed behind Labour, and J. Ramsay MacDonald became Britain's first Labour Prime Minister. For a few months Addis absented himself from the depressing problems of Europe and the British economy by agreeing to serve on a special banking commission to Brazil.

THE MONTAGU MISSION TO BRAZIL

In 1923 the Brazilian government requested a £25m long-term loan from Rothschilds 'to liquidate the floating debt and set Brazilian finances in order'.[102] Rothschilds' and Brazil's other major creditors (Barings and Schroders) insisted that a financial mission should assess the situation before it would consider such a loan.[103] Lionel de Rothschild asked E. S. Montagu, a former Cabinet Minister in the Lloyd George government who had recently retired from politics, to head the mission. In all likelihood, Norman recommended Addis as a member of the commission, but the recommendation might also have come from Revelstoke.[104]

Doubtless a factor in Addis's decision to accept the offer (which would require a long absence from his family) was the fee of £2000, plus expenses. Throughout his career, lacking any inherited wealth, Addis felt pressured by the expenses of having a large family to support and educate. By 1923 he was beginning to feel that time was running out, remarking that even though he was retired, there was little leisure. Then he continued: 'But one must work for the shadows are lengthening and the day grows shorter.'[105]

The Montagu Mission, which included Hartley Withers, the former editor of *The Economist*, Sir William McLintock, a partner of one of the largest British accounting and auditing firms, and Lord Lovat, who owned cotton plantations in Brazil, sailed on 14 December 1923. Addis wrote that he liked his companions but did not feel one of them, since 'they liked to gamble, and sports played such a large part of their existence'.[106] Of course the days in Brazil were not wholly devoted to work, but were filled with travel and the inevitable receptions, sumptuous luncheons and dinners.

As had been the case with China's debt, the 'crux of the question', as Montagu informed Rothschild, was whether or not the Brazilians would submit to 'some form of control of the finances'.[107] Montagu rejected Addis's moderate proposal as 'very timid'.[108] He was determined to separate the Banco de Brasil from political influence. But Rothschild thought foreign ownership of the bank would be too unpopular.[109] After considerable negotiation and pressure from Montagu, the mission succeeded in persuading the government officials to accept the terms required before it agreed to recommend a loan.[110]

After returning to London in March the Commission submitted a thirty-eight-page report recommending a loan to Brazil.[111] However, because of the unofficial embargo on foreign issues, no loan for Brazil could be floated, despite the bankers' concern that American investments were replacing British in Brazil.[112] The Americans floated $60m in two issues in May and June, 1926.[113] The recommendations of the Montagu Mission provide further evidence of the similarity of investment bankers' views and goals, whether in China, South America or Europe – they sought to avoid political influence and to preserve investment opportunities.

Afterwards Montagu thanked Addis for his participation:

> I recognised from the outset how difficult a position I had been invited to fill and how anomalous it was to have asked me to lead a mission which you, with all your experience and the position that you have earned in the City, were the vital part. That difficulty could not have been overcome except by your unremitting loyalty and consideration.[114]

For Addis, the trip must have provided a needed respite from the perplexing European problems, to which he returned that spring of 1924.

THE DAWES SETTLEMENT, 1924

Hardly was Addis back from Brazil than he became immersed in the report of the Expert Reparations Committee, chaired by the American banker, Charles G. Dawes.[115] The Reparations Committee had appointed two Committees of Experts to make recommendations for a reparations settlement after the French occupation of the Ruhr in 1923 had proved disastrous to both France and Germany.[116] The most important of the two committees (that chaired by Dawes) was charged with considering means to balance the German budget and stabilise the German currency. The second committee (headed by McKenna) was asked to estimate 'the amount of exported German capital' and to consider ways 'to ensure the return of this capital to the Reich for productive use'.[117]

Addis praised the report in effusive language: 'A new birth lies here for Europe, if only France has the will to do justly . . . Christ is risen, Can you drink of his cup? Let France answer, "We are able." '[118] But neither the British Treasury nor Norman shared Addis's enthusiasm. Norman had hoped to link the new German currency to sterling rather than the dollar. However the Americans had other ideas, seeing this as the ideal opportunity 'to complete our position as world bankers'.[119] A. N. Young, an economic adviser to the State Department, and Professor Kemmerer, the American currency expert, had specifically warned the State Department that if Norman succeeded in his plans for Germany to keep its reserves in London, American business would suffer.[120]

In addition to the concern about sterling, there was doubt as to whether a large loan to Germany was either necessary or beneficial to international financial stability. Bradbury (the British delegate on the Reparations Commission) warned: 'any considerable international credit operations in favour of either France or Germany are likely to lead to a further entanglement of the international exchanges without permanent advantage to anyone'. Niemeyer agreed.[121] Yet, ignoring Treasury opinion, Norman deferred to Strong's and Morgans' wishes.[122] Although Strong and Morgans recognised that the Dawes Plan was only an interim solution, they did not foresee the explosion of American lending to Germany which would follow; they deluded themselves that economics and politics could be kept separate.[123] Morgans warned the Germans that they must accept the Dawes Plan before they could hope to get American loans.[124]

The Dawes Plan denationalised the German railways and provided for the establishment of a railway company controlled by a combination of private interests, the German Government and a foreign director. It also specified that an American Agent General for Reparations would oversee the reparations machinery and the German economy.[125] In addition it established international control of the Reichsbank, which was placed under a General Council (one half of which was to be German, one-half foreign) which had powers regarding note issue, reserve requirements and appointment of the President.[126]

One goal of the bankers was thwarted by the American expert, Owen Young, who proved capable of standing up to the bankers.[127] Young, the President of General Electric, impressed everybody that spring with his ability to harmonise conflicting views.[128] According to Young's secretary (Stuart Crocker) Lamont and Norman had threatened not to support the Dawes loan unless the Reparations Commission was extinguished.[129] Young thereupon threatened to give the loan to the American investment banker, Clarence Dillon.[130] At that point Norman and Lamont changed their minds.[131]

In addition to the question of whether the mark would be based on a sterling or gold currency, there was the question of security for the loan. Both Lamont and Norman claimed to be worried about the marketability of the bonds to the American public.[132] While one specialist on this subject (Professor Schuker) concludes that these fears were sincere, another (Professor Sayers) is sceptical. The latter comments: 'it is permissible to wonder whether the Bank and its Governor need in August 1924 have been so worried about the appetite of investors'.[133] Niemeyer suggested his real opinion of the Dawes proposals by referring to the Dawes Report as 'the Americans' beastly plan'.[134] Certainly the British position was not strengthened by its current political leader, Labour Prime Minister J. Ramsay MacDonald, who only barely comprehended high finance.[135]

Whether needed or not, the bonds proved to be enormously popular and profitable, and were oversubscribed in both New York and London, since they yielded two to three times the return on domestic bonds.[136] Young personally had assured investors that the loan would have 'first charge in Germany ahead of reparation and all other payments'.[137] With the Dawes Plan in operation, the Americans had finally been persuaded to re-enter European finance – but on their own terms.

Although Addis had no part in the drafting of the Dawes Plan, he soon became part of its implementation, when he was invited to become the British Director of the Reichsbank. Governor Norman and Chancellor of the Exchequer Philip Snowden had opposed Bradbury, who seemed the most qualified for the position, because he was a member of the Reparations Commission, which Norman felt subjected him to too much political influence.[138] It did not take long for Addis to learn just how badly the new arrangement would work against British interests. Arriving in Berlin for the first meeting of the Reichsbank Council, Addis consulted with Owen Young, the Acting Agent-General, who told him that he favoured giving the German loan priority over reparations.[139] Since the other Directors supported Young, there was little Addis could do except to enter an official disagreement in the minutes.[140] With the German reparations question settled for the moment at least, British and American leaders once more turned their attention to Britain's return to the gold standard, a step long anticipated.

BRITAIN'S RETURN TO GOLD, 1923–5

As we have seen, British and American financial leaders agreed that only a return to the gold standard and central bank cooperation would ensure international stability. Prior to his trip to Brazil, Addis had further evidence of the dangers to the Empire caused by uncertaintly over monetary policy when A. Stephen (Chief Manager of the HSBC) warned that 'the elimination of the risk of exchange to the merchant is the factor that counts. We shall have to wait for a stabilised exchange between New York and London before the London accepting houses regain the business in the East.'[141] In October 1923 Addis was appointed Treasury Representative on the Imperial Conference Currency Committee.[142] Niemeyer suggested that he use the Imperial Economic Conference as 'the occasion to preach central banking to the Antipodes . . . I don't think it would take much time and no one could speak more fruitfully to the savages'. He indicated that 'the foreign bankers [to whom] I have spoken heartily agree' and said he hoped that 'S. Africa will put on Strakosch so there will be a good nucleus to work on'.[143] After meeting Canadian Prime Minister MacKenzie King, Addis noted his concern about Canadians getting 'too much under control of US financiers. They ought to borrow here.'[144]

The issue of Britain's return to gold was given a full-scale public debate in the spring of 1924 at the same time as the Dawes Plan was being negotiated. The debate was held as part of the annual meeting of the Royal Economic Society at the London School of Economics. Participants included Professor Cannan of the University of London, Keynes, Hawtrey and Addis. By this time, the issues had been widely discussed in the press and financial journals, after the publication of Keynes's *A Tract on Monetary Reform* and Addis's Edinburgh speech.[145] During the debate Addis reiterated his conviction that British prices must go down further if Britain were to regain her standing as the centre of international trade and finance. He argued that gold represented stability and that the 'worst thing was uncertainty.'[146] These views seem inconsistent with Addis's earlier opposition to bank rate increase and concern for industry, which he had expressed in his memo for Norman. Perhaps the explanation lies in the audience, or perhaps in the changed situation of 1924. Or most likely, Addis was suggesting that all other concerns must take second place to preservation of the Empire.

Keynes responded with a devastating critique of both Addis's and

Hawtrey's arguments, specifying that his most serious disagreement was with Addis: 'I am afraid there is no room for agreement between us and Sir Charles Addis if Sir Charles insists on immediate deflation.'[147] Afterwards Addis described the event to Mills: 'We had a great debate on Monetary Reform at the Economic Society. All the big guns were among the audience. Jenks from America, LeGroot from Holland, etc. Milner in the chair. Cannan and I one side of him. Keynes & Hawtrey on the other.' He wrote that Hawtrey and he were now agreed and that 'Keynes is wobbling. The Gold Standard is saved.'[148] Such comments demonstrate again how emotional the gold-standard question had become, resembling more a religious crusade than debate over economic policy.

The attempt to understand the relations between prices and currency was of course still in its infancy in 1924. Addis noted the confusion in the Committee of Treasury meetings about the gold standard in his diary, commenting that 'the gold question is evolved into a duel between the Governor and me. The others say little and scarcely understand the question and its bearings.'[149] Earlier, Strong had asked Addis: 'are you certain that: (a) advance of 12 per cent in American price level *must* be accompanied by equal advance in $ value of pound or (b) there *could be* a 12 per cent price advance in America w/o [without] a considerable price advance here?'[150]

That spring the government appointed a committee (chaired by Austen Chamberlain) officially to consider the amalgamation of the note issue but with the underlying purpose of discussing Britain's return to gold.[151] The Committee (which included Bradbury, Niemeyer, Professor Pigou and Gaspard Farrar) began holding hearings at the end of June. Appearing as the first witness Norman said that the first thing to do to restore the gold standard was to 'decide a date on which the export [of gold] should be permitted and I think the next thing to do is to announce it as a fixed and immutable date beyond all possibility of change and to leave me to work toward it.' Norman favoured fixing a long period, up to three years. But Addis (who testified next) felt that it was more important to fix a maximum period of eighteen months, and while recognising that some sacrifice would be entailed, felt it 'would not be too high a price to pay for the substantial benefit of the trade of this country and its working classes, and also, although I put it last, for the recovery by the City of London of its former position as the world's financial centre.'[152]

In supporting the return to gold, Addis emphasised its effect on the continued unity of the empire. He explained to Keynes that there was a 'tendency to fly from sterling, not only on the Continent but also in Egypt and Siam', as well as the Dominions. He felt that only by returning to gold could Britain hope to preserve her empire.[153] Thus the question of Britain's return to gold, like the reparations question and the Brazil loan, was part and parcel of the ongoing Anglo-American competition.

The discussion concerning the return to gold continued through the summer and autumn of 1924.[154] Although Keynes's articles in the *Nation* and the *Athenaeum* were brilliant, they could not sway the majority of financial opinion for whom the traditional, orthodox views of Addis inspired greater confidence. Hawtrey wrote to Addis on 29 July 1924: 'There is no one in the length & breadth of the City whose opinion I value more highly than yours and I am not peculiar in that respect.'[155] Addis explained why he felt the return should not be postponed, saying 'We must be prepared to use the Bank rate boldly if necessary. I do not think it will be necessary to raise it at present and it might not be necessary at all. It would depend on the relative mutation of prices here and in the U[nited]S[tates]'.[156] In reply Keynes warned Addis of the dangers ahead to the British economy and predicted: 'To risk all these misfortunes merely for the sake of linking up the London and New York money markets, and so facilitating the work of international financiers – for this in my judgment is all it comes to – is going to lay the City and the Bank of England open to popular attacks the violence of which might be very great.' Next he appealed to Addis, saying:

> Do not be the Louis XVI of the monetary revolution. For surely it is certain that enormous changes will come in the next twenty years, and they will be bad changes, unwisely and even disastrously carried out, if those of us who are at least agreed in our ultimate objects and are aiming at the stability of society cannot agree in putting forward safe and sound reforms.[157]

But Keynes could not convince Addis. Meanwhile the Bank of England monitored the exchange, hoping that the pound would reach the old parity against the dollar.[158] As 1924 wore on, the real questions that emerged were not *if*, but *when*, and *how*?

The Committee on Currency and Bank of England Note Issues (Chamberlain–Bradbury–Committee) suggested in September 1924 that the Government wait for up to twelve months for a rise in American prices (so as to avoid painful deflation) and that the whole situation be looked at again 'not later than the early autumn of 1925' since the embargo on the support of gold would expire at the end of that year.[159] But new developments that autumn convinced Norman of the urgent need to make a decision. The decisive victory of the Conservative Party in the October election was one factor that convinced Norman that the opportunity for action had arrived.[160] But more important was American pressure.

Both Lamont and the international lawyer, John Foster Dulles, had warned the American government that unless Britain returned to gold, she might threaten American trade, and the United States could be left 'with a huge pile of yellow metal'.[161] In April, Strong, who was visiting Norman, reported to Jay:

> Very confidentially, I have a strong conviction, after an all-afternoon discussion with Norman, Revelstoke and Addis (the real ones here) that if the Dawes Report is accepted, we can find a way to deal with the London–New York exchange that will finally do the job. But it is all in [the] future and depends upon that big 'if'.[162]

Strong described Addis as being on 'the extreme Right of British monetary opinion'.[163]

Even more important was a November visit from the Dutch Banker and currency expert, Vissering, and the American economist, Kemmerer, who were *en route* to South Africa to advise that government on its return to gold. At a dinner-party which Strakosch gave for Kemmerer to meet Norman and Niemeyer, Kemmerer became aware of the British bankers' 'pro-sterling' views.[164] Norman strongly opposed South Africa acting independently, and resented that government's inviting outside advisers.[165] It seems likely that Kemmerer's mission was an attempt to encourage the British to return to gold.

Norman and Strong began to lay plans for a credit in the United States and in December Norman informed Niemeyer of his intention 'to go to New York to consult Strong and Morgan re support in America if [we] return to gold to maintain the dollar exchange'. Norman suggested to the Treasury that a cushion be established to protect the exchange.[166] Niemeyer did not like the idea, writing:

> The more I think of the cushion, the less I like it . . . to go back – because that is what it amount to – to war methods of maintaining exchange is to me a loathsome prospect . . . Is not the proper method rather cooperation with the central banks of other nations

ready to return to gold? In particular ought not US – *much* interested in gold – to cooperate without requiring us to go to the pawnshop? Can gold be restored, if she doesn't cooperate? (e.g. encourage loans, long and short, by US: encourage Federal Reserve Banks to give European credits)

Niemeyer felt that the 'cushion' would 'simply put into people's heads fears which (not being J. P. M.) they probably wouldn't themselves think of?' He concluded that 'if the return is to be done, it can only be done on *"l'audace et toujours l'audace."*'[167]

Yet, despite Niemeyer's opposition, Norman proceeded to New York and arranged with the Federal Reserve Bank and Morgans for a revolving credit of $500m, divided into portions of $200m and $300m for use for two years.[168] Niemeyer again expressed his opposition, both to Lubbock, the Deputy Governor of the Bank of England, and to Sir Warren Fisher, the permanent head of the Treasury, writing to the latter, 'the more I hear of this the less I like it'.[169]

Fisher shared Niemeyer's concern, writing: 'I find Monty's [Norman's] cables very disquieting. Neither the gold standard nor anything else is worth having on sufferance of another country or of their institutions – we might find ourselves at mercy, & be out of the frying pan into the fire.'[170] Addis who agreed with Niemeyer and Fisher, wrote a long memorandum regarding Norman's proposals:

1. In our judgement the restoration of the Gold Standard should follow and not precede the conditions of trade appropriate to the maintenance of a stable exchange.
2. It would be a mistake to anticipate a return to the free exports of gold before conditions warrant it. The risk would be too great and the consequences of failure too grave for us to recommend it. We must be satisfied that the exchange situation is such as to afford reasonable grounds for believing that the parity of exchange, having once been reached, could be maintained by the natural play of the market forces of supply and demand without resort to any artifical aids such as Gov. credits.
3. The essential condition is a balance of international payments in favour of this country.
4. We think there is some ground for believing that this condition already exists, but we think it would be unsafe to rely upon its

permanence until it has been tested by a period of comparatively stable exchange.

5. Temporary or seasonal fluctuations in exchange would no doubt have to be provided for, but these variations could more effectively be countered by shipments of bullion than by credits, the ultimate effect of which must be to weaken exchange and to increase the difficulty of a return to parity.

6. . . . we do not believe credits are either necessary or expedient and we should still prefer to rely on our own resources.[171]

Addis also testified to this effect before the Bradbury Committee on 28 January 1925, where he referred to Norman's proposals as 'this adventure'.[172]

Thus Addis's position on the return to gold had changed significantly since the past summer and now corresponded more with Treasury views than with those of Norman.[173] In addition Addis seems to have been influenced by the criticisms of the academic economists, industrialists and Liberal Party leaders who opposed Gold Restoration. Addis described a Tuesday Club discussion to Mills, indicating that Keynes, Stamp, Layton, Henderson, Brand, Strakosch, Kiddy, Hawtrey, Falk and Robertson all took part, and commented: 'From the van I have passed to the rear, now trying to prevent premature restoration before underlying condition ascertained to assure maintenance of gold.'[174] Addis's views resembled those of C. Goodenough, the Chairman of Barclays.[175] Addis was also thinking about the possibility of stabilising at a ratio of 4.6 dollars to the pound.[176]

Yet despite this strong opposition from his most trusted advisers, Norman refused to reconsider. Disregarding the opinions and advice of Fisher, Niemeyer and Addis, Norman persisted in making arrangements for the 'cushion' in New York. After returning, he convinced Churchill, the newly appointed and financially inexperienced Chancellor of the Exchequer, to accept his recommendations.[177] As Professor Sayers has observed, this indeed was 'near autocracy'.[178]

The timing of the British government's decision was doubtless affected by South Africa's decision to return to gold. Norman, who was furious that Vissering and Kemmerer had persuaded the South African government to act independently of London, refused to see Kemmerer on his return to London.[179] Such a move by South Africa appeared as yet another threat to Imperial unity.

Another important consideration for the Treasury was the war debt payment of $68 000 000, due to the United States in June 1925.

The problem for the Treasury was to find the dollars.[180] If the value of the pound was set where the exchange suggested it should be, it would be 10 per cent less than its prewar value, therefore, since the war-debt payments had been set in gold, it would mean paying 10 per cent more.

For his part, although Addis continued to oppose the 'cushion' and felt there was no necessity to rush the return, once the decision was made he went along. He and Norman agreed to differ on such things as the cushion and the temporary suspension of note convertability, which Addis opposed.[181] On 14 April Addis wrote to Strong that he was 'thankful to have escaped managed currency'.[182] And as one scholar has argued recently, British opinion was over-whelmingly in favour of a return to the gold standard.[183]

While much has been written about Britain's return to gold, little has been said about the increased dependence upon Morgans and the American financial market which Norman's arrangements created. Nor have historians devoted much attention to the increased influence which Morgans gained from the triple victory of the debt settlement, the Dawes plan and the return to gold. Both Keynes and Niemeyer expressed concern about the dependence on the United States but Niemeyer felt the return would 'diminish our dependence'.[184] Morgans charged a commission of 1 per cent the first year, and if not used, half that the second year which, while not an excessive rate, yet represented a sizeable income for credit which never proved necessary. The Federal Reserve Bank did not charge unless the credit was used.[185] Niemeyer, Fischer and Addis proved to be correct regarding the so-called 'cushion' since it was not used.

What most needs to be recognised is the fact that while Morgans was performing the functions of a central bank in providing credits to governments, it was in fact a private bank which was free from public control. While it is true that the Bank of England was also a private institution, its public role and responsibility had been so well developed over a century of time that the situation was quite different.[186] Most significantly, the role of the Bank of England as a central bank was accepted by the British government and the British people, whereas Morgans' role was neither defined nor accepted by either Congress or the American people.

Given Britain's continued dependence on Morgans' cooperation and support, it should not be surprising that little specific complaint or criticism can be found in Treasury records, since no one likes to record mistakes. But anyone reading extensively in these documents comes away with the distinct sense of how deeply the British resented their treatment from the Americans, as will be seen more fully later. However, British officials found it difficult to believe that good relations with Morgans would not necessarily ensure good relations with Washington. But the American system of government was so different from the British in terms of the legislature's ability to thwart the will of the Executive, that no Administration had the political power to produce the debt cancellation for which the British Treasury hoped. One entry in the Norman Diary is both suggestive and puzzling. On 7 April 1925 Norman recorded a visit from F. Schuster (a prominent banking authority) who indicated that 'Cl [Colonel House] House proposal as to Earmarking gold as meagre and ungenerous, but the best they will do'.[187] While there were adverse comments in the press about Morgans' rate of interest and some suggestion that Chancellor of the Exchequer Churchill questioned it privately, in public he accepted it.[188] One interesting aspect of this whole arrangement was Strong's insistence that the management of the Bank of England remain unchanged for two years.[189]

As it turned out, Keynes's predictions proved valid, the pound was overvalued, the British economy remained stagnant, and unemployment continued to grow.[190] Naturally Britain's economic problems did not all originate in monetary policy.[191] But there is little doubt that the return to gold at the prewar parity made the solution of those problems more difficult. To avoid further labour unrest, the Baldwin government provided unemployment insurance, while wages remained high for those working. All this meant that British goods were not competitive on the world market, which resulted in the unfavourable balance of trade leading to a continued drain of gold from the Bank of England.

THE ADDIS–NORMAN RELATIONSHIP AND THE BANK OF ENGLAND

One of the most fascinating aspects of this whole question was the independence demonstrated by Norman, despite significant opposition both within the Bank and from the Treasury. Here Addis's support was probably crucial. For the evidence in the Addis papers suggests that the dissatisfaction within the Court might have been sufficient to lead to Norman's replacement, had Addis not remained loyal. As early as 5 November 1923 Revelstoke had sounded Addis as to his interest in becoming Governor. Later that same month Addis talked with Grenfell regarding the Governor's successor, recording that Grenfell said 'no' to Lubbock.[192]

The tradition in the Bank was for a two-year rotation of Governors, so in 1925 Norman was already overdue for replacement. Professor Sayers wrote that the tradition had not been observed in the early 1920s because of the economic and international crises and also because the particular Directors in line for succession were ruled out as 'money-market Directors'.[193] In 1924 the Court decided that rotation would be resumed in 1927 with Alan Anderson (the Deputy Governor) to succeed Norman. However before the year was out this plan broke down and the dispute over the succession continued to be a matter of controversy over the next few years.

In September 1926 Addis wrote a seven-page memorandum outlining his reasons why Norman should continue as Governor. The proposal was to return to the prewar system of rotation of governors. Another idea being suggested was to 'separate the position into domestic and international'. Addis felt that they had:

> reached a critical stage. The convention of central banks, the stabilisation of continental currencies, the amalgamation of our own note issues, are problems which are all ripe or at least ripening for settlement during the coming year.

Because of this situation, Addis felt it unwise to resume rotation, or to divide the administration of the Bank into two separate departments, one for foreign affairs and the other for home affairs, with a director in charge of one and the Governor in charge of the other. He continued: 'In this double role of negotiator at home and abroad the present Governor has found an appropriate field for the exercise of his remarkable powers of courage and imagination and statesmanship.' Addis therefore recommended that the Court must 'allow a craftsman to complete his own work'.[194] In February 1927 Addis told a special committee that he favoured a return to the prewar system of rotation as soon as it was expedient, in three to five years.[195]

One reason why Addis continued to back Norman as Governor lies in the feeling of trust which existed between the two bankers. For both Addis and Norman, character was the most important consideration, and Addis found it difficult to believe in 1925 that anyone like Keynes, who advocated such radical ideas as a managed currency or who said that it was necessary to pay off the national debt could be considered trustworthy.[196] As seasoned bankers, both

Addis and Norman relied on personal relationships rather than official structures, academic theory or statistics in making decisions. For instance, Norman advised Gates McGarragh, the American director of the Reichsbank, to 'depend on his personal relationship with Schacht not on statutes.'[197] The consequences of these personal relationships for Britain were enormous.

Perhaps most important was the fact that while Norman and Addis disagreed about many issues, they shared a common view of the world's problems and how these could best be solved. They recognised 'the correlation of external and internal finance' and the impossibility of separating them.[198] Both men remained confident that if the politicians would leave the financiers alone, they could solve the world's economic problems. Each felt a sense of mission, a commitment to the country's national interest and the firm assurance that they knew best what that interest was. A Christmas note which Addis sent to Strong in 1926 clearly conveys these themes of commitment, mission and duty. Addis hoped that Strong was feeling better so that he could rejoin the 'task where you have already accomplished so much of redressing the ills of an impoverished and distracted world'.[199]

While one can concede that Addis, Norman and Strong were undoubtedly dedicated, well-intentioned and honourable men, one must also recognise that they were unrealistic in believing that decisions which affected the economic well-being of all of their countrymen and the world, could or should remain solely in the secret control of Anglo-American bankers, no matter how superior their knowledge and experience, or how exceptional their moral rectitude. Their cult of secrecy caused suspicion and resentment both at home and abroad.[200] One scholar notes that 'Even the Chancellor of the Exchequer was kept in the dark about certain crucial facts of the Bank of England's operations.'[201] By keeping critical information secret even from the Treasury, the Bank of England prevented those responsible for government economic and financial policy from knowing the full range of facts necessary to carry out their responsibilities, as well as placing them in the embarrassing position of appearing to misrepresent Britain's situation in international affairs.[202]

Furthermore, recognising and acknowledging the commitment and integrity of the men does not permit the historian to ignore or discount the role which personal ambition or vanity played in their decision-making. Obviously these bankers enjoyed playing the role of Kings, and were guilty of arrogance in believing that they could force the other governments of the world to adopt the 'sound banking practices' which Norman and Strong advocated.[203] Nevertheless, right or wrong, it was this task to which Strong, Norman and Addis turned their attention once the gold question had been settled. No doubt the desire to proceed with this work to a large degree explains Addis's continuing support for Norman.

Evidence of the extent to which Norman continued to rely on Addis is provided by Addis's trip to the United States in the autumn of 1925, ostensibly to attend a Consortium Council meeting, but also to consult with Strong on currency matters. Norman cabled to Strong: 'Please consult Addis freely', and three days later added: 'I hope Addis will have talked freely with you as I asked him to do. But though he knows much and is helpful, he is not easily forthcoming.'[204]

Over the next few years the Addis–Norman friendship survived many disagreements. In fact, Addis seems to have taken disagreement for granted. For instance, on 10 February 1926, he noted: 'A long Treasury Committee. Discussed guaranteed bills till 1.50 p.m. The Governor & I arguing on opposite sides as usual.'[205] A year later Addis recorded another controversy with Norman over the question of an Expert Governor.[206] Addis told his fellow-directors that:

> The proper place for an expert is not in the Chair but behind it. It is for him to assist and advise, but it is for the Merchant Directors to determine the policy of the Bank, and it is the belief that the policy is so determined which has won for the Bank its traditional authority and prestige.[207]

In 1928 some of the Bank of England Directors undertook a serious effort to unseat Norman.[208] Speaking to the Court in June, Addis said:

> The result of our long discussion has been to throw into sharp relief two divergent and, I fear, irreconcilable policies. Those who advocate the first are convinced that, owing to the changed conditions in Europe, the administration of the Bank should in future be carried on by an expert Governor whose tenure of office should be permanent, or, if that is too strong a word, indeterminate. Those in favour of the second policy believe that European conditions which render a temporary suspension of the former system expedient have passed, or are passing, and that a return, not precipitately or prematurely but as soon as possible, should be made to the traditional practice of a non-expert Governor supported by an adequate body of export assistants, with a term of office rotating every two years.

Addis said that the Governor had suggested a compromise – not what I like but 'as much as I am likely to get'. The Governor's tenure was to end in 1931.[209] A heated debate among the Directors ensued, and Addis recorded: 'Once more Court discussed return to rotation. I spoke I think effectively. Some heat generated with Kindersley Grenfell & Booth. Booth says he once thought I was all brains & no heart. Now he thinks I am all heart and no brains.'[210] Early in October Addis noted that Booth had sounded him out as to whether he would be willing to succeed the Governor if he backed down. 'It is urged against it that I am not popular in the city. Interesting to hear that. I should dread popularity.'[211] At the next week's meeting of the Court, Addis spoke against what he considered to be a 'wrecking resolution' put forth by Lord Cullen (formerly Sir Brien Cokayne) which was an attempt to rescind an earlier compromise resolution that the system of rotation would resume in 1931.[212]

Addis's chief counter-argument was that there was no one else both capable and willing to take on the job, which suggests that he himself refused to undertake it.[213] Finally, after much more discussion, the confirmation of Norman was carried unanimously by the Court on 25 October 1928, marking a victory both for Norman and Addis. By this time, plans for a new reparations conference were well developed, which further explains Addis's insistence that Norman continue as Governor.

THE REICHSBANK, MONETARY POLICY AND EUROPEAN POLITICS, 1925–8

The appointment to the Reichsbank Council deepened Addis's involvement in European politics and provided him with new expertise regarding reparations questions. At the age of 65 he began studying German. Like everything else he did, Addis attacked German vocabulary with such determination and perserverance that before long, he was able to read German novels.[214] His daughters can still recall seeing their father memorising his vocabulary by positioning a German grammar book on a corner shelf next to the mirror while shaving with a straight razor.[215]

The monthly meetings of the Reichsbank Council in Berlin brought Addis into close contact with Reichsbank President Schacht, and with the American Agent-General, Parker Gilbert, who was responsible for the transfer of all reparation funds. Since Norman frequently accompanied Addis to these meetings, the two had the opportunity for long talks on the train or aboard ship. On 26 October 1924, Addis described one passage: 'Norman would take no risks and went straight to his cabin. We had seats together on the train to Paris and had much talk. I love him.'[216] After one of the first meetings of the Council Addis sadly recalled a similar meeting in 1911 when 'we French, German, American and English sat and Herr Urbig in an eloquent speech looked down a vista of international peace! The irony of events!'[217] Addis hoped to avoid another such disaster.

Between 1925 and 1929, Addis became well acquainted with Schacht, and the Americans – Gilbert and his assistants, Pierre Jay and Shepard Morgan. Addis admired Gilbert, calling him 'a great man who has done great works by sheer force of character'.[218] He often dined with Gilbert and his family while in Berlin. Although Schacht was a difficult person to get along with, Addis described him as 'an intelligible, able man' and liked him.[219] While they sometimes had serious disagreements, the two preserved their mutual respect.[220] The Reichsbank appointment also brought Addis into increased contact with British Treasury views on reparations, and with Leith-Ross, the Deputy Controller, who had charge of such matters.[221]

When the Dawes settlement was arranged in 1924, all recognised that it was only a temporary settlement, since it had not set any final reparations figure. The British and Germans continued to hope that ultimately the burden of German debt payments might be reduced, either through American willingness to cancel war debts or through world-wide economic expansion.[222] However these expectations were not fulfilled. The effect of Britain's return to gold produced further deflation and by 1926 the economic situation was increasingly troubling to the Treasury, where the indomitable Winston Churchill (having returned to the Conservative Party) reigned as Chancellor of the Exchequer.[223]

At this time the General Strike of 1926, while not successful, had alarmed British political leaders about the state of popular discontent and its future implications. Addis wrote to Mills that he sympathised with the strikers' demand for a larger share of the wealth: 'it is only because I do not believe in the Socialism which is proposed as a substitute, that I go on tinkering with the old system in the hope of ameliorating if not abolishing, its manifest injustice'.[224]

Within the Treasury, Churchill expressed concern about the relationship of high bank rate to unemployment, and let Bank of England officials know of his displeasure when they raised the rate to 5 per cent on 3 December 1925.[225] Earlier Addis had argued at the Committee of Treasury meeting in July 1925 for a reduction in Bank Rate because of the state of trade, but he did not convince his fellow-Directors until August, when the bank rate was reduced to 4½ per cent, followed by a further reduction to 4 per cent in October.[226] But the outflow of gold late in 1925 forced the rate back up to 5 per cent on 3 December, leading to Churchill's complaint.[227] As Professor Sayers observes: 'Everyone knew that the political interest was derived from, and would last as long as, the obstinate million in the unemployment figures.'[228]

Norman and Addis continued to differ over the issue of bank rate. After returning from the United States, Norman discussed bank rate with the Committee of Treasury and 'Blackett's move towards a full Gold Standard for India'.[229] Addis tried to get the rate reduced in January 1927 but was defeated, with the Committee of Treasury deciding to leave it at 5 per cent 'in view of gold shipment to Russia'.[230] The other members of the Committee of Treasury did not demonstrate much interest in the problem.[231]

In addition to Norman, Addis was consulting Hawtrey at the Treasury, who the previous December had given a series of lectures on the Gold Standard.[232] Addis admired Hawtrey, commenting on his 'Problem of Economics': 'His philosophical exposition of familiar market conditions is most lucid and interesting.'[233] Later he remarked: 'I love his genial sensitive nature and his subtle delicately poised mind.'[234] Lacking a University education, Addis felt honoured to be included on the Economic Society Council with such distinguished economists as Keynes, D. H. MacGregor, a Professor of Political Economy at Oxford, A. L. Bowley, a Professor of Statistics at the University of London, Hawtrey and Dr James Bonar, an economist.[235]

Addis had gained further insight into British economic problems through his service on the Committee on National Debt and Taxation which had been created by the Treasury in March 1924. Chaired by Lord Colwyn, the Committee was asked to report on the effect of the National Debt and taxation on trade, employment, industry and national credit. Despite three years of discussions, the members were unable to reach agreement and submitted majority and minority reports, with Addis siding with the majority, but both majority and minority agreed on the necessity for a sinking fund.[236] Keynes discussed the Colwyn Committee's recommendations at the Tuesday Club meeting of 9 March 1927, when McKenna, Sir John Anderson and Leith-Ross all took part.[237] The Minority Report of the Colwyn Committee on National Debt and Taxation pointed out that:

> The external debt obliges the taxpayers of this country to make payments to the Governments of our creditor countries, giving the latter a claim upon the world's production which would otherwise have been exercised by and for some British citizen or institution.[238]

Chancellor of the Exchequer Churchill expressed concern to Niemeyer that the debt kept getting larger, while Germany and France had no government debt. Furthermore he worried that 'the policy of the Treasury and the Bank favours the Capitalists' interests and in particular the *rentier* class', and expressed the fear that a political campaign on the debt issue might ensue.[239]

The way that the gold standard was affecting prices was a matter of serious concern to economists in 1927. Addis had testified before the Indian Currency Committee where it first became clear that there was likely to be a shortage of gold if India went on a full gold standard and established a central bank as the Commission recommended.[240] The question at issue was the stabilisation of the rupee at a fixed rate in relation to gold or sterling. Addis advised that it was 'better to wait until further progress has been made in the stabilisation of European currencies, and until the reconstruction of the economic life of Europe permits of some sort of reasonable estimate being taken of the future course of world prices.' He continued by explaining that once the European governments had stabilised, then the central bank cooperation provided for by the Genoa resolutions would 'come into play' and 'a deliberate and concerted attempt will then be made by the Central Banks of Europe to prevent undue fluctuations in the future value of gold'.[241]

However, the expected Central Bank cooperation never materialised and British prices continued to fall. In June 1927 Keynes demonstrated to the Colwyn Committee how falling prices had increased the weight of the national debt.[242] In December 1927 Addis warned that:

> The general return to a gold standard in Europe has sharpened the demand for gold and the greatest caution and economy in its use is imperative if a fall in the general level of prices, with its lamentable consequences to the gold-using nations, is to be prevented.[243]

Also of concern was the increased weight of the American debt payments. Never one to suppress his views, Churchill made no secret of his resentment of American war debt policy toward Britain. Churchill blamed Britain's situation on the wealthy Americans who insisted on debt collection.[244] Such statements hardly improved Anglo-American relations.

Not surprisingly, the view from the other side of the Atlantic was quite different. Under-secretary of the Treasury Garrard Winston, who had visited London in 1925, discussed Churchill's accusations, saying that he had 'seldom seen such persistent effort on the part of any European Statesman to put this country in [the] wrong as Churchill's'. The American official denounced Churchill as 'gratuitous in his slurs on our harsh treatment of our debtors' and continued:

> I should like nothing more than the opportunity to tell the facts with reference to England's treatment of her relief debtors and ours; of England's confiscation of private German property; of England's divvy with France of the Russian gold surrendered by Germany; of England's abstraction of our army costs paid by Germany.

He admitted that 'the burden of the English debt settlement to America is a bit unfair considering that England was the first to come up and settle' and felt that 'there may in the future come an opportunity to effect a readjustment'. But then he observed that 'England has treated no debtor as leniently as we have, and her grandstand play that she is willing to cancel what is owed her if we will cancel what she owes us, won't bear analysis' and concluded with the comment: 'Who would not be willing to release a bankrupt debtor if one's creditors would release us in a like amount. This may sound a bit warm tempered; it is.'[245] Shortly thereafter, Garrard Winston adopted a more conciliatory tone, admitting that 'if a sentiment for war-debt cancellation arises in America sufficiently strong to influence Congress, and we voluntarily offer to cancel the debts, then I believe that we here could stand the expense and that the world would be better off.' But he added that repudiation would simply halt new investment.[246] However, the 'sentiment for war-debt cancellation' never developed in the United States.

Niemeyer articulated the British Treasury's view in 1927:

> America came into [the] war to protect her own interests. Could not provide military aid for 18 mo. [months], while Europe held the line she provided money and saved her gore and her wealth in man power . . . did nothing to help to straighten the world (except

since 1923 to lend money on exceedingly good commercial terms). She did not even honour (though we and France did) the pledge on war debt given to Belgium by Wilson, Lloyd George and Clemenceau . . . We feel in fact that America has pretty badly let the world down.[247]

Treasury bitterness at the Americans no doubt partly resulted from domestic conditions – the difficulties it was experiencing in dealing with the problems of unemployment and managing the debt. Nine-tenths of the external debt was owed to the United States.[248]

In 1927 the Bank of England began its consideration of the amalgamation of the currency and appointed a committee which included Addis.[249] In a memorandum to the Report of the Special Committee appointed to report on the Amalgamation of the Note Issues and the Bank's profits, Addis emphasised his fear that the new provision would 'change the whole face of our currency system . . . Gold would be sterilised . . . currency would become a managed currency indeed.' He warned that there was not too much gold but too little. 'I confess I view with misgiving the growing tendency to curtail the freedom of the national money market and to manage its operations in the supposed interests of international finance.'[250] Sayers interprets Addis's comment narrowly, as indicating that Addis opposed Norman's manipulation of the gold standard. However, it seems more likely that Addis's concerns were similar to those which Keynes expressed – that the Amalgamation Act made British currency vulnerable to foreign influence.

In an article in *The Times* of 12 May 1928 Keynes explained his opposition:

> To compel the Bank of England to measure its margin of safety by the volume of the note issue is therefore to compel it to pay more attention to a particular symptom than the Bank, left to itself, would deem reasonable, and to do something which to its own untrammelled judgement seems unwise. In particular, when employment is reviving and the wages bill increasing, such a provision has the effect of putting pressure on the Bank of England to terminate the reviving prosperity, even though the Bank, left to itself, may see no reason in the world for doing such a thing.[251]

But Addis was not able to convince his fellow-members of the Committee of Treasury and the 1928 Amalgamation Act was submitted to Parliament, which approved it with little debate and no doubt even less understanding.[252]

Meanwhile criticism of the government's monetary policy increased.[253] Early in 1928, Addis took Walter Stewart (the American adviser to the Bank of England) to the Tuesday Club, where Hubert Henderson, the editor of the *Nation*, opened a discussion of the Liberal Party's Report on Britain's Industrial Future.[254] Obviously it would help the domestic economy if the debt could be reduced and if the American government could somehow be persuaded to forgive the war debts.

Another possible cure for the problem of high rates was to implement the Genoa recommendations for central bank cooperation. Late in 1927, Sir Henry Strakosch (who had served on the Royal Indian Commission) attempted to convince Strong that there was 'an impending shortage of monetary gold' which would lead to 'high discount rates, contracting credit and falling world commodity prices' and that the remedy for these circumstances was 'an extensive and formal development of the gold exchange standard'.[255] But Strong was not at all convinced, describing Strakosch as a '100 per cent "quantity" theory man', who 'holds Cassel's views in regard to the world's gold position'.[256] Strong had encouraged talk of the gold exchange standard only until the British stabilised in 1925. After that, Strong ceased to cooperate with plans for Central Bank cooperation to ensure exchange stability.

Nor did Strong accept Strakosch's recommendation that the Financial Section of the League of Nations should begin a study of the gold problem. Instead, Strong told Strakosch that he did not share Cassel's fears, that he did not believe in the 'quantity theory of prices', that he thought the 'gold exchange as now developing was hazardous in the extreme', and that he was opposed to 'a meeting of the banks of issue in the immediate future'. Strong stated that the Genoa resolution 'was no longer operative'.[257] He was utterly opposed to the idea that 'manipulation of gold and credit can be employed as a regulator of prices at all times and under all circumstances' as he felt Strakosch was suggesting. After this long summary of his discussion with Strakosch, Strong asked for Norman's views.

Norman replied on 11 April 1928, writing that he was in agreement:

> with most of what you write, particularly as regards unlimited further development of the gold exchange standard and the wisdom of allowing the Dawes Plan to work itself out a good deal further before any formal action by Central Banks or meeting between them.

He continued that he was:

> sceptical as to how far it would be practicable and how far it would
> be wise for the Central Banks to admit in any way that they can
> regulate prices through their gold and credit policies: or, in other
> words, how far the power of fixing prices (which would likely be
> taken to cover particular commodities as well as the general
> average) could or should come within the admitted purview of any
> Central Bank.[258]

Thus by 1928 the question of managing the gold standard had
become immersed in political controversies which Norman refused
to acknowledge.

Norman's personal relations with the French (which had never
been good) had been further exacerbated in the spring of 1928 by
the controversy over Roumanian stabilisation, which Norman insisted
must come under the League of Nations, while the Governor of the
Bank of France, Emile Moreau, attempted to persuade Strong to
support a private arrangement.[259] At issue here were both personal
and national rivalries; questions of principle became intertwined with
personal vanity. While Strong and Norman succeeded in patching up
their disagreements in June 1928, in the future this personal friendship
was no longer able to bridge the gap of international misunderstand-
ings, since in October 1928, Strong died. With Strong gone, the hope
for continuing Anglo-American financial cooperation diminished, not
because his successor, George Harrison, failed to understand its
importance, but because Harrison never enjoyed Strong's authority
over the Federal Reserve Board in Washington.[260]

In 1928 the British Treasury launched a new effort to change
American policy. Although the Dawes Plan had unleashed a flood
of American loans to Germany, which had temporarily created an
aura of stability and prosperity in Europe, by 1928 it was clear to
financial leaders that some final arrangement for establishing the total
amount of German reparations must be made. Agent General Gilbert
told Addis in March 1928 that it was urgent to fix the amount of
German reparations.[261] The French government refused to evacuate
its troops from the Rhineland without a settlement and also refused
to ratify the French war-debt settlement with the United States.
Unless ratification was completed by 1 August 1929, The French
Treasury would have to pay Washington $400m.[262] Naturally the
French Government wished to settle the amount it would receive

from Germany before ratifying the debt settlements with the United States and Great Britain.[263]

Early in 1928 Niemeyer had paid a visit to Strong to discuss the war-debt question. Strong told Niemeyer that the reparations question must be settled with no assurances that inter-Allied debts would be revised.[264] Strong also wrote Norman to the same effect.[265] Without such American assurances, Chancellor of the Exchequer Churchill refused to agree to a final settlement, indicating that he would not adopt an 'obsequious' attitude toward the United States.[266] Churchill and Prime Minister Baldwin had agreed to accept a revision of the Dawes Plan *on condition* that Britain be assured of an annuity sufficient to cover her debt to America, but Leith-Ross, opposed the decision.[267]

Faced with a possible new reparations crisis, the League of Nations Council decided in September 1928 that a review of the Dawes Plan should take place.[268] In October Addis discussed the League resolution with Gilbert, who told him that he would like Addis and Sir Josiah Stamp, one of the British authors of the Dawes Plan, to be the English members of a new Expert Committee, which was to have the American industrial, Owen Young, as Chairman. Addis commented in his diary: 'But will the Treasury want me? I doubt it.'[269] Perhaps Addis felt that the Treasury would prefer a less independent representative. However, the Treasury did after all approve Addis, who was appointed as an alternate with Blackett, to Revelstoke and Stamp. Certainly in terms of experience with the participants as well as with the subject matter, no one could have been better qualified than Addis.

The years between 1922 and 1928 had hardly fulfilled British expectations that central bank cooperation would lead to economic recovery and international financial stability. While Britain had funded her debts to the United States and returned to the gold standard, thus conforming to the accepted rules for international behaviour, the results had not proved beneficial to Britain's economy, where unemployment still numbered over a million. While the Dawes Plan had eased political tension and released American investments to Europe, a final settlement had yet to be reached.

In the meantime France, which had achieved a remarkable economic recovery, having stabilised with an undervalued franc, had acquired large reserves of gold and was demonstrating its determination to enforce its own point of view. For the French, the primary concern continued to be obtaining security against a resurgent

Germany, which translated into a determination to keep Germany weak. American leaders, facing a Presidential election in 1928, were more determined than ever to avoid involvement in European political problems, while Norman had lost his best American friend – Benjamin Strong. Thus the outlook for a new Reparations Conference was not auspicious.

7 An End to Reparations and the Gold Standard, 1929–31

'[The Americans] must be considered the greatest profiteers that the World has ever seen'.–Lord Revelstoke, 14 February 1929.

'Monetary stabilisation means international peace'.—Addis, 17 December 1930.

During the years between 1929 and 1931 the European powers undertook another major effort to solve the issue of reparations and war debts. In May 1929 after long months of negotiations the independent experts at Paris came to a final agreement, known as the Young Plan, which established total reparation assessments on Germany, provided for their division among the Allies and connected both reparations and inter-Allied debts to the European debts to America. Unfortunately the achievement did not win American support – the new Bank for International Settlements, which the Young Plan created and which Addis hoped would provide a means for credit expansion and central bank coordination – was never able to carry out this role.[1]

Briefly stated, events overtook solutions: the American stock market crash of October 1929 ended the period of economic expansion; the emergence of the Nazi party in Germany terrified the French; the collapse of the Austrian bank (the Credit Anstalt) in May 1931 triggered a financial crisis which ultimately forced Britain to leave the gold standard in September 1931. All these events were interconnected – all reflected the failure of the European powers and the United States to reach agreement on economic cooperation.[2]

Between 1929 and 1931 Addis devoted most of his time to trying to persuade the Americans to cooperate in solving the world's financial problems. First at Paris, then at the Hague and Baden-Baden, he helped to draft agreements aimed at solving the problem of reparations and war debts. In 1930 he travelled to Washington and New York in an effort to convince the Federal Reserve bankers and the Hoover administration of the seriousness of the international situation. But the Americans remained unconvinced of the need to cooperate and suspicious of British motives. Although experiencing an outflow of sterling, Addis and a small group of British financial leaders neverthless refused an offered loan from France in July because of the political demands which accompanied the offer. Instead they tried to force the Hoover Administration to cancel war debts and reparations. The gamble failed and Britain left the gold standard.

What is now clear is that these years between 1929 and 1931 marked a critical turning-point in the interwar period. Unfortunately, the turn was towards that economic warfare which Addis had both predicted and sought to avoid.

THE REPARATIONS CONFERENCE, 1929[3]

As the experts assembled in Paris in January and February, the most critical question was: would the United States government cooperate in reaching a final settlement on the war-debts–reparation imbroglio? A new concern was the bull market which was developing on Wall Street, causing the withdrawal of capital from Europe.[4] Addis noted that the Tuesday Club had discussed the Stock Exchange position on 14 November 1928, with Keynes, Robertson, Strakosch, Falk and himself participating: 'Rather a brilliant evening', he observed.[5]

After the death of Strong (in October 1928) no central banker emerged in the United States with sufficient authority to deal with the impending stock-market crisis. The domestic American economy's need for credit-tightening differed from Europe's need for cheap money.[6] Thus the Federal Reserve Board failed to break the market early in 1929 before the damage was done.[7] Then in November 1928 the Americans elected as President the political leader most hostile to Britain – Herbert Hoover.[8]

As the experts assembled in Paris Addis emphasised how much depended on finding a solution to the reparations–war-debts impasse. 'I can't bear to think of a failure and all it might involve politically. It might put peace back for a decade. We *must* get something arranged'.[9]

In theory, the Committee of Experts had been appointed by the Reparations Commission and was independent of political control. In fact, all its members kept closely in contact with their respective

governments.[10] Before Young left Washington the Hoover administration gave orders that the American members 'should under no
circumstances agree to discuss Allied indebtedness'.[11] It was thought
essential to have the Morgan partners on hand because (as Leith-
Ross later explained) no one knew what the Germans could pay and
the ultimate solution must be determined by the loan which the
market could provide.[12] Lamont indicated that neither the Hoover
Administration nor the British Treasury were particularly happy at
this admission of Morgans' power and observed:

> For a Government that declares that it has no connection with this
> whole affair and sticks its head into the sand whenever anybody
> points a finger at it, our Washington friends are taking an extraordi-
> nary interest in the whole proceeding.

To this he added a postscript: 'I think Jack [Morgan] perhaps noted
that there was no great enthusiasm evinced at London over his
appointment'.[13]

Lamont's comment suggests the ambiguous position which Morgans
occupied, both with Whitehall and in American politics. While each
succeeding Republican administration knew that it could not do
without Morgans' cooperation, no politician dared to admit this fact
to the American people. However, it seems likely that President-
elect Hoover (who had far more international experience than his
predecessors) was less easily intimidated by Morgans. Whatever the
explanation for its make-up, the American delegation included Owen
Young, Morgan and Lamont.

Although Addis feigned reluctance to accept the appointment, one
senses that he was both honoured and happy to have an opportunity
to help to solve this fundamental problem with which he had been
concerned since 1919. Certainly one can detect a touch of enthusiasm
in his diary entry: 'Preliminary papers for Reparations Committee
received. To work!'[14] The two official British delegates were Stamp
and Revelstoke. Stamp had been politically active in the Liberal
Party's proposals for solving unemployment, which promised to be a
major issue in the forthcoming election. His election as a Director of
the Bank of England in 1928 was meant 'to assuage' those critics who
saw the Bank as dominated by international bankers.[15] Addis later
described Stamp as 'a tower of strength in knowledge, acuteness,
adroitness and versatility'.[16] Revelstoke was probably selected for
the enormous influence and authority he commanded in the City as

the leader of Barings, and perhaps because Morgan requested his appointment.[17]

Early in January Dulles (the American international lawyer) sent a new and highly secret proposal to Frank Tiarks (a Director of the Bank of England and of the merchant banking firm, J. Henry Schroder) which offered a possible solution to the problem of Britain's debt to the United States.[18] Tiarks wrote that he had shown the letter 'to Monty [Norman]) and Addis, otherwise to no one'. Discussing the inter-Allied debts, Dulles wrote: 'it is probably politically impracticable to change the existing debt settlements by merely reducing the amounts of the annuities now provided for'. However, he predicted that it would be 'politically possible to discount the annuities on some favorable basis and discharge them entirely by a present cash payment'. Dulles continued that he had had the debt owed by the Allies to the United States calculated as at 15 June 1929: 'discounting on a 6 per cent semi-annual basis, the aggregate of such then present value would be $4 932 000 000'. He felt that Congress 'would agree to $4 000 000 000'.[19] These views were regarded as authoritative because Dulles (who was the nephew of former Secretary of State Robert Lansing and had been an adviser to the American Mission at Versailles) had since served as special counsel to Bankers Trust, the American underwriters of the Dawes loan.[20] The significance of this secret proposal was that it promised American cooperation in a scheme to solve the war-debts–reparations issue. After ten years of refusal, the British naturally were sceptical.

Before meeting with the other British experts and Treasury officials Revelstoke talked with the British Ambassador to France, Sir William Tyrrell, concerning Morgan's views and the position of the American government. The memorandum which Revelstoke made of his conversation with Tyrrell provides a rare insight into the real feelings of British investment bankers, as well as revealing the strategy they decided to adopt.

T. [Tyrrell] knows that I have known J. P. M. [Morgan] for thirty or forty years, and my opinion of him as a great, big, large-hearted, generous man, w/o [without] many personal antipathies, with a character which is remarkable for straight-dealing – with perhaps a trace of that innocence which is characteristic of Americans who have not been steeped in European tradition, who are convinced that the American Eagle does indeed rule the world, and who are 'fresh' (to use their own language) in the sense that, owing to their power of money, they count on an immediate and satisfactory solution of matters which appear more complicated to a tired European who has eaten more of the apple of knowledge, and who is sadly aware that all is vanity: that he was eminently proud, as he has told me more than once since he has been here, of the acclaim with which his nomination to the Committee has been welcomed: and that he is intensely desirous for his own credit's sake, to be the leader of a satisfactory settlement.

Revelstoke was so convinced that he told Tyrrell 'that *I cannot help thinking that J. P. M. very possibly has some authorization from Coolidge and Hoover to make some kind of concession to Europe. Otherwise it is difficult to explain J. P. M's extreme and continued optimism*'. He said that Tyrrell agreed with him when he 'lamented the tremendous power of the US' and when he 'called his attention to the sad position necessarily occupied by Gt. Brit., who in spite of their loss of blood and treasure since 1914, find themselves ground under the iron heel of the insolent wealth of a trans-Atlantic people who *must be considered the greatest profiteers that the World has ever seen*'. Revelstoke warned Tyrrell that Morgan 'must be handled with care and with all simplicity, so as to retain his confidence and not hurry him'.[21]

The next day Revelstoke noted that Morgan said 'with all modesty that he supposed that the ultimate result would lie with him & me, and that he was glad to say that it was not the first time we had done a big business together'. He added that Frederick Leith-Ross 'looks on J. P. M. as a "Crusader" and [Leith-Ross] is disinclined to listen to any suggestion of commercialization. However, the role for Gt. Brit. . . is to realise that we have already declared satisfied with Balfour Note conditions'.[22]

After Stamp had discussed with Sir Warren Fisher and Sir Richard Hopkins (the Controller of Finance) the possible commercialisation of the German debt (which meant issuing bonds) the British experts met on 14 February in Paris with Treasury officials G. H. S. Pinsent and Leith-Ross.[23] Addis pointed out that the discussion inevitably led back to the question whether any concessions were obtainable from the US Government. Blackett observed that commercialisation 'is only useful as part of a scheme which includes an offer by the US to allow discounting of debts'.[24] They also discussed Revelstoke's conversation of the previous day with Morgan, in which the American banker had 'proposed the prompt issue of a certain large quantity of

Bonds bearing 6 per cent interest and 1 per cent Sinking Fund'.[25] Morgan had told Revelstoke that 'he was thinking of an issue being made of German bonds on the markets of Europe and the US. He would be willing to make himself responsible for $500 000 000. Total issue of $1 000m, bonds bearing 6.5 per cent interest, 1 per cent sinking fund, redeemable at 105 and issued at about 95'.[26]

Afterwards Addis noted that Germany's economic position was still the topic of discussion and that 'the British policy is to sit tight and wait till we get to realities'.[27] The next day, after meetings with Lamont, Morgan, Young and Revelstoke, Addis noted that the 'Americans were out for a loan with prospect of discounting US debt. 6 per cent would do but can we get it?'[28] Addis described Morgan as 'a great personality and a big man in outlook as well as in bulk'.[29]

Revelstoke had harsh words for British Treasury officials, commenting to Norman that 'the Treasury people were hidebound in their ideas, and that I hoped they might be induced to have a little more elasticity'. Three days later he told Norman that the Treasury Representatives 'with their supercilious manner and sneering attitude for the whole of the rest of mankind, had such impossibly inelastic preconceptions'.[30] Somewhat later Norman described Leith-Ross as having been 'sandbagged into acquiescence' by Fisher on the Reparation question, but Norman recognised that Leith-Ross 'knew more about principles and details of the affair than anyone else, and was powerful in this respect, antipathetic as might be his personality to Frenchmen'.[31] The Treasury officials told Revelstoke they did not want to have daily reports, 'lest they have to tell Winston [Churchill]'.[32]

For the British experts, the aim remained the same as it had been since the war – to ensure that Britain would have sufficient income from reparations and allied war debts to pay its war debts to America. Since there was little likelihood that the Hoover administration would recognise any connection between these two topics, some way must be found at Paris to achieve this aim in disguise. Since Morgan's words seemed to confirm Dulles's earlier letter, the most promising strategy was to humour and control Morgan, whom Revelstoke described as 'easily subdued and led'.[33] The British officials and bankers could not conceive of the lack of communication which actually existed in the United States between different centres of power, which was so different from London. But the fact that there was no understanding soon became all too clear.

The new technique devised at Paris was to create a Bank for

International Settlements (BIS), which was to replace the transfer committee in handling the reparations payments, as well as to arrange the loan for the commercialisation of the German debt. Emile Francqui, the Belgian representative, described the provisional plan as 'an American intrigue to force Great Britain to commercialize its debt, and thus enter into engagements which cannot be modified later'.[34] Franqui seems to have been the chief architect of the Bank for International Settlements.[35] In March Revelstoke commented that he had 'no knowledge myself of this scheme: but I conceive that if, as I am told, the matter has been referred to Burgess, Stewart and Quesnay, they are not likely to endorse a project which may be a chimera'.[36] Later he informed Hopkins that the 'scheme on the Bank was not primarily American at all'.[37] Clearly by March the British experts had accepted the idea of the BIS for Addis described his first major task as 'to pilot the new International Bank scheme through the Sub.-Committee'.[38]

An early indication of the reception which lay ahead for the BIS in the United States was the *Chicago Tribune*'s denunciation of the bank as 'a sinister plot of the international bankers for cancelling the war debts, or restoring London's financial supremacy, or both',[39] Nor could Young (a Democrat who in the elections of 1928 had supported both Al Smith for President and Franklin D. Roosevelt for Governor of New York) count on help from President-elect Hoover, despite their old friendship.[40]

While the plans for the Bank were being drawn up, the task of calculating the final figure for German reparations continued, with Reichsbank President Schacht behaving in a most alarming manner.[41] Throughout March there was much manoeuvring, rumour and suspicion, charges and countercharges. At the March meeting of the Reichsbank Council which Addis and Schacht attended, Schacht said that the 'discrepancy between the Creditor nations and Germany was so large that settlement [was] impossible'. Addis wrote that when he disagreed with Schacht's statement, the latter 'seemed touched'.[42]

The French (who suspected the British experts of being pro-German) were particularly hostile to Governor Norman, who had maintained a close friendship with Schacht. In addition Revelstoke suggested that 'some of the French intrigues against Norman might probably be traced to the jealousies of the Lazard lot, who would give a good deal to see M. N. [Norman] deposed from his present position'.[43]

Although Addis liked Schacht, with whom he had had many

pleasant contacts over the previous four years, and sympathised with the difficulties of his position, he became impatient with him at Paris. Schacht tried to make the return of Germany's colonies and the Polish corridor a condition for cooperation.[44] He felt that Young had made a mistake by allowing the experts to present their claims to Schacht secretly, because the aggregate turned out to be 'absurdly large'.[45] Afterwards Addis described to his wife how Schacht received the proposals:

> Suspense. Proposals tabled at yesterday's meeting. Any observations? Dr Schacht? No Sir. Shall we adjourn meeting, Dr Schacht: I have no objection, Sir. Meeting adjourned till Monday. I make no comment. The whole thing is too humiliating. First £24 thousand millions and 'Hang the Kaiser' at Versailles. Then the London Conference of 1922 with £6600 millions. We have now got down to below £2000 millions and still have got nowhere. Was ever a great issue handled in so pettyfogging a fashion?[46]

It was typical of Addis that in the midst of all this controversy, he took time to write a reassuring letter to his wife concerning her worry about the choice of career of their son, George. Using one of his favourite quotations, he reminded her: 'All service ranks the same with God. It is the way we do it that he cares about'.[47]

Then, just when the Conference was at the point of complete breakdown, Revelstoke died suddenly. His death provided the excuse for a postponement of a final session until 22 April. One of Revelstoke's last comments was: 'It is obviously to the interest of the whole committee, and to the particular interest of Great Britain that the American representatives should not again be allowed to "run out" and again leave us in the lurch'. He described the American representatives as 'admirable', but observed: 'They cannot control the antics and the disloyalties of the US Government'.[48]

When the British Cabinet met to appoint a successor to Revelstoke, it chose Addis rather than Blackett, the other alternate. Reporting the appointment to his wife, Addis wrote:

> It is absurd to rank me alongside a man who is a genius in his way and bears the authority and prestige of an Indian Minister of Finance. However, the Cabinet met yesterday and decided otherwise and I have, reluctantly and distressed, accepted the post. Stamp was insistent. He would not agree to any other appointment.[49]

In the meantime, Schacht had gone to Berlin, where he was

persuaded to adopt a more conciliatory attitude. Young was authorised to prepare a new schedule of payments, and the negotiations
continued.

By 1 May Addis described the situation as

> the most painful phrase of our negotiations. We are all on edge
> and with failure probably impending, personal animosities and
> recriminations have broken loose. Even Gilbert. But I like to
> add that in writing to Winston Churchill that his patience and
> everybody's patience was really exhausted Stamp made an
> exception – 'but I suspect', he wrote, 'that the imperturbable Addis
> still has some reserve in store'.[50]

On 3 May the German Cabinet, bowing to Schacht's insistence that
acceptance be a government responsibility, agreed to the Young
compromise, because 'they saw no alternative'.[51]

The next step was to persuade the creditors to reduce their claims.
A week later Addis exclaimed:

> It can't go on like this! Owen Young is at the fainting stage; he
> looks awful. Even Stamp all nerves; face twitching; sleeping badly.
> French at their worst making accusations of English complicity
> with Germans, and Anglo-American–Germanic plot, etc. Moreau
> attacked me savagely yesterday in his room. I sent for Stamp and
> asked Moreau to repeat what he said in the presence of witnesses.
> We ended by shaking hands, but it was a painful and anxious
> exhibition of his state of mind.[52]

That same day, Young's assistant, Stuart Crocker, noted in his
diary: 'To think that this whole question of repartition would be
settled if Hoover had courage enough to come out and say that the
United States would waive her army costs'.[53] Crocker's comment
suggests the disenchantment of the American experts with President
Hoover and Secretary of State Stimson, who had not only failed to
support them but had actually criticised their proposals. Young might
have resigned, had Morgan not insisted that he continue.[54] Morgan
and Lamont not only encouraged Young to keep going but intervened
with the Germans, letting the German bankers know that if there
was no settlement, there would be no further credits. Similar methods
were used to influence the French experts.[55] At this point, Moreau
was appointed to bring the Belgians into line and Addis was asked
to persuade the Italians to accept the new schedule.[56]

Meanwhile, the British press was attacking Young for the amount of reparations assigned to Britain. Crocker quoted Young as saying:

> if anybody should give up anything to make a settlement possible
> it should be England, and mentioned again the fact that the English
> group were all embarrassed, realizing that everybody knew that
> they had in their treasury unheralded pounds which they had
> received from the sale of sequestered properties. We all have not
> very much sympathy with the English position since their dirty
> double-crossing of Mr Young in making him unjustly and
> untruthfully responsible for cutting the percentage which England
> was to receive under the Spa agreement.[57]

Lamont was bitter at Stamp and Addis 'for permitting attack [the]
on Young in [the] English press'.[58] As we have seen, Revelstoke
himself had criticised the British Treasury officials' 'inelasticity and
arrogance', and he conceded that the British could not insist upon
both the Dominion participation and the arrears.[59] But it is clear that
Addis had not only deliberately released the information to the press
but was pleased with its effect, which he rather smugly described to
his wife:

> I hope you realize the power of the Press. For nearly three months
> . . . I have held them in steadily. On Monday I let them go. They
> responded like well-broken horses and have produced the effect
> intended. Our patience and conciliation were being mistaken for
> weakness. Now they know that we can stand a lot without flinching
> but that when we do strike we strike hard. The effect has been
> extraordinary all over the world. 'Addis's hot stuff' it is called in
> America. . . We have cleared the air and produced a sobering
> effect on the Latins and Yankees which is all to the good. I am
> satisfied with what we have done.[60]

This revealing comment provides a rare instance when Addis let
down his guard, demonstrating his resentment of both the Americans
and the French as well as his tough determination to assert British
interests.

One of the explanations for Addis's manoeuvre may have been
political: the British were holding general elections, and the
Government Bench were 'building their fences'.[61] Churchill was
apprehensive that the Conservatives would lose.[62] Labour leader
Philip Snowden had told the House of Commons in April that Labour
favoured an all-round cancellation of war debts.[63] While it is true that
the reparations question did not play any direct role in the election,

neverthless, any major settlement could have political ramifications on the eve of an election.[64] Obviously no government would wish to appear to be outmanoeuvred at Paris, and the Conservative government naturally would have welcomed a resounding success. Yet such a victory was not to be won. When Baldwin failed to win a clear majority in parliament, he resigned and MacDonald returned to Downing Street as Prime Minister of the second Labour government.

At the same time (on 30 May) Addis was reporting that the French had given way 'on the figures and repartition' and that the Germans had agreed. he warned that 'We may still break on the conditions, but subject to these we are now all agreed on the *amount of the annuity* and the *division of proceeds*. It is a great step. We take fresh heart of grace and go on in hope'.[65] According to Addis's diary, Young had virtually collapsed at this point. 'All leadership is gone. We are wallowing in the trough of the waves'.[66]

By 8 June, the Conference had finally come to an end as an agreement had been reached. At the last session, Addis chaired the meeting from noon until 6.00p.m., 'when Owen Young resumed the chair and the report was unanimously signed. Thank God. The long struggle is over'.[67] Writing later, Schacht claimed that:

It was evident to each of us – with the exception of a few fanatics – that from an economic point the Young Plan was completely crazy. The decision whether or not to sign did not depend on the economic workability of the plan. The question at issue was whether one was justified in refusing to sign, since to do so would give rise to new political entanglements; or whether, having signed, one should continue steadily to resist reparations in general until the occasion arose which would enable them to be put to an end once and for all.

Schacht wrote that he had decided in favour of the second method.[68]

Schacht's comment accords with other telling evidence, suggesting that few believed the Young Plan workable. Months earlier Carl Melchior (the German banker who had served on the German delegation at Genoa and was a member of the League of Nations financial section) advised ter Meulen: 'the best course would be to give in to any conditions imposed, however unreasonable they might think them, and to look forward to a crash within the next three years'.[69]

Addis, however, still hoped that the BIS might yet provide a means for solving the war debts and reparations question. The next task was to convince the Treasury – a task he and Stamp began after only a few days of rest.

THE YOUNG PLAN AND THE BANK FOR INTERNATIONAL SETTLEMENTS, 1929–30

After the exhausting weeks and months of negotiations, with a settlement finally achieved, how depressing it was to return to England to find, not appreciation and approval, but instead criticism and rejection. Yet that was what Stamp and Addis received from the Labour Government. Addis noted that he and Stamp went to 10 Downing Street 'where we were heckled for a couple of hours on the Young Plan report by the Prime Minister, Ramsay MacDonald, and his colleagues, Arthur Henderson and W. Graham'.[70] Leith-Ross in the Treasury was advising Snowden, the Chancellor of the Exchequer, to 'fight for the [Spa] percentages'.[71]

There were really two issues involved in the government's unhappiness with the Young Plan. One concerned the Bank of England and the BIS, specifically, their independence from political control. The other question concerned Britain's national interests: did the Young Plan assure Great Britain the best solution obtainable for the problem of war debts and reparations?

The first issue involved the matter of interest rates. Chancellor of the Exchequer Snowden suspected the Bank of England of sacrificing British interests to those of international finance, hardly a surprising suspicion from a Labour government elected on the pledge to solve Britain's economic crisis. As early as 12 February 1929 (when the Baldwin government was still in power) F. W. Pethick Lawrence (an MP, who became Financial Secretary of the Treasury under Snowden) had asked the Chancellor of the Exchquer for a remedy for high rates 'to prevent the industry of this country from being at the mercy of speculators in America or in any other foreign country'.[72] Churchill had responded to this criticism by requesting the Deputy Governor to see him.[73] On 9 February Lubbock (the Deputy Governor) wrote to Hopkins that he doubted whether he had given the Chancellor 'as full as exposition of our reasons for raising the Bank rate as I should have done', and he continued that 'the essence of the situation is that we are not only a free gold market but also a free international money market, meaning that borrowers go where the money is the cheapest'.[74] Sir Frederick Phillips (in the Treasury) had informed

Hopkins that the 'Fed was trying to gain control over speculation, which seriously endangers [the] situation here'. To relieve the strain on the exchanges he suggested: '(a) increase the amount of the Fiduciary Issue under the Bank Notes Act of last year, by say, £25m so as to enable an equivalent amount of gold to be exported to American w/o [without] effect on our economic position. (b) & (c) sell securities'.[75] Shortly thereafter, Hopkins explained to Churchill that the 'exchange was low, money market nervous, future obscure. We are of course buying no dollars for the American Debt though this is the normal season for obtaining them'.[76] Despite an increase in the bank rate that spring, gold continued to flow out, leading to fears that a further increase might be necessary.

Norman hoped to avoid any increase until after the Hague Conference (scheduled for August) to consider the Young Plan. But he feared that without an increase, England might be forced off the gold standard.[77] Hopkins, who was also concerned about the political effects of an increase in bank rate, conferred with Norman, who agreed to try to prevent an increase 'which might embarrass the British claims. If a [diplomatic] break should occur at the Hague: these things are so largely psychological that the conditions after the break must depend very largely on the atmosphere in which a break occurs'.[78] Norman consulted with Addis and Grenfell concerning the possibility of a crisis in Germany, which might put Britain off the gold standard. Addis, who was leaving for the Hague the next day, felt it 'was only a risk'.[79]

On the second issue of reparations and war debts, Snowden continued to follow established Treasury policy, which was to ensure that the Young Plan provided sufficient income to pay the debts owed to America, but he adamantly opposed the reduction in the Spa percentages.[80] One analysis of the Young Plan acknowledged that:

> the scheme does give HM Government the means, securely guaranteed, of meeting year by year the payments to the US Gov. and to the Dominions, which (once the claim for arrears had been abandoned) is all that they [the Dominions] have been asking for.[81]

This analysis also recognised the 'disastrous political effects if Plan rejected'.

Stamp and Addis collaborated in their attempt to persuade Whitehall to support the Young Plan, drawing up two memoranda for the Prime Minister. One concluded that the Bank for International

Settlements would have as a by-product, 'European cooperation in the *control of gold* – something of far greater value to civilization and particularly to British interests, than the whole question of reparations and debts'.[82] In the summer of 1929 Addis and Stamp were both concerned about deflation, which they believed was caused by American and French hoarding of gold, and they viewed the BIS as a way of implementing the gold exchange standard which had been recommended by the Genoa resolutions.[83]

During July Addis had met with Leith-Ross and Niemeyer to discuss the organisation of the BIS. Addis observed: 'Snowden is very stiff and doesn't want Organization Committee set up "till after conference of Powers"'.[84] Stamp reported to Young that the Foreign Office favoured 'outright acceptance' of the Young Plan but that the Cabinet agreed to Snowden 'having a go on his own at the conference to put matters right'. Stamp remarked that 'Mac[Donald] always thinks he can do better than anyone else!' and added that S. [Snowden] was 'so bitter about Italy getting so much that I fear there will be a real row'. He concluded: 'I do not think any of these political fellows appreciate that we saved a complete breakdown of the reparation machine and of course one can't talk much about it. One must just grin and bear it!'[85] Leith-Ross later explained the intricate details of the conditional and unconditional payments:

> The [Young Plan] Report provided for the payment by Germany of reichsmarks to an average value of £100 million for thirty-seven years, but of these payments only £30 million a year were to be unconditional and these payments were to be mobilised by a projected new Bank for International Settlements, the organization and functions of which were outlined in the report. The German reparation liabilities were intended to cover the Allied liabilities for war debts, but the report provided for a modification in the method of distribution as between the Allies of the receipts obtained from Germany and furthermore, gave France and Italy a prior claim on the bulk of unconditional annuities. Thus the British share of receipts from Germany was to be reduced by £2 400 000 a year and something like 90 per cent of our total share would depend on the transfer of the 'conditional' annuities.[86]

The Treasury instructions for the British Delegation to the Hague Conference were quite clear:

> Whatever we may say in public or from a legal point of view, we do, in fact, want to ensure that *the security of our payments to*

USA will be no better than that of German payments to us. To do
this we ought not to issue German Bonds unless we can use the
proceeds to pay off our indebtedness to the USA *on the same basis
of interest.*[87]

On 30 July, Addis (after meeting with Lamont, Hawtrey, Niemeyer
and Stamp) described Stamp as being 'very cast down'.[88]

While plans for the Conference were being made Lamont attempted
personal diplomacy with Snowden, an attempt which backfired,
confirming Snowden's suspicions that the international bankers were
trying to put something over on him. Accompanied by American
Ambassador to England, Charles Dawes, Lamont told the Prime
Minister that he should have 'members of the Expert Committee,
like Lamont, Stamp, Addis, present to reach agreement'.[89] Despite
a personal appeal to Chancellor Snowden, Lamont was not invited
to the Hague.[90]

Undaunted by the snub, Lamont wrote a seven-page personal
letter to Snowden, expressing concern about the rumours regarding
political control of the BIS. He predicted that such control would
make the BIS a 'new and glorified Reparations Commission' and
warned 'America will not cooperate if the Bank is politically controlled'. Lamont advised that 'Cooperation in international affairs can
best be established not by action of the treasuries but by cooperation
among the leading men of affairs the world over'.[91]

Snowden's response to Lamont revealed the fundamental difference
between the British leaders and the American bankers. He denied
any intention 'to put the Bank of International Settlements under
the control of the Treasuries' but added 'the Governments must, of
course, decide what discretion they are prepared to entrust to the
Bank with reference to reparations, as contemplated in the Young
Plan'. Snowden emphasised that the governments 'must be satisfied
that the general powers of the Bank are so delimited as not to
affect adversely the national economic interests for which they are
responsible', and expressed his determination to ensure that the Bank
would not 'be made an instrument of reactionary policy in these
matters.'.[92] Meanwhile Norman spent 10 August with the Prime
Minister and Lamont at Lossiemouth, MacDonald's home in Scotland.[93]

Across the Atlantic, an adviser to the Hoover Administration was
also warning about the political powers of the BIS and the danger of
allowing Morgans to exercise monopoly influence over American

The parents of Charles Stewart Addis:

1. (*above*) The Reverend Thomas Addis, DD, 23 December 1813–18 July 1899
   Horsburgh, Edinburgh

2. (*left*) Robina Scott Addis (née Thorburn), 31 August 1822–3 April 1900
   Horsburgh, Edinburgh

4. (*above*) The Hong Kong and Shanghai Bank in Hong Kong, North façade c. 1900, after completion of the Praya reclamation.
The Hong Kong and Shanghai Bank, Hong Kong

5. (*right*) Ah Yeung Wai, who taught Charles Addis Chinese in Hong Kong

6. (*above*) Lt Dudley Mills, Charles Addis and Gershom Stewart
   R. Forbes, Dublin
7. (*below*) Charles Addis and Miss Denby at Hill Temple, 1887

9

8

8. and 9. Eba McIsaac and Charles Addis, on their wedding day, 6 June 1894

10. Second Annual Dinner, Hong Kong and Shanghai Bank, at the Trocadero Restaurant, London, Wednesday, 13 January 1909. Charles Addis is circled.

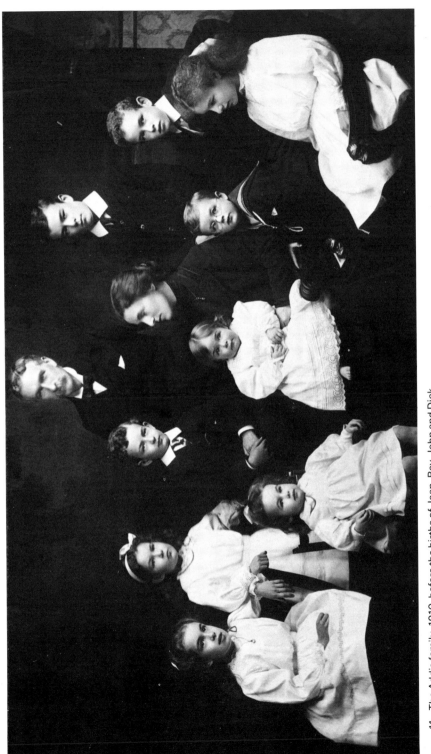

11. The Addis family, 1910, before the births of Jean, Ray, John and Dick. From L. to R. are: Robina, Sue, Hetty, Bill, Charles S. Addis, Margie, Eba Addis, Tom (standing), George (seated), Charlie and Betty

12. The Committee of Treasury of the Bank of England, 1928. Mural at the Bank of England
The Governor and Company of The Bank of England

COMMITTEE OF TREASURY 1928
BY A.K. LAWRENCE, R.A.

1. LORD CULLEN OF ASHBOURNE
2. SIR ALAN ANDERSON
3. SIR CHARLES ADDIS
4. H.A. TROTTER, ESQ.
5. LORD REVELSTOKE
6. ARTHUR WHITWORTH, ESQ.

7. R.C.G. DALE, Secretary
8. THE HON. ALEXANDER SHAW
9. THE RT. HON. M.C. NORMAN
10. SIR ERNEST HARVEY
11. CECIL LUBBOCK

FREDERICK W. STEVENS,
New American Group.
Representative at Peking.

FREDERICK W. ALLEN,
Lee Higginson & Cº

HENRI MAZOT,
French Group.

RÉNÉ THION DE LA CHAUME,
French Delegate.

CHARLES E. MITCHELL,
Pres. National City Cº

GEORGES PICOT,
French Delegate.

MORTIMER L. SCHIFF,
Kuhn Loeb & Cº

BURNETT WALKER,
Vice President Guaranty Cº
Representing
Guaranty Trust Cº of N.Y.

JOHN A. ABBOTT,
Vice President Continental
and Commercial Trust.

THOMAS W. LAMONT,
Chairman of American Trust.

SIR CHARLES ADDIS,
Chairman of British Group.

KIMPEI TAKEUCHI,
Japanese Delegate.

W. E. LEVESON,
British Secretary
of Conference.

J. ROSS TILFORD,
American Secretary
of Conference.

R. C. WITT,
British Group.

ALBERT H. WIGGIN,
Chairman Chase National
Bank of New York.

MALCOLM D. SIMPSON,
Secretary American Group.

R. INCHINOMIYA,
Japanese Delegate.

SYDNEY F. MAYERS,
British Delegate.

13. The Second China Consortium, New York, October 1920

14. The Conference held at Baden Baden, October 1929

15a. (*above*) Hotel George V, Paris. Signing the Experts Report, Reparations Conference, 1929

15b. (*below*) The first meeting of the Board of Directors of the Bank for International Settlements (Young Plan) Basle, May 1930
Note: 1 is Sir Charles Addis
      2 is Lord Norman

16 Sir Charles Addis and Lord Norman, Bank of England, c. 1930. *The Governor and Company of The Bank of England*

Commission on Banking

THOMAS WHITE, FORMER ~~FINAN~~CE MINISTER ~~OF~~ CANADA.

PREMIER J.E. BROWNLEE OF ALBERTA

SIR CHARLES ADDIS, DIRECTOR OF THE BANK OF ENGLAND.

MR. BEAUDRY LEMAN GEN. MANAGER AND DIRECTOR OF THE BANQUE CANADIENNE NATIONALE

LORD MACMILLAN, CHAIRMAN OF THE ROYAL COMMISSION.

CANADA'S BANKING SYSTEM

Sketched by Jack Boothe at Victoria on Sunday. *13 Aug 1933.*

17. (*above*) Royal Banking Commission for Canada, 1933
Jack Boothe, at Victoria on Sunday

18. (*below*) On the way home from Canada, Quebec, 30 September 1933

19. The Addis family at Woodside, Frant, 1939

20. The Addis family at Woodside, Frant, D Day, 6 June 1944

21. Sir Charles Addis, 1930
The National Portrait Gallery

participation.[94] After a lengthy analysis of the potential of the BIS, this memorandum recommended that either the Administration insist that the BIS deal only with reparations, or if an expanded role were permitted for the BIS, then the Administration 'reserve in some manner the right to substitute the Federal Reserve Bank for the House of Morgan at any time in the future they might deem it advisable'.[95] Judging by what followed, the Hoover Administration decided to approve the BIS only as an agent for reparation payments.

Lamont's British partners, Grenfell and Vivian Smith, had held up the delivery of Lamont's letter to Snowden until they could let Norman read it. They also showed it to Addis.[96] Although Lamont did not succeed in getting himself invited to the Conference, Addis was appointed to serve on the subcommittee on Bank Law.[97]

While the Hague Conference was in session, Young summarised American attitudes, saying that although Washington disliked the Young Plan, 'It has not dared to exhibit its unfriendliness except on the question of participation of the Federal Reserve in the International Bank'.[98] Young suggested that 'the want of enthusiasm at Washington has served more or less as an encouragement to Snowden. In any event, there has been no influence from Washington to deter it notwithstanding the fact that *we are the largest beneficiaries of the settlement.*'[99]

One reason why Young regarded the United States as 'the largest beneficiary' was because the Young Plan confirmed the fact that 'Article 248 of the Versailles Treaty which made reparations a first obligation of the German Government had effectively been laid to rest'.[100] Little wonder then that the British Treasury was not pleased, and still determined that it would not pay the United States more than it received from Germany, France and Italy. However, since the Treasury recognised that the BIS would lead to 'real & continuous cooperation between the Central Banks in the management of credit', it argued that the proposal for the bank was 'our only hope and it represents the culmination of the efforts which have been made during the last ten years by the Governor of the Bank of England to establish closer relation between Central Banks'. The Treasury felt that 'the enormous work which he [Norman] has done in this sphere is beginning to be recognised throughout the world, and represents the best asset that we have'. Furthermore it recognised that:

the Treasury cannot dictate international monetary policy. Facts have shown only too clearly our inability to withstand pressures from other centres, particularly America, and the possibility of future progress depends on our persuading the other Banks to adopt a more enlightened policy.[101]

While Snowden made one last effort at the Hague to increase Britain's share of the reparations settlement, Addis sat back and enjoyed the politicians' discomfort. During a conversation with Graham, he observed that 'the politicians seemed to be no more adroit than the experts in agreeing among themselves'.[102] Unlike Snowden, Foreign Secretary Henderson believed that 'the price of acceptance of the Young Report was worth paying in order to get a settlement in the Rhineland'.[103]

A letter to his wife indicates Addis's more philosophical state of mind:

> I watched the moon rise threading its way through some mazy clouds. The moon went slowly up the sky and nowhere did abide. Slowly she was going up and a star or two beside. It was all wonderfully still and beautiful and awful. It seemed an answer to all our interminable wranglings and disputations of the day. The night cometh. *Still* there abides a peace of time man did not make and cannot mar.[104]

Despite all Snowden's bold talk, he found that there was little to be gained at the Hague. The only way to get more funds for Britain was to raise what Germany had to pay.[105] While this was accomplished at The Hague, it did not achieve the results expected, as will be seen.[106] However, the government leaders' assertion of their authority had made Norman hesitant to make appointments to the organising committee for the BIS.[107]

At some point Snowden must have become convinced of Addis's reliability, for he agreed to appoint Addis and Walter Layton as British representatives to the organising committee for the BIS. Layton, an economist, was familiar with the American debt question, having served with the Balfour mission to the United States in 1917 when the war loans were negotiated, and later as a Director of the Economic and Financial Section of the League of Nations.[108] Snowden at the same time emphasised to the Treasury that he opposed 'autocracy' and felt that the BIS should not be wholly free of government control.[109] Not only Snowden but also Sir Arthur Salter, the highly respected British League of Nations official, who had been consulted by the Treasury, opposed the arbitrary power of the BIS. Salter recommended that it be 'placed in proper relation to League'.

But the Treasury realised that the United States would never cooperate under these circumstances.[110] Despite this internal dispute between Snowden and the bankers about the control of the BIS, the British leaders agreed that the most urgent problem was to obtain American cooperation, for if an open break should occur at The Hague, it might lead to a rapid withdrawal of gold from Britain, which would force Britain off the gold standard, an outcome all wished to avoid.[111]

Once the Hague Conference was successfully completed, the bank rate was raised to $6^{1}/_{2}$ per cent on 26 September.[112] However, the Treasury continued to worry about the political effect of raising the bank rate. One *Daily Express* comment, addressed to Governor Norman in September, claimed that raising the bank rate benefited Norman's colleagues 'who are closely identified with large foreign interests'.[113] One official in the Treasury, in attempting to explain the transfers of French balances from London to New York, wrote that 'The coming into power of a Labour Government had perhaps more repercussions abroad than in England itself, and for the rest the high rates of interest in America had worked in the same direction'.[114]

By 19 September, Addis, Fisher, and Snowden seem to have reached a meeting of minds on the BIS, for Addis wrote to his wife that he had had a long talk with the Chancellor and with Fisher and that his mind was 'much easier'.[115] Leith-Ross's strategy was 'to provide a mechanism in the BIS statutes which would connect the American debt payments to the reparations amounts and provide for the *non-payment of both*'.[116] Such a comment suggests Leith Ross's determination to eliminate reparations and war debts, once and forever.

BADEN-BADEN AND THE SECOND HAGUE
CONFERENCE

The Hague Conference had adjourned temporarily while the experts met at Baden-Baden to draft the statutes of the BIS. The participants in the Organisation Committee included many of those individuals who had been working on international finance since the war, including Pierre Jay, ter Meulen, and C. F. Whigham.[117] From Baden-Baden, Addis described to Norman the 'general spirit of goodwill and accommodation which prevails – in striking contrast to that inferno of Paris – makes me hopeful (but, you know, I am always sanguine)'.[118] Addis continued to carry the major part of the work as Layton was forced to return to London.[119]

The question of the extent to which the government should influence the great financial questions continued to cause friction. Addis seemed satisfied, writing to Norman that 'we have secured for the Governments the due measure of influence and initiative to which they are entitled, and at the same time obtained for the Bank, with due safeguards against their abuse, the requisite freedom and elasticity to enable it to act as a nucleus of Central Banking co-operation'.[120] Neither Norman nor Morgans were willing to acknowledge the authority of the Treasury. The Morgan Grenfell partners complained to J. P. Morgan that Addis 'does not seem to have the requisite authority to deal with Mr Pinsent (a British Treasury official) at Baden any more successfully than Sir Josiah Stamp did at Paris'. When Grenfell discussed this problem with Norman, Norman replied that the Treasury officials 'were servants of Addis and should not communicate with Treasury'.[121] Norman's views were extreme, representing Morgans' approach more than Addis's.

How to provide for the British debt to the United States still presented the most difficult problem. Addis wrote to Norman on 3 November that 'The inter-European debts present no difficulty since the German annuities are sufficient to provide the means for a common settlement, with the possible exception of Romania'. But he indicated that the debt to the United States was different, since:

the dates of the annuity receipts and the debt payments do not coincide, the former being met in equal monthly amounts throughout the year, while the latter are payable twice a year in unequal amounts. The result of this is that in June and December the deficit, taking 1933/34 as a specimen year, will amount to as much as RM300 millions, and the deplorable fact is that the Governments have not agreed among themselves how this gap is to be filled.

Addis recognised that:

HMG will not sign any trust Agreement which does not make provision for the full execution of Article 6 of the Hague Protocol. The Chairman [Jackson Reynolds] on the other hand, is determined that nothing shall go into the Trust Agreement which is not precise and in conformity with sound backing practice. There is our dilemma.

He felt that:

> our best tactic is to lie low, say nothing about the decision of HMG and coax, if we can, the Chairman into admitting a clause in which the operative part could be inserted if and when the Powers have agreed among themselves how the deficit is to be financed. I am not w/o [without] hopes of succeeding, although the Chairman is very obstinate and I think has been fortified in his views by consultation with his friends in America.[122]

A week later the Chairman (Jackson Reynolds, the head of the First National Bank of New York) received a telegram from Morgans which indicated that 'if the English text of Clause IV(a) providing for Debt Settlements was included in the Trust Deed, it would be impossible for the American Group to participate in the new Bank'.[123]

Under these circumstances, Addis proposed to leave the issue for the Governors of the respective Central Banks to decide. The Italians and the Japanese went along but the French refused, suggesting instead that they should deal with other American bankers.[124] Addis complained 'Those tiresome French are still holding out'.[125] After reporting this, Addis wrote that he thought it would be 'impolitic to exchange Morgan Group for Dillon Read & Co., and if the French propose to break on the Debt Clause they will have to do it by themselves'. He continued: 'I regard American participation as essential, if the BIS is to fulfil the functions we expect of it'.[126] H. A. Siepmann, an adviser to the Bank of England, took a night train to London to confer with the Governor; after returning, he reported that the French had accepted Addis's view and that the Governor was satisfied.[127]

Addis's efforts were much appreciated at the Bank of England. Lubbock described a Court meeting in which the Governor 'spoke of the immense debt of gratitude we all owe you for what you have done & his words were received with that subdued murmur of applause which the Court only gives when it is really and heartily in accord with what is said'.[128] The Governor followed this with a personal letter:

> I have watched you standing fairly and patiently, and sometimes alone while the Latins and the Teutons have surged up and down, eventually to come back to where they left you. So accept my thanks and now take it easy; and let me add that just what I am

saying for myself Jack Morgan wished me to say to you from him.[129]

For a few months it looked as though solutions were still possible. With hardly a moment to catch his breath, Addis returned to the City, to meet all manner of visitors and committees.[130]

In a frank and revealing speech on 28 November at Cambridge about the BIS and German reparations, Addis made some startling admissions and proposals. He suggested the possible development of an international unit of currency which he said would enable the BIS to economise on the issue of gold. He described the origins of the BIS, saying that: the original conception had expanded to aim at 'securing the cooperative action of Central Banks, of facilitating international exchange and of developing international trade'. After describing the organisation of the Bank and the means by which reparations and war debt payments were to be made, Addis stated frankly:

> The effect of this will be to link up the German annuities to the debts due to the United States by Europe. Germany will in fact take upon her own shoulders the burden of discharging for account of the European Powers the entire amount of their debt to the United States by an annual payment through the BIS of say £80 millions. The disclosure of this fact, for fact it is, can scarcely be congenial to the American mind and may even give rise to doubts as to whether so one-sided an arrangement can be wholly beneficial to the sole creditor, and whether a situation so utterly at variance with all our previous experience of international trade relations is likely to be permanent. It is possibly an inkling of this which has led the debtor Powers to agree that if and when any abatement is made of the United States claim it shall enure, to the extent of two-thirds and three-fourths, to the benefit not of themselves but of Germany.

Addis then went on to discuss the larger possibilities of the BIS, explaining 'The appreciation of gold, or what is the same thing, the downward trend of prices, has become a serious menace and, if allowed to go unchecked, must inevitably check enterprise and retard economic recovery'. Next he asked:

> What is to be done? Obviously we must economise the issue of gold . . . with the adoption of an international unit of currency, not a coin but a money of account, the dealers in foreign exchange

would find their occupation gone, since the BIS would be prepared to make transfers of the international unit to or from any part of the world at par, just as the Federal Reserve Bank transfers dollars at par to or from any point within the United States.[131]

Although from today's perspective, these proposals seemed Utopian, Addis was serious about them and proceeded to seek support.

Next he was off to Berlin for a meeting of the General Council of the Reichsbank. In a dinner speech Addis challenged the Council:

to build up . . . an institution whose foundation should be laid on the broad principle of the substitution of international cooperation for international competition, in which Representatives of the great central banks could work together and would be content to subordinate their international interests and ambitions in a common effort to undo the ravages of war and to restore to a distracted world the blessings of peace.[132]

In January Addis returned to The Hague, where the government representatives met to make the final arrangements for implementing the Young Plan. Aside from a brief rebellion by Schacht, the plans proceeded swiftly, with the official text ready for signature by 18 January.[133] Meanwhile, the British Treasury, which had decided 'to accept the French contention that the allocation of the unconditional annuity was irrevocable', reached a secret understanding with the French 'to cooperate in ensuring German annuity would not total less than 950–1000 million Reichsmarks'. The French made a similar agreement with Belgium at The Hague in January.[134] Addis evidently did not approve of this secret agreement, for he told Norman to refuse to enter into any secret agreement with the French.[135] Addis was assigned the task of setting up the BIS when Jackson Reynolds, the American Chairman of the Organisation Committee, returned to the United States.

Despite the hope of the central bankers that henceforth political issues could be kept out of the reparations question, events soon demonstrated that his goal was both unrealistic and unattainable. The British Treasury's primary concern was the continuing burden of the American debt.[136] The Americans recognised the determination of the British Treasury to obtain debt-cancellation and were determined to frustrate every move. From Berlin Gilbert warned President Hoover and Secretary of State Stimson that:

The fundamental object of Snowden and the British Treasury is the same already stubbornly pursued for many years by the British Treasury, *viz.*, to bring about at the expense of the United States what they call the all-around cancellation of war debts and reparations. For this reason Snowden and the treasury have always opposed the Mellon-Baldwin debt-funding agreement and the Dawes Plan, the two principal commitments to the policy of debt collection.

Gilbert continued this analysis with the charge that the British were hoping for an economic crisis in Germany so that the whole question could be reopened, and he advised Washington to put pressure on the MacDonald government to conclude The Hague Conference before the Naval disarmament conference begins. Gilbert also suggested that the French government make the proposal, 'as the French premier must attend both conferences and as the French reparations policy is most closely in harmony with the American debt-collection policy'.[137]

Parker Gilbert's warning (which was not far off the mark) suggested that there was little hope for Anglo-American accommodation. Leith-Ross argued that the government should announce its decision to postpone the American-debt-payment, saying that such action was a contractual right under the Young Plan.[138] In addition there was disagreement between the Treasury and Morgans about whether the American debt payments should be entrusted to the BIS, with Morgans threatening that if this were done, 'no shares in the Bank would be held or issued by J. P. Morgan & Co., and there was no prospect whatever of the future cooperation of the Federal Reserve system'.[139] While Addis did not want to oppose openly the American bankers' views, he thought financial arrangements could be made to achieve the Treasury's aim.

At the end of January Addis went to Berlin for a meeting of the Reichsbank Council and conferred with Gilbert and Schacht. He gave the Council a summary of the BIS provisions for the Reichsbank Council, informing them that the Reichsbank would be compelled by law to join the BIS and that the foreign members of the Council would be eliminated.[140] Despite Addis's efforts to persuade Schacht to welcome the Reichsbank's participation in the BIS, Schacht refused. Addis therefore withdrew his resolution, hardly a good omen for the future.[141] In March 1930 Schacht resigned from the Reichsbank.[142]

Addis hoped that American cooperation with the BIS might be

achieved by appointing American bankers to its management. In February he discussed with Norman and Grenfell the appointment of Gates McGarragh and Leon Fraser.[143] By May agreement was reached that McGarragh would be President of the Bank and Addis Vice-President. Addis described McGarragh as 'a good man but slow; not a strong man I fear'.[144] With the organisation of the BIS at last accomplished, Addis turned to the task of winning support for this new international institution.

MONETARY POLICY, 1930: THE TREASURY VS. NORMAN

While the plans for the BIS were being made, the Labour Government of Prime Minister MacDonald launched Britain's first attempt at securing professional economic advice, through the appointment of an Economic Advisory Committee, which included Keynes and Hubert Henderson.[145] In addition, it sought to meet growing public criticism through the appointment of a Committee to Investigate Finance and Industry, chaired by H. P. Macmillan. During this same period, the League of Nations and the Royal Institute of International Affairs (RIIA) both established committees to investigate the question of the gold shortage. Addis chaired the RIIA committee, which included Hawtrey and S. D. Waley from the Treasury, Brand and Keynes from the Macmillan Committee, and Niemeyer and Sprague from the Bank of England.[146]

The Royal Institute for International Affairs had its origins at the Paris Peace Conference where several American and British representatives decided to found organisations aimed at international understanding and particularly Anglo-American cooperation. Its American counterpart was the Council on Foreign Relations.[147] At first the organisation was known as the British Institute of International Affairs but after the purchase of Chatham House (the former home of three British Prime Ministers) in 1923, it became the Royal Institute of International Affairs, but was (and is) often referred to as Chatham House.[148] Addis was one of the original members. By the mid-1920s various groups had been organised to study particular geographical areas (such as the Far East) or problems (such as 'the gold question'). These study groups held regular discussions and presented papers, some of which were subsequently published.[149] Addis participated in both the Gold Study group and the China group.[150]

All the Labour government's efforts in appointing these special committees were attempts to find the causes of unemployment and a means to restore British trade and prosperity. All reflected a growing recognition that government could not stand aside while its industries collapsed and gold continued to flow out of the country. As Mac-Donald and Snowden searched for solutions to unemployment, monetary policy increasingly became the focus of attention. Complicating the picture was the secrecy which surrounded the Bank of England, particularly its Governor. More and more, the Bank was being blamed for Britain's problems.[151] In a memorandum for the Prime Minister in November 1929, Keynes called for cheap money, accusing the Bank of England of reducing the national wealth by £500 000 000![152]

When the Macmillan Committee began its hearings (in November 1929) the question of the relationship of the Bank of England and the British Treasury emerged as one of the major issues.[153] Two of the Bank's most vocal critics, Keynes and McKenna, were members of the Committee. It seems likely that the criticism and suspicion of the Bank contributed to Norman's breakdown at this point, since it was expected that the Macmillan Committee Report 'would recommend moderate if not radical changes in the constitution of the Bank of England'.[154] Stamp informed Young: 'You will be sorry to learn that Monty Norman has had a breakdown and won't be back till the New Year at the earliest. The chief drawback of this is that his evidence was to be the foundation of the work of the new Committee on Finance & Credit'.[155]

By early 1930 Addis and Norman held different views on monetary policy and the future role of the BIS. Perhaps Addis's close contacts with both Treasury officials and economists such as Keynes, Stamp, and Henderson, had convinced him of the urgency for easing credit by late 1929. As noted above, he and Stamp had both mentioned their concern the previous summer about the shortage of gold. Addis's speech at Cambridge that autumn also demonstrated his support for the Treasury view, which placed the entire responsibility for the war debts and reparations impasse on the Americans; his actions at Baden-Baden and The Hague demonstrated his willingness to cooperate with the Treasury in devising a solution, even if this solution did not find favour in the United States.

In contrast, Norman continued to defer to Morgans' view that government should keep its hands off banking decisions. This attitude – this refusal to communicate with elected officials or respond to the criticisms of economists – had led to the demand for a government take-over of the Bank of England – a possibility which Norman greatly feared. As Professor Sayers makes clear, Governor Norman privately was much more concerned about the conditions of industry than his public image suggested, and was attempting to meet its needs.[156] Since the Governor recognised the critical role that Morgans played in exchange questions, it seems possible that Norman was attempting to humour Morgans' known antipathy for government intervention, for above all Norman sought to maintain confidence in the pound.

Addis was less willing to defer to the Americans. Clearly the gold standard which Norman and he had envisioned in the early 1920s was not functioning as they had hoped; it was in fact harming British trade. It seems significant that while Norman was on one of his periodic visits to the United States the Treasury sought Addis's help in easing credit conditions. The Wall Street crash had brought the discount rate of the Federal Reserve Bank of New York down to $4\frac{1}{2}$ per cent.[157] Hopkins had written to P. J. Grigg, Snowden's secretary, early in January that 'the market expected a moderation of Bank Rate last Thursday but the Bank thought it prudent to wait'. He predicted that 'we will have $4\frac{1}{2}$ quite soon' if the situation did not change.[158] On 5 February Addis noted that he had 'a long talk with Hawtrey at the Treasury on discount policy. We are in general agreement about lowering the rate'.[159] However Addis and Stamp could not convince their fellow-members of the Bank of England's Committee of Treasury who were reluctant to take action while Norman was away.[160]

The announcement of a visit by George Harrison to London led Hawtrey to appeal again to Addis, saying that he hoped Harrison's visit 'does not mean fresh obstacles in the way of a reduction of Bank rate'. Hawtrey felt that 'even a mere postponement till next week on the ground that he is on his way would be deplorable, now that the market is fully ripe for 4 per cent'. He feared that the Bank of England 'may tie its hands in some way by an agreement with him', and emphasised that the 'lag of Bank rate behind the market rate has already done immense harm'.[161] Grigg complained to Hopkins that 'the Bank's policy seems to me quite inexplicable except by an unreasoning terror of cheap money'.[162] On 5 March Addis noted: '[Bank] rate reduced to 4 per cent at last!'[163]

A further explanation for Addis's views can be found in his Chatham House contacts on the gold study committee. These discussions helped to confirm the view which Addis had already stated in his Cambridge speech, namely, that the shortage of gold was the cause of Britain's economic crisis.[164] However there was considerable disagreement among British financial leaders as to the ability of the BIS to solve the problem of the gold shortage. Niemeyer was sceptical, but Hawtrey described Niemeyer as a 'black pessimist'.[165] Norman continued to endure the strain of conflicting loyalties – torn between his American friends and his British critics.[166]

In 1930 the expectation was that Norman would shortly cease to be Governor. The previous October he had written to Addis, referring to an earlier conversation, saying that he had asked the Committee of Treasury 'to settle on my successor so that he should be my alternate on the Board of the BIS for the first year, while you would also kindly serve for a period of one year'.[167] However, when the Committee of Treasury could not agree as to who should succeed Norman, no change occurred, despite the fact that Norman was showing exhaustion from the heavy responsibilities he had carried for ten years.[168] Meanwhile the Macmillan Committee continued its hearings. When Norman finally made his appearance, his testimony – far from clarifying and defending Bank policy – instead had the effect of deepening public suspicions.[169] On 31 March Addis noted that he had talked with Harvey and Lubbock 'about Governor's evidence before Macmillan's Committee. It fills us with consternation. It is deplorable. Difficulty is how to revise it'.[170] Early in May he noted: 'Norman grows more & more temperamental, freakish & paradoxical'.[171]

In a speech to the Institute of Bankers early in April, Addis publicly revealed how dramatically his ideas had changed since 1925 and how much they differed from those of his American counterparts. He warned that the downward trend in prices had become a 'serious menace' which, if left unhindered, would check enterprise and retard recovery. He described the persistent fall as 'crippling industry', indicating that over the previous five years prices had fallen by 25 per cent. Since the monetary factor was the most important in this fall, Addis favoured a 'moderate dose of temporary inflation' in order to maintain the commodity value of gold.[172]

The American bankers sharply disagreed, both with Addis's diagnosis and with his prescription for a cure. Commenting on Addis's speech, Randolph Burgess, Deputy Governor of the Federal Reserve Bank in New York, described Addis as going 'much further in two respects than I should. The first is in blaming the recent decline in commodity prices so fully upon gold, and the second is in carrying the description of future developments of the BIS as far as he does.'[173] At the same time, Melvin Traylor, President of the First National Bank of Chicago, speaking before the American Committee of the International Chamber of Commerce, painted a much different picture of the BIS. He emphasised that the BIS was not 'a reflection of the desire of international bankers or political intriguers to involve the world and especially the United States in some kind of a mysterious financial oligarchy. . . . it has no power to inflate or contract the world's available credit'. He reassured his American colleagues that 'the Bank is not an international financial octopus, threatening the economy of any country, . . . it is not part of or an adjunct to any other international group or association'[174] Traylor seemed to claim that the BIS was not the institution which Addis was advocating it should become!

In June Addis recorded a discussion on BIS policy, in which he and Norman 'differ as usual'.[175] Although there does not seem to be any precise outline of Norman's views, the fact that Addis recorded a difference suggests that Norman shared the American point of view that the BIS could serve as a means for reparation payments and a place for central bankers to exchange views.[176] Meanwhile Addis continued to campaign, both in Great Britain and the United States, to gain support for a BIS with enlarged responsibilities, a view which no doubt only increased the Hoover administration's suspicions. Hirst, Addis's old and influential friend, published *Wall Street and Lombard Street* in 1931, quoting Addis's ideas on the BIS as offering a way to economic recovery.[177]

And so Britain approached a severe economic crisis with Bank of England Directors divided as to what policies would best serve their country's interests. While the evidence suggests that Addis and Stamp leaned more toward the views advanced by Keynes, Strakosch, and Hawtrey, favouring cheap money, Addis refused to defy his chief or betray his personal friendship to Norman by cooperating with those who wished to replace him as Governor.[178]

The refusal of the Hoover administration to permit the Federal Reserve Banks to cooperate with the BIS forced the Europeans' continued dependence on Morgans to support the forthcoming bond issues for the BIS and the German Reparations loan. Norman recorded in his Diary on 19 May 1930: C. F. Whigham will talk to Anderson & J. P. M. [Morgan] as to atmosphere there & price for Germ mob[ilisation] issue'.[179] Bonds for the BIS were sold in May.[180]

Next Addis and Norman began planning for the £60m note ($300m) Reparations issue, two thirds of which was to go to the Allies and one-third to Germany. The bonds were to be secured on the annuities payable to Great Britain and the proceeds were to go to the Treasury.[181] Addis and Norman discussed the Reparations loan with Leith-Ross, Waley and Hopkins at the Treasury.[182] However, unlike the Dawes Plan issue, the Young Plan loan was never popular: Rothschild told Norman later that summer that no one wanted the bonds.[183] The amount of funds actually mobilised 'was equivalent to only about one-tenth of the unconditional annuities'.[184] One unfortunate effect of the Young Plan bond flotation was the withdrawal of gold by French banks from the Bank of England.[185] When Leith-Ross consulted French monetary authorities, he was told that the withdrawals were 'due to nervousness as to our being able to maintain the value of sterling'.[186]

In the Foreign Office, E. H. Carr blamed the Bank of England and Addis for the 'bad start' which the BIS made. He repeated the comment of a member of the French delegation to The Hague Conference who had told him that 'Sir C. Addis was doubtless an excellent banker and a worthy man, but that a capacity for defending the British standpoint was not one of his qualifications'. Carr continued that everyone but the Bank of England recognised this fact and complained about Addis's appointment as the Bank's representative 'in all the intricate negotiations which followed'. He felt that the Bank of England had 'lamentably failed to grasp that what was needed for these conferences and committees was not a first-class theorist on international banking, but a negotiator whose personality and experience made him a match for quick-witted and politically-minded Frenchmen like M. Quesnay'. As a result, Carr said, 'in every question regarding the establishment of the bank which was left to the bankers we have been completely "*roules*". M. Quesnay is an intelligent, energetic and not over-scrupulous man of 35. Sir C. Addis is 69'.[187] Carr argued that the Treasury 'should have had more say over issue which is political'. Not to be outdone, Owen O'Malley, who had negotiated with the Chinese Nationalists in 1927, added: 'I have often come across Sir C. Addis's tracks in China and my humble opinion of his sagacity is, unlike that of this office, on the whole a low one'.[188]

In the Foreign Office and Treasury view, the real 'defect' in Addis's character, seems to have been that he was too principled, too international-minded, perhaps too far-sighted, preferring to sacrifice immediate gains in order to obtain the long-term goal of international cooperation rather than the immediate profit of the British Treasury. Certainly neither Addis nor Norman believed that Germany should continue to be treated as a conquered enemy. Time would show that Addis was right even about immediate profits. In 1941 after Europe was once again at war, Addis described the result of Snowden's intervention with the Young Plan provisions, saying that 'a majority of the delegates were bent for political reasons, upon holding her [Germany] in subjection'. He continued that the British delegation was sharply criticised by Snowden, but the Chancellor's triumph at The Hague was shortlived. 'The later annuities were never paid and the only practical result of his intervention was that Great Britain received less *in cash* than she would otherwise have done had the original scheme of the British Delegates been adhered to'.[189] Addis still hoped to keep political factors, that is, French hatred for Germany, from preventing economic recovery, but the economic conditions in the United States were making this hope more difficult to fulfil.

Meanwhile, the Gold Delegation of the League of Nations had brought in its first interim report in June 1930, placing the blame for the world's financial crisis squarely on the United States and France for their policies of hoarding gold.[190] In commenting on the report, the *Economist* (edited by Layton) said that the only alternative to coordinated action was 'to break the link between the currencies of the world', or in other words, abandon the gold standard.[191]

Neither Norman nor his American advisers (Sprague and Stewart) were happy about the Gold Study report, in which Strakosch had played a large role.[192] Strakosch wrote to Leith-Ross that he had 'purposely refrained from seeing' Norman until Hopkins indicated 'how the land lies'.[193] In September the Committee of Treasury was informed that publication of the interim Gold Study report would be 'likely to harm cooperation of Fed with European Central Banks'.[194] The Committee also heard that Strakosch favoured publication and complained that the Gold Study Committee had been boycotted by the Bank of England. The Committee of Treasury 'decided to make no change'. Leith-Ross, who shared Strakosch's views, urged Salter to publish the final report of the League's Gold delegation promptly.[195] He felt that 'The economic situation throu'out the world is becoming so seriously strained that some practical action ought to be set on foot as soon as possible'.[196]

In October 1930 Addis chaired the Chatham House session where

C. H. Kisch spoke on 'Central Bank Reserves'.[197] After Kisch's speech, Addis commented that 'the obvious remedy is cooperation of the central banks in order to correct an evil which is worldwide'.[198] How to secure such cooperation remained the problem. At this same discussion, Hawtrey (in a comment which can be interpreted either as prophetic or as a warning) informed his colleagues that countries suspend gold payments when the 'necessary monetary contraction or credit contraction is greater than their economic system can stand'.[199] Layton and Hawtrey's comments in 1930, like Norman and Treasury fears in 1929, reveal the ongoing concern of British financial experts that the gold standard could not be maintained.

Although Norman and Addis continued to work closely together, travelling back and forth to Basle for the monthly BIS meetings, they continued to disagree on the functions of the BIS. Addis wrote that he thought Norman 'confuses in thought policies and methods. But we shall never agree'.[200] While the official Treasury view was that 'Britain could not act alone' on the gold question, the Treasury's intentions are indicated in Leith-Ross's comment to Hopkins concerning the appointment of a British representative to a Special Advisory Committee to the Young Plan.

The purpose of the Special Advisory Committee was to notify other governments when Germany was unable to transfer reparation payment.[201] Leith-Ross suggested possibly Keynes, McKenna or Salter, 'the latter not because of his fighting qualities, but because of his greater experience of international intrigue'. Leith-Ross emphasised that 'Whatever the Plan may pretend, the question of reparations has always been, and always will be, as much a political as an economic question, and it would be a disaster if the British expert were to recommend proposals which were unacceptable to his Government'. He added that 'at some stage we shall have to inform the British representative of the confidential arrangements made between us and the French at the Hague, which have never been published. I do not think that we need go into the details about this with the Governor, but it is important to arrange with him that the Brit[ish] rep[resentative] should keep in close contact with us'.[202] This comment suggests that Leith-Ross was anticipating the breakdown of the Young Plan arrangements and attempting to plan for what would follow if the United States did not cancel war debts.

Further evidence of the expectation that Germany would soon announce its inability to make reparation payments was provided by the Committee of Treasury in December 1930. Norman discussed the appointment of a British representative to the Special Advisory Committee and the Committee agreed that 'if & when the need arises', Layton would be invited to serve.[203]

ONE LAST ATTEMPT IN AMERICA

By the autumn of 1930 (faced with high unemployment, a deficit budget and a continuing drain of gold) the choice for British leaders seemed to lie between protection or devaluation. According to one estimate, over the course of 1930 unemployment rose from 12 to 20 per cent of the insured labour force.[204] The seriousness of the situation convinced even former free-traders such as Keynes to change their positions and become advocates of some type of tariff.[205] In addition there was growing support for efforts to promote trade within the Empire, as demonstrated by the publication in July 1930 of a 'Bankers' Manifesto', signed by McKenna and two Bank of England Directors, Anderson and Whigham.[206]

To show his continued opposition, Addis joined prominent Liberal leaders in a free-trade reply in September, but the ranks of free-traders were thinning. Nonetheless, Addis never wavered from his support for free trade. During this same period he was engaged in a heated debate with his fellow-members of the China Subcommittee of the Economic Advisory Committee, over the issue of Boxer Indemnity Funds being tied to purchases in Britain, which he unsuccessfully opposed.[207] Late in October Addis spoke to a Chamber of Commerce luncheon in Edinburgh, warning of the danger of economic war and proclaiming: 'I am old-fashioned enough to believe that free trade is the handmaid of peace'.[208]

Given the seriousness of the economic situation, Addis once more travelled to the United States, ostensibly for the purpose of giving a lecture to the American Academy of Political Science's annual meeting (whose entire programme was to be devoted to the BIS) but one suspects with a larger purpose of seeking support from the Federal Reserve Board and the Hoover administration for the BIS. Speaking before the Bond Club of New York on 24 November, Addis argued that the fall of prices was a major cause of the depression and advocated policies which would keep prices fairly steady, saying that this was 'an international problem, which the BIS could help to solve'.[209] In his address on 'The Young Plan and the World's Credit Structure', Addis warned his audience that the problem was urgent, and in prophetic words commented:

Disaster, if we continue to drift, is not far off. The remedy will
not brook delay. Whatever difficulties may lurk in the way they
must be faced. The problem presses for solution. It is imperative
that it should be tackled, and tackled at once. It is simply intolerable
to sit any longer with folded hands like idle spectators at the play,
while the sorry spectacle goes on and the trade and industry of the
world continue to be made the sport of our ineffectual monetary
systems.

He concluded with the challenge: 'We must be masters in our own
house, the rulers and not the slaves of money'.[210] Addis sounded this
same note of urgency in his address to the British Empire Chamber
of Commerce in the United States of America, again emphasising
the importance of continuing a policy of free trade and advocating
an expanded role for the Bank for International Settlements in helping
to achieve stability in exchange. He called upon the commercial men
to follow the example of the world financiers in adopting a policy of
cooperation and warned that 'Unless some such arrangements are
made, unless it is possible for those rival industrial groups to come
to some kind of arrangement in the international field, in the same
way [as] we are doing in the field of finance. I think the world will
be running a very great danger'. Referring to the recent signing of
the Kellogg–Briand Peace Pact, he said: 'the spirit of militarism is
only scotched – it is not killed; and I am not sure whether it would
really be less disastrous if the spirit which has been laid to rest within
the orbit of military affairs should once more be revived in the form
of economic war.'[211]

During their time in New York Addis and his wife stayed with the
Lamonts, while the Federal Reserve Bank provided Addis with a
room where he was able to talk with the various officers, including
Eugene Meyer, the Governor of the Federal Reserve Board.[212] The
next week Addis went to Washington where he discussed silver with
Senator Pittman and 'Barney' Baruch, lunched at India House with
two former Secretaries of State – Charles Evans Hughes and Frank
Kellogg – and spoke to the Council of Foreign Relations on the gold
question.[213]

The silver question had become an important political issue in the
United States because of the continued decline in the price of silver
after India established a central bank.[214] When Governor Harrison
expressed his concern to Norman the previous spring, he was informed
that the price was likely to continue to decline since there was a large

surplus.[215] One suggestion under consideration in some British circles was to pay the war debts to America in silver.[216] Throughout the spring of 1931 (after his return to London) Addis continued to be asked about the possible 'rehabilitation of silver'.[217]

President Hoover was exploring the idea of calling some kind of conference on silver, but Leith-Ross had no sympathy for the proposal. He wrote to Hopkins 'Nothing short of a general raising of commodity prices therefore should be considered'. He felt that only a conference covering 'the whole ground, i.e. tariffs, debts, reparations, gold as well as silver' would be useful and then remarked: 'There is no reason why we should pull chestnuts for Mr Hoover by encouraging or agreeing to participate in a conference on silver alone.'[218]

After further meetings with various international bankers in Washington, Addis went to Chicago by train to speak to a Foreign Relations lunch.[219] Addis explained to Lamont that 'Between ourselves Melvin Traylor was not very happy over here, and if a visit from me would be of any comfort to him (as I think it would be) I should not like to withhold it'.[220] While in Chicago, Addis lunched at the Continental Bank and was entertained by Rufus Dawes, the brother of Charles Dawes. Then back to New York and Washington for more speeches and talks with Treasury Secretary Mellon and finally, President Hoover himself. Addis found the President 'depressed, talked Gold (a fetish) & China'.[221] It is interesting that Addis should refer to gold as 'a fetish', which suggests the degree to which his ideas had changed since 1925. Hawtrey used the same term the next month.[222]

After a farewell lunch attended by Walter Stewart, Morgan and Lamont, the Addises set sail on 29 November. Addis wrote 'It has been without alloy a precious happy memory.'[223] However, while the trip may have been personally pleasant, Addis had failed in this final attempt to convince American leaders of the urgent necessity for joint action in solving the world's financial problems.

Meanwhile the European political situation continued to deteriorate. In the German elections of September 1930, the Nazis had advanced from being a minority party to becoming a major national party. The Nazis made no pretence of their intention to scrap the Versailles Treaty provisions, including reparations. In the months that followed, the Reichsbank lost some $250m in gold and foreign exchange.[224] The Bruning government, backed by the army (which had been ruling by decree since October 1930) was desperate for domestic political support.[225]

The underlying cause of international economic problems continued to be mutual suspicion and competition among the French, Germans, Americans and British which precluded genuine cooperation. The French suspected the Germans and British of conspiring against them, while Hoover remained determined that the British would not be let off the hook of paying their war debts. In the months that followed, the French attempted to use their financial strength to gain British support for their German policy, by insisting upon political conditions for loans. But Norman refused to accept French proposals.[226] Thus by 1931 Germany's refusal to continue reparation payments seemed a foregone conclusion. The British Treasury, under Leith-Ross's and Hopkin's continuing influence, remained equally determined not to pay America more than it received in reparations. Only if the BIS could provide a solution to this problem could a breakdown be prevented.[227]

After returning from the United States, Addis spoke to the Kensington branch of the League of Nations Union in December concerning the maldistribution of gold, which he bluntly described as being 'locked up in the vaults of the United States and France'. He said the maldistribution was one of the predominant causes of the continuous fall in prices. Addis suggested that the BIS might 'contribute by the use of credit to the development of the world of international finance and to act as a factor in stabilising exchanges and in eliminating the unnecessary risk of expense incurred in the shipping and re-shipping of gold.'[228] In addition Addis said the BIS would contribute to the world of international finance 'by the use of its credit to the opening up of new markets'. As we have seen, these were exactly the type of activities which the Americans opposed.

Britain's economic situation gave great alarm. After a Committee of Treasury meeting on 7 January, Addis noted that Norman was 'very nervous and depressed at business situation'.[229] Norman had learned from Moret, the Governor of the Bank of France, that the French would not cooperate in stopping 'what they regard as the natural flow of gold'.[230] Even Addis was having difficulty sleeping, a condition his doctor ascribed to overwork.[231]

In January the idea of using the BIS to solve the world's credit problems was incorporated into a formal proposal, which became known as the Kindersley Plan.[232]. Its origins date from a memorandum which Norman presented to the Committee of Treasury on 7 January 1931, providing for the issue of ten-year guaranteed loans in Paris and New York.[233] The objective was 'To finance the world by means of a corporation with a capital of £100 000 000 subscribed in England, France & US to raise funds by issue of Debentures up to £200 000 000 for making loans to foreign countries.[234] Initially, this scheme was considered impractical, but the Treasury took up a modified version of the proposal. Leith-Ross described the essential purpose of the plan as an inducement for the Americans and French to convert their balance of payments surpluses 'by lending their surplus abroad instead of absorbing monetary gold'.[235] Leith-Ross indicated that Norman had given the plan his blessing. At the Committee of Treasury meeting on 25 February 1931 Norman proposed that if the BIS would support the plan, the Bank of England would 'undertake to underwrite 100 per cent capital not exceeding £5 000 000'.[236] The corporation directors were to be appointed by the BIS.

Not surprisingly, the Americans and the French did not support this proposal, which Norman explained to Harrison would enable the BIS to carry out the larger functions which Addis had envisioned and the Germans favoured.[237] Despite the lack of American and French support for such a plan, Addis and Kindersley pushed ahead. On 23 February Addis noted that 'Kindersley, Siepmann & the Gov. saw me on BIS development scheme', and on 24 February: 'Much telephoning with Kindersley & Brand about the BIS & the 'K' scheme. Kindersley off to Paris.'[238] At the BIS meeting on 9 March Addis found the Germans 'very depressed' and the French (Moret) 'very trying'.[239] Since France and the United States possessed the vast majority of the world's gold reserves, their cooperation would be essential to any implementation of the Kindersley proposal.

In February the French asked Leith-Ross to formulate a common policy on war debts, if, as anticipated, the Germans suspended reparations.[240] But the Committee of Treasury refused to commit the country to a definite policy, deciding instead to 'wait to decide if & when'.[241] It is difficult to conclude that a breakdown in the system was not inevitable unless the United States agreed to a cancellation of reparations and war debts. In March the German government asked for relief from reparation payments, a request expected in London, perhaps even encouraged.[242]

The announcement in mid-March by the Bruning government of plans to form a customs union with Austria (a step forbidden by the First World War settlement) further heightened tension between France and Germany. No solution to the impending financial crisis emerged. In the midst of this depressing situation, Addis recorded his last election at the Bank of England: 'It was not without some emotion that I made my declaration for the last time. The shadows are lengthening.'[243]

THE BANK CRISIS OF 1931: 'PLAYING THE GAME AT ALL COSTS'

In the spring of 1931 the only escape Addis found from the constant pressure and sense of impending doom was a two-week trip to Morocco at the end of April. He regretfully declined Stamp's offer of a directorship of the Abbey Road Society, commenting: 'It is worth £1400 a year but I cannot do more than I am doing'.[244] The intricate fabric of international finance which Addis and his colleagues had so carefully woven was beginning to unravel.

The BIS, which had decided to explore the possibility of providing middle- and long-term credits to Germany, in May appointed a committee to be chaired by Franqui.[245] That same month the failure of the Credit Anstalt, Austria's largest commerical bank, initiated the series of events which ultimately took Britain off the gold standard. More than £5m of British deposits became unavailable.[246] The Bank of England's Committee of Treasury discussed the Austrian situation on 27 May as well as the 'Francqui Credit at Brussels'.[247] On 1 June Addis met Kindersley at the Bank of England and agreed to take his place at Brussels 'on the Middle & Long Term Credit Committee with Francqui Melchior Revelstoke', since Kindersley could not leave the Austrian Kreditanstalt Committee.[248] Two days later at an all-day session at Brussels, Addis found that the French were 'not to be moved. They do not want anything done with long-term credits at present except in Paris.'[249]

The French insisted that the Austrians abandon the Customs Union as the price for their assistance, but the British refused to cooperate in enforcing such requirements.[250] From Brussels Addis went to Basle, where he, Siepmann, Rodd and Quesnay discussed Austria.[251] The next day the BIS agreed on remedial measures for Austria and passed the Brussels report which Addis, substituting for Kindersley, who was in Austria, had arranged with Francqui, Melchior, and Revelstoke.[252] Addis described the Germans as 'pleased with the Brussels report'.[253] On 16 June a Special Court at the Bank of England approved the granting of a £4 300 000 credit to Austria.[254] All these events and negotiations reveal the interdependence of European finances.

The Austrian requirement for credit was hardly met when the Germans appealed to the Bank of England. The Reichsbank lost some $250m in gold and foreign exchange in the first three weeks of June.[255] Feeling the strain, Norman telephoned to Harrison on 18 June and told him that 'Unless somebody grasps the problem of reparations and debts we cannot emerge from this mess'. When Harrison asked him what he meant Norman replied that he thought the emergency was 'so great that all reparations & debts should be remitted for five years'.[256]

But on 20 June President Hoover granted only a disappointing one-year moratorium on inter-governmental debts, despite a strong warning from Dulles that 'there was danger of the whole system breaking down'.[257] Hoover was determined that the Germans should not use the postponement procedures built into the Young Plan, which would have enabled the British to suspend their war-debt payments.[258] On 23 June, the Committee of Treasury of the Bank of England agreed to join the Federal Reserve Bank in granting £20m credit to Germany.[259] The French however insisted that the Germans continue to pay reparations and that they would then loan the money back to them, a policy which infuriated the British.[260]

In the midst of this crisis, Addis found solace in a brief Edinburgh holiday, whence he wrote to Eba: 'I stood by the garden gate through which I led my bride-to-be seven and thirty years ago with mother smiling welcome at the door and the old man stooping to pluck a nosegay of wallflowers for his future daughter-in-law'. He recalled all the years which had passed:

What a flood of memories well up as I look back! Thoughts grateful, thankful and I trust humble in the confidence that the goodness and mercy which have preserved us all the long way will keep us steadfast to the end.

At my bedroom window I see Edinburgh lying open to the sea with her background of encircling hills, old as time. Where I write I look up to the Pentlands and the Dalmahoys and Craiglockart. Peace on the hills and in my heart. I am glad I have come.[261]

Perhaps this respite provided Addis with the opportunity to consider the difficult decisions which the Committee of Treasury faced: British financial leaders were about to take their most serious gamble since the return to gold in 1925.[262]

Early in July a run on the German banks led to a new effort by the Reichsbank to secure large credits. The Committee of Treasury accepted Norman's view that Luther's request was 'a political matter'. At the same time it agreed that Kindersley should meet with the Clearing Bankers to make plans 'in readiness for any emergency that may arise'.[263] Next, in a critically important conversation on 9 July, Norman, speaking by transatlantic telephone to Harrison in New York, informed the Federal Reserve banker that he had turned against the idea of further credits to the Reichsbank.[264] Norman said that the Bank of England directors 'did not wish to participate in a credit that would facilitate the continued payment of reparations to France'.[265] Norman's conversation with Harrison and the Committee of Treasury decision provide evidence of a decisive policy shift by Bank of England leaders. Although the leading authority on this topic suggests that it demonstrated that Norman and Snowden were 'working for a new order' which would eliminate reparations and war debts, it seems quite possible that Snowden had not been fully informed.[266]

The small group of Bank of England Directors and Treasury officials who had decided to force a showdown on the reparations–war-debt issue, even if it meant risking the gold standard, included the Bank of England officials Norman, Addis, Harvey, Siepmann, Lubbock, and Kindersley; the British representative on the BIS, Rodd; and Treasury officials Hopkins, Leith-Ross and Hawtrey.

Perhaps Keynes's trip in June to the United States (where he met President Hoover and Federal Reserve officials) was a last attempt to find out if anything more than a one-year moratorium was possible. If so, it failed, even though Keynes found some agreement for his advocacy of cheap money. When Keynes returned to England on 11 July, he circulated a memorandum on the United States situation to the members of the EAC and in addition to Addis, Harvey, Lubbock, Layton and Rodd.[267]

Simply stated, this decision not to provide further credits to Germany, was tantamount to a decision to risk being forced off the gold standard, which depended in the last resort, on confidence in sterling.[268] The Committee of Treasury and the Treasury officials, determined to put an end to the whole structure of war debts and reparations, were gambling that the United States, if pressed hard enough, would ultimately accept the necessity for cancellation rather than permit an international financial crisis. As Addis had emphasised in 1929 at Cambridge, the whole structure of the Young Plan emphasised that American policy was the key component.

British financial leaders believed that their responsibility in maintaining confidence lay in persuading the Labour government to balance the budget.[269] The argument used to convince the politicians was that budget cuts were essential to the preservation of the gold standard. But leaders like Leith-Ross and Addis knew that balancing the budget would not be enough; Britain was too heavily involved in European finances to escape the effect of the crisis there. The war-debt–reparation issue must be settled before the flight from sterling would cease. In March Snowden had told Norman that he was 'constantly hearing it stated that no matter what action he may take this country will inevitably "slide off" the Gold Standard before very long'. In response, Norman had assured Snowden that the Bank 'was prepared to take any steps that may be necessary, however drastic, to prevent that taking place'. However, he had also informed Snowden 'that no financial position, however good, could be maintained indefinitely against worsening fiscal and industrial conditions'.[270]

Evidence that Addis and his colleagues at the Bank of England and the BIS had concluded that the situation was beyond the ability of the banks to solve is provided by his diary entries and correspondence of the period. At the BIS meeting on 11 July, Hans Luther (Schacht's successor as President of the Reichsbank) convinced the bankers of the 'gravity of the situation' but no one devised a solution.[271] Addis wrote to his wife: 'We talked last night, Walter Stewart, Siepmann, Rodd and I, until this morning was well on its way. The situation has developed for the worse. It is doubtful if it can be saved now. If so, it will be a sad end to all our plans. Paris, Baden, the Hague.'[272] Nor did further telephone conversations between Harrison in New York and Norman at Basle provide any answers.[273]

Several factors explain why these leaders were willing to take such a gamble. First, as we have seen, by this time various investigations demonstrated that the gold standard was enabling the United States and France to acquire huge stocks of gold, which they refused to lend out except on unacceptable terms.[274]

Second, they believed that the gold standard had led to the decline in prices, which had created economic crisis at home and vastly increased the burden of the war debt and reparation payments. Devaluation was one method of curing Britain's economic problems. Both Ernest Bevin, the powerful Labour leader, and Lord Bradbury revealed in their discussions on the Macmillan Committee that they preferred devaluation to protection.[275] And Hubert Henderson had warned of the inevitability of devaluation if world prices continued to fall while British costs proved inflexible. It seems likely that Addis preferred risking the gold standard to imposing a tariff.[276] Hankey noted that Lord d'Abernon, the former British Ambassador to Germany, favoured an inflationary policy rather than supporting sterling.[277] While it is true – as many scholars of the 1931 crisis have mentioned – that the Macmillan Report, finished in June and published in July 1931, officially rejected devaluation, this official statement could well have been calculated to reassure international opinion. Furthermore, two members wrote an addendum in which they expressed a preference for devaluation.[278]

Third, Leith-Ross had favoured a showdown on reparations and war debts since January 1930, when he first suggested that the postponement clause of the Young Plan be put into effect. He reminded Hopkins: 'Ever since the Balfour Note, it has been the policy of successive British Gov's to link debts and reparations together'. Leith-Ross emphasised:

> This principle was finally endorsed and implemented by the Young Plan, which made the conditional annuities payable by Germany to the Allied Powers correspond precisely with the Allied debts to America and gave Germany similar rights of postponement for two years to those which America had given the Allied Powers.[279]

Layton (whom the Bank, appointed the British representative on the BIS Special Advisory Committee in July) reported in August that he favoured 'complete cancellation of war debts and reparations'.[280] After receiving the Layton report, Hopkins expressed his conviction that reparation payments were 'the cause of the present economic depression, since these intergovernmental payments are eventually received by the United States and by France and give rise to the abnormal import of gold to those countries leading to restriction of credit and loss of purchasing power in the rest of the world'.[281] He therefore advised the Chancellor that 'if the United States refuses to cancel, then Britain must refuse to pay on grounds that "we never believed in the [Young] Plan but were forced to accept it largely under American pressure"'.[282] Hopkins knew that any such refusal to pay would result in a further flight from sterling.

Naturally, a decision to take such risks could not be stated publicly, lest it precipitate a run on sterling. Nevertheless the decision to refuse further loans to Germany implied such an understanding.[283] Faced with a continuing outflow of gold, a budget badly out of balance, and unemployment of 23 per cent, drastic action was necessary.

The most important task before British financial leaders was to ensure that confidence in sterling be preserved. They knew that achievement of such confidence would require painful actions on the part of the government, namely budget cuts.[284] If the British government was to be forced off gold, the world must first be convinced that it had no other option.

On 13 July the German banking system was forced to close, reopening only after the imposition of exchange controls.[285] A few days later Addis noted that he met the Governor, Harvey, Stamp and Lubbock at the Bank of England and learned that 'Lazards have lost £8 million in Brussels. Kindersley a ruined man'. The next day the Bank agreed to loan Lazards £3m 'to keep them going'.[286] At the same time, the publication of the Macmillan Committee Report on 13 July and the May Committee on Economy Report at the end of the month revealed to the world the seriousness of Britain's financial plight.[287]

In late July, the Bank of England lost one quarter of its official reserves and raised the bank rate from $2^{1}/_{2}$ per cent to $3^{1}/_{2}$ per cent on 23 July and to $4^{1}/_{2}$ per cent on 30 July.[288] A meeting of government representatives from seven countries had been assembled in London to try to solve the German problem, but the Conference broke down - in Hankey's words, 'because the French tried to impose unacceptable political conditions'.[289] Next the Governments asked that the BIS appoint a committee of experts to make recommendations, while Norman began conferring with J. P. Morgan, who had arrived in London on 26 July, about the possibility of a loan.[290] At the same time plans were made for increasing the fiduciary issue and arrangements were made for credits in Paris and New York.[291] Yet in late July, as Parliament adjourned and Ministers began their holidays, few political leaders grasped the seriousness of the situation or understood the implications of the Bank of England's decision to cease supporting German reparation payments to France.[292]

Early in August the flight from the pound became alarming. The Deputy Governor, Harvey, warned the Chancellor that the reserves would soon be exhausted and that foreigners expected a 'readjustment of the budgetary position'.[293] Keynes, speaking as Chairman of the Economic Advisory Committee to the Cabinet and the chief drafter of the Macmillan Committee Report, informed Prime Minister MacDonald on 5 August that devaluation was inevitable.[294] At the height of this financial crisis, Norman collapsed and had to leave for a long rest.[295] On 11 August Addis was called back to London to learn that 'We have lost £20 million in gold to devisen [outflow of gold] since May, £50 million last 5 weeks'.[296] In the days which followed, the Cabinet and King returned to London.

Addis was one of the small handful of financial leaders who worked closely with those recommending to the MacDonald government budget changes aimed at stemming the flight from the pound. The first task for the government was to reach agreement on sufficient reductions in spending and increases in taxes as to satisfy the New York bankers and persuade them to provide further loans to support the pound.[297] When several of the Labour ministers refused to accept a cut of 10 per cent in the unemployment benefit, MacDonald agreed on 24 August to head a National Government. 'The new Government agreed to a programme of cuts on 27 August. Two days later the Government raised loans totalling £85 million in New York and Paris'.[298]

Addis described the crisis: 'Yesterday was a day of meetings – Cabinet, Opposition, Bank. I was there all day up till 9 p.m. when Grenfell, Peacock & I went off to dine at a cosy little restaurant in Dover Street . . . Bank meets again at 2.30.' He continued by saying that the Cabinet was to meet that evening in the 'hope of arriving at a plan acceptable to the three political parties and to the Bank. If not Ramsay will go at once to the King, who, as you know, has returned to town.' The next day Addis reported to his wife that 'This is Basle over again, only ten times worse. Politicians are the devil and all.' He hoped a coalition government would be formed 'with Ramsay as Premier. It is only an emergency government and will not last long. The split in the Labour party goes too deep. A general election is probably not far off'. On 27 August Addis noted that 'Harvey, Peacock and I have to see some of the new Cabinet Ministers at 5.30.'[299]

Yet, despite the formation of the National Government and the imposition of drastic economies, the financial crisis was only arrested, not cured. Speculation on the pound forced continued loss of gold until 18 September, when the Bank of England reported to the Government that it 'could no longer hold the exchange rate beyond the close of trading on Saturday morning'.[300] On Monday, 21 September, the Gold Standard (Amendment) Bill was approved.

Addis (who had been recalled to London on 18 September) described most of his days as being 'spent at the Bank'.[301] At no point did Addis register either surprise or dismay at the decisions reached, suggesting that he, like Keynes, recognised the advantages of devaluation.[302] In other words, Addis and his colleagues on the Committee of Treasury had already made the critical decision in July – to stop supporting German reparation payments to France – one which involved not only the possibility of leaving the gold standard but abandoning the American cooperation as well. This decision was the first step in the development of a new and independent monetary policy.

When every possible measure had been adopted to support the pound and the loss of gold continued, devaluation became inevitable, since the Hoover administration refused any further action on war debts and reparations. Having cut the budget and formed a National Government, British leaders could now face the decision with a clear conscience. As Treasury officials proceeded to draft the Gold Standard (Amendment) Bill, Peacock, the Bank of England Director who had been in close contact with the King throughout the crisis, told the Prime Minister on 18 September 1931: 'no one could accuse this country of not having made every effort before letting the pound go, and it was pointed out that by having balanced the Budget whatever happened, this country had at least demonstrated her will to play the game at all costs'.[303] After Britain went off gold Niemeyer (who had been in Australia) recommended adopting Keynes's earlier suggestion of forming a sterling block.[304]

Naturally historians of the Crisis of 1931 have been concerned with the charge that it was a 'bankers' ramp' aimed at removing the Labour government, and economists have analysed whether it was a balance-of-payments crisis or an exchange crisis.[305] But fully to explain the financial crisis of 1931, it is necessary to assume an international political perspective – to view the devaluation as the inevitable result of the Powers' inability to harmonise their objectives. Behind the United States' refusal to cooperate with the BIS lay distrust over a number of issues – war-debt payments, China policy, disarmament. In addition there was the continuing French–German impasse over reparations and the Austrian credit union, among other items. Houghton, the former American Ambassador to Germany, told a Pittsburgh audience in June 1931, that 'while the debtor nations were spending to the tune of $12 billion a year (on armaments) it was difficult to believe that the 200-odd millions coming to us is between them and prosperity'.[306] Houghton's comment demonstrates that underlying Britain and Germany's financial problems were political issues for which no solution had been found. After British attempts for ten years to follow 'the rules of the game' and to resolve these international differences through cooperation had left the country's economy weaker than ever, one can understand the British leaders' willingness to risk the gold standard. One can also understand why this decision was so carefully (and successfully) camouflaged.

Part III
A Return to Sterling

Overview: A Sterling Strategy

The essence of a successful strategy is the ability to change; to adapt tactics and resources to new circumstances. When Britain's leaders left the gold standard in September 1931 no one knew what the next steps would be. The assumption of many was that the move was temporary – Britain would soon return to gold. However when Treasury leaders found that devaluation benefited British trade, they did not return to the gold standard but instead developed a sterling strategy. Because they viewed their primary task as ensuring the continued value of the pound, they sought to convince as many trading partners as possible to peg their currencies to sterling, both within and without the Commonwealth. In the 1930s Addis helped to devise and implement the new sterling strategy, serving the government in several different capacities.

At the Bank of England he served on a Committee to make recommendations for future monetary policy. At Chatham House he chaired a committee dealing with the future of gold. After his retirement from the Bank of England (in the spring of 1932) the Prime Minister appointed him to chair a Cabinet advisory committee whose charge was to make recommendations for the World Economic Conference, set to meet in London in June 1933. Until the conference British leaders clung to the hope that the new Roosevelt administration might cancel war debts and cooperate in international economic policy. After that hope was disappointed, Addis was dispatched to Canada as the member of a Royal Banking Commission whose primary purpose was to advise Canadian leaders on the creation of a Central Bank and to ensure that Canada was not wooed away from sterling by her American neighbour. Following his return, he helped with Britain's last attempts to solve the American debt problem. When Congress forbad any modification, the Treasury finally defaulted on its payment due in 1934, a humiliating decision for Whitehall and one which may have strengthened British resolve to ensure that China became part of the sterling area.

The hope for Anglo-American cooperation in East Asia steadily diminished after the conclusion of the Washington Conference in

1922. During the mid-1920s, Addis kept in close touch with his Consortium partners and with the Foreign Office on China policy, but all efforts to make the Peking government viable proved unsuccessful.

Meanwhile the Soviet Union's aid to the Chinese Nationalist cause created great apprehension in both London and Washington but no agreement on what to do about it. When negotiations at the Tariff Conference of 1925 broke down and an anti-British boycott by the Chinese nationalists badly damaged British trade, Addis recommended that the government recognise the Canton government. In December 1926 Foreign Secretary Austen Chamberlain unilaterally announced that Britain would seek to reach agreement with the Southern Nationalists. Chamberlain's memorandum was regarded as marking the end of Anglo-American cooperation in China. During the next months, until Chiang K'ai-shek established control over Peking in 1928, the political situation in China was too confusing to make any policy possible.

Addis's position appeared ambiguous and somewhat contradictory. Despite the demise of Peking, he insisted on the preservation of the Consortium even though the Foreign Office and Treasury felt it no longer served any purpose. This insistence caused the government officials to suspect that Addis was motivated only by self-interest; that he sought to ensure the continued dominance of the HSBC over China investments. During this same period however, Addis (in his capacity as a member of the Boxer Indemnity Advisory Committee) advocated a very liberal approach to China questions, insisting that the Foreign Office recognise the Chinese right to use these revenues as they saw fit. This viewpoint brought Addis into direct conflict with the Treasury determination to enforce a policy of tied loans, which would mean that the Chinese government be required to spend Boxer indemnity funds in Great Britain.

Furthermore through his Chatham House activities, Addis led the movement supporting a more liberal response toward Chinese nationalism. In 1927 when the Kuomintang forces seized Hankow and attacked foreigners in Nanking, Addis advised the Cabinet to adopt a policy of restraint and conciliation which helped to bring about a peaceful resolution of Anglo-Chinese differences and the recognition of the Nationalist government of Chiang K'ai-shek in 1929. Addis also supported the new Inspector-General, Frederick Maze, when he insisted that the Nationalists had the right to control their own revenues. At the same time however, he refused to allow the Consortium to grant loans without control and insisted that the

Consortium be continued, despite the Nationalists' expressed hatred for it.

The China situation became even more complicated in the early 1930s when the Japanese moved to annex Manchuria. Once again Addis and the Foreign Office came into conflict, with Addis arguing for League action and the Foreign Office reluctant to antagonise Japan. When (in 1932) Addis joined with Lord Cecil and others in a public condemnation of Japanese actions, he was dismissed as Chairman of the London Committee of the HSBC. By 1933 (with his retirement from the Bank of England, the BIS, and the London Committee of the HSBC) it seemed reasonable to expect that Addis's influence over international affairs had come to an end. But such was not to be the case. When Chinese Finance Minister T. V. Soong came to London in the summer of 1933 to seek assistance against Japanese aggression in Manchuria, Governor Norman supported Addis in blocking Soong, since his proposals bypassed the Consortium.

While there were some in the British government who advocated reaching an agreement with Japan which would recognise her predominant position in China, Norman and Addis did not agree. Instead they began to devise a new plan for a loan to the Nationalists which would tie China's currency to sterling. By late 1934 the HSBC, the British Treasury and the Bank of England were cooperating on a new scheme for Chinese currency reform. When in late 1934 the Chinese Nationalists finally indicated their willingness to accept Addis's terms for a loan, the way seemed clear for a new Anglo-Chinese partnership.

In 1935 the Cabinet appointed Leith-Ross to head a special Far Eastern mission, one of its central purposes being to bring about Chinese currency reform. With British assistance, the Nanking government created a new paper unit of exchange which was linked with sterling. After this significant breakthrough, Addis aided Leith-Ross in gaining the City's acceptance for railway loan agreements, and agreed to ask his Consortium partners for permission to issue an independent loan to the Nationalists.

Unlikely as it may seem from today's perspective, in 1937 British leaders believed that they were on the threshold of a promising new era in China relations. In the final decade of his life, Addis found himself absorbed in the same questions with which he had begun his career – loans for Chinese currency reform and railways. The euphoria was brief. In 1938, as Japanese troops swept over the coast of China and the Roosevelt Administration began to provide direct financing to Chiang K'ai-shek's government, the unreality of British plans became only too obvious. Although Addis preserved the structure of the Consortium until his death, like the sterling strategy it could no longer contain either the Japanese or the American avalanche in China.

8 Towards a Sterling Bloc, 1931–4

'Any international policy in which one nation seeks to promote its own national advantage at the expense of its neighbours is doomed to failure.' — Addis, April 1934

In the spring of 1932 Addis retired from the Court of the Bank of England, thus ending his direct involvement as a formulator of Britain's monetary policy. However he continued to influence policy indirectly as a government advisor until he had to undergo surgery in October 1934. In addition he became chairman of an important Chatham House study group on international monetary policy and remained active in such opinion-making organisations as the Tuesday Club and the Political Economy Club, where he met regularly with financial policy-makers such as Leith-Ross, Keynes, Layton, Henderson, Strakosch, Blackett and Brand.

Initially Addis opposed the government's adoption of economic nationalism. But when the World Economic Conference (June 1933) failed to produce any understanding with the United States, Addis accepted the necessity for the development of a sterling strategy.

MANAGING CURRENCY AND RETIREMENT FROM THE BANK OF ENGLAND, 1931–2

Following the departure from the gold standard the immediate question facing the Bank of England was 'what to do next?' since the Bank lacked instructions from the government.[1] This was a time of uncertainty for the financial leaders who all their lives had believed and preached the indispensability of the gold standard. While the initial expectation, both in Britain and abroad, was that the departure was temporary, the evidence suggests that the Treasury deliberately allowed this mistaken impression to continue, in order to encourage the stability of the pound, which was the real objective.[2] Since there was general agreement that the pound could not be restored at the old parity, the first task was to regulate the pound.[3]

When the Bank of England's Court of Directors met to deal with the emergency on Sunday, 20 September 1931, they appointed two new special committees 'to deal with (1) "questions of currency" (Lubbock [Chairman], Addis, Blackett, Sprague and Clay). (2) "matters relating to credit and possible facilities to banks etc."'[4] The meetings took place almost daily.[5] The Currency Committee, and the Foreign Exchange Committee monitored the exchange closely through the autumn of 1931 until the creation of the Exchange Equalisation Account in April 1932 made it easier for the Bank to regulate exchange.[6]

The election of the National government in late October helped to increase confidence in sterling. Addis noted that he had 'voted for the first time in my life for a Conservative'.[7] Although MacDonald stayed on as Prime Minister, the majority of Cabinet positions in the National government went to Conservatives, with Neville Chamberlain becoming Chancellor of the Exchequer, and Baldwin the Lord President of the Council.[8]

While the Bank of England managed the day-to-day exchange problems the Prime Minister appointed an Advisory Committee on Financial Questions (which he chaired) to make long-term recommendations. In addition to Addis, this Advisory Committee included many of the same people as had served on the Chatham House Gold Study Committee, individuals who regularly met at the Political Economy Club, namely, Brand, Layton, McKenna, Macmillan, Stamp, Salter, Keynes and Henderson.[9] Addis noted that the Political Economy Club was supposed to hear Henderson lead a debate on 'What to do with the Pound?' on 4 November, but Henderson and Keynes were both ill. Addis described the discussion as 'long and interesting' saying 'nothing very new, perhaps, but talk helps to clear the air'.[10] In November the Advisory Committee considered a memorandum which Keynes (at the request of Leith-Ross) had prepared on 'The Currency Question', in which Keynes proposed the calling of an Imperial Currency Conference in order to form an Empire sterling standard, and suggested ways to manage it.[11] Blackett also favoured a sterling standard.[12] Although the Advisory Committee did not discuss at length Keynes's suggestions, they were to become the basis for the Treasury's policies in 1932, under the guidance of Hopkins and Sir Frederick Phillips in the Treasury.[13] Keynes informed Leith-Ross: 'the present may be an exceptional opportunity for uniting the whole Empire . . . on a reformed sterling standard'.[14] In March 1932 the Committee on Financial Questions recommended the consolidation of the sterling group and also the possible adoption of a common monetary policy for the British Empire.[15]

The most immediate concern for the Advisory Committee was the forthcoming Reparations Conference to be held at Lausanne, Switzerland. The Committee believed that 'a likely and perhaps a desirable outcome of the Reparations Conference would be that Germany would announce her inability to continue to pay reparations'.[16] For the Treasury and the Bank of England, the real objective at this time was to avoid inflation and a subsequent flight from sterling. What made this task difficult to achieve was Britain's lack of reserves and her large outstanding obligations.[17] In such a situation secrecy (both with regard to intentions and conditions) was critical if confidence in the pound were to be preserved. This was why the issue of reparations and war debts assumed such importance, since any doubt as to Britain's intention to continue payment to America would further weaken sterling.[18] Since neither the Treasury nor the Bank of England intended to continue war-debt payments without income from reparations, they continued to seek cancellation from Washington.[19]

At Germany's request the BIS convened a Special Advisory Committee to investigate Germany's capacity to pay.[20] This Committee (which included Layton, Stewart, Melchior and Franqui) reported that Germany could not make the payment which was due in July 1932.[21] The Committee called for the adjustment of all intergovernmental debts without delay.[22] On 9 January 1932 German Chancellor Bruning announced that Germany could not resume reparations payments after the expiration of the Hoover Moratorium. Addis noted on 21 January 1932 that Leith-Ross was at the Bank lunch, 'very tired after his long Paris reparation negotiations'.[23] There seems little doubt that British financial leaders were unanimous in their determination to eliminate war debts and reparations. But they still hoped to avoid the odium of default.[24]

One of the ways Addis proved useful to the Bank of England at this juncture was to arrange for the HSBC to purchase gold in India for the account of the Bank of England.[25] The arrangement provided that 'The Bank of England will undertake to finance the Hong Kong Bank free of interest for all shipments destined for the Bank, paying all necessary charges plus a reasonable commission to the Hong Kong Bank for carrying out the transaction.' In addition, it specified that:

the Hong Kong Bank will use its discretion in competing for the gold so as to get the best possible price for the Bank of England without unduly competing with the other English shippers and without making it apparent that there is any special buying taking place.[26]

Meanwhile Norman and the Treasury continued to disagree, with Addis supporting the Treasury advocacy of cheap money, which they felt would encourage industrial recovery and enable the government to refinance its debt. Until February the Governor insisted on a rate of 6 per cent. But on 17 February 1932, Addis noted: 'At last we go down to 5 per cent for which I have long contended.'[27]

For some time after his return from the United States on 28 September, Norman behaved erratically, convincing Addis that the time had come for the Governor's retirement.[28] He and Lubbock collaborated on a retirement statement meant to force the Governor's retirement in April 1932. But apparently Norman succeeded in outmanoeuvring them, for the Bank Court re-elected Norman and Harvey (as Deputy) for another year in November 1931.[29]

This was the last time Addis was able directly to influence the management of the Bank since he had notified both the Governor and the BIS that he would be retiring in the spring following his seventieth birthday.[30] Although Professor Sayers does not mention any attempt to unseat Norman in 1931, it seems possible that the evidence may have been destroyed; that instead Addis's retirement was encouraged (or at least not *discouraged*) by the Governor. The Peacock Committee on Bank organisation had recommended that 'all should be liable to retire at 70 "unless otherwise requested by the Court"'.[31] That Addis, who had been so close to the Governor and played such a large role on the Committee of Treasury, was not so requested, suggests a rift, which the Addis diary confirms, but to date no other documentation verifies this event.

As he prepared to surrender his responsibilities at the Bank of England and the BIS, one of the last major issues in which Addis was involved concerned the question of indemnification of the BIS for the losses it suffered through the depreciation of sterling. Since all countries having sterling deposits in London suffered from the 1931 devaluation, Leigh-Ross felt that if the government agreed to indemnify the BIS, then other depositors would demand the same treatment.[32] Siepmann also opposed the suggestion, on the grounds of expenditure.[33] Nonetheless, Addis characteristically refused to give in, either to the Treasury or Siepmann, stating that indemnifying the BIS was 'right in principle and on ground of expediency, otherwise will not become "Bankers Bank" hoped for but simply agent of reparations payments'.[34] This comment demonstrates that Addis still hoped that his plan for an international currency administered by the BIS might become a reality; that he believed a chance still existed to solve the world's international credit policies. In what must be regarded as a significant demonstration of his influence, Addis succeeded in convincing his fellow-directors and the Treasury to indemnify the BIS 'as a special case', providing 'other members agree not to demand similar concessions. Loss to be suffered exclusively by [Bank of England].'[35]

As the time approached when he must retire from the Bank of England and the BIS, there was no doubt that Addis regretted leaving the centre of decision-making. Speaking for the last time as the Vice-president of the BIS, Addis tried to reassure his colleagues that their efforts had not been in vain. Addis recognised that:

It may be that some of us are disheartened at times by the meagre results which appear to have followed our prolonged labours. It is true that the high hopes we cherished on setting out on this high adventure have not yet been realised.

He continued by suggesting that:

It may be that we have to expiate the wrongs done by statesmen, in permitting their political action to be influenced by the one-sided economic discrimination against which the Central Bankers, in this respect more advanced than they, expressly warned them in the conclusion to the Paris Report as certain to delay indefinitely economic recovery.

Drawing upon the idealistic phrases reminiscent of his youth, Addis assured his fellow-bankers that:

the world is governed by moral as well as material forces. The condition precedent to economic recovery is a change of heart. The opportunities for what must necessarily be a slow process are to be found in the monthly meeting of the BIS. I verily believe that if the BIS were dissolved tomorrow you would have to set about constructing a similar institution the day after. It is the one indispensable instrument of international cooperation.

In ringing terms he challenged his colleagues to continue their efforts:

In your hands it is safe. You will not falter in your task until the

high hopes with which you set out have found their complete
fulfilment in a world raised to a higher level of economic stability
and of mutual confidence, on which it may be possible to establish
the foundations of universal peace.[36]

After returning home, Addis reflected: 'It all seems like a dream.
No more BIS. The monthly journeys to the continent which began
in October 1924 with Berlin and reparations are now at an end: *sic
transit!*'[37] After his last meeting with the Committee of Treasury of
the Bank of England, Addis admitted: 'Now that the tie is severed I
realise how much the [Bank of England] is interwoven with the roots
of my life during the last 14 years.'[38]

Addis evidently slipped away quickly after his final attendance at
the Court, for Norman missed speaking to him. Afterwards, in a
personal note, the Governor expressed the hope that Addis would
come 'often and freely for luncheon', and on a rather plaintive note
continued: 'Of course the past is passed – & perhaps the less said
about it the better – but I shall ever remember it & yourself with
thankfulness.'[39] While the tone of this note suggested the strain which
had marked these friends' relationship in recent years, it also conveyed
the deeper ties of respect and personal affection which continued to
bind the two central bankers together. This relationship ensured that
Norman continued to seek Addis's advice on international affairs.

REPARATIONS, WAR DEBTS AND THE WORLD
ECONOMIC CONFERENCE, 1932–3

While Addis was bidding farewell to his associates at the Bank of
England and the Bank for International Settlements, Henderson was
preparing a proposal for the Reparations Conference, scheduled for
April in Lausanne, Switzerland. Henderson's proposals very much
resembled the ideas Addis had been advocating since the autumn of
1929, namely, that 'the BIS issue notes to governments which would
be the equivalent of gold, thus increasing international liquidity and
allowing countries to repay debts or engage in expansionary domestic
policies'.[40]

Meeting at Lausanne, the European Powers (Britain, France,
Belgium and Italy) agreed to cancel reparations in return for which
Germany was to deposit £150m with the BIS in the form of bonds to
be held without interest for three years, then offered for sale to the
public. Keynes had first proposed a similar plan in November 1931.[41]

The Lausanne agreements also provided for the calling of an International Monetary and Economic Conference. In the hope that Washington might yet make concessions, the French and British Prime Ministers signed a 'gentlemen's agreement' not to ratify the Lausanne agreement until the war-debts question was settled.[42]

On 29 July 1932 Prime Minister MacDonald appointed Addis to chair a Committee on International Economic Policy which was 'to consider the programme of subjects to be discussed at the forthcoming International Monetary and Economic Conference and to advise personally as to points to which British policy should be specifically directed.'[43] The other members were Lord Astor (the proprietor of *The Times*) Blackett, Lord Essendon, Keynes, Layton, Salter and Stamp.[44] Reporting in October 1932, the Committee on International Economic Policy concluded that the British Government could not contemplate the return to gold 'under such unstable conditions as now prevail'. In substitute for gold as a medium of international exchange, it recommended that the BIS be authorised to issue International certificates in return for advances.[45]

Despite the fact that many Congressional leaders remained bitterly opposed to any revision, Hoover (who was campaigning for re-election) indicated that he might trade debt payments for economic concessions from the Europeans.[46] But when the British asked that the war-debt payment due in December be suspended, they were informed that the President was not authorised to do so.[47] Reluctantly, the Treasury paid another instalment on the war debt, but the French defaulted.[48]

In addition to chairing the Committee on International Economic Policy, Addis had also been asked in 1932 to chair a Study Group on International Monetary Problems for Chatham House. This group included Salter, Professor Henry Clay, Henderson, Professor Denis Robertson, Pethick Lawrence, and secretaries Stephen King-Hall and A. T. K. Grant.[49] Blackett, who was angry at not being included in the Chatham House currency group, told Addis he thought Norman was 'at the bottom of it', which suggests that Norman continued to oppose 'managed money'.[50]

The election of the Democratic candidate, Franklin D. Roosevelt, as President of the United States in November 1932 created fresh hopes in Europe for a new, more cooperative attitude in Washington. Shortly thereafter, Addis chaired a Chatham House lecture by Schacht on 'Freedom of International Payments', at which he expressed the hope that at the forthcoming International Economic Conference:

There would be an opportunity for revising the whole fiscal scheme of tariffs by the removal of those excrescences which had been adopted not as part of a definite policy of protection but as emergency measures aggravated by still more mischievous quotas and exchange restrictions for safeguarding budgets and currency.

Addis stated that the adoption of some form of international currency was not a novel proposal, citing Adam Smith's chapter on the Bank of Amsterdam.[51]

Two months later, openly criticising government policy, Addis (speaking at the Union Discount Company dinner) commented on the disagreement among economists concerning the cure for problems and the exhaustion of the politicians. Of the latter he observed: 'Thinking – never an easy task – has become an intolerable burden to them.' Addis predicted that 'fundamental economic forces, led by an invisible hand, are slowly and silently working out their saving effect' and claimed that the outlook was encouraging 'for the restoration of London to its former predominance over the international market'.[52]

Meanwhile, a British Treasury memorandum observed that:

practically all the continental Governments are agreed it is futile to convene the [Economic] Conference unless some prior arrangement has been arrived at at least for the suspension of War Debt payments . . . It rests with Mr Roosevelt to decide whether to force us into a default which we are most anxious to avoid, or to agree that payment should be suspended.[53]

The strategy aimed at conducting stabilisation talks concurrently with the Economic Conference. The problem was that no one, either in London or in Washington, was certain what the President had in mind, since he himself could not decide.[54]

The Committee on International Economic Policy felt it was 'essential to attempt' to establish an international note issue, even though the Treasury felt it was impractical.[55] Prior to leaving for Washington for talks on disarmament and finance, MacDonald thanked Addis for the second report of the Committee on International Economic Policy, telling him he would hear from him after his return from America.[56] But there seemed little reason for optimism. One of Roosevelt's advisers (Herbert Feis) had told the British that an international monetary fund was politically impractical because Congress, resentful of war-debt defaults, would refuse to grant new credits.[57]

Roosevelt quickly demonstrated the folly of European hopes for cooperation when, on 18 April, he halted all support for the gold standard and allowed the dollar to depreciate.[58] In Leith-Ross's words: 'this made nonsense of all the plans for the World Economic Conference', since one of its chief aims was to restore financial stability.[59] Nevertheless, Whitehall kept trying to convince the Americans of the necessity of cooperation. Although the charming and affable American President assured MacDonald of his sympathy for war-debt revision and promised to ask Congress for authority to deal with this problem as well as his interest in stabilisation, nothing came of these assurances.[60]

In Washington, Leith-Ross (who accompanied the Prime Minister) held five meetings with his American counterparts in which he asked for cancellation but the Americans refused.[61] Leith-Ross discussed a complicated proposal made by James Paul Warburg (the son of the former Federal Reserve banker who was serving Roosevelt as an expert adviser) and with Dean Acheson (the Under-secretary of the Treasury) but found little enthusiasm for it on either side of the Atlantic. Norman was emphatic as to 'impossibility of cooperation between Bank of England & US Treasury', urging Leith-Ross 'to come away at once, or otherwise the US will try to involve him and us in the blame for what they are at'.[62] In the Treasury, Phillips derided the Warburg plan for war debts as 'such obvious camouflage that it would be surprising if even the middle West was deceived by it'.[63] And Leith-Ross sent a telegram to Hopkins that Warburg was 'doubtful of settlement', and advised him to 'go slow'.[64]

After MacDonald returned Addis met him and Henderson, but found it difficult to discuss the currency question with the Prime Minister, since he had 'no grasp of financial problems'.[65] Henderson volunteered to draft a letter to the Prime Minister for Addis 'to explain how Currency Committee's findings have been modified by the US going off gold'.[66] Meanwhile a trusted Roosevelt adviser informed the State Department that the British government 'with the possible exception of MacDonald has now little real faith or interest in achieving economic cooperation with the United States'.[67] Thus, although Roosevelt sent a delegation to the London Conference, given the chaotic nature of Roosevelt's policy-making and the inadequacy of the preparation, there seemed little possibility that anything positive could come from the conference.

As the delegates were assembling, Addis again chaired a session at Chatham House where Pierre-Etienne Flandin (the former French

Minister of Commerce and Finance) spoke on 'The Problem of the Gold Standard'. In his preliminary remarks, Addis first posed the question of whether or not there was a real shortage of gold. He admitted that a managed gold standard was necessary; that Britain had stabilised too high in 1925 and France too low in 1928; that what was most needed was an exchange agreement and the establishment of an international currency. He concluded with the warning: 'For the alternative is to sink deeper into the abyss of international competition in currency depreciation. It is to prevent such a disaster that the energies of the delegates at the forthcoming Economic Conference should be sedulously directed.'[68]

However, the continuing American suspicion of British ambition coupled with Roosevelt's primary concentration on domestic concerns in 1933, resulted in an American delegation which was divided among itself and without any clear instructions or authority.[69] Nor was any agreement reached on war debts at a time when American opinion was most favourable to revision. Although the delegates to the World Economic Conference (representing sixty-six nations) received great hospitality, including a welcome at the London School of Economics, a reception at Chatham House, and a dinner at the Grosvenor Hotel, the Conference accomplished little.[70] Despite the agreement reached by representatives of the three central banks and the Treasuries from the United States, France and Great Britain, Roosevelt's statement to the press on 2 July 1933 opposing 'any proposal of a purely artificial and temporary experiment affecting the monetary exchange of a few nations', destroyed the Conference and with it the hope for economic and financial cooperation.[71] Instead 'the gold bloc, the sterling area, and the United States each moved in its own way to solve its special economic problems'.[72]

After Roosevelt's so-called 'bombshell', Keynes commented in the *Daily Mail*, that the United States was 'magnificently right' in forcing nations to choose one policy or another. He himself left no doubt that Britain should adopt expansionary methods within the Empire arguing that:

> Of all countries in the world we are afflicted by the heaviest burden of our War and post-war debt at almost the pre-war price level. A rise of prices and incomes for their own sake is indispensable for us, precisely because we, alone of the European participants in the War, have not yet devalued our currency in the appropriate degree.
>
> . . . it would be excessively imprudent to link sterling to currencies

already devalued by two-thirds or more. On the other hand, we should feel grateful to Mr Roosevelt for making it easier for us to perform what our vital interests demand.[73]

Since it was now certain that the French and the British could expect no help from the United States either on stabilising exchange or revision of war debts, the immediate problem for the British Treasury was to pay the next instalment on the war debt, due in December 1933. On 13 June, Hopkins and Phillips from the Treasury and Whigham discussed with Addis the possibility of paying the US debt in silver. Addis told them that the HSBC 'could supply them with 20 million at once'.[74] The upshot of all these conversations was that the Americans agreed to accept Indian silver even though it could not arrive in San Francisco before 30 June.[75] In a conversation which suggests the complexity of the problems as well as the reason why Addis was so valuable to the Treasury and the Bank of England, Addis advised Hopkins and Norman to 'buy spot and sell forward with Hongkong [Bank] – cover spot Bombay thro' India office paying what price they require over $19\frac{7}{16}$, even up to 23 Executed to avoid being short of silver and able to rate purchase complete'.[76] This was to be merely a 'token payment' of $10m, which was followed by one more token payment in December 1933. After that Congress passed a resolution precluding the President from accepting any further 'token payments', and Britain finally defaulted on the debt to America in June 1934. Thus ended the long struggle, begun at the Paris Peace Conference, to achieve an Anglo-American financial partnership.[77]

It seems certain that the British Treasury could have met its war-debt payment to the United States had it so desired, since at this time Britain had accumulated a gold balance in New York of £60m. But the Treasury and the Bank of England wished to keep the existence of this gold as a secret reserve to protect sterling.[78] The Treasury therefore had the New York gold gradually shipped to Paris, 'the better to obscure its ownership'.[79] In the face of what they regarded as American intransigence, British leaders proceeded to develop a sterling bloc of trading partners.

One critically important component of the sterling group was Canada, which had not yet linked its currency to the pound. In August 1933 the government announced the appointment of a Royal Banking Commission for Canada, to be chaired by Lord Macmillan and to include as the British representative Sir Charles Addis.[80]

THE ROYAL BANKING COMMISSION FOR CANADA

The Canadian Prime Minister, R. B. Bennett (who was in London to attend the World Economic Conference) invited Addis to serve as one of two British Representatives on a Royal Banking Commission in July.[81] Addis and Macmillan had previously worked together on the University of London Investment Committee.[82] In urging Addis to accept the appointment, Macmillan frankly admitted: 'I shall certainly need all the expert assistance I can get for, as Bennett with engaging and accurate candour reminded me, I am no economist and my role is to be that of the lay chairman.'[83]

The stated charge of the Commission was to review every aspect of the banking and currency and credit system and consider the advisability of setting up a central bank, but its overall purpose can best be understood as the attempt of the British government to ensure imperial unity.[84] One Canadian historian who accompanied the mission, later explained:

> The desire in England for a chain of Empire central banks was a latter-day expression of financial imperialism. The terminology was changed and the word 'cooperation' figured more than formerly, but the essential purpose was the same: the maintenance and extension of London's influence and control.[85]

By keeping their reserves in London, the Dominions provided the Bank of England with much-needed gold. Before leaving England, Macmillan had met Norman who stressed the 'imperial concept if Canada should fail to establish C[entral] B[ank] & so be sucked into financial domination of F[ederal] R[eserve] Banks more and more'.[86] On the other side of the Atlantic, Dulles warned the Roosevelt administration that Canada was being lured back to the London market.[87] All the British Commonwealth nations had tied their currencies to sterling except Canada.[88]

Eba (who accompanied her husband on the mission) kept a journal of their travels, which between 9 and 24 August included Ottawa, Winnipeg, Edmonton, Vancouver, Victoria, Calgary, Lake Louise, Saskatoon, and Regina. The Commission held hearings and conferred with local financial and political leaders.[89] After one lengthy hearing (in summer heat reaching 90°) Eba observed that 'Lord [Macmillan] thought it good policy to let him [a crank] have his say out, but Charlie would long ago have chopped him.'[90]

After all the testimony and discussion was completed, the Commission found itself unable to reach agreement. Macmillan and Addis recommended a central bank for Canada (which would be linked to sterling) while two other members, Sir Thomas White, Canada's wartime Finance Minister, and a Mr Lennon, dissented.[91] It seems clear that both Addis and Norman viewed Canada as a colony, a place for investment and development, not as an independent country. The possibility that Canadian interests might be better served by alliance to the American dollar was simply not considered as a viable option. But there were many Canadians who did not agree.[92] Macmillan's and Addis's recommendations for private ownership of the central bank went 'directly in conflict with weight of evidence taken in Canada'.[93] Although Canada established a central bank in 1935, it was not the independent or private institution recommended by Addis and favoured by Norman. The Canadians recognised from the beginning that control of currency was a political rather than a private matter and were determined to assert their independence of both Britain and the United States.[94]

Nowhere does Addis's commitment to the defence of the British Empire become more clear than in his approach to Canadian central banking. After his return to London he spoke to the Canada Club Dinner in October, expressing optimism concerning Canadian loyalty to the British Empire.[95] In April 1934 speaking to the Lombard Association of Foreign Bankers on 'Canada and Its Banks', Addis stated frankly why he recommended a central bank for Canada, saying that he felt Canada should tie itself to sterling.[96]

INTERNATIONAL MONETARY POLICY, 1933–4

After returning to England Addis resumed his work as Chairman of the Chatham House study group on International Monetary Problems and on the Committee on International Economic Policy. After meeting Henderson, Layton and Stamp, he agreed to advise the Prime Minister that a proposed letter to the Powers was 'premature. Better wait till US currency policy is more clearly defined.'[97] On 8 December 1933 he noted that after lunching with Hawtrey he 'saw the Prime Minister for an hour with Stamp, [Sir Arthur] Balfour, [Sir Alfred] Lewis, & Erdman re [Economic Conference].' By March 1934, Addis and the Chatham House Secretaries (A. T. K. Grant and Commander Stephen King-Hall) had a draft report ready for discussion.[98] In addition Addis continued the informal exchange of views at the Tuesday Club dinners and at the Political Economy Club.[99]

One of the continuing topics of discussion was the question if, and when, Britain would return to the gold standard. Addis resigned from the Sound Money Association after refusing to approve its pamphlet on *The Return to Gold*.[100] But in contrast to most of the members of the Chatham House Committee, Addis continued to argue that 'a return to gold should be the immediate objective of British monetary policy'. When the Study Group's report was published in 1934, Addis, N. F. Hall, and O. R. Hobson expressed their dissent from the view that restoration should be postponed. They specified that 'by restoration we do not imply that it should embody the more unfortunate features of the gold standard in the past'. They argued that 'an opportunity of securing a general stabilisation of exchanges is likely to arise in the early future', and stated that 'many of the difficulties of an international standard could be solved through the development of the Bank for International Settlements'. They optimistically predicted that 'Britain will be in a position to secure such developments as the price of her adherence to an international standard.'[101] Thus (as this committee's report makes clear) Addis continued to hope that the Bank for International Settlements might develop into an international institution capable of meeting the world's credit problems.[102]

But by 1934 many of Addis's views must have seemed increasingly anachronistic – more appropriate to British experience and power in the nineteenth than the twentieth century. For instance, Addis continued to support free trade which the government had abandoned in favour of Imperial Preference. A general tariff of 10 per cent *ad valorum* was imposed in February 1932.[103] Yet on 22 March 1934 (speaking to the Cornhill Club) Addis declared himself an 'impenitent Free-trader'. At the same time he denied that tariffs were the cause of the Depression. Instead he described the causes as belonging 'in the moral rather than the material sphere, in the mind and in the heart of man'. He continued:

> Any international policy in which one nation seeks to promote its own national advantage at the expense of its neighbours is doomed to failure. Any policy in which a national section seeks to make itself an exception to the international whole is doomed to failure.

At the same time Addis also denounced the notion that overproduction was at fault, taking a swipe at:

an American administrator who is having the fight of his life – and I hope he may lose it – in an attempt to raise wages by 10 per cent and reduce the hours of labour by a corresponding amount! All these fantastic devices have only one thing in common – to encourage people to pursue the popular policy of doing the minimum amount of work for the maximum amount of pay.

He asked his audience:

Until we are content to reverse that policy and take up again the burden of a fair day's work for a fair day's pay, what hope can there be of recovery?

Addis finished his speech by reiterating his faith in the moral government of the universe and in the:

invisible hand which will lead the 2 billion people of the earth back from devious ways to the paths of sanity, liberty and peace. They will not always be content to believe that they will grow fat by snuffing up the east wind of nationalism run mad.

He therefore called upon his listeners to:

cherish a cheerful faith. The change may be coming more quickly than we think.[104]

Mills wrote that he had persuaded the editor of the *Manchester Guardian* to print excerpts of the speech, while Lamont sent the speech to his partners with the comment: 'It is my idea of the old-time religion, and I like it.'[105]

But the 'old-time religion' could not convert Britain's new leaders. While Addis may have continued to inspire investment bankers, he no longer exercised his former influence in the Treasury. More and more, he now had time to spend with Eba, reading aloud and walking in the countryside. In the autumn of 1934, he was busy preparing an address for the London Missionary Conference at Newcastle, in honour of the Morrison Centenary.

Addis told the Conference of his belief, which he had held since his early days in China, that Morrison's life 'is a perpetual reminder that we are all missionaries, whether we like it or not, living epistles to be read and known of all men and by none more keenly than the subtle and curious Chinese'. He asked: 'Merchant *or* Missionary, Merchant *and* Missionary. Is the difference so great as we are sometimes tempted to think? Shall we not rather say, 'All service ranks the same with God?'[106] Despite his enthusiasm for the idealism of the missionary, Addis's fundamental objectives continued to be those of the British merchant – an eagerness to take advantage of the new opportunities in China which seemed at last to present themselves.

While much of Addis's time in the past ten years had been devoted to monetary and economic concerns, he had not abandoned his interest or involvement in China questions, continuing to support the Consortium policy. However the optimism concerning China's future (which he had expressed in 1922) had not proved any more realistic than had his hopes for central bank cooperation.

9 Addis and British China Policy, 1923–9: The Resumption of Anglo-American Competition

'We must show the Chinese we have something better to offer than Bolshevism.' — Addis, December 1926

There are several reasons why the cooperative policy in China failed. First and foremost, the policy of giving exclusive support for the Peking government presupposed a political unity in China which did not exist and could not be imposed by the foreigners. Chinese nationalism insisted upon the abolition of the old treaty system – a fact which Addis and the Foreign Office were slow to accept.

Second, when an anti-Japanese government was established in Peking in 1922 Japan refused to support a Consortium loan. Since Japan had been accepted as an equal partner of the other Consortium Powers, her views had to be considered. By the time a pro-Japanese government took over Peking (October 1924) the Canton government had become a force which Britain could not afford to ignore.

Third, since the major share of British investments were in central and south China, Britain could not antagonise the Kuomintang Party leaders who were demanding recognition as the National government of China. This became very clear in 1925, when an outbreak of Chinese nationalism (the May 30 Movement) led to a boycott of British goods and the demand that the 'unequal treaties' be abolished. Unable to reach agreement with Washington and Japan on a common response, Whitehall decided to initiate a new, independent China policy.

As we have seen, Addis had argued as early as 1922 that some concessions must be made to the demands of the Southern Chinese leaders. Four years later he supported recognition of the Kuomintang. At the same time however the Kuomintang's attacks on British citizens and property in Hankow and Nanking led many British leaders to call for military action in China. Throughout this period

Addis counselled a policy of restraint and accommodation. After Generalissimo Chiang K'ai-shek purged the Kuomintang of Communists and conquered Peking, the British recognised his Nanking government. Addis's major achievement was to preserve the Consortium, despite the change in policy.

THE CONSORTIUM AND THE PEKING GOVERNMENT, 1923–4

In October 1922 the Foreign Office decided to send Wellesley (the Chief of the Far Eastern section of the Foreign Office) to Washington for some preliminary conversations on China.[1] After several meetings with Wellesley before he left for the United States, Addis commented: 'Another jaw at FO with that softy Wellesley. It grows tedious.'[2] To Acheson (the Chinese Maritime Customs Representative in London) he explained that he:

> favoured a Consortium loan for unsecured debts provided the British Government said that they considered there was in Peking the nucleus for a stable government in the future and would give some sort of written assurance to the Consortium that they really meant to see this matter of future stable government through.

Otherwise Addis said he felt that 'a loan would do more harm than good'.[3]

The problem of course was that times had changed, and gunboat diplomacy could not be conducted with impunity as it had been in the nineteenth century. The Foreign Office feared that American public opinion would not support force in China, since Americans liked to think of themselves as the protectors of China. However, neither did the Foreign Office believe that it could win Japanese cooperation in financing a Peking administration hostile to Japan. Simply stated, the Western bankers did not believe any loans to Peking were secure investments unless the Japanese supported such loans.

Additional opposition to the Consortium policy came from the British Inspector General, Sir Francis Aglen, who believed both Sir John Jordan and Addis were out of touch with events in China. Writing with some bitterness, Aglen said: 'The FO will of course follow Sir John blindly: once you establish an oracle you can't very well ignore him.'[4] Aglen had become committed to the Peking government through his administration of the Domestic Loan Fund (established by Presidential Mandate in 1921) which required that all surplus revenues be deposited in this fund to serve as security for the Domestic Loans. Because he wished to protect the Domestic Loans, Aglen opposed Addis's and Jordan's suggestion that some of the foreign-controlled revenues be shared with the provincial governments. In Aglen's opinion, this so-called 'federal solution' would undermine the security of the Domestic Loan bonds which Aglen had guaranteed. As the months passed, Aglen grew increasingly hostile to the Consortium. Curiously enough, Addis and the Foreign Office seized upon a kidnapping incident in China as an opportunity to 'get the Consortium to work'.

In May 1923 Chinese bandits held up a train at Lincheng, Shantung, and kidnapped the foreign passengers.[5] The unfortunate event coincided with the assembly of the Consortium Council in Paris. The Group Managers (Addis, Lamont, de la Chaume and K. Yano) agreed at Paris that the Lincheng incident provided, in Addis's words, a perfect excuse for overcoming:

the Chinese objection to an amalgamated railway system under effective foreign managers and technical experts. We think this may be done by proposing the increase of foreign supervision over each individual line with a view to a composite railway loan secured on the revenues of all Government railways.[6]

Addis estimated that under efficient management, the Chinese railways could 'show a net profit, after paying the service of their respective loans, of over $35 000 000.' He suggested that 'foreign control might be extended to cover the appointments of Chief Engineers, traffic managers, Chief Accountants and Police Officers on all railways'.[7]

The British Foreign Office enthusiastically recommended these proposals to Washington and Tokyo. Wellesley minuted: 'At least we have got the Consortium to work and we can give it our blessing.'[8] The Foreign Office incorporated Addis's suggestions in its instructions to the Peking Legation for the Group Representatives, stressing: 'It should be made clear at the outset that cash advances can only be considered as part of, or as a sequel to, a completed scheme, and that only by facilitating and expediting such a scheme can the Chinese Government hope to obtain the advances they require.'[9]

In order to provide additional incentive to the American Group to participate, Addis suggested that the Group Representatives examine 'the possibility of opening up new and hitherto untried sources of revenue. It would appear possible that the absence of vested interests might render such sources, if available, particularly suitable for foreign control.'[10] One particular area Addis had in mind was the Wine and Tobacco Tax, which he thought might be reorganised as the Salt Administration had been after the Reorganisation Loan of 1913.[11] The American Group had long been interested in the Wine and Tobacco tax, since it had been used as security for American wartime loans. In Lamont's words, 'There has always been a feeling that in due course of time it would be appropriate for an American to handle the wine and tobacco revenue just as the citizens of other nationalities handle these other revenues.'[12]

But while British policy-makers and the American Group were enthusiastic about Addis's proposals, the State Department expressed misgivings. Secretary of State Hughes wrote to President Coolidge:

> Certain details of the plan of the British Minister, as set forth in the telegram from Peking, appear to be obviously designed, not merely to provide for the organization and proper functioning of a force of railway police, but also to obtain a rather complete and undue control over both the finances and the operation of the Chinese Railway system.

For this reason, Hughes persuaded President Coolidge to oppose the British proposals.[13]

Without American diplomatic support, the ambitious Consortium plans (largely formulated by Addis) had little hope of success. No Peking government would willingly accept the Consortium's terms and the US government refused to force them on Peking. Without such acceptance, the Hongkong and Shanghai Bank would not provide advances to Peking.[14]

Washington proved to be more cooperative regarding reprisals against the Canton government. When Sun Yat-sen threatened to seize the Customs at Canton, American warships joined the other foreign Powers in a joint demonstration of force in Canton harbour, which forced Sun Yat-sen to reconsider. However this foreign demonstration also showed Sun that the Washington Treaty Powers' professions of support for Chinese sovereignty were not sincere. He concluded that they had no intention of surrendering their privileges voluntarily and that the United States was as imperialistic as were the other foreign powers. In an emotional address to Chinese students, Sun announced: 'Only Russia will help us.'[15] Thus the

Canton demonstration of November 1923 paved the way for Sun's alliance of the Kuomintang with the Soviet Union in 1924.[16]

For the time being, Addis's attentions were diverted from China to Brazil, as he accepted an invitation to serve on the financial mission, from which he did not return to Britain until April 1924.

Meanwhile, as the Southern Nationalists moved closer to their Bolshevik advisers, both the British and American diplomats began to reconsider their attitude towards Chang Tso-lin, the Manchurian warlord whom they had earlier regarded as a Japanese puppet and therefore unacceptable for support. When Wellesley learned that F. S. Mayers of the B&C Corporation had persuaded Chang Tso-lin to supply trains from Peking to Mukden and also to the Kailan mines, he commented: 'Possibly he is a better man than Wu Pei-fu after all.'[17] As early as August 1923 the American Group Representative predicted that Chang Tso-lin would make a move soon 'either to break away completely from China or to extend effective control over Peking and North China'.[18] Neither the Americans nor the British had any illusions about Chang Tso-lin's close relations with the Japanese, but with Soviet agents gaining influence over both the Peking and Canton governments and the Consortium seemingly impotent, Japanese influence in North China no longer seemed as objectionable as it had in 1919.[19]

In all likelihood the purpose of Liang Shih-yi's visit to London in the spring of 1924 was to lay the groundwork for Chang Tso-lin's future take-over of the Peking government.[20] Addis had last seen Liang in Tientsin, two years earlier, when they had formulated the abortive plans for a coalition with Sun Yat-sen. After Wu Pei-fu's victory over Chang (in 1922) Liang had retired to Hong Kong.[21] Addis arranged that Liang Shih-yi and his party should meet the Deputy Governor and have a tour of the Bank of England.[22] On 30 April, the B&C Corporation sponsored a dinner in Liang's honour, attended by fifty English and Chinese.[23] Since Addis had hosted many of the same individuals at a dinner-party two weeks earlier to meet Major Walter Nathan CMG (the new Chairman of the B&C Corporation) it seems likely that new negotiations were underway.[24]

While Liang was in London, Nathan prepared a memorandum suggesting that the individual Consortium Groups 'have liberty to go ahead with railway loans in which it has mortgage rights, with the consent of the other groups'.[25] The State Department denounced this proposal, since it seemed to confirm American suspicions of British plans in China – namely that they intended to keep American capital out.

While there is no record of Liang and the British discussing General Feng Yu-hsiang's future coup, in view of Addis's earlier discussions with Liang in 1922, and the occurrence of such a coup the following October (which favoured Chang Tso-lin and was financed by Japanese sources) it seems reasonable to suspect that at least preliminary discussions took place. The leading foreign bankers were all in London at this time, holding a Consortium Council meeting and making plans for the Dawes Plan loan.

Certainly Aglen was mystified by the welcome and reception Liang received in London, describing him as 'a back number' in China. Aglen saw 'no prospect of his emerging again for some time to come'.[26] Further evidence of British intentions can be found in a Foreign Office minute by S. P. Waterlow (who had replaced Wellesley when he was promoted to Under Secretary). Waterlow described Chang Tso-lin as having a small and efficient army and indicated that he was 'only waiting to consolidate his force and to give his rivals time to exhaust themselves'.[27] Aglen condemned the Consortium as 'trying to flog a dead horse into life by having a meeting in London . . . To my mind this is pure waste of time. So far as China is concerned the Consortium is dead and buried.'[28]

Needless to say, Addis took a much different view. At a Consortium Dinner on 14 July he delivered a welcoming toast:

> I know there are some who will regard these remarks as too idealistic, impractical, unbusinesslike, and, if we were living in normal times, I should be disposed to agree with them. But Gentlemen, we are not living in normal times. The world is floundering in the throes of transition from a war to a peace status. You cannot segregate China and practise there a policy of isolation.

Addis continued by saying that 'We should be stultifying ourselves if, while we are to combine together for the restoration of Europe, we were to leave the rehabilitation of China to the competitive forces of rival and independent international policies.'[29]

But the IG was not the only British leader questioning the role of the Consortium in Britain's China policy. Waterlow informed Addis that the new Labour Prime Minister, MacDonald, 'saw objections to the Consortium policy and did not wish to commit himself'. Waterlow asked Addis for a statement on the Consortium 'suitable for Prime Ministerial consumption'.[30] Meanwhile the plans for the overthrow of the Peking government were proceeding.

Scholars who have studied General Feng Yu-hsiang's coup of October 1924 have concluded that the Japanese planned and paid for this betrayal.[31] Once a Peking government friendly to Japan was established, Washington and London hoped that a Consortium loan to Peking might finally be arranged.[32] However, as in the past, Chinese nationalists soon exposed the futility of such hopes.

PEKING vs CANTON, 1925–6

Officially the Foreign Office and the State Department were still committed to exclusive support for the Peking government. In fiscal terms, this meant that all the revenues collected by the Maritime Customs Administration – namely the salt tax and the customs revenues – officially belonged to Peking and were channelled to that government by the HSBC and the Diplomatic Body. By 1924 the Foreign Office, alarmed at increased Soviet influence over the Kuomintang government in Canton (as demonstrated not only by Soviet advisers but also by the establishment of a Central bank in Canton under Finance Minister T. V. Soong with a $10m loan from the USSR) had begun its search for some alternative scheme which would satisfy the Southern provinces.[33] In the meantime Addis (who was being kept fully briefed on Foreign Office discussions) approached Lamont about a possible change of China policy.

The American Group wanted the revenues from the proposed tariff increase to be used to pay off China's past debts to Americans (which had defaulted in 1921) whereas Addis (as head of the British Group) continued to insist that any additional revenues should be used for new railway development.[34] Lamont informed Addis that the American Group 'favored negotiations of railway contracts only with the Central Government'. In other words, he opposed the new British proposal.[35] At this point events in China began to outpace British planning.

In May 1925 the shooting of Chinese student demonstrators by a British officer in Shanghai led to the outbreak of what became known as 'The May 30 movement', a nationalistic uprising involving a wide cross-section of the Chinese people and a more effective mobilisation than had ever occurred.[36] In retaliation for the Shanghai killings, the Chinese nationalists began an anti-British boycott which soon badly damaged British trade and the port of Hong Kong.[37] Demands for tariff autonomy and an end to extra-territoriality were heard everywhere in China.

Addis's initial response to this latest outbreak of anti-foreignism in China was to call for decisive action by the United States and Great Britain. He wrote to Grenfell:

> In my judgement the present disorders in China if left unchecked may lead to consequences unparalleled since 1900. Immediate concerted action by the Powers is imperative and I have no doubt T. W. Lamont is representing to his State Department as I am doing to mine the urgency of cooperating in such measures as may be required for the prompt restoration of order in China.[38]

Lamont responded with the information that Kellogg's views on China were 'similar to those of Addis'.[39]

For the first time since the Paris Peace Conference, Chinese demands were receiving a sympathetic hearing in Washington, where Secretary of State, Frank Kellogg, and a new Chief of the Far Eastern Division, Nelson T. Johnson, showed signs of abandoning the cooperative policy.[40] Even though conservative Chinese leaders such as Liang Shih-yi advised the foreigners to meet demands for treaty revision with promises, Johnson (who recently had returned from China) recognised that the situation demanded more than promises.[41] Perhaps by 'decisive action', Addis meant not force but a convening of the Tariff Conference to find some solution for Chinese demands. If so, the Peking government ended the debate over when to hold the conference by itself issuing invitations for October 1925.

Certainly by the autumn of 1925 Addis was advising a policy of conciliation. He worked closely with the Foreign Office in preparing the British delegation to the Tariff Conference.[42] He succeeded in convincing Foreign Secretary Austen Chamberlain that the Conference should avoid the appearance of a debt-collecting agency, but he was less successful with the Americans and Japanese.[43] While the Tariff Conference delegations assembled in Peking, Addis travelled to New York for a meeting of the Consortium Council. At a dinner which Lamont gave in his honour at the Metropolitan Club, Addis, urged 'a spirit of conciliation in Chinese negotiations'. He warned that it was 'dangerous to attempt to bluff China and not possible to force her'.[44] Afterwards Addis described the event to his wife: 'The speech went off well. A little high-pitched but I meant every word of it . . . More has been accomplished than I dared to hope for . . . It has been a struggle but I am satisfied.'[45] Nelson T. Johnson informed Lamont and his partner, Anderson, at this same dinner that he was opposed to any attempt at foreign financial control of China.

Despite Addis's optimistic words in New York, the Tariff Conference turned out to be the disaster for Anglo-American relations which Wellesley had predicted.[46] Ongoing military strife between the various factions of the Warlords and disagreement among the foreign delegates made agreement impossible.[47] By March 1926, after conferring with Wellesley, Lampson, Pratt, and Mounsey concerning China policy, Addis admitted: 'It is a baffling problem.'[48] The Americans refused to support the British position that some of any Customs increase must be given to the provinces or else Canton would unilaterally seize the Customs revenues.[49]

In 1926 Addis recommended that the British government recognise the Canton government. British officials in Hong Kong (where trade had been badly affected by the boycott) had adopted this position, and they were already initiating steps to reach accommodation with the Kuomintang leaders. The problem in 1926, however, was knowing who was in fact in command of the Kuomintang.

Since Sun Yat-sen's death in 1925 various nationalists had competed for leadership of the Kuomintang.[50] In 1926 it was still not clear who would emerge as Sun's successor, but conversations were underway with the commander of the Whampoa Military Academy, Chiang K'ai-shek, as one of the most likely candidates.[51] The Kuomintang forces launched a Northern Expedition in July 1926 from Canton which succeeded in bringing most of China south of the Yangtze under their control.[52] However the Kuomintang was still not united. In 1927 the Nationalists split, with the more radical faction located in Wuhan, and the more conservative leaders concentrated in Nanking.[53] At this time, Hong Kong Governor Cecil Clementi (who replaced Sir Reginald Stubbs in November 1925) reported to Matthew Nathan (a brother of Walter Nathan and a former Governor of Hong Kong): 'Chiang Kai-shek is now practically dictator in Canton.' He continued that Chiang wanted to 'get rid of the boycott and the strike Committee organization' and that he had instructed Eugene Chen (the Foreign Minister) to negotiate a settlement with Hong Kong. Clementi felt that the Russians were 'still a danger' and that Britain 'should abandon the idea of a central government and negotiate with local leaders'.[54]

Further evidence of the new proposals came from a variety of sources. Aglen wrote to Bowra: 'Your idea that the Canton Government should be bribed with the Customs revenue is not feasible.'[55] Addis noted in his diary on 26 May 1926 that Sir James

Jamieson was home from Canton and that he had 'changed his opinions and now backs the Kuomintang and advocates independent negotiations with the Governor of Canton'.

The Foreign Office faced a real dilemma: the new recommendations from British leaders in South China were the opposite of the views of the IG in Peking as well as the cooperative policy with America. What were they to do? Warnings that Aglen would resist a new policy alarmed the Far Eastern experts. G. E. Hubbard (the Peking agent of the HSBC) warned on 1 April 1926 that Aglen intended 'to tap the stream before it reaches the banks' and worried that the 'Chinese might see a new opportunity – a decidedly dangerous precedent.'[56] What Hubbard's warning meant was that Aglen might block the automatic flow of Chinese Customs revenues into foreign banks, which would undermine foreign financial control, threatening at once and the same time, the future of two pillars of British power in China – the HSBC and the IG.

The Foreign Office was very annoyed by Aglen's attitude. Mounsey wrote to Minister Macleay:

> He has, with undeniable skill, achieved for himself a position of complete control over the whole of China's Customs Revenues, but I think you will agree that he has at times exercised this control in a manner which was not altogether fair to China's foreign creditors and against which the Diplomatic body have for years past registered ineffectual protests . . . we sometimes wonder whether something very like juggling with figures may not be taking place.[57]

Aglen reciprocated these feelings, writing: 'I seriously distrust the gentlemen who are now running China policy at your end.'[58]

Faced with such fundamental differences of opinion among British leaders themselves, and unable to reach a common policy with their American or Japanese colleagues at the Tariff Conference, the government ordered the British delegation home. Meanwhile, the officially recognised Peking government had virtually ceased to function in the midst of civil war. Stanley Hornbeck, who had served as an American expert at the Tariff Conference and who soon after became Chief of the Far Eastern Division of the State Department, interpreted the British withdrawal from the Conference in May 1926 as a signal that London was abandoning the cooperative policy in China.[59] Hornbeck was correct.

BOXER INDEMNITY FUNDS AND BRITAIN'S NEW CHINA POLICY, 1925-7

At the same time as the Tariff Conference was meeting, Addis was appointed to the China Indemnity Advisory Committee (established by the Boxer Indemnity Act of 30 June 1925 and chaired by Lord Buxton) which was charged with recommending a way in which the Boxer Indemnity Funds could be used for 'mutually beneficial purposes'. The Boxer payments had been resumed in 1922 after a five-year remission given to Peking in exchange for its entrance into the First World War on the Allied side. Instead of being paid to the credit of the British Government, these payments were deposited in the HSBC, where they had accumulated by 1925 to the amount of £7m principal and £4 250 000 interest.[60]

While this amount does not seem sufficiently large to create great controversy, if one remembers the shortage of investment capital in Britain at this time, one can understand the dispute which followed. From the beginning there had been serious disagreements within the government as to the use of the Boxer Indemnity funds. The Treasury (which was never convinced that Britain should give up the indemnity) conducted an ongoing campaign to ensure that the funds would be used to promote British trade and industry.[61] In 1925 a subcommittee of three members was appointed to investigate possible uses of the revenues in China. This subcommittee was headed by Lord Willingdon, his two colleagues being Dame Adelaide Anderson and Professor W. E. Soothill.[62] The Willingdon subcommittee (which left Britain for China in January 1926) spent the next several months travelling and hearing various proposals for the use of the funds. The Governor of Hong Kong suggested that the funds be used for bargaining purposes with the Canton government, to complete the loop-line extending the Hankow–Canton Railway to Kowloon.[63]

Addis (who adamantly opposed using the Boxer funds for railways) met Lord Buxton at the FO with Mounsey and Ashton-Gwatkin and drafted a telegram to Willingdon 'putting him right on applying Indemnity funds to railways'.[64] But the supporters of this proposal were not easily dissuaded. The final report recommended that 'the Boxer Funds be used to create an Investment Fund which could invest in Chinese Government or other Government securities'.[65] Addis was not happy with the report, describing it as 'a series of compromises'.[66]

Meanwhile Addis continued to press for the adoption of a new

China policy. He and John T. Pratt (who had recently been recalled from China to provide his expertise in the Foreign Office) agreed that the threat of Bolshevism to China was exaggerated.[67] In July Addis gave a dinner for Sidney Peel, HMG's representative to the Tariff Conference, who had recently returned from Peking. The dinner included leading bankers and government officials, such as Lord Gosford, H. A. Trotter (a Director of the Bank of England) Wellesley, Clark, and Niemeyer.[68]

Addis opposed the proposal of Lady Clementi, wife of the Governor-General of Hong Kong, to revert to the Anglo-Japanese Alliance, since it ignored the Washington Conference resolutions and was 'based on the fallacy that it is possible to isolate our policy in China instead of regarding it as part of our general foreign policy'.[69] He felt that 'Sun Yat-sen's government is the only one that has persisted in China' and said that he had 'long urged its recognition – *de facto* – with conditions imposing *pro rata* immediate responsibility for national debts and, ultimately, provision for incorporation in a union of federal government'. He described Lampson as 'blocking the way, hesitating naturally, to go against the considered policy of Macleay in the North and Jamieson in the South'. Addis continued that 'Jamieson has now been removed to Tientsin and Macleay has been recalled. Lampson is to take his place. The recognition of the South is begun. The Hong Kong Government is negotiating with Canton. What will Lampson do?'[70]

At a dinner at Lord Revelstoke's Addis discussed the situation with Lord Balfour.[71] After this talk, he summarised his view:

> Has the time not come to recognise them as the *de facto* Government of China? That would not be incompatible with maintaining the official recognition of the Government of the North as a sort of Chinese Ulster. Oppose the Bolshevik element in the Kuomingtan [*sic*] and you fan it into flame. Refuse to allow it to be an obstacle to recognition and thereby give heart to the Moderate Section of the party.[72]

Addis conveyed much the same view to Lamont and the FO.[73] In his 'Notes for the Chairman's Speech', in December 1926, Addis wrote: 'We must show the Chinese that we have something better to offer them than Bolshevism.'[74]

While Addis was conducting these unofficial efforts outside the government, Pratt had launched a similar drive within the Foreign Office, writing a series of memoranda in favour of support for the southerners and the policy of permitting the Chinese 'to be masters in their own house'.[75] Pratt particularly opposed the policies of Aglen, which he believed led directly to the crisis with the Kuomintang.[76] Pratt claimed that: 'something of this sort was certain to happen in consequence of Sir F. Aglen's attempt to make himself the master of the Chinese instead of their servant and his hostile attitude towards Canton ever since he identified himself with the northern militarists by assuming responsibility for the domestic loans.'[77]

The influence of Addis and Pratt, in combination with other factors persuaded Foreign Secretary Austen Chamberlain to adopt a new China policy, which he announced in the famous December Memorandum of 1926.[78] This policy demonstrated a willingness to consider Chinese demands for tariff autonomy, to negotiate with the southerners and to resist pressure from the old China hands who wished to use force. In issuing it independently of the other Powers, Chamberlain demonstrated that Britain had broken with the postwar cooperative policy in China.[79] Needless to say, Chamberlain's independent announcement caused resentment in the United States, for it appeared to be an attempt to woo the Chinese nationalists away from the Americans. From Hong Kong, Lampson reported that the British there favoured recognition of the South. Chamberlain commented: 'The more he sees of the South on his way North the better I shall be pleased.'[80] While the Foreign Office had reached agreement on the necessity for reaching accommodation with the southern leaders, the question of which leaders as well as the nature of the accommodation still remained to be solved.

It is easy to understand why the Foreign Office found the situation in China puzzling and the future uncertain: Chiang K'ai-shek had not yet achieved real control over the Kuomintang, nor had the question of the Communists' influence within the party been resolved. Since 1923, the Soviet Union had furnished both advisers and military aid to the Kuomintang, and Chinese Communists had been included within the membership.[81] But despite the fact that Chiang had spent some time in the Soviet Union, he was determined to expel the Communists from both the Kuomintang and China.

Chiang owed his rise to power and influence to his connections with China's infamous Green Gang, a secret society which controlled China's extensive underworld and which was allied to the banking empire of H. H. Kung.[82] Kung (whose family had made its fortune first in pawnbroking in the western province of Shansi, then in facilitating agreements for Standard Oil) after competing his University education in the United States, returned to China to become an adviser of warlord Yen Hsi-shan.[83] During the war Kung married Ai-ling Soong, a member of the famous Soong family. Madame Kung's brother, T. V. Soong, was China's finance minister, while one sister, Ching-ling, was married to Sun Yat-sen. The other sister, May-ling, later became the wife of Chiang K'ai-shek.

In 1926–7, Chiang (still dependent upon his Communist advisers for aid and support) had not made his own views public. How much the British knew of his connections with the Green Gang is uncertain. Seagrave concludes that during Chiang's prewar career in Shanghai, he 'was basically a hit man for the mob running Shanghai, to whom the role of "revolutionary" was often just a convenient excuse for murder, armed robbery, and extortion'.[84] Chiang's successful deception of both the Russian and Chinese Communists is one of the most remarkable and significant stories of the twentieth century.

RECONCILIATION WITH THE NATIONALISTS, 1927–9

While Lampson and Owen O'Malley (the First Secretary in the Peking legation) were conducting negotiations in China, Addis continued to seek public support for the Chinese Nationalists. In November 1926 Addis chaired a session at Chatham House where Dr Hu Shih (one of China's most prominent intellectuals) spoke. After the address, Addis cautioned the audience concerning the difficulties of knowing what was going on in a country where Western journalists did not know the language and advised a policy of patience and conciliation. Praising Hu Shih, he said: 'He shows us a young and modern China being reborn. Its leaders, perhaps, are inclined to go farther and faster than some of us older heads would like, but on the whole they are alive, with a definite purpose in view.' Addis pointed out that these new leaders had:

> the faults of youth, but also its merits. There are mong them men of undoubted character and competence, of genuine patriotism, who have furnished the country for the first time with a party as opposed to a personal following; a party which has managed to continue in being under great difficulties, which has contrived to perform the functions of a *de facto* government in levying taxation and in equipping an army.

Addis advised his countrymen that 'It will not do to dismiss a movement of this kind merely by attaching the label of "Red" to one section of it and of "Anti-Red" to the other.'[85]

In addition to this public speech, Addis entertained at a dinner for Hu Shih, to which he invited influential members of the press, such as Dr Harold William, the foreign editor of *The Times*.[86] The next month Addis chaired another discussion on China at Chatham House, preceded by a dinner at the Reform Club, to which he invited prominent businessmen and leaders.[87]

Despite Addis's and Chamberlain's efforts at conciliation, much pressure was being put on the government to take military action in China in response to the take-over of the foreign concession in Hankow and concern about the security of Shanghai. On 13 January 1927 Addis noted that the Cabinet had asked that the Imperial Defence Committee should consult him 'about the expediency of using a financial blockade as a means of bringing the Chinese to their senses'. Addis 'advised strongly against any financial reprisals as futile and likely to hurt us more than the Chinese'.[88] A few days later he commented: 'It is suggested that an economic blockade should be instituted and compensation paid to British merchants and bankers by H.Gov't! Bosh, I say, as to blockade and compensation both.'[89]

As the violence against foreigners in China increased, so too did the pressure on those British officials in charge of China policy. The Nationalist troops seized Hankow in January, attacked Nanking in late March and called for a General Strike in April.[90] Such violence and lawlessness naturally caused a sense of crisis, even panic, in Whitehall.[91] Despite O'Malley's success in negotiating an agreement with Chinese Foreign Minister Eugene Ch'en in January, the future was uncertain since deep divisions within the Nationalist leadership resulted in a situation resembling anarchy. While a split in the KMT leadership between the more extremist forces at Wuhan and Chiang K'ai-shek's government at Nanking had been rumoured, no one was certain how to interpret the various rumours and allegations.[92] In the face of such violence and political uncertainty, the temptation to take military action was strong; a policy advocated by Chancellor of the Exchequer Churchill and Lord Birkenhead, the Secretary for India.[93]

Despite the uncertainty and fear, Addis continued to advise restraint.[94] When the Generalissimo purged the unions, arresting and slaughtering Communists in Shanghai in April, the British government felt reassured that Chiang was not under Moscow's control.[95] The Cabinet therefore decided to instruct Lampson that 'since Chiang Kai-shek has acted with vigour against the extremists and so has somewhat relieved the tension at Shanghai and Canton and even somewhat improved the situation at Nanking . . . It would appear therefore unwise to do anything to antagonise or weaken him.' However, the Foreign Office felt it was 'too early yet to found a policy upon his final success or even upon his good will if successful'.[96] The extent to which foreign bankers aided Chiang remains obscure, but there seem to be little doubt that the Generalissimo had foreign support in his purge of the Communists.[97]

One thing is certain – Addis's counselling of patience helped to restrain the British Cabinet. On 27 April Chamberlain informed the Cabinet that:

> while he favoured reoccupation of Hankow, Sir Charles Addis, the former Chairman of the Hong-Kong Shanghai Bank and a great authority on China, was a strong partisan of the policy of patience hitherto pursued by HMG and although unaware that the project was seriously under consideration, had expressed disapproval of the proposal to reoccupy the Hankow Concession.[98]

Addis confided to Mills that he had 'spent the last two days at FO counselling restraint'; he had as well advocated 'approaching Chiang Kai-shek with a view to setting up a commission on which the North would be represented with which we could deal provisionally pending the formation of the national government'.[99]

Addis's views were not typical of the old China Hands group, whom Addis labelled 'Diehards'. Mentioning such people as Stabb and Landale he said, 'they want force. I am for patience and mediation'.[100] Nor was he happy with his fellow-board-members' proposals regarding British railway interests in Manchuria. In May the Cabinet discussed a proposal of Major Walter Nathan 'to finance Chang Tso-lin under the guise of an industrial loan'. Rather than oppose such proposals (as the Foreign Office formerly had done) members of the Cabinet stated that they need not:

> discourage financial assistance from private sources to Chang Tso-lin, who had at least shown himself less unreasonable and less anti-British than the Nationalist Government whom he was fighting and who were receiving support in arms & money from the Soviet Government.[101]

The evidence suggests that Sir Newton Stabb and Nathan were not informing Addis of their activities. In the autumn of 1927 Addis discussed a B&C Corporation proposal 'for transferring British railway interests to Japan' with Wellesley and Pratt, indicating that he did not approve it.[102] Whether this proposal was the reason for Nathan's being removed from the Chairmanship of the B&C Corporation is not certain, but (using exceptionally strong language) Addis wrote that Nathan 'had disgusted all his colleagues as Chairman of the B&C'.[103] On 14 December Nathan resigned as Chairman in favour of Sydney Mayers. At this same time Morgans was also negotiating a loan with the Japanese government for the South Manchuria Railway, despite the opposition of the State Department.[104]

The significance of these Manchurian railway arrangements is that they represented further encroachment by the Japanese in China, aided by British and American finance. In other words, they mark the beginning of the return to the system of spheres of influence (in which each Power's special interests would be respected) rather than the development of the Chinese economy on a cooperative basis. The chief problem in returning to a system of spheres of influence was the preservation of the Chinese Maritime Administration. If Great Britain recognised the Nanking government, could she continue to insist that the nationality of the Inspector General continue to be British? While concern about this matter had been voiced for several years in the Foreign Office, Peking's dismissal of Aglen as Inspector General in January 1927 made the issue urgent.

MAINTAINING CONTROL OF THE CUSTOMS, 1927–9

Despite Aglen's removal the problem of how Britain could recognise the Nanking government and at the same time preserve the integrity of the Chinese Maritime Customs remained. If the revenues were awarded to the Nanking government, what would become of the domestic loans? Between 1927 and 1929, some complicated financial manoeuvres were carried out to solve this problem.

The first task was to ensure that A. H. F. Edwardes (who had been appointed Acting IG after Aglen's dismissal) continued in power.[105] Aglen had transferred £404 000 'to a special account in London with a view to providing cover for an overdraft'. Hubbard (the HSBC agent in Peking) indicated that since the Chinese Ministry was unaware of this transfer of funds, he foresaw a 'big explosion when the Chinese discover that this large sum has been taken by Aglen out of the Domestic Loan account, leaving as I understand, insufficient to provide for the 9th Year Internal Loan drawing next month'.[106]

In March Addis took steps to ensure that Edwardes did not meet with Aglen's fate. In order to avoid 'the risk that the new IG may be sacked & a new Japanese successor might break up the whole Customs system', Stabb (the London Manager of the HSBC) agreed to advance funds for the payment of the 1896 China Loan coupon, if necessary.[107] However, while the HSBC could provide this type of temporary coverage, the larger task of winning the Kuomintang's support for continued British management of the Customs presented a far more difficult challenge.

Earlier (when Edwardes was Commissioner of Customs at Canton) he had antagonised the Kuomintang leaders by ignoring Foreign Minister C. C. Wu's instruction to open the Custom House.[108] In contrast, Southern leaders had enjoyed good relations with Frederick Maze (the Customs Commissioner at Shanghai) who was a nephew of the famous IG, Sir Robert Hart. Maze claimed that the British Consul-General in Shanghai (Sir Sidney Barton) had asked him 'to cooperate in smashing the Nanking gov[ernment] Surtax organiz-ation', but that he had refused.[109]

The big breakthrough came in July 1927 when Chang Kia-ngao, the Vice-President of the Bank of China in Shanghai, informed Maze that the Kuomintang Government at Nanking would be willing to maintain the Consolidated Loan Service.[110] Acting IG Edwardes opposed Chang's proposal, indicating that he could not agree to any 'modification whatever of existing Loan Service' until the Presidential Mandate of March 1921 was rescinded.[111] Nevertheless, in 1927 T. V. Soong (who had become the Governor of the Central Bank of China) created a sinking fund for domestic loans, using the 2.5 per cent surtax acceded to by the British government.[112] Chinese bankers then helped to finance the new Nationalist government by buying its bonds, which were secured on these funds.[113]

Unable to achieve unity, Chiang K'ai-shek resigned from the government in August 1927 but shortly thereafter returned to power and proceeded to conquer Peking. In July 1928 the United States accorded Chiang's government *de facto* recognition.[114] Meanwhile in his capacity as Finance Minister, T. V. Soong convened a National Economic Conference in Shanghai (in June 1928) which was attended by bankers Chang Kia-ngau and Li Ming.[115] At the same time, Maze wrote to C. T. Wang (the Nationalist Foreign Minister) that he would 'try to have customs formerly sent to Peking to Nanking but Nat[ional]

Gov[ernment] does not recognize officiating IG'.[116]

It is difficult to interpret this offer as anything else than an attempt by Maze to gain the appointment of IG for himself. His support for the Southerners had won the enmity of Lampson, who refused to leave the Peking legation.[117] While Maze had the reputation of being an 'excellent Chinese scholar' and one who 'understands Chinese psychology and successfully cultivates the best possible personal relations with the Chinese', his sympathy with the Nationalists made him unpopular with the British community in China.[118]

When Edwardes was fired in January 1929 and Maze named Inspector General by the Nanking government, the announcement was not welcomed by either Lampson or the British press in China.[119] The English language newspapers subsequently launched a campaign to discredit the new IG.[120] At first the Foreign Office considered suggesting that the Chinese appoint someone else.[121] The HSBC Agent warned that Maze would be 'merely a puppet of the Chinese by appointment and so exit foreign control'.[122] Fortunately for Maze as well as for British interests in China, both Addis and Pratt supported Maze in the spring of 1929. Addis had heard Maze's views a year earlier from a colleague in the Customs, L. A. Lyall, who supported Chinese tariff autonomy when he spoke to Chatham House in April 1928.[123]

Maze wrote directly to both Addis and Pratt, criticising the policies of Sir Francis Aglen in guaranteeing the domestic loans and arguing that since 'the foreign liabilities no longer absorb half the revenue, the foreign powers have no right to decide what is to be done with the other half'.[124] Pratt arranged secretly to keep in touch with Maze. The outcome of this dispute was that Wellesley (who had at first sympathised with Lampson's position) concluded that Maze had been 'the victim of misrepresentation' and that he had 'probably saved the Customs'; he admitted that Maze was 'brilliant and able' but possessed a 'rather unpleasant personality'.[125]

One further concession which Maze agreed to was the provision that the Nationalist Government would have the right to deposit part of the Customs Revenues in the Central Bank of China, instead of using the HSBC exclusively, as had been the case since the war. Maze asked in August 1929: 'How can the IG or anybody else, legally hypothecate or control moneys belonging to a third party?'[126] With Maze as IG, the British were well-equipped to compete against the Americans and the Germans, each of whom was wooing the Nanking government.[127]

It seems likely that the Chinese Nationalist leaders hoped to use this continuing foreign competition in China to escape from the financial controls which the Consortium insisted upon (or so the British leaders believed). Addis gave a dinner in his home in honour of Kuomintang leaders Hu Han-min and Sun Fo. He continued to meet regularly with Far Eastern specialists in the FO, and in December 1928, he took Aglen, Mayers and Col. Malone as his guests to the Tuesday Club, where the discussion was on China.[128] Sun Fo (the son of Sun Yat-sen) had told American representatives in China that the Nationalists distrusted the Japanese and the HSBC and wanted to negotiate an independent loan from the United States. However, after visiting the United States, Sun Fo found that 'no new funds would be available until the whole financial structure of the Govt. [Government] had been reorganized'. In preparation for such a reorganisation he invited the United States to send a financial mission to Nanking.[129]

In 1929 Professor Kemmerer and his assistant, A. N. Young, arrived in China. Addis seems not to have been alarmed by the Kemmerer Mission, assuming that any agreement reached would be shared with the other Consortium Powers. In his 'Notes for the Chairman's Speech' in December 1928, Addis indicated that the situation in China was 'more promising than at any time in this generation', and he spoke of the recent visit of Avenol, the Deputy Secretary General of the League of Nations, and the prospects for a central bank for China.[130] From the Reparations Conference at Paris Addis wrote to Frank Ashton-Gwatkin (in the FO) that he recognised that the Chinese did not like the Consortium:

> Nor do I. But both of us know in our hearts that in a weak, divided and politically corrupt country like China, as described by Lampson, the alternative to the Consortium is a return to the welter of international competition with, as experience shows, its inevitable tendency to a re-opening of the noxious policy of spheres of interest.[131]

After lengthy conversations, Addis and Pratt persuaded the Foreign Office to recommend that the Boxer Indemnity Funds be returned to China without conditions.[132] Addis continued to be confident that through patience and perseverance the conflicts in China could be peaceably resolved and British interests preserved.

This confidence soon proved to be too optimistic. While it was true that the transition from the Peking government to the Nanking government had been achieved, none of the parties involved was satisfied. As the KMT attempted to assert its authority over all of China, the fragility of the structure soon became all too apparent.

10 Japan vs China, 1929–34

'Sir Charles Addis's position in the City of London is unique.' —
Revelstoke to Grayburn, 27 October 1932

Following Britain's recognition of the Nanking government (in 1929)
both the Foreign Office and the Treasury were anxious to reach new
loan agreements with that government in order to ensure the
continuation of British influence in China. Since the Consortium
seemed to hinder these efforts – in fact created friction rather than
understanding because it provided that all loans must be offered to
all four members and Nanking refused to deal with Japan – the
British Labour government decided to dissolve the Consortium. Not
surprisingly Addis opposed this decision, insisting instead on a
continuation of the cooperative policy.

Once again Addis demonstrated his formidable authority in the City
for China was unable to obtain loans. However Addis antagonised the
Far Eastern experts who accused him of senility. Addis added to his
unpopularity when (after Japan's invasion of Manchuria in 1931) he
publicly condemned Japanese aggression and called for action by the
League of Nations. The management of the HSBC responded by
asking for his resignation.

The evidence suggests that in the early 1930s the Foreign Office
may have been attempting to return to the old system of spheres of
influence in East Asia, in effect re-establishing a system which would
accept Japan's domination in North China, while seeking British
paramountcy over central and southern China. If this were the
Foreign Office plan, then Addis clearly sabotaged it. Only after the
failure of the World Economic Conference in 1933 and Japan's
annexation of Manchuria did Addis finally agree to cooperate with
the government in financing new independent loans to China.

COPING WITH JAPAN, 1929–32

In 1929 The Kemmerer Commission recommended that China go on
the gold standard.[1] But to do this, China would need a foreign loan,
and the Consortium (led by Addis) refused to grant such loans until
the Nationalists paid off their old defaulted bonds.[2] Whitehall

continued to worry that the Americans were displacing British influence in China, especially since the Nanking government had so many American advisers. In April 1929 Sir Miles Lampson received a warning that American interests were 'working hard' to secure the contract for the completion of the Canton–Hankow Railway and that 'hesitancy on our part would unquestionably result in the contract going to the United States'.[3]

The MacDonald government was anxious to win trade agreements with China as a means to alleviate Britain's economic woes. Leith-Ross asked Ashton-Gwatkin in July 1929: 'are there no possible schemes for new construction of Railways, Bridges, etc., where our hands are free to secure the placing of orders unconditionally in this country?' He thought if that were the case, 'HMG are surely entitled to stipulate that the [Boxer] Indemnity Fund should be applied primarily if not exclusively, for such schemes and the rehabilitation of other Railways must wait till they can be financed in the market.' He continued: 'I am assuming throughout that the policy of HMG is to secure preference for British goods if possible.'[4]

But Addis strongly opposed Leith-Ross's proposal, observing that 'it is comparatively easy to induce the Chinese by persuasion to buy British goods; it is impossible to compel them to do so'. He warned that 'An attempt to impose a limitation in selecting their market is in itself sufficient to suggest evasion, and at evasion the Chinese are adepts.' Addis's second objection was based on the Nine Power Treaty and its promise of equal opportunity. He felt that 'The proposal is so important to the continuity of our national policy in China that I venture to express the hope that it will not be adopted before being submitted to the cabinet for decision.'[5] If one recalls that at this same time, Addis also reaped criticism for the Young Plan agreement, one can appreciate how annoying he must have been to the government. Nevertheless, his authority in the City was so great that his views could not be ignored. That autumn the Nanking government dispatched Jun Ke Chou (the Railway Minister) to London for discussions with Addis.[6]

The Foreign Office had no illusions about the extent of the Nanking Government's authority in China, or its wish to divide the Powers. Pratt cynically observed that 'Sun Fo has failed to get money in America and is now trying to wheedle us . . . no need to rush into Mr Choy's arms but at the same time it is evident that the sooner we withdraw from the Consortium, the better.'[7] Wellesley reserved decision until he could discuss the whole question of the Consortium with Addis.[8] Addis believed that Nanking's real reason was that it did not want Consortium control.[9]

In fact, neither Whitehall nor the State Department were optimistic concerning the future of the Nationalist government; both tended to regard Chiang K'ai-shek as simply another warlord.[10] Furthermore, the aggressive nature of the Japanese army's behaviour in Manchuria – including the assassination of Chang Tso-lin in 1928, and the take-over of the Chinese Eastern Railway in 1929 – left no doubt in either Whitehall or Washington of Japanese determination to control Manchuria, regardless of Nanking's claims.[11]

In July 1930 Foreign Secretary Arthur Henderson revealed the government's increased interest in China when, speaking to the first annual dinner of Chatham House, he devoted about one third of his speech to China.[12] That same month Hubbard told a section meeting of Chatham House that it was improbable that either the League of Nations or any financial group outside the Consortium would be able to finance Chinese development.[13] A week after Hubbard's speech MacDonald appointed Addis to a special China subcommittee of the Economic Advisory Council (EAC) to 'prepare an appreciation of the Chinese situation and to submit recommendations as to possible steps which could be taken to develop British trade in the Far East'.[14] When the Committee met in November Addis opposed Leith-Ross's recommendation that loans to China be tied to purchase agreements.

While the subcommittee continued its work, Addis went to New York to seek support for the Bank for International Settlements and also to discuss China with the American group. After returning to England he reported that the Americans were opposed to excluding railways from the scope of the Consortium.[15] As a result of the impasse regarding the use of Boxer Indemnity funds, the China subcommittee submitted a majority and minority report.[16] Despite Addis's opposition, the Cabinet approved and Parliament passed the second Boxer Indemnity Act, which stipulated that purchases must be made in Britain.[17] Addis's refusal to compromise, and the public protest which his assistant, W. E. Leveson, made in *The Times* could not have endeared him to the government.[18] Addis commented to Harvey (the Deputy Governor of the Bank of England) that the second Boxer Indemnity Act had retarded 'the growth of British prestige in China which of late has shown encouraging signs of recovery'.[19]

Not surprisingly, the China experts in the Foreign Office resented Addis's refusal to follow their lead, denouncing him as being 'disingenuous & artful', questioning his true motives, and raising the possibility that he was growing senile.[20] But Addis's influence succeeded in blocking any loan. At the Bank of England's Committee of Treasury meeting on 4 March 1931, Norman reported that the Treasury had sought his advice concerning a loan to China. The Committee (no doubt deferring to Addis) decided to wait for the report of Salter, whom the League of Nations had sent to China.[21]

Preoccupied by the financial crisis that summer, the MacDonald government could not have given too much thought to China. This then was the situation when (in September 1931) the Japanese invaded Manchuria, using a bombing incident at Mukden as their excuse for moving large numbers of troops into the area.[22] China responded to Japanese aggression by appealing to the League of Nations, which appointed a committee (to be chaired by Lord Lytton) to investigate Chinese charges.

By early 1932 Addis was disappointed at the Foreign Office's failure to take a stronger stand opposing the Japanese aggression in Manchuria. While the Lytton Commission was investigating China's charges against Japan, and Japanese planes were bombing Shanghai, Lord Cecil – the British representative at the League of Nations – had launched his own initiative to put pressure on the Cabinet to condemn Japanese aggression. Addis agreed to sign Lord Cecil's letter to *The Times*, in February 1932 which asserted: 'It is time that British opinion faced the fact that the Japanese Government has committed itself to a course which seems to be directed towards the military domination of China as a whole.' The authors (who, in addition to Cecil and Addis, included Salter, Arthur Hayworth, A. D. Lindsay and Gilbert Murray) claimed that Japan's actions were 'a threat to the peace of the world', and they called for the cooperation of the United States and the League of Nations 'to exert all the diplomatic and economic pressure which may be necessary to secure from Japan respect for the collective system and the sanctity of treaties'. The letter concluded with the warning: 'There is certainly no escape from danger by neglect of our honour and duty.'[23]

Although Addis agreed to sign the letter, he refused Cecil's invitation to meet with Members of Parliament regarding 'the Chinese–Japanese imbroglio', preferring instead to follow his more traditional role of exerting influence behind the scenes, through such organisations as Chatham House. At the Chatham House discussion on China, Addis noted that he was 'in the chair and spoke for 20 minutes'.[24] Meanwhile, faced with economic crisis at home and

German–French conflict in Europe, with nothing by way of action except words from the Americans, the MacDonald National government resisted proposals for decisive action which might provoke Japan.[25]

By April 1932 Addis had become thoroughly discouraged with the Foreign Office, feeling that there was no policy; that instead the government was 'simply drifting'.[26] After meeting with Lamont (who was in London) Addis wrote a long memo on the Sino-Japanese dispute, intending that Morgans should pass it on to Secretary of State Stimson. The memo proposed that 'the Economic Committee of the League should operate through a Commissioner General for China with previous experience of such work, plus an international staff, on the lines familiar in the reconstruction of Europe'. Addis suggested that 'a start might be made with the railways' and reaffirmed his belief that 'There is no doubt that the development of communications would do more to enhance the authority and prestige of the recognised Government of China than anything else. All reconstructive work would soon pay for itself and create fresh credit.' He felt that although 'Manchuria would of course fall within the zone of the Commissioner General' he would 'use a considerable proportion of Japanese personnel there, the distribution of a due proportion of non-Japanese personnel in Manchuria, and of Japanese personnel in the provinces south of the Great Wall, forming part of a League policy of distributed responsibility'.[27] Since Addis had no illusion that Britain could expect 'equal opportunity for our trade in Manchuria under a Japanese regime', he suggested that since the results of the Nine Power Treaty had 'proved disappointing', it was no longer safe 'to leave China alone to work out her own salvation'. As a substitute for the old policy, Addis proposed that China 'apply to the Economic Committee of the League for the services of a Commissioner General', and warned that '*otherwise Chinese may lose Manchuria and more*'.[28]

When Addis submitted this memorandum to the Foreign Office, he encountered the same kind of scepticism and derision awarded his views on the Boxer Indemnity and the Consortium a year earlier. Pratt commented: 'The search for a complete and logical scheme for the salvation of China is a waste of time. That goal can only be reached by a very arduous and uphill road where we are lucky if we can see even one step ahead at a time.'[29] And when Lampson returned from China in July, he irritably remarked: 'I am frankly not impressed by Sir C. Addis's paper. It betrays considerable lack of appreciation of the hard *facts* of the situation. In fact, to use a colloquialism, it is largely "hot air" to my mind if I may be allowed to say so.' Lampson continued that he was alarmed by the trend of Addis's and Mayer's views: 'And *note* how they *both* harp on railways. That is a curious coincidence and suggests ulterior motives – which we of course know are there.' Not to be outdone, Wellesley added: 'I entirely share Sir M. Lampson's views.'[30]

Clearly the Far Eastern specialists did not believe Addis had any motive but self-interest; his credibility in the Foreign Office apparently had vanished. And yet one wonders who was really avoiding responsibility here. The facts of the case suggest that the diplomats may have been lashing out at Addis partly in frustration at their own inability to take any significant action. In such a powerless situation, they naturally resented being reminded of their duty to support principles, especially from a HSBC banker.

When the League condemned Japan as the aggressor, the Japanese withdrew from the League of Nations and proceeded to establish the puppet state of Manchukuo.[31] Whether or not the Powers would recognise Manchukuo remained to be seen.

During this period Addis further annoyed the Foreign Office in a matter concerning the endowment of chairs in British universities from Boxer Indemnity funds. The incident provides further insight into Addis's refusal to conform to political dictates and his determination to protect what he believed to be the genuine interests of China. As Treasurer of the Universities China Committee, Addis protested against the proposed allocation, writing to the Chairman (A. D. Lindsay) 'that the allocation of so disproportionate an amount as £3000 for University Chairs, out of the comparatively slender balance of income left over (after deduction is made for administrative expenses in London and China and for Chinese scholarships, etc.) must have the effect of impoverishing the efforts of the Committee on behalf of the Chinese students in this country, and of diverting the main body of the expenditure from the purposes for which it was originally designed.'[32]

When Addis's recommendation was defeated, he angrily resigned from the committee, sending a letter of protest to the Foreign Office. Pratt (who was also on the Committee) wrote a long minute describing the proceedings, characterising Addis's manner as 'aggressive, indeed violent'.[33] Even though the clerks who reviewed this whole question concluded that Addis was right about the terms of the arrangement, Charles Orde nevertheless complained: 'If Sir C. Addis had been a little more pliant the amount [would] have been £500 less.'[34]

The significance of the Universities China Committee dispute is that it clearly reveals Addis as a person devoted to principle, a man capable of seeing beyond his own country's interests and determined to carry out a trust assigned to him, despite the unpopularity which such resolution produced. In contrast, the Foreign Office personnel hardly show up so favourably at this juncture, and their irritation with Addis appears to have stemmed from resentment at his defiance of their wishes. Nor does their suspicion that Addis sought only the selfish interests of the B&C Corporation seem warranted since he had earlier opposed Nathan's attempt to reach a separate arrangement with the Japanese. Finally, the accusations of senility sound more like the excuses of younger men whose poor judgement had been exposed and who were retaliating. The further protests from Addis in November regarding Japanese loans to Manchuria were similarly ignored.[35]

In addition to his unsuccessful efforts to galvanise the Foreign Office and State Department into taking a stand against Japan, Addis sought to influence the Japanese government through protests to his Japanese banking friends. He wrote to Nohara (the London representative of the Japanese Group of the Consortium) who was with the Yokohama Specie Bank, regarding the reported loan of 20 million yen to Manchukuo by Mitsui and Mitsubishi Banks (both members of the Consortium) claiming that the security for the loan would be a 'contravention of the agreed policy of the Consortium'.[36]

The Foreign Office welcomed this protest with the suggestion that it might serve as an excuse to dissolve the Consortium but the State Department rejected the suggestion that the Consortium policy had failed. Furthermore, while the Americans thought there might be merit in the League approach suggested by Addis, they suspected that the League would call on the United States 'for capital but not for supplies'.[37] Thus Addis's efforts to contain Japanese expansion in Manchuria proved unsuccessful. All that he had accomplished was to arouse the suspicions of all three parties involved – the British, the Japanese and the American State Department. The fact of the matter was that in the international atmosphere of fear, suspicion and economic crisis which characterised the early 1930s, the kind of cooperation which Addis favoured – in fact had achieved in the 1920s – was no longer possible.[38] As if to conform the decline of Addis's influence, the new HSBC Manager (Sir Vandeleur Grayburn) informed Addis in October that he would have to retire as Chairman of the Bank's London Consultative Committee.[39]

REMOVAL FROM THE LONDON COMMITTEE, HSBC

Astounded and humiliated by Grayburn's unexpected action, Addis determined not to accept the decision without a fight. He wrote back immediately, protesting against the Directors making the decision 'retrospective': 'To make the rule retrospective in my case amounts to my summary dismissal from every post I hold in the Bank.' He added that he would have expected at least one year's notice: 'The action now taken is so contrary to the usage I have always received that I find it difficult to believe it was the intention of the Directors to treat me in this summary fashion and I respectfully ask them to reconsider their decision.'[40]

When Addis informed the London Committee, they indignantly passed a minute insisting that the ruling should not apply to the incumbent. Lord Revelstoke, the senior member of the London Committee and a powerful voice in the City, assumed the leadership in Addis's defence, telling H. O. C. Jones (the London Manager of the HSBC) that 'if Addis goes, he 'Revelstoke' goes too'.[41] In addition to the cable sent to Hong Kong by the London Committee, Revelstoke wrote a personal note to Grayburn, observing that:

Sir Charles Addis's position in the City of London is unique. Both in business and official circles he has established, throughout a long period of active work, contacts of a delicate nature which must be of the utmost value to the Bank. The nature of the tie which unites him to the members of the London Committee is one of great strength and intimacy.

Revelstoke added that

we should, in the business interests of the Bank, view with disfavour and anxiety any sudden relinquishment on his part of the other posts which, as the Bank's representative, he has filled with such conspicuous ability.

Revelstoke asked that:

your Board will see their way to defer definite action until such time as your presence in London has made it possible to discuss this matter in the way which, in our opinion, it deserves.[42]

Despite this forceful protest, when the Directors of the HSBC met in November they refused either to be intimidated or influenced by the appeals from London. Instead, they resolved that their decision would stand, adding that henceforth 'no one should be advertised as Chairman of the London Committee but that the London Manager should take the chair at all meetings, and be in a position to counsel the Committee when he wished to do so'. Furthermore, they resolved 'that the Bank's representative on the Board of the B&C Corporation should be the London Manager in place of Sir Charles Addis'.[43]

However, Grayburn did write Addis a personal letter of apology, asking him to say on as Manager of the British Group of the Consortium and explaining that the Bank could not afford 'to pay you the extravagant amount we have been paying the last 11 years while earnings via the Consortium have been practially nil'. He continued that 'no discourtesy was intended in the slightest degree'.[44] After receiving Grayburn's letter, Addis noted: 'A frank manly letter. If only he had written that first I should have understood.'[45] However, despite subsequent letters of apology from Grayburn for his 'clumsy treatment of a delicate issue', nothing altered the reality that by the end of March 1933, Addis had chaired his last meeting of the London Consultative Committee.[46] On 30 March Addis sadly noted: 'Tomorrow my salary drops from £5000 to £2000. Well, I am glad it is over.'[47]

At Addis's final meeting Charles Whigham (a partner of Morgan Grenfell) paid a very handsome tribute to Addis, saying that he had had the privilege of working with him since 1910, serving as a link between the British and the American groups of the China Consortium, and regretting that the Bank was to be deprived of his services 'while his physical and mental abilities are still unabated and apparently likely to be so for many years to come'. Whigham stated that Addis had 'done more than any other to uphold and enhance the prestige of this great institution not only in London but throughout the various countries to which the Bank's operations and Sir Charles's activities have extended'. He continued: 'as each task succeeded another the breadth of his vision and of his idealism in the services of humanity grew, transgressing the boundaries of nationality and aiming in its final stages at serving all the peoples of the world'.[48]

As the minutes of the Directors suggest, the Hong Kong leadership of the Bank undoubtedly resented the authority, prestige and independence which Addis enjoyed while nominally in their employ. Especially trying was the tendency of all and sundry to refer to Addis as the Chairman of the Bank![49]

But the issues were larger than personal vanity and really concerned Britain's future relations with Japan. Addis's signing of the 'Cecil letter' had met with disfavour with the Hong Kong management, which did not wish to antagonise Tokyo.[50] Then there was the question of the Consortium and Addis's insistence on the principle of open tender. Stabb wrote that the Bank 'would have preferred the Consortium to confine its activities to purely financial loans leaving industrial loans alone. It was too one-sided for the Bank to supply the money and for other countries to secure most of the orders for material under the system of open tender.'[51]

Thus is seems clear than that there were both personal jealousies and matters of policy involved in Addis's dismissal. No doubt the Directors in Hong Kong wished to demonstrate just who was in charge of their bank, but more importantly, they wished neither to antagonise Japan nor lose potential business because of open-tender stipulations. Far better to dissolve the Consortium, an institution which no one except Addis and the Americans seemed to like. However, in asserting their authority in the face of specific warnings from Lord Revelstoke, the HSBC Directors and Grayburn underestimated the importance of Addis's connections in the City and the advantages these connections had provided the HSBC over the previous thirty years. When Grayburn arrived in London that spring, he discovered just how significant Addis's authority was. In all likelihood, both the Foreign Office and the Hong Kong Directors expected Addis to retire quietly to the country home at Woodside (which he had recently purchased) and spend his last years in peace and contentment, as his age suggested he should do. Before long, however, they found that they needed Addis more than he needed them.

As we have seen, the British government was anxious to secure some business with the Chinese and frustrated by the Consortium's blocking of independent agreements. Early in 1933 a way to get around the problem was finally devised. The previous December, the Foreign Office began sounding Addis as to whether the 'Chinese could borrow elsewhere if the Consortium was unwilling to provide a loan'. Addis responded: 'Technically, yes, but bondholders for Hukuang railways would have prior claim to security.' Orde, who was apparently attempting to discern the possibility of such a protest, minuted that Addis was 'properly cautious'.[52]

In the spring (as preparations were being made for the World Economic Conference and Prime Minister MacDonald and Leith-Ross journeyed to Washington to appeal for cancellation of the war debts) the HSBC and the Foreign Office, with Addis's help, finally succeeded in devising a way to finance the Canton–Hankow railway. The new proposal came from Hubbard, who, with the support of the British legation, suggested that the HSBC join with the Bank of China to issue a sterling loan of £1 000 000, secured on the British Boxer Indemnity.[53] Addis explained to Orde that 'a Chinese loan, raised in China, in a foreign currency is a new departure which we shall watch with sympathetic interest'.[54] In his reply to Hubbard, Addis indicated that the 'Consortium Agreement does not relate to loans floated in China. I consider therefore that HSBC is free to act as you suggest without reference to other groups.'[55]

Thus, early in 1933, the HSBC took the initial steps in what would become a new British approach to China – cooperating with the Bank of China rather than with the Consortium Banks. In March *The Times* announced the decision to proceed with the completion of the Shiukwan–Changsha gap out of the British Boxer Indemnity Fund' as giving 'much satisfaction'. While the *Times* article acknowledged that actual material benefit was small, it stressed that the real significance of the contract was the evidence it provided of the cementing of Sino-British cooperation.[56] In July 1933, a contract was signed for the completion of the Canton–Hankow Railway.[57] But the greater question of how Britain would respond to Japanese claims in China had yet to be addressed.

T. V. SOONG'S MISSION, 1933

In the spring of 1933 China's Finance Minister T. V. Soong began an attempt to win Western support for China's resistance to Japanese aggression. Frustrated by Chiang K'ai-shek's policy of appeasement (as demonstrated by the signing in May 1933 of the Tangku Truce which established a demilitarised zone separating China and Manchuria) T. V. Soong travelled first to the United States to seek backing for an anti-Japanese campaign (a policy which Chiang K'ai-shek refused to undertake). Chiang preferred instead to fight the Chinese Communists who at this time were concentrated in Kiangsi province.[58] In a surprise move the Roosevelt administration agreed to provide Soong with a $50m credit, to be spent on wheat and cotton.[59] Needless to say, Soong's success in gaining American financing for China, free of Consortium control, did not improve Anglo-American relations, still strained from the failure to adopt a common policy regarding the Mukden crisis.[60] Morgans told Addis that they had not been informed about the loan.[61] Soong had appointed Kuhn Loeb as his US financial agent.

Thus when Soong arrived in London he encountered a certain degree of suspicion. On 8 June 1933 Addis recorded that 'Bob Kindersley called to inform me of negotiations of his firm [Lazard's] with T. V. Soong meant (I think) to get rid of the Consortium.'[62] Not surprisingly, Addis did not greet this news warmly. Officially Soong came to London to represent his government at the World Economic Conference. He told the plenary session that China would 'welcome Western capital and skill' but emphasised the importance of 'political and economic independence'.[63] Meeting with members of the Board of Trade, Soong explained his purpose quite frankly as seeking help in opposing Japan. He suggested that 'now was the time for the Chinese and the United Kingdom Governments to cooperate in dealing with Japanese competition'. He also affirmed his opposition to the Japanese proposal 'for the allocation of markets so as to avoid undue competition between Japanese and United Kingdom interests'.[64]

Commenting on Soong's remarks, Orde warned that 'if Chinese suspected that we had entered into a bargain with Japan to share the profits of the China trade, we fear that they would very likely try to boycott us both as they have boycotted the Consortium'. While he felt it was 'very desirable to secure mutual accommodation with the Japanese in regard to all foreign markets' Orde recognised that 'when we come to the Chinese market there are foreseeable political complications'.[65]

Orde next discussed Soong's visit with Addis. There were actually two distinct proposals. One was to form an international consultative committee to secure long-range credits for large industrial and railway projects in China. No doubt hoping to avoid Consortium opposition to these credits, Soong invited Addis and Lamont to serve as advisers on the committee which was to be chaired by the French financier, Jean Monnet.[66] The other proposal was for the Exports Credit Department to guarantee credits for the purchase of 600 000 spindles and river and coastal vessels. Foreign Office officials acknowledged that such an agreement would be 'as much a breach of the spirit of the Consortium Agreement as the American Wheat and Cotton loan', while one cynic observed: 'We could not even claim to be acting from humanitarian motives.'[67]

After discussing Soong's proposals with Orde, Addis met with Soong, Brand, Kindersley, Monnet and Dennys at Lazards.[68] Shortly thereafter he told the government officials that Soong's real objective was to 'break up the Consortium which the Chinese disliked', emphasising that 'Mr Soong and his colleagues were opposed to foreign control and were trying to play off one foreign country against another . . . The Consortium was "ready & anxious" to admit a Chinese group on terms of complete equality.'[69]

Prime Minister MacDonald expressed the rather naive hope that Addis would find the 'ways & means of backing up Mr Soong', but the Foreign Office did not pretend to agree.[70] Instead it urged Addis not to serve on Soong's Advisory Committee. Addis met Pratt on 14 July and Wellesley on 19 July. Of Wellesley he observed: 'it was like meeting a jelly fish'.[71] Despite Soong's pressure to announce the formation of an advisory committee, Addis wrote that he was 'still hanging back'. At first he agreed to join 'subject to the consent of the Government and the Consortium Groups'.[72] But after Addis and Lamont talked with various Japanese diplomats and bankers, as well as British officials, they decided not to cooperate with Soong.[73] On 26 July Addis reported to Kindersley that he would 'like to accept Soong's invitation' but could not do so 'at the expense of alienating his Japanese partners in the Consortium'.[74]

One of the most decisive influences on Addis may have been Governor Norman. Norman wrote to Addis on 8 July regarding the reports that Salter was going to China to advise the Finance Minister and warned him: 'You may need to take up an offensive × defensive [*sic*] position.'[75] Norman seems to have been determined to prevent the League of Nations from displacing British paramountcy in China. In July 1933 the League Council appointed a special committee on technical cooperation between the League and China.[76]

Soong's unsuccessful mission to London demonstrated several realities of Far Eastern politics in 1933. First, both Addis and the Foreign Office regarded Soong's resistance to Japanese control of Manchuria as futile, advising him 'to acquiesce tacitly in the Manchukuo regime'.[77]

Second, although Monnet and Salter proceeded to China, Soong had failed to secure British financial support for resistance to Japanese aggression in China. When the Finance Minister returned to China with little to show for his long absence, Chiang K'ai-shek compelled him to issue new domestic loan bonds to fund the continuing war against the Chinese Communists. When Soong resigned in protest, Chiang replaced him with his other brother-in-law, the more compliant H. H. Kung.[78] With the resumption of deficit financing in 1934, the Nanking government lost any hope for true independence. Before long it came, cap in hand, to the Consortium.

Third, Norman and Addis, in resisting Soong's proposals to work with Salter and Monnet, were showing their determination to preserve the predominant position of the HSBC in China. When Addis returned from his Canadian Banking Mission that autumn, he informed Orde of Norman's views. Norman had told Grayburn that summer that 'the Consortium should be kept going at all costs'. When Grayburn told the Governor that he thought 'it was dead and never could do any good owing to the intense dislike of the Chinese for it', that therefore it would be better 'to abandon it and let each country act on its own', Norman replied that such a course 'was impossible as England would not be in a position to lend money to any country outside the British Empire for a number of years yet'. Grayburn, who had described this interview in a long letter to Addis, appealed for further explanation, writing: 'I gather from him that Salter, a Frenchman, and another man were going out as advisers to Soong and their joint intention would be to break the Consortium which Norman said we must resist to the utmost and the burden of resistance would and must fall on the HSBC'.

Grayburn wrote to Addis that he could not 'see where our power of resistance come in if the authorities are definitely against authorising the issue of a new loan even suppose we could find security, which is doubtful'. Then the Chief Manager asked: 'How are we to act now?' Grayburn felt:

that the Consortium is no good to the HSBC except that, as Norman said, it brings us prestige. Of course I quite see that the Consortium has for some time done good work or shall we say prevented bad work, by stopping indiscriminate lending to China, but how long can that blocking system go on? I cannot help feeling that some link will give if the strain is continued too long.

He concluded by confessing that he was:

somewhat worried over the whole thing as I cannot imagine that Norman would have been so insistent unless there is a great deal in what he said, but it leaves me with the uneasy feeling that I have been advised of serious dangers surrounding the H&SBC without knowing exactly what they are and how to cope with them.

He asked Addis for his advice.[79]

This humble appeal must have filled Addis with a sense of sweet vengeance, coming from the man who had so abruptly dismissed him a year earlier. Before replying, Addis consulted Orde and A. Stevenson, the London representative of the Chinese Maritime Customs. Addis told Orde that the HSBC 'could not cope with China loans unaided' and also conceded that the Consortium would 'not aim at weakening exclusive rights in Manchukuo'.[80] To Grayburn, Addis replied: 'For various reasons, racial and geographical, it is probable that Japan will ultimately acquire a predominant position in China. That is a danger to British trade which it would be folly for us to underestimate or ignore.' He continued that Japan's real objective 'has always been by a variety of fiscal and other devices, to shut the door on foreign competition'. Nevertheless, Addis favoured cooperation rather than competition with Japan 'as far as that is possible'. Finally he admonished Grayburn that 'the Bank could afford to take a long view'.[81]

Shortly after this letter was written, the Japanese attacked Chahar in January 1934 and then issued the 'Amau Declaration' (in April) indicating Japan's intention to establish a protectorate over all China.[82] These events confirmed Britain's worst fears. But whether the government would accede to Japan's claims in East Asia remained to be seen.

CHINA AND THE SILVER CRISIS, 1934

As the Japanese became more threatening in China in 1934, the Nationalists and the British drew closer together. Salter and Monnet's negotiations in China had led to the formation of a syndicate between the B&C Corporation and the China Development Finance Corporation, created to float a CN$16m loan on the Shanghai market to rehabilitate the Shanghai–Hangchow–Ningpo Railway.[83] When Salter returned from China he met both Addis and Norman.[84] In all likelihood these meetings led to the plans for Chinese currency reform.[85] Monnet later told Lamont that 'a key British official had hinted that Chinese currency reform should be handled by the Consortium'.[86]

At the same time, American policy on silver led to a new crisis in China. The Silver Purchase Act (which Congress passed in June 1934) drove the world price of silver up and led to a drain on silver from China.[87] Initially, the British Treasury attempted to cooperate with Washington in dealing with the silver crisis. However, when

American Treasury Secretary Henry Morgenthau refused British overtures, Whitehall adopted a unilateral approach to the issue.[88] Following appeals from the HSBC and the Bank of China Norman 'persuaded' the Chancellor of the Exchequor to set up an inter-departmental committee to examine China's needs.[89]

However much he desired to preserve good relations with Japan, Addis opposed the abandonment of Britain's position in China. But he continued his attempts to continue friendships with both the Chinese and the Japanese, attending their receptions and entertaining each country's diplomats and banking representatives.[90] Addis had also begun a series of meetings with Viscount Kano, the Japanese Group Representative, regarding the future of the Consortium. At this time Kano reaffirmed his government's support for cooperation with Nanking, but he and Addis differed as to whether the cooperative policy could best be pursued through political or economic means.[91] Kano expressed concern about the plans of the Chinese Development Finance Corporation (organised by Monnet and T. V. Soong) for Chinese railways and Addis agreed to explore the topic further after talking to Monnet.[92]

China's movement towards sterling accelerated with the visit of Li Ming, a Director of the Bank of China, to London in June 1934.[93] After lunching with Li Ming at the HSBC, Addis described him as 'frank and intelligent'.[94] Two days later Addis took the Chinese banker to see Norman 'who showed much interest & friendliness'. In the afternoon Addis and Li Ming visited the Foreign Office meeting first Pratt and then Wellesley. Addis was struck with the difference between Norman's and Wellesley's reception of Li Ming, writing of Wellesley: 'He sat like a sphinx and showed neither interest nor curiosity. What a contrast to Norman!'[95] After meeting with Lamont to discuss the Far Eastern situation, Addis lunched with Li Ming again and attended a farewell luncheon for him at the Chinese Embassy. The B&C Corporation demonstrated its interest in the Chinese banker by hosting a luncheon for him.[96]

During the summer of 1934 fundamental differences emerged among British policy-makers concerning Britain's future policy in East Asia. The Foreign Office continued to favour support for China, while Chancellor of the Exchequer Neville Chamberlain (who feared the possibility of Japan and Germany coming together) suggested a direct approach to Japan with perhaps agreed areas of investment.[97] Sir Charles Seligman, a member of the Board of Trade's Export Credit's Guarantee Department, believed that the best policy was to accept Japan's role as trustee for China rather than risk war. Seligman went to Japan as part of a Federation of British Industries Mission.[98] Before leaving, Seligman met both Addis and Norman only to find that neither agreed with him.[99] Norman told Seligman frankly that his mission was political though 'dressed as industrial'.[100] During this same period, Addis also discussed Far Eastern policy with Evelyn Fitzgerald and Anthony Eden (then a junior in the Foreign Office).[101]

Governor Norman's increased involvement in China matters stemmed from several areas of concern. British bondholders appealed to the Governor for protection of their interests when loans defaulted.[102] To meet this complaint, a British bondholders' Committee had been created. Another point of concern related to exchange. Since Britain had gone off the gold standard in 1931, the Bank of England had the authority to veto foreign loans.[103] Then too, as we have seen, Norman's continuing effort to promote London as the world's financial centre meant that he favoured China linking its currency to sterling rather than the dollar (as the Kemmerer Commission had recommended). For all these reasons, Norman was keeping in close touch with the China situation in 1934.

Late in August, Addis met with Monnet and his assistant, David Drummond, to discuss their plans 'for rehabilitating Chinese railways'. Although Addis did not quite trust Monnet, describing him as 'a clever debater but perhaps just a little too adroit', he agreed to study their plan 'and see how far I can discuss it with him without reference to Consortium'.[104]

These developments explain why, when Sir Frederick Maze (the Inspector General) came to him in October with an ambitious proposal for a loan to China, Addis did not turn him down flat, even though he thought the sum of which Maze proposed was ridiculous. Afterwards Addis frankly described the interview to Norman remarking: 'Why we couldn't issue £15 000 000'. He continued: 'the bribe is British IG for duration of loan'.[105]

Despite the unrealistic size of the proposed loan, Addis was pleased that at last the Chinese Nationalists seemed reconciled to the necessity of dealing with the Consortium and accepting the terms demanded. Although he did not think a large loan was possible, he suggested to Grayburn that a Railway conversion loan might be arranged, and recommended 'passing over the collection of the Railway Revenues to the control of the Chinese Maritime Customs'.[106] Norman confirmed the Treasury's opposition to a loan to China at that time: 'I write to tell you of the agreement of the Treasury that a cold douche should be administered on every occasion to the Chinese project which you associated with the name of Sir Frederick Maze in our conversation on Friday last.' Norman felt that Addis would be relieved and emphasised that 'no other attitude is possible'.[107]

For the time being, Addis could do no more about China loans, since he entered the hospital for surgery to remove his gall bladder. Thus during the remainder of 1934 and early 1935, as new plans were being devised for linking the Chinese currency to sterling, Addis was forced to sit on the sidelines, a rare position for this elderly financier, now approaching his seventy-third year. In December Norman wrote: 'I should like your advice about China and Silver, which seems more and more perplexing the oftener I hear about it as a problem which may need a solution.'[108] And Pratt (while inquiring about Addis's health) wrote to Eba: 'We have been struggling with a silver crisis in China and his wise counsel was badly needed.'[109]

There is no doubt that with the advancing years, Addis had a sense that 'the sands are running out'.[110] But while the surgery put a final end to Addis's involvement with the government's monetary policy, before long he was back in the thick of China negotiations.

11 A New British Initiative in China, 1935–41

'We are on a very good wicket here and we ought to take full advantage of it.' — Knatchbull-Hugessen to Cadogan, 3 March 1937

The refusal of the Roosevelt administration in 1933–4 to assume any responsibility for the world's economic health, combined with its reluctance to cooperate with the British Treasury on silver policy in China, encouraged the British government to adopt a unilateral, forward policy in China, one which increasingly placed it in the role of China's defender against the Japanese. Norman's influence ensured that the Foreign Office and the Treasury cooperated with the HSBC. When the London Manager of the HSBC (O. J. Barnes) frankly confessed to being 'out of his depth' regarding matters of China loans and currency,[1] the Government turned once again to Addis, whose unrivalled expertise and experience with China loans and Chinese railways made him indispensable.

In 1935 the Leith-Ross Mission to China succeeded in arranging for currency reform and payment of defaulted railway loans. For a brief period British leaders believed that a new era of Anglo-Chinese cooperation was dawning. But the Japanese invasion of China proper in the autumn of 1937 destroyed this illusion. As the Chinese retreated Addis worked to achieve some kind of compromise between the two Asian Powers. Instead the Nationalist leadership turned to the Americans, who in 1938 finally granted the Kuomintang what they wanted – loans without supervision or control.

THE LEITH-ROSS MISSION, 1935–6

When Addis learned from Inspector General Maze in October 1934 that Chiang K'ai-shek's government was willing to deal with the Consortium, the way was cleared for the long-delayed Consortium loan. Although his operation forced Addis to retire from the scene temporarily, Norman and the Treasury began making plans for bringing China into the sterling area. The previous August, Phillips had observed: 'If other countries base their currencies in sterling the prestige of sterling is increased and trading & financial relations between those countries and the UK are strengthened.'[2]

In November 1934 Sir Alexander Cadogan (the British Minister in Peking) forwarded to the Foreign Office a plan by Pei Tsu-i (the Manager of the Bank of China in Shanghai) to control exchange by a credit in London from the HSBC and the Chartered Bank. Both Grayburn and A. S. Henchman (the Manager of the Shanghai branch of the HSBC) recommended the plan but the HSBC insisted on receiving diplomatic support.[3] In December 1934 Phillips (the Chairman of a special Treasury China Committee) began meeting representatives of the India Office, Foreign Office and the Bank of England to consider the problems and opportunities created by the silver crisis.[4]

At the same time Chinese Finance Minister H. H. Kung put T. V. Soong in charge of arrangements for the relief of China's financial situation. Soong had initially proposed a loan of £20m for the rehabilitation of China by the Consortium but was turned down because the proposal did not involve currency reform.[5]

In January 1935 the special China committee agreed to adopt the plan for Chinese currency reform proposed by the Bank of England's representative, R. N. Kershaw. It provided that the United States would be asked to buy silver which was to be surrendered for a new paper currency, and that an Order in Council would be obtained to ensure the cooperation of British banks.[6] The Chinese reasoned that the 'US Treasury are bound to support the price of silver and therefore to buy whatever silver is offered'.[7] The special committee's discussions and those taking place in China between various British banking and diplomatic representatives produced an agreement to establish a sterling exchange system for China.[8] Grayburn informed the Treasury that the Chinese Government had instructed Soong 'to carry through negotiations. A. S. Henchman holds signed authority from [the Ministry] of Finance to conduct negotiations with Soong with his full support'.[9] In March 1935 Kung announced the government take-over of the Bank of China and the Bank of Communications, and he dismissed its chief officers, Chang Kia-ngau and Li Ming.[10]

At the same time, the British Cabinet announced the appointment of a financial expert to be attached to the British legation in Shanghai and in June it appointed Leith-Ross to head a special mission to China.[11] Although the purposes of Leith-Ross's mission were never fully explained by the government, Professors Endicott and Trotter make clear that the Cabinet hoped Leith-Ross would be able both to reassure the Japanese (whom he visited first) of continued British friendship and at the same time bring the Chinese Nationalist government into closer economic relations with Great Britain through currency reform. Not a small challenge!

In terms of overall worldwide strategy Whitehall sought to stabilise the Far East in order to strengthen its position in Europe, where loomed the threat of war with Germany.[12] Norman described the international scene to Addis in April 1935, saying that when he was in Basle there was 'only one subject of conversation – war, war, when, where, how'. But Norman continued that he and Schacht believed it 'to be as remote as the millenium'. Norman described the United States, 'on whom we *all* depend for international health', as 'more autarchic than ever – decoyed in one direction by a strange President & buffeted in the other by a wicked Congress'.[13] A week later Norman responded enthusiastically to the news of Addis's recovery, saying: 'about a week ago Kershaw suddenly broke and stepped from being as effective as he was essential on to the shelf where he will stay, I fear, for some months'.[14]

Anticipating opposition from the Americans and Japanese, the Foreign Office invited the other Consortium Powers to send financial advisers to China. Norman (who was visiting Lamont at Bar Harbor in August 1935) asked him to send someone from the Consortium and someone from the State Department or Treasury, 'at once to China to stay & cooperate with FWLR' [Leith-Ross].[15] But the United States refused. Later, Norman told Lamont that he 'regretted US [government] failure to send financial expert to China'.[16]

American Secretary of the Treasury Morgenthau was both ignorant of China affairs and highly suspicious of the British. He therefore foolishly ignored the advice of the most experienced China expert in the State Department – Stanley Hornbeck – that Anglo-American cooperation in China was desirable.[17] Morgenthau left little doubt that rather than cooperate, he intended to displace the British in China.[18] In the autumn of 1935 when the Chinese asked the Treasury to buy 200 million ounces of silver, Morgenthau naively informed the President: 'This is our chance, if they are down low enough, to hook them up to the dollar instead of the pound sterling.'[19] While Morgenthau correctly perceived that China was 'the bone in the middle' between the United States, Japan and Britain, he over-estimated his ability to capture the prize. In matters of Chinese loans and currency reform, Addis, Norman and Leith-Ross were years ahead of Morgenthau. The Japanese were equally suspicious of British intentions, but, unlike the Americans, they were prepared to use force if necessary to preserve their interests.[20]

After Leith-Ross's appointment, Addis wrote suggesting that he read the report of the Economic Advisory Committee on China of 1930, claiming that its recommendations 'are as applicable today as on the day they were printed'.[21] Leith-Ross replied that he had read the report but did not think the Consortium agreement was adapted to present conditions, because the 'provision about open tender is a bar to loans in London'.[22] He reminded Addis that the proceeds of any foreign loans must be spent in the United Kingdom.

As we have seen, Addis and Leith-Ross had been arguing about open tender since 1929. Addis observed that without such a provision, 'China is deprived of the benefit, to which she is entitled, of access to the cheapest world market.' He stated that in practice, it was not possible to do this 'without bribing and corrupting the Chinese officials' and advised Leith-Ross as he had Grayburn: 'In China it is necessary to take the long view.'[23]

While Addis emphasised the moral aspects of the open tender obligation, Norman and his deputy, Professor Henry Clay, explained the realities of Chinese finance to Leigh-Ross. Initially Leith-Ross intended to end the influence of the HSBC over China loans, but he soon discovered that Norman was giving his full support to both the HSBC and the Consortium.[24] Clay explained that the Consortium must be continued because: 'over a long period London cannot, unaided, finance the capital development of China, and that the USA is the greatest potential reservoir of credit'. Therefore, he argued: 'if we terminate now the agreement by which the Americans undertake to share the market with us, we may be without the means of securing for ourselves a reasonable share of the business there in competition with them, if and when they resume foreign lending'.[25]

Norman defended the primacy of the HSBC in China finance, explaining that while a 'number of loans were issued in London before the old consortium came into existence in 1909, but the HSBC were then almost the only issuers and indeed they are responsible for practically all the important loans floated here at any time'. He promised Leith-Ross that once he had time to become oriented to China, he would 'broach the matter with the Hongkong Bank' if Leith-Ross wanted representation of the bondholders in London.[26] Thus Norman and Clay decisively intervened in favour of the Consortium and the HSBC.

By November a Chinese Bondholders Committee had been formed.[27] Norman's diary makes clear that he was consulting Addis regarding the China Consortium and the proposed Bondholders Committee.[28] Before Leith-Ross left England Addis assured him that he would not let his private views on open tender 'interfere with loyal efforts to give effect to HM Government's change of policy'.[29] Nevertheless, he continued his attempt to persuade the Treasury that such a policy would mar the Consortium relationship, unless the other Groups agreed to make an exception, as Addis thought might be possible.[30]

FINANCING THE KMT

Leith-Ross's conversations in Tokyo (where he stopped *en route* to China) had not encouraged the hope that the Japanese might cooperate with British proposals for Chinese currency reform.[31] Nevertheless, after he arrived in Shanghai, Leith-Ross and T. V. Soong proceeded to put into effect the stabilisation plan for Chinese currency which British and Chinese financiers had been working on over the previous year.[32] All silver was to be surrendered and exchanged for a paper currency, *fapi*; and a King's Regulation ordered British banks to cooperate with the Chinese Currency Decree of 4 November 1935.[33] The Treasury explained that because the Chinese had 'launched their currency reform scheme on their own responsibility', it was not possible 'to insist on reforms to the same extent as could have been done if our approval of a loan had been simultaneous with the currency reform scheme'.[34] However, Leith-Ross sent a telegram saying that the Chinese wanted to keep the agreement secret, noting that 'If we sponsor a sterling scheme without cooperation we affront Japan on her most sensitive spot (her position in North China) and the United States in their most sensitive spot (the Silver Policy).'[35] Obviously, Leith-Ross understood the risks they were taking.

With the currency crisis solved, at least for the moment, Leith-Ross could turn to the question of China's defaulted loans, hoping that a settlement of these would pave the way for new railway loans. Leith-Ross clearly aimed at an overall settlement with Chiang K'ai-shek's government, which would assure the continuation of British influence in China through a large reconstruction loan and continued British management of the Customs.[36]

In April 1936 Leith-Ross appealed from Peking to Addis to help to 'expedite' the settlement of the Tientsin–Pukow and Hukuang loans, indicating that China needed finance for new railway development and that Germany was 'showing both imagination and authority'.[37] Addis consulted the Morgan Grenfell partners (Charlie Whigham and Francis Rodd) about possible American protests.[38] Leith-Ross encouraged Addis 'to fight for a British engineer on Chinese railways', leading him to comment that Leith-Ross was 'as rabidly nationalist as ever!'[39] The Americans' demand that the American Hukuang railway bonds be given precedence over the Tietsin–Pukow bonds irritated Addis. He complained: 'the Americans as usual are making trouble'.[40] But Addis did not let American objections stand in his way. Nor did he fail to cooperate when the Foreign Office formally asked him to revoke the open tender resolution of the Consortium, in order to facilitate new railway loans to China.[41]

Perhaps because of Leith-Ross's deferral to Addis, the HSBC management began treating Addis more cordially. He noted in his diary in February: 'Barnes has today asked me to lunch whenever I am in town, a mark of friendship I value and of returning confidence as shown in a friendly note from Grayburn.'[42] Grayburn commented: 'I think 1935 will have to rank as one of the most amazing in the history of the Bank, certainly as far as Hongkong and Shanghai are concerned – I would not say that we came out unscathed but I can safely say that we found ample balm to cure any bruises we received.'[43]

Addis's recommendation to the bondholders proved very decisive. Practical businessman that he was, he recognised that 'the B&C will have to make enormous sacrifices of arrears or be faced with the alternative of – repudiation' and reasoned, 'Better half a loaf than no bread.'[44] Although Addis succeeded in persuading the British Bondholders Committee to accept the settlement recommended by Leith-Ross, he was not so fortunate in reconciling his American Consortium partners to the new developments.[45]

While Addis did not seem too concerned about the American objections he did warn Leith-Ross (in June 1936) of the power of Japan 'to thwart our endeavours'. He predicted: 'Unless we can come to terms with them I see no hope of our being able to carry out a constructive policy in China; the Japanese will foil us at every turn.'[46] When Leith-Ross returned to Japan in June he found the atmosphere 'more cordial' but did not gain any major concession on China except agreement to have a British Inspector General and a Japanese Deputy Inspector of the Chinese Customs.[47]

Meanwhile, recognising that 'it would be easier to market a large loan to China with Japanese cooperation', the FO asked Addis if he would explore the topic with Viscount Kano.[48] When Leith-Ross made the request Addis and Eba were on holiday in Scotland whence Addis replied:

> I am here on a sentimental quest – to revisit past scenes of delight; in particular, the cottage up the glen where I led my wife as a bride two and forty years ago. It is unchanged; and I might say the same, I believe, of my affection. This by the way.

Addis agreed to contact Kano and thanked Leith-Ross 'for paving the way to an interview with Kano by your word to the Japanese Ambassador'.[49]

Despite the new tensions in the Far East, Addis continued to enjoy good relations with Japanese representatives in London. In July Yoshida Shigeru (the new Japanese Ambassador to the Court of St James) had visited Woodside to discuss China policy.[50] When Kano and Addis met in November the Japanese banker told Addis that his Government 'including the Military Party, were satisfied that . . . the division into North and South, which had formerly been part of the Japanese policy with regard to China, was now recognised as impracticable'.[51] After Addis's memorandum was forwarded to Sir Hugh Knatchbull-Hugessen (the British Ambassador to China) the Ambassador replied that Suma Yakichiro (the Japanese Consul-General) felt that Addis's approach to the Yokahama Specie Bank was 'premature'. Pratt commented that he feared Suma's views better reflected the Japanese Government's attitude.[52]

Despite this pessimism, Foreign Secretary Anthony Eden urged the continuation of the Addis–Kano talks.[53] When Kano suggested that their talks be incorporated into Anglo-Japanese economic negotiations, Addis declined, saying that such talks would be 'beyond my competence as involving political considerations'. To Orde in the FO Addis commented that he suspected the Japanese of 'merely wanting to pump him as to British plans' and said that he 'was not inclined to indulge them'.[54] Both Addis and Leith-Ross believed that they should 'let the Japs take next step'.[55] After a visit to Yoshida Shigeru at the Japanese Embassy, Addis briefly noted: 'Words, words, words!'[56] Addis reported that Yoshida 'advocates independent action by England & Japan as the only two Powers who could effectively intervene in the reconstruction of China.[57]

The success of Leith-Ross's mission in stabilising the currency and reaching agreement on defaulted loans, coupled with internal political developments in China in 1936, at last convinced Whitehall and the City that the long-awaited British opportunity to establish predominant influence with the Nationalist government had arrived. The B&C Chairman's speech (which Addis wrote for his son-in-law, Dan Bernard) sounded a new optimism: 'The Tu-chuns are now held in check. The cloud of Communism has been broken up. Civil war has ceased throughout the length and breadth of China . . . We have staked our reputation on the word of China.'[58] Late in June Bernard hosted a dinner for the Chinese Ambassador (Quo Tai-chi) which Addis and his daughter Robina attended with the Cadogans, the Knatchbull-Hugessens and the Crowes.[59]

In order to understand the new enthusiasm concerning China which began to influence British policy in late 1936 and early 1937, one must recall the perspective of those years. To the investor, Leith-Ross's mission suggested that the old tried-and-true policies of the past might work again, namely, close cooperation between the British government and the HSBC; continuation of British management of the Chinese Maritime Customs through a British Inspector General, and foreign supervision of loan proceeds, through the appointment of British financial advisers, accountants and engineers.[60] Norman had outlined these terms to Leith-Ross before he left on his mission.[61] After spending almost a year in China, Leith-Ross returned convinced that the terms would be met. However, Leith-Ross warned that 'a reorganization of the whole railway system of China under the control of a Board of first-class foreign experts has not the sightest chance of the Chinese Government adopting it'.[62] Once the old railway debts had been settled, there were new revenues that could be tapped, as Leith-Ross pointed out: 'It should be borne in mind however, that Salt revenues produced at present annual revenues of 184 million dollars with actual foreign loan charges of only 11 millions, so that Salt is far less encumbered than Customs.'[63]

Of course it should be recognised that, in addition to the new cooperative attitude of the Nationalist officials, there were solid indications that the Chinese government's popular support had become more widespread by 1937. After Chiang K'ai-shek was kidnapped at Sian by Chinese Communist soldiers in December 1936, he agreed to form a united front with the Chinese Communists to oppose Japanese aggression.[64] One sinologist argues that with

Nanking's success in suppressing the revolt of Kwangtung and Kwangsi, 'China for the first time since 1916 appeared to be unified.'[65]

Thus the reason the Foreign Office was encouraging Addis to facilitate a new, large loan to Chiang K'ai-shek (despite the anticipated opposition of the other Consortium Groups) was that the Far Eastern experts thought that British opportunities in China were the best since the war. As Ashton-Gwatkin explained: 'owing to hatred of Japan, Canton is "pro-British" for the first time in a hundred years'. Therefore, he continued, 'there is an opportunity which we should not lightly miss'.[66] One scholar explains that Cantonese fears and objections that the Canton–Meishien would make Canton a 'way-station' were overcome in 1936 by the greater fear of Japan.[67] From Peking, Ambassador Knatchbull-Hugessen wrote a long, personal letter to his predecessor, Cadogan:

> The progress of our own political and commercial policy is slow, but if only we can get the Reserve Bank on its feet and make certain of a sound currency we may make some advance . . . We have got one or two big things in a fair way of settlement, the Canton Waterworks and the trolley bus business, and I hope we shall be able to get ahead with the Canton–Meihsien Railway.

With considerable enthusiasm, the Ambassador continued:

> We are on a very good wicket here and we ought to take full advantage of it. It is not just a question of goods. We are now being asked by the Chinese to supply advisers of various sorts, and I hope it will be possible to supply the best type of man.[68]

For investors, the most significant influence was the ledger sheet. Addis noted in March 1937: 'We have made so much money by sales of investments principally, that the distribution of profits is becoming embarrassing.'[69] Bernard told the B&C Corporation stockholders at the annual meeting that the past year had been 'the most useful and most hopeful for the industries and trade of China since the check due to the Great War'.[70] During the first four months of 1937, the Customs receipts showed a surplus of $50m over loan charges.[71]

With the Chinese and British ready to do business the next task was to gain the Consortium members' consent to waive their rights to equal shares of any agreement reached, since the Chinese refused to deal with the Japanese. While Addis proceeded to ask the other members for permission unilaterally to provide a loan to build the Canton–Meihsien railway (an extension of the Canton–Kowloon line) the Foreign Office recognised that the 'Addis approach was only a manoeuvre, whatever answer Addis received, the money would be lent somehow, provided security was accurate'.[72] Addis addressed a letter to the other Group representatives in London, asking them to waive their objections and assuring them that:

> the permission, if granted, would be confined to the special emergency which it is designed to meet, and would not in any event be cited as a precedent for any undertakings which may fall within the purview of the Consortium in the future.

Working closely with the Bank of England and the Treasury, Addis succeeded in arranging for the issuance of the Canton–Meishien railway loan in London which, in Addis's phrase, made China 'a member of the sterling area'.[73]

Between April and May 1937 the expectation that the Consortium would be dissolved gave way to plans for expanding its membership. Chinese Finance Minister Kung announced that he was interested in a large currency loan and would be ready to discuss terms when he visited London to attend the coronation of George VI.[74] Leith-Ross informed Addis that the currency loan was most desirable because it gave the British 'the means of securing (a) the reform of the central Bank (b) the maintenance of British influence in the Customs'.[75] However, while Leith-Ross was very eager to take advantage of Kung's visit to London to work out the details of the long-desired currency loan, he emphasised that they did not want the currency loan discussions 'to obstruct the proposals for a consolidated railway loan which Addis is putting forward'.[76]

After having succeeded in gaining the other Group Representatives' consent to issue unilaterally the Canton–Meihsien loan, Addis exclaimed: 'A burden which has been weighing on me for the last six months is lifted.'[77] Addis now faced the task of proposing a 'Consolidated railway loan'.[78] Late in May Addis wrote to the other Group Representatives, telling them that 'The Canton–Meihsien project (£2 700 000) has been carried a step further' and proposing additional extensions amounting to a £15 000 000 Consolidated Railway Loan.[79] Not surprisingly the other bankers were 'taken aback' at this new proposal, since Addis had earlier assured them that the Canton–Meihsien arrangement was to be a unique situation.[80] Nonetheless, Addis did not apologise but instead remarked: 'after having long suffered obloquy for upholding the Consortium I should now be reviled when I come to the assistance of those who have long been trying to pull it down. I do not repine.'[81] One can understand why both the Japanese and the Americans might have been suspicious of British intentions in China. Undaunted by the protests, Addis proceeded to move ahead with the negotiations with Kung.

What seems unmistakably clear from these complicated manoeuvres is the unanimity of purpose shared by Leith-Ross, Addis and Norman. After these three British financiers had met Kung, Leith-Ross predicted to Norman: 'I have the impression that Dr Kung will eventually accept our conditions as he has apparently set his heart on obtaining a Currency Loan, but the negotiations will take some time.'[82] Leith-Ross harboured no illusions, about Kung, describing him as 'a great nuisance', but he did not want to antagonise him but rather to convince him that 'his interest is to collaborate with us in getting things to work efficiently'.[83]

One cannot help but wonder: 'What about Japan?' How could British leaders expect the Japanese to accept passively this new wave of British loans to China? The answer seems to be that arrogant Treasury officials such as Leith-Ross and Sir Warren Fisher, trained in finance rather than diplomacy, still believed that an agreement could be reached with Tokyo, ignoring the contrary advice of their Foreign Office colleagues. While Leith-Ross and his assistant in Shanghai, Edmund Hall-Patch, recognised that Japan would be suspicious of a currency loan, they both believed that it was important enough to British interests to justify the risk.[84] Writing from Shanghai, Hall-Patch explained: 'a sterling loan would diminish Chinese reliance on America and delete undue American influence in China's currency affairs'. Although he recognised that 'this loan may lead to difficulties with Japanese' he felt that, 'provided that a formal acceptance of every condition is obtained it is perhaps justifiable as our contribution to consolidation of existing stability through establishment of a sound Central Bank and continuous foreign guidance in the Customs under British Inspector General.'[85]

From a post-Second-World-War perspective the above comments may seem fantastic, but one must remember that British officials and bankers had been cooperating with the Japanese since 1901 on similar ventures, so perhaps their optimism was not so unrealistic as it now appears.[86] What was stranger was Leith-Ross's belief that the Chinese would accept the kind of terms he demanded, since Chinese nationalists had consistently resisted such infringements on their sovereignty since the war. Moreover, both Pratt and Cadogan repeatedly warned Leith-Ross of the likelihood of such resistance. Cadogan advised:

It is impossible to ignore the lesson of the Reorganization Loan and the Nishihara loans which is briefly that any Chinese Government which attempts to retrieve a deteriorating position with foreign support and foreign money merely accelerates its own downfall, most of all if foreign tutelage is mixed up with it.

But the confident and impatient Leith-Ross dismissed Cadogan's warning as 'a long grouse which doesn't seem to amount to anything' and undeterred, ordered Waley in the Treasury to: 'get in touch with the Hongkong Bank and see if they are prepared to draw up a draft Loan Agreement in respect of the currency loan'. He claimed: 'Kung would very much like to have such an Agreement' and predicted: 'I think he is in a mood to be accommodating.' Leith-Ross acknowledged that 'the agreement might have to leave open not only the price and time of issue but also the details as to security'.[87] At this juncture, Barnes 'had a nervous collapse' and Addis once again stepped into the breach, writing out terms for both the Canton–Meihsien railway loan and the currency loan.[88]

Japan's full-scale invasion of China, which began with the Marco Polo bridge incident (in July 1937) ultimately made all the negotiations pointless and punctured British illusions. The market soon demonstrated that loans could not be floated for a government threatened with extinction. By the middle of August, Addis commented: 'This awful Sino-Japanese fighting in Shanghai has brought business to a standstill. Nothing to do in the City.' By 7 September he observed that 'Depression in City amounts to stagnation. All securities (Eastern) heavily marked down.'[89] Faced with the probable defeat of Chiang K'ai-shek's government, the question in London was, what to do next?

APPEASEMENT OR WAR? 1938–41

Early in 1938 Dan Bernard told his father-in-law that Tony Keswick of Jardine Matheson saw 'no future for the JM Co. in China' and talked of 'gradual liquidation of the firm'.[90] Leith-Ross wrote to Hall-Patch that he anticipated a 'possible complete defeat of China,' and felt that 'there is a lot to be said for trying to negotiate a settlement, provided that this is on the basis of the maintenance of China's integrity and sovereignty; and then use any credit which China can have to reconstruct after the war'.[91] Addis clearly was thinking along the same lines. In November 1937 he proposed the revival of the

Bankers' Committee, which in 1912 had taken control of the Maritime Customs receipts after the Republican Revolution. However this time the Americans refused to participate.[92] When the Bank of China withdrew from Shanghai (in October 1937) to avoid the Japanese take over of that city, Maze arranged for the deposit of all Customs Revenues (save those of Tientsin and Chinwantao) in the HSBC.[93]

Unlike the Treasury, the Foreign Office sought ways to help the Chinese to resist the Japanese invasion and lashed out at the HSBC for its apparent lack of sympathy at the Chinese plight. Cadogan wrote an angry letter to Leith-Ross, enclosing a letter from Barnes to the Foreign Office, which he felt provided 'further confirmation of the rumour that the Hongkong and Shanghai Bank had made up its mind that it must work in with the Japanese'. Cadogan felt that since the Consortium Group 'enjoys the complete support of His Majesty's Government the question arises – whether Bank should be clued in'. Cadogan continued that he was disturbed that Addis 'speaking for the Consortium group, adopts a policy which in effect amounts to putting financial pressure upon the Chinese Government with a view to forcing them to abandon resistance, cease hostilities and seek a compromise with Japan'. He said 'this is directly contrary to the policy of HMG which aims at giving China every possible encouragement and support'. The Permanent Under-Secretary of State concluded this frank and emotional letter with the suggestion that the HSBC be influenced by the Bank of England and the Treasury.[94]

While Cadogan's sympathies for the Chinese are clear, it is not certain that the government agreed with him. Leith-Ross had already contracted the Bank of England, saying that a 'sell-out was opposed', only to be told that the HSBC's policy was 'their own affair' and that it was not possible to take any useful action in London. Instead the Bank of England suggested that HM Ambassador in Shanghai was 'the proper person to drop a hint in the desired quarter'.[95] When the new Ambassador to China (Sir A. Clark-Kerr) consulted Grayburn, the Chief Manager denied that he was pro-Japanese and indicated that he was willing to help China, but insisted on a guaranteed loan.[96] Privately Leith-Ross recognised the justification for the HSBC's requiring a government guarantee, observing that 'The security offered by the Chinese Gov[ernment] is sound enough *provided China survives the war* but some guarantee might be wanted in case this condition were not fulfilled.'[97] Since such a guarantee would require parliamentary approval and thus involve publicity, the government was reluctant to take such action, anticipating that Japan 'would react with fury against Great Britain'.[98] Given the continuing deterioration of the European political situation in 1938, Government leaders were understandably reluctant to antagonise the Japanese.

As all the coastal cities of China fell to the Japanese in the autumn of 1938 and the Nationalist government retreated to Chungking, the British government continued to resist pressure for a loan to China.[99] Addis was more convinced than ever that the Powers should mediate the dispute.[100] In November 1938 Addis had lunch with Ambassador Shigemitsu Mamoru to discuss the Chinese situation. Addis suggested that a public announcement by Japan 'that there was no intention on the part of Japan of interfering in the Administration of the Customs might . . . allay public anxiety'.[101] In a speech for the Chinese Relief Fund, Addis predicted that the policy of neutrality 'should greatly strengthen the hands of our Government, when the time comes, as come it will, perhaps sooner than we expect, to mediate an honourable peace between the two great nations of the Orient'.[102]

Disappointed with London, the Chinese sought support in Washington where, despite the determined opposition of Secretary of State Cordell Hull, Morgenthau succeeded in persuading President Roosevelt to give aid to the Nationalists if they would continue to resist Japan. In a highly revealing dispatch, one of the Chinese negotiators in Washington informed Kung that the $25m the Americans granted was:

> only the beginning . . . Further large sums can be expected . . . this is a political loan . . . America has definitely thrown in her lot and cannot withdraw. We will have two years [of a] sympathetic Washington administration, possible six. Our political outlook is now brighter.[103]

In other words, the Chinese Nationalist government had at last obtained its objective – loans with no strings attached. Only after the Americans had taken such decisive action did the Chancellor of the Exchequer finally agree (in March 1939) to provide a guaranteed loan to China.[104] By this time, with war in Europe now almost a certainty, Whitehall had become resigned to letting the Americans lead in China.[105] In a memo on 'The Future of the British & Chinese Corporation Ltd.', Pratt (who had become Chairman of the B&C Corporation in 1939 after his retirement from the FO) predicted that the influence of the Americans in China would have an adverse influence on the Corporation's interests.[106]

Addis's final effort on behalf of the Chungking government was to arrange a loan for the Burma–Szechuan Railway.[107] A syndicate of French banks, known as the Groupe Unie des Banques Francaises, the B&C Corporation and the China Development Finance Corporation reached agreement in November 1938 to cooperate in building this line.[108] Showing signs of a guilty conscience, Addis informed the Morgan Grenfell partners ahead of time about the agreement, explaining that he 'wanted the American Group to hear from me before they hear it from China'.[109] Perhaps as a result of this announcement, Thomas Lamont gave notice in December 1938 of the American Group's intention to withdraw from the Consortium.[110]

Once again Addis moved quickly to prevent the Consortium's dissolution by persuading Norman that the Bank should pay the Americans' Consortium fee to the HSBC.[111] In doing so, he preserved the appearance of cooperation a little longer. But the shell of the Consortium could no longer hide the strife occurring among its members. Soon the former partners' troops would be slaughtering each other.

Conclusion

'there is nothing more helpful in the life of a great man than his weakness.' — Addis, 1896

FINAL YEARS

Upon reaching his late seventies Addis at last found time for the interests he most enjoyed – music, literature, nature and, especially, family gatherings at Woodside. Apparently experiencing little reduction of his critical faculties, he continued his wide range of readings. In June 1936 these included Fisher's third volume of the *History of Europe*, Kellerman's *Lied der Freindshaft*, Bentham's *Principles of Morals* and Charles Morgan's *Sparkenbroke*. On the latter he commented: 'It leaves a bad taste in my mouth. For all his cleverness and his poetic sense, it is a corrupt book, a glorification of the senses, a cowardly shrinking from the truth, that the wages of sin is death.'[1] A few years earlier, after reading a biography of Bismarck, Addis had commented: 'I want to see a man at his best. Landing is always poking in to the dark places where jealousy and envy lurk. Bismarck is too big for him.'[2] After seeing Ibsen's play, *A Doll's House*, Addis commented: 'It is an impressive play, uncompromising, unsparing in laying bare human nature as seen in a marriage based on union instead of communion.'[3] Comments such as these suggest that Addis remained sensitive to the complexities of human relationships and took a generous attitude toward human frailities.

It is clear that Addis remained idealistic to the end of his life and that he was unashamed of showing emotion – even of shedding tears when moved – whether at a play, concert or in church.[4] In 1939 Addis told the prizewinners at the Technical Institute, Tunbridge Wells: 'there is no force in the world to compare with the power of an ideal in directing and controlling the destiny of man. Without ideals we will never get anywhere.'[5] In giving the toast 'The Immortal Memory' at the Burns Dinner in 1940 in Tunbridge Wells, Addis emphasised that the worth of a man's life should be 'reckoned by what he has done for others'.[6]

Addis's marital happiness was the source of his inner contentment and peace in the midst of great stress. The letters to Eba (which

Addis continued to write every day when they were apart) reveal the depth of their marital love and give evidence that their relationship was indeed one of communion. When Addis and his wife returned to Scotland in 1936, he gave an indication of this marital joy in his comment: 'Another grand day. White clouds on the wing – like our hearts!'[7] He and Eba continued their practice of reading aloud together before dinner, finishing *War and Peace* in September 1937 and beginning Disraeli's *Coningsby*. As the year came to a close, he still found it possible to write: 'Sunshine & shadow on my path on which the shadows are lengthening. The best is yet to be!'[8] The elderly couple celebrated their golden (fiftieth) wedding anniversary in June 1944, just as the Allies were launching the Normandy invasion.[9]

The diary entries reveal the 'inner Addis' as a humble man, one who did not crave the limelight or public acclaim. No matter how busy, Addis tried to return home each afternoon for tea with his family, to hear about the children's various activities and problems, which were then duly listed in the diary. After becoming a grandfather (in 1926) Addis took great delight in the presence of ever-growing numbers of grandchildren at Woodside. After walking up the lane with some small children, Addis quoted: 'My heart for better lore would seldom yearn could I but teach the hundredth part of what from thee I learn.'[10] He had turned down the suggestion of a peerage in 1923 and when Revelstoke consulted him in November 1923 concerning the Governorship of the Bank of England, Addis replied that he thought he could 'serve the Bank better as I am'.[11]

Occasional comments in his diary indicate his impatience with pride, pretence and arrogance, especially that displayed by the young Foreign Office and Treasury clerks, fresh from Oxford or Cambridge. Addis described one of the young members of the Montagu Mission as 'a typical Cambridge young man who has been in Treasury, full of pose and conceit and cynicism, clever and stimulating'.[12] In all likelihood Addis was especially sensitive to such assumptions of superiority, since he himself had not enjoyed the privilege of a University education.

Yet to the 'juniors' at the HSBC, Addis appeared to display that same arrogance which he despised in others. One famous story about Addis, frequently recalled by retired employees of the HSBC recounts an incident at the HSBC Bank when Addis was waiting for the elevator. When it arrived with several young women employees inside, they were told to leave, while Addis, in top hat and tails, rode up in solitary splendour to his office.[13] Such a story (as well as the fact that it became a legend) not only demonstrates how regal Addis appeared to younger members of the staff, but also suggests the degree to which customs had changed from the late nineteenth century, when such an event would not have attracted attention, let alone produced sufficient astonishment to cause the story to be retold over the next few decades.

Among the greatest pleasures of the final years were the visits to old friends. While Addis gradually regained his former intellectual curiosity and keenness, sadly, such was not the case with his life-long friend, Col. Mills, who visited Woodside in June 1936. Addis found Mills 'much aged' with his 'memory going' but still 'a dear fellow'.[14] That summer Addis also resumed with great pleasure the monthly lunches at the Bank of England, where he enjoyed talking with many of his former associates – 'Niemeyer, whom I love, Siepmann and Gladstone'.[15] In November 1937 Addis noted that Kindersley had discussed the question of Norman's successor with him. Addis thought Niemeyer was 'the best man obtainable but Kindersley is strongly against on account of his German origin'.[16] Delighted at the welcome he received at the Bank of England lunches, Addis exclaimed: 'How good they all are to an old buffer like me!'[17]

Addis was still frequently asked to give public speeches, both to local groups in Tunbridge Wells and to more influential assemblages. He outlined his political philosophy in an address to the Rotary Club of Tunbridge Wells, choosing its motto for his topic – 'Service Above Self'. He told the members that while he sympathised with the aims and aspirations of socialism, especially 'a more equitable distribution of the national income', he doubted that a socialist system could 'deliver the goods'. Instead, he agreed with Adam Smith that self-interest 'is the mainspring of economic activity'.[18]

Early in 1937 Addis spoke as the guest of honour at a luncheon of the American Club in Paris where he commented on the recently concluded Tripartite Agreement which stabilised the exchange value of the currencies of the United States, Great Britain and France.[19] He surveyed the economic changes since 1931, conceding that 'The old order *has* changed. We are entering on a new world to which we must learn to accommodate our old notions if we are to master and not be mastered by the new conditions.' Addis argued that despite the changes, 'the economic man of today . . . does not appear to differ materially from his fellow-men before the War'. He warned that 'salvation is not to be found in political machinery' and stated his belief that permanent financial stability required that currency be based on gold.[20] In conclusion he called for a *'via media* along which Capitalism and Socialism might travel together without jostling each other into the gutter'.[21] Addis affirmed his own political priorities when he gave a tribute to his long-time friend and colleague, Sir Josiah Stamp, upon Stamp's introduction to the House of Lords. Addis praised Stamp for putting the 'interests of his own country first, but not without due regard for the rights of other countries'.[22]

As one reads Addis's comments as he approached 80 years of age, one is struck by their similarity to the views he had expounded with such fervour fifty years earlier. In other words, despite the enormous success and wide experience which Addis had achieved, his basic beliefs, values and goals remained very similar to those of his youth. This continuity accounts both for the remarkable integrity and strength of the man and for the esteem which he enjoyed. The Calvinist heritage, combined with the practical experience in East Asia, had endowed him with faith and self-confidence which remained unshaken through war and economic crisis. His wide experience in the business world and with government officials freed him from illusions as to how the individual and the system functioned.

Addis continued to believe in a rational and ordered universe; to expect that Britain's troubles were temporary and would ultimately right themselves. Perhaps it is in this respect that Addis most clearly belonged to the Victorian era – his faith prevented him from recognising that the old system of empire was doomed. Most of all, Addis sought to prevent another war. Despite all the signs to the contrary, he refused to accept that war could not be avoided. In an article published in the *Spectator*, entitled 'A Liberal Economy', Addis described himself as 'an impenitent believer in a liberal economy' and decried the growing powers of the state. He optimistically predicted that 'liberalism is passing through an eclipse from which it will surely emerge'.[23] Nonetheless, his concern deepened in the late 1930s. After visiting the German and Russian pavilions at the International Exposition in Paris, he wrote to Eba: 'This glorification of materialism is disquieting and makes peace seem farther off than ever.'[24]

By late 1937 one senses that Addis's faith had come under great strain. He described the international outlook as 'gloomy indeed. Mussolini and Hitler portents of evil and opposed to them – mediocrities.'[25] However, even after Hitler forced the union of Austria and Germany in the Anschluss in March 1938 and Prime

Minister Chamberlain at Munich agreed to a plebiscite in the Sudentenland of Czechoslovakia in September, Addis still clung to the hope that war could be avoided, applauding the policy of appeasement.[26] By April 1939 he reported 'great anxiety in the City; fears that Roosevelt's peace message will be rejected by Hitler & Mussolini & that war may be imminent. I am not convinced.'[27] This time however Addis's faith in the rationality of his fellow-man had underestimated the insanity which gripped Germany. By September England was at war. On 7 September 1939 the elderly banker wrote: 'At night I repeat the 91st Psalm. It is a great comfort. Eba's Psalm I call it. She says it saved her life when I left her mortally ill, at Hankow in 1896 . . . Truly the Lord has led us in a marvellous way. Surely He will not fail us now.'[28]

While Addis had hoped to avoid war he was not prepared to accept peace at any price. After Finland signed a treaty with Russia in 1940, he wrote: 'Finland has made peace with Russia on heavy terms. It is to me a national humiliation. For all our fine words what have we done to avert the fall of Manchuria, Abyssinia, Czecho-Slovakia, Poland, etc. And now Finland!'[29] Two months later, as German troops invaded France, he quoted Bernard Shaw's words: 'We are in a very tight corner, faced with surrender or dying in the last ditch', and with defiance remarked: 'I think we prefer to die in the last ditch.'[30]

Even after Britain declared war in September 1939 Addis continued to hope that the Chinese would reach some accommodation with Japan, speaking in favour of a negotiated agreement and maintaining his contacts with the Japanese Ambassador, Shigemitsu Mamoru, and the Consortium representative, Kano, almost until Pearl Harbor.[31] Despite the war Addis succeeded in keeping the Consortium from being abrogated.[32] His objective was clear – to assure that no matter what the outcome in East Asia, Britain would preserve her influence there. Thus Addis continued to help the HSBC, the B&C Corporation and the FO with arrangements for loans to China and continued to attend state functions for Chinese officials such as Ambassador Wellington Koo.[33] He also advised the Bank of England and the government on the new Commission to Chunking, which Niemeyer headed.[34]

There is no doubt that though he knew he should retire, Addis hated to relinquish his position on various Boards. He accepted reappointment for a third term as the Crown Member of the University Court, University of London, but when his old friend,

Lord Macmillan, turned down reappointment, Addis admitted that
Macmillan's decision was: 'a signal to me. I grow deafer & duller!
But I do not like to give in.'[35] He continued to enjoy the Royal
Economic Society meetings almost to the end of his life.[36]

After suffering a stroke in April 1943 Addis never fully regained
his strength. By 1944 his declining health made resignations from the
B&C Corporation, the P&O Board and the University Court, and
as Censor to the State Bank of Morocco, essential.[37] Though weak,
Addis remained clear in mind until his death in December 1945.[38]
He was buried at the small village church graveyard at Frant where
he had served as churchwarden.

AN ASSESSMENT

An assessment of a life and a career as long and eventful as that of
Addis's necessitates choices. One can evaluate the political effect –
on both national and international history, particularly in China and
on the Anglo-American relationship. In addition one should estimate
the career's economic impact, in terms of banking history and
monetary policy, considering such matters as Addis's contribution to
decision-making within the HSBC, the Bank of England and the
Bank for International Settlements, on such major questions as the
Consortium, debt-funding, the gold standard and reparations policy.
Nor should one overlook the influence which Addis exerted over
trade policy. On the more personal level the biographer should
acknowledge the influence which an individual exerts on those around
him, as friend, model, benefactor or opponent. Obviously any hope
for a complete assessment is unrealistic. My aim is more modest –
to explain Addis's success, suggest some of his most significant
accomplishments and briefly discuss the relationship between the
beliefs and practice – the extent to which Addis lived up to the values
and ideals which he preached.

Any attempt to explain Addis's remarkable rise from bank clerk
to Bank of England Director, lacking the usual qualifications of
wealth, University education, or family status, must acknowledge the
rare combination of intellectual and personality traits which Addis
possessed. Not the least of these was language ability. One former
associate (A. S. Henchman) recalled that Addis was 'the only man
in the Bank I can remember who could compose beautiful flowery
English'.[39] And the daughter of Sir Thomas Jackson described Addis

as 'quite the most scholarly of all the men I have met in the Bank'.[40]

Other outstanding characteristics which contributed to Addis's success were his ability to work with people, his broad-minded acceptance of diversity, his faith in the essential goodness of human nature, his ability to see the other person's point of view and to emphasise what united people rather than those things which divided them. For example, after reading Vansittart's *Black Record* about the German record (in February 1941) he commented: 'Brilliant invective but I could not help wondering whether a German equally gifted might not have made at least a plausible case against the English (in the plural) on many of the same grounds.'[41] These traits – impartiality, fairness, scepticism, rationality, and patience in reconciling opposing points of view – most account for Addis's success. In short, people trusted him – he inspired confidence.

Despite the fact that Addis tended toward certainty, he was not inflexible; when convinced he was wrong he demonstrated willingness to change, to admit mistakes. One instance which shows this flexibility concerned the question of the gold standard. As we have seen, Addis was a major advocate of Britain's return to the gold standard, but in 1929 he recognised his mistake, admitted that Britain had stabilised too high, changed his views and supported inflation and the creation of a new international currency. After having worked so hard for Anglo-American cooperation, he admitted its failure in 1933 and cooperated with the government's pursuit of a sterling strategy.

Other personality traits evident from the beginning were ambition, self-discipline, and determination. Addis possessed a clear sense of direction – he always knew what he wanted and had the initiative to pursue his objective. Furthermore he knew how to distinguish between ends and means, making it possible for him to compromise. One must conclude that for the most part this Scotsman deserves to be credited with his own success; he was a self-made man.

This much acknowledged, one should not overlook outside influence in his career. The contacts with people like Jackson, Cameron, Michie, Revelstoke and Norman were most important in determining his success. While the evidence is not conclusive, it seems likely that Revelstoke was responsible for Addis's election to the Court of the Bank of England and also for his appointment as British expert to the Reparations Conference in 1929. One charge which might be made, is that Addis should be understood simply as the agent of the large merchant bankers, such as the HSBC and Barings. To describe him thus would be simplistic; would contradict the evidence of a lifetime of fierce independence and controversy. Certainly Addis sought to promote the interests of the HSBC, he would not deny such an obvious fact. But in doing so, he sought to serve the larger interests of the nation and the world. Certainly he promoted interests such as free trade, which favoured concerns such as Barings. But he was not a man who could be bought; he followed his own star. Addis did not pursue power for selfish purposes, in the sense of fame or personal profit. When he could easily have devoted his time and ability to amassing great personal wealth, he chose instead to devote his skills to national and international interests.

Turning then to Addis's influence on events and people, it is clear that many individuals felt that Addis had greatly influenced their lives.[42] After Addis submitted his resignation to the Tuesday Club in July 1935, O. T. Falk (the original organiser) wrote: 'You probably don't appreciate how much I owe to you personally'. Falk recalled that 'at the original dinner . . . I said that I felt rather like an office boy who had invited his directors to dinner . . . From that day forward you have shown me unfailing kindness, and what has been all too necessary, I fear, toleration; toleration with an addition of wisdom which I shall never forget.'[43]

When Addis proposed a toast to Lord Stamp in 1938, Stamp responded by telling his audience that he had first known Addis 'as a sage economist and financier at economic and dining clubs such as the Tuesday Club'. He continued by saying that after he joined the Bank of England 'he was my model both in Court and in the Treasury Committee. His calm judgement and delightful powers of exposition in speech greatly impressed me . . . But it was our experiences in Paris . . . that made me understand and appreciate him most . . . he never failed in wisdom or courage'.[44]

This personal influence on others continued almost to the end of his life. Late in 1938, Layton wrote to Addis, thanking him for a letter and saying: 'it said what I wanted someone with your wisdom and understanding to say to me. And that is that in spite of one defeat after another of the things that are right and decent and just it has been worth while to fight on.'[45] It seems clear that Addis served as model and inspiration for many of his contemporaries, both at home and abroad.

After Addis's death Dr G. W. J. Bruins (who had worked with Addis at the BIS) wrote to Lady Addis saying that Sir Charles had impressed him 'by his sincerity, his good heart, his alertness, and as was necessary many times with Dr Schacht, his tenacity and the precise way he expressed his views. In this international milieu he was easily the outstanding figure whose leadership was accepted as a matter of course'. Dr Bruins continued that he would never forget Addis's speeches, especially 'the one he delivered at the farewell dinner, a most eloquent and almost passionate appeal to the large numbers of Germans present for international goodwill and peace'.[46] In surveying a career of over fifty years' duration, this theme – a passion for international goodwill and peace – well defines Addis's primary goal – the motivation which fuelled his efforts. That he did not achieve it, was not for want of effort or vision.

Addis's greatest strength was at the same time his most serious weakness – his self-confidence and certainty that he was right provided endurance, sustained him and enabled him to persevere while others fell by the wayside. But at the same time this sureness blinded him to such realities as the fact that American politics did not operate like the British system, that Morgans and the Federal Reserve Bank of New York could not control the government's financial policy, or that control over Chinese finance could no longer ensure stable government in China. Similarly, it allowed him to ignore the contradictions between advocating free trade while seeking special government treatment for the HSBC.

It is in the area of Anglo-American cooperation that Addis is most vulnerable to the charge of hypocrisy. For while preaching (and the verb is deliberate) its necessity, he unilaterally pursued policies in China aimed at preserving British interests and keeping the Americans out, utilising tactics which were bitterly resented in the United States and which undermined Foreign Office policy. One cannot call for a 'change in heart' or blame discord on 'misunderstanding and mistrust', when the real problem is that one's professed partner understands all too well that he is being short-changed. Addis's trip to China in 1921–2, and the arrangements he made there on his own authority, leave no doubt that he was capable of ignoring the wishes of both his American partners and the Foreign Office.

Similarly Addis's independent negotiations with H. H. Kung in 1937 for a Reorganisation Loan must have appeared to both Morgans and the US State Department (not to mention the French or the Japanese) as a betrayal of the Consortium principle of equal opportunity. After insisting on full cooperation in China loans since 1920, Addis proceeded to negotiate and sign secret agreements, informing his Consortium partners only after the fact.

Of course in his defence one can argue that the Far Eastern

situation had changed so radically by 1937 that the old rules no longer applied. One could point to the fact that prior to Japan's annexation of Manchuria, Addis had refused Whitehall's appeals for independent action in China. While there is some truth in this explanation, the whole history of the Consortium suggests that from the beginning, it was primarily a device to protect and perpetuate British predominance in China. The frank explanations which Addis wrote to Grayburn in 1934 and Norman and Clay gave Leith-Ross in 1935 as to why the Consortium must be continued, leave little doubt on this topic.[47] Thus to a degree Addis remained to the end the shrewd businessman whose authority Morrison and Bland had so bitterly resented in the early 1900s, keen to defend British interests and those of the HSBC from competition, both at home and abroad. His success in achieving this goal marks one of the major accomplishments of his career.

The issue of war debts provides another instance where Addis sacrificed personal principle for the larger interests of Empire. Although Austen Chamberlain, Blackett and Grigg all believed that it was both wiser and more honourable to fund the American debt and unilaterally forgive the debts which France, Italy and Russia owed Britain, Addis supported Norman and Lloyd George in refusing to pay the United States more than Britain received from her allies.

If free trade was only a mask for protection and cooperation was a cover-up for competition and exclusion, must we then conclude that Addis was a hypocrite?

I think it fairer to describe him as an English imperialist who (along with most of the British governing élite) believed (with some justification) that the British were the only rulers capable of assuring world stability. Addis must be understood and judged as a nineteenth-century Victorian statesman who had come to maturity during the era of Britain's greatness. In Hawtrey's phrase, he 'was the embodiment of the qualities of the great epoch into which he was born'.[48] The central theme of Addis's career was to defend the Empire. One can understand – even sympathise with – his desire to re-establish the system which he and his colleagues assumed was responsible for the remarkable peace and stability of the prewar era. It was inconceivable to them that Britain would not regain her former position as the financial centre of the world. After the First World War, he recognised the need for cooperation with the United States in international affairs, but, to quote Willard Straight again: 'The Englishman's notion of cooperation is that we provide the money and they do the management.' (Of course Addis was a Scotsman, but here the distinction did not matter.)

Quite naturally, the Americans resented this attitude and refused to 'play the game'. Thus the hoped-for postwar Anglo-American cooperation, which financial leaders in both countries knew to be essential for world peace, was never fully achieved. One must conclude that the blame for this failure can be equally shared: the British were not convinced that they must take second place; the Americans were not prepared to assume world leadership.[49] What Norman and Addis, Lamont and Strong understood only too well was the futility of war and revolution – that after any future slaughter, the bankers and diplomats would ultimately be the ones charged with restoring order since they alone knew how to make the system work.

One major criticism of Addis's (as well as Strong's, Lamont's and Norman's thinking) lay in their assumption that a few individuals can be permitted to control the world's monetary policy, virtually free from political control. Here it must be recognised that distrust of government's role in economic affairs was a prevailing assumption in both the United States and Great Britain prior to the Second World War. While the financiers' suspicion, distrust and derision of political leaders may have been well justified in many instances, the fact remains that governments which allow such fundamental powers to be exercised free of public control are ruled by élites, not by the electorate. While Addis repeatedly recognised the inevitable connection between finance and empire, he never devised a solution to the problem of assuring public control, no doubt because he did not see it in those terms. His proposals for the BIS, if implemented, might have provided a solution. Addis was typical of his time and his class in being an élitist who was confident that personal integrity would prevent abuse of public responsibilities.

One can admit that the British system had been remarkably successful in inculcating and achieving this notion of public service among its upper classes but such was not the case in the United States. The failure of Addis, Norman and British Treasury officials to recognise the difference between the two systems of government represented a major mistake in strategy, from which the only apparent beneficiary was the firm of J. P. Morgan & Co. Conflict of interest constitutes a major threat to the democratic process and cannot be ignored. Addis and Norman preferred informal controls, which operated effectively under their administration in Great Britain but were not suitable to the much larger and more complex American economic system.

Perhaps one of the most interesting and important aspects of Addis's life was his friendship with Montagu Norman. Had Addis not supported Norman in the 1920s, history could have been quite different. For a moment, let us speculate as to what might have been if Britain had *not* funded its debt in 1923 (as Addis opposed), or if (as Niemeyer argued) the Dawes Plan had *not* been put into effect, giving the Americans first claim on German resources and unleashing the frenzy of investments which led to the stock-market crash of 1929. Or if Britain had *not* returned to gold in 1925 under the arrangements for a 'cushion' supplied by Morgans (which Addis and Niemeyer both opposed). Or suppose that the British had decided to force the showdown on reparations and war debts with the Americans in 1927 instead of 1929, when Strong was still alive and Coolidge (not Hoover) in the White House and before the great bull market was underway. Or what if Addis had cooperated with the efforts to unseat Norman between 1926 and 1928, and had himself agreed to take the helm, and cooperated with the Treasury in lowering rates? Would such measures have prevented the disasters of the 1930s?

Certainly we must recognise that historical events are not inevitable, that particular decisions, individual personalities as well as chance play a large part. Conceivably, had Addis known in 1927 what he knew in 1929, he might have opposed Norman's re-election then, as he did in 1931 when it was too late. In any event, the responsibility of the historian is to discover who actually exercises authority and to explain how decisions were made. Such information is essential if government in service of the public interest is to be more than a myth, if future wars are to be avoided.

Addis believed that human progress must be made slowly, through education and compromise, not through violent change. More than most of his contemporaries, he took the long view of issues, sought to resolve disputes peaceably, practised and advised restraint and mediation, whether in discussing policy toward China or Germany. Had his advice on German reparations been taken in 1919, much of the postwar economic problems could have been avoided. Had it been ignored in China in 1927, Britain could have found herself at war with the Kuomintang. Similarly, we will never know what might have happened if Addis's proposals for League action in China in the early 1930s had been accepted by Whitehall and the State Department. There seems at least a possibility that a Pacific war might have been avoided.[50]

Addis's awareness of the interconnectedness of all areas of the world was probably his most distinctive insight and contribution to policy-making. His recognition that the major Powers must exercise international control over loans to weak states if peace is to be preserved has proved valid (despite the fact that the Consortium system also preserved British interests in China). Certainly world conflicts since Addis's death – Vietnam in the 1960s, Iran in the 1970s, Lebanon and Nicaragua in the 1980s – all demonstrate that violence and tragedy result when major Powers finance rival regimes in weak nations.

Above all, the Addis career reveals the way in which private international bankers influenced government and the decision-making process, chiefly as a result of their expertise and control of capital. Working together after the First World War, Addis, the Foreign Office and the Treasury, with the cooperation of Morgans, succeeded in blocking the State Department's initiative in China because they were able to utilize the resources of the Hongkong and Shanghai Bank and the revenues of the Chinese Maritime Customs. In contrast, the British effort to frustrate American financial expansion in Europe failed, because Britain was unable to control German or Austrian revenues. In Europe, Morgans cooperated with the State Department, not the Foreign Office. Thus this study suggests that the competition between large investment houses may be more fundamental to understanding history than is the political competition which historians' generally emphasise.

Addis and his colleagues recognised that no debtor nation could hope to remain a major Power and that since the United States was not only Britain's creditor but the World's, she must be persuaded to cooperate in international finance. But Norman and Addis's success in winning Strong's support for Central Bank cooperation was only temporary. One can understand why the British felt in 1931 that they alone had 'played the game'; why they so bitterly resented the American insistence on war debt collection. Addis and Norman knew that only Anglo-American cooperation could preserve world peace after the First World War. When that cooperation broke down, war was probably inevitable. Even though the British and Americans once again fought as allies, the source of the international instability between the war was these two Powers' failure to work out a new relationship reflecting their changed financial status.

One cannot but be struck by the similarities between the problems of the 1930s and those of today. Obviously Addis was way ahead of his time in advocating that the Bank for International Settlements create an international currency as the means of preventing the speculation which creates exchange instability. How far ahead is vividly demonstrated by the failure of the world to solve this problem fifty years later.[51] Although the need for international cooperation to prevent trade wars and to promote financial stability is universally recognised today, these goals still remain elusive, as the financial world reels in the face of the American Stock Market crash of October 1987 and the effects of the declining dollar.[52] Today, as in the interwar period, elected officials 'have only an imperfect understanding of the economics of trade and payments'.[53]

One of the purposes of studying history is to help us understand the significance of present events. The historian must always keep in mind that although the text ends, the process continues. The overall process at work in Addis's life (which has accelerated in the present) was the declining influence of the nation-state – the decreasing ability of national governments to control the decisions affecting their peoples' destiny. Future historians seeking to explain the sources of world conflict will have to focus on the struggles between giant conglomerates whose power and influence transcend national boundaries. As Americans in the late 1980s witness the yen supplanting the dollar, see their government forced by its creditors to balance its budget and raise taxes, and face a reduced standard of living, they are likely to have more sympathy for the British experience since 1919.[54]

Like most mortals, Addis sought to reconcile that which is human with that which is divine. On balance I would say he did rather well. Since he fought throughout his life for improved education and wider understanding as methods for achieving peaceful relations among the world's peoples, he surely would be pleased if his biography contributed to this essential if immensely difficult effort.

Appendix: The Speeches and Writings of Sir Charles Addis

In the late 1880s and early 1890s, Addis contributed articles to the *Chinese Times* (Tientsin) and the *North China Herald* and *North China Daily News* (Shanghai) which were unsigned. In addition he wrote a column called 'Peking Notes' in the *Chinese Times* and 'Notes by Quidnunc' in the *China Daily News*. However since other individuals contributed to these columns as well, the authorship is not always certain. Listed below, in chronological order, are those articles where the evidence of Addis's authorship is certain. Many of these can be found in the Addis scrapbook, /673 or elsewhere in the collection. Most are also listed in the *Catalogue of the Papers of Sir Charles Addis*.

'Genius', a speech at Burns Dinner, 22 April 1880.
'The Wedding Rice', *Chinese Times*, 4 June 1887.
'Exchange', ibid, 9 November 1889.
'New Railroads in China', ibid, 16 November 1889.
'Railways in China', *Contemporary Review*, May 1889.
'Notes by Quidnunc', *North China Daily News*, March–December 1890.
'Education in China', *China Review*, January 1890.
'The Opium Question, A Rejoinder', *Indian Evangelical Review*, October 1891.
'Corea under the Russians: The Issacher of the East', *United Services Magazine*, 15 June 1897.
Speech to students at St John's College, Shanghai, *St John's Echo*, March 1901.
'Individual Character as Political Force', SDCGK publication, August, September, October 1901.
'Memorandum on Chinese currency', prepared for the American Commissioners in Shanghai, 1902.
'The Relation of the Foreign Community to the Education of the Chinese', extracts published in the *Journal of the American Asiatic Association*, July 1902.
'The Daily Exchange Quotations', speech to Literary and Debating Society, Shanghai, 4 February 1903. Printed as a pamphlet by *North China Herald*.
Addis reply to a speech by A. J. Barry on 'Railway Development in China', *Journal of the Royal Society of Arts*, May 1909.
'Western Culture as a Means of Chinese Reform', speech to Stepney Readers' Union, 1911.
'Memorandum for Conference between the Right Hon. Walter Runciman and the Right Hon. Sir John Simon on British Wartime Trading with German Firms in China, 4 May 1915.

'A British Trade Bank', *Economic Journal*, 26 (December 1916).
'Vote of thanks' for President's address to the Institute of Bankers, *Journal* (December 1916).
Introduction to *Silver: Its History and Romance* by Benjamin White (August 1917).
'Bank Reserves and Depreciation' *Economic Journal*, 27 (September 1917).
'Problems of British Banking', *Edinburgh Review*, 228 (July 1918).
'Policy and Finance in China', *International Review* (February 1919).
'The Economics of a War Indemnity', *Journal of the Institute of Bankers* (1919) and *Nation*, 108 (12 April 1919).
'What Should Germany Pay', *International Review* (May 1919).
'European Policy and Finance in China', *Living Age*, 350 (28 June 1919).
'The Victory Loan', *Review of Reviews*, 60 (July 1919).
'British Overseas Banking', *International Review*, July 1919.
'Finance of China', *Edinburgh Review*, 230 (October 1919).
'The China Consortium', *Times*, 14 October 1920.
Review of *Foreign Financial Control in China* by T. W. Overlach, *Economic Journal*, XXX (1920) pp. 96–9.
Memorandum on the bank rate and inflation, 1920.
'The Chinese Republic and the International Consortium', speech to Professor Kemmerer's students at Princeton University, October 1920.
'Speech on post-war reconstruction' at Paish dinner, 1921.
'Two Fallacies and a Great Truth', speech to the London Missionary Society, 11 May 1921.
'The China Consortium', speech at the Reform Club, 20 May 1921.
'Reconstruction – a problem in prices', Oxford Economic Society, 1921.
'Inaugural Address of the President', 8 November 1921, *Journal of the Institute of Bankers*.
Speech at Hong Kong University on receiving an honorary degree, 1922.
'Changes in China in the past Twenty Year', *Bankers Magazine*, 104 (May 1922).
Obituary of Murray Stewart, *China Express*, 1922.
'Memorandum of the Formation of a Reserve in Connexion with the British Debt to the United States', 11 May 1923.
'Back to the Gold Standard', *Accountants' Magazine*, 28 (January 1924).
'Discussion on Monetary Reform', *Economic Journal*, 34 (June 1924).
Obituary of Stephen of the HSBC, *Times*, 1924.
'The Call of China', speech at St Katherine's Royal Chapel, 14 March 1926.
'Chinese Tariff Revision', *Times*, 26 November 1925.
'Comments on Hu Shih speech', *Journal of the Royal Institute of International Affairs*, 5 (9 November 1926).
'Toast to Sir Frederik Whyte', 23 February 1928.
Speech at China Society Dinner, 24 May 1928.
Speech at Dinner to Hu Han-min, 24 July 1928.
'Notes for [HSBC] Chairman's Speech, 1928–9.
Speech at Cambridge on the Bank for International Settlements, 28 November 1929.
'How International Bank Can Aid in World Finance', 3 April 1930, *Journal of the Institute of Bankers*, 51 (May 1930).

'Free Trade and World Trade', speech to Edinburgh Chamber of Commerce, 27 October 1930, *Bulletin Periodique of the Societe Belge d'Etudes at d'Expansion*.

'The Outlook for International Cooperation in Finance', speech to the New York Academy of Political Science, 14 November 1930, *Proceedings of the Academy of Political Science*, 14 (January 1931).

'Free Trade' speech given to the British Empire Chamber of Commerce in New York and printed in their *Monthly Journal* (November 1930).

Speech on current financial situation to the Bond Club, New York, *Coupon*, 1930.

'The Small Investor', Toast at National Savings Committee Dinner, 7 January 1931.

'The Young Plan and the World's Credit Structure', speech to League of Nations meeting, *Journal of the Institute of Bankers* (January 1931).

'Memorandum on Chinese Railways', 4 October 1932.

Comment on Schacht speech on 'Freedom of International Payments', 6 December 1932, Chatham House.

Introduction to Flandin Address on 'The Gold Standard', 7 June 1933, Chatham House.

Speech at Canada Club Dinner, 23 October 1933.

Obituary of Cecil Baring, Lord Revelstoke, *Banker*, 1934.

Speech on 'Canada and its Banks', made in Oxford and at a dinner for the Lombard Association of Foreign Banks, London, 1934, *Quarterly Review* (July 1934).

Introduction to *Credit and International Trade* by Barnard Ellinger (London; Macmillan, 1934).

Speech to London Missionary Society Conference, Newcastle, on Robert Morrison, 1934.

'Service above Self', Speech at Tunbridge Wells Rotary Club, 1936.

'The New Monetary Technique', speech to the American Club in Paris, *Quarterly Review*, 269 (July 1937).

'The Future of Gold', January 1938, *Daily Telegraph*, Financial Supplement.

'A Liberal Economy', *Spectator*, 160 (4 Febuary 1938).

Speech on Lord Stamp's elevation to the Peerage, *Abbey Road Monthly Review*, IX (August 1938).

'China and Japan – A Contrast', 31 October 1938, speech to the Rotarians, Tunbridge Wells and to the Lombard Association, 16 November 1938.

Speech to the prizewinners, Technical Institute, 19 January 1939, Tunbridge Wells.

Appeal on behalf of the British Fund for the Relief of Distress in China, 31 March 1939.

Toast to 'The Immortal Memory' at Tunbridge Wells Burns night dinner, 1940 and again in 1941.

Speech on 'Post-War Policies, Mercantile and Monetary' for the Tunbridge Wells Institute of Bankers, 11 March 1941.

Notes

Preface and Acknowledgements

1. 'Struggle for China: The Anglo-American Relationship, 1917–25', unpublished Ph.D. dissertation at the State University of New York, Buffalo, 1972.
2. Professor Clarence Davis told me about the Addis papers
3. C. P. Addis, 'Thomas Addis (1813–1899)', 1974; 'William Addis (1844–1917)', 1975; 'The Thorburns', 1978.
4. Priscilla Norman's *In the Way of Understanding*, describes her friendship with Miss Addis.
5. Margaret Harcourt Williams' *Catalogue of the Papers of Sir Charles Addis*, does not include a 1986 discovery of materials, mainly letters to Addis from Murray Stewart, Dudley Mills and Alexander Michie. See Rosemary Seton's Introduction to the *Catalogue*, p. xix.
6. 'The Young Charles S. Addis: Poet or Banker', in F. H. H. King (ed.) *Eastern Banking: Essays in the History of the Hongkong and Shanghai Banking Corporation.*

Introduction

1. *Bankers and Diplomats in China 1917–1925: The Anglo-American Relationship*, was finished in 1976 but not published until 1981.
2. A. Salter *et al.*, *The World's Economic Crisis*.
3. 21 October 1921, *DBFP*, 1st series, XIV, p. 450.
4. B. J. C. McKercher, *The Second Baldwin Government and the United States, 1924–1929.*
5. Richard Sayers, *The Bank of England*, p. 597.
6. B. J. C. McKercher (ed.) *Struggle for Supremacy.*
7. See the pioneering work of Carl Parrini, *Heir to Empire: United States Economic Diplomacy, 1916–1923* and the current writing of D. Cameron Watt, *Succeeding John Bull.*
8. For instance, Secretary of State Cordell Hull wrote that if the Anglo-American Trade Agreement of 1938 had been signed four years earlier, The Second World War might not have occurred. Cited in Watt, *Succeeding John Bull*, p. 65.
9. Alec Cairncross and Barry Eichengreen, *Sterling in Decline*, p. 23, define the 'sterling area' as made up of 'countries that endeavour to keep their currencies pegged to the pound, invoice the bulk of their trade in sterling, and maintain the largest portion of their foreign exchange reserves in the form of sterling balances held in London.'
10. For recent discussion of the relationship between investment bankers and their governments, see David McLean, 'International Banking and its Political Implications: The Hongkong and Shanghai Banking Corporation and the Imperial Bank of Persia, 1889–1914', in F. H. H.

King, *Eastern Banking*; Pat Thane, 'Financiers and the British State: The Case of Sir Ernest Cassel', *Business History*, XXVIII (1986) pp. 80–99; R. C. Michie, 'Options, Concessions, Syndicates, and the Provision of Venture Capital, 1880–1913', *Business History*, XXIII (1981) pp. 147–64.

PART I THE DEVELOPMENT OF A MAN AND HIS CAREER

1 The young Charles Addis, 1861–95

1. C. P. Addis, 'William Addis, 1844–1917' (1975).
2. C. P. Addis, 'Thomas Addis, 1818–1899' (1974); 'William Addis' (1975). See also *Annals of the Free Church of Scotland 1843–1900*. Kindly supplied by Olive Checkland.
3. Charles's brothers were William, George, Thomas, David, Robert. His sisters were Anne, Susan, Henrietta, Jane and Robina (Croppie). One sister (an earlier Robina), died in childhood.
4. Addis to Aunt Mansfield, 7 May 1886, speaks of Uncle Robert and Uncle John coming to China in 1847, Addis papers.
5. Addis to Susan, 4 September 1886, Addis papers. Robina earned the nickname 'Croppie' when she cut her hair with a pair of nail scissors (Miss Addis to author, August 1984).
6. Diary, September 1887–September 1889, Addis papers.
7. Addis's oldest brother, William, studied theology at Oxford; his brother George was a banker.
8. Diary, 1887–1889.
9. Addis to Miss Turnbull, 30 May 1889, Addis papers.
10. 18 March 1932, Addis papers.
11. Sydney and Olive Checkland, *Industry and Ethos: Scotland 1832–1914*.
12. Mills to mother, 1889, Addis papers, /200.
13. Addis to Susan, 18 July 1887, Addis papers.
14. C. P. Addis, 'William Addis'.
15. Diary, September 1887–September 1889, Addis papers.
16. 11 March 1880, Addis papers, /101.
17. Fleming to Addis, 17 November 1881, Addis papers, /130.
18. George Addis to Charles, 26 November 1880, Addis papers, /70; Addis to Manager, HSBC, January 1880, Addis papers.
19. Ronald Robinson and John Gallagher, 'The Imperialism of Free Trade', *Economic History Review*, 2nd series, VI (1953) pp. 1–15.
20. J. K. Fairbank and K. C. Liu (eds) CHC, II, Part II.
21. Maurice Collis, *Foreign Mud: The Opium Imbroglio at Canton and the Anglo-Chinese War*.
22. For the Chinese point of view, see Arthur Waley, *The Opium War through Chinese Eyes*.
23. Hsin-pao Chang, *Commissioner Lin and the Opium War*.
24. Michael Greenberg, *British Trade and the Opening of China 1800–1842*;

326 *Notes*

John K. Fairbank, *Trade and Diplomacy on the China Coast: The Opening of the Treaty Ports 1842–1854.*
25. Britten Dean, *China and Great Britain: The Diplomacy of Commercial Relations, 1860–1864.*
26. A. Michie, *The Englishman in China*, vol. II, p. 157.
27. Masataka Banno, *China and the West, 1858–1961: The Origins of the Tsungli Yamen*, chs. I and II.
28. Mary Wright, *The Last Stand of Chinese Conservatism: The T'ung-Chih Restoration, 1862–1974.*
29. K. C. Liu, 'Li Hung-chang in Chihli: The Emergence of a Policy, 1870–1875', in A. Feuerwerker, R. Murphey and Mary Wright (eds) *Approaches to Modern Chinese History*, pp. 68–104. For Hart, see S. F. Wright, *Hart and the Chinese Customs.*
30. Jonathan Spence, *To Change China: Western Advisers in China, 1620–1960*, pp. 94–5.
31. J. K. Fairbank, K. F. Bruner, E. M. Matheson (eds) *The IG in Peking: Letters of Robert Hart, Chinese Maritime Customs, 1868–1907*, 2 vols.
32. Michie, *The Englishman in China*, vol. II, p. 165.
33. D. McLean, 'Commerce, Finance and British Diplomatic Support in China, 1885–6', *Economic History Review*, 2nd series, XXVI (1973) pp. 464–77.
34. F. H. H. King, 'Establishing the Hongkong Bank: The Role of the Directors and their Managers', in F. H. H. King (ed.) *Eastern Banking: Essays in the History of the Hongkong and Shanghai Banking Corporation*, pp. 230–64.
35. Ibid, pp. 43–4.
36. Yen-P'ing Hao, *The Comprador in Nineteenth Century China: Bridge Between East and West*; C. T. Smith, 'Compradores of the Hongkong Bank', King (ed.) *Eastern Banking*, pp. 93–111.
37. Diary, 1887–1889, Addis papers.
38. Account of Miss Addis to author.
39. Diary, 24 January; 24 April; August–November 1881.
40. C. S. Addis, 'Peking in the Eighties, II', Addis papers. This was classical Chinese. Later the instruction would emphasise commercial Chinese.
41. Charles Davis to Addis, 3 October 1883, Addis papers, /103.
42. H. M. Thomsett to Addis, 16 May 1883, Addis papers, /103.
43. Jackson, who was knighted in 1889, served as Chief Manager three different times. See King (ed.) *Eastern Banking*.
44. Addis to father, 27 January 1886, Addis papers.
45. Addis to Grayburn, 8 November 1933, Addis papers.
46. Cameron was awarded the KCMG in 1900.
47. Addis to mother, 8 January 1886, Addis papers.
48. Quoted in Catherine King, 'The First Trip East – P&O via Suez', in King (ed.) *Eastern Banking*, pp. 225–6.
49. Addis to sister Annie, 23 January 1886.
50. Addis to mother, 22 November 1886, Addis papers.
51. Addis to sister Susan, 15 June 1886, Addis papers.
52. Addis to sister Etta, 1 March 1886, Addis papers. The pigtail or *queue*, had been imposed on the Chinese by the Manchus.

53. The portrait remains in the Addis study at Woodside.
54. Addis to Annie, 23 January 1886, Addis papers.
55. F. Barry Smith, 'Sexuality in Britain, 1800–1900: Some Suggested Revisions', in Martha Vicinus (ed.) *A Widening Sphere: Changing Roles of Victorian Women*, pp. 182–99.
56. 14 June 1883, Addis papers, /103.
57. Charles Davis to Addis, 28 November 1884, Addis papers, /104.
58. Fleming to Addis, 11 June 1885, Addis papers, /130.
59. See views on prostitutes and concubinage below.
60. Mills's father had been a Member of Parliament, 1875–80.
61. Addis to Susan, 15 March 1886, Addis papers.
62. 'The Curse of China', Mills's speech in Newcastle, 14 March 1889 reported in the *Chinese Times*, 25 May 1889.
63. Addis to Mills, 9 March 1887, Addis papers.
64. Mills to Addis, 5 December 1923, Addis papers.
65. Recollections of Miss Addis as told to author.
66. Mills to Addis, 22 December 1927, Addis papers, /216.
67. Addis could speak and understand some Chinese but it was Cantonese (used in Hong Kong), not the Mandarin dialect used in Peking.
68. Addis to father, 4 April 1886, Addis papers.
69. Addis to father, 11 May 1886, Addis papers.
70. Addis to Lockhart, 13 June 1886, Addis papers. Jordan served as Minister to Peking from 1906 to 1920.
71. K. C. Liu, 'Li Hung-chang in Chihli: The Emergence of a Policy, 1870–1875', in A. Feuerwerker, R. Murphey and Mary Wright (eds). *Approaches to Modern Chinese History*, pp. 68–104.
72. George Woodcock, *The British in the Far East*.
73. Addis to brother Tom, 4 July 1886, Addis papers.
74. Addis to father, 4 April 1886, Addis papers.
75. Edward Le Fevour, *Western Enterprise in Late Ch'ing China: A Selective Survey of Jardine, Matheson & Company's Operations, 1842–1895*, pp. 64–5.
76. Addis to Fleming, 22 May 1886, Addis papers.
77. Addis to Craig, 4 July 1886, Addis papers.
78. Addis to Leith, 31 May 1886, Addis papers. See also David King, 'China's First Public Loan: The Hongkong Bank and the Chinese Imperial Government "Foochow" Loan of 1874', in King (ed.) *Eastern Banking*, pp. 230–64.
79. Addis to Gershom Stewart, 23 June 1886, Addis papers.
80. Addis to Cameron, 16 June 1886. Nicholas R. O'Conor was the British Chargé d'Affaires of the legation in Peking. The *shroff*, a term coming from India, was the Chinese official who determined the value of coins. The *tael* was a unit of account. See Frank H. H. King, *Money and Monetary Policy in China*, pp. 70–81.
81. Addis to Tom, 4 July 1886, Addis papers.
82. Addis to Mills, 3 January 1892, Addis papers, /153. The Marquis Tseng had been Minister to Britain, 1879–85.
83. Addis to Tom, 4 July 1886, Addis papers.
84. Michie to Addis, 4 December 1886, Addis papers, /132.

85. 'Peking Notes', *Chinese Times*, December 1886.
86. Le Fevour, *Western Enterprise*, *passim*.
87. Addis to mother, 27 October 1887, Addis papers.
88. 'Peking Notes', *Chinese Times*, January, February, May, June, 1887, and *passim*.
89. Michie to Addis, 2, 20, 31 May 1887, Addis papers, /133.
90. Michie to Addis, 5, 22 June 1887, Addis papers, /133.
91. Addis to Aunt Mansfield, 25 November 1886, Addis papers.
92. Sundius to Addis, 1889, Addis papers, /111.
93. *Chinese Times*, 12 February 1887, p. 225.
94. Addis to J. L. Chalmers, 17 April 1887, Addis papers; 'Peking Notes', *Chinese Times*, 16 April 1887.
95. Michie to Addis, 12, 25, 26 June 1887, Addis papers, /133.
96. Addis to Mills, 28 June 1887, Addis papers.
97. *Chinese Times*, 25 June, 16, 30 July, 20 August 1887.
98. Addis to father, 4 October 1886, Addis papers.
99. Addis to George, 27 September 1886, Addis papers.
100. Addis to Etta, 20 September 1887, Addis papers.
101. Addis to Lockhart, 10 September 1887, Addis papers.
102. Lockhart to Addis, 27 December 1886, Addis papers, /131.
103. See three-page description of the fluctuations of the London Market quotations of the Mexican dollar which Addis wrote for Jordan, 15 December 1886, Addis papers.
104. Addis to sister-in-law, Elsie, 10 May 1887, Addis papers.
105. Charles Denby served as Minister to Peking for fourteen years. He wrote *China and her People: Being the Observations, Reminiscences, and Conclusions of an American Diplomat*. His two sons, Charles Jr., and Edwin, later held political appointments in the USA.
106. Addis to Etta, 24 December 1886.
107. Diary, 22 April 1888.
108. Miss Denby to Mr Addis, 9 September 1888, Addis papers, /108.
109. Michie to Addis, 5 April 1888, Addis papers, /134.
110. Michie to Addis, 19 April 1888, Addis papers, /134.
111. Addis to Mills, 2, 3 December 1888, Addis papers.
112. Ralph W. Huenemann, *The Dragon and the Iron Horse: The Economics of Railroads in China, 1876–1937*, p. 40.
113. Ibid, p. 43.
114. 'Railways in China', *Contemporary Review*, LV (1889) pp. 742–51.
115. Addis to sister-in-law Carnie, 17 May 1889, Addis papers.
116. Aglen joined the Customs in 1888.
117. Diary, June, July, August 1889. Michie, *The Englishman in China*, II, p. 154.
118. 'Exchange', *The Chinese Times*, 9 November 1889; 'New Railroads in China', *The Chinese Times*, 16 November 1889.
119. 'Exchange', *The Chinese Times*, 9 November 1889.
120. Ibid.
121. Michie to Addis, 3 March 1890, Addis papers, /136.
122. Michie to Addis, 17 February 1890, Addis papers, /136.
123. Addis to Tom, 26 September 1889, Addis papers.

124. Addis to Croppie, 27 October 1889, Addis papers.
125. Addis to Mills, 14 January 1890, Addis papers. For the SDCGK see Murray Rubenstein, 'Propagating the Democratic Gospel'.
126. Michie to Addis, 7 February 1891, Addis papers, /137.
127. C. S. Addis, 'On Educating the Chinese', manuscript in Addis papers, reported in *North China Daily News*, 16 May 1890.
128. Addis to Mills, 15 June 1890, Addis papers.
129. Addis to Mills, 20 April 1890, Addis papers.
130. Mills to Addis, 16 May 1891, Addis papers.
131. Russell & Co. made Addis an offer through his Uncle John. The other offer came from Vincent Smith. See Addis to George, 15 February 1890; Addis to Crop, 22 February 1890, Addis papers.
132. Addis to George, 15 February 1890, Addis papers.
133. Ibid.
134. Addis to Susan, 23 August 1890, Addis papers.
135. Addis to Mills, 20 February 1891 indicates that originally he had been appointed to Saigon but that was changed at the last minute. Addis papers.
136. Diary, 31 March, April 1891.
137. 10 May 1891, Addis papers.
138. Addis to Mills, 14 April 1891, Addis papers.
139. Addis to Croppie, 11 June 1891. Addis papers. The quotation is from Robert Browning, 'Pippa Passes'.
140. Addis to Mills, 6 July 1892, Addis papers, and Diary, 10 June 1892.
141. Addis often recounted the experience to his children (Miss Addis to author, August, 1984).
142. Addis to Croppie, 14 July 1893, Addis papers, /292.
143. Diary, 22 October to 3 November 1892.
144. Addis to Mills, 6 November 1892, Addis papers, /153.
145. Diary, 14 December 1892.
146. 'Leaves from a Young Man's Journal in Rangoon', 12 September 1893, Addis papers, /154.
147. Addis to Croppie, 14 July 1892, Addis papers.
148. Addis to Mills, 29 June 1893, Addis papers, /159.
149. Addis to Wallop, 13 July 1887, Addis papers.
150. 10 May 1891, Addis papers.
151. Addis to Eba, 10 March 1894, Addis papers.
152. Lockhart to Addis, 4 March 1888, Addis papers, /131.
153. Leith to Addis, 19 February 1893, Addis papers, /116.
154. Diary, 24 November–27 December 1893.
155. The Provost was similar to the Mayor of a village.
156. Diary, 15 January 1894. Eba's real name was Elizabeth.
157. Diary, 16 January 1894.
158. Diary, 14 February 1894.
159. Diary, 24–27 February 1894.
160. Addis to Eba, 7 March 1894, Addis papers.
161. Diary, 7, 16 March 1894; Addis to Miss Eba, 17 March 1894, Addis papers.
162. Diary, 11 April 1894.

163. Diary, 28 April 1894.
164. Addis to Mills, 24 September 1894, Addis papers.
165. Diary, 1 January 1895.
166. Diary, 31 December 1895.
167. Timothy Richards to Charles Addis, 30 November 1894. Timothy Richards was born in Wales and served in the Baptist Missionary Society, London. See *Forty-five Years in China: Reminiscences by Timothy Richard.*
168. Diary, 3, 10, 11 January, 8 February 1895.
169. Diary, 2 October 1895, Eba writing.
170. Addis to wife, 4 October 1895, Addis papers.
171. Diary, 9 March 1896, Eba writing.

2 Widening Horizons 1895–1904

1. The explanation for the differing response of Japan and China is a subject much discussed and still debated by Asian specialists.
2. The Treaty of Shimonoseki is in John van Antwerp MacMurray (ed.) *Treaties and Agreements with and concerning China, 1894–1919*, I, pp. 18–24.
3. Hosea Ballou Morse, *The International Relations of the Chinese Empire*, vol. III.
4. William Langer, *The Diplomacy of Imperialism*, I, p. 167, indicates that England controlled 65 per cent of Chinese foreign trade and 85 per cent of all imports and exports were carried in British ships. See also C. F. Remer, *Foreign Investments in China.*
5. C. J. Lowe, *The Reluctant Imperialists*, pp. 230–2; J. A. S. Grenville, *Lord Salisbury and Foreign Policy: The Close of the Nineteenth Century.*
6. Addis to father, 4 March 1895, Addis papers.
7. Addis to Mills, 20 July 1895, Addis papers. O'Connor was Minister to Peking, 1892–5.
8. Addis to Mills, 20 July 1895, Addis papers. See also David McLean, 'The Foreign Office and the First Chinese Indemnity Loan, 1895', *Historical Journal*, XVI, (1973) pp. 303–21.
9. Addis to father, 4 March 1895, Addis papers, /292.
10. Ibid.
11. Addis to Townsend, 15 May 1898, Addis papers.
12. Addis to Mills, 28 July 1895, Addis papers.
13. For an insightful discussion of late Victorian expansion see Ronald Robinson, John Gallagher and Alice Denny, *Africa and the Victorians: The Climax of Imperialism*, ch. 1.
14. D. C. M. Platt, *Finance, Trade and Politics in British Foreign Policy 1815–1914.*
15. For the relations between the HSBC and Germany, see D. J. S. King, 'The Hamburg Branch: The German Period, 1889–1920', in King (ed.) *Eastern Banking*, pp. 517–44.
16. Inscribing the bonds added to the creditworthiness of the bonds which could be exchanged for Bank of England Stock 'free of all expense'.

See 'Prospectus – Chinese Imperial Government 5 per cent Gold Loan of 1896', Bank of England.

17. 1 July 1896, Private letterbook, 1895–7, Addis papers. Addis wrote Murray Stewart, 9 September 1898 that it was a mistake to guarantee the loan. /227.

18. Quoted in David McLean, 'British Banking and Government in China: The Foreign Office and the Hongkong and Shanghai Bank 1895–1913', unpublished doctoral dissertation at Cambridge University, 1972.

19. Hart to Campbell, 8 March 1896, in Fairbank *et al.* (eds.) *The IG in Peking*, p. 1011.

20. *North China Herald*, 21 February 1896.

21. Addis to Mills, 30 March 1896, Addis papers.

22. *North China Herald*, 27 March 1896, p. 477.

23. Memorandum in Addis papers, undated but probably 1896.

24. Ross Terrill, *Flowers on an Iron Tree*, pp. 233–5.

25. Ibid, p. 245. For the missionary influence, see Edmund S. Wehrle, *Britain, China and the Antimissionary Riots 1891–1900*.

26. Diary, April 1896, Eba writing.

27. Eba to Addis, 18 August 1896, Addis papers, /286.

28. Addis to Mills, 29 July 1896, Addis papers.

29. Addis to Mills, 21 October 1896, Addis papers. John McLeavy Brown was the Chief Commissioner of Korean Customs, a subsidiary of the Chinese Customs, and Financial Adviser to the King of Korea. See Lo Hui-min (ed.) *The Correspondence of G. E. Morrison, I, 1895–1912*, p. 71, n. 2.

30. Addis to Gard'ner, 17 November 1896, Addis papers, /164.

31. Diary, 18 January 1897.

32. Diary, Eba writing, January 1897.

33. Addis asked Mills to submit the manuscript to 'Michie's, Blackwood, Grove's Contemporary or Macmillans'. (27 February 1897, Addis papers).

34. 'Korea Under the Russians', *United Services Magazine*, 1897, Addis papers.

35. Diary, 5 February 1897.

36. Diary, 8 June 1897.

37. Diary, Eba writing, 11, 23, 31 August 1897.

38. Addis to Mills, 10 February 1897, Addis papers.

39. Diary, 6 May 1897.

40. Diary, 27 February 1898. I assume these were Hong Kong dollars, which fluctuated but were generally equivalent to half a gold dollar. If not specified, dollar loans issued in China or Hong Kong are likely to be Hong Kong dollars, worth only half the gold or American dollar.

41. Diary, 9 February 1898.

42. Diary, April 1898.

43. Diary, May, July 1898.

44. McLean, 'British Banking and Government in China', p. 346.

45. Addis to Mills, September 1898, Addis papers.

46. For the 1898 attempt at reform, see Maribeth Cameron, *The Reform Movement in China, 1898–1912*.

47. Diary, 4, 7, October 1898.
48. Addis to Mills, 19 October 1898, Addis papers.
49. Diary, 8, 17, November 1899 and Addis to Mills, 14 February 1899, Addis papers. Beresford refers to Addis in *The Break-up of China*, p. 354.
50. Langer, *The Diplomacy of Imperialism*.
51. Huenemann, *The Dragon and the Iron Horse*, pp. 47–60.
52. Addis to Mills, 11 October 1898, Addis papers.
53. Huenemann, *The Dragon and the Iron Horse*, p. 57.
54. Addis to Mills, 14 February 1899, Addis papers.
55. A. L. Rosenbaum, 'The Manchurian Bridgehead, Anglo-Russian Rivalry and the Imperial Railways of North China, 1897–1902', *Modern Asian Studies* (1976) pp. 41–64.
56. Huenemann, *The Dragon and the Iron Horse*, p. 57.
57. Beresford to Morrison, 7 May 1901, in Lo Hui-min, (ed.) *Morrison*, pp. 161–2.
58. Minutes of Meetings held at New Court, St Swithin's Lane, London, 1, 2 September 1898, HSBC archives, Hong Kong.
59. Quoted in L. K. Young, *British Policy in China*, p. 55; Hicks-Beach to Salisbury, 27 December 1897, Salisbury papers.
60. Young, *British Policy in China*, pp. 51–63.
61. February 1898, quoted in Young, *British Policy in China*, p. 64.
62. Young, *British Policy in China*, p. 83.
63. C. S. Addis, 'How to Spend Money', 17 February 1896, in *North China Herald*, 6 March 1896, pp. 372–6.
64. Addis to M. Stewart, 9 January 1897, Addis papers.
65. Diary, 1 January 1899, Eba writing.
66. Eba to Addis, 11, 12 August 1896, Addis papers, /286.
67. Eba to Addis, 9 February 1897, Addis papers, /287.
68. Diary, 19 January 1899.
69. Addis to Mills, 22 October 1899, Addis papers, /167.
70. Addis to Mills, May 1900, Addis papers.
71. Addis to Mills, 10 May 1900, Addis papers, /168.
72. Diary, 9 July 1900.
73. Addis to Eba, 9 August 1900, Addis papers, /285.
74. Ibid.
75. Addis to Eba, 10 August 1900, Addis papers. The State Department records do not mention Addis but do refer to the dispute. See MacArthur to Adjutant General, 9 August 1900, Record Group 350, file 808/37.
76. Emily S. Rosenberg, 'Foundations of United States International Financial Power: Gold Standard Diplomacy, 1900–1905', *Business History Review*, vol. 59 (1985) pp. 169–202.
77. Addis to Mills, 23 November 1900, Addis papers, /168. James Bryce was the British Ambassador to the United States.
78. Addis to Mills, 23, 25 November 1900, Addis papers, /168.
79. Diary.
80. Diary, 19 November 1899.

81. Chester Tan, *The Boxer Catastrophe*; Victor Purcell, *The Boxer Uprising*.
82. HSBC archives, G1/2; Daniel H. Bays, *China Enters the Twentieth Century*, pp. 72–5.
83. The ability of the British to use Indian rather than English soldiers enabled the British people to escape paying the human costs of colonialism. However, the Boer War in South Africa led to anti-imperialism in Great Britain. See D. K. Fieldhouse, *Economics and Empire, 1830–1914*.
84. Addis to Mills, 20, 26 December 1900, Addis papers.
85. Addis to Mills, 21 February 1901. See also 'Leaves from a Diary', 20 December 1900, Addis papers, /67.
86. Addis to Mills, 11 December 1901, Addis papers.
87. 1 October 1901, Addis papers, /143. James Mackay later became the first Earl of Inchcape. See *DBB*, IV, pp. 27–31.
88. *North China Herald*, 19 February 1902, p. 338.
89. Addis to Mills, 13 August 1902, Addis papers.
90. Addis to Tom, 5 May 1902, Addis papers.
91. 19 December 1901, Addis papers, /232.
92. 3 February 1901, Addis papers, /232.
93. Addis to Murray Stewart, 2 May 1902, Addis papers.
94. Addis wrote to Mills: 'As usual my speech pleases nobody.' 27 December 1903, Addis papers.
95. 27 December 1903. Addis to Tom, 23 August 1903, Addis papers.
96. *North China Herald*, 17 December 1902.
97. Printed as a pamphlet by the *North China Herald*. The Cambridge professor of Political Economy, Alfred Marshall, emphasised ethics in his *Principles of Economics*, published in 1890.
98. 30 January 1902, Addis papers, /233. Stewart was becoming a close family friend and 'bachelor uncle' to the Addis children whom he visited in Shanghai that spring.
99. The Anglo-Chinese Commercial Treaty of 1902 provided for unification of the Chinese currency system by the Ch'ing. See Takeshi Hamashita, 'The International Financial Relations behind the 1911 Revolution'.
100. 21 July 1902, Addis papers, /233. Walter Bagehot was a well-known nineteenth-century banking historian. For Chinese currency negotiations, see Chapter 3. 'Addis Memorandum on Chinese Currency', 5 June 1902, Addis papers, /480.
101. Diary, 28 January 1904, Eba writing: 'He is much pleased & I am happy he is happy.' Again, though not specified, I assume these are Hong Kong dollars.
102. Addis to Smith, 13 July 1903, Addis papers.
103. Diary, 15 April 1904.

3 From Eastern Banker to Financial Diplomat, 1904–14

1. For Japanese motives, see James Crowley, 'Japan's Military Foreign Policies', in James Morley (ed.), *Japan's Foreign Policy, 1868–1941: A Research Guide*, p. 14.

2. Diary, 13 May 1904.
3. Ian Nish, *The Anglo-Japanese Alliance*.
4. Addis to Murray Stewart, 28 November 1905, Addis papers.
5. Andrew Malozemoff, *Russian Far Eastern Policy 1881–1904*.
6. McLean, 'British Banking and Government in China', p. 122.
7. Steven MacKinnon, *Power and Politics in Late Imperial China*, p. 68.
8. Jack Gray (ed.) *Modern China's Search for a Political Form* and Mary Wright (ed.) *China in Revolution*.
9. Addis to Mills, 15 November 1905, Addis papers.
10. 'Leaves from a Diary', 22 January 1906, Addis papers.
11. Smith to Addis, July 1904, Addis papers.
12. Addis to Cameron, 4 November 1904, Addis papers, /352.
13. Diary, 28 February 1905.
14. Diary, 1 March 1905, Eba writing.
15. HSBC article on the new office, 1913, p. 738, HSBC archives, Hong Kong.
16. Addis to Mills, 25 April 1906, Addis papers.
17. Thomas, b. 1895; Elizabeth, b. 1897; Charles, b. 1898; Robina, b. 1900; William, b. 1901; Susan, b. 1903.
18. Diary, 27 May 1905.
19. Diary, 25 June 1905, Eba writing.
20. Addis to Mills, n.d., but probably 1905, Addis papers.
21. Zara Steiner, *Britain and the Origins of the First World War*, pp. 39–41.
22. Morrison to Chirol, 8 June 1905, Lo Hui-min (ed.) *The Correspondence of G. E. Morrison*, I, p. 316.
23. C. P. Fitzgerald, 'Dr George Morrison and his Correspondence', in Lo Hui-min (ed.) *Morrison*, pp. vii–xiv.
24. Addis to Mills, 25 April 1909, Addis papers, /177.
25. Diary, 27 October 1905.
26. Minutes of Meeting held at Hotel Metropole, Brussels, 4 October 1905, HSBC archives, Hong Kong.
27. McLean, 'British Banking and Government in China', ch. 6.
28. 28 November 1905, Addis papers.
29. Ibid.
30. 'Our Guests', Toast at China Association Dinner, 31 October 1905, Addis papers.
31. *Times* (London) 31 December 1905.
32. E. W. Edwards, 'The Origins of British Financial Cooperation with France in China, 1903–6', *English Historical Review* (1971) 285–317.
33. Madeleine Chi, 'Shanghai–Hangchow–Ningpo Railway Loan: A Case Study of the Rights Recovery Movement', *Modern Asian Studies*, 7 (1973) p. 86.
34. Roger Des Forges, *Hsi-liang*, parts 2 and 3; Bays, *China Enters the Twentieth Century*, ch. 8.
35. Here the Chinese revolution is considered as an ongoing event which continued until 1949.
36. M. Young, *Rhetoric of Empire*, p. 251, n. 29.
37. William R. Braisted, 'The United States and the American China

Development Company', *Far Eastern Quarterly*, II (1952) pp. 142–65.

38. Lee En-han, *China's Quest For Railway Autonomy, 1904–1911*, pp. 65–78.
39. E. Tseu-Zen Sun, *Chinese Railways and British Interests, 1893–1911*.
40. E. Rhodes, *China's Republican Revolution*, p. 94. See also Bland to Addis, 16 January 1907 and Addis to Bland, 27 December 1906, box 23, Bland papers; Viceroy Chang Chih-tung to Consul-General Fraser, 9 September 1905, Addis papers, /372.
41. Lee En Han, *China's Quest*, pp. 162–9.
42. Diary, March–May 1908; Huenemann, *The Dragon and the Iron Horse*, pp. 70–3.
43. Diary, 19 June 1908.
44. Diary, 7 July 1908.
45. Lee En-Han, *China's Quest*, provides the best guide through this thicket of railway negotiations and conflicting interests.
46. 28 November 1905. Bland had requested the appointment on 22 June 1905.
47. Morrison to Chirol, 8 September 1906, Lo Hui-min (ed.) *Morrison*, I, p. 375. For the swindle, see E. C. Carlson, *The Kaiping Mines* and George H. Nash, *The Life of Herbert Hoover*, chs. 8–11.
48. Addis to Bland, 24 November 1908; Bland to Addis, 5 September; 17 December 1908, Bland papers, box 23; Diary, Eba writing, 21 July, 27 August 1908; Addis to Mills, 25 July 1908, Addis papers.
49. Murray Stewart to Addis, 29 May 1909, Addis papers, /240.
50. Stewart to Addis, 17 July, 13 October 1909.
51. Addis papers, /228. For Chang Chih-tung's refusal to deal with Bland, see E. Tsu-Zen Sun, *Chinese Railways and British Interests*, pp. 98–110.
52. Addis to Mills, 7 December 1908. William Keswick, one of the senior partners of the B&C Corp., had been a partner of Jardine Mathesons in Shanghai in the 1880s and 1890s.
53. The whole controversy can be studied in the Addis and Bland papers.
54. Murray Stewart to Addis, 10 July 1910, Addis papers, /241.
55. Diary.
56. Walter V. Scholes and Marie V. Scholes, *The Foreign Policies of the Taft Administration*, pp. 119–20; Michael Hunt, *Frontier Defence and the Open Door: Manchuria in Chinese–American Relations, 1895–1911*.
57. See next section.
58. For Lord ffrench, see *DBB*, II, pp. 350–3.
59. Diary.
60. See exchange of letters between the Bank of England and the Foreign Office, November/December 1908, Addis papers, Bank of England ADM 16/8; 'Leaves from Diary', 26 December 1908, Addis papers.
61. Diary, 25 February 1909.
62. Diary; McLean, 'British Banking and Government in China'.
63. Charles Vevier, *The United States and China 1906–1913: A Study of Finance and Diplomacy*, pp. 18–24.
64. Chirol to Morrison, 19 August 1909, Lo Hui-min, (ed.) *Morrison*, I, p. 514.

65. Morrison to C. Clementi Smith, 13 February 1911, in Lo Hui-min (ed.) *Morrison I*, p. 575.
66. Stewart to Addis, 22 July 1909, Addis papers, /240.
67. Scholes, *The Foreign Policies of the Taft Administration*, pp. 142–7.
68. Diary, 17 May 1910.
69. Scholes, *The Foreign Policies of the Taft Administration*, p. 156, and Chs. 9, 10, 11.
70. Diary, 10 November 1910. C. S. Addis to Morgan Grenfell, 10 November 1910, HSBC archives, Hong Kong.
71. Hunt, *Frontier Defence*; Helen Kahn, 'The Great Game of Empire: Willard Straight and American Far Eastern Policy', unpublished doctoral dissertation, Cornell University; Addis diary, Eba writing, 17 March 1911.
72. Scholes, *Taft Administration*, ch. 12; Vevier, *The United States and China*.
73. Leffingwell to Long, 24 December 1918, SDF 893.51/2085, indicates Morgans loaned Japan $100 000 000.
74. Professor Jenks taught political economy at Cornell University. See Emily Rosenberg, 'Foundations of United States International Financial Power'.
75. Charles Conant, 'Putting China on the Gold Standard', *North American Review*, 177 (1903) pp. 691–704. The recommendations are in Hamashita, 'The International Financial Relations behind the 1911 Revolution', pp. 19–20.
76. Hamashita, 'The International Financial Relations', pp. 21–2.
77. Ibid, p. 23.
78. MacMurray (ed.) *Treaties and Agreements*, I, pp. 841–9.
79. Addis diary, 25 May 1911, indicates that the French, Russian and Japanese Ambassadors had all called at the FO regarding the currency negotiations.
80. Addis to FO, 10, 12 May 1911, supplied to author by Professor F. H. H. King.
81. Diary, September 1911; Addis to wife, 11, 14, 22, 23 September 1911.
82. Addis to Sir Francis Campbell, 3 October 1911, CO 129/385, kindly furnished to author by Professor King.
83. Huang Hsing, quoted in K. S. Liew, *Struggle for Democracy: Sung Chiao-jen and the 1911 Chinese Revolution*, pp. 87–8.
84. MacMurray (ed.) *Treaties and Agreements*.
85. Liew, *Struggle for Democracy*, ch. 8; Vidya P. Dutt, 'The First Week of Revolution: The Wuchang Uprising', in Wright (ed.) *China in Revolution*, pp. 383–416.
86. John G. Reid, *The Manchu Abdication and the Powers, 1908–1912*, pp. 244–5; Peter Lowe, *Great Britain and Japan, 1911–1915: A Study of British Far Eastern Policy*, pp. 69–74.
87. Diary, 8 November 1911. Addis described Jack Morgan, the American representative, as 'a chip off the old block'.
88. Harold Z. Schiffrin, *Sun Yat-sen and the Origins of the Chinese Revolution*, ch. 5.
89. Marius Jansen, *The Japanese and Sun Yat-sen*; Michael Gasster,

'The Republican Revolutionary Movement', in Wright (ed.) *China in Revolution*, pp. 486–530.

90. Diary, 11 November 1911.
91. Diary, 13 November 1911, Eba writing.
92. Diary, Eba writing, 14 November 1911, 7 December 1911.
93. Diary, 8 December 1911.
94. Scholes, *Taft*, p. 224.
95. Diary, 7 November 1911; K. C. Chan, 'British Policy in the Reorganization Loan to China 1912–1913', *Modern Asian Studies*, V (1971).
96. Ernest P. Young, *The Presidency of Yuan Shih-k'ai*, p. 50; Edward Friedman, *Backward Toward Revolution*, p. 23. The term 'Morgans' follows British practice and probably reflects the plural nature of the firm.
97. Tang Shao-yi (whose father had been the comprador of Jardine Mathesons) had studied at Columbia University in New York. See MacKinnon, *Power and Politics in Late Imperial China*, p. 67.
98. Aide-Memoire, marked 'Strictly private', 23 March 1912, HSBC archives, G1/4.
99. Diary, 17 February 1912.
100. Scholes, *Taft*, chs. 10–12.
101. Marie Bergère, 'The Role of the Bourgeoisie', in Wright (ed.) *China in Revolution*, p. 293.
102. Maurice Collis, *Wayfoong*, p. 134; Jerome Ch'en, *Yuan Shih-k'ai*, p. 119.
103. Diary, 5 March 1912. See also Addis to FO, 6 March 1912, 'Correspondence respecting Chinese Loan Negotiations, 1912–13' (Cmd 6446) and account of interview with Sir Edward Grey, Diary, 9 March 1912.
104. 'Preliminary Agreement for Crisp Loan', 12 July 1912, MacMurray (ed.) *Treaties and Agreements*, II, pp. 972–3. For Crisp see *DBB*, I, pp. 822–6.
105. Yuan was also negotiating with German bankers. See Friedman, *Backward Toward Revolution*, p. 180.
106. Morrison to Jordon, 1 November 1912, Lo Hui-min (ed.) *Morrison*, II, pp. 43–6.
107. Grey to Jordan, 23 August 1912, Cmd. 6446.
108. The cancellation of the Crisp agreement is in MacMurray (ed.) *Treaties and Agreements*, II, pp. 972–3. See also Straight Diary, 27 April 1916.
109. McLean, 'British Banking and Government in China', p. 201.
110. British Group Agreement, 14 December 1912, HSBC archives, G1/4.
111. Diary, 7 June 1912; FO to Eastern Bank, 25 May 1912, Cmd. 6446, explained why HSBC should be 'sole issuing bank'.
112. Diary, 6 June 1912.
113. Minutes of Adjourned Meeting of the Six Groups held at the Banque de l'Indochine, Paris, 18, 19, 20 June 1912, HSBC archives, G1/4. Inter-Bank Conference Minutes, 6 groups, 7 June 1912, Paris, Addis papers, /370.
114. Diary, 7 February 1913.
115. McLean 'British Banking and Government in China'.
116. Diary, 6 March 1913: 'Interview with Chinese Minister. Impressed

on him the futility of further attempts to borrow outside 6 Power Consortium.'

117. Ernest Young, 'Politics in the Aftermath of Revolution: The Era of Yuan Shih-K'ai, 1912–16', *Cambridge History of China*, XII, pt. 1, pp. 208–36.
118. Liew, *Struggle for Democracy*, pp. 182–90.
119. Jonathan Spence, *The Gate of Heavenly Peace*, p. 132.
120. Diary, 26 April 1913.
121. Minutes, Inter-Bank Agreement, 26 April 1913, HSBC archives, G4.
122. Diary, 9 May 1913, Eba writing.
123. Roy Watson Curry, *Woodrow Wilson and Far Eastern Policy*; Li Tien-yi, *Woodrow Wilson's China Policy, 1913–1917*.
124. 'Statement of American government in regard to support requested by the American Group', 18 March 1913, MacMurray (ed.) *Treaties and Agreements*, II, p. 1025; Grey quotation in Diary, 20 March 1913.
125. Noel Pugach, *Paul Reinsch, passim*; Jerry Israel, *Progressivism and the Open Door*, ch. 5.
126. Diary, 20 May 1913. Mills to Addis, 14 May 1913 refers to Addis's protests against loan.
127. Young, 'Politics in the Aftermath of Revolution', *CHC*, XII, pt. 1, p. 235.
128. For budget figures, see Ch'en, *Yuan Shih-k'ai*, p. 147.
129. 'Arrangement for the establishment of a Commission of Bankers to receive the customs revenues for the service of the foreign debt charges thereon', 30 January 1913, MacMurray (ed.) *Treaties and Agreements*, II, pp. 946–7 (my emphasis).
130. Grey to Addis, 2 October 1913, handwritten. Industrial loans included loans to railways.
131. *The Times* (London), 23 October 1913; Addis diary, 21 October 1913.
132. Diary, 23 October 1913.
133. Diary, 25 October 1913.
134. 'The Hongkong and Shanghai Banking Corporation', the *Bankers Magazine*, December 1913, including picture of Sir Charles Addis and comments on his career.
135. Hillier passed this correspondence to Morrison, who commented on it in Morrison to E. G. Hillier, 19 May 1914, Lo Hui-min (ed.) *Morrison*, II, p. 317.
136. Stabb to Addis, 12 December 1910, Addis papers.
137. Diary, 11 January 1912.
138. Jackson to Stabb, 11 January 1912.
139. Diary, 15 February 1912, Addis papers.
140. Diary, 30 October, 12 December 1912. For Barings see Stanley Chapman, *The Rise of Merchant Banking*.
141. Addis noted that at a concert they were attending, Lord Revelstoke had presented him to the King. 26 February 1913, Diary.
142. Schiller to Addis, 28 November 1899, 2 February 1900, 17 April 1901, 3 November 1902, 15 September 1902, Addis papers, /117 and /118.
143. Addis to Schiller, 28 November 1903, Addis papers, /280. The reference is not given.

144. E. M. Forster, *Goldsworthy Lowes Dickinson*, p. viii.
145. See R. F. Harrod's discussion of 'The Apostles', in *The Life of John Maynard Keynes*, pp. 87–8.
146. Peter Clarke, *Liberals and Social Democrats* provides a description of a wider group of Britain's pre-war liberal intellectuals, chs. 1–4.
147. Diary, 13 December 1906.
148. Proctor (ed.) *The Autobiography of G. Lowes Dickinson*, pp. 105–12, describes Dickinson's homosexual love for Schiller, which Schiller, a heterosexual, could only answer with friendship.
149. G. Lowes Dickinson, *Justice and Liberty: A Political Dialogue*, 1908; 'Leaves from a Diary', 10 December 1908, Addis papers, /176. Dickinson had earlier published *A Modern Symposium* which was reissued in 1907 and translated into several languages. His first important work was *The Greek View of Life*, 1896.
150. Miss Addis recalls that her father's face always broke into a warm smile when 'Goldie's' name was mentioned.
151. Harrod, *Keynes*, p. 88.
152. Addis to Mills, 22 October 1899, Addis papers, /167.
153. Diary, 16 March 1910.
154. Diary, 5 August 1908.
155. 22 August 1908, Addis papers, /176. Miss Addis recalls that her parents found they must join the Anglican Church in Shanghai in order to take communion, and since there was no Free Church of Scotland in Shanghai at that time, they became Anglican.
156. Diary, 27 January 1910.
157. For comment on Chinese coolies in South Africa, see Addis to Murray Stewart, 28 November 1905, Addis papers.
158. Diary, 20 January 1911, Eba commenting. Addis sent the manuscript to the *Contemporary* but it was rejected. Diary, 3, 7 February 1911.
159. Forster, *Dickinson*, p. 145. Dickinson published *Letters from John Chinaman* afterwards.
160. Diary, 8, 13 June 1914. The speech does not seem to have survived.
161. Diary.
162. By 1910 Addis had ten children. Three more were born in the next four years.
163. Diary, 21 January 1910.
164. Diary.
165. Speech by F. N. Schiller at HSBC dinner, autumn, 1912, Addis papers.
166. For examples, see R. P. T. Davenport-Hines, *Dudley Docker*, ch. 4.
167. 12 December 1912, Addis papers.
168. See reference to Sir Edward Holden's attack on the South Manchurian loan. Diary, 2 January 1911.
169. Quoted in Harrod from 'Paper on the Indian Currency Question' for the Royal Economic Society, 1911, *Keynes*, p. 193.
170. Addis Diary, 2 December 1913.
171. Addis diary, 29 November–15 December 1913; Felix Schuster to Addis, May 1913, Addis papers, /372. Schuster succeeded Lord Inchcape as Chairman of the Finance Committee of the Indian Council.
172. Diary, 5 December 1913.

173. Addis to Mills, 7 March 1914, Addis papers, /182.

4 Becoming a Central Banker, 1914–19

1. Addis confidently predicted: 'There will be no occasion for war for another six years anyway' Addis to Mills, 7 April 1914, Addis papers, /182.
2. Diary, 7 August 1914; R. S. Sayers, *Bank of England*, pp. 66–78.
3. Addis to Mills, 9 August 1914, Addis papers.
4. Diary, 15 August 1914 and Addis to wife, 10 August 1914, Addis papers.
5. Diary, 14 August 1914.
6. Sayers, *Bank of England*, pp. 64–5.
7. Robert Skidelsky, *John Maynard Keynes*, I, pp. 289–93.
8. Sayers, *Bank of England*, pp. 72–8; Harrod, *Keynes*, pp. 237–9, quoting Blackett diary, 2–5 August 1914.
9. E. V. Morgan, *Studies in British Financial Policy*, 1914–25, pp. 1–59.
10. Diary, 16 September 1914; Kathleen Burk, 'The Treasury: From Impotence to Power', in K. Burk (ed.) *War and the State*, pp. 84–7.
11. 14 September 1914. Lord St Aldwyn was Michael Hicks-Beach, Chancellor of the Exchequer 1895–1902; Lord Inchcape was Chairman of the Peninsular & Oriental Steamship Co. (P&O); Sir Edward Holden was Chairman, London City and Midland Bank, 1908–19.
12. Diary, 11 December 1914.
13. 20 December 1914. For discussions with Langley and Alston in the FO, see Diary, 2 December 1914.
14. Diary, 17 March 1915. The British, French and Russians had agreed to pool their resources. See J. M. Keynes, *The Collected Writings of John Maynard Keynes* (*JMK*) XVI, p. 67.
15. Straight Diary, 9 March 1915, quoting Grenfell. See also Nicholas Davenport, 'Keynes in The City', in Milo Keynes (ed.) *Essays on John Maynard Keynes*, pp. 224–9.
16. Diary, 8, 15, 22, 29 November 1915; 6, 13 December 1915.
17. Diary, 29 November 1915.
18. Speech on War Savings, 3 June 1915, Addis papers.
19. 19 June 1916. See *The Times* (London) account, 1 July 1916 of Addis speech on War Savings, p. 5; Addis scrapbook, Scrapbook, /673.
20. *Scottish Bankers Magazine*, VII, April 1915, no. 235, pp. 1–2, accompanied by a full-page picture.
21. Diary, 30 June 1915.
22. Lester Chandler, *Benjamin Strong, Central Banker*.
23. Strong Diary of trip of Europe, May–June, 1914, Strong papers.
24. Addis to Stabb, 29 July 1915, HSBC archives, Hong Kong.
25. Sir Henry Clay, *Lord Norman*, pp. 97–100.
26. Roberta Dayer, 'Strange Bedfellows: J. P. Morgan & Co., Whitehall and the Wilson Administration during World War I', *Business History*, XVIII (1976) pp. 127–51.
27. Straight diary, 7 March 1915, Straight papers.

28. See for instance, E. C. Grenfell to McKenna, the Chancellor of the Exchequer, 22 January 1916, T170/122.
29. See Morgan testimony, 7 January 1936, *Hearings Before the Special Committee Investigating the Munitions Industry* (Nye Committee) US Senate, 2nd session, 73rd Congress, Part 25, pp. 7488–96.
30. J. P. Morgan Jr wrote to Morgan Grenfell requesting names of English relatives who might help influence families like the 'Vanderbilts, Goulds, Astors, Marshall Field'. 29 September 1915, T170/122.
31. Charles Seymour, (ed.) *The Intimate papers of Colonel House*; Thomas Lamont, *Henry P. Davison*.
32. Chandler, *Strong*, pp. 258–76.
33. Clay, *Norman*, p. 93; Andrew Boyle, *Montagu Norman*, ch. 2.
34. *JMK*, XVI, chs. 2, 3.
35. British Treasury Papers, T176/1B.
36. Addis to Stabb, 1 February 1916, HSBC archives, Hong Kong.
37. Diary; Sayers, *Bank of England*, I, pp. 90 and III, Appendix 4, pp. 46–50.
38. Addis to Stabb, 1 February 1916, HSBC archives, Hong Kong, vol. 320.
39. Diary, 25 February 1916.
40. Diary, 2 March 1916.
41. Diary, 16 August 1916.
42. See *below*.
43. For American ambitions, see Burton I. Kaufman, *Efficiency and Expansion: Foreign Trade Organization in the Wilson Administration, 1913–1921*; Pugach, *Reinsch*, chs. 7–11.
44. Strong Diary, 13 March 1916.
45. Diary, 28 March 1916.
46. Henry N. Scheiber, 'World War I as Entrepreneurial Opportunity: Willard Straight and the American International Corporation', *Political Science Quarterly*, LXXXIV (1969) pp. 486–511.
47. Straight Diary, 29 March 1916. See also Strong–Straight correspondence regarding the AIC. July–September 1916, Strong papers.
48. Straight to T. N. Perkins, 24 April 1916, Straight papers. See also Straight memorandum of London visit, 22 April 1916.
49. Straight to E. V. Morgan, 1 June 1916, Straight papers.
50. Clarence Davis, 'The Defensive Diplomacy of British Imperialism in the Far East, 1915–1922: Japan and the United States as Partners and Rivals', unpublished doctoral dissertation at the University of Wisconsin, 1972.
51. 15 January 1915 letter concerning British banks in China. Quoted in Claude Fivel-Demoret notes from French archives, kindly supplied to author.
52. Memorandum, Board of Trade, 4 May 1915, Addis papers. For the Board of Trade's attitude, see Richard Davenport-Hines, *Dudley Docker*, ch. 7.
53. 1 September 1915, Addis papers, /183.
54. See de Hoyer of the Russo-Asiatic Bank, 5 January 1916, Claude Fivel-Demoret summary for author from French archives.
55. See also undated report by the Peking agency of the Banque de

l'Indochine which is very hostile toward Addis, Fivel-Demoret Summary.

56. Diary, 2 December 1915.
57. Addis to Stabb, 15 February 1916, HSBC archives, Hong Kong. Diary, 21 September 1916, regarding Carl Myer's expulsion from the London Committee because of his German ancestry.
58. Young, *The Presidency of Yuan Shih-K'ai*, chs. 6, 7.
59. Ibid, ch. 8.
60. Addis papers. Stabb relied on Addis to write the part of the Chairman's speech on the international situation.
61. Diary, 3 October 1916.
62. Jordan to Langley, 24 November 1914, quoted in S. A. M. Adshead, *The Modernization of the Chinese Salt Administration*, p. 4.
63. Addis to Stabb, 30 May 1916, HSBC archives, vol. 320, Hong Kong.
64. Addis to Stabb, 8 December 1916, Addis papers.
65. G. C. Allen and Audrey G. Donnithorne, *Western Enterprise in Far Eastern Economic Development: China and Japan*, p. 115.
66. For these charges, see Davenport-Hines, *Docker*, pp. 149–50. For anti-German feelings, see Robert E. Bunselmeyer, *The Cost of the War 1914–1919: British Economic War Aims and the Origin of Reparation*.
67. Davenport-Hines, *Docker*, p. 133.
68. For Hirst's early career, see F. W. Hirst, *In The Golden Days*. Hirst's publications included *Free Trade and Other Fundamental Doctrines of the Manchester School*.
69. 'Free Trade, Office and Principle', *Economist*, 26 February 1916, p. 395.
70. Ibid.
71. 12 April 1916, Addis papers, /184.
72. 'A British Trade Bank', *Economic Journal*, 26 December 1916, p. 489.
73. For Faringdon, see *DBB*, III, pp. 153–6.
74. Diary, 12 December 1918.
75. Tuesday Club memoir by O. T. Falk, 23 May 1950, Marshall Library, Cambridge University. See also 'Recollections by Mr A. T. K. Grant – "From the Thirties to the Fifties"', 27 June 1967, kindly furnished by Professor Donald Moggridge.
76. 'The First Twenty Years', unsigned, but perhaps by Richard Kahn. Undated, but around 1968, furnished by Professor Moggridge.
77. Falk memoir, from Professor Moggridge. R. H. Brand joined in 1918 and Blackett in 1919, Schuster in 1920, Josiah Stamp, Walter Layton, Henry Strakosch, Dennis Robertson and H. D. Henderson in 1922, Otto Niemeyer in 1923, Richard Hopkins in 1928, Leith-Ross and Sir Arthur Salter in 1933 and Alexander Shaw in the early 1930s. With the exception of Shaw, all these people are important in the following pages.
78. Carl P. Parrini, *Heir to Empire: United States Economic Diplomacy, 1916–1923*, ch. 2.
79. Addis's Vote of Thanks to President on his inaugural address, 8 November 1916, *Journal of the Institute of Bankers*, XXXVII (1916)

pp. 422–5. For the Institute of Bankers, see Edwin Green, *Debtors to Their Profession*.

80. See Straight warning to Gilbert Parker of the US Treasury, June, 1916, quoted in Scheiber, 'World War I as Entrepreneurial Opportunity', p. 504.
81. *JMK*, XVI, pp. 197–210.
82. Arthur Link, *Campaigns for Progressivism and Peace, 1916–1917*, pp. 200–3.
83. E. C. Grenfell to Chancellor of the Exchequer, McKenna, 28 November 1916, T170/122.
84. Sir Hardman Lever Diary, 22 March 1917, T172/429. Lever served as a British Treasury agent in Washington.
85. The FO warned the Cabinet of this danger. See Bunselmeyer, *The Cost of the War*, pp. 45–6.
86. W. B. Fowler, *British–American Relations, 1917–1918: The Role of Sir William Wiseman*.
87. Addis to Mills, 10 April 1917, Addis papers.
88. Addis to Mills, 9 July 1917, Addis papers, /176.
89. Forster, *G. Lowes Dickinson*, pp. 162–74; Proctor (ed.) *Autobiography*, pp. 3–24, 190–5.
90. Dayer, 'Strange Bedfellows'.
91. Lever's Diary, 17 April 1917, T172/429.
92. *JMK*, XVI, p. 287. Law became Chancellor of the Exchequer when Lloyd George formed his War Cabinet in December 1916.
93. 'Bank Reserves and Depreciation', *Economic Journal*, XXVII, pp. 414–17.
94. Sayers, *Bank of England*, III, p. 57, indicates that planning for this committee began in October 1917.
95. Other members were R. Beckett, G. C. Cassels, G. Farrer, H. Gibbs, W. H. N. Goschen, Lord Inchcape, R. W. Jeans, G. F. Stewart and W. Wallace.
96. Sayers, *Bank of England*, p. 58.
97. Diary, 18, 25, 26 February; 13 March; 8, 9 April; 6, 7 May 1918.
98. The first interim report was made in August 1918 and the final report in December 1919. Cd. 9182, London, 1918.
99. Diary, 9 April 1918.
100. Diary, 14 August 1918.
101. 'Note re modification of Bank Act of 1844', 20, 21 June 1918, Addis papers.
102. Diary, 1 May 1918.
103. 28 May 1918, Addis papers, /460. See comment in Sayers, *Bank of England*, p. 597.
104. Diary.
105. Diary, 15 January 1918; Cox to Addis, 16 February 1918, Addis papers.
106. Diary, 6 April, 8 May 1918.
107. 'The Problems of British Banking', *Edinburgh Review*, 228 (1918) 56.
108. For City views, see S. G. Checkland, 'The Mind of the City 1870–1914', *Oxford Economic Papers*, new series, (October 1957) pp. 261–79.

109. Diary, 17 July 1918; *Times*, 22 July 1918, p. 10.
110. Addis to Mills, 5 August, Addis papers.
111. HSBC archives, vol. 95. Diary, 20 June, 27 August, 27, 28 September 1917.
112. HSBC archives, Hong Kong.
113. Arthur F. Sewall, 'Key Pittman and the Quest for the China Market, 1933–40', *Pacific Historical Review* (August 1975) pp. 354–5.
114. Diary, 31 July 1918.
115. Addis to Stabb, 1 August 1918, HSBC archives, Hong Kong.
116. E. C. Grenfell to Bonar Law, 13 December 1916, T170/122.
117. Richard Ullman, *Anglo-Soviet Relations, 1917–1921*, 3 vols. For gold question, see T170/122. Tsarist bonds were still being negotiated in 1986.
118. Jacqueline D. St John, 'John F. Stevens: American Assistance to Russian and Siberian Railroads, 1917–1922', unpublished doctoral dissertation at the University of Oklahoma Library, 1969, p. 96.
119. Ullman, *Intervention and the War*, p. 87.
120. Drummond to Reading, 19 April 1918, Balfour Papers, Add. MSS., 49741; Ullman *Intervention*, pp. 129–207.
121. Fowler, *British–American Relations*; Betty Untermeyer, *America's Siberian Expedition*.
122. Lloyd C. Gardner, *Safe for Democracy: The Anglo-American Response to Revolution, 1913–1923*, ch. 6.
123. William Appleman Williams, *American–Russian Relations*.
124. Robert Rhodes James, *Churchill: A Study in Failure 1900–1939*, pp. 132–60.
125. N. Gordon Levin Jr, *Woodrow Wilson and World Politics: America's Response to War and Revolution*; Arno J. Mayer, *Wilson vs Lenin*.
126. Wiseman to Drummond, 4 February 1918, Balfour Papers, Add. MSS. 49741. See also Ullman, *Britain and the Russian Civil War*, pp. 82–102; Burton Beers, *Vain Endeavor*, pp. 128–9.
127. Ullman, *Intervention and the War*, pp. 248–61. See also 'Memo on Siberia', *DBFP*, III, 1st series, pp. 724–25.
128. Morris to Lansing, 25 October 1918, Breckenridge Long papers, Box 179.
129. Ullman, *Intervention*, p. 262.
130. Collis, *Wayfoong*, p. 176.
131. Ibid, p. 177.
132. For the Kolchak policy, see *DBFP*, 1st series, III, p. 700.
133. Sayers, *Bank of England*, pp. 597–8.
134. Whitham Report on Neutralization of Transportation in China, SDF 893.77/1851.
135. Dayer, *Bankers and Diplomats*, pp. 57–64.
136. Addis to Stabb, December 1917, HSBC archives, Hong Kong.
137. Stabb to Addis, 9 February 1918, HSBC archives, vol. 97.
138. For American group, see Gardner, *Safe for Democracy*, pp. 224–6.
139. Madeleine Chi, 'Ts'ao Ju-lin (1876–1966): His Japanese Connections', in Akira Iriye (ed.) *The Chinese and the Japanese*, pp. 140–61.

140. Pugach, *Reinsch*, ch. XI; Israel, *Progressivism and the Open Door*, ch. 6.
141. Dayer, *Bankers and Diplomats*, ch. 2.
142. MacMurray to Lansing, 10 September 1918, SDF 893.00/2887.
143. Jack [Morgan] (Paris) to Lamont, 23 August 1918, Lamont papers, pp. 183–3.
144. Strong to Norman, 22 November 1918, Strong–Norman Correspondence, Hoover Presidential Library.
145. Whitham report, SDF 893.77/1852.
146. MacMurray to Long, 11 February 1919, SDF 893.51/2112. For Lamont, see Thomas W. Lamont, *Across World Frontiers*.
147. Dayer, *Bankers and Diplomats*, pp. 49–73.
148. Addis to Stabb, 16 May 1919, HSBC archives, vol. 329, Hong Kong. See also Charles Drage, *Taikoo*, p. 240.
149. See Box 71, Hornbeck papers.
150. Russell Fifield, *Woodrow Wilson and the Far East: The Diplomacy of the Shantung Question*.
151. Diary, February 1919.
152. Diary, March 1919.
153. Diary, 19 March 1919.
154. Diary, February 1919, refers to Carsun and Yeh Kung Cho. The latter was the Vice-Minister of Communications, while 'Carsun' was probably Carsun Chang, the older brother of Chang Kia-ngau, the Assistant General Manager of the Bank of China in Peking.
155. Diary, 10–12 May 1919; Minutes of Inter Group Conference, 12 May 1919, Paris, MacMurray papers, Box A2; Morgan to Secretary of State, 22 May 1919, SDF 893.51/2222.
156. Lamont to Long, 25 June 1919, Long papers.
157. Fifield, *The Diplomacy of the Shantung Question*.
158. The demonstrations in Peking began the May Fourth movement. See Chow Tse-tsung, *The May Fourth Movement: Intellectual Revolution in Modern China*.
159. *JMK*, XVI, pp. 313–34.
160. Skidelsky, *Keynes*, pp. 354–7.
161. Diary, 5 December 1918; Addis to Mills, 1918, Addis papers.
162. Addis speech at Cambridge, 28 November 1929, Addis papers.
163. *JMK*, XVI, p. 337. Although this reference does not name Addis, it corresponds with evidence from the Addis papers.
164. Ibid, p. 336.
165. *Journal*, Institute of Bankers.
166. Sir B. Mallet, reviewing the *Political Economy Club: Centenary Volume, The Economic Journal*, XXXI (1921) p. 496.
167. *Morning Post*, 6 March 1919; the speech was printed in the *Nation*, vol 108, April 1919 and in the *International Review*, as 'What Should Germany Pay', no. 68 (1919) pp. 353–9.
168. Ibid, p. 355.
169. Ibid, p. 357.
170. Addis's comment on the use of German indemnity bonds suggests his knowledge of Keynes's proposal at Versailles.

171. Addis to Mills, 22 April 1918, Addis papers.
172. Mayer, *Politics and Diplomacy of Peacemaking*, ch. 5. The phrase was that of Sir Eric Geddes, First Lord of the Admiralty.
173. *JMK*, XVI, pp. 429–74.
174. Skidelsky, *Keynes*, I, p. 369; Michael J. Hogan, 'Thomas W. Lamont and European Recovery: The Diplomacy of Privatism in a Corporatist Age', in K. P. Jones (ed.) *US Diplomats in Europe, 1919–1941*.
175. Seth P.Tillman, *Anglo-American Relations at the Paris Peace Conference of 1919*.
176. Addis to Mills, 17 May 1919, Addis papers.
177. Ferdinand Czernin, *Versailles, 1919*, ch. IX.
178. Addis to Mills, 22 June 1919, Addis papers. For Lansdowne proposal, see A. J. P. Taylor, *English History 1914–1945*, pp. 65–6.

PART II ATTEMPTS AT ANGLO-AMERICAN COOPERATION

Overview: British Postwar Strategy

1. Dan P. Silverman, *Reconstructing Europe After The Great War*, ch. 2; Parrini, *Heir to Empire*, ch. 3; Michael J. Hogan, *Informal Entente*, ch. 2.
2. Henry Roseveare, *The Treasury*, ch. 6.
3. Blackett was Controller of Finance, 1919–22; Niemeyer was Principal Assistant Secretary and then Controller of Finance until 1927; Hawtrey was Director of Financial Enquiries; Bradbury was British delegate on the Reparations Commission; Leith-Ross became Deputy Controller in 1925.
4. Russell Leffingwell, Assistant Secretary of the Treasury, 1917–20, became a partner in J. P. Morgan & Co. in 1923; S. Parker Gilbert, Assistant Secretary of the Treasury, 1921–3, first became Agent General for Reparation payments, then joined Morgans in 1931.
5. See Chapters 2 and 3 above.
6. D. C. Watt, *Personalities and Policies, passim*.
7. Sayers, *Bank of England*, p. 200, and *passim*.
8. Priscilla Norman, *In the Way of Understanding*, pp. 70–128.
9. Sayers, *Bank of England*, pp. 626–38.
10. Strong's report of Addis's views, Strong Journal, 25 July 1919, Hoover Presidential Library, container 4.
11. *Review of Reviews*, LX, pp. 26–8.
12. D. E. Moggridge, *British Monetary Policy*, pp. 3–14; Barry Eichengreen's introduction to *The Gold Standard* surveys current opinion on this controversial subject.
13. Brian McKercher (ed.) *The Struggle for Supremacy* (forthcoming).
14. Michael Hogan, 'Thomas W. Lamont and European Recovery', in K. P. Jones, *U. S. Diplomats in Europe, 1919–1941*, pp. 8–9.

15. Stephen Schuker's 1984 comment on an earlier draft of this chapter.
16. Strong Journal, 25 July 1919, Strong papers.
17. Strong to Leffingwell, 31 July 1919, Strong papers.
18. Strong Journal, 8, 9 September 1919; Strong memorandum, 30 August 1919, Hoover Presidential Library, container 4 1000.3(2).
19. Grey to Curzon, 29 September 1919, Lloyd George papers, F/60/3/6.
20. Grey to Curzon, 17 November 1919, *DBFP*, 1st series, V, p. 1022.
21. Dayer, *Bankers and Diplomats*, ch. 4.
22. See Garrard Winston, 'American War Debt Policy', June 1928, box 220, RG39.
23. For the purpose of a Central Bank, see Ernest Harvey's testimony before the Macmillan Committee in 1929 in Sayers, *Bank of England*, III, pp. 119–21.
24. The Strong and Norman diaries and their correspondence record the friendship and views. Kathleen Burk, 'Diplomacy and the Private Banker: The Case of the House of Morgan', *Konstellationen Internationaler Politik 1924–1932*, pp. 25–40.
25. Silverman, *Reconstructing Europe*, ch. 6; Stephen A. Schuker, *The End of French Predominance in Europe*, pp. 141–2 and *passim*. Schuker does not agree fully with this interpretation.
26. Thomas W. Lamont, *Henry P. Davison: The Record of a Useful Life*.
27. Parrini, *Heir to Empire*, ch. III, and *passim*.

5   Competition vs Cooperation, 1919–22

1. Diary, June 1919. The children were: Thomas (1895), Elizabeth (1897), Charles (1898), Robina (1900), William (1901), Susan (1903), George (1904), Henrietta (1906), Margaret (1908), Jean (1910), Rachael (1912), John (1914), Richard (1916).
2. Addis to Mills, 22 June 1919, Addis papers.
3. Strong Journal, 8 August–15 September 1919.
4. Sayers, *Bank of England*, p. 200; Chandler, *Strong*, pp. 140–8.
5. *JMK*, XVII, p. 128; Silverman, *Reconstructing Europe*, p. 272.
6. Chandler, *Strong*, p. 43. See also Melvin Leffler, 'The Origins of Republican War Debt Policy 1921–1923', *Journal of American History*, LIX (1972) 591.
7. *JMK*, XVII, p. 136. Brand was a managing director, Lazard Bros. & Co. Ltd. See *DBB*, 437–9.
8. *JMK*, XVIII, p. 139.
9. Silverman, *Reconstructing Europe*, p. 274.
10. *JMK*, pp. 147–9.
11. Skidelsky, *Keynes*, pp. 393–400. Skidelsky tends to underestimate the damage caused by Keynes's book.
12. Diary, 31 December 1919.
13. Addis to Mills, 19 January 1920, Addis papers. Silverman, *Reconstructing Europe*, notes that the French published the Memorial later.
14. Diary, 26 January, 3 February 1920; Addis to Eba, 2 February 1920,

Addis papers. Cecil was one of the founders of the League of Nations Union in Britain.

15. Chamberlain to Bradbury, 24 March 1920, T194/272.
16. Kent papers, Princeton, box 28.
17. Diary, 7 May 1920; Norman to Chancellor Austen Chamberlain, 7 May 1920, T172/1108. Brand and Sir Robert Kindersley (Chairman of Lazards) attended instead. See Clay, *Norman*, p. 136.
18. For earlier negotiations, see Silverman, *Reconstructing Europe*, pp. 30–1.
19. Norman diary, 4, 5, 9 February 1920, Bank of England.
20. Norman diary, 19 February 1920, Bank of England.
21. Norman diary, 17, 18, 21 May 1920, Bank of England.
22. Memorandum, unsigned, 21 May 1920, Addis papers, Bank of England ADM16/2.
23. Cabinet Minutes, 10 May 1921, C37/21 CAB 23; Chamberlain memorandum, May 1920, CP1259, Austen Chamberlain papers, AC34/107.
24. Lansing to Davis, 11 October 1919, SDF 893.51/2451.
25. Addis to Stabb, 8 July 1919, HSBC archives, Hong Kong.
26. It is not clear which Turner this is, but probably the George Turner who had interests in Chinese railways. See Lo Hui-min, *Morrison*, II, p. 54, n. 2.
27. Diary, 3 June 1919.
28. Davenport-Hines, *Docker*, p. 146.
29. Marshall to Long, quoting Lamont, 12 June 1919, Breckenridge Long papers, box 180.
30. *Living Age*, 301 (1919) p. 818.
31. Long to Lamont, 20 December 1919, box 180, Long papers. For full discussion see Dayer, *Bankers and Diplomats*, pp. 76–9.
32. Lamont to State, 26 March 1920, SDF 893.51/2738; Alston to FO, 28 March 1920, FO371 F314/2/10.
33. Telephone message from Simpson [of J. P. Morgan] to Lamont, Breckenridge Long papers, box 180; Addis diary, 10, 17, April 1920.
34. *DBFP*, 1st series, VI, p. 1030.
35. Dayer, *Bankers and Diplomats*, pp. 76–9.
36. Treasury to Geddes, 1 June 1920, T172/460.
37. William Jones (of HSBC) to Strong, 26 February 1920, Addis to Strong, 18 February 1920, Strong papers. Strong was in Japan from May until late July 1920 and then in Paris and London until December 1920. Chandler, *Strong*, p. 165.
38. Lamont's preliminary report on trip to Asia, 14 May 1920, Lamont papers, 185/22.
39. Strong to Pierre Jay, 11 May, 4, 21 July 1920; Strong to J. H. Case, 29 May 1920, Strong papers.
40. Diary, 8 July 1919.
41. Dayer, *Bankers and Diplomats*, pp. 81–2.
42. Diary, 30 March and 1 April 1920.
43. Addis to Stabb, 6 April 1920, HSBC archives, Hong Kong.
44. Addis papers, /662.
45. 30 September 1920, FO371 A7021/182/45.

46. Treasury (Seymour) to FO, 4 October 1920, FO371 A7024/182/45.
47. Diary, 9 September 1920.
48. The *Morning Post* reported on this speech on 22 January 1921, Addis papers, /662.
49. Addis to Eba, 4 October 1920, Addis papers.
50. Addis to Eba, 12 October 1920, Addis papers.
51. Addis to Eba, 14 October 1920, Addis papers.
52. Addis to Eba, 13 October 1920, Addis papers.
53. Consortium Agreement, MacMurray Papers, box A2.
54. *Times*, 14 October 1920, Addis papers.
55. 'Minutes of an adjourned meeting, China Consortium', 15 October 1920, Breckenridge Long papers, box 161.
56. J. P. Morgan to Secretary of State, 29 October 1920, SDF893.51/3027.
57. Peking Legation to State, 2 December 1920, SDF 893.00/3697.
58. 'The Chinese Republic and the International Consortium', 6 October 1920, delivered 22 October 1920; Kemmerer to Addis, 28 October 1920, Addis papers. Kemmerer and Addis had corresponded earlier regarding currency and central banking.
59. Lamont to Norman Davis, 18 October 1920, *FRUS 1920*, I, p. 723.
60. Case to Strong, 21 October 1920, mentions that Addis had called with an introduction from Norman, Strong papers. J. Herbert Case was the Deputy Governor.
61. 15 October 1920, Addis papers.
62. Case to Strong, 21 October 1920, Strong papers.
63. Jay to Strong, 26 November 1920, Strong papers.
64. Geddes to FO, 22 October 1920, FO371 A7431/182/45, vol. 4563. See also Geddes to Curzon, 18 October 1920, Lloyd George papers, F/60/4/8.
65. Curzon to Geddes, 5 November 1920, FO371 A7472/182/45. This is known as 'commercialising the debt'.
66. Walter A. Adams, Vice-Consul in China, Canton, 29 November 1920, Price papers, box 9. Crane to Secretary of State, 16 March 1921, SDF 893.00/3845.
67. Lamont to F. W. Stevens, 10 February 1921, Lamont papers, 185–2.
68. Lamont to Davison, 2 March 1921, Lamont papers, 91–4.
69. Arnold to MacMurray, 5 April 1921, MacMurray Papers, Box 62. For Wireless struggle, see Michael J. Hogan, *Informal Entente*, ch. 6.
70. Hoover to Denby, 23 April 1921, Secretary of Commerce Official File, Hoover papers, box 109. Denby was Harriet's brother whom Addis knew in Peking.
71. *Hearings before the Committee on Foreign Relations*, US Senate, 67th Congress, 1st session, 29 April 1921, in MacMurray papers, Box A2.
72. Dayer, *Bankers and Diplomats*, pp. 93–6.
73. A. Stephen to Addis, 20 May 1921, Addis papers.
74. *Times*, 3 June 1921, p. 12.
75. Ibid, 18 June 1921, p. 15.
76. Addis to son Charles, 30 July 1921, Addis papers.
77. Diary, 21, 23, 26 December 1920; 4 January 1921; Norman Diary, 16 November 1920, Bank of England.

78. For Brussels Conference, see H. A. Siepmann account, *Economic Journal*, XXX (1920).
79. Diary, 30 December 1920.
80. These were offered by Lord Inchcape on 8 November 1920.
81. Addis to Mills, 30 March 1921, Addis papers.
82. 'Problems of Reconstruction', Sir George Paish's dinner, Savoy Hotel, 16 March 1921, Addis papers; Diary, 16 March 1921.
83. 12 Mary 1921, Addis papers, /394.
84. Norman diary, 21 May 1921, Bank of England.
85. Addis diary, 24, 26 May 1921.
86. Norman to Strong, 23 May 1921, Strong–Norman correspondence, Hoover Presidential Library.
87. See Addis diary and Norman personal diary, Bank of England.
88. R. Dayer, 'The British War Debts to the United States and the Anglo-Japanese Alliance', *Pacific Historical Review*, XLV (1976) pp. 569–95.
89. Addis diary, 20 May 1921. The *London Morning Post*, 23 May 1921, reports on the Lamont dinner given by Addis.
90. Diary, 16 March 1921.
91. Addis to Mills, 28 March 1921, Addis papers, /189.
92. Norman to Strong, 13 July 1921, Strong–Norman Correspondence, Hoover Presidential Library.
93. Lamont to Hughes, 18 August 1921, Lamont papers.
94. Addis diary, 23, 24 August 1921.
95. Addis to wife, 24 August 1921, Addis papers.
96. Addis to Wellesley, 22 September 1921, FO371 F3540/45/10.
97. Roberta Dayer, 'Struggle for China: The Anglo-American Relationship, 1917–25', unpublished doctoral dissertation at the State University of New York, Buffalo, 1972, ch. 3.
98. Strong to Addis, 13 September 1921, Strong papers. See also Strong to Jay, 15 September 1921 and Norman to Strong, 15 September 1921, Strong papers.
99. 1 September 1921, Lamont papers, 111–13. Eliot Wadsworth was the Secretary of the World War Foreign Debt Commission. See *BDI*.
100. Norman diary, Bank of England, 17 October 1921. The subrogated securities were those which the American Treasury had demanded from the British as collateral for loans during the First World War.
101. Leffler, 'Origins of Republican War Debt Policy', p. 592; Hogan, *Informal Entente*, pp. 42–3.
102. Hearings in re Refunding of Obligations of Foreign Governments, before US Senate Committee on Finance, 29 June 1921, box 220, RG39 'Country File', US Treasury.
103. Referred to in letter by M. Stewart to Addis, 7 October 1921, Addis papers, /253.
104. Diary, 20, 28 September 1921.
105. 15 November 1921, Addis papers.
106. Addis diary, 26 October 1921. See also Sayers, *Bank of England*, p. 175.
107. Norman diary, 17 November 1921, Bank of England.

108. Jay to Norman, 16 December 1921, Strong–Norman Correspondence, Hoover Presidential Library.
109. Norman diary, 27 November–16 December 1921. See also Norman to Strong and Strong to Norman, 1 November 1921, Strong–Norman papers.
110. Norman to Strong, 28 October 1921, Strong–Norman Correspondence, Hoover Presidential Library.
111. Lampson memo, 19 July 1921, FO371 F2599/45/10; Wellesley to Addis, 23 July 1921, FO371 F2599/15/10. Ira Klein, 'Whitehall, Washington and the Anglo-Japanese Alliance, 1919–21', *Pacific Historical Review*, XLI (1972) pp. 460–83.
112. Dayer, 'The British War Debts to the United States and the Anglo-Japanese Alliance'.
113. Addis to Mills, 15 November 1921, Addis papers.
114. Addis to Mills, 31 October 1921, Addis papers.
115. Addis diary, 18 October 1921.
116. Diary, 31 October 1921.
117. *Times*, 9 November 1921, including picture. While in China, Elizabeth met and married Dallas Bernard.
118. Addis to Robina, 16 November 1921, Addis papers.
119. Addis to Tom, 17 December 1921, Addis papers.
120. Diary, 18–20 December 1921.
121. Diary, 27–30 December 1921.
122. James Sheridan, *China in Disintegration*, pp. 150–1.
123. Consul-Gen. Jamieson to FO, 14 March 1922, FO371 F1496/927/10.
124. 17 March 1922, FO371 F1577/927/10.
125. Colonial Office to FO, 29 March 1922, FO371 F1284/927/10.
126. 6 March 1922, FO371 F1529/917/10.
127. Alston to FO, 7 April 1922, FO371 F13944/927/10, with attached minutes by Archer and Campbell.
128. Diary, 4–9 January 1922.
129. Peking to Hughes, 23 February 1922, Hornbeck papers, Box 71; F. W. Stevens to Lamont, 6 February 1922, SDF 893.51/3784.
130. Hornbeck notes on Atherton memorandum of 23 February 1922, Hornbeck papers, Box 71.
131. *Times*, 30 January 1922, p. 17.
132. F. W. Stevens to Lamont, 19 February 1922, SDF 893.51/3784; *North China Daily News*, 28 January 1922, quoting Addis speech to Union Club, Addis papers /624.
133. Acheson report on Wellesley conversation to Aglen, 5 January 1922, Aglen papers; Alston to FO, 2 January 1922, FO371 F59/59/10.
134. Alston to Curzon, 3 March 1922, FO371 F1424/59/10.
135. Stevens to E. G. Hillier, S. F. Mayers, Henry Mazot, K. Takeuchi, SDF 893.51/3784.
136. Hong Kong University speech on receiving LL.D., 11 January 1922, Addis papers.
137. This report of Addis's speech is marked 'Reuters Agency', Addis papers /624.
138. 'Anglo-American Cooperation', *Peking and Tientsin Times*, 14 February

1922, included in Ruddock to Hughes, 23 February 1922, SDF 893.51/3780.

139. Diary, 22 January–18 February 1922. For Liang Shih-i, see Howard Boorman (ed.) *Biographical Dictionary of Republican China*, II, pp. 354–6.

140. Schurman to State, 28 February 1922, SDF 893.00/4239; Diary, February 1922. For the warlord struggles, see Hsi-Sheng Ch'i, *Warlord Politics in China 1916–1928*.

141. F. W. Stevens to Lamont, 20 February 1922, SDF 893.51/3784.

142. Diary, 19 February–3 March 1922.

143. In 'Murray Stewart: An Appreciation', *China Express*, 7 June 1922, Addis papers, Addis said: 'It is character that counts'.

144. Diary, 24 March 1922.

145. Addis to Hillier, 29 March 1922, SDF 893.00/4710. Hillier had cabled Addis on 22 March that the scheme was progressing according to plan.

146. MacMurray Memorandum, 1 April 1922, SDF 893.00/4710, includes Addis memorandum of conversation with premier Liang Shih-yi at Tientsin, 18 February 1922.

147. 'Nine Power Treaty', *FRUS*, 1922, I, pp. 278–9.

148. E. T. Williams Diary, 1 December 1921, Williams papers.

149. See Rodney Gilbert's articles in the *North China Daily News*, included in Cunningham to Hughes, 3 March 1922, SDF 893.51/3774. See also the William Hurd article for Cosmopolitan News Service (part of the Hearst publications) 9 march 1922, Lamont papers, 185–8.

150. *Financial News*, 4 November 1921, reported that Lamont had offered a loan of $16m to the Peking government to cover the repayment of the $5½m due on 21 November to the Continental Commercial Bank and $5m payable to the Pacific Development Loan on 1 December but that the Chinese would not accept Lamont's terms.

151. Dayer, *Bankers and Diplomats*, pp. 130–6.

152. Alston to FO, 3 March 1922, FO371 F931/59/10.

153. 'Changes in China in Past Twenty Years', *Bankers Magazine*, 104 (1922) pp. 849–55.

154. Ruddock to Hughes, 10 April 1922, SDF 893.51/3822.

155. Hughes to Lamont, 13 April 1922, Hornbeck papers, box 71, SDF 893.51/3788.

156. Hornbeck Memorandum, 9 May 1922, Hornbeck papers, box 71.

157. See minutes by E. H. Carr and W. Tyrrell, on Addis to Wellesley, 11 April 1922, FO371 F1463/59/10.

158. Schurman to Hughes, 31 May 1922, SDF 893.51/3846.

159. Sokolsky to Lamont, 18 April 1922, Lamont papers, 183–17. For Sokolsky, see Warren Cohen, *The Chinese Connection*, ch. 3.

160. 15 July 1922, SDF 893.51/4248, included in Ruddock to MacMurray, 14 August 1922.

161. Aglen to Acheson, 31 July 1922, which was a response to Acheson's account of a conversation with Addis, Aglen papers.

162. Stewart to Addis, 3 January 1922, Addis papers, /256.

163. Diary, 29 March 1922; Norman to Addis, 29 March 1922, Addis papers.

6 Monetary Policy and European Reconstruction, 1920–8

1. Sayers, *Bank of England*, ch. 8; Chandler, *Strong*, ch. 7; Stephen V. O. Clarke, *Central Bank Cooperation: 1924–31*, ch. 3; Clay, *Norman*, ch. 5.
2. The above authors deal in depth with monetary policy, as do Moggridge and Howson who are cited below. However, only Clarke shows the influence of the reparations question and none of them adequately examine the way the war-debts-reparations question affected monetary policy.
3. Susan Howson, *Domestic Monetary Management in Britain, 1919–38*, p. 9. See also A. J. Youngson, *The British Economy 1920–57*, p. 25.
4. *JMK*, XVII, p. 180.
5. Addis to Eba, 8 February 1920, Addis papers.
6. Diary, 6 February 1920.
7. 'Memorandum on currency and fiscal policy', 8 February 1920, 6 pp. Addis papers. An unsigned published version of this, dated 10 February is in Sayers, *Bank of England*, III, pp. 65–8.
8. Ibid.
9. *JMK*, XVII, p. 150. See also the discussions of bank rate at The Tuesday Club on 8 July 1920, p. 184, and Howson, *Monetary Management*, pp. 9–23.
10. Sayers, *Bank of England*, p. 123.
11. Ibid and *JMK*, XVII, pp. 184–5.
12. The Cunliffe Commission made its final report in 1919.
13. Silverman, *Reconstructing Europe*, pp. 40–7, 52–6.
14. Ibid, pp. 55–6.
15. Addis to wife, 25 July 1919, Addis papers.
16. Silverman, *Reconstructing Europe*, citing Norman's views, p. 50.
17. Speech to Oxford Economic Society, 11 June 1921, Addis papers /524. A press clipping indicates that the title was 'Reconstruction – A Problem of Currency'. Addis papers, /622.
18. The memorandum is undated and unsigned, but includes identical language to that used in the Oxford speech quoted above. Addis papers /524.
19. Norman diary, 3 July 1921, Bank of England.
20. Quoted in Davenport-Hines, *Dudley Docker*, p. 130.
21. 'Inaugural Address of the President, Sir Charles Addis, KCMG, to the Institute of Bankers, 8 November 1921, *Journal of The Institute of Bankers.*
22. Hawtrey to Addis, 27 October 1921. Professor Pigou's handwritten reply, dated 13 October 1921, is almost impossible to read. Addis papers /397.
23. Keynes to Addis, 26 October 1921, Addis papers.
24. *Christian Science Monitor*, 15 December 1921, Addis papers.
25. *The Empire Review and Journal of British Trade*, December 1921; *Scottish Bankers Magazine*, January 1922; *Financial News*, 9 November 1921; *Bank of Liverpool & Martins Ltd. Monthly Circular*, 14 November 1921, Addis papers /622.

26. *Economist*, 12 November 1921, Addis papers /622; *Financier*, 11 November 1921; *Scotsman*, 9 November 1921; Addis papers /526 and /622.
27. *Manchester Guardian*, 9 November 1921; *Statist*, 12 November 1921; *Spectator*, 12 November 1921, Addis papers /526.
28. Major E. S. Grogan, DSO, 'Financial Policy', *Times Annual Financial Review*, 31 December 1921, Addis papers /622. Grogan was identified as 'a forceful critic' of the Cunliffe policy and the author of *The Economic Calculus*.
29. *Referee*, 30 July 1922, Addis papers /623.
30. Stewart to Addis, 3 January 1922, Addis papers /256.
31. Silverman, *Reconstructing Europe*, ch. 2.
32. For background to Genoa, see Stephen V. O. Clarke, *The Reconstruction of the International Monetary System: The Attempts of 1922 and 1933*, pp. 4–8; Clay, *Norman*, pp. 200–4.
33. P. J. Grigg, *Prejudice and Judgment*, pp. 74–7; *FRUS, 1922*, I, p. 384.
34. Carole Fink, *The Genoa Conference: European Diplomacy, 1921–22*.
35. Chamberlain to Prime Minister, 23 March 1922, Austen Chamberlain papers, AC23/6/20. See also Lord Beaverbrook, *The Decline and Fall of Lloyd George*, Appendix 51, p. 293.
36. For the Bankers Committee, see Stephen Schuker, *The End of French Predominance in Europe: The Financial Crisis of 1924 and the Adoption of the Dawes Plan*, p. 178, which accepts at face value Morgan's 'reluctance to become involved'.
37. Harjes to Lamont, 15 May 1922; Lamont to Harjes, 17 May 1922, Lamont papers, pp. 122–18.
38. Washington had an unofficial observer. See Hogan, *Informal Entente*, pp. 45–6; *FRUS, 1922*, I, pp. 386–93.
39. W. A. Williams, *American–Russian Relations*, pp. 193–7; Frank Costigliola, 'The Politics of Financial Stabilization: American Reconstruction Policy in Europe 1924–30', unpublished doctoral dissertation at Cornell University, 1973, pp. 54–5.
40. Susan Howson, 'Monetary Theory and Policy in the 20th Century: The Career of R. G. Hawtrey', in M. Flinn (ed.) *Proceedings of the Seventh International Economic History Congress*, p. 507.
41. R. G. Hawtrey, *The Art of Central Banking*, p. xiii.
42. Diary, 18 April 1922; *JMK*, XVII, p. 380; Clay, *Norman*, p. 137; Fink, *The Genoa Conference*, pp. 232–42.
43. For Peacock, see *DBB*, IV, pp. 559–67.
44. Norman to Addis, 18 April 1922, Addis papers, Bank of England, ADM16/2.
45. Norman personal diary, 4 May 1922; Addis diary, 19 April 1922.
46. 'Resolutions proposed for adoption by the Central and Reserve Banks represented at meetings to be held at the Bank of England', Addis papers, Bank of England, ADM16/2.
47. *DBEP*, 1st series, XIX, p. 724; *JMK*, XVII, p. 380.
48. 'Notes on Governor Norman's talk to Committee on Foreign Affairs', 5 January 1926, FRBNY.

49. Norman evidence to Trotter Committee, 29 December 1926, Appendix 16, Sayers, *Bank of England*, III, p. 92.
50. Silverman, *Reconstructing Europe*, ch. 2.
51. S. V. O. Clarke, *Reconstruction of the International Monetary System*, pp. 17–18.
52. Harold G. Moulton and Leo Pasvolsky, *War Debts and World Prosperity*, pp. 80–1.
53. Cabinet Minutes, 23 May 1922, C29/22; 16 June 1922, C35/22; 7 July 1922, C 38/22. (CAB 23); Grigg, *Prejudice and Judgment*, p. 30.
54. 26 June 1922, Lamont papers, 96–12.
55. Sir Edward Grigg to Lloyd George, 6 July 1922, Lloyd George papers, F86/2/4.
56. B.F.B. [Blackett] to Chancellor of Exchequer, 12 July 1922, T176/8. Norman alerted Strong to the forthcoming Balfour Note on 26 July 1922, Strong papers.
57. Balfour to Saint-Aulaire, 1 August 1922, *FRUS, 1922*, I, pp. 406–9; Kenneth Morgan, *Consensus and Disunity: The Lloyd George Coalition Government 1918–22*, pp. 317–18.
58. Costigliola, 'Financial Stabilization', p. 258; Dayer, 'British War Debts', p. 589.
59. For Lloyd George's overthrow, see Beaverbrook, *Decline and Fall of Lloyd George*, pp. 170–203 and Keith Middlemas and John Barnes, *Baldwin*, ch. 6.
60. Norman to Strong, 17 August 1922, Strong papers.
61. Addis to Lamont, 13 October 1922, Lamont papers, 80/9.
62. Diary, 18 October 1922.
63. Norman diary, Bank of England, 3 October 1922.
64. Norman diary, Bank of England, 8 August 1922.
65. 20 October 1922, Strong Papers; Costigliola, *Awkward Dominion*, p. 107.
66. *JMK*, XIX, pt. 1, pp. 6–76.
67. 5 December 1922, *JMK*, XVIII, pp. 101–2.
68. Keynes to Paul Cravath, 23 November 1922, *JMK*, XVIII, pp. 44–5.
69. Diary, 15 November 1922.
70. 'Sir John Bradbury's Scheme for a Comprehensive Settlement of European Inter-Allied Debts', 15 December 1922, Bradbury to Baldwin, T194/263.
71. Diary. For expectations, see Middlemas and Barnes, *Baldwin*, pp. 136–41; Robert Blake, *Unrepentant Tory*, p. 486; Boyle, *Montagu Norman*, p. 155.
72. Diary, 31 December 1922.
73. Norman personal diary, 18 January 1923, lunch with Strong. Middlemas and Barnes, *Baldwin*, pp. 139–42.
74. Cabinet Minutes, 15 January 1923, (CAB 23).
75. Diary, 29 January 1923.
76. *JMK*, XVIII, p. 103.
77. Loose sheets from notebook, Addis papers, /126.
78. Diary. The best account of the Cabinet crisis is in Robert Rhodes

James, *Memoirs of a Conservative: J. C. C. Davidson's Memoirs and Papers*, pp. 142–3.

79. *JMK*, XVIII, pp. 103–4; Beaverbrook, *Decline and Fall of Lloyd George*, pp. 231–2.
80. Grigg, *Prejudice and Judgment*, p. 102; Middlemas and Barnes, *Baldwin*, pp. 146–7; Blake, *Unrepentant Tory*, p. 493.
81. Strong to Gilbert, 6 March 1923, Strong papers.
82. Minute on Geddes to FO, 2 February 1923, FO371 A665/136/45. See also Cabinet Minutes, 31 January 1923 (CAB 23).
83. Howson, *Domestic Monetary Management*, pp. 23–9; Donald E. Moggridge, *British Monetary Policy 1924–1931*, chs. 1 and 2.
84. Norman diary, 31 January 1923. Howson indicates Hawtrey was the source of this idea. *Domestic Monetary Management*, p. 508. See also Sayers, *Bank of England*, pp. 126–7.
85. Diary, 31 January 1923.
86. Clay, *Norman*, pp. 146–7; Norman diary, 13 March 1923, Bank of England.
87. Diary.
88. Norman to Addis, 29 March 1923, Addis papers, Bank of England ADM16/3.
89. 'Memorandum on the Formation of a Reserve in Connexion with the British Debt to the United States', 11 May 1923. An enlarged version of this memorandum, dated 21 May, is also in the Addis papers. The memorandum is cited in Sayers, *Bank of England*, III, p. 380n.
90. Diary, 15, 21 March 1923.
91. Norman diary, 8 May 1923, Bank of England.
92. Diary, 7, 8, 9, 11, 16 May 1923. Sayers's account of this dispute emphasises Bradbury's opposition, *Bank of England*, pp. 126–9. See also Clay, *Norman*, pp. 146–8.
93. Niemeyer to Governor, 23 June 1923, T172/13.
94. Norman Diary, April and June 1923, Bank of England.
95. Addis memo on Bank rate, 7 April 1923, Addis papers, Bank of England, ADM16/3.
96. Sayers, *Bank of England*, p. 130, cites Addis dissent. Niemeyer to Governor, 23 June 1923, T176/13. Niemeyer succeeded Blackett in 1922 as Controller of Finance when Blackett went to India as Finance member of the Viceroy's Council.
97. 'Welcome and Comment on Professor Cassel's address to Institute of Bankers', 25 June 1923, Addis papers.
98. Howson, *Domestic Monetary Management*, p. 30.
99. *JMK*, XIX, Pt. 2, p. 163.
100. *Accountants Magazine*, January 1924. The speech is also in the *Scottish Bankers Magazine*, XV (1924).
101. 'Gold and Sir Charles', *Spectator*, 132 (19 January 1924) pp. 78–80. Philip Williamson suggests these initials may be those of Strachey.
102. W. Fritsch, 'Aspects of Brazilian Economic Policy Under the First Republic, 1889–1930', p. 131, unpublished doctoral dissertation at Cambridge University, 1983.
103. Addis diary, 21 November 1923.

104. E. S. Montagu saw Governor Norman on 3 October and on 11 December 1923. Norman diary, Bank of England. Addis diary, 21 November 1923, records Revelstoke's request.
105. Diary, 3 November 1923.
106. Diary, 20 December 1923.
107. Quoted in Fritsch, 'Aspects of Brazilian Economic Policy', p. 143.
108. Ibid, p. 143, n.1.
109. Ibid, p. 145.
110. Ibid, pp. 145–53.
111. 'Brazil Commission Report', Addis papers. This was the public report. Fritsch indicates that there was a private report for the bankers, but it is not among the Addis papers.
112. Fritsch, 'Aspects of Brazilian Economic policy', pp. 158–82.
113. For a discussion of the informal embargo, see Moggridge, *British Monetary Policy*, ch. 7.
114. E. S. Montagu to Addis, 26 March 1924, Addis papers.
115. Dawes was the only mid-Western banker to support the Anglo-French loan of 1915. See Dayer, 'Strange Bedfellows'.
116. Schuker, *End of French Predominance*, pp. 20–8, 179–81.
117. Ibid, p. 181.
118. Diary, 20 April 1924. For Dawes Plan negotiations and report, see Schuker, *The End of French Predominance*, ch. 6; Beerits memo in Hughes Papers, container 172.
119. Warburg to Young, quoted in Costigliola, 'Financial Stabilization', p. 120.
120. Ibid, pp. 33, 119; Parrini, *Heir to Empire*, p. 119.
121. Bradbury to Chancellor of Exchequer, 27 February 1924; OEN memorandum 29 February 1924, T194/261.
122. This differs from that of K. P. Jones, 'Discord and Collaboration: Choosing an Agent-General for Reparations', *Diplomatic History* (Spring 1977), 137–8, which pictures Morgan as being used by Norman.
123. Norman personal diary, Bank of England.
124. Costigliola, 'Financial Stabilization', pp. 127–32; Schuker, *End of French Predominance*, p. 152.
125. Frank Costigliola, 'US and Reconstruction of Germany in the 1920s', *Business History Review* (1976) p. 487, n. 41.
126. Sayers, *Bank of England*, p. 182.
127. Sayers credits Josiah Stamp and Andrew McFadyean for drafting the Dawes Report, *Bank of England*, p. 180, n. 1.
128. Josephine Young Case and Everett Needham Case, *Owen D. Young and American Enterprise*, chs. 16, 17.
129. Crocker later recalled the event in his notes, 11 February 1929, Owen Young papers.
130. John M. Carroll, 'Owen D. Young and German Reparations: The Diplomacy of an Enlightened Businessman', in K. P. Jones (ed.) *US Diplomats in Europe, 1919–1941*, pp. 43–62.
131. Norman's private diary records frequent meetings with Lamont and J. P. Morgan in August 1924. Bank of England.
132. Addis noted on 28 April 1924 that J. P. Morgan 'seems fairly hopeful about the projected German loan for £40m.' Diary.

133. Sayers, *Bank of England*, p. 183; Schuker, *End of French Predominance*, p. 381, n. 17.
134. Quoted in Schuker, *End of French Predominance*, pp. 379–80.
135. David Marquand, *Ramsay MacDonald*, pp. 344–5 and *passim*.
136. Costigliola, 'Financial Stabilization', p. 134; Boyle, *Norman*, p. 177; Lamont to Hughes, 23 October 1924, Box 62, Hughes papers.
137. Case and Case, *Owen Young*, p. 311.
138. Norman to Addis, 21 August 1924; Addis to Mills, 15 September 1924; Kindersley to Addis, 16 August 1924; Addis to Kindersley, 18 August 1924, Addis papers.
139. Addis minutes of Reichsbank General Council, T188/5; also in Addis papers, 29 November 1924. Young was replaced by Parker Gilbert.
140. Addis minutes of Reichsbank General Council, T188/5.
141. Stephen to Addis, 20 September 1923, Addis papers.
142. Addis diary, 23 October 1923.
143. Niemeyer to Addis, 22 October 1923, Addis papers.
144. Addis diary, 25 October 1923.
145. 'A Tract on Monetary Reform', *JMK*, IV, ch. 2.
146. *Economic Journal*, 34 (1924) pp. 166–9.
147. *JMK*, XIX, Pt. 1, p. 212.
148. Addis to Mills, 20 April 1924, Addis papers.
149. Diary, 18 June 1924.
150. Strong to Addis, May 1924, Addis papers. See also Strong–Norman exchange in Moggridge, *British Monetary Policy*, p. 55.
151. Moggridge, *British Monetary Policy*, pp. 37–9.
152. Ibid, Norman and Addis testimony quoted, pp. 40–2.
153. Addis to Keynes, July 1924. Norman also had emphasised this feature in his testimony to the Chamberlain–Bradbury Committee. See also L. S. Pressnell, '1925: The Burden of Sterling', *Economic History Review* (February 1978) pp. 77–8.
154. For debate, see *JMK*, XIX, Pt. 1, pp. 238–356.
155. Addis papers.
156. Addis to Keynes, 21 July 1924, Addis papers.
157. Keynes to Addis, Addis papers. Keynes also testified to the Chamberlain–Bradbury Committee in July 1924. See Moggridge, *British Monetary Policy*, pp. 42–3.
158. The Bank of England's Exchange Committee included Addis, Pease, Whigham and Niemeyer from the Treasury. See Norman diary, 1923, 1924, Bank of England.
159. Quoted in Moggridge, *British Monetary Policy*, p. 50. Bradbury became Chairman after Chamberlain retired.
160. Ibid, p. 56.
161. Costigliola, *Awkward Dominion*, pp. 101–2.
162. Quoted in Moggridge, *British Monetary Policy*, p. 51.
163. Ibid, p. 89. Norman's private diary records a meeting with Pierre Jay on 26 October 1924, Bank of England.
164. Bruce R. Dalgaard, *South Africa's Impact on Britain's Return To Gold, 1925*, p. 75; Norman diary, 19, 21 November 1924, Bank of England.
165. Dalgaard, *South Africa's Impact*, pp. 76, 147–50.

166. Norman to Niemeyer, 4 December 1924, T172/1500a. Norman suggested the cushion to the Committee of Treasury in November. See Clay, *Norman*, p. 151.
167. Niemeyer to Norman, 8 December 1924, T172/1500a. Norman's diary of 8 December 1924 indicates that Gaspard Farrar approved of a £100m 'cushion'. Bank of England.
168. Lubbock to Niemeyer, 7 January 1925, T172/1500a.
169. Niemeyer to Mr Deputy, 9 January 1925; OEN to Warren [Fisher] 9 January 1925, T172/1500a.
170. WNEF [Fisher] to Otto, [Niemeyer] 12 January 1925, T172/1500a.
171. Addis's memorandum was sent under Lubbocks's name by telegram to Norman, 9 January 1925. Addis papers, Bank of England, ADM16/3.
172. See 'Hearings, Committee on the Currency and Bank of England Note issues', 28 January 1925, pp. 17–40, Marshall Library, Cambridge University. Kindly supplied by Professor Moggridge.
173. Diary, 28 January 1925; 16 April 1925.
174. Addis to Mills, 16 January 1925. Addis wrote that the only 'Die-Hards' were Falk and Robertson; Diary, January 1925.
175. Robert Skidelski, 'Gold Standard and Churchill: The Truth', *Times*, 17 March 1969, p. 25.
176. Diary.
177. For Churchill's doubts and Treasury response, see Moggridge, *British Monetary Policy*, pp. 64–79.
178. Sayers, *Bank of England*, p. 152.
179. Dalgaard, *South Africa's Impact*, pp. 152–77.
180. Sydney-Turner to Waley, 5 December 1924, T172/1500a.
181. Diary, 16 April 1925.
182. Strong papers.
183. Philip Williamson, 'Financiers, the Gold Standard and British Politics, 1925–1931', in John Turner (ed.) *Businessmen and Politics*, pp. 105–8.
184. Moggridge, *British Monetary Policy*, p. 266.
185. Strong memorandum of meeting with Norman and Sir Alan Anderson re Britain's return to gold, 11 January 1925, FRBNY papers, Hoover Presidential Library, container 1. See also S. V. O. Clarke, *Central Bank Cooperation*, p. 82.
186. Williamson, 'Financiers, the Gold Standard and British Politics', pp. 108–29.
187. Norman diary, 7 April 1925, Bank of England.
188. Norman diary, 8 May 1925, Bank of England. See extract from Hansard, 14 May 1925 in T172/1500a.
189. Sayers, *Bank of England*, p. 147, n. 1.
190. Moggridge, *British Monetary Policy*, pp. 228–42; Clay, *Norman*, pp. 151–4; Howson, *Domestic Monetary Management*, discusses other views of the causes of Britain's economic woes.
191. N. H. Dimsdale, 'British Monetary Policy and the Exchange Rate 1920–38', *Oxford Economic Papers*, vol. 33 (1981) Supplement, pp. 328–43.
192. Diary, 5, 20 November 1923. It is not clear if this means Lubbock's succession, but since he was Deputy, that seems likely.
193. Sayers, *Bank of England*, pp. 647–8 referring to Revelstoke, Tiarks, Kindersley and Grenfell.

194. Addis memorandum, 28 September 1926, Addis papers /454; Sayers, *Bank of England*, p. 649.
195. 'Notes of evidence given by Sir Charles Addis before Special Committee on Wednesday, 23 February 1927', Addis papers /455; Sayers, *Bank of England*, pp. 650–1.
196. See Addis–Keynes exchange during the Colwyn Committee on the National Debt Hearings, October 1924 and May 1925, in *JMK*, XIX, Pt. 1, pp. 295–320; Pt. 2, pp. 839–47.
197. Norman diary, 4 December 1924, Bank of England.
198. Addis notes, 28 September 1926, Addis papers /454.
199. 24 December 1926, Strong papers.
200. Sayers comments on the unreality of the Central Bankers' attempt to draw 'a rigid line between central banking and international politics', *Bank of England*, p. 180.
201. S. V. O. Clarke, *Central Bank Cooperation*, p. 142.
202. Moggridge, *British Monetary Policy*, pp. 183–5; Williamson, 'Financiers, the Gold Standard and British Politics', pp. 109–14.
203. Silverman, *Reconstructing Europe*, ch. 2.
204. Norman to Strong, 15, 18 October 1925, Strong papers, Hoover Presidential Library, container 6.
205. Diary.
206. Diary, 28 December 1927.
207. 'Notes of speech at Bank Court on 17 May 1928', Addis papers /456.
208. Sayers, *Bank of England*, pp. 651–2.
209. 'Addis statement to Court, Bank of England', 14 June 1928, Addis papers /456.
210. Diary, 7 June 1928. Booth was a Director from 1915 to 1946.
211. Diary, 12 October 1928.
212. 'Notes of Speech at Bank Court on 17 May 1928' and additional material on the Bank of England, May–October, 1928, Addis papers.
213. Statement in the Addis papers, October 1928; Sayers, *Bank of England*, pp. 650–1.
214. Thomas Mann's *Buddenbrooks* was the most challenging. See diary.
215. Author's interviews with Addis's daughters, 1979–81.
216. Addis papers.
217. Addis to wife, 24 March 1925, Addis papers.
218. Addis diary, 30 September 1926. For description of Gilbert see *BDI*.
219. Diary, 2 August 1926.
220. For disagreement over Goldiskontbank, see Commissioner's Report, Berlin, 31 January, 1 February, 28 March 1927, T188/5. For Schacht's view of Addis, see H. Schacht, *My First Seventy-Six Years*, p. 216.
221. Diary, 9 December 1927, 20 July 1928, 1, 5 July 1929. Addis submitted minutes of the Council meetings to Leith-Ross, which are in T188/5.
222. Leffler, *Elusive Quest*, pp. 100–12; Schuker, *End of French Predominance*, pp. 182–6; Clarke, *Central Bank Cooperation*.
223. Robert Rhodes James, *Churchill: A Study in Failure, 1900–1939*, p. 227.
224. Addis to Mills, 12 May 1926, Addis papers.
225. Leith-Ross memo, 3 December 1925, T176/13. See also Norman–Niemeyer exchange in July, T176/13.

226. Diary, 29 July, August, 1925. Hawtrey wrote a 12 page memo (11 July 1925, T176/13) in favour of reducing bank rate.
227. Diary, December 1925; Strong to Norman, 22 October 1925; Addis to Strong, 22 October 1925, Bank of England ADM 16/3; Norman to Strong, 28 October 1925, Strong papers, Hoover Presidential Library.
228. Sayers, *Bank of England*, pp. 215–16.
229. Addis diary, 27 January 1926. Dalgaard discusses the interrelationship between events in India and South Africa in *South Africa's Impact.*
230. Diary, 17, 19 January 1927. The rate was reduced to $4\frac{1}{2}$ in April 1927.
231. Diary, 9 March 1927.
232. Diary, 15, 23 November 1926. Addis was in the Chair at the opening lecture.
233. Diary, 21 January 1926. Addis noted that he, Hawtrey, J. A. Hobson and Hirst 'had a great talk.' For Hobson, see *BDI.*
234. Diary, 18 March 1926.
235. Diary, 20 October 1927.
236. Diary, 21 October 1926, Addis wrote: 'a three year's job done.'
237. Diary. Sir John Anderson was a Director of the Bank of England.
238. Minority Report, 15 November 1926, Colwyn Committee, p. 355. Signed by Bowen, Hall, Lees-Smith and Wooten.
239. Churchill to Niemeyer, 26 January 1927, T176/39.
240. Norman and Addis gave joint evidence in March 1926. Diary, 5, 29 March 1926. See Sayers, *Bank of England*, p. 347.
241. 'Minutes of Evidence taken in London before the Royal Commission on Indian currency and Finance', vol. V, 1926, Addis papers/660; Report of the Royal Commission on Indian Currency and Finance, 1926 Cmd 2687.
242. 'The Colwyn Report on National Debt and Taxation', *Economic Journal*, June 1927, in *JMK*, XIX, Pt. 2, pp. 675–95.
243. 'Notes for the Chairman's speech', 13 December 1927–8, Addis papers.
244. Churchill speech, 24 March 1926, quoted in Costigliola, 'Financial Stabilization', p. 259.
245. Garrard Winston to Strong, 18 July 1926, Strong papers. For an American analysis of British war costs which concludes that the United Kingdom was a net beneficiary from the war, see 'Memorandum', 9 March 1931, Hoover Presidential Library, Presidential Papers–FA–Financial–British Debt. See also Leffler, *Elusive Quest*, p. 181, who finds flaws in this view.
246. Winston to Strong, 30 August 1926, Strong papers.
247. Niemeyer to Brand, 19 May 1927, T188/13. In 1927, Niemeyer left the Treasury and went to the Bank of England. On 2 April Niemeyer informed Whigham that the Treasury would not renew its Morgan credit. T172/1500A.
248. Minority Report, Colwyn Committee.
249. Sayers, *Bank of England*, ch. 12.
250. Addis papers, Bank of England, ADM 16/4, 24 November 1927.
251. *JMK*, XIX, Pt. 2, pp. 744–5. S. V. O. Clarke, *Central Banking*, pp. 139–41, analyses what the authors of the legislation intended.
252. S. V. O. Clarke, *Central Bank Cooperation*, p. 141, notes some criticism.

253. See Howson, *Domestic Monetary Management* for statistics; Williamson, 'Financiers, The Gold Standard and British Politics', pp. 112–13 for politics.
254. Diary, 8 February 1928. See *JMK*, XIX, Pt. 2, pp. 731.
255. Strong to Norman, 27 March 1928, Strong–Norman Correspondence, Hoover Presidential Library, box 6.
256. Ibid.
257. Ibid.
258. Norman to Strong, 11 April 1928, ibid. These discussions are not mentioned in either Clay or Chandler, which devote their attention to the Strong–Norman differences over Roumanian stabilisation.
259. Chandler, *Strong*, pp. 403–15; Clay, *Norman*, pp. 260–5.
260. S. V. O. Clarke, *Central Bank Cooperation*, pp. 151–2.
261. Diary, 28 March 1928.
262. Jon Jacobson, *Locarno Diplomacy*, pp. 159–60.
263. S. V. O. Clarke, *Central Bank Cooperation*, p. 145 and n. 1, which shows that Governor Moreau had worked out a scheme for a new loan to Germany in March 1928.
264. Costigliola, 'Financial Stabilization', p. 441.
265. 3 March 1928, Strong papers, Hoover Presidential Library, Container 6.
266. Quoted in Costigliola, 'Financial Stabilization', p. 449. See also Hogan, *Informal Entente*, p. 220.
267. Costigliola, 'Financial Stabilization', p. 451. In July 1928, Addis noted that Leith-Ross was at the Bank of England lunch and that he 'had much talk with him about reparations'. (Diary, 20 July 1928.)
268. The Geneva Communiqué is in Jacobson, *Locarno Diplomacy*, pp. 199–200.
269. Diary, 16 October 1928. Norman discussed the composition of the Reparations Committee with Gilbert, Sir Ronald Lindsay, Warren Fisher and Richard Hopkins on 15 October 1928. Norman Diary, Bank of England.

7 An End to Reparations and the Gold Standard, 1929–31

1. The standard work is Eleanor Lansing Dulles, *The Bank for International Settlements at Work*.
2. Charles P. Kindleberger, *The World in Depression 1929–1939*.
3. For pictures of the delegates, see *Current History*, 30 (1929) p. 725.
4. S. V. O. Clarke, *Central Bank Cooperation*, pp. 147–68.
5. Diary.
6. S. V. O. Clarke, *Central Bank Cooperation*, pp. 150–8.
7. Sayers also discusses the American situation, see *Bank of England*, pp. 225–8, 345–6. Stephen Schuker indicates that the Europeans were using American loans to speculate or to buy gold. See 'Owen D. Young, American Foreign Policy and the New Reparation plan, 1929', in Gustav Schmidt (ed.) *Konstellationen Internationaler Politik 1924–1932*.
8. Hoover's hostility may have originated in the early 1900s when he was involved in Chinese mines and the Burmah Oil Company. See Nash, *The Life of Herbert Hoover*, chs. 8–24.

9. Addis to Eba, 18 February 1929, Addis papers.
10. Jacobson, *Locarno Diplomacy*, pp. 222–35; Case and Case, *Owen Young*, ch. 24.
11. Schuker, 'Owen D. Young, American Foreign Policy, and the New Reparation Plan, 1929'.
12. Leith-Ross to Ernest Rowe-Dutton, the Treasury representative in Paris, 19 June 1928, quoted in Leith-Ross, *Money Talks*, p. 105.
13. Lamont papers, 178–14.
14. Addis diary. See also 3 January 1929.
15. Sayers, *Bank of England*, pp. 324, 327. For Stamp views on appreciation of gold, see *JMK*, XIX, Pt. 1, p. 420.
16. Addis to wife, 28 February 1929. See Young comment on delegates, Memo dictated abroad the 'Acquitania', 11 June 1929, file -34, Young papers.
17. Revelstoke diary, 9 February 1929, p. 9.
18. Tiarks to Revelstoke, 4 January 1929, including Dulles letter, which he asks to be returned to Major Pam of Schroeders. Revelstoke papers, DPP2.4.1–2. For Major Pam, see *DBB*, IV.
19. Tiarks to Revelstoke, 4 January 1929.
20. For Dulles, see Louis Gerson, *John Foster Dulles*, pp. 11–21; Ronald W. Pruessen, *John Foster Dulles: The Road to Power*.
21. Revelstoke Diary, 14 February 1929. My emphasis.
22. Ibid, 15 February 1929. One wonders if Revelstoke's reference to modesty was made sarcastically.
23. For changes in the Treasury at this time see Leith-Ross, *Money Talks*, pp. 106–7.
24. Revelstoke Diary, 14 February 1929.
25. Revelstoke Diary, 13 February 1929, DPP2.4, 3–4.
26. Revelstoke Diary, 14 February 1929, memorandum of interview with Morgan.
27. Diary, 14 February 1929.
28. Diary, 15 February 1929.
29. Addis to Eba, 6 March 1929, Addis papers.
30. Revelstoke Diary, 23, 25 February 1929.
31. Revelstoke Diary, 9 March 1929, p. 83. Stamp had found Fisher more helpful than Leith-Ross (Revelstoke Diary, 4 March 1929, p. 63.) The issue referred to was commercialisation which the French favoured.
32. Revelstoke Diary, 22 February 1929, p. 47.
33. Revelstoke Diary, 6 March 1929.
34. Revelstoke Diary, 22 February 1929, p. 43.
35. Case and Case, *Owen Young*, pp. 436–7 credits Francqui and Schact, with Young's help.
36. Revelstoke Diary, 2 March 1929, p. 58. W. R. Burgess became Deputy Governor of the Federal Reserve Bank of New York in 1930. Walter Stewart was the American adviser to the Bank of England, Pierre Quesnay was the General Manager of the Bank of France.
37. 13 March 1929, Revelstoke Diary, p. 93.
38. Addis diary, 15 March 1929.
39. Quoted in Case and Case, *Owen Young*, p. 438.

40. Everett Case suggested that some people thought Hoover feared Young as a potential political rival in the next Presidential campaign. Author's interview with Everett Case.
41. 'Notes on meeting of General Council', 30 November, 1 December 1928, T188/5.
42. Ibid, 23 March 1929.
43. Revelstoke Diary, conversation with Tyrrell, 4 March 1929, p. 66. See below for evidence of Lazard competition with Consortium, 1933 and Costigliola, 'Financial Stabilization', pp. 268–76.
44. Schuker, 'Owen Young'.
45. Diary, 6 April 1929; Jacobson, *Locarno Diplomacy*, p. 253; Case and Case, *Owen Young*, pp. 441–4.
46. Addis to daughter, Robina, 14 April 1929, Addis papers. For detailed description, see Jacobson, *Locarno Diplomacy*, pp. 253–6.
47. Addis to Eba, 14 April 1929, Addis papers.
48. Revelstoke diary, 17 April 1929.
49. Addis to Eba, 20 April 1929. Blackett, who (through the influence of Addis and Norman) had been chosen as the head of Cables and Wireless, had not spent much time in Paris.
50. Addis to wife, 1 May 1929, from Berlin. Addis papers.
51. Jacobson, *Locarno Diplomacy*, pp. 261–7. Addis was in Berlin that weekend. See Addis to son, John, 3 May 1929, Addis papers.
52. Addis to wife, 11 May 1929, Addis papers. Moreau was the Govenror of the Bank of France.
53. Crocker diary, 11 May 1929, Owen Young papers. These were the occupation costs, which by the terms of the Dawes Plan, had priority. See Leffler, *The Elusive Quest*, p. 209.
54. Case and Case, *Owen Young*, pp. 444–9; J. D. Forbes, *J. P. Morgan, Jr*, p. 165.
55. Crocker notes, 26 April 1929, Young papers; Jacobson, *Locarno Diplomacy*, pp. 265–6.
56. Addis to Eba, 15 May 1929, Addis papers; Crocker notes, 15 May 1929, pp. 238–9, Young papers.
57. Crocker notes, 22 May 1929, p. 282, Young papers. The Spa agreement of 1920 provided the percentages of reparations which each Allied Power was to receive. See *JMK*, XVIII, pp. 336–41.
58. Crocker notes, 18 May 1929, p. 263, Young papers.
59. Revelstoke Diary, 11 April 1929, pp. 160–2.
60. Addis to Eba, 9 May 1929, Addis papers.
61. Crocker notes, 8 May 1929, Young papers.
62. Martin Gilbert, *Winston Churchill*, pp. 17–19.
63. Philip Snowden, *Autobiography*, pp. 748–9.
64. For the 1929 election see Philip Williamson, '"Safety First": Baldwin, The Conservative Party, and the 1929 General Election', *Historical Journal*, 1982.
65. Addis to wife, 30 May 1929, Addis papers.
66. Diary, 27 May 1929. Case and Case, *Owen Young*, suggest Young's despair but do not picture him as unable to function.
67. Diary, 7 June 1929.

68. Quoted in Boyle, *Norman*, p. 243.
69. Quoted in Revelstoke Diary, 6 March 1929, p. 69. Keynes's analysis is in *JMK*, XVIII, pp. 342–7. Stephen Clarke believes everything depended upon the continued expansion of the world economy. Letter to author, April 1985.
70. Diary, 25 June 1929. Henderson was Foreign Secretary, Graham was President of the Board of Trade.
71. O. G. Sargent Memorandum, 9 July 1929 and FLR comment, 11 July 1929 on proposed Conference to consider Young Plan, T172/1694.
72. T176/13.
73. Hopkin's notes, 19 February 1929, T176/13. Norman was in New York and Washington returning to London 15 February 1929. Norman private diary, 29 January–15 February 1929, Bank of England.
74. Lubbock to Hopkins, 9 February 1929, T176/13.
75. Phillips to Hopkins, 9 March 1929, T176/13.
76. Hopkins to Churchill, 18 March 1929, T176/13.
77. Sayers, *Bank of England*, p. 228.
78. Hopkins to Grigg, 19 August 1929, T172/13.
79. Ibid. See also Leith-Ross memo, 26 August 1929, T172/1694, kindly supplied by Philip Williamson.
80. *Times*, 25 July 1929.
81. O. G. Sargent memorandum on Young Plan, 17 June 1929, PREM 1/83.
82. Stamp to PM, 4 July 1929, PREM 1/83. My emphasis.
83. Robert Boyce, 'British leadership in the International Economic System', pp. 20–1. A paper presented at a Conference on the 1931 Crisis and its Aftermath', Clare College, Cambridge, 1982.
84. Diary, 5 July 1929.
85. Stamp to Young, 26 July 1929, Young papers, box 4–35.
86. Leith-Ross, *Money Talks*, pp. 119–20.
87. Reparation Conference, 1929, British Delegation – Financial note #6, Cab 29/116.
88. Addis to wife, 30 July 1929, Addis papers.
89. Dawes, *Journal as Ambassador*, p. 44.
90. Lamont to Snowden, 14 August 1929, T172/1656.
91. Ibid, 20 August 1929.
92. Snowden to Lamont, 23 August 1929, T172/656.
93. Norman personal diary, Bank of England.
94. 'The Young Reparations Plan: A Hasty Analysis', by John Calvin Brown, 24 July 1929, prepared at request of James F. Burke. Hoover Presidential Library, Presidential Foreign Affairs, p. 295.
95. Ibid, p. 6.
96. Grenfell to Jack Morgan, 22 August 1929; Grenfell to Addis, 23 August 1929, Morgan Grenfell papers.
97. British delegation (The Hague) to FO, 19 August 1929, FO371 C6465/1/8.
98. The Federal Reserve Bank was prohibited from joining. See S. V. O. Clarke, *Central Bank Cooperation*, p. 147.
99. Young to Stamp, 26 August 1929, Young papers, box 4–35. My emphasis.

100. Robert Olds to Dulles, 11 June 1929, Quoted in Costigliola, 'Financial Stabilization', p. 474.
101. 'Prices and Credit Policy', n.d., T175/146.
102. Addis to Eba, 25 August 1929, Addis papers.
103. Quoted in Stephen Roskill, *Hankey: Man of Secrets*, II, p. 481.
104. Addis to wife, 23 August 1929, Addis papers.
105. Leith-Ross, *Money Talks*, pp. 125–6; Addis to Mills, 5 September 1929, Addis papers.
106. Roskill, *Hankey*, II, p. 489, n. 3; Boyce, 'British Leadership in the International System', p. 18.
107. S. P. Gilbert to Young, 3 September 1929, Young Papers, box R–34.
108. Earlier Layton had taught economics at Cambridge.
109. PS to Sir Warren Fisher, 14 September 1929, T172/1656.
110. Waley to Fisher, 30 September 1929, T172/1656. For Salter, see *BDI*.
111. Snowden believed in the gold standard more fervently than did Churchill. See Williamson, 'Financiers, The Gold Standard and British Politics'.
112. The Treasury expected, in addition to a bank rate increase, a request to increase the fiduciary issue. See Phillips Memo, 13 September 1929, T176/13 (kindly furnished by Philip Williamson.)
113. Included in Phillips to Fisher, 30 September 1929, T176/13.
114. M. Sergent, 30 September, 1 October 1929, T188/5.
115. Addis papers.
116. Leith-Ross to Waley, 1 October 1929; G. H. S. Pinsent memorandum, 21 October 1929, T172/1656, my emphasis.
117. Jay was Deputy Agent-General; Whigham was a Morgan partner; ter Meulen was a Dutch banker. Addis to Eba, 4 October 1929, Addis papers.
118. Addis to Norman, 12 October 1929, Addis papers at Bank of England ADM 16/1.
119. Layton apologised to Addis for leaving him 'single-handed', n.d. Addis papers.
120. Addis to Norman, 31 October 1929, Addis papers, Bank of England, ADM 16/1.
121. Morgan Grenfell to J. P. Morgan, 31 October 1929, Morgan Grenfell papers, kindly furnished to author by Dr Kathleen Burk.
122. Addis to Norman, 3 November 1929, Addis papers.
123. Addis to Norman, 10 November 1929, ibid.
124. Addis diary, 9, 10, 12 November 1929.
125. Addis wrote in a similar vein to his son John, 12 November 1929, Addis papers.
126. Ibid. For further evidence of competition between Morgans and Dillon, see J. P. Morgan for S. P. Gilbert, 17 December 1929; J. P. Morgan to Morgan & Cie, 19 December 1929, Morgan Grenfell papers, kindly furnished to author by Dr Kathleen Burk.
127. Siepmann to Addis, 12 November 1929, ibid. See also de Sanchez (for Reynolds) to Morgan Grenfell, 9 November 1929; J. P. Morgan to Reynolds, 9 November 1929. Morgan was in London. Morgan Grenfell papers, Burk copy.

128. Lubbock to Addis, 14 November 1929, Addis papers.
129. Norman to Addis, 15 November 1929, Addis papers.
130. Diary, 27 November 1929. For international financial situation, see S. V. O. Clarke, *Central Bank Cooperation*, pp. 168–71.
131. Addis speech at Cambridge, 28 November 1929, Addis papers, /569, which is very similar to his speech to the Institute of Bankers the following April (see below).
132. Speech at Dinner given by German provincial members of the General Council of the Reichsbank at Hotel Adlon, Berlin, 1 December 1929, Addis papers.
133. Addis diary, 12–18 January 1930; Addis to wife, 14, 15 January 1930, Addis papers.
134. Leith-Ross memorandum, December 1930–November 1931, Germany II, T188/16. Addis's diary records a meeting at the Treasury, 12 December 1929, with Leith-Ross, Waley and Pinsent where they discussed the Trust Agreement and made progress 'towards agreement with the French'.
135. Diary, 4 February 1930.
136. For figures on UK deficit in 1929, see Alec Cairncross and Barry Eichengreen, *Sterling in Decline*, pp. 47–9.
137. Gilbert to State Department, 13 December 1929, Hoover Presidential Library, Presidential foreign affairs, box 1015. Gilbert became a partner in J. P. Morgan & Co. in 1931.
138. Leith-Ross memo, 3 pp. 'Postponement of British War Debt to USA', January 1930, T188/16. See also Leith-Ross to Hopkins, n.d., T188/16.
139. 'Financial Note #3, BIS, The Hague Conference, 1930', British Delegation, Cab 29/116.
140. 'Notes on the Meetings of the General Council of the Reichsbank at Berlin', 2 December 1929, 31 January, 1 February 1930.
141. Diary, 30, 31 January, 1 February 1930.
142. Henry A. Turner, Jr, *German Big Business and the Rise of Hitler*, p. 103; E. Dulles, *The Bank for International Settlements*, p. 363.
143. Diary, 3 February 1930.
144. Diary, 8 April 1930. Both Lamont and Young had suggested Addis for President of the BIS. See Lamont to Morgan, 5 November 1929, Morgan Grenfell papers, furnished to author by Dr Kathleen Burk. For Fraser, see *BDI*.
145. Susan Howson and Donald Winch, *The Economic Advisory Council 1930–1939*, pp. 5–29.
146. For League Gold committee, see Sayers, *Bank of England*, pp. 346–51; *JMK*, XIX, pt. 2, pp. 775–80. For Chatham House Committee, see RIIA, *The International Gold Problem: A Record of the Discussions of a Study Group of Members of the RIIA, 1929–1931*.
147. Hamilton Fish Armstrong, *Peace and Counterpeace*, p. 5.
148. Lionel Curtis, *The Capital Question of China*, preface. Curtis was one of the founders of Chatham House. See also Stephen King-Hall, *Chatham House*.
149. The official publication was first called the *Journal of the British Institute of International Affairs, 1922–6*, then the *Royal Institute of International*

Affairs Journal from 1927 to 1930. Thereafter the publication became *International Affairs*.
150. Diary.
151. Sayers, *Bank of England*, p. 360.
152. *JMK*, XX, p. 19.
153. 'Relation of the Bank to the Treasury', Draft notes for evidence'; 'Gold Standard and Rationalization', Notes, RVNH [Hopkins' with Sir O. E. Niemeyer's compliments, T175/46. The Evidence of bank officials is in Sayers, *Bank of England*, III, Appendix 21. Keynes's evidence is in *JMK*, XX, pp. 38–309.
154. Sayers, *Bank of England*, pp. 371–2.
155. Stamp to Young, 29 November 1929, Young papers.
156. Sayers, *Bank of England*.
157. S. V. O. Clarke, *Central Bank Cooperation*, pp. 168–9.
158. Hopkins to Grigg, 13 January 1930, T176/13.
159. Addis diary, 5 February 1930.
160. Diary, 12, 25 February 1930.
161. Hawtrey to Addis, 25 February 1930, Addis papers, Bank of England ADM 16/5; T176/13.
162. Grigg to Hopkins, 28 February 1930, T176/13.
163. Diary, 27 February, 5 March 1930. See also Sayers's discussion of the Bank's market operations, *Bank of England*, pp. 309–13; Howson, *Domestic Monetary Management*, pp. 66–71.
164. Diary, 5, 12 December 1929. See Chatham House lecture by Sir Josiah Stamp on 'The International Functions of Gold', 5 December 1929, *The International Gold Problem*, pp. 1–17.
165. RIIA, *The International Gold Problem*, pp. 90–108.
166. Sayers, *Bank of England*, pp. 346–51.
167. Norman to Addis, 17 October 1929, Addis papers, *Bank of England*, ADM 16/1.
168. 'Extract from Minutes of the Committee of Treasury of 16 October 1929', Addis papers, *Bank of England*, ADM 16/1.
169. Sayers, *Bank of England*, pp. 368–71.
170. Diary, 31 March 1930.
171. Diary, May 1930.
172. 'The Bank for International Settlements', 3 April 1930, *Institute of Bankers' Journal*; 'Sir Charles Addis on Gold and Prices', *Times*, 4 April 1930, p. 22; the *Bankers' Magazine* (May 1930) reprints the speech with a picture of Addis.
173. Burgess to Osborne, 23 April 1930, FRBNY papers, C797.3.
174. Address of Melvin A. Traylor, Bank for International Settlements, *Documents*, pp. 155–72.
175. Diary, 7 May, 23 June 1930.
176. Boyce, 'British Leadership in the International Economic System', p. 21.
177. Francis W. Hirst, *Wall Street and Lombard Street: The Stock Exchange Slump of 1929 and the Trade Depression of 1930*, pp. 161–7. Hirst (who was in the United States during the Stock Market crash) quotes from a series of lectures which he gave on the BBC in the summer of 1930.

178. See exchange of views between Niemeyer, Strakosch and Hawtrey, 9 April 1930, RIIA, *The International Gold Problem*, pp. 84–115.
179. Norman diary, *Bank of England*.
180. Sayers, *Bank of England*, pp. 356–7; Dulles, *The Bank for International Settlements at Work*, p. 56.
181. Diary, 12, 20 May 1930. The Committee of Treasury Minutes of 9 April 1930 indicate that the issue was to be made by the Bank of England.
182. Diary, 9 May 1930. Leith-Ross, *Money Talks*, p. 127.
183. Boyle, *Norman*, p. 254; Clay, *Norman*, pp. 366–7.
184. Dulles, *Bank for International Settlements*, p. 366; Roger Auboin, *The Bank for International Settlements*, p. 8 indicates $300m raised.
185. Leith-Ross to Waley, 30 May 1930; Leith-Ross to Hopkins, Snowden, 1930, T160/430/12317/1; kindly furnished by Philip Williamson.
186. Leith-Ross memo, 28 July 1930, Ramsay MacDonald papers, /257, kindly furnished by Philip Williamson.
187. E. H. Carr minute, 23 May 1930, on Francis Rodd to Sir Robert Vansittart, 20 May 1930, FO371 C3974/658/62.
188. Ibid.
189. Addis to H. Henderson, 25 June 1941, Addis papers, /441.
190. Leith-Ross, *Money Talks*, p. 130; Sayers, *Bank of England*, pp. 351–1; *JMK*, XIX, pt. 2, pp. 775–80.
191. *Economist*, 27 September 1930, p. 556.
192. Leith-Ross to Brand, 21 July 1930, Brand papers, 28, enclosing memo on 'Probabilities of Government action in Regard to the recent fall in world prices', 20 July 1930, PRO 30/69/2/257, kindly furnished by Philip Williamson.
193. Strakosch to Leith-Ross, 25 August 1930, T188/274 H 16/17.
194. Committee of Treasury Minutes, 3 September 1930, Bank of England. Jeremiah Smith (Lamont's assistant) was quoted.
195. Leith-Ross to Hawtrey, Phillips, Waley, 2 December 1930; Leith-Ross to Strakosch, 11 December 1930, T188/15 b, kindly furnished by Philip Williamson.
196. Leith-Ross to Strakosch, 11 December 1930, as n. 195.
197. RIIA, *The International Gold Problem*, pp. 141–53. For Kisch, see *BDI*.
198. Ibid, 29 October 1930, pp. 153–4.
199. Ibid, p. 159.
200. Diary, 25 September 1930.
201. Dulles, *Bank for International Settlements*.
202. Leith-Ross to Sir R. Hopkins, 29 December 1930, T188/16.
203. Committee of Treasury Minutes, 10 December 1930, Bank of England.
204. Barry Eichengreen, *Sterling and the Tariff*, p. 17.
205. Howson and Winch, *Economic Advisory Council*, pp. 43, 56–8, 68, 72; *JMK*, XX, pp. 470–82.
206. Williamson, 'Financiers, The Gold Standard and British Politics', p. 119.
207. See Ch. 9 below.
208. 'Address of C. S. A., 27 October 1930, *Monthly Journal of the British Empire Chamber of Commerce* (November 1930) pp. 11–14; also

printed in French in *Société Belge d'Etudes et d'Expansion*, no. 78 (December 1930) pp. 526–33. The *Economist*, 1 November 1930, referred to Addis's 'sturdy free-trade declaration'.
209. 'Addis for Control of World Prices', *New York Times*, 25 November 1930, p. 41; The address is in *The Coupon* (December 1930) no. 41, pp. 24–31.
210. *Institute of Bankers' Journal* (1931) pp. 1–12. Addis's speech to the Academy was on 14 November 1930. See *Proceedings of the Academy of Political Science*, XIV (1931).
211. *Monthly Journal of the British Empire Chamber of Commerce in the United States of America*, X (1930) pp. 11–14.
212. Diary, 12 November 1930.
213. Diary, 17 November 1930. For proposals regarding silver, see Williamson, 'Financiers, the Gold Standard and British Politics', pp. 117–18.
214. For rupee problem, see B. R. Tomlinson, 'Britain and the Indian Currency Crisis, 1930–32', *Economic History Review*, XXXII (1979) pp. 88–99.
215. Harrison to Norman, 12 June 1930, 'Notes of a conversation with Addis regarding Harrison Cable', 18 June 1930; Cattern to Addis, 1 July 1930; Harvey to Harrison, 27 June 1930, Addis papers, Bank of England ADM 16/5.
216. Archibald Rose to Snowden, 13 January 1931, T172/1505. Rose (a Director of the British–American Tobacco Co.) was working with Addis on the China Subcommittee.
217. Diary, 30 January to 20 July 1931.
218. Leith-Ross to RVNH/PS, 6 February 1931, T175/53, followed by 'Norman agrees' (kindly supplied to author by Philip Williamson).
219. Diary, 19, 20 November 1930.
220. 31 October 1930, Lamont papers, 80/10.
221. Diary, 26 November 1930.
222. See Streat Diary, 15 January 1931. Reference supplied by Philip Williamson. For American political situation, see Leffler, *Elusive Quest*, ch. 7; Eliot Rosen, *Hoover, Roosevelt, and the Brains Trust*, ch. 4.
223. Diary, 5 December 1930.
224. S. V. O. Clarke, *Central Bank Cooperation*, pp. 172, 174, 177.
225. Turner, *German Big Business*, pp. 100–11.
226. S. V. O. Clarke, *Central Bank Cooperation*, pp. 178–9.
227. Sayers, *Bank of England*, p. 408, n. 2, indicates that the 'first substantial talk on the Continent of a possibility of British departure from gold' began in January 1931. See also Henderson's comment to Keynes in February 1931, *JMK*, XX, p. 483.
228. *Times*, 18 December 1930. See also *Financial News*, 17 December 1930.
229. Diary, 7 January 1931.
230. Committee of Treasury Minutes, 10 December 1930, *Bank of England*.
231. Diary, 24 January 1931.
232. Diary, 30 January 1931. *Manchester Guardian*, 13 April 1931, identified Kindersley and Addis as the authors of this plan. See Edward W. Bennett, *Germany and the Diplomacy of the Financial Crisis, 1931*, p. 106, n. 41.

233. Committee of Treasury Minutes, 7 January 1931, Bank of England.
234. Ibid.
235. 30 January 1931, T160/398 F12377 (reference kindly furnished by Philip Williamson).
236. Committee of Treasury Minutes, 25 February 1931, Bank of England. See also S. V. O. Clarke, *Central Bank Cooperation*, pp. 179–80.
237. Leith-Ross to Rowe-Dutton, 24 February 1931, T160/398/F12377 (reference supplied by Philip Williamson).
238. Diary.
239. Diary.
240. Leith-Ross to Hopkins, 2 February 1931, T160/404 F557/01 1 (reference supplied by Philip Williamson).
241. Committee of Treasury Minutes, 4 February 1931, Bank of England.
242. S. V. O. Clarke, *Central Bank Cooperation*, p. 184.
243. Diary, 22 April 1931.
244. Diary, 25 February 1931. The Abbey Road Society was a Building Society which provided mortgages for homes.
245. *Times*, 5, 27 May 1931; Dulles, *Bank for International Settlements*, p. 240.
246. Cairncross and Eichengreen, *Sterling in Decline*, p. 62.
247. Addis noted 'Endless talk with Norman, Stamp, Kindersley, Mayers, Henderson.' Diary, 27 May 1931.
248. Diary, 1 June 1931.
249. Diary, 3 June 1931.
250. S. V. O. Clarke, *Central Bank Cooperation*, p. 188; Marquand, *MacDonald*, pp. 17–19.
251. Diary, 7 June 1931.
252. Diary, 27 May, 1–4 June 1931.
253. Addis to Eba, 3, 5 June 1931. This must have recommended BIS credits for Germany. Henry H. Schloss, *The Bank for International Settlements*, p. 81, indicates the BIS, in cooperation with other central banks, granted a 'twenty-day rediscount credit to the Reichsbank of $100m.'
254. Diary, 16 June 1931. S. V. O. Clarke reports that total grants of $14m were inadequate, *Central Bank Cooperation*, pp. 186–8.
255. Ibid, pp. 190–1. For the diplomatic negotiations, see Bennett, *Germany and the Diplomacy of the Financial Crisis, 1931*, ch. V.
256. Norman to Harrison, 18 June 1931, Harrison papers, FRBNY.
257. S. V. O. Clarke, *Central Bank Cooperation*, p. 189; Pruessen, *Dulles*, p. 108.
258. Schuker, 'Owen D. Young, American Foreign Policy and the New Reparation Plan, 1929', p. 7.
259. Diary, 23 June 1931; Clarke, *Central Bank Cooperation*, pp. 191–2, indicates that the credit undertaken by US, UK, France and BIS was for $25m each.
260. David Carlton, *MacDonald versus Henderson*, p. 199.
261. Addis to Eba, 4 July 1931, Addis papers.
262. Addis noted on 8 July 1931: 'Alan Anderson, Runciman, D. Simon and others dined with me at the Athenaeum before going on to Chatham House where, Stamp in the Chair, Anderson opened a discussion on "The US Tariff and World Prices."'

263. Committee of Treasury Minutes, 9 July 1931, Bank of England.
264. S. V. O. Clarke, *Central Bank Cooperation*, pp. 194–6.
265. Ibid, p. 196.
266. Ibid. What follows must be considered a hypothesis, since it is based on circumstantial rather than definitive evidence.
267. *JMK*, XX, pp. 561–88. Addis's diary records a meeting with Layton on 17 July 1931.
268. Cairncross and Eichengreen, *Sterling in Decline*, emphasise the importance of confidence in maintaining currency stability.
269. Committee of Treasury Minutes, 29 July 1931, Bank of England. See also the press Notice explaining the suspension of gold payments on 20 September 1931, in Sayers, *Bank of England*, p. 265.
270. Committee of Treasury Minutes, 4 March 1931, Bank of England.
271. Diary, 11, 13 July 1931.
272. Addis to wife, 12 July 1931, Addis papers. Norman and Moret (the Governor of the Bank of France) were to meet in Basle to discuss the German crisis. Rodd, an assistant to Norman at the Bank of England, spent 20 months at the BIS.
273. S. V. O. Clarke, *Central Banking*, pp. 198–9.
274. Gold losses from the Bank of England to the Bank of France resumed in May 1930. Howson, *Domestic Monetary Management*, p. 65.
275. Howson and Winch, *Economic Advisory Council*, pp. 80–1.
276. Addis seems undismayed throughout the crisis, suggesting that he may have welcomed – or at least have accepted the need for – devaluation.
277. Roskill, *Hankey*, II, p. 552.
278. Cairncross and Eichengreen, *Sterling in Decline*, pp. 54–5, 61.
279. Leith-Ross to Hopkins and Chancellor of Exchequer, T188/16.
280. Addis records a meeting with Layton on 5 August 1931.
281. Hopkins memorandum on Layton report, 28 August 1931, T188/16.
282. Hopkins to Chancellor of Exchequer, August 1931, T188/16.
283. See discussion in Cairncross and Eichengreen, *Sterling in Decline*, pp. 224–9.
284. Sayers, *Bank of England*, ch. 17, repeatedly emphasises the agreement of financial opinion on the necessity for such cuts.
285. Howson, *Domestic Monetary Management*, p. 85.
286. Diary, 17, 18 July 1931.
287. Williamson, 'A "Bankers' Ramp"?', pp. 783–5.
288. Howson, *Domestic Monetary Management*, p. 85.
289. Roskill, *Hankey*, II, p. 542.
290. Sayers, *Bank of England*, pp. 391–4; Williamson, 'A "Bankers' Ramp"?'.
291. Committee of Treasury Minutes, 29 July 1931, Bank of England.
292. An excellent suggestion of Ministers' ignorance concerning the international financial situation and its implications for Britain is provided by the Diary of Sir Maurice Hankey who was one of the best informed of Britain's government officials. See Roskill, *Hankey*, II, pp. 542–5; Marquand, *MacDonald*, chs. 25 and 26.
293. Quoted in Williamson, 'A Bankers' Ramp"?', pp. 786–7.

294. Howson and Winch, *Economic Advisory Council*, p. 89; *JMK*, XX, p. 591.
295. Diary, 5, 12 August 1931; Sayers, *Bank of England*, p. 394.
296. Diary, 12 August 1931.
297. Williamson, 'A "Bankers' Ramp"?', pp. 787–96.
298. *JMK*, XX, p. 595; For the terms, see Sayers, *Bank of England*, III, pp. 257–61.
299. Addis to wife, 23, 24 August 1931; Diary, 27 August 1931.
300. Committee of Treasury Minutes, 17, 18 September 1931, Bank of England.
301. Diary, 18, 19, 23 September 1931.
302. See Sayers's analysis of Norman's feigned surprise when he returned to England, *Bank of England*, p. 415, n. 1.
303. Quoted in Howson, *Domestic Monetary Management*, p. 78.
304. Howson, *Domestic Monetary Management*, p. 79.
305. Cairncross and Eichengreen, *Sterling in Decline*, pp. 73–83; Williamson, 'A "Bankers' Ramp"?', *passim*.
306. *Times*, 15 June 1931, p. 19.

PART III   A RETURN TO STERLING

8   Towards a Sterling Bloc, 1931–4

1. Howson, *Domestic Monetary Management*, pp. 79–81; Sayers, *Bank of England*, p. 416.
2. Sayers, *Bank of England*, pp. 416–19; Susan Howson, *Sterling's Managed Float: The Operations of the Exchange Equalisation Account, 1932–39*, p. 45.
3. Howson, *Domestic Monetary Management*, pp. 82–6.
4. Quoted in Sayers, *Bank of England*, p. 412, n. 4.
5. Diary, 24 September–6 October 1931.
6. Sayers, *Bank of England*, pp. 419–25 and III, pp. 266–73.
7. Diary, 27 October 1931.
8. A. J. P. Taylor, *English History*, pp. 321–8.
9. T175/56; Howson and Winch, *The Economic Advisory Council*, p. 368; *JMK*, XXI, p. 29.
10. Diary, 4 November 1931. On 2 December Addis chaired the discussion, opened by Salter, on 'The Future of the Pound'.
11. *JMK*, XXI, pp. 16–28; Howson, *Domestic Monetary Management*, p. 174.
12. *Economist*, January 1932.
13. Ibid, pp. 29–32; Howson, *Domestic Monetary Management*, pp. 82–6 and Appendix 4, which quotes evidence.
14. 16 November 1931, *JMK*, XXI, p. 17. See also Norman to Keynes, 27 November 1931, Ibid, p. 28.
15. Cab. 58/169, in Howson and Winch, *Economic Advisory Council*, p. 258. Pressnell, 'The Burden of Sterling', shows that an imperial currency had first been proposed in 1917.

16. 26 November 1931, T175/56. See Keynes memorandum on 'German Riddle', 30 November 1931, *JMK*, XVIII, pp. 358–63.
17. See Treasury discussions in Howson, *Domestic Monetary Management*, Appendix 4.
18. Sayers, *Bank of England*, p. 424, indicates a rise in confidence when the December war-debt payment was made.
19. Chancellor of the Exchequer, Chamberlain, announced this on 19 February 1932. See *JMK*, XVIII, p. 370.
20. Ibid, p. 365.
21. *JMK*, XVIII, p. 365. Alexander Shaw, a Director of the Bank of England, informed Keynes that the BIS meeting concurred with his views. Ibid, 15 January 1932, p. 369.
22. 'Report of the Young Plan Advisory Committee with Annexes', Supplement to the *Economist*, 2 January 1932, pp. 6–7.
23. Diary.
24. The steps leading to Lausanne can be followed in *JMK*, XVIII, pp. 370–8; Rosen, *Hoover, Roosevelt and the Brains Trust*, pp. 81–91.
25. Memorandum, 20 January 1932, Addis papers, Bank of England, ADM 16/6.
26. Ibid.
27. Diary. For Treasury views, see Howson, *Domestic Monetary Management*, p. 87. Sayers indicates that Blackett, Stamp and Kindersley all argued for rate reduction. *Bank of England*, pp. 424–5.
28. Diary, 8–13 October 1931.
29. Diary, 28 October–12 November 1931; Lubbock to Addis, 2 November 1931; Lubbock to Addis, 4 November 1931, Addis papers. Clay does not mention this dissent in *Norman*, pp. 312–7.
30. Addis to Norman, 17 October 1931; Bank of England Secretary to Addis, 29 October 1931, Addis papers.
31. Quoted in Sayers, *Bank of England*, p. 601.
32. Leith-Ross to Sir Richard Hopkins, 30 October 1931, T175/46.
33. Siepmann to Addis, 16 November 1931, Addis papers, Bank of England, ADM 16/1.
34. Addis to Siepmann, 17 November 1931, ibid; Addis diary, 20, 24 November, 3 December 1931.
35. Hopkins memorandum, 6 pp. 'Depreciation of the Sterling Balances of the BIS', 9 December 1931, T175/56; See also Roger Auboin, *Bank for International Settlements*, pp. 8–11; Leith-Ross, *Money Talks*, p. 140.
36. 8 May 1932, Basle, Addis papers.
37. Diary, 12 May 1932.
38. Diary, 6 April 1932.
39. Norman to Addis, 7 April 1932, Addis papers.
40. 'A Monetary Proposal for Lausanne', summarised in *JMK*, XXI, p. 203, and XVIII, p. 378.
41. 'A Note on the German Riddle', *JMK*, XVIII, pp. 358–63.
42. Roskill, *Hankey*, III, pp. 46–50. For discussions of strategy, see *JMK*, XVIII, pp. 273–80. See also Leffler, *Elusive Quest*, pp. 288–95.
43. First Report, 11 October 1932, 32 pp., T188/48 EAC(H)153. See also Howson and Winch, *Economic Advisory Council*, p. 370.

44. Layton discussed the Lausanne arrangements with Addis at the Tuesday Club meeting in July. Diary, 13 July 1932.
45. Ibid. This report is also in Cab 58/183. See also Addis diary, September 1932 to March 1933.
46. Leffler, *Elusive Quest*, p. 294.
47. Ibid, pp. 306–10; *JMK*, XVIII, pp. 380–90.
48. Roskill, *Hankey*, III, p. 50.
49. Diary, 11 July 1932, 12 October 1932, 16 January 1933.
50. Diary, 13 July 1932.
51. Addis comments, 6 December 1932, Chatham House, Addis papers. Addis diary, 6 December 1932.
52. 'Toast to Union Discount Co.', 24 February 1933, Addis papers. In 1932 at Ottawa, the MacDonald government had adopted a programme of imperial protection, which caused Snowden, the Lord Privy Seal, to resign.
53. 'The Preparatory Committee and War Debts', 27 March 1933, T175/79.
54. Leffler, *Elusive Quest*, pp. 323–46.
55. 2nd report, 6 April 1933, Cab 58/183.
56. Ibid.
57. Clarke, *The Reconstruction of the International Monetary System*, p. 29.
58. Ibid, p. 18.
59. Leith-Ross, *Money Talks*, p. 160.
60. Leffler, *Elusive Quest*, pp. 333–46.
61. Leith-Ross, *Money Talks*, p. 163.
62. Exchange of telegrams between Hopkins and Leith-Ross, 2–10 May 1933, T175/79.
63. 4 May 1933, Phillips minute on Leith-Ross to Treasury, 2 May 1933, T175/79.
64. Ibid, 10 May 1933. See also Sayers, *Bank of England*, III, appendix 27.
65. Diary, 18 May 1933.
66. Diary, 31 May 1933.
67. Norman Davis to Cordell Hull, 19 May 1933, quoted in Clarke, *Reconstruction of the International Monetary System*, pp. 29–30. Davis chaired the American delegation to the Disarmament Conference.
68. Addis introduction to Flandin address, Chatham House, 7 June 1933, Addis papers. The Chatham Committee's first report was published as *Monetary Policy and the Depression* in the hope of influencing the World Economic Conference.
69. Leffler, *Elusive Quest*, pp. 345–59; Rosen, *Hoover, Roosevelt, and the Brains Trust*, pp. 369–80.
70. Diary, 29, 30 May, 12 June 1933.
71. Clarke, *Reconstruction of the International Monetary System*, pp. 30–3.
72. Ibid, pp. 354–9; Sayers, *Bank of England*, pp. 456–7.
73. 'Shall We Follow the Dollar or the Franc?', *Daily Mail*, 14 July 1933, *JMK*, XXI, p. 279.
74. Diary, 13 June 1933. Norman indicates that Whigham was to see Addis and telephone New York. Norman Diary, 13 June 1933, Bank of England.

75. Hopkins to Chancellor of Exchequer, 14 June 1933; Hopkins to Norman, 14 June 1933, T177/17; Addis diary, 14 June 1933; Norman diary, 14 June 1933, Bank of England.
76. Norman diary, 13 June, 1933, Bank of England.
77. Leith-Ross, *Money Talks*, pp. 171–9; Leffler, *Elusive Quest*, pp. 352–60.
78. Sayers, *Bank of England*, pp. 463–8.
79. Hopkins to Chancellor of Exchequer, 13 July 1933, T175/71. Lamont had a long conversation with Norman two days earlier. See Norman diary, 11 July 1933, Bank of England.
80. *Times*, 2 August 1933.
81. Diary, 22 July 1933.
82. Diary, 1, 7 March 1933.
83. Macmillan to Addis, 25 July 1933, Addis papers.
84. *Times*, 2 August 1933, p. 10; Sayers, *Bank of England*, pp. 514–15.
85. A. F. W. Plumptre, *Central Banking in the Dominions*, p. 193. See also A. F. W. Plumptre, 'The Evidence Presented to the Canadian Macmillan Commission', *Canadian Journal of Economics and Political Science*, II (1936) pp. 54–67, which mentions Addis's 'penetrating analysis'.
86. Norman diary, 28 July 1933, Bank of England.
87. Pruessen, *Dulles*, p. 142.
88. Eichengreen, *Sterling and the Tariff*, p. 26.
89. 'Notes on Canadian visit', kept by Eba, 31 July–27 September 1933, Addis papers. Peacock also accompanied the mission. See diary, 30 July 1933.
90. Diary, 25 September 1933, Ottawa. Before leaving Canada, Addis was awarded an honorary LL.D. by Kingston University.
91. *Times* (London) 16 September 1933, reported Addis's condemnation of the recommendations of Canadian Bankers Association.
92. Sayers, *Bank of England*, p. 515.
93. Ibid.
94. C. A. Curtis, 'The Canadian Macmillan Commission', *Economic Journal*, 44 (1934) p. 53.
95. 23 October 1933, Savoy Hotel, Addis papers. E. R. Peacock presided. See *Times*, 24 October 1933.
96. Diary, 11 April 1934; 'Canada and Its Banks', *Quarterly Review* (1934) pp. 43–55, reviewed in *Times*, 26 July 1934, p. 19.
97. Diary, 29 November 1933. One assumes this referred to stabilisation suggestions.
98. Diary, 21 March 1934.
99. Diary, 11 October, 8 November 1933. Salter, Rodd and Leith-Ross were elected to the Tuesday Club in January 1933. See diary, 11 January 1933.
100. Diary, 1 February 1934.
101. RIIA, *The Future of Monetary Policy*, pp. 26–7.
102. Ibid, ch XVI.
103. Eichengreen, *Sterling and the Tariff*, p. 1.
104. 'A Fantastic Economic World', *Manchester Guardian*, 3 April 1934,

sent by Lamont to his partners, 3 May 1934; Addis diary, 22 March 1934, 4 April 1934. A copy of the speech is in the Addis papers.
105. Mills to Addis, 26 March 1934, Addis papers, /223; Lamont papers, 80/9.
106. 'Morrison Centenary Address', 3 October 1934, 10 pp., Addis papers. Morrison was the first British missionary to go to China.

9 Addis and British China Policy, 1923–9; The Resumption of Anglo-American Competition

1. Wellesley Memorandum on China Consortium, 23 October 1922, SDF 893.51/4038; Acheson to Aglen, 9 November 1922, Aglen papers; Geddes to FO, 20 November 1922, FO371 F3532/59/10.
2. Diary, 10 November 1922.
3. Acheson to Aglen, 9 November 1922, Aglen papers.
4. Aglen to Acheson, 25 October 1922, Aglen papers.
5. Chan Lau Kit-Ching, 'The Lincheng Incident', *Journal of Oriental Studies*, X (1972) pp. 172–86.
6. Part of Minutes of Consortium Meeting, 28 May 1923, first included in British proposed agenda for meeting and sent to FO by Addis on 25 May 1923, FO371 F1603/81/10. Also in Morgan to Hughes, 1 June 1923, SDF 893.51/4314. Addis's diary shows that much of his time in April 1923 was devoted to the China loan question.
7. Addis to Whigham, 23 May 1923, Morgan Grenfell papers.
8. Wellesley minute on Addis to FO, 2 June 1923, FO371 F1667/81/10.
9. Ibid, and F1702/81/10.
10. Wellesley to the Chinese Consortium, 6 June 1923, FO371 F1667/81/10.
11. Addis to Whigham, 16 July 1923, included in Morgan to Hughes, 14 November 1923, SDF 893.51/4425.
12. Lamont to C. R. Bennett, 3 August 1923, included in Morgan to Hughes, 14 November 1923, SDF 893.51/4425.
13. Hughes to President, 25 August 1923, SDF 893.00/5152a; Coolidge to Hughes, 24 August 1923, SDF 893.00/5153.
14. Malcolm Simpson to MacMurray, 27 September 1923, SDF 893.51/4412, including Group correspondence.
15. Quoted in C. Martin Wilbur, *Sun Yat-sen: Frustrated Patriot*; Dayer, *Bankers and Diplomats*, pp. 161–6.
16. C. Martin Wilbur, 'The Nationalist Revolution: From Canton to Nanking, 1923–28', *CHC*, XII, pt. 1, pp. 528–47.
17. Alston to FO, 7 September 1922, FO371 F3339/84/10, with Wellesley minute.
18. Lamont to Whigham, 4 August 1923, Morgan Grenfell papers.
19. Minutes by Waterlow and Wellesley, 18 June 1924, on Macleay to FO, 24 May 1924, FO371 F1989/19/10; Wellesley minute on William Jones (of Hong Kong Bank) to Wellesley, 4 September 1922, FO371 F2868/84/10.
20. C. Bowra (the new Chinese Customs Agent in London) wrote to Aglen that Liang was coming to London and enquired as to how he should be received (Bowra to Aglen, 6 March 1924, Aglen papers).
21. Liang was a leader of the Communications Clique, and head of the

Domestic Bond Bureau, see A. J. Nathan, *Peking Politics*, p. 87.

22. 'Arrangements made by the Bank with Mr Paish of the Dept. of Overseas Trade on the occasion of the visit of Mr Liang Shih-Yi & party', 24 April 1924, Addis papers, Bank of England, ADM 16/3.

23. Bowra to Aglen, 1 May 1924, Aglen papers.

24. Dinner list, 15 April 1924, Addis papers. Addis to Whigham, 23 May 1924, included in Morgan to Hughes, SDF 893.51/4628.

25. Nathan to Mayers, 12 May 1924, included in Morgan to Hughes, SDF 893.51/4628.

26. Aglen to Bowra, 15 April, 27 May 1924, Aglen papers.

27. Minute to Macleay to FO, 7 May 1924, FO371 F1989/19/10.

28. Aglen to Bowra, 8 July 1924, Aglen papers.

29. Addis toast, 14 July 1924, Addis papers.

30. Addis papers. A five-page memorandum on 'The China Consortium', dated 1 September 1924, is in the HSBC archives, Hong Kong.

31. Gavan McCormick, *Chang Tso-Lin*, pp. 254–6; James Sheridan, *Chinese Warlord: The Career of Feng Yu-hsiang*, pp. 136–47.

32. Dayer, *Bankers and Diplomats*, pp. 185–91.

33. For T. V. Soong, see Sterling Seagrave, *The Soong Dynasty*, pp. 192–3 and *passim*.

34. Dayer, *Bankers and Diplomats*, pp. 203–10.

35. Addis to Waterlow, 4 May 1925, FO371 F1794/190/10.

36. Richard Rigby, *The May 30 Movement*, chs. 1 and 2; Wilbur, 'The Nationalist Revolution', pp. 548–53.

37. William J. Megginson, III, 'Britain's Response to Chinese Nationalism 1925–1927: The Foreign Office Search for a New Policy', unpublished doctoral dissertation at the George Washington University, 1973.

38. Lamont to Kellogg, 26 June 1925, including Addis to Grenfell, SDF 893.00/6364.

39. Lamont to Whigham, 9 July 1924, Lamont papers, 111–12.

40. Dorothy Borg, *American Policy and the Chinese Revolution*, ch. 11.

41. J. P. Morgan to Kellogg, 17 August 1925, SDF 893.00/6537, forwarding account of conversation between Sidney Mayers and Chao Ching Hua, who gave Liang Shih-i's views.

42. Megginson, 'Britain's Response to Chinese Nationalism', p. 230.

43. Addis to Wellesley, 2 September 1925, FO371 F4372/190/10; Chamberlain to Eliot, 29 August 1925, FO800/255.

44. N. T. Johnson Memorandum of Lamont dinner, 21 October 1925, SDF 893.00/6692. Addis's speech was enclosed in FO371 F5323/190/10.

45. Addis to Eba, 21 October 1925, Addis papers.

46. Wellesley memorandum, 1 March 1925, FO371 F952/190/10; Megginson, 'Britain's Response', ch. x.

47. Megginson, 'Britain's Response', ch. XII.

48. Diary, 2 March 1926.

49. 'Notes on discussion between K. D. Stewart of British Delegation and Hornbeck concerning attitude of Provinces toward a treaty negotiated with Peking, 10 March 1926', M. F. Perkins, 11 March 1926, Hornbeck papers, box 107.

50. Wilbur, 'The Nationalist Revolution', pp. 553–81.

51. For background on Chiang K'ai-shek, see Seagrave, *The Soong Dynasty*, pp. 152–97.
52. Donald Jordan, *The Northern Expedition: China's National Revolution of 1926–1928*.
53. Lloyd Eastman, *The Abortive Revolution: China under Nationalist Rule, 1927–1937*.
54. Clementi to Nathan, 3 July 1926. See also Clementi to Nathan, 16 January 1926. Matthew Nathan Papers, Rhodes House, box 351–352, Oxford University.
55. Aglen to Bowra, 13 March 1926, Aglen papers.
56. Hubbard to Stitt (Shanghai HSBC Agent), 1 April 1926, HSBC archives, Hong Kong.
57. Mounsey to Macleay, 15 June 1926, FO371 F2127/255/10.
58. Aglen to Bowra, 7 June 1926, Aglen papers.
59. Hornbeck to MacMurray, 21 March 1929, Hornbeck papers, box 284.
60. Report of the China Indemnity Advisory Committee, Cmd. 2766, p. 9.
61. O. E. Niemeyer to Sir W. H. C. Clarke, 7 December 1922, T160, box 374, F.3607/1.
62. Megginson, 'Britain's Response', p. 244; Cmd. 2766.
63. Wellesley to Macleay, 20 March 1926, FO371 F1051/1/10.
64. Diary, 6 June 1926.
65. Buxton Committee Report, Cmd. 2766, p. 16.
66. Diary, 18 October 1926.
67. Addis diary shows him dining with Pratt on 19 June 1926.
68. Diary, 22 July 1926. Lord Gosford Address, 15 July 1926, in RIIA *Journal*, September 1926, pp. 239–44.
69. Addis to Mills, 15 October 1926, Addis papers.
70. Addis to Mills, 11 September 1926, Addis papers. Addis attended at least two dinners in Lampson's honour that autumn and was one of a small group to see him off for China on 22 October (Diary, 5, 11, 22 October 1926).
71. Diary, 15 November 1926.
72. Addis to Mills, 17 November 1926, Addis papers.
73. Addis to Lamont, 18 November 1926, included in Lamont to N. T. Johnson, 21 December 1926, SDF 893.51/4998; J. P. Morgan to Kellogg, 4 November 1926, SDF 893.00/7808, including extract from private letter of Addis to Lamont. Acknowledged by N. T. Johnson on 10 November 1926.
74. Addis papers.
75. Pratt memos, FO371 F4938/10/10; minute on Macleay to FO, 22 November 1926, FO371 F4964/10/10.
76. Wilbur, 'The Nationalist Revolution', pp. 599–603.
77. Minute, 27 November on Macleay to FO, 26 November 1926, FO371 F5112/10/10.
78. The memorandum was sent by Chamberlain to Barton for Lampson on 2 December 1926. Lampson was instructed to gain the other Ministers' views. FO371 F5233/10/10. See also D. C. Wilson, 'Britain and the Kuomintang, 1924–1928: A Study of the Interaction of Official Policies and Perceptions in Britain and China', unpublished doctoral dissertation, University of London, 1973, pp. 421–6.

79. Chamberlain minute, 21 December 1926, on FO to Lampson, 8 December 1926, FO371 F5269/1/10.
80. Chamberlain minute on Lampson to FO, 27 November 1926, FO371 F5215/10/10.
81. Allen S. Whiting, *Soviet Policies in China, 1917–1924*; Conrad Brandt, *Stalin's Failure in China, 1924–1927*; Robert C. North, *Moscow and Chinese Communists*.
82. Parks Coble, *The Shanghai Capitalists and the Nationalist Government, 1922–1937*, pp. 36–7; Seagrave, *The Soong Dynasty*, pp. 150–65.
83. Seagrave, *The Soong Dynasty*, pp. 130–6.
84. Ibid, p. 480, n. 156.
85. *Journal of RIIA*, November 1926, p. 282.
86. Diary, 4 November 1926.
87. Diary.
88. Diary, 13 January 1927; Cabinet 1 (27) 12 January 1927, Cab 23.
89. Diary, 17 January 1927. See also Cab 2 (27) 17 January 1927, Cab 23.
90. Wilbur, 'The Nationalist Revolution', pp. 614–20.
91. Megginson, 'Britain's Response', pt. III; Wilson, 'Britain and the Kuomintang', pp. 550–82.
92. Edmund S. Fung, 'Anti-Imperialism and the Left Guomindang', *Modern China* (January 1985) pp. 39–76.
93. Megginson, 'Britain's Response', p. 591. Birkenhead (F. E. Smith), was Secretary for India.
94. Diary, 14 February, 30 March, 18 April, 7 May 1927.
95. Harold Isaacs, *The Tragedy of the Chinese Revolution*, ch. 11; Seagrave, *The Soong Dynasty*, pp. 218–33.
96. FO to Lampson, 26 April 1927; Appendix III to Cab 28 (27) 27 April 1927, Cab 23. See also Edmund S. K. Fung, 'The Sino-British Rapprochement, 1927–1931', *Modern Asian Studies*, 17 (1983) pp. 79–105.
97. Coble, *Shanghai Capitalists*, pp. 29–30; Seagrave, *Soong Dynasty*, ch. 10. Megginson, 'Britain's Response', p. 603, concludes that the FO did not support Chiang.
98. Cab 28 (27) 27 April 1927, Cab 23.
99. Addis to Mills, 29 April 1927, Addis papers.
100. Diary, 8 July 1927.
101. Cabinet 31 (27) 11 May 1927, Cab 23.
102. Diary, 27 October 1927.
103. Diary, 8 December 1927. Addis discussed his removal with Landale, Mayers and Stabb on 7 December 1927.
104. Dayer, *Bankers and Diplomats*, p. 238.
105. According to Wellington Koo's account of this episode, when Lampson balked at Edwardes' appointment, Koo threatened to appoint Frederick Maze (Wellington Koo Papers). Edwardes later became the financial adviser to Manchukuo and to the FBI Mission in 1934 (see below).
106. Hubbard to Stabb, 15 February 1927, HSBC archives, Hong Kong.
107. Diary, 9, 17, 23 March 1927.
108. *Shih Shih Hsin Pao* abstract, 3 August 1928, Maze papers.
109. Maze to Addis 22 February 1929, Maze papers.
110. Chang Kia-ngao to Maze, 18 July 1927, Maze papers, II, 1926–9. See

Andrea McElderry, 'Robber Barons or Nationalist Capitalists: Shanghai Bankers in Republican China', *Republican China*, XI (November 1985). An interview with Chang (who was of course very elderly) at Stanford in 1978 did not produce any really useful information.

111. 20 July 1927.
112. Soong was originally part of the left KMT camp at Wuhan. See Y. C. Wang, *Chinese Intellectuals and the West*, pp. 438–47.
113. Andrea McElderry, *Shanghai Old-Style Banks*, p. 165.
114. The American Minister, MacMurray, negotiated a Tariff Treaty with T. V. Soong.
115. Coble, *Shanghai Capitalists*, p. 49.
116. Maze to C. T. Wang, 20 June 1928, Maze papers.
117. 'Six Years of Political Life in Peking', Typescript interview with Wellington Koo, 13 August 1962, box 1, Wellington Koo papers.
118. G. Mounsey minute on interview with Stephenson concerning Edwarde's resignation and possible successor, 1 January 1929, FO371 F142/52/10.
119. Maze to Tyler, 19 October 1929, Maze papers.
120. Parks Coble notes that the Maze appointment was not welcomed by many Chinese who preferred a Chinese IG (comment on earlier draft of this chapter).
121. Lampson to FO, 2 January 1929, FO371 F52/52/10; Maze to Stephenson, 10 January 1929, FO371 F208/52/10, with minutes by Mounsey, Wellesley and Chamberlain.
122. A. B. Lowson to Hubbard, 18 December 1928, HSBC archives, Hong Kong.
123. Addis diary, 2 April 1928. *International Affairs* lists but does not publish Lyall's speech.
124. Lyall memorandum, 28 May 1927, Maze papers. Maze to Pratt, 15 May 1929; Maze to Addis, 22 February 1929.
125. Wellesley memorandum, 11 March 1929, 29 pp., FO371 F911/52/10.
126. Maze to Stephenson, 31 August 1929, Maze papers.
127. W. Kirby, *Germany and Republican China*, ch. 3.
128. Diary.
129. Hornbeck to MacMurray, 1 August 1929, Hornbeck papers, box 284.
130. 'Notes for Chairman's Speech 1928–29', Addis papers, /568. Avenol is described in Christopher Thorne, *The Limits of Foreign Policy*, p. 112, as 'essentially an opportunist and a cynic'. See *BDI*.
131. Addis to Ashton-Gwatkin, 2 March 1929, FO371 F1147/57/10. (annexed to F4271/57/10). Ashton-Gwatkin was a boyhood friend of Montagu Norman; see Boyle, *Norman*, p. 308.
132. Diary, 12, 19 June 1929; Pratt minute, 16 July 1929 on Addis to Ashton-Gwatkin, 5 July 1929, FO371 F3436/57/10.

10 Japan vs China, 1929–34

1. 'Memorandum on loans to China', 6 April 1929, Kemmerer papers, Box 25; Conference with T. V. Soong, 18 March 1929, Kemmerer papers, box 16.

2. Julean Arnold memorandum on Kemmerer Commission, Hornbeck to MacMurray, 1 August 1929, Hornbeck papers, box 284; J. T. Pratt minute, 9 September 1929, on Lampson to FO, 3 September 1929, FO371 F4603/31/10.
3. B. Lauder Lewis to Lampson, 30 April 1929, included in Newton to FO, 26 June 1929, FO371 F3505/57/10.
4. Leith-Ross to Ashton-Gwatkin, 3 July 1929, FO371 F3483/57/10.
5. Addis to Ashton-Gwatkin, 5 July 1929, FO371 F34367/57/10; Leith-Ross to Ashton-Gwatkin, 3 July 1929, FO371 F3482/57/10; Diary, 12, 19 June 1929.
6. Diary, 19 November, 19 December 1929; Addis to Wellesley, 12 December 1929, with enclosed notes of conversations and Pratt minute, FO371 F6685/3745/10.
7. J. T. Pratt minute, September 1929, on Lampson to FO, 3 September 1929, FO371 F4603/31/10. This minute also mentioned that Mayers was consolidating interests in five British railways in China.
8. Wellesley minute on Lampson to FO, 15 November 1929, FO371 F5834/3745/10.
9. Wellesley minute on Lampson to FO, 15 November 1929, FO371 F5834/3745/10; Addis to Wellesley, 12 December 1929, F6685 ibid.
10. Akira Iriye, *After Imperialism*, pp. 271–5; Ian Nish, 'Japan in Britain's View, 1919–37', in Nish, *Anglo-Japanese Alienation, 1919–1952*, p. 38.
11. Ian Nish, *Some Foreign Attitudes to Republican China*; McCormack, *Chang Tso-lin*, p. 248.
12. Diary, 16 July 1930.
13. G. E. Hubbard, 'Financial Reconstruction for China', *RIIA Journal*, IX (1930) pp. 636–51.
14. Howson and Winch, *The Economic Advisory Council, 1930–1939*, p. 360.
15. Note by Addis on meeting with American Group, 18 November 1930, EAC, Committee on Chinese Situation, 3rd meeting, Cab 58/155. Addis submitted this memorandum on 12 December 1930.
16. Report of Committee on Chinese Situation, Economic Advisory Council, 18 December 1930. Cab 58/155.
17. Cabinet 6 (31) 14 January 1931, Cab 23; Lionel Curtis, *The Capital Question of China*, ch. 26.
18. *Times*, 19 December 1930. See also Leveson's denunciation of the government at the China Association meeting, 24 March 1931, Nathan papers, box 351–2.
19. 16 April 1931, Addis papers, Bank of England, ADM 16/6.
20. See minutes on Wellesley to Addis, 9 May 1931, FO371 F1500/10/10; Pratt minute, 15 June, Wellesley minute, 23 June 1931, on Addis to Wellesley, 28 May 1931, FO371 F2941/10/10.
21. Committee of Treasury minutes, 4 March 1931, Bank of England.
22. Christopher Thorne, *The Limits of Foreign Policy*, ch. 5.
23. *Times*, 18 February 1932, p. 13; Addis diary, 19 February 1932.
24. Diary, 9, 17, 25 February 1933.
25. Thorne, *The Limits of Foreign Policy*, pp. 217–18; Rennell Rodd, MP,

Letter to *Times*, 23 February 1932, gives the government's point of view.
26. Diary, 8 April 1932.
27. Addis to Lamont, 28 April 1932, Hornbeck papers, box 272; Diary, 26, 28 April 1932.
28. Addis to Lamont, 28 April, 1932, Hornbeck papers, box 272.
29. Pratt minute, 12 May 1932, on Addis to Wellesley, 2 May 1932, FO371 F3963/3163/10, including Addis to Lamont, 28 April 1932.
30. Lampson minute, 5 July 1932, Wellesley minute, 7 July 1932, on Lampson minute. For Lampson, see D. Steeds, 'The British Approach to China during the Lampson period, 1926–1933', in Ian Nish (ed.) *Foreign Attitudes*, p. 51.
31. Shimada Toshihiko, 'Designs on North China, 1933–1937', in James W. Morley (ed.) *The China Quagmire*, p. 15.
32. Addis was the Crown nominee on the University Court from 1926. See Diary, 28 May, 25 June, 12 July 1932. Lindsay was the Master of Balliol College at Oxford (Minutes of the Universities China Committee, Nathan papers, boxes 349–351/2).
33. Pratt minute, 19 July 1932, FO371, F5524/82/10.
34. Minutes on Addis letter of resignation, FO371 F6132/82/10.
35. Addis to Wellesley, 16 November 1932, FO371 F8073/3142/10.
36. Addis to Nohara, 6 April 1932, FO371 F3329/3142/10, included in Addis to Wellesley, 19 April 1932, FO371 F3574/3142/10.
37. Hornbeck to Lamont, 22 September 1932, giving Far Eastern division comments on Addis proposal of 28 April. Hornbeck papers, box 272.
38. Hosoya Chihiro, 'Britain and the US in Japan's View of the International System, 1919–1937', in Nish (ed.) *Alienation*, p. 16.
39. Addis diary, 18 October 1932.
40. Addis to Grayburn, 19 October 1932, HSBC archives, Hong Kong.
41. Diary, 20, 24, 27 October 1932.
42. Revelstoke to Grayburn, December 1932, HSBC papers, Hong Kong.
43. 'Extracts from HSBC minutes', 29 November 1932, HSBC papers.
44. Grayburn to Addis, 1 December 1932, HSBC archives. Grayburn also replied on similar lines to Revelstoke the same day.
45. Diary.
46. Diary, 15 February 1933.
47. Diary, 30 March 1933.
48. 'Extract from Minutes of London Consultative Committee of the HSBC, 5 pp. 30 March 1933, Addis papers.
49. See for example, *Economist*, 1 November 1930.
50. 'Extract from Grayburn papers', HSBC archives.
51. Stabb to Grayburn, 12 June 1932, HSBC archives. The British, French, American and Japanese groups each paid the Bank £750 a year to defray the cost of the special work entailed (Barnes to Grayburn, 10 January 1933, HSBC archives).
52. Sir C. Addis to Orde, 3 January 1933, FO371 F109/4/10 with Orde minute, 19 January 1933.
53. Addis to Orde, 7 February 1933, FO371 F912/4/10. Addis may have

devised this procedure in his earlier talks with Tsu-i Pei. See diary, 2 July 1931.

54. Ibid.
55. Addis to Hubbard, 6 February 1933, Addis papers.
56. 'Canton River Bridged', *Times*, 23 March 1933, p. 13.
57. Ling Hung-Hsun, 'A Decade of Chinese Railway Construction', in Paul K. T. Sih (ed.) *The Strenuous Decade*, p. 266.
58. Coble, *Shanghai Capitalists*, pp. 124–9.
59. Dorothy Borg, *The United States and the Far Eastern Crisis of 1933–8*.
60. Thorne, *Limits of Foreign Policy*, ch. 10.
61. Diary, 6 June 1933.
62. Diary, 8, 12 June 1933.
63. Quoted in Endicott, *Diplomacy and Enterprise*, p. 35.
64. Quintin-Hill (BOT) to Orde, 12 June 1933, FO371 F3937/2712/10.
65. Orde to Quintin-Hill, 20 June 1933; See also D. C. Watt, 'Brit, US and Japan in 1934', *Personalities and Politics*, pp. 83–99.
66. Orde minute of meeting with Addis, 13 June 1933, FO371 F3972/2712/10.
67. Harrison minute, 16 June 1933 on the Orde-Addis meeting.
68. Diary, 14, 23 June 1933.
69. Minute of meeting, 20 June 1933: Orde, Pratt, BOT, DOT, HKSB–Grayburn, Addis, Barnes, Exports Credits Guarantee Department FO371 F4142/2712/10. Orde was sceptical about the Consortium's admission of a Chinese group.
70. MacDonald quoted 29 July 1933 in Endicott, *Diplomacy and Enterprise*, p. 35, n. 36. FO views are in Ann Trotter, *Britain and East Asia*, p. 67.
71. Diary, 19 July 1933.
72. Diary, 10, 11 July 1933, on meeting with Soong, Lamont and Salter.
73. Diary, 13, 14, 19, 20, 24 July 1933.
74. Diary, 26 July 1933; Norman Diary, 27 July 1933, Bank of England.
75. Addis papers.
76. Jurgen Osterhammel, 'Technical cooperation between the League of Nations and China', *Modern Asian Studies* (1979).
77. Orde minute on conversation with Addis, 27 October 1933, FO371 F6845/2678/10.
78. Coble, *Shanghai Capitalism*, pp. 127–38; Endicott. *Diplomacy and Enterprise*, ch. 2.
79. V. M. Grayburn to Addis, 27 September 1933, Bank of England, ADM16/6.
80. Orde minute on conversation with Addis, 27 October 1933. Orde reported his conversation to Waley in the Treasury, FO371 F6845/2678/10.
81. Addis to Grayburn, 8 November 1933, HSBC archives; Diary, 3 November 1933.
82. Nish, *Japanese Foreign Policy*, p. 210.
83. Endicott, *Diplomacy and Enterprise*, pp. 38–42; Chang Kia-ngau, *China's Struggle for Railroad Development*, pp. 93–9.
84. Diary, 6, 20 April, 7 May 1934; Norman Diary, 20 April 1934, Bank of England.

85. Sir Arthur Salter's report, *China and Silver*, recommends new loans to China. For his comments on Chinese leaders, see Salter, *Personality and Politics*, Ch. XV.
86. Quoted in Lloyd Gardner, 'The Role of the Commerce and Treasury Departments' in Dorothy Borg and Shumpei Okamoto (eds) *Pearl Harbor as History*, p. 271.
87. Coble, *Shanghai Capitalists*, pp. 141–7; RIIA, *The Future of Monetary Policy*, pp. 202–5.
88. Gardner, 'The Role of the Commerce and Treasury Departments', pp. 268–75.
89. Clay, *Norman*, p. 455.
90. For example, Addis entertained the Chinese diplomat, Alfred Sze, and his family at tea at Woodside on 29 July 1934 and attended a reception at the Japanese Embassy for the Matsudairas on 24 July, See Diary.
91. 'Memorandum of conversation between Addis and Viscount H. Kano', 5 June 1934, sent to Pratt, 29 August 1934, FO371 F5300/42/10, in T188/151. Addis apologised for taking so long to send this memo to the FO. It was forwarded to Waley on 22 May 1935, and includes a note from Waley to Leith-Ross, 23 November 1934, anticipating Japanese opposition to Monnet's proposals.
92. Addis to Kano, 10 August 1934, T188/151.
93. Li Ming earlier floated a loan for H. H. Kung. See Coble, *Shanghai Capitalists*, pp. 164, 306, n. 10.
94. Diary, 19 June 1934.
95. Diary, 21 June 1934.
96. Diary, 3, 18 July 1934.
97. Ann Trotter, 'Tentative Steps for an Anglo-Japanese Rapproachment in 1934', *Modern Asian Studies*, 8 (1974) pp. 67–74; William Roger Louis, *British Strategy in the Far East*, ch. VII.
98. Trotter, *Britain and East Asia*, ch. 7.
99. Diary, 14 August 1934.
100. Norman diary, 23 August 1934, Bank of England.
101. Diary, 26 July 1934.
102. Clay, *Norman*, ch. X.
103. Sayers, *The Bank of England*, chs. 18–20.
104. Diary, 21, 22 August 1934. Addis met Monnet, Drummond and Morris again in October. Drummond was the son of Sir Eric Drummond, the former Secretary-General of the League of Nations.
105. Diary, 12, 15 October 1934.
106. Addis to Grayburn, 18 October 1934, including memoranda and Maze telegram to Kung. HSBC archives.
107. Norman to Addis, 17 October 1934, Addis papers, Bank of England, ADM 16/6.
108. Norman to Addis, 13 December 1934, Addis papers.
109. Pratt to Lady Addis, 28 January 1935, Addis papers.
110. Diary, 13 July 1934.

11   A New British Initiative in China, 1935–41

1. Norman diary, 31 December 1934, Bank of England.
2. F. Phillips to Hopkins, 29 August 1934, T175/71.
3. Cadogan to FO, 30 November 1934, T177/21, pt. 1.
4. First meeting of Treasury China Committee, 19 December 1934, T177/21, pt. 1.
5. Trotter, *Britain and East Asia*, pp. 134–5.
6. Second meeting of Treasury China Committee, 2 January 1935, T177/21, pt. 1, Waley in Chair.
7. October 1935, T175/91.
8. Waley to F. Phillips, 12 January 1935, T177/21, pt. 2; Waley to Phillips, Leith-Ross, Hopkins, 7 January 1935, T177/21, pt. 1; Kershaw to Waley, 11 January 1935, T177/21, pt. 2.
9. Grayburn to Treasury, 9 January 1935, T177/21, pt. 2.
10. Coble, *Shanghai Capitalists*, p. 180. Chang did not think the government needed a loan. See Endicott, *Diplomacy and Enterprise*, p. 86, n. 19.
11. Endicott, *Diplomacy and Enterprise*, chs. 5 and 6; Trotter, *Britain and East Asia*, ch. 9.
12. Borg, *US and Far Eastern Crisis*, p. 129.
13. Norman to Addis, 14 April 1935, Addis papers /459.
14. Norman to Addis, 20 April 1935, Addis papers.
15. Norman personal diary, 26 August 1935, Bank of England; 'Memorandum of Hornbeck–Lamont conversation', 9 September 1935, Hornbeck papers, box 272.
16. Addis to Lamont, 2 March 1936, T188/139.
17. Gardner, 'The Role of the Commerce and Treasury Departments', pp. 270–1.
18. Borg, *The United States and the Far Eastern Crisis*, pp. 126–31.
19. Quoted in Gardner, 'The Role of the Commerce and Treasury Departments', p. 273.
20. Nish, *Japanese Foreign Policy*, pp. 213–14.
21. Addis to Leith-Ross, 23 June 1935, T188/151.
22. Leith-Ross to Addis, 1 July 1935; Leith-Ross to Pratt, 22 July 1935; Leith-Ross to Waley, 3 July 1935, T188/151.
23. Addis to Leith-Ross, 31 July 1935, T188/151. Addis lunched with Leith-Ross, Hall-Patch and W. C. Cassels (the political adviser to the Bank) at the HSBC on 19 July 1935 to discuss 'Leith-Ross's China currency mission' (Diary, 19 July 1935).
24. Phillips to Waley, 16 October 1935, T175/91. In *Money Talks*, p. 206, Leith-Ross claimed that the HSBC was at first unwilling to cooperate with the Chinese.
25. Clay to Leith-Ross, 1 August 1935, T188/151.
26. Norman to Leith-Ross, T188/151.
27. Norman diary, 4 November 1935, Bank of England. For Leith-Ross's criticism of the HSBC, see Stephen L. Endicott, 'British Financial Diplomacy in China: The Leith-Ross Mission, 1935–37', *Pacific Affairs*, 46 (1973–74) p. 488.

28. Norman diary, 18 September 1935, Bank of England. See also E. L. Hall-Patch to Leith-Ross, 3 August 1935, 188/151.
29. Addis to Leith-Ross, 31 July 1935, HSBC archives.
30. Addis to Waley (draft) 4 November 1935, Addis papers.
31. Leith-Ross's account of his mission is in *Money Talks*, p. 206. Trotter, *Britain and East Asia*, pp. 150 and 244, n. 10, describes the proposal for a loan to China.
32. Ibid, and Endicott, *Diplomacy and Enterprise*, p. 114.
33. For the importance of currency reform in helping Chinese resistance, see Usi Katsumi, 'The Politics of War', in Morley (ed.) *The China Quagmire*, pp. 355–63.
34. November 1935, T175/91.
35. Leith-Ross to Treasury, November 1935, T175/91.
36. See draft report, December 1935, marked 'never published', T188/284; Philips to Waley, 16 October 1935, T175/91.
37. Leith-Ross to Addis, 8 April 1936, Addis papers. For the German relationship with the KMT, see Kirby, *Germany and Republican China*; Jurgen Osterhammell, 'Imperialism in Transition: British Big Business and the Chinese Authorities, 1931–1937', *China Quarterly*, 260–86.
38. Diary, 24, 25, 30 March, 2, 6 April 1936. Rodd took over Whigham's position in the Consortium in 1938.
39. Diary, 29 April 1936.
40. Addis diary, 4 March, 5 June 1936.
41. FO to Addis, 12 August 1936; Addis to FO, 17 August 1936, HSBC archives. Addis diary, 26, 27 August 1936.
42. Diary, 6, 12 February 1936.
43. Grayburn to Addis, 9 January 1936, Addis papers, /436.
44. Addis diary, 18 February 1936.
45. Diary, 24, 25 February, 5 March 1936. See Addis diary in May 1936 for steering of Hangchow completion loan.
46. Addis to Leith-Ross, 3 June 1936, Addis papers. Also T188/152.
47. Trotter, *Britain and East Asia*, pp 181–5; Leith-Ross, *Money Talks*, p. 221.
48. Leith-Ross to Addis, 9 October 1936, T188/152.
49. Addis to Leith-Ross, 12 October 1936, T188/152.
50. Diary, 10 July 1936.
51. 'Memorandum of a conversation between Viscount Kano and Sir Charles Addis at No. 1 St Michael's Alley', 3 November 1936, included in Leith-Ross to Cadogan, 5 November 1936, T188/152; Addis diary, 3, 4 November 1936.
52. H. Knatchbull-Hugessen to FO, 10 November 1936, FO371. F6891/38/10 and Pratt minute, 12 November 1936.
53. Diary, 9 December 1936.
54. Addis to Orde, 10 December 1936, FO371 F626/38/10, and Orde minute, 19 December 1936.
55. Diary, 14 December 1936.
56. Diary, 15 December 1936. For Yoshida-Eden talks, see Nish, 'Japan in Britain's view, 1919–37', and Trotter, *Britain and East Asia*, pp. 191–203.

57. Addis to Leith-Ross, 16 December 1936, T188/152.
58. B&C Corporation Chairman's Speech, 24 May 1936, delivered in June. Addis papers; Diary, 10, 11, 15 June 1936.
59. Diary, 22 June 1936. Sir Alexander Cadogan, who had been Minister to Peking, replaced Sir Edward Crowe as Deputy Permanent Under-Secretary in the FO in 1936.
60. Leith-Ross to Kung, 1 June 1935, T188/139, including 'Memorandum from Bondholders' Committee'.
61. Endicott, *Diplomacy and Enterprise*, p. 107.
62. Leith-Ross to Mr Woods, 4 November 1936, T188/152.
63. Leith-Ross to FO, 27 March 1936, T188/139. For details on the settlements, see A. N. Young, *China's Nation Building*, pp. 129–39.
64. Borg, *US and Far East*, pp. 218–26.
65. Lloyd E. Eastman, *China Under Nationalist Rule*, p. 65.
66. Ashton-Gwatkin minute, 11 January 1937, on Knatchbull-Hugessen to FO, 14 November 1936, FO371 F7999/33/10.
67. Ling Hung-Hsun, 'A Decade of Chinese Railway construction', in Sih (ed.) *The Strenuous Decade*, p. 268.
68. Knatchbull-Huggessen (Nanking) to Cadogan, 3 March 1937, FO800/294.
69. Addis diary, 8 March 1937.
70. Dallas Bernard's report, *Times*, 6 May 1937, p. 25. Addis was very pleased when Bernard was elected to the Court of the Bank of England, commenting: 'It is the highest distinction the City can confer.' (Diary, 20 March 1936.) Norman earlier discussed the possibility of Bernard's election with Addis.
71. 'Notes on a conversation with Dr Kung', 5 May 1937, by Leith-Ross, T188/187.
72. Quoted in Endicott, *Diplomacy and Enterprise*, p. 142.
73. Diary, 14 January 1937.
74. Addis to Orde, 2 April 1937; Leith-Ross to Orde, 7 May 1937, T188/151.
75. Leith-Ross to Addis, 20 May 1937, T188/152.
76. Chang Kia-ngau did not want the railway loan to come under Kung's control. See Louis Beale to Sir E. Crowe, 3 June 1937, T188/188.
77. Addis diary, 6 May 1937.
78. Addis to Leith-Ross, 26 May 1937, T188/151, including letter to the Group Representatives. Diary, 21 May 1937.
79. Ibid.
80. Leith-Ross to Waley, 28 May 1937; Leith-Ross to Addis, 31 May 1937; Cable from J. P. Morgan, 31 May 1937, T188/151.
81. Addis to Leith-Ross, 1 June 1937, T188/151.
82. Leith-Ross to Norman, 24 May 1937, T188/188.
83. Leith-Ross to Hall-Patch, 7 June 1937, T188/188. Later Ambassador to China Clark Kerr called H. H. Kung 'a cancer in the belly of China'. Quoted in Thorne, *Allies of a Kind*, p. 65.
84. Leith-Ross to Cadogan, 26 May 1937, T188/188.
85. Hall-Patch to Treasury, 15 July 1937, T188/188. For Hall-Patch, see *BDI*.
86. Nish, 'Japan in Britain's View' in Nish (ed.) *Alienation*, p. 51, which emphasises the German factor.

87. Cadogan to Leith-Ross, 20 July 1937; Leith-Ross to Waley, 21 July 1937, T188/188.
88. Diary, 20 July 1937.
89. Diary, August and 7 September 1937.
90. Diary, 16 January 1938.
91. Enclosed in Leith-Ross to Sir F. Phillips, 19 January 1938, T188/205.
92. Diary, 18 November 1937.
93. Nicholas Clifford, 'Sir Frederick Maze and the Chinese Maritime Customs, 1937–1941', *Journal of Modern History*, XXXVII (1965) pp. 18–34. See also Usui Katsumi, 'The Politics of War', in Morley (ed.) *The China Quagmire*, p. 341.
94. Cadogan to Leith-Ross, 9 February 1938, T188/205.
95. Leith-Ross to J. L. Fisher, 19 January 1938; J. Fisher to Sir Frederick Phillips, 24 January 1938, T188/205.
96. Clark-Kerr to FO, 19 February 1938, T188/205; Leith-Ross to Waley, 11 March 1938, Waley to Sir F. Phillips, 14 March 1938, T188/207.
97. Leith-Ross to Sir F. Phillips, 12 January 1938, T188/205, my emphasis.
98. The prediction was made by the Ambassador to Japan, Sir Robert Craigie. Leith-Ross to N. E. Young, 12 May 1938, T188/224. See also Peter Lowe, *Great Britain and the Origins of the Pacific War*.
99. FO to Craigie, 27 July 1938, T188/224; Aron Shai, *Origins of the War in the East*, p. 204, n. 117.
100. Diary, 4 October 1938. See also Addis speech on 'China and Japan' to the Lombard Association, 16 November 1938, Addis papers.
101. 'Note on some observations by the Japanese Ambassador', 16 November 1938, Addis papers, /438.
102. 13 March 1939, Tunbridge Wells, Addis papers. The collaboration between Chiang's government and the Japanese may have affected Addis's views. See Lloyd Eastman, 'Facets of an Ambivalent Relationship', in Akira Iriye (ed.) *The Chinese and the Japanese*.
103. Quoted in Michael Schaller, *The United States Crusade in China, 1938–1945*, p. 29.
104. Frank H. H. King, 'Defending the Chinese Currency: the Role of the Hongkong and Shanghai Banking Corporation, 1938–1941', in F. H. H. King (ed.) *Eastern Banking*, pp. 279–320; Thorne, *Allies of a Kind*, pp. 53–4.
105. Nicholas Clifford, *Retreat from China*, p. 133; David Reynolds, *The Creation of the Anglo-American Alliance 1937–41*, p. 60; Bradford A. Lee, *Britain and the Sino-Japanese War, 1937–1939*.
106. File RIIA, Pratt papers.
107. Diary, 13, 20 October, 1 November 1937, 21 November 1938.
108. P. Lowe, *Great Britain and the Origins of Pacific War*, Appendix D, p. 295.
109. Diary, 25 November 1938; Leith-Ross to Addis, 4 December 1938, T188/226.
110. Diary, 21 December 1938, 18 January 1939; Cohen, *The Chinese Connection*, pp. 218–19.
111. Diary, 29 July, August, October, 22 November, 28 December 1939; Leith-Ross to Waley, 28 January 1939, T188/151; Norman to Addis, 4 January 1940, Addis papers.

Conclusion: Final Years and an Assessment

1. Diary, 4 June 1936.
2. Diary, 20 January 1928.
3. Diary, 23 June 1926.
4. Interviews with family members and friends.
5. Seven-page untitled speech to congratulate the prize-winners, 19 January 1939, Addis papers.
6. 27 January 1940, Addis papers.
7. Diary, 12 October 1936. 'White Clouds on the Wing', from 'A Memory' by William Allingham.
8. Diary, 31 December 1937.
9. Diary, 6, 10 June 1944.
10. Diary, 9 March 1936.
11. Diary, 5 November 1923. The reference to the peerage was in the newspaper while Addis was in Brazil. See Acheson to Aglen, 18 January 1924, Aglen papers.
12. Diary, 2 January 1924.
13. Told to author by retired employee of HSBC at the Conference on the History of the HSBC in Hong Kong, 1981.
14. Diary, 17, 18 June 1936. Mills died in 1937.
15. Diary, 14 August, 22 September 1936; 12 March 1937. Sir Albert Charles Gladstone was a Director, 1924–47.
16. Diary, 24 November 1937.
17. Diary, 21 February 1940.
18. 'Service Above Self', 20 April 1936, Tunbridge Wells, Addis papers; Diary, 13, 17, 20 April 1936.
19. Diary 2, 6, 16, 18 March 1937. For the Tripartite Agreement, see Clarke, *Exchange-Rate Stabilization in the Mid-1930s: Negotiating the Tripartite Agreement*; and Ian M. Drummond, *London, Washington, and the Management of the Franc, 1936–39*.
20. 'The New Monetary Technique', speech to American Club, Paris, 1937, Addis papers. See also Addis article on 'The Future of Gold', which he wrote for a financial supplement to the *Daily Telegraph*, January 1938, Addis papers.
21. 'The New Monetary Technique', *Quarterly Review* (July 1937) pp. 64–73.
22. 'Tribute to Lord Stamp' at Dorchester House after his introduction to the House of Lords, *Abbey Road Monthly Review* (August 1938), Addis papers.
23. *Spectator*, 160 (1938) pp. 173–4; Diary, 30 December 1937, 6 January 1938.
24. Addis to Eba, 31 May 1937, Addis papers.
25. Diary, 11 October 1937.
26. Diary.
27. Diary, 17 April 1939.
28. Diary, 7 September 1939.
29. Diary, 13 March 1940.

30. Diary, 24 May 1940.
31. Diary, 12, 17 January; 29 May, 27 November 1940; 26 February, 22 June 1941.
32. Diary, 2, 4 February, 27, 29 May 1942.
33. Diary, 4, 6, 27 March, 12 April 1940; 22, 29 July 1941.
34. Diary, 1941 and January 1942.
35. Diary, 5 June 1941; Diary, 10 February 1943, notes that Macmillan and Addis were the two remaining original Government Court members.
36. Diary, 28 April 1941, 23 March 1942.
37. Diary, 25, 28 June 1944.
38. Interview, Miss Robina Addis, August 1985. The Diary entries are very sparse after 1943. Addis received radiation treatments in 1944 for cancer of the prostate.
39. Henchman to Jones, 2 December 1952, H&SBC Blue Book, HSBC archives, Hong Kong.
40. Mrs Lloyd to Jones, 4 July 1951, HSBC archives, Hong Kong.
41. Diary, 7 February 1941. Sir Robert Vansittart was the Permanent Under-Secretary in the Foreign Office.
42. The esteem in which he was held was demonstrated by his election to the Athenaeum Club in 1923 as one of the distinguished people whose entrance fees are waived. 'Notice of Election', 19 April 1923, Addis papers, /320.
43. 3 July 1935, Addis papers.
44. Tribute to Lord Stamp at Dorchester House after his introduction to the House of Lords, *Abbey Road Monthly Review* (August 1938) Addis papers.
45. 26 October 1938, Addis papers, /84–108. See also W. F. Spaulding to Addis, 29 March 1939, Addis papers, /103.
46. 20 January 1946, excerpt to HSBC archives, Hong Kong.
47. See above and Addis to Grayburn, 1934, Addis papers.
48. Sir Ralph Hawtrey, 'Obituary: Sir Charles Addis', *Economic Journal*, 56 (1946) pp. 507–10.
49. I am particularly indebted to Stephen Clarke for discussion of this topic.
50. Gardner, 'The Role of the Commerce and Treasury Departments' discusses the possibility of such an understanding. See also Kyozo Sato's review of Nish, *Anglo-Japanese Alienation*, in *Modern Asian Studies*, XX (1986) pp. 375–87.
51. Austin Robinson, 'A Personal View', in Milo Keynes (ed.) *Essays on John Maynard Keynes*, p. 20.
52. Lionel Robins, *Economic Planning and International Order*, pp. 279–305; Felix Rohatyn, 'What Next?', *The New York Review of Books*, xxxiv (3 December 1987) pp. 3–5.
53. Cairncross and Eichengreen, *Sterling in Decline*, p. 224.
54. Stephen V. O. Clarke, 'Has The United States Caught The British Disease?', *Tocqueville Research Parallels* (August 1987) pp. 1–9.

Bibliography

ADDIS, C. P., 'Thomas Addis (1813–1899)', 1974.
ADDIS, C. P., 'William Addis (1844–1917)', 1975.
ADDIS, C. S. See appendix.
ADDIS, C. S., Papers. Library, School of Oriental and African Studies, London.
ADSHEAD, S. A. M., *The Modernization of the Chinese Salt Administration, 1900–1920* (Cambridge, Massachusetts: East Asian Research Center, Harvard University, 1970).
AGLEN, SIR FRANCIS, Papers. Library, School of Oriental and African Studies, London.
ALLEN, G. C. and DONNITHORNE, AUDREY G., *Western Enterprise in Far Eastern Economic Development: China and Japan* (London: Allen & Unwin, 1954).
ARMSTRONG, HAMILTON FISH, *Peace and Counterpeace: From Wilson to Hitler* (New York: Harper & Row, 1971).
AUBOIN, ROGER, *The Bank for International Settlements, 1930–55* (Essays in International Finance, Princeton, New Jersey: Princeton University, 1955).
BALFOUR, A. J., Papers, Additional MSS. British Library, London.
BANK FOR INTERNATIONAL SETTLEMENTS: *Documents* (Chicago: The First National Bank of Chicago and First Union Trust and Savings Bank, 1930).
BANNO, MASATAKA, *China and the West, 1858–1861: The Origins of the Tsungli Yamen* (Cambridge, Massachusetts: East Asian Research Center, Harvard University, 1964).
BAYS, DANIEL H., *China Enters the Twentieth Century: Chang Chih-tung and the Issues of a New Age, 1895–1909* (Ann Arbor: University of Michigan Press, 1978).
BEAVERBROOK, LORD, *Decline and Fall of Lloyd George* (New York: Collins, 1963).
BEERS, BURTON F., *Vain Endeavor: Robert Lansing's Attempts to End the American–Japanese Rivalry* (Durham, North Carolina: Duke University Press, 1962).
BENNETT, EDWARD W., *Germany and the Diplomacy of the Financial Crisis, 1931* (Cambridge, Massachusetts: Harvard University Press, 1962).
BERESFORD, CHARLES, *The Break-up of China* (New York: Harper & Bros., 1899).
BERGÈRE, MARIE, 'The Role of the Bourgeoisie', in Mary Wright (ed.) *China in Revolution*.
BIX, HERBERT, 'Japanese Imperialism and the Manchurian Economy, 1900–31', *The China Quarterly*, 51 (1972) pp. 425–43.
BLAKE, ROBERT, *Unrepentant Tory: The Life and Times of Andrew Bonar Law, 1858–1923* (New York: St Martin's Press, 1956).

BLAND, J. O. P. Papers. Thomas Fisher Rare Books Library, University of Toronto, Toronto, Canada.

BOORMAN, HOWARD L. (ed.) *Biographical Dictionary of Republican China*, 4 vols. (New York: Columbia University Press, 1967–1971).

BORG, DOROTHY, *The United States and the Far Eastern Crisis of 1933–38* (Cambridge, Massachusetts: Harvard University Press, 1964).

BORG, DOROTHY, *American Policy and the Chinese Revolution* (New York: Macmillan, 1947).

BORG, DOROTHY and OKAMOTO, SHUMPEI (eds) *Pearl Harbor as History: Japanese–American Relations, 1931–41* (New York: Columbia University Press, 1973).

BOYCE, ROBERT, 'British Leadership in the International Economic System 1925–1931', a paper presented at a Conference on the 1931 Crisis and Its Aftermath, Clare College, Cambridge, 1982.

BOYLE, ANDREW, *Montague Norman: A Biography* (New York: Weybright & Talley, 1967).

BOYLE, JOHN H., *China and Japan at War, 1937–1945: The Politics of Collaboration* (Stanford: Stanford University Press, 1972).

BRADBURY, SIR JOHN, Papers. T170. Public Record Office, Kew, England.

BRAISTED, WILLIAM R., 'The United States and the American China Development Company', *Far Eastern Quarterly*, II (1952) pp. 42–65.

BRANDT, CONRAD, *Stalin's Failure in China, 1924–1927* (New York: W. W. Norton & Co., 1966) first published, 1958.

BRIDGES, LORD, *The Treasury* (London, 1964).

BUNSELMEYER, ROBERT E. *The Cost of the War, 1914–1919: British Economic War Aims and the Origins of Reparation* (Hamden, Connecticut: Archon Books, 1975).

BURK, KATHLEEN, 'The Treasury: from Impotence to Power', in Kathleen Burk (ed.) *War and the State: The Transformation of British Government, 1914–1919* (London: George Allen & Unwin, 1982).

BURK, KATHLEEN, *Britain, America and the Sinews of War, 1914–1918*, (London: George Allen & Unwin, 1983).

BURK, KATHLEEN, 'Diplomacy and the Private Banker: The Case of the House of Morgan', in Gustav Schmidt (ed.) *Konstellationen Internationaler Politik 1924–1932*.

BURNS, RICHARD DEAN and BENNETT, EDWARD M. (eds) *Diplomats in Crisis: United States–Chinese–Japanese Relations, 1919–1941* (Santa Barbara, California: ABC–CLIO, Inc., 1976).

CAIRNCROSS, SIR ALEC and EICHENGREEN, BARRY, *Sterling in Decline: The Devaluations of 1932, 1949 and 1967* (Oxford: Basil Blackwell, 1983).

CAMERON, MARIBETH, *The Reform Movement in China, 1898–1912* (Stanford: Stanford University Press, 1931).

CAPIE, FORREST, *Depression and Protectionism: Britain Between the Wars* (London: George Allen & Unwin, 1983).

CARLSON, E. C. *The Kaiping Mines (1877–1912)*(Cambridge, Massachusetts: East Asian Research Center, Harvard University, 1971) 2nd edn., first published 1957.

394 *Bibliography*

CARROLL, JOHN M., 'The Paris Bankers' Conference of 1922 and America's Design for a Peaceful Europe', *International Review of History and Political Science*, 10 (1973) pp. 39–47.

CARROLL, JOHN M., 'Owen D. Young and German Reparations: The Diplomacy of an Enlightened Businessman', in K. P. Jones (ed.) *U.S. Diplomats in Europe, 1919–1941*.

CASE, JOSEPHINE YOUNG and CASE, EVERETT NEEDHAM, *Owen D. Young and American Enterprise* (Boston: David R. Godine, 1982).

CHAMBERLAIN, SIR AUSTEN, Papers. Library, University of Birmingham, Birmingham.

CHAN, L. C., 'British Policy in the Reorganization Loan to China, 1912–1913', *Modern Asian Studies*, V (1971).

CHAN, LAU KIT-CHING, 'The Lincheng Incident – A Case Study of British Policy in China Between the Washington Conference (1921–22) and the First Nationalist Revolution (1925–28)', *Journal of Oriental Studies*, X (1972) pp. 172–86.

CHANDLER, LESTER V., *Benjamin Strong, Central Banker* (Washington, DC: The Brookings Institution, 1958).

CHANG, HSIN-PAO, *Commissioner Lin and the Opium War* (Cambridge, Massachusetts: East Asian Research Center, Harvard University, 1964).

CHANG, KIA–NGAU, *China's Struggle for Railroad Development* (New York: John Day, 1943).

CHAPMAN, STANLEY, *The Rise of Merchant Banking* (London: George Allen & Unwin, 1984).

CHECKLAND, SYDNEY and OLIVE, *Industry and Ethos: Scotland, 1832–1914* (London: Edward Arnold, 1984).

CHECKLAND, S. G. 'The Mind of the City 1870–1914', *Oxford Economic Papers*, new series (October 1957) pp. 261–79.

CH'EN, JEROME, *Yuan Shih-k'ai, 1859–1916: Brutus Assumes the Purple* (Stanford: Stanford University Press, 1972) 2nd edn, first published 1961.

CHEONG, W. E., *Mandarins and Merchants: Jardine Matheson & Co., A China Agency of the Early Nineteenth Century* (London and Malmo: Curzon Press, 1979).

CHI, MADELEINE, 'The Shanghai–Hangchow–Ningpo Railway Loan: A Case Study of the Rights Recovery Movement', *Modern Asian Studies*, 7 (1973).

CHI, MADELEINE, 'Ts'ao Ju-lin (1876–1966): His Japanese Connections', in Akira Iriye (ed.) *The Chinese and the Japanese*.

CHI-MING HOU, *Foreign Investment and Economic Development in China, 1840–1937* (Cambridge, Massachusetts: East Asian Research Center, Harvard University, 1965).

CHOW TSE-TSUNG, *The May Fourth Movement: Intellectual Revolution in Modern China* (Cambridge, Massachusetts: East Asian Research Center, Harvard University, 1960).

CLARKE, PETER, *Liberals and Social Democrats* (Cambridge: Cambridge University Press, 1978).

CLARKE, STEPHEN V. O., *Central Bank Cooperation: 1924–31* (New York: Federal Reserve Bank of New York, 1967).

CLARKE, STEPHEN V. O., *The Reconstruction of the International*

Monetary System: The Attempts of 1922 and 1933 (Princeton, New Jersey: International Finance Section, Princeton University, 1973).

CLARKE, STEPHEN V. O., *Exchange-Rate Stabilization in the mid-1930s: Negotiating the Tripartite Agreement* (Princeton, New Jersey: International Finance Section, Princeton University, 1977).

CLARKE, STEPHEN V. O., 'Has the United States Caught the British Disease?' *Tocqueville Research Parallels* (August 1987) pp. 1–9.

CLAY, SIR HENRY, *Lord Norman* (London: Macmillan, 1957).

CLIFFORD, NICHOLAS, R., *Retreat from China: British Policy in the Far East, 1937–1941* (Seattle: University of Washington Press, 1967).

CLIFFORD, NICHOLAS R., 'Sir Frederick Maze and the Chinese Maritime Customs, 1937–1941', *Journal of Modern History*, XXXVII (1965) pp. 18–34.

COBLE, PARKS M., *The Shanghai Capitalists and the Nationalist Government, 1927–1937* (Cambridge, Massachusetts: Council on East Asian Studies, Harvard University, 1980).

COHEN, WARREN I. and KWAN WAI SO, *Essays in the History of China and Chinese–American Relations* (East Lansing: Asian Studies Center, Michigan State University, 1982).

COHEN, WARREN, *The Chinese Connection: Roger S. Greene, Thomas W. Lamont, George E. Sokolsky and American–East Asian Relations* (New York: Columbia University Press, 1978).

COLLIS, MAURICE, *Foreign Mud: The Opium Imbroglio at Canton and the Anglo-Chinese War* (New York: J. W. Norton, 1968) first published 1946.

COLLIS, MAURICE, *Wayfoong: The Hongkong and Shanghai Banking Corporation* (London: Faber & Faber, 1965).

COMMITTEE OF TREASURY MINUTES, Bank of England, 1930–1.

COMMITTEE ON THE CURRENCY AND BANK OF ENGLAND AND NOTE ISSUES, Hearings, 28 January 1925, Marshall Library, Cambridge University.

COMMITTEE ON CURRENCY AND FOREIGN EXCHANGES AFTER THE WAR, 1918–19 (Cunliffe Committee) T185.

COMMITTEE ON NATIONAL DEBT AND TAXATION (Colwyn Committee) *Report*, Cmd. 2800, 1927.

CONANT, CHARLES, 'Putting China on the Gold Standard', *North American Review*, 177 (1903) pp. 691–704.

CORRESPONDENCE respecting Chinese Loan Negotiations, Cmd. 6446.

COSTIGLIOLA, FRANK C., 'The Politics of Financial Stabilization: American Reconstruction Policy in Europe, 1924–30', unpublished Ph.D. dissertation at Cornell University, 1973.

COSTIGLIOLA, FRANK C. 'The US and Reconstruction of Germany in the 1920s', *Business History Review*, 50 (1976) pp. 477–502.

COSTIGLIOLA, FRANK C. *Awkward Dominion: American Political, Economic, and Cultural Relations with Europe, 1919–1933* (Ithaca: Cornell University Press, 1984).

CROWLEY, JAMES (ed.) *Modern East Asia: Essays in Interpretation* (New York: Harcourt Brace & World Inc., 1970).

CROWLEY, JAMES, 'Japan's Military Foreign Policies', in James Morley (ed.) *Japan's Foreign Policy, 1868–1941*.

CURRY, ROY WATSON, *Woodrow Wilson and Far Eastern Policy, 1913– 1921* (New York: Bookman Associates, 1957).

CURTIS, C. A., 'The Canadian Macmillan Commission', *Economic Journal*, 44 (1934) pp. 48–59.

CURTIS, LIONEL, *The Capital Question of China* (London: Macmillan, 1932).

CZERNIN, FERDINAND, *Versailles, 1919* (New York: Capricorn Books, 1965).

DALGAARD, BRUCE, R., *Sotuh Africa's Impact on Britain's Return to Gold, 1925* (New York: Arno Press, 1981).

DAVENPORT, NICHOLAS, 'Keynes in the City', in Milo Keynes (ed.) *Essays on John Maynard Keynes.*

DAVENPORT-HINES, R. P. T., *Dudley Docker: The Life and Times of a Trade Warrior* (Cambridge: Cambridge University Press, 1984).

DAVIS, CLARENCE, 'The Defensive Diplomacy of British Imperialism in the Far East, 1915–1922: Japan and the United States as Partners and Rivals', unpublished Ph.D. dissertation at the University of Wisconsin, 1972.

DAVIS, CLARENCE, 'Limits of Effacement: Britain and the Problem of American Cooperation and Competition in China, 1915–1917', *Pacific Historical Review, XLVIII* (February 1979), pp. 47–63.

DAVIS, CLARENCE, 'Financing Imperialism: British and American Bankers as Vectors of Imperial Expansion in China, 1908–1920', *Business History Review*, LVI (Summer 1982) pp. 236–64.

DAWES, CHARLES, *Journal As Ambassador to Great Britain* (New York: Macmillan, 1939).

DAYER, ROBERTA A., 'Struggle for China: The Anglo-American Relationship, 1917–25', unpublished Ph.D. dissertation at the State University of New York at Buffalo, 1972.

DAYER, ROBERTA A., 'Strange Bedfellows: J. P. Morgan & Co., Whitehall and the Wilson Adminstration during World War I', *Business History* XVIII (1976) pp. 127–51.

DAYER, ROBERTA A., 'The British War Debts to the United States and the Anglo-Japanese Alliance, 1920–1923', *Pacific Historical Review*, XLV (1976) pp. 569–77.

DAYER, ROBERTA A., *Bankers and Diplomats in China, 1917–1925: The Anglo-American Relationship* (London: Frank Cass, 1981).

DAYER, ROBERTA A., 'The Young Charles S. Addis: Poet or Banker', in F. H. H. King (ed.) *Eastern Banking*, pp. 14–31.

DEAN, BRITTEN, *China and Great Britain: The Diplomacy of Commercial Relations, 1860–1864* (Cambridge, Massachusetts: East Asian Research Center, Harvard University, 1974).

DES FORGES, ROGER V., *Hsi-liang and the Chinese National Revolution* (New Haven: Yale University Press, 1973).

DICKINSON, GOLDSWORTHY LOWES, *Justice and Liberty: A Political Dialogue* (New York: Doubleday Page, 1908).

DICKINSON, GOLDSWORTHY LOWES, *The Choice Before Us* (New York: Dodd, Mead & Co., 1917).

DIMSDALE, N. H., 'British Monetary Policy and the Exchange Rate, 1920– 38', *Oxford Economic Papers*, 33 (1981) Supplement, pp. 328–43.

DINGMAN, ROGER, *Power in the Pacific: The Origins of Naval Arms Limitation, 1914–1922* (Chicago: University of Chicago Press, 1976).

Documents on British Foreign Policy, 1919–1939, edited by Rohan Butler, J. P. T. Bury, and M. E. Lambert, 1st series, vols. III, V, VI, XIX.

DRAGE, CHARLES, *Taikoo* (London: Constable, 1970).

DRUMMOND, IAN M., *London, Washington, and the Management of the Franc, 1936–39* (Princeton: International Finance Section, Princeton University, 1977).

DULLES, ELEANOR LANSING, *The Bank for International Settlements at Work* (New York: Macmillan, 1932).

DUTT, VIDYA P., 'The First Week of Revolution: The Wuchang Uprising', in Mary Wright (ed.) *China in Revolution.*

EASTMAN, LLOYD, 'China Under Nationalist Rule, 1927–1937', a draft of a chapter for *The Cambridge History of China*, vol. 13, edited by John K. Fairbank and Albert Feuerwerker.

EASTMAN, LLOYD, 'Facets of an Ambivalent Relationship', in Akira Iriye (ed.) *The Chinese and the Japanese.*

EASTMAN, LLOYD, *The Abortive Revolution: China Under Nationalist Rule, 1927–1937.*

EDWARDS, E. W., 'The Origins of British Financial Cooperation with France in China, 1903–6', *English Historical Review*, 86 (1971) pp. 285–317.

EICHENGREEN, BARRY J., *Sterling and the Tariff, 1929–32* (Princeton: International Finance Section, Department of Economics, Princeton University, 1981).

EICHENGREEN, BARRY J. (ed.) *The Gold Standard in Theory and History* (New York: Methuen, 1985).

ENDICOTT, STEPHEN L., *Diplomacy and Enterprise: British China Policy, 1933–1937* (Victoria: University of British Columbia Press, 1975).

ENDICOTT, STEPHEN L., 'British Financial Diplomacy in China: The Leith–Ross Mission, 1935–37', *Pacific Affairs*, 46 (1973–4).

FAIRBANK, JOHN K., *Trade and Diplomacy on the China Coast: The Opening of the Treaty Ports, 1842–1854* (Cambridge, Massachusetts: Harvard University Press, 1954).

FAIRBANK, J. K., BRUNER, K. F. and MATHESON, E. M. (eds) *The I. G. in Peking: Letters of Robert Hart, Chinese Maritime Customs, 1868–1907*, 2 vols (Cambridge, Massachusetts: Harvard University Press, 1975).

FAIRBANK, J. K. and TWITCHETT, DENIS (eds) *The Cambridge History of China*, vol. II, pt. 2, vol. XII, pt. 1. (Cambridge: Cambridge University Press, 1980–3).

FEDERAL RESERVE BANK OF NEW YORK, Papers.

FEUERWERKER, ALBERT, *China's Early Industrialization: Sheng Hsuan-huai (1944–1916) and Mandarin Enterprise* (Cambridge, Massachusetts: Harvard University Press, 1958).

FEUERWERKER, ALBERT, *The Foreign Establishment in China in the Early Twentieth Century* (Ann Arbor: Michigan University Press, 1976).

FIELDHOUSE, D. K., *Economics and Empire, 1830–1914* (Ithaca: Cornell University Press, 1973).

FIFIELD, RUSSELL, *Woodrow Wilson and the Far East: The Diplomacy of the Shantung Question* (New York: Crowell, 1952).

FINK, CAROLE, *The Genoa Conference: European Diplomacy, 1921–1922* (Chapel Hill: The University of North Carolina Press, 1984).

FISCHER, LOUIS, *The Soviets in World Affairs: A History of the Relations between the Soviet Union and the Rest of the World, 1917–1929* (New York: Vintage Books, 1960) abridged by author; first published in two volumes, 1930.

FORSTER, E. M., *Goldsworthy Lowes Dickinson* (New York: Harcourt Brace Jovanovich, 1934).

FOWLER, W. B., *British–American Relations, 1917–1918: The Role of Sir William Wiseman* (Princeton: Princeton University Press, 1969).

FRIEDMAN, EDWARD, *Backward Toward Revolution: The Chinese Revolutionary Party* (Berkeley: University of California Press, 1974).

FRITSCH, W., 'Aspects of Brazilian Economic Policy Under the First Republic, 1889–1930', unpublished Ph.D. dissertation at Cambridge University, 1983.

FUNG, EDMUND S., 'The Sino-British Rapproachment, 1927–1931', *Modern Asian Studies*, 17 (1983) pp. 79–105.

FUNG, EDMUND S., 'Anti-Imperialism and the Left Guomindang', *Modern China*, 19 (1985) pp. 39–76.

GAGNIER, D., 'French Loans to China, 1895–1914: The Alliance of International Finance and Diplomacy', *Australian Journal of Politics and History*, 18 (1972) pp. 229–49.

GARDNER, LLOYD, C., 'The Role of the Commerce and Treasury Departments', in Dorothy Borg and Shumpei Okamoto (eds) *Pearl Harbor as History*, pp. 261–86.

GARDNER, LLOYD C., *Safe for Democracy: The Anglo–American Response to Revolution, 1913–1923* (New York: Oxford University Press, 1984).

GASSTER, MICHAEL, 'The Republican Revolutionary Movement', in *Cambridge History of China*, XI, pt. 2.

GERSON, LOUIS, *John Foster Dulles* (New York: Cooper Square Publishers, 1967).

GILBERT, MARTIN, *Winston Churchill: The Wilderness Years* (London: Macmillan, 1981).

GRAY, JACK (ed.) *Modern China's Search for a Political Form* (New York: Oxford University Press, 1969).

GREAT BRITAIN, GOVERNMENT DOCUMENTS, Public Record Office, Kew.
Foreign Office Records: FO371, F0800.
Treasury Office Records: T160, T172.
Cabinet Office Records: Cab 23, Cab 58, Cab 27. PREM 1.

GREEN, EDWIN, *Debtors to Their Profession: A History of the Institute of Bankers, 1879–1979* (London: Methuen, 1979).

GREENBERG, MICHAEL, *British Trade and the Opening of China, 1800–42* (Cambridge: Cambridge University Press, 1951).

GRENFELL, MORGAN, Papers, London.

GRENVILLE, J. A. S., *Lord Salisbury and Foreign Policy: The Close of the Nineteenth Century* (London: Athlone Press, 1964).

GRIGG, P. J., *Prejudice and Judgment* (London: Jonathan Cape, 1948).

HAMASHITA, T., 'The International Financial Relations Behind the 1911 Revolution', a paper presented at the International Conference on the 1911 Revolution Commemorating the 70th anniversary, Peking, 1981.

HAO, YEN-P'ING, *The Comprador in Nineteenth Century China: Bridge Between East and West* (Cambridge, Massachusetts: Harvard University Press, 1970).

HARRISON, GEORGE L., Papers. Federal Reserve Bank of New York.

HARROD, R. F., *The Life of John Maynard Keynes* (New York: St Martin's Press, 1951) Avon edition.

HAWTREY, SIR RALPH G., *A Century of Bank Rate* (London: Frank Cass, 1962) 2nd edn; first published in 1938.

HAWTREY, SIR RALPH G., *The Art of Central Banking* (London: Longmans, Green, 1932).

HAWTREY, SIR RALPH G., 'Obituary: Sir Charles Addis', *Economic Journal*, 56 (1946) pp. 507–10.

HEARINGS BEFORE THE SPECIAL COMMITTEE INVESTIGATING THE MUNITIONS INDUSTRY, (Nye Committee) Washington, DC, US Senate, 2nd session, 73rd Congress.

HIRST, F. W., *In the Golden Days* (London: Muller, 1947).

HIRST, F. W., *Wall Street and Lombard Street: The Stock Exchange Slump of 1929 and the Trade Depression of 1930* (New York: Macmillan, 1931).

HOGAN, MICHAEL J., *Informal Entente: The Private Structure of Cooperation in Anglo-American Economic Diplomacy, 1918–1928* (Columbia, Missouri: University of Missouri Press, 1977).

HOGAN, MICHAEL J., 'Thomas W. Lamont and European Recovery: The Diplomacy of Privatism in a Corporatist Age', in K. P. Jones (ed.) *US Diplomats in Europe, 1919–1941*.

HONGKONG AND SHANGHAI BANKING CORPORATION, Papers, Hong Kong.

HOOVER, HERBERT, Papers. Hoover Presidential Library, West Branch, Iowa.

HOPKINS, SIR RICHARD, Papers. T175, Public Record Office, Kew.

HORNBECK, STANLEY, Papers. Hoover Institute, Stanford, California.

HOSOYA, CHIHIRO, 'Britain and the US in Japan's View of the International System, 1919–1937', in Ian Nish (ed.) *Anglo-Japanese Alienation, 1919–1952*.

HOWSON, SUSAN, *Domestic Monetary Management in Britain, 1919–38* (Cambridge: Cambridge University Press, 1975).

HOWSON, SUSAN, '*Monetary Theory and Policy in the 20th Century: the Career of R. G. Hawtrey*', in M. Flinn (ed.) Proceedings of the Seventh International Economic History Congress, Edinburgh, 1978.

HOWSON, SUSAN, *Sterling's Managed Float: The Operations of the Exchange Equalisation Account, 1932–39* (Princeton: International Finance Section, Department of Economics, Princeton University, 1980).

HOWSON, SUSAN and WINCH, DONALD J., *The Economic Advisory Council, 1930–1939* (Cambridge: Cambridge University Press, 1977).

HSIEH, WINSTON, 'A Symposium on the 1911 Revolution', *Modern China*, II (1976).

HSI-SHENG CH'I, *Warlord Politics in China, 1916–1928* (Stanford: Stanford University Press, 1976).

HSU, IMMANUEL C. Y., *China's Entrance into the Family of Nations: The Diplomatic Phase, 1858–1880* (Cambridge, Massachusetts: Harvard University Press, 1960).

HUBBARD, G. E., 'Financial Reconstruction for China', *RIIA Journal*, IX (1930) pp. 636–51.

HUENEMANN, RALPH, W., *The Dragon and the Iron Horse: The Economics of Railroads in China, 1876–1937* (Cambridge, Massachusetts: The Council on East Asian Studies, Harvard University, 1984).

HUGHES, CHARLES EVANS, Papers. Library of Congress, Washington DC.

HUNT, MICHAEL, *Frontier Defence and the Open Door: Manchuria in Chinese–American Relations, 1895–1911* (New Haven: Yale University Press, 1973).

HURD, DOUGLAS, *The Arrow War: An Anglo-Chinese Confusion, 1856–1860* (New York: Macmillan, 1967).

ICHIKO, CHUZO, 'Political and Institutional Reform, 1901–11', in *Cambridge History of China*, Late Ch'ing (1800–1911), vol. II, pt. 2, pp. 375–415.

IRIYE, AKIRA, *After Imperialism: The Search for a New Order in the Far East, 1921–1931* (Cambridge, Massachusetts: East Asian Research Center, Harvard University, 1965).

IRIYE, AKIRA, 'Imperialism in East Asia', in James B. Crowley (ed.) *Modern East Asia: Essays in Interpretation* (San Francisco: Harcourt Brace & World, Inc., 1970).

IRIYE, AKIRA (ed.) *The Chinese and the Japanese: Essays in Political and Cultural Interactions* (Princeton: Princeton University Press, 1980).

ISAACS, HAROLD, *The Tragedy of the Chinese Revolution* (New York: Atheneum, 1968) 2nd revised edn; first published, 1938.

ISRAEL, JERRY, *Progressivism and the Open Door: America and China, 1905–1912* (Pittsburgh: University of Pittsburgh Press, 1971).

JACOBSON, JON., *Locarno Diplomacy: Germany and the West, 1925–1929* (Princeton: Princeton University Press, 1972).

JAMES, ROBERT RHODES, *Memoirs of a Conservative: J. C. C. Davidson's Memoirs and Papers* (London: 1969).

JAMES, ROBERT RHODES, *Churchill: A Study in Failure, 1900–1939* (London: Weidenfeld & Nicolson, 1970 and Penguin) Penguin edn.

JANSEN, MARIUS, *The Japanese and Sun Yat-sen* (Cambridge, Massachusetts: Harvard University Press, 1954).

JEREMY, DAVID J. (ed.) *Dictionary of Business Biography*, 5 vols. (London: Butterworth, 1984–6).

JONES, K. P., 'Discord and Collaboration: Choosing an Agent-General for Reparations', *Diplomatic History*, (Spring 1977).

JONES, K. P. (ed.) *US Diplomats in Europe, 1919–1941* (Santa Barbara, California: ABC–CLIO, 1981).

JORDAN, DONALD, *The Northern Expedition: China's National Revolution of 1926–1928* (Honolulu: University Press of Hawaii, 1976).

KAHN, HELEN, 'The Great Game of Empire: Willard Straight and American Far Eastern Policy', unpublished Ph.D. dissertation, Cornell University, 1968.

KAHN, RICHARD F., *The Making of Keynes' General Theory* (Cambridge: Cambridge University Press, 1984).

KAUFMAN, BURTON I., *Efficiency and Expansion: Foreign Trade Organisation in the Wilson Administration, 1913–1921* (Westport, Connecticut: Greenwood Press, 1974).

KEMMERER, EDWIN W., Papers. Princeton University, Princeton, New Jersey.

KENT, FRED, Papers. Princeton University, Princeton, New Jersey.

KEYNES, JOHN MAYNARD, *The Collected Writings*, vols. 16–21, edited by Elizabeth Johnson and Donald Moggridge (London: Macmillan, 1971–82).

KEYNES, MILO (ed.) *Essays on John Maynard Keynes* (Cambridge: Cambridge University Press, 1975).

KINDLEBERGER, CHARLES P., *The World in Depression, 1929–1939* (London: Allen Lane, The Penguin Press, 1973).

KING, CATHERINE, 'The First Trip East – P&O via Suez', in F. H. H. King (ed.), *Eastern Banking*.

KING, DAVID, 'China's First Public Loan: The Hongkong Bank and the Chinese Imperial Government "Foochow" Loan of 1874', in F. H. H. King (ed.), *Eastern Banking*.

KING, DAVID, 'The Hamburg Branch: The German Period, 1889–1920', in F. H. H. King (ed.), *Eastern Banking*.

KING, FRANK H. H., *Money and Monetary Policy in China, 1845–1895* (Cambridge, Massachusetts: East Asian Research Center, Harvard University, 1965).

KING, FRANK H. H., 'Defending the Chinese Currency: the Role of the Hongkong and Shanghai Banking Corporation, 1938–1941', in F. H. H. King (ed.) *Eastern Banking: Essays in the History of the Hongkong and Shanghai Banking Corporation* (London: Athlone Press, 1983).

KING-HALL, STEPHEN, *Chatham House* (Oxford: Oxford University Press, 1937).

KIRBY, WILLIAM C., *Germany and Republican China* (Stanford: Stanford University Press, 1984).

KLEIN, IRA, 'Whitehall, Washington, and the Anglo-Japanese Alliance, 1919–1921', *Pacific Historical Review*, XLI (1972) pp. 460–83.

KOO, V. K. WELLINGTON, Papers. Butler Library, Columbia University, New York City.

KUEHL, WARREN F. (ed.) *Biographical Dictionary of Internationalists* (Westport, Connecticut: Greenwood Press, 1983).

LAMONT, THOMAS W., *Henry P. Davison: The Record of a Useful Life* (New York: Harper & Bros., 1933).

LAMONT, THOMAS W., *Across World Frontiers* (New York: Harcourt Brace, 1951).

LAMONT, THOMAS W., Papers. Baker Library, Harvard University, Cambridge, Massachusetts.

LANGER, WILLIAM, *The Diplomacy of Imperialism*, 2 vols. (New York: Knopt, 1951) 2nd edn; first published 1935.

LEE, BRADFORD A., *Britain and the Sino-Japanese War, 1937–1939* (Stanford: Stanford University Press, 1973).

LEE, EN-HAN, *China's Quest for Railway Autonomy, 1904–1911* (Singapore: Singapore University Press, 1977).

LEFFLER, MELVYN P., 'The Origins of Republican War Debt Policy, 1921–1923', *The Journal of American History*, LIX (1972) pp. 585–601.

LEFFLER, MELVYN P., *The Elusive Quest: America's Pursuit of European Stability and French Security, 1919–1933* (Chapel Hill: University of North Carolina Press, 1979).

LE FEVOUR, EDWARD, *Western Enterprise in Late Ch'ing China: A Selective Survey of Jardine, Matheson & Company's Operations, 1842–1895* (Cambridge, Massachusetts: Harvard University Press, 1968).

LEITH-ROSS, SIR FREDERICK, *Money Talks: Fifty Years of International Finance* (London: Hutchinson, 1968).

LEITH-ROSS, SIR FREDERICK, Papers. T188, Public Record Office, Kew.

LEVIN, N. GORDON JR., *Woodrow Wilson and World Politics: America's Response to War and Revolution* (Oxford: Oxford University Press, 1968).

LIEW, K. S. *Struggle for Democracy: Sung Chiao-jen and the 1911 Revolution* (Berkeley: University of California Press, 1971).

LING HUNG-HSUN, 'A Decade of Chinese Railway Construction', in Paul K. T. Sih (ed.) *The Strenuous Decade: China's Nation-Building Efforts, 1927–1937* (Jamaica, New York: St John's University Press, 1970).

LINK, ARTHUR, *Campaigns for Progressivism and Peace, 1916–1917* (Princeton: Princeton University Press, 1965).

LI TIEN-YI, *Woodrow Wilson's China Policy, 1913–1917* (New York: Twayne, 1952).

LIU, K. C., 'Li Hung-chang in Chihil: The Emergence of a Policy, 1870–1875', in A. Feuerwerker, R. Murphey and M. Wright (eds) *Approaches to Modern Chinese History* (Berkeley: University of California Press, 1967).

LLOYD GEORGE, DAVID, Papers, House of Lords, London.

LO HUI-MIN (ed.) *The Correspondence of G. E. Morrison*, 2 vols (Cambridge: Cambridge University Press, 1976–8).

LONG, BRECKENRIDGE, Papers. Library of Congress, Washington, DC.

LOUIS, WILLIAM ROGER, *British Strategy in the Far East, 1919–1939* (Oxford: Clarendon Press, 1971).

LOWE, C. J., *The Reluctant Imperialists: British Foreign Policy, 1878–1902* (London: Routledge & Kegan Paul, 1967).

LOWE, PETER, *Great Britain and Japan, 1911–1915: A Study of British Far Eastern Policy* (London: Macmillan, 1969).

LOWE, PETER, *Great Britain and the Origins of the Pacific War* (Oxford: Clarendon Press, 1977).

McCORMICK, GAVAN, *Chang Tso-lin in North-east China, 1911–1928: China, Japan and the Manchuria Idea* (Stanford: Stanford University Press, 1977).

McELDERRY, ANDREA, *Shanghai Old-Style Banks (Ch'en-Chuang), 1800–1935* (Ann Arbor: Michigan Papers in Chinese Studies, University of Michigan Press, 1976).

McELDERRY, ANDREA, 'Robber Barons or Nationalist Capitalists: Shanghai Bankers in Republican China', *Republican China*, XI (1985).

McKERCHER, B. J. C., *The Second Baldwin Government and the United*

States, 1924–1929: Attitudes and Diplomacy (Cambridge: Cambridge University Press, 1984).

McKERCHER, B. J. C., 'A Sane and Sensible Diplomacy: Austen Chamberlain, Japan, and The Naval Balance of Power in the Pacific Ocean, 1924–29', *Canadian Journal of History*, XXI (1986) pp. 187–213.

McKERCHER, B. J. C. (ed.) *The Struggle for Supremacy* (London: Macmillan, forthcoming).

McKERCHER, B. J. C. and MOSS, D. J. (eds) *Shadow and Substance in British Foreign Policy, 1895–1939* (Edmonton: University of Alberta Press, 1984).

MacKINNON, STEVEN, *Power and Politics in Late Imperial China: Yuan Ship-kai in Beijing and Tianjin, 1901–1908* (Berkeley: University of California Press, 1980).

McLEAN, DAVID, 'British Banking and Government in China: The Foreign Office and the Hongkong and Shanghai Bank, 1895–1913', unpublished Ph.D. dissertation at Cambridge University, 1972.

McLEAN, DAVID, 'Commerce, Finance and British Diplomatic Support in China, 1885–6', *Economic History Review*, second series, XXVI (1973) pp. 464–77.

McLEAN, DAVID, 'The Foreign Office and the First Chinese Indemnity Loan, 1895', *The Historical Journal*, 2 (1973) pp. 303–21.

McLEAN, DAVID, 'Chinese Railways and the Townley Agreement of 1903', *Modern Asian Studies*, 7 (1973) pp. 145–64.

McLEAN, DAVID, 'International Banking and its Political Implications: The Hongkong and Shanghai Banking Corporation and The Imperial Bank of Persia, 1889–1914', in F. H. H. King (ed.) *Eastern Banking*, pp. 1–13.

MacMURRAY, JOHN VAN ANTWERP (ed.) *Treaties and Agreements with and concerning China, 1894–1919*, 2 vols (New York: Oxford University Press, 1921).

MacMURRAY, JOHN VAN ANTWERP, Papers. Princeton University, Princeton, New Jersey.

MALOZEMOFF, ANDREW, *Russian Far Eastern Policy, 1881–1904* (Berkeley: University of California Press, 1958).

MARQUAND, DAVID, *Ramsay MacDonald* (London: Jonathan Cape, 1977).

MARSHALL, ALFRED, *Principles of Economics* (London: Macmillan, 1961), 9th edition.

MAYER, ARNO J., *Wilson vs Lenin: Political Origins of the New Diplomacy, 1917–1918* (New Haven: Yale University Press, 1959).

MAYER, ARNO J., *Politics and Diplomacy of Peacemaking: Containment and Counterrevolution at Versailles, 1918–1919* (New York: Alfred A. Knopf, 1967).

MAZE, SIR FREDERICK, Papers. Library, School of Oriental and African Studies, London.

MEGGINSON, WILLIAM JAMES, 'Britain's Response to Chinese Nationalism, 1925–1927: The Foreign Office Search for a New Policy', unpublished Ph.D. dissertation at the George Washington University, 1973.

MICHIE, ALEXANDER, *The Englishman in China during the Victorian*

Era as illustrated in the Career of Sir Rutherford Alcock, KCB, DCL, 2 vols (Edinburgh: Blackwood, 1900).

MICHIE, R. C., 'Options, Concessions, Syndicates, and the Provision of Venture Capital, 1880–1913', *Business History*, XXIII (1981) pp. 147–64.

MIDDLEMAS, KEITH and BARNES, JOHN, *Baldwin: A Biography* (London: Macmillan, 1969).

MOGGRIDGE, DONALD E., *British Monetary Policy, 1924–1931: The Norman Conquest of $4.86* (Cambridge: Cambridge University Press, 1972).

MOGGRIDGE, DONALD E., '1931 Financial Crisis – A New View', *The Banker* (1970).

MORGAN, E. V., *Studies in British Financial Policy, 1914–25* (London: Macmillan, 1952).

MORGAN, KENNETH, *Consensus and Disunity: The Lloyd George Coalition Government, 1918–22* (Oxford: Oxford University Press, 1979).

MORLEY, JAMES W. (ed.) *Japan's Foreign Policy, 1868–1941: A Research Guide* (New York: Columbia University Press, 1974).

MORLEY, JAMES W. (ed.) *The China Quagmire: Japan's Expansion on the Asian Continent, 1933–1941* (New York: Columbia University Press, 1983).

MORSE, HOSEA BALLOU, *The International Relations of the Chinese Empire*, 3 vols (London: Longmans, Green & Company, 1910–1918).

MOULTON, HAROLD G. and PASVOLSKY, LEO, *War Debts and World Prosperity* (Washington, DC: Brookings Institution, 1932).

NASH, GEORGE H., *The Life of Herbert Hoover: The Engineer, 1874–1914* (New York: W. W. Norton, 1983).

NATHAN, ANDREW J., *Peking Politics, 1918–1923: Factionalism and the Failure of Constitutionalism* (Berkeley: University of California Press, 1976).

NATHAN, ANDREW J., 'A Constitutional Republic', in *Cambridge History of China*, XII, pt. 1.

NATHAN, MATTHEW, Papers. Rhodes House, Oxford University, Oxford.

NAYLOR, JOHN F., *A Man and an Institution: Sir Maurice Hankey, the Cabinet Secretariat and the Custody of Cabinet Secrecy* (Cambridge: Cambridge University Press, 1984).

NIEMEYER, SIR OTTO, Papers. T176, Public Record Office, Kew.

NISH, IAN H., *The Anglo-Japanese Alliance: The Diplomacy of Two Island Empires, 1984–1907* (London: University of London, 1966).

NISH, IAN H., *Alliance in Decline: A Study in Anglo-Japanese Relations, 1908–1923* (London: University of London, 1972).

NISH, IAN H., *Japanese Foreign Policy, 1869–1942: Kasumigaseki to Miyakezaka* (London: Routledge & Kegan Paul, 1977).

NISH, IAN H. (ed.) *Some Foreign Attitudes to Republican China* (London: London School of Economics, 1981).

NISH, IAN H. (ed.) *The Russian Problem in East Asia* (London: London School of Economics, 1981).

NISH, IAN H., *Anglo-Japanese Alienation, 1919–1952* (Cambridge: Cambridge University Press, 1982).

NORMAN, MONTAGU, Diaries, personal and office, Bank of England, London.

NORMAN, PRISCILLA, *In the Way of Understanding* (Surrey: Foxbury Press, 1982).

North China Daily News, 1890s.

North China Herald, 1890s.

NORTH, ROBERT C., *Moscow and Chinese Communists* (Stanford: Stanford University Press, 1953).

OSTERHAMMEL, JURGEN, 'Technical cooperation between the League of Nations and China', *Modern Asian Studies* (1979).

OSTERHAMMEL, JURGEN, 'Imperialism in Transition: British Big Business and the Chinese Authorities, 1931–1937', *China Quarterly* (1984) pp. 260–86.

PARRINI, CARL P., *Heir to Empire: United States Economic Diplomacy, 1916–1923* (Pittsburgh: University of Pittsburgh Press, 1969).

PEDEN, G. C., *British Rearmament and the Treasury, 1932–39* (Edinburgh: Scottish Academic Press, 1979).

PLATT, D. C., *Finance, Trade and Politics in British Foreign Policy, 1815–1914* (London: University of London, 1968).

PLUMPTRE, ARTHUR F. W., *Central Banking in the British Dominions* (Toronto: University of Toronto Press, 1940).

PLUMPTRE, ARTHUR, F. W., 'The Evidence presented to the Canadian Macmillan Commission', *Canadian Journal of Economics and Political Science*, II (1936) pp. 54–67.

PRATT, SIR JOHN T., *War and Politics in China* (London: Jonathan Cape, 1943).

PRESSNEL, L. S., '1925: The Burden of Sterling', *Economic History Review* (February 1978).

PRICE, ERNEST B., Papers. Hoover Institute, Stanford University, Stanford, California.

PROCTOR, DENNIS (ed.) *The Autobiography of G. Lowes Dickinson and Other Unpublished Writings* (London: Duckworth, 1973).

PRUESSEN, RONALD W., *John Foster Dulles: The Road to Power* (New York: The Free Press, 1982).

PUGACH, NOEL, *Paul S. Reinsch: Open Door Diplomat in Action* (Millwood, New York: KTO Press, 1979).

PURCELL, VICTOR, *The Boxer Uprising. A Background Study* (Cambridge: Cambridge University Press, 1963).

REICH, CARY, *Financier, The Biography of André Meyer* (New York: William Morrow, 1983).

REID, JOHN G., *The Manchu Abdication and the Powers, 1908–1912* (Berkeley: University of California Press, 1935).

REMER, C. F., *Foreign Investments in China* (New York, Macmillan, 1933).

REVELSTOKE, LORD, Papers. Barings, London.

REYNOLDS, DAVID, *The Creation of the Anglo-American Alliance, 1937–41: A Study in Competitive Co-operation* (London: Europa, 1981).

RHOADS, EDWARD J. M., *China's Republican Revolution: The Case of Kwangtung, 1895–1913* (Cambridge, Massachusetts: East Asian Research Center, Harvard University, 1975).

RICHARD, TIMOTHY, *Forty-five Years in China: Reminiscences by Timothy Richard* (London: T. Fisher Unwin, 1916).

RIGBY, RICHARD W., *The May 30 Movement: Events and Themes* (Canberra: Australian National University Press, 1980).

ROBBINS, LIONEL, *Economic Planning and International Order* (London: Macmillan, 1937).

ROBINSON, AUSTIN, 'A Personal View', in Milo Keynes (ed.) *Essays on John Maynard Keynes*.

ROBINSON, RONALD and GALLAGHER, JOHN, 'The Imperialism of Free Trade', *Economic History Review*, 2nd Series, VI (1953) pp. 1–15.

ROBINSON, RONALD, GALLAGHER, JOHN and DENNY, ALICE, *Africa and the Victorians: The Climax of Imperialism* (New York, St Martin's Press, 1961) Anchor Book edition.

ROHATYN, FELIX, 'What Next?' *The New York Review of Books*, xxxiv (3 December, 1987) pp. 3–5.

ROSEN, ELIOT A., *Hoover, Roosevelt, and the Brains Trust: from Depression to New Deal* (New York: Columbia University Press, 1977).

ROSENBAUM, A. L., 'The Manchurian Bridgehead, Anglo-Russian Rivalry and the Imperial Railways of North China, 1897–1902', *Modern Asian Studies* (1976) pp. 41–64.

ROSENBERG, EMILY S., 'Foundations of United States International Financial Power: Gold Standard Diplomacy, 1900–1905', *Business History Review*, 59 (1985) pp. 169–202.

ROSEVEARE, HENRY, *The Treasury: The Evolution of a British Institution* (New York: Columbia University Press, 1969).

ROSKILL, STEPHEN, *Hankey, Man of Secrets* (London: Collins, 1970).

ROYAL INSTITUTE OF INTERNATIONAL AFFAIRS, *The International Gold Problem: Collected Papers* (Oxford: Oxford University Press, 1931).

ROYAL INSTITUTE OF INTERNATIONAL AFFAIRS, *Monetary Policy and the Depression* (Oxford: Oxford University Press, 1933).

ROYAL INSTITUTE OF INTERNATIONAL AFFAIRS, *The Future of Monetary Policy* (Oxford: Oxford University Press, 1935).

RUBENSTEIN, MURRAY, 'Propagating the Democratic Gospel: Western Missionaries and the Diffusion of Western Thought in China, 1830–1848' (unpublished).

SALTER, SIR ARTHUR, *et al.*, *The World's Economic Crisis and the Way of Escape* (New York: Century, 1931).

SALTER, SIR ARTHUR, *Recovery: The Second Effort* (New York: Century, 1932).

SALTER, SIR ARTHUR, *China and Silver* (London: 1934).

SALTER, SIR ARTHUR, *Personality in Politics: Studies of Contemporary Statesmen* (London: Faber & Faber, 1947).

SAYERS, RICHARD S., *The Bank of England, 1891–1944*, 3 vols (Cambridge: Cambridge University Press, 1976).

SCHACHT, H., *My First Seventy-Six Years* (London: Wingate, 1955).

SCHALLER, MICHAEL, *The United States Crusade in China, 1938–1945* (New York: Columbia University Press, 1979).

SCHEIBER, HENRY N., 'World War I as Entrepreneurial Opportunity:

Willard Straight and the American International Corporation', *Political Science Quarterly*, LXXXIV (1969) pp. 486–511.

SCHIFFRIN, HAROLD, *Sun Yat-sen and the Origins of the Chinese Revolution* (Berkeley: University of Califorņa Press, 1970).

SCHLOSS, HENRY HANS, *The Bank for International Settlements* (Amsterdam: North-Holland Publishing Co., 1958).

SCHMIDT, GUSTAV (ed.) *Konstellationen Internationaler Politik, 1924–1932* (Boehurn: Studienwerlag Dr. N. Brookmeyer, 1983).

SCHOLES, WALTER V. and SCHOLES, MARIE V., *The Foreign Policies of the Taft Administration* (Columbia, Missouri: University of Missouri Press, 1970).

SCHUKER, STEPHEN, *The End of French Predominance in Europe: The Financial Crisis of 1924 and the Adoption of the Dawes Plan* (Chapel Hill: The University of North Carolina Press, 1976).

SCHUKER, STEPHEN, 'Owen D. Young, American Foreign Policy and the New Reparation Plan, 1929', in Gustav Schmidt (ed.) *Konstellationen Internationaler Politik, 1924–1932*.

SEAGRAVE, STERLING, *The Soong Dynasty* (New York: Harper & Row, 1985).

SEWALL, ARTHUR F., 'Key Pittman and the Quest for the China Market, 1933–1940', *Pacific Historical Review* (1975).

SEYMOUR, CHARLES (ed.) *The Intimate Papers of Colonel House* (Boston: Houghton Mifflin, 1928).

SHAI, ARON, *Origins of the War in the East: Britain, China and Japan, 1937–39* (London: Croom Helm, 1976).

SHERIDAN, JAMES, *Chinese Warlord: The Career of Feng Yu-hsiang* (Stanford: Stanford University Press, 1966).

SHERIDAN, JAMES, *China in Disintegration: The Republican Era in Chinese History, 1912–1949* (New York: Free Press, 1975).

SILVERMAN, DAN P., *Reconstructing Europe after the Great War* (Cambridge, Massachusetts: Harvard University Press, 1982).

SKIDELSKY, ROBERT, *John Maynard Keynes* (London: Macmillan, 1983) vol. I.

SKIDELSKY, ROBERT, 'The Gold Standard and Churchill: the Truth', *The Times* (London) 17 March 1969, p. 25.

SMITH, CARL T., 'Compradores of the Hongkong Bank', in F. H. H. King (ed.) *Eastern Banking*.

SMITH, F. BARRY, 'Sexuality in Britain, 1800–1900: Some Suggested Revisions', in Martha Vicinus (ed.) *A Widening Sphere: Changing Roles of Victorian Women* (Bloomington: Indiana University Press, 1980).

SNOWDEN, VISCOUNT PHILIP, *An Autobiography*, 2 vols (London: 1934).

SPECTOR, STANLEY, *Li Hung-chang and the Huai Army: A Study in Nineteenth Century Chinese Regionalism* (Seattle: University of Washington Press, 1964).

SPENCE, JONATHAN, *To Change China: Western Advisors in China, 1620–1960* (Boston: Little, Brown, 1969).

SPENCE, JONATHAN, *The Gate of Heavenly Peace: The Chinese and*

Their Revolution, 1895–1980 (New York: The Viking Press, 1981 and Penguin).

ST JOHN, JACQUELINE D., 'John F. Stevens: American Assistance to Russian and Siberian Railroads, 1917–1922', unpublished Ph.D. dissertation at the University of Oklahoma Library, 1969.

STEEDS, DAVID, 'The British Approach to China during the Lampson Period, 1926–1933', in Ian Nish (ed.) *Some Foreign Attitudes to Republican China*.

STEEDS, DAVID, 'The Ending of Highly Discreditable Enterprise – Miles Lampson in Siberia, 1919–1920', in Ian Nish (ed.) *The Russian Problem in East Asia*.

STEINER, ZARA S., *Britain and the Origins of the First World War* (New York: St Martin's Press, 1977).

STRAIGHT, WILLARD, Papers. Cornell University, Ithaca, New York.

STRONG, BENJAMIN, Papers. Federal Reserve Bank of New York.

STRONG–NORMAN, Correspondence, Federal Reserve Bank of New York and Hoover Presidental Library, West Branch, Iowa.

SUN, E. TSU-ZEN, *Chinese Railways and British Interests, 1898–1911* (New York: Columbia University Press, 1954).

TAN, CHESTER, *The Boxer Catastrophe* (New York: Columbia University Press, 1955).

TAYLOR, A. J. P., *English History, 1914–1945* (Oxford: Clarendon Press, 1965).

TERRILL, ROSS, *Flowers on an Iron Tree: Five Cities of China* (Boston: Little, Brown, 1975).

THANE, PAT, 'Financiers and the British State: The Case of Sir Ernest Cassel', *Business History*, XXVIII (1986) pp. 80–99.

The Chinese Times, 1886–1890.

THORNE, CHRISTOPHER G., *The Limits of Foreign Policy: The West, the League and the Far Eastern Crisis of 1931–1933* (New York: G. P. Putnam's Sons, 1973).

THORNE, CHRISTOPHER G., *Allies of a Kind: The United States, Britain and the War against Japan, 1941–1945* (New York: Oxford University Press, 1978).

TILLMAN, SETH P., *Anglo–American Relations at the Paris Peace Conference of 1919* (Princeton: Princeton University Press, 1961).

TOMLINSON, B. R., 'Britain and the Indian Currency Crisis, 1930–32', *Economic History Review*, XXXII (1979) pp. 88–99.

TROTTER, ANN, *Britain and East Asia, 1933–1937* (Cambridge: Cambridge University Press, 1975).

TURNER, HENRY A. JR., *German Big Business and the Rise of Hitler* (New York: Oxford University Press, 1985).

TURNER, JOHN (ed.) *Businessmen and Politics: Studies of Business activity in British Politics, 1900–1945* (London: Heinemann, 1984),

ULLMAN, RICHARD H., *Intervention and the War*, vol. I of *Anglo-Soviet Relations, 1917–1921*, 1961, and *Britain and the Russian Civil War, November 1918–February 1920*, vol II, 1968 (Princeton: Princeton University Press).

UNITED STATES GOVERNMENT DOCUMENTS, National Archives,

Washington, DC State Department Record Group 59 and 350; Treasury Record Group 39.

UNTERMEYER, BETTY, *America's Siberian Expedition, 1918–1920: A Study of National Policy* (Durham, North Carolina: Duke University Press, 1956).

USUI KATSUMI, 'The Politics of War, 1937–1941', in Morley (ed.) *The China Quagmire.*

VEVIER, CHARLES, *The United States and China, 1906–1913: A Study of Finance and Diplomacy* (New York: Greenwood Press, 1968) first published, 1955).

WALEY, ARTHUR, *The Opium War Through Chinese Eyes* (Stanford: Stanford University Press, 1968) first published, 1958).

WANG, YEH-CHIEN, *Land Taxation in Imperial China, 1750–1911* (Cambridge, Massachusetts: East Asian Research Center, Harvard University, 1973).

WANG, Y. C., *Chinese Intellectuals and the West, 1872–1949* (Chapel Hill: University of N. Carolina Press, 1966).

WATT, D. C., *Personalities and Policies: Studies in the Formulation of British Foreign Policy in the Twentieth Century* (Notre Dame, Indiana: University of Notre Dame Press, 1965).

WATT, D. C., *Succeeding John Bull: America in Britain's Place, 1900–1975* (Cambridge: Cambridge University Press, 1984).

WEHRLE, EDMUND S., *Britain, China and the Antimissionary Riots, 1891–1900* (Minneapolis: University of Minnesota Press, 1966).

WHITING, ALLEN S., *Soviet Policies in China, 1917–1924* (Stanford: Stanford University Press, 1968).

WILBUR, C. MARTIN, *Sun Yat-sen: Frustrated Patriot* (New York: Columbia University Press, 1976).

WILBUR, C. MARTIN, 'Military Separatism and the process of Reunification under the Nationalist Regime', in Ping-ti Ho and Tang Tsou (eds) *China in Crisis*, I (Chicago: 1968).

WILBUR, C. MARTIN, *The Nationalist Revolution in China, 1923–1938* (Cambridge: Cambridge University Press, 1983) first published as chapter 11 of the *Cambridge History of China, vol. 12.*

WILBUR, C. MARTIN and HOW, JULIA (eds) *Documents on Communism, Nationalism and Soviet Advisers in China, 1918–1927* (New York: Columbia University Press, 1956).

WILLIAMS, E. T., Papers. University of California, Berkeley, California.

WILLIAMS, MARGARET HARCOURT, *Catalogue of the Papers of Sir Charles Addis* (London: School of Oriental and African Studies, 1986).

WILLIAMS, WILLIAM APPLEMAN, *American–Russian Relations, 1781–1947* (New York: Rhinehart, 1952).

WILLIAMSON, PHILIP, 'Financiers, the Gold Standard and British Politics, 1925–1931', in John Turner (ed.) *Businessmen and Politics.*

WILLIAMSON, PHILIP, ' "Safety First": Baldwin, The Conservative Party, and the 1929 General Election', *The Historical Journal*, 1982.

WILLIAMSON, PHILIP, 'A "Bankers' Ramp"? Financiers and the British Political Crisis of August 1931', *English Historical Review* (XCIX) 1984.

WILLOUGHBY, W. W., *Foreign Rights and Interests in China*, 2 vols (Baltimore: John Hopkins Press, 1927).

WINCH, DONALD, *Economics and Policy: A Historical Study* (New York: Walker, 1969).

WOODCOCK, GEORGE, *The British in the Far East* (New York: Atheneum, 1969).

WRIGHT, MARY, *The Last Stand of Chinese Conservatism: The T'ung-Chih Restoration, 1862–1974* (Stanford: Stanford University Press, 1957).

WRIGHT, MARY (ed.) *China in Revolution: The First Phase, 1900–1913* (New Haven: Yale University Press, 1968).

WRIGHT, STANLEY F., *Hart and the Chinese Customs* (Belfast: Wm. Mullan, 1950).

YOUNG, ARTHUR N., *China and the Helping Hand, 1937–1945* (Cambridge, Massachusetts: Harvard University Press, 1963).

YOUNG, ARTHUR N., *China's Nation-Building Effort, 1927–1937*, (Stanford University: Hoover Institution Press, 1971).

YOUNG, ERNEST P., *The Presidency of Yuan Shih-k'ai: Liberalism and Dictatorship in Early Republican China* (Ann Arbor: University of Michigan Press, 1977).

YOUNG, ERNEST P., 'Politics in the Aftermath of Revolution: The Era of Yuan Shih-k'ai, 1912–16', in *Cambridge History of China*, XII, pt. 1, pp. 208–36.

YOUNG, L. K., *British Policy in China, 1895–1902* (Oxford: Oxford University Press, 1970).

YOUNG, MARILYN, *Rhetoric of Empire: American China Policy, 1895–1901* (Cambridge, Massachusetts: Harvard University Press, 1968).

YOUNG, OWEN, Papers, Van Hornesville, New York.

YOUNGSON, A. J., *The British Economy, 1920–57* (Cambridge, Massachusetts: Harvard University Press, 1960).

Index

411

Addis, Sir Charles Stewart – *continued*
and speech to Lombard Association
(1934), 249
and Union Discount speech (1933), 244
and Lin-ch'eng incident, 255
and China Indemnity Advisory
Committee, 263
and Boxer Indemnity funds, 234, 263,
272, 275
and comments at RIIA (1926), 266–7
and advice to Cabinet (1927), 267
and China policy (1927), 234, 254, 260,
264–8, 272
on Consortium, 234, 254, 258, 260, 274
and Chinese Nationalists, 234, 254
and Liang Shih-yi's visit (1924), 257
and Maritime Customs administration,
270
and Japanese bankers (1932), 280
and criticism of FO (1932), 277
and Cecil letter, 1932, 277
memo on Sino-Japanese dispute
(1932), 278, 280
and China subcommittee, EAC (1930),
276
as link with Americans, 259
and retirement, Bank of England, 237
and dismissal from HSBC (1932), 280–
3
and Grayburn, 287–8
denounced by FO, 278–9
opposes Leith-Ross, 275–6
as Treasurer, Universities China
Committee, 279
and sterling loan with Bank of China,
284
and Soong proposals (1933), 284–8
and Japanese in China, 288, 290, 297–
8
discusses Chinese railways with
Monnet, 290
and Maze proposals (1934), 290–2
and surgery (1934), 291
and Leith-Ross mission, 295, 297, 302
and defaulted bonds, 297
and open tender, 295–6
and Canton-Meishien railway loan,
300, 303
and Consortium partners, 300
and Consolidated railway loan, (1937),
301–2
and currency loan, 303
and Sino-Japanese War, 303–5
and China's future, 303–5

and speech for Chinese Relief Fund,
305
and Burma-Szechuan Railway, 306
and article, 'A Liberal Economy',
(1938), 310
and refusal of peerage, 308
and refusal to become Governor, Bank
of England, 308
and comment on FO and Treasury
clerks, 308
and Rotary Club speech (1936), 309
and speech to Technical Institute
(1939), 307
and golden wedding anniversary, 308
and speech to the American Club
(1937) on *The New Monetary
Technique*, 309–10
and stroke (1943), 312
and Toast at Burns Dinner (1940), 307
and tribute to Sir Josiah Stamp (1938),
310
and Victorian era, 310, 316
and appeasement, 311
and influence on others, 312–15
and characteristics, 312–13
and hypocrisy, 315–16
and resignation from Boards, 311–12
and death, 312
Addis, Charles Thorburn, 42
Addis, Croppie (sister of C. S. Addis),
5–6
Addis, David (brother of C. S. Addis),
5
Addis, Lady Eba McIsaac, 43, 54, 74
illness (1898), 42
to Japan, 189
relationship with husband, 40, 42, 46,
55, 68, 70, 75, 88, 193, 298, 311
in Seoul, 41
in New York, 48
and Bland affair, 60
describes Sun Yat-sen, 65
accompanies husband to Far East, 141
and Canadian mission, 248–9
Addis, Elizabeth, 42, 136
Addis, George (C. S. Addis's brother),
7, 10, 21, 28
Addis, George (C. S. Addis's son), 193
Addis, Henrietta (Charles S. Addis's
sister), 4
Addis, Robina (Croppie) (Mrs Robert
Adamson), 4, 5, 29, 30, 32
Addis, Robina Scott (Charles S. Addis's
daughter), 47, 136

Mellon, Andrew, US Secretary of the
  Treasury, 133–4, 155, 219
Mellon-Baldwin agreement, 208
Memorial on International Finance and
  Currency (1920), *see* International
  Memorial
Meyer, Eugene, 218
Michie, Alexander, 37, 49
  editor, *The Chinese Times*, 19, 20, 21
  views on Addis, 19, 20, 23, 32
  advice to Addis, 23
Mill, John Stuart, 26
Mills, Col. Dudley, 21, 27
  description of Addis family, 5–6
  friendship with Addis, 14, 23, 29–31,
    36–7, 40, 44, 47, 49, 53, 55, 73–4,
    77, 80, 81, 85, 88, 90, 94, 103–4,
    131–4, 168, 177, 251
  in France, 191
missionaries, 21
Mitsui and Mitsubishi Bankers, 280
monetary policy, 111, 146
monetary theory, 151
Monnet, Jean
  Addis opinion of, 290
  and Chinese currency reform, 288
  and International Memorial, 119
  and Soong mission, 285
  and trip to China, 286
  and Chinese railways, 290
Montagu, E. S., 161–2
Montagu mission, 161–2
Moreau, Émile, 183, 194
Moret, Governor, Bank of France, 220
Morgan Grenfell & Co., 65, 204, 306
Morgan, House of, 58, 201
Morgan, J. P. Jr,
  and Addis, 219
  negotiating Consortium agreement,
    100
  and Bankers' Committee, 151
  and British war debts, 155
  and Revelstoke opinion of, 189–90
  and Committee of Experts (1929), 188,
    191, 194
  and BIS, 200–1, 204, 213
  and 1931 crisis, 227
Morgans, 84, 110
  and Russo-Japanese War, 62
  and China Consortium, 65
  named British fiscal agent, 82
  loans to Britain, 82, 89, 90, 95
  and Anglo-French loan, 82, 121
  McAdoo's criticisms of (1917), 91

on Warburgs (1916), 89
opposition to Kuhn Loeb, 90
interests in China, 100
comment on Addis, 134
and British relationship, 115–16, 134,
  171–2
and relationship with Strong, 116, 132,
  134, 168–9
and relationship with Norman, 135,
  152, 169
and limits of power, 116
and Americans' suspicion of, 123
and Chinese Eastern Railway, 124, 134
and loan to Austria, 132
and terms for loan to Germany (1921),
  135
and Britain's return to gold, 169
as central bank, 171
and British war debts, 123
and BIS, 208
and American and British attitude
  toward (1929), 188
and European credits, 213
and loan to SMR, 269
and Manchurian crisis, 278
and Soong loan, 284–5
Morgenthau, Henry Jr, US Secretary of
  the Treasury, 289, 294, 305
Morrison, George E., 44, 55, 61
Morrison Centenary, 251
Mounsey, George, 261, 263
Muller, Max, 66
Murray, Gilbert, 277

Nanking, 65, 68
Nanking government, 235, 267
  and British Foreign Office views, 275
  and Consortium, 287
  and Japan, 289
  and Chinese unity, 300
Nathan, Matthew, 261
Nathan, Walter
  and Addis dinner for, 257
  and removal from B&C Corp., 269,
    280
  and Chang Tso-lin, 268
National City Bank, 61, 84
National government (British 1931), 228
Nationalist government of China, 288
  and customs revenues, 271
  and defaulted bonds, 274
  and American advisors, 275
  and retreat to Chungking, 305
  and American loan, 305

Straight, Willard, 60, 62, 67, 80, 84, 85
Strakosch, Sir Henry
  at Genoa, 152
  and Addis, 156
  and South Africa, 165, 168
  and Gold Restoration, 170
  and visit to Strong (1927), 182
  and Stock Exchange, 187
  and cheap money, 213
  and League gold study report, 215
Strong, Benjamin
  and Addis, 81, 113–15, 119, 131, 145,
    146, 171, 174
  and Norman, 82, 115, 168, 172, 174,
    183
  and Blackett, 113
  and central bank cooperation, 83, 115,
    174, 182
  war debt plan (1919), 113–14
  and Morgans, 116, 125, 155
  visit to Tokyo (1920), 124
  and Japanese bankers, 125
  and war debts, 155
  and Dawes Plan, 163
  differs with Strakosch, 182
  and monetary views, 168
  and death (1928), 183
Stubbs, Sir Reginald, 138, 143
Suma Yakichiro, 298
Sun Fo, 138, 272, 275
Sundius, A. J., 32
Sun Yat-sen
  as revolutionary, 64–5
  flight to Japan (1913), 68
  and Southern Revolutionaries, 86
  and Bolshevism, 137
  and *The International Development of
    China*, 138
  and coalition with Chang Tso-lin, 141
  and Customs crisis (1923), 256
  and alliance with Russia, 257
  and recognition, 264
  and death, 1925
Sung Chiao-jen, 68

Taft, William Howard, US President, 61,
  68
Taiping Rebellion, 9
Tang Shao-yi, 65
Tariff Conference, 260, 264
ter Meulen, C. E., 118–19, 196, 203
ter Meulen scheme, 131
Thomas, J. H., 120

Thomsett, Harry M., 10
Thorburn, Rev. David, 3
Thorburn, Robina Scott, 3
Tiarks, F. C., 189
Tientsin Notes, 25
Tientsin-Pukow Railway, 58, 297
Townsend, A. M., 47, 55, 70
Tract Society, 21
Trans-Siberian Railway, 95
Traylor, Melvin, 213, 219
Treaty of Brest-Litovsk, 94, 124
Treaty of Nanking, 8
Treaty of Shimonoseki, 35
Treaty of Tientsin, 8–9
Treaty system (in China), 8, 253
Trotter, Professor Ann, 294
Trotter, H. A., 264
Tsar Alexander II, 95
Tsarist gold, 95, 97, 124–5
Tseng Chi-tse, Marquis, 18
Tseng Kuo-fan, Viceroy, 16, 18
Ts'u, Hsi, Empress Dowager, 15, 43, 49,
  53, 63–4
Tuan Ch'i-jui, 98
Tuesday Club, 89, 93
  and war debts, 132, 156
  and Gold Restoration, 170
  and Britain's Industrial Future, 182
Turner, George, 123
Tyrrell, Sir William, 58, 114, 189–90

Union of London-Smith Bank, 71
United States
  and British debt, 112–13
  as world's creditor, 112, 117, 245
  and Norman description, 294
United States Chamber of Commerce,
  119
United States House of Representatives,
  134
United States Senate, 113
United States State Department, 191
  and Russian gold, 125
  and dissatisfaction with Consortium,
    143
  and Genoa Conference, 152
United States Treasury
  and views and strategy on reparations,
    114
  and refusal to issue loans, 119
  and silver policy, 293
Universities China Committee, 279
University Court, University of London,
  74